FOURTH EDITION

CRIMINAL COURTS

STRUCTURE, PROCESS, AND ISSUES

Richard D. Hartley
University of Texas San Antonio

Gary A. Rabe
Minot State University

Dean John Champion

 Pearson

330 Hudson Street, NY, NY 10013

Vice President, Portfolio Management:
Andrew Gilfillan
Portfolio Manager: Gary Bauer
Editorial Assistant: Lynda Cramer
Senior Vice President, Marketing: David Gesell
Field Marketing Manager: Thomas Hayward
Product Marketing Manager: Kaylee Carlson
Senior Marketing Coordinator: Les Roberts
Director, Digital Studio and Content Production:
Brian Hyland
Managing Producer: Cynthia Zonneveld
Managing Producer: Jennifer Sargunar

Content Producer: Purnima Narayanan
Manager, Rights Management: Johanna Burke
Operations Specialist: Deidra Smith
Cover Designer: StudioMontage
Cover Art: Aleksandar Radovanovic/123RF
Full-Service Project Management:
Rakhshinda Chishty
Composition: iEnergizer Aptara®, Ltd.
Printer/Binder: LSC Communications
Cover Printer: LSC Communications
Text Font: ITC Garamond Std

Library of Congress Cataloging-in-Publication Data

Names: Hartley, Richard D., author. | Rabe, Gary A., author. | Champion, Dean
J., author.
Title: Criminal courts : structure, process, and issues / Richard D. Hartley,
University of Texas San Antonio; Gary A. Rabe, Minot State University;
Dean John Champion.
Description: Fourth edition. | Boston : Pearson, 2017. | Includes
bibliographical references and index.
Identifiers: LCCN 2017007640| ISBN 9780133779745 | ISBN 0133779742
Subjects: LCSH: Criminal justice, Administration of—United States. |
Criminal courts—United States.
Classification: LCC KF8700 .R33 2017 | DDC 345.73/01—dc23 LC record available at
https://lccn.loc.gov/2017007640

ISBN 10:   0-13-377974-2
ISBN 13: 978-0-13-377974-5

Contents

Chapter 10   Judicial Sentencing Options, Sentencing Disparities, and Appeals   238

Criminal Courts: Structure, Process, and Issues (fourth edition) is a comprehensive examination of the U.S. Criminal Court systems, to include discussion of actors in the system with decision-making power, and case processing from the point when offenders are arrested and charged with crimes through the sentencing and appeals process. This book also deals with issues confronting the system from historical, philosophical, sociological, and psychological perspectives. Some of these include judicial activism and the Supreme Court, prosecutorial and judicial discretion, the right to legal representation, judicial misconduct, jury nullification, diversion and alternative programs, specialty courts, and the role of plea bargaining in our system of justice. Finally, throughout this work, there are comparisons of court ideals with actual court functioning. This is to give students a more straightforward look at how the courts in our criminal justice system operate as well as how the persons who work in the system sometimes follow the rules, and at other times they bend the rules. This is not to say that our system of laws and justice can be manipulated, even though that sometimes happens, but that much of the law is broad and ambiguous and actors in the system are given discretion to interpret it. The reality of the criminal justice system, including the criminal courts, is that often limited human and financial resources hinder actors' ability to invoke the formal legal system to its full extent. It is through this ideal versus reality lens that students will learn much about the structure and function of the U.S. Criminal Courts.

The opening chapter begins with an examination of law and its social and political origins as well as where and how courts and the legal system fit into the criminal justice system. Despite the different periods or eras into which world history has been divided by scholars, the pervasiveness and continuity of law are apparent. Laws have always existed in some form or another, but largely intended to fulfill the same general purposes regardless of the culture we choose to examine. The major functions of law are social control, dispute resolution, and social change. Over time, technological changes have occurred and social ideas have evolved, and this has contributed to new thinking about how persons should orient themselves to others. The courts have made landmark decisions related to what the constitution guarantees to persons and many social and legal issues have been addressed and restructured via the law; in some instances, liberating persons and their beliefs, and in others restricting previously tolerated behaviors.

Laws can also be differentiated according to whether they pertain to civil or criminal matters. Statements about what the law says and how we should comport ourselves in our daily lives or out in the community in the company of others are referred to as substantive law. In less complex social systems, substantive law tended to be espoused by the courts in the form of common law. Common law is based on traditions, dependent upon the particular needs and desires of groups of people living together in cities or towns. As our social systems have become increasingly complex, we have devised more elaborate legal schemes and more formal mechanisms to maintain the social order and regulate human conduct. How the law should be applied is the province of procedural law. The United States has one of the most complex and contrived legal systems. Today, there are all types of law pertaining to different aspects of our society. These laws are either civil or criminal, and increasingly, a whole body of law focuses upon administrative law.

It is a legal reality that the early applications of the law favored particular interests over others. Some persons believe that our laws have been created to preserve the status quo for those who possess political and economic power. Thus, there have been inherent disparities existing in how the law is applied and for whom it is implemented. Those suffering the most from legal disparities historically have been women, children, and minorities. In recent decades, sociolegal movements have prompted substantial social changes in response to disparate treatment of certain groups, and still there are groups today who believe their interests are not reflected in the current application of the law.

Understanding the laws of the United States begins with a critical examination and description of the dual court system that is present in the United States. The principal components of the dual court system are federal and state court apparatuses. Chapter 2 describes federal and state court organization, and various functions of these different types of courts. There are diverse court systems, and there is little continuity among the states concerning what these different courts should be called. We do not have a universal nomenclature that can be applied to all state and local courts at various levels. However, there is considerable continuity within the federal court system. Federal and state court jurisdictions are distinguished, and the processes and functions of different types of courts are described and discussed.

The court workgroup consists of the same types of actors, regardless of whether we are discussing federal or state jurisdictions. Whenever one or more laws are violated, prosecutors at the state or federal level act against alleged offenders to bring them to justice. Thus, Chapters 3 and 4 examine prosecutors and defense counsels in some detail, identifying their principal functions and duties. The U.S. Constitution and the Bill of Rights have vested all citizens with particular rights to ensure that they will be treated equally under the law. All persons who are charged with a criminal offense are entitled to counsel if they are obligated to appear in court to answer criminal charges. Under particular circumstances, anyone may enjoy the right to a jury trial comprised of one's peers. These are due process rights afforded to those accused of criminal acts. These due process rights and the roles and functions of both prosecutors and defense counsels are examined and discussed.

The judge is often seen as the most important actor in the court system. Judges oversee all court proceedings and make important decisions. Several types of systems are used for judicial selection. These systems are described. While legal backgrounds are strongly recommended for persons functioning as judges, it is not necessarily true that all judges have law degrees or legal training. Thus, different methods for selecting judges are explained, together with the strengths and weaknesses of these methods. Merit selection of judges now seems to be favored in many jurisdictions to try and seat the best qualified candidates as judges. There is still, however, a segment of the judiciary clearly lacking the qualifications and commitment to make good decisions. Judicial misconduct of various kinds will be described, and some of the remedies available to the public for recalling bad judges will be examined.

At the heart of our legal system is the jury process despite the fact that a very small percentage of cases actually result in a jury trial. In fact, juries account for only about 10 percent of all criminal cases that are pursued. Nevertheless, considerable time is devoted to examining the jury process and how jurors are selected. Juries are comprised of persons from the general population. Methods of jury selection vary greatly among jurisdictions. Both prosecutors and defense counsel conduct *voir dires* or oral questioning of prospective juries from a list of veniremen or a *venire*. Sometimes experts are used to assist as consultants, since some persons believe that jury selection can enhance the chances of a conviction or an acquittal. Various methods for discharging prospective jurors are examined, including challenges for cause and peremptory challenges. Various standards among the states and the federal system are described to show that there are different criteria applied for determining the appropriate jury size and the process of jury decision making. The decision-making process of juries is examined in some detail, and the important topics of jury nullification and juror misconduct are explored.

For offenders who are prosecuted criminally for violating the law, the arrest and booking process are described in Chapter 7. The issue of bail is also discussed. An overview of bail decision making and bail bondspersons is provided. Bail has always been a controversial issue and critics assert that it is punishment against poor offenders who often cannot afford bail. The purposes and practices of bail, therefore, are also discussed in detail. Changing sentiments in some jurisdictions has led to bail reform in order that bail might be more affordable to all offenders and that jail and detention overcrowding might be alleviated.

The actual trial process is also illustrated. Those charged with crimes may undergo either bench or jury trials, where either a judge will decide their case or a jury will deliberate. The criminal trial process is described in some detail with various fictional scenarios that have paralleled some actual legal cases in the recent past. In any criminal trial, due process requires that we consider any defendant innocent of a crime until proved guilty beyond a reasonable doubt. This is a difficult standard to achieve in many cases. Prosecutors who pursue criminal cases against particular suspects believe that they can convince juries of the defendant's guilt. However, the defendant is represented by counsel who attempts to show that the defendant is innocent. Various witnesses are brought forth and testify, either for or against particular defendants. Some of these witnesses are eyewitnesses, while others are expert witnesses who testify about the quality and significance of collected evidence. Juries deliberate and decide one's guilt or innocence.

One, however, must also keep in mind that the most frequently used resolution strategy for criminal offenders is not a trial but plea bargaining, which is discussed in Chapter 8. Plea bargaining is a preconviction agreement between prosecutors, defense counsels, and their clients where guilty pleas are entered to criminal charges in exchange for some type of leniency. Plea bargaining results in a criminal conviction, but the penalties imposed are often less harsh compared with the penalties imposed through trial convictions. Different types of plea bargaining will be discussed. The pros and cons of plea bargaining are listed. Furthermore, some jurisdictions have abolished plea bargaining, and their reasons for doing so will be examined.

Regardless of whether offenders plead guilty through some type of plea bargain or are found guilty at trial, they will have a sentencing hearing. Sentencing hearings are conducted by trial judges. Sentencing hearings permit victims or relatives of victims to make victim impact statements in either verbal or written form. Others testify on behalf of defendants. Judges are the final arbiters and impose different sentences, depending upon the seriousness of the crime, one's prior record, and other factors. Several different types of sentencing systems that are used by U.S. courts today will be discussed. Chapter 9 examines these systems as well as the goals of punishment. In the event that convicted offenders are dissatisfied with the verdict, they are entitled to appeal their cases to higher courts. Judicial sentencing options, disparity in sentencing, and the appellate process are discussed in Chapter 10. Featured are death penalty cases, which are always automatically appealed. The appeals process is especially lengthy, and even those who are sentenced to death in states with capital punishment laws may not be executed for ten or more years.

A parallel system of justice exists for juvenile offenders. Thus, Chapters 11 and 12 examine the juvenile justice system with particular emphasis upon how the juvenile court system is structured and operated. A different language applies to juvenile processing, and various comparisons are made between the juvenile and criminal justice systems. Several important landmark juvenile cases are cited where they have been granted certain constitutional rights by the U.S. Supreme Court. Over time, juvenile courts have taken on the characteristics of criminal courts. Some persons believe that in several years, the juvenile court may be abolished and that a unified court for both juveniles and adults will emerge.

Not all persons charged with crimes are ultimately processed by the criminal justice system. Chapter 13 discusses how some offenders are diverted to civil courts or into civil dispute resolution programs where their cases can be concluded in noncriminal ways. Victims and offenders are often brought together in alternative dispute resolution actions, where victim compensation and restorative justice are sought as remedies for wrongdoing. In some states, various laws are being scrutinized for the purpose of changing them and causing criminal acts to become decriminalized through legislative changes. Thus, the process of alternative dispute resolution, pretrial diversion, and specialty courts will be examined.

Chapter 14 concludes with an examination of how the court process is influenced by the media. As our society has become increasingly complex in a technological sense, we have mastered ways of delivering information to more people through different mediums such as television and the Internet. At the same time that we have been increasingly exposed to what goes on in the courtroom, a major litigation explosion has occurred, where increasing numbers of lawsuits are filed. We have evolved into a very litigious society. One reason for the great increase in litigation is the great publicity derived from courtroom coverage by the media and the sensationalization of particular cases. Media in the courtroom will be explored, and the pros and cons of media coverage will be examined in terms of how public opinion is shaped.

Ancillaries and desirable features of this book include critical thinking exercises, a case study decision-making exercise, and numerous concept review questions at the end of each chapter. Key terms are boldfaced and listed in the margins throughout the text and revisited again at the end of the chapter; a comprehensive glossary of these and other terms is found in an appendix. Recently published readings are also suggested at the end of each chapter so that those interested in learning more about particular subjects can locate further reading for their edification and education. An up-to-date bibliography of both research publications and legal cases is provided in the end-of-book references to facilitate one's research and general study. A new feature to this edition is the use of boxed sections which discuss key cases and legal issues in each chapter. These are included to feature landmark cases and current issues or events that complement the text itself. Some of these key cases are considered landmark decisions which have had a great impact on criminal justice in action, and the real people and real events that take place in society every day. Chapter openers have also been included to heighten student interest in learning more about our court system and to provide them with real stories or snapshots of important knowledge about courts and the law.

While this book is coauthored, it is acknowledged that the final result is the work of many persons. We wish to thank Gary Bauer, Lynda Cramer and Jennifer Sargunar from Pearson for their patience and help in getting this fourth edition together. We are also indebted to the many reviewers who have made helpful suggestions and constructive criticisms for all editions of this work (Stephen Brodt, Ball State University–Muncie; Kristine Mullendore, Grand Valley State University–Grand Rapids; Timothy Garner, Ball State University–Muncie; Sylvia Blake-Larson, Tarrant County College; Scott Donaldson, Tarrant County College; Robert Greenwood, Madonna University; and Julie Raines, Marist College). Finally, special thanks to Judge Catherine Torres-Stahl for her comments and suggestions on this fourth edition, and UTSA Masters students Michelle Hill, Johannes Laven, and Thomas Garza for their assistance in finding sources, references, and suggested reading materials.

▶ New to the 4th edition

- A revised introductory chapter discusses the criminal courts and their functions in the context of the larger criminal justice system to include a section on the relationship between the courts, and police and corrections agencies.

- Many new chapter openers have been added to introduce students to the main topic of the chapter.
- Boxed items in each chapter have been added under the themes of key cases and legal issues. Key cases succinctly list and describe the most important landmark cases that have been influential to the process and functioning of the courts and its key actors. Legal Issues boxes describe contemporary problems confronting the courts and ask students to opine about the best course of action for both policy and practice.
- Definitions for key terms are now listed in the margins of the chapters.
- Chapter summaries have been reorganized by learning objectives.
- New "What Do You Think" feature in each chapter prompts students to use critical thinking skills with real-world application.
- Policy-oriented critical thinking exercises and case study decision-making exercises have been added to complement the concept review questions at each chapter's end.
- Findings from contemporary and classic empirical research studies have been interspersed throughout the text to provide students with the knowledge of real-world functioning of courts and the criminal justice system.

—Richard D. Hartley
Gary A. Rabe
Dean John Champion

Richard D. Hartley is an associate professor in the Department of Criminal Justice at the University of Texas at San Antonio. He holds a Ph.D. from the School of Criminology and Criminal Justice at the University of Nebraska at Omaha. He teaches courses relating to criminal courts and the administration of justice, as well as research methods for criminology and criminal justice. Dr. Hartley's research interests include prosecutorial and judicial discretion, and extralegal determinants of court decision-making practices. He has been involved with a number of National Institute of Justice-funded research projects for which he analyzed court outcomes, especially those for federal narcotics and immigration offenders, as well as the impact of veterans treatment courts on justice involved veterans. He holds professional memberships in the American Society of Criminology, the Academy of Criminal Justice Sciences, the Society for Empirical Legal Studies, and the European Society of Criminology. Dr. Hartley has also given lectures and collected data on court decisions in international venues in both Colombia and Spain. Some of his recent peer-reviewed publications appear in *Criminal Justice and Behavior, Criminal Justice Policy Review, Crime & Delinquency*, and *Justice Quarterly*.

Gary A. Rabe After serving for five years as the Vice President for Academic Affairs at Minot State University (MSU), Dr. Gary A. Rabe has returned to his academic appointment as a professor within the Department of Criminal Justice.

Dr. Rabe earned a Ph.D. in Criminology from the University Delaware, an M.A. in Criminology and Corrections from Sam Houston State University, and a B.S. in Criminal Justice from MSU. His professional experience includes Executive Director of the Rural Crime and Justice Center (MSU), Department Chair and Associate Professor of the Criminal Justice Center (MSU), Interim Dean of the College of Arts and Sciences (MSU), and Director of the Rural Law Enforcement Education Project at MSU. As Director of the Rural Crime and Justice Center, he was successful in obtaining over $8 million dollars in grants and contracts.

Dr. Rabe's professional memberships and services have included the National Consortium for White Collar Crime Research, the American Society of Criminology, the Law and Society Association, and the Academy of Criminal Justice Sciences. Dr. Rabe has served as a consultant to the Federal Law Enforcement Training Center and the National White Collar Crime Center, and served on the editorial board for the *Journal of Crime and Justice*. Dr. Rabe was recently reappointed by the Governor to a second consecutive four-year term on the North Dakota Commission on Alternatives to Incarceration. Dr. Rabe's academic areas of specialization include Criminological Theory, Criminal Justice Policy Evaluation, Rural Crime, Criminology, Corporate Crime and Sentencing, Courts, and Sociology of Law. He has coauthored three books and published several book chapters, articles, and technical reports.

Dean John Champion (1940–2009) was Professor of Criminal Justice at several universities, including Texas A&M International University, Minot State University, California State University-Long Beach, and the University of Tennessee-Knoxville. He received his Ph.D. from Purdue University and B.S. and M.A. degrees from Brigham Young University. He also completed several years of law school at the Nashville School of Law. Dr. Champion

was a prolific writer and has over 40 texts and/or edited works to his credit, a few of which were internationally recognized having been translated into Russian, Portuguese, Chinese, and Spanish.

He maintained membership in 11 professional organizations and was a lifetime member of the American Society of Criminology, Academy of Criminal Justice Sciences, and the American Sociological Association. He was a former editor of the Academy of Criminal Justice Sciences/Anderson Publishing Company Series on *Issues in Crime and Justice* and the *Journal of Crime and Justice*, and a contributing author for the *Encarta Encyclopedia 2000* for Microsoft. He was also a former Visiting Scholar for the National Center for Juvenile Justice and president of the Midwestern Criminal Justice Association.

Some of his published books for Prentice-Hall include *Crime Prevention in America* (2007); *Research Methods for Criminal Justice and Criminology 3/e* (2006); *The Juvenile Justice System: Delinquency, Processing, and the Law 5/e* (2007); *Corrections in the United States: A Contemporary Perspective 4/e* (2005); *Probation, Parole, and Community Corrections 5/e* (2008). His specialty interests included juvenile justice, criminal justice administration, corrections, and statistics/methods. Dr. Champion was a great advocate of student education and will be missed by all who knew him. His absence will especially be felt in the classroom and at the association annual meetings.

▶ Instructor Supplements

Instructor's Manual with Test Bank. Includes content outlines for classroom discussion, teaching suggestions, and answers to selected end-of-chapter questions from the text.

This also contains a Word document version of the test bank.

TestGen. This computerized test generation system gives you maximum flexibility in creating and administering tests on paper, electronically, or online. It provides state-of-the-art features for viewing and editing test bank questions, dragging a selected question into a test you are creating, and printing sleek, formatted tests in a variety of layouts. Select test items from test banks included with TestGen for quick test creation, or write your own questions from scratch. TestGen's random generator provides the option to display different text or calculated number values each time questions are used.

PowerPoint Presentations. Our presentations are clear and straightforward. Photos, illustrations, charts, and tables from the book are included in the presentations when applicable.

To access supplementary materials online, instructors need to request an instructor access code. Go to **www.pearsonhighered.com/irc**, where you can register for an instructor access code. Within 48 hours after registering, you will receive a confirming email, including an instructor access code. Once you have received your code, go to the site and log on for full instructions on downloading the materials you wish to use.

▶ Alternate Versions

eBooks This text is also available in multiple eBook formats. These are an exciting new choice for students looking to save money. As an alternative to purchasing the printed textbook, students can purchase an electronic version of the same content. With an eTextbook, students can search the text, make notes online, print out reading assignments that incorporate lecture notes, and bookmark important passages for later review. For more information, visit your favorite online eBook reseller or visit www.mypearsonstore.com.

1 Law

The Legal Battlefield

LEARNING OBJECTIVES

As a result of reading this chapter, you will have accomplished the following objectives:

1 *Apply your knowledge of what the law is and the role that courts play in various facets of our daily lives.*

2 *Compare and contrast the different functions of law, including social control, dispute resolution, and social change.*

3 *Understand the evolution of disputes and the formal resolution of them.*

4 *Identify the difference between substantive law and procedural law.*

5 *Summarize the different types of law, including common law, civil law, and criminal and administrative laws.*

6 *Draw appropriate conclusions about the different sociolegal perspectives on law, such as sociological jurisprudence, legal realism, critical legal studies, and feminist legal theory.*

Recently, a nonprofit organization called the Texas Sons of Confederate Veterans (Texas SCV) applied to the state to make available a specialty license plate that would be issued by the Texas DMV. The state rejected their application because the license plate proposed included confederate flags on it. The Texas DMV had a policy that it can refuse specialty license plates if they might offend some persons. The nonprofit sued, stating that their First Amendment rights were violated. The DMV argued, however, that license plates are considered "government speech," and therefore, the state can decide what messages to display on license plates. The Fifth Circuit Court of Appeals sided with the Texas SCV, ruling that the DMV discriminated against them by not approving their application to make the license plates available. The Supreme Court weighed in after appeal from the DMV and determined in a 5–4 decision that license plates are government speech, and therefore, the Texas DMV had the right to refuse the design submitted by the Texas SCV. Should states be able to determine what types of license plates they will issue? Does this, in your opinion, violate an individual's right to free speech? How is it that two different courts could come to two different decisions about this matter? Why did the Supreme Court have to make the decision in this case? What do you think? Was this about the nonprofit's ability to raise money through the license plate or was it truly that they wanted persons to be able to express their viewpoints through the specialty license plate? Couldn't the nonprofit sell bumper stickers that individuals could display next to their Texas license plates? Why are license plates regulated by the courts and bumper stickers not?

▶ Introduction

When most persons think of the law, they conjure up ideas about rules of conduct for behavior that have been written down. This is what we would refer to as substantive law. The law, however, also is the structures, procedures, and persons who have the authority to put the law into practice. The law can mean different things for different people. Some might see the law as an avenue for redress of social ills in society. Others might believe that the law is used only as a means to maintain the *status quo* and the power of those in the ruling class. The law is both, and can be viewed in many ways by many different people. The law may be liberating to some and at the same time oppressive to others (Vago 2006). Indeed, in the United States, the law enabled and eliminated slavery, controlled and liberated women, and ruled for and against government control of people's lives. In the introductory example, the Supreme Court weighed in on what is allowable to be displayed on a state license plate. A Texas nonprofit felt that the state violated their First Amendment rights when it rejected their specialty license plate application because the design included confederate flags on it. The federal courts have the authority to decide disputes between the states as well as between the states and individuals, and private or nonprofit organizations. This example also shows that courts decide not only matters of crime and justice, but also matters about constitutional rights. Remember that the U.S. Constitution is the supreme law of the land, and the federal courts have the right to determine whether the rights and freedoms enumerated in the constitution have been violated by state laws, city and county rules, and even governmental and private institutions' policies. No matter how one views the law, the criminal courts are both the institution and the structure that bring the law to life, and the courts make important decisions that affect society and the lives of its citizens.

The criminal court system in the United States is very complex and can be a confusing system to study and understand. The federal government and each state have their own court structure and rules of procedure for implementation of the law. There are also different punishment structures; there are indeterminate and determinate sentencing structures, as well as guideline-based systems, and depending on the court or the crime, there may also be statutes in place that guide punishment, such as habitual offender laws, truth in sentencing, or mandatory minimums. To be even more confusing, criminal courts may not be the only option for administering justice. Throughout the United States, there are also military courts, tribal courts, juvenile courts, and specialty courts such as drug courts or veterans courts. There is no uniformity in the courts and the sentencing structures they employ among the jurisdictions across the country, and therefore, the U.S. criminal court system can sometimes be very confusing.

The functions of criminal courts are more straightforward; most persons believe that the primary function of law is to maintain social order, and indeed, the law and court structure are charged with maintaining order. This is accomplished through the adversary system that characterizes the U.S. courts, and its adjudicative function. Throughout societies, the law vests considerable power in judges to impose punishment on convicted offenders. The instrument of law and punishment is the criminal justice system whose actors are responsible for apprehending offenders, charging them with crimes, ascertaining guilt, and meting out punishments. The adversary system of justice pits the prosecution against the defense in a search for the truth. Some, however, might question whether the system is adversarial as the relationship between the prosecution and defense seems to be more reciprocal than adversarial. In other words, the prosecution, defense, and judge (the courtroom workgroup) have broader common interests to efficiently process the court's caseload than to argue and search for the truth. This is exemplified by the fact that roughly 90 percent of cases are plea bargained rather than settled at trial. This notion of prosecution, defense, and judge being cooperative rather than adversarial is based upon the idea that the actors who practice the law must work together to efficiently process cases. Eisenstein and Jacob (1977) assert that the courtroom workgroup has many shared goals, and thus, working together is incentivized. The courtroom workgroup is more than just prosecution, defense, and judge, however, and includes bailiffs, clerks, and even defendants whose interactions on a daily basis affect court outcomes.

There are two broad philosophies regarding how courts function. One portrays a legal institution that focuses on rules and procedures and where justice is the ultimate goal, and the other depicts a community where interdependent actors rely on one another to perform their roles and where the nature of these relationships will influence processes and practices. Indeed, the formal rules and procedures are in place to guide the administration of justice, but courts are complex political institutions and different courtroom communities may dispense different kinds of justice.

Notwithstanding the manner in which one views the role and function of courts in society, there are several different kinds of laws or rules that attempt to govern our behavior and the way the citizenry conduct their lives. There are laws against many violations we may or may not know exist but are in place to protect us from things that may harm or injure us. Law is dynamic and has many definitions. What is against the law in one place or at one time may not be a violation in another place or at another time. What elements of a crime need to be proved to meet the different evidentiary standards? Different states and the federal government define crimes in particular ways. There is much variation among the states about the nature and seriousness of different types of offenses. There is also variation among different jurisdictions in the application of laws, even if they have the same or similar laws. This is referred to as interdistrict disparity. For example, if two persons commit the same federal narcotics violation and have similar backgrounds, but one is being convicted in district court in Texas and the other in district court in North Dakota, their sentences may be very different because of local court contexts (plea bargaining, departure rates, and prison overcrowding) even though they violated the same federal law.

There are also many definitional differences of criminal law in various places and also at various times. While these definitions are important to learn, it is also important to understand the different functions of law for a society as well as the consistency and inconsistency with which the law is applied. This chapter examines various perspectives regarding the purposes and functions of law. Law can be used as a means to regulate the behavior of society, it can be used to settle disputes between grieving parties, and it can be used to elicit change in current practices or ideas. This chapter also provides a framework for the evolution of disputes and their formal resolution. There are different stages in the evolution of disputes. Persons investigating this evolution are concerned with developing a conceptual framework in order to better understand which disputes will reach the courts for formal resolution. Different types of law are also described—substantive versus procedural law, common law, civil law, administrative law, and criminal law. Another section describes some of the more important contributions of sociolegal scholars like Oliver Wendell Holmes, Roscoe Pound, Karl Llewellyn, and Roberto Unger, as well as some feminist legal theorists who have investigated the interplay between law and society. Finally, some theoretical perspectives related to court decision-making processes and practices are offered.

▶ What Is Law?

law the body of rules of specific conduct, prescribed by existing, legitimate authority in a particular jurisdiction and at a particular point in time.

Law is a set of rules defining behavior for a particular place and at a particular time. Law has been argued by some as an expression of the needs of the ruling class. Depending on your particular view of the legal system, law might be perceived as either liberating or oppressive, preserving the *status quo*, or providing the means and opportunity to challenge the existing social order. Law has been used to both perpetuate and eliminate slavery, dominate and liberate women, and convict and acquit the innocent. Law is related closely to all of these different definitions (Vago 2006).

The *Dred Scott* Case and the Law

The role of law was very apparent in the *Dred Scott* case, in which the slavery issue was challenged. This case was more about citizenship than slavery. Dred Scott was the slave of an army officer. The officer took Scott from Missouri, to Wisconsin, and eventually to Illinois. When Scott returned to Missouri, he claimed that he was no longer a slave because slavery was not recognized in either Wisconsin or Illinois. Therefore, an important constitutional question arose as to whether citizenship and freedom were vested in former slaves as the result of their relocating in states where slavery was prohibited. The U.S. Supreme Court heard and decided the case in 1857. Recognizing the rights of individual states, the U.S. Supreme Court held that citizenship was not a federal issue. Rather, the issue of slavery was to be determined by the individual states. Thus, according to this decision, Dred Scott was still considered a slave, since the U.S. Supreme Court chose not to interfere in states' rights. This decision encouraged antislave activists to make federal citizenship take priority over state citizenship. Subsequently, the efforts of these antislave activists resulted in the ratification of the Fourteenth Amendment. The Fourteenth Amendment established the primacy of federal citizenship and became the foundation by which many legal and social issues have been addressed by the U.S. Supreme Court (Vago 2006).

The Courts and the Criminal Justice System

Crime has been considered to be a major problem in society for some time and has been the focus of numerous government efforts throughout the history of the United States.

Even though crime, especially violent crime, has declined in the past three decades, crime and the criminal justice system still eat up a large portion of federal and state budgets. The cost for public safety in communities around the country as well as for incarcerating those who have been convicted of violating the law continues to rise, forcing many jurisdictions around the nation to rethink the administration of justice. Indeed, the criminal justice system is a major institution in society and is generally thought of as being made up of three entities: the police, the courts, and corrections. Of course, many more agencies and entities are involved in criminal justice, from bail bonding companies to substance abuse and mental health treatment providers, who all play important roles in ensuring that the system continues to operate. There is also interdependence among the agencies involved in the criminal justice system even though each entity's goals, objectives, and responsibilities might be different. The courts play a critical role in the criminal justice system because actions by the police and corrections agencies require, or are the result of, actions from the courts. Likewise, actions by the courts may be influenced by processes that the police and corrections undertake or implement. In this sense, the criminal justice system is a system that is codependent on the entities and actors involved for its continued functioning.

On the other hand, one could argue that the criminal justice system is very disjointed. The police, courts, and corrections rely on each other to do their jobs; however, there is no articulated coordination among them, and each has its own large hierarchical organization that is bureaucratic in nature. Each makes decisions that will affect its own workload and implements rules and procedures to achieve its particular goals. Each also competes for resources from the government and local counties and municipalities. Resources are usually in limited supply and each has to justify requests for increasing budgets. Police agencies want more police officers, courts want more prosecutors and judges, and corrections wants more jail and prison guards, and probation and parole officers.

Oftentimes, these fights are more political than logical or need-based. Since the terrorist attacks in 2001, for example, an increasingly larger share of the crime and justice budget has gone to law enforcement to combat terrorism and other crimes that fund criminal organizations. Meanwhile, many districts at the federal level are in need of increased numbers of judges, and many judgeships sit vacant as Congress is not moving to confirm the President's nominations. Funding for prisons and incarceration is also being reduced as many jurisdictions around the country are realizing the effects of an increased incarceration population and lengthy prison sentences. The get-tough movement and crime control era of the late 1980s and 1990s saw increasingly harsh and even draconian sentences meted out by the courts (truth in sentencing, three strikes, mandatory minimums, and habitual offender statutes are just a few of the tools that were enacted and utilized in an effort to curb crime by increasing punishment). This meant an exploding prison population, and now a recognition that incarceration is expensive, and not that effective, with recidivism rates somewhere around 66 percent for those released from prison. Now many jurisdictions are rethinking their responses to certain offenses, and increasingly using diversion, alternative dispute resolution, and treatment for certain offenders. As the focus of how to respond to crime shifts, so do the courts. Many jurisdictions now have several specialty, or problem-solving, courts to process certain types of cases or offenders as an alternative to traditional criminal court case processing.

The public has also become increasingly distrustful of the amount of tax dollars that are being spent by the criminal justice system with seemingly little effect on future crime and public safety. Criticisms of the way the criminal justice system operates and functions are nothing new, and have focused on one or more of the different components at different times. Although the current focus of criticisms is on discretion and its use and misuse and abuse by law enforcement, for the previous 25 years it was focused on the courts. Namely, judges and their wide-ranging discretion to hand out punishments that they deemed appropriate were the focus of major reforms at both the federal and state court levels. Prosecutors have also been the recipients of much scrutiny aimed at the great deal of power they hold as the gatekeepers of the criminal justice system and their wide-ranging discretion over liberty, and in some cases, life.

Courts have also been a very political subject regarding the extent to which they make decisions that intrude on the lives of the citizenry; critics have accused some judges of legislating from the bench. Some recent SCOTUS (Supreme Court of the United States) decisions give examples of decisions that have an impact on society. For example, in *Evenwel v. Abbott*, the court decided that under the Equal Protection Clause of the Fourteenth Amendment, states can draw their legislative districts based on population, and in *Fischer v. The University of Texas*, the court decided that using race as a factor in the University's admission process did not violate the Fourteenth Amendment's Equal Protection Clause. In *Holt v. Hobbs*, the court decided that a restriction against prisoners growing beards violated inmates' rights to exercise their religion, and in *Obergefell v. Hodges*, the court decided that states were required to license and recognize same-sex marriages under the Fourteenth Amendment. All of these decisions will have some effect on people and what they can and cannot legally do in society. Often, these decisions also affect how some aspect of the criminal justice system will operate.

Determining precisely what the law should and should not be has proved to be elusive. Adamson Hoebel (1954) has said that seeking a precise definition of law is like the quest for the Holy Grail. Legislators, prosecutors, defense attorneys, judges, defendants, businesspersons, consumers, parents, students, priests, the wealthy, and the poor all have different perspectives about what the law is and how it should be applied. Despite these diverse views of the law, there are several fundamental assumptions about the functions of law.

▶ The Functions of Law

Various legal scholars have studied the functions of law in different social systems and at different points in time. Their many observations about the functions of law can be classified as (1) social control, (2) dispute resolution, and (3) social change.

Social Control

> **social control** informal and formal methods of getting members of society to conform to existing norms.

Social control consists of efforts by society to regulate the behavior of its members. The most visible form of social control is the application of the law (e.g., being arrested, prosecuted, and sentenced). For most citizens, this method of control is often the subject matter of the evening news and only happens to other people who they believe deserve to be controlled by the state. We seldom realize that we are subject to these same social controls in our daily lives.

Legal scholars distinguish between informal and formal social controls. Informal social controls are an integral feature of the socialization process. From early childhood, we are constantly taught the norms of behavior that our parents and the social world expect of us. These norms are a product of cultural expectations regarding dress, language, and behavior and our biological capacity to comprehend and adapt to these expectations. These informal social controls are effective because we are rewarded or punished by people who are important to us. Such persons are known as significant others in our lives. Parents, teachers, and even friends and acquaintances are essential in developing a person's sense of right or wrong and will ultimately guide and form our future behaviors. It is through a system of rewards and punishments that these informal social controls become the tools that stop most people from engaging in behavior that would require invoking formal social control mechanisms. Formal social controls include the police, the courts, and corrections. The formal social controls most people think of include being arrested by the police and being prosecuted, convicted, and sentenced by the courts. For most citizens, these formal social control mechanisms will never have to be utilized. This is because informal social controls and the socialization processes they foment are enough to keep most citizens law abiding.

Dispute Resolution

A second function of law is dispute resolution. Persons frequently engage in disputes with others. Spouses might disagree about the division of labor in their household. Employees may disagree with their employers about their work effectiveness and quality. Sometimes, disagreements occur among total strangers about how to drive on the interstate highways or how we or our children should behave in shopping centers or stores. Historically, persons involved in disputes have relied on informal methods for dispute resolution. In colonial times, families or individuals relied on their village elders to settle disputes. Not so long ago, disputes about many issues were considered private matters settled in nonlegal ways. In more recent decades, informal nonlegal resolutions of disputes have changed considerably. Increasingly, disputants rely on the legal system to resolve issues that once were settled privately. A major change in our social dynamics is largely responsible for this shift. Informal methods for dispute resolution used to be more effective in small, closely knit homogeneous societies. Often, the members of these communities were more closely related either through family ties or economically. Therefore, disputes were quite disruptive to the stability of the community and had to be resolved quickly. It was not deemed necessary to use legal means for resolving disputes because these disputes rarely rose to such formal levels.

> **dispute resolution** civil action intended to resolve conflicts between two parties.

> **disputants** opposing sides in a civil action or case.

One additional benefit of nonlegal methods to resolve disputes is that agreements are usually reached that are satisfactory to both parties. In traditional courtroom litigation, legal dispute resolution results in winners and losers. One side is usually dissatisfied with whatever decision was rendered, but tradition called for accepting that decision without further argument. However, as social systems became increasingly complex and heterogeneous, informal dispute resolution methods were less effective. There was no clear interdependence among the disputants, and the authority attempting to resolve the dispute was unclear. This social evolution generated more formal methods for dispute resolution, which gradually replaced less formal methods. Although formal, legal methods may settle the disputes to the satisfaction of the legal system, this doesn't necessarily mean that the dispute will never recur. It has been claimed, for instance, that a legal resolution of a conflict does not necessarily result in a reduction of tension or antagonism between the aggrieved parties (Vago 2006, 20). However, it is unlikely that most disputes are ever fully resolved; rather, they are temporarily quelled but eventually are resurrected into new conflicts and disputes.

Social Change

Social change is another important function of law. Social change is the use of the law to modify ideas and practices, either actively or passively through natural forces or deliberate social actions. Law is the principal avenue through which social ills and biases are resolved. Legislative bodies are responsible for most of the laws that society abides by, but the courts have been the mechanism by which the law is put into practice. In this sense, the judicial branch of the government plays an important part in the functioning of society. Judges decide what evidence will be admissible in court, and whether persons have violated the law. Circuit court and Supreme Court judges also produce social change with their legal decision making. Appellate court decisions decide correct interpretations and applications of the U.S. Constitution and other legal rules. Court rulings therefore sometimes establish precedents to which subsequent decisions must

> **social change** process whereby ideas and/or practices are modified either actively or passively or naturally.

adhere. These precedents then become the foundation for establishment or transformation of social policy. Under common law and the principle of *stare decisis*, decisions become law. *Stare decisis* literally means to stand by that which has been decided. This does not mean that all cases will be decided the same way, nor that a higher court cannot overturn the precedent. It simply means that courts will abide by the latest ruling on any given issue.

History is replete with examples of law used to effect social changes of various kinds. State legislatures continually implement new laws to change the existing social order. Legislative actions are diverse and change our lives in various ways. For instance, new laws passed by legislatures may require us to wear seat belts or pay increased taxes, may raise or lower the speed limit, or may declare new national holidays. Judges also create social change through their own interpretations of the law and how it should be applied. Thus, the precedents established by judges have formed the bases of changes in various social policies. These changes are the functional equivalent of law-making. Legislators regard this activity as judicial activism and are opposed to it, since they believe that legislatures, not the judiciary, should have the exclusive authority to make law. Beyond this, law is also a method by which to initiate broader societal changes. These processes demonstrate that the relationship between the law and the citizenry is not static but rather dynamic, and that social change arises out of continual iterations of policy and practice.

> **judicial activism**
> judges' use of their
> power to accomplish
> social goals.

▶ The Evolution of Disputes

Disputes occur frequently, perhaps many times a day among individuals. We may have disputes with our spouses, children, coworkers, and bosses; however, we rarely rely on the legal system to resolve or settle these types of disputes. It is important to realize that many disputes follow particular patterns, and that a process for seeking legal remedies occurs only when several important factors converge. Some researchers have conceptualized the dispute process as consisting of various stages.

Naming, Blaming, and Claiming

Felstiner, Abel, and Sarat (1980) identify three stages in the evolution of disputes: (1) naming, (2) blaming, and (3) claiming. These researchers were concerned with developing a conceptual framework to understand the evolution of disputes before they reach the courts for formalized resolution. Their view of disputes starts with classifying injuries into either perceived or unperceived. For instance, sometimes we are victimized or injured but aren't aware that we have been victimized or suffering any loss or injury. If we never realize we have been victimized, then we cannot consider bringing a dispute. Have you ever wondered why all of the gasoline prices are the same in your neighborhood? Perhaps this reflects a free and open market where competition has driven gas prices down as far as the local market forces can sustain. Or maybe, all of the gas station owners have secretly conspired to set fuel prices at fixed levels so that they can all benefit from higher prices. The point is that you never know when this situation actually occurs and whether you are being victimized. Each time you refuel your vehicle, you may be benefitting from the free-market system, or you may be being victimized through price-fixing. Thus, you may be the unwitting victim of a crime. When this occurs, even though you are a victim, no dispute arises. However, when you are able to identify yourself as a victim through naming, this is the first stage in formulating a legitimate dispute. The second stage in the dispute process is blaming. This stage involves translating your victimization into a formal grievance. In order for this event to occur, you must blame someone else for your victimization. For example, smokers move from naming to

> **naming** identifying a
> party in a legal action.

> **blaming** a step in the
> dispute process whereby
> the victim singles out
> someone as a potential
> target for legal action.

blaming when they allege that the tobacco companies have failed to inform them about the hazards of smoking. The final stage in the formulation of disputes is claiming. This occurs whenever victims believe that they have been injured, have identified a particular victimizer (someone to blame), and formally express a grievance against the person or organization responsible for their victimization. In most cases, victims seek monetary remedies. These claims ultimately evolve into disputes when the claim is initially rejected by another person or an organization. Not surprisingly, most disputes do not result into formal lawsuits. Most injuries are never perceived, and if they are, it is difficult to identify a particular victimizer. Therefore, the courts are faced with and address only a small fraction of the disputes that evolve into formal complaints and where those involved seek legal remedies.

A similar typology of disputes has been developed by Nader and Todd (1978) and Nader (1979). Like Felstiner, Abel, and Sarat (1980), Nader and Todd describe three stages in the dispute process: (1) the grievance or pre-conflict stage, (2) the conflict stage, and (3) the dispute stage. The grievance or pre-conflict stage requires that individuals or groups must perceive that they have been involved in an unfair or unjust situation. If the grievance is not resolved at this stage, then it progresses to a conflict stage where the victims confront the party they believe is the cause of their victimization. The dispute fully evolves when it reaches the dispute stage and the dispute is made public.

▶ Types of Law

Typologies of law are both important and necessary. Law varies according to who prosecutes, the nature and types of existing penalties, and a law's particular historical origins. A broadly applicable typology is difficult to develop that includes all types of law. A common distinction is made between substantive law and procedural law.

Substantive Law

Substantive law is the law in books. Substantive law is what the law says. Basically, this is the compilation of local, state, and federal laws created by legislatures. A law exists that defines when someone is under the influence of alcohol when operating a motor vehicle. All states now have .08 BAC as the intoxication standard. Thus, if a motorist has a BAC of .08 or higher, then the motorist is legally intoxicated. If the motorist has a BAC level of .07 or lower, then the motorist is not legally intoxicated. Persons who take money from others by force commit robbery. If they use a dangerous weapon in order to take money from others by force, they commit armed robbery. Laws exist that define these and other criminal acts. Many additional laws combine to form the substance of substantive law.

Procedural Law

Procedural law or the process of law pertains to how the law is applied. Procedural law is also called the law in action. Procedural law specifies how police officers must obtain and execute a search warrant. It also details how witnesses should be sworn when testifying in court, how evidence should be admitted in the courtroom, and how jurors should return their verdicts.

For example, Rule 4(b)(1) of the Federal Rules of Criminal Procedure regarding warrants states that a warrant must:

(A) contain the defendant's name or, if it is unknown, a name or description by which the defendant can be identified with reasonable certainty; (B) describe the offense charged in

claiming the process in a dispute where a grievance is expressed and a cause of action is cited.

grievance, grievance procedure formalized arrangements whereby institutionalized individuals have the opportunity to register complaints about the conditions of their confinement.

pre-conflict stage perception by individuals or groups that they are involved in a conflict situation where a legal resolution is sought.

conflict stage either a pretrial or an alternative dispute resolution phase where a plaintiff and a defendant confront one another and an accusation is made.

dispute stage public revelation of a dispute by filing of a legal action.

substantive law body of law that defines and prescribes the rights and obligations of each person in society.

procedural law rules that specify how the law should be implemented and applied against those who violate the law.

the complaint; (C) command that the defendant be arrested and brought without unnecessary delay before a magistrate judge or, if none is reasonably available, before a state or local judicial officer; and (D) be signed by a judge.

And, Rule 31, related to jury verdict, states:

(a) Return. The jury must return its verdict to a judge in open court. The verdict must be unanimous.

(b) Partial Verdicts, Mistrial, and Retrial.
    (1) *Multiple Defendants.* If there are multiple defendants, the jury may return a verdict at any time during its deliberations as to any defendant about whom it has agreed.
    (2) *Multiple Counts.* If the jury cannot agree on all counts as to any defendant, the jury may return a verdict on those counts on which it has agreed.
    (3) *Mistrial and Retrial.* If the jury cannot agree on a verdict on one or more counts, the court may declare a mistrial on those counts. The government may retry any defendant on any count on which the jury could not agree.

(c) Lesser Offense or Attempt. A defendant may be found guilty of any of the following:
    (1) an offense necessarily included in the offense charged;
    (2) an attempt to commit the offense charged; or
    (3) an attempt to commit an offense necessarily included in the offense charged, if the attempt is an offense in its own right.

(d) Jury Poll. After a verdict is returned but before the jury is discharged, the court must on a party's request, or may on its own, poll the jurors individually. If the poll reveals a lack of unanimity, the court may direct the jury to deliberate further or may declare a mistrial and discharge the jury.

Common Law

common law laws determined by judges in accordance with their rulings.

Another type of law is **common law**. Common law is whatever is prevalent, traditional, or customary in a given jurisdiction. It is the law of precedent. There are no specific statutes that govern particular situations. Judges decide cases by common law on the basis of whatever is customary or traditional, not what is written down or codified.

Common law originated in England. Common law is judicially created law compared with law made by legislatures. English judges would travel to different cities and towns and decide cases on their circuits. Their decisions and the sentences they imposed were a combination of existing precedent and local custom. Because customs vary, common law varies among jurisdictions. For example, a judge in one jurisdiction may find that local residents are very tolerant of political dissent. If a defendant is arrested and charged with political dissent in this jurisdiction, it may be customary for the judge to impose a lenient sentence. The judge will probably not impose a harsh sentence because the citizenry would oppose it. However, in another jurisdiction where political dissension is unpopular, a judge might impose a harsh sentence upon a political dissident and have substantial community approval.

Although American society has become formalized and the laws at all jurisdictional levels are largely codified, it is not the case that common law has ceased to exist. In the United States, more than a few jurisdictions have common law and utilize it. Also, they might supplement their common law with codified statutory law. For example, many urban areas do not condone prostitution, although some prostitution exists and is accepted informally. There is a certain area of town where prostitution exists. If prostitutes are arrested, they are fined a nominal amount and are soon back on the street engaging in more prostitution. In many rural areas of the United States, prostitution might be treated quite

BOX 1-1

LEGAL ISSUES: COMMON LAW IN ACTION

The Case of Ghen, the Whale Hunter

It happened in Massachusetts Bay. A whale hunter, Ghen, shot a whale with a bomb lance off the coast and the whale swam away and died about 25 miles from where it had been shot. Rich, a wandering beachcomber, came upon the dead whale lying on the beach. He stripped the blubber from the beached whale and converted the fat to oil, which he later sold at a nearby market. Subsequently, he bragged about his luck to others, and eventually, word reached Ghen about where his whale had gone. Ghen tracked down Rich and accused him of converting the whale remains for profit, thus denying Ghen any revenue from the whale he had shot. Rich refused to turn over the money he had received from the whale remains, arguing that he had found the whale, didn't know it was someone else's property, and did a lot of work converting the remains to fat. Ghen sued Rich, seeking to recover damages.

An interesting case was presented to the presiding judge. In the Cape Cod area, there were *no laws* governing whale rights. However, it was customary for those finding whales to alert the whale hunters where the whale had washed ashore so that the whale hunters could obtain the blubber and make valuable oil from the remains. The bomb lances used by different whalers were thus marked distinctively, so that anyone familiar with whaling knew whose lance it was and, thus, who owned the whale. In Massachusetts, the custom was that the original whale hunter who shot a whale possessed it through a type of ownership, regardless of where the whale eventually swam or washed ashore. When Rich found the beached whale, he either knew or should have known the proper procedure to follow regarding turning the whale remains over to the rightful owner. In this case, he ignored custom and precedent and converted the whale remains for his own benefit. Thus, the judge ruled against Rich and in favor of Ghen, who was subsequently reimbursed for his loss by Rich.

The Case of Bradbury's Dead Sister

Bradbury lived in a large two-story building with his sister, Harriet, in a Maine community. During a particularly severe winter, his sister became ill and died in the apartment. Bradbury had little money and could not afford to pay for a funeral for his sister. Therefore, he concluded, he could dispose of his sister in the large apartment house furnace in the basement. He dragged her body to the basement, where he cremated it in the large furnace. Neighbors detected a foul odor and called police, who investigated. They determined what Bradbury had done and arrested him. At the time, there was no law or written statute prohibiting anyone from disposing of a dead body in an apartment furnace. However, the court determined that Bradbury had violated the common law, which spoke against indecent burials of dead bodies. The fact that Bradbury had indecently disposed of his sister's body and had not given her a decent Christian burial was sufficient to find him in violation of the prevailing common law.

In both the *Ghen* and *Bradbury* cases, no statutes existed during those times that prohibited the specific conduct described. In both cases, judges decided these matters strictly on the basis of prevailing precedent established by common agreement through common law. Today, in the United States, many states continue to have common laws, although statutory law has replaced much of it. At the federal level, there is no common law anymore, replaced entirely by statutory law.

Electra Kay-Smith/Fotolia

Sources: From *Ghen v. Rich*, 8 F. 159 (1881) and *State v. Bradbury*, 136 Me. 347 (1939).

differently. If police arrested a prostitute, the prosecutor would be expected by the community to pursue the case against the prostitute as a serious crime. Therefore, certain crimes vary in their seriousness according to jurisdictional variations and prevailing customs and definitions of criminal conduct.

Civil Law

civil law all state and federal law pertaining to noncriminal activities, law that pertains to private rights and remedies.

Civil law originated in ancient Roman law. Contrasted with common law, civil law stresses codification. Early civil law existed as compilations of rules and laws that were made under the emperor Justinian. Rather than rely on local custom to resolve disputes, common-law judges would refer to the written law when deciding cases. Civil law in America is used to resolve disputes between private parties. Unlike criminal law, the private party originates a case against another person or an organization rather than the prosecutor. The penalties sought are typically monetary. If one party is found to be at fault, damages are assessed. These damages are largely financial. Another feature of civil law is the standard of proof. In a civil case, the plaintiff must prove that the defendant was negligent by a preponderance of the evidence, which means more than 50 percent. Most Americans were made aware of this difference in the case of O. J. Simpson. While O. J. Simpson was acquitted of murder charges in a criminal case in California in 1995, subsequently he was found at fault in the wrongful deaths of his former wife, Nicole Brown Simpson, and a friend, Ronald Goldman, in the civil case that followed. The media attributed the different outcomes in the two trials to the different standards of proof required for criminal and civil cases. In O. J. Simpson's criminal case, the more difficult standard of beyond a reasonable doubt caused jurors to question the evidence against him and find him not guilty of the crimes. However, in the civil case that followed, another jury believed the plaintiffs who asserted that Simpson was responsible for the two deaths. In the latter case, Simpson's culpability was demonstrated according to the civil standard of the preponderance of evidence or weight of the evidence, not the criminal standard of beyond a reasonable doubt.

preponderance of the evidence civil standard whereby the greater weight of the information is in favor of or against the defendant.

beyond a reasonable doubt standard used in criminal courts to establish guilt of criminal defendant.

Criminal Law

For many citizens, the evening news on television is their primary source of information about how the criminal justice system operates. Television dramas such as *Law and Order*, *CSI*, and *N.Y.P.D. Blue* feature stories about the legal system and do much to shape our views about criminal law. We might see a story where an offender is sentenced in California to life in prison because he stole golf clubs, or a story where a serial sex offender released by a parole board subsequently commits a new sex crime. For most people, the efficacy of the justice system is measured by the sound application of criminal laws or the poor application of these laws.

criminal law body of law that defines criminal offenses and prescribes punishments (substantive law) and that delineates criminal procedure (procedural law).

Criminal law is differentiated from civil law according to the following criteria:

	Criminal law	Civil law
Who is the victim	State	Individual
Who prosecutes	State	Individual
Possible punishments	Fine, probation, or imprisonment	Monetary awards

In both civil and criminal laws, the victim is a person or class of persons, such as an aggregate of smokers, inmates in a jail or prison facility, or persons who use marijuana. However, in criminal law the offense is regarded as so disruptive to the social order that society as a whole is the nebulous victim. This is because under criminal law, society is considered harmed by someone's illegal actions. In civil law, someone is the victim and brings suit against the victimizer. Punishments under criminal law are more severe than the punishments prescribed under civil law. Persons convicted of crimes may be fined and/or incarcerated. The most severe form of criminal punishment is the death penalty. In civil cases, however, victimizers who are found liable are not imprisoned or put to death. In most instances, they are obligated to compensate victims for their losses and suffering. These penalties are monetary judgments or awards for damages.

Again, the O. J. Simpson case demonstrates this difference. If Simpson had been convicted in that criminal case, he would have been sentenced to prison. In the subsequent civil case against him, Simpson was found liable and ordered to pay damages. He was ordered by the court to pay $25 million in punitive damages, which were intended to punish him for his conduct, and he was further ordered to pay $8.5 million in compensatory damages, which were intended to compensate the families of his victims for their pain and suffering.

Administrative Law

Administrative law are rules and regulations that administrative agencies have set up to govern procedures for organizational behavior. While the other forms of law may not directly affect us in our daily lives, administrative law is pervasive and affects all of us in various ways. There are over 50 federal regulatory agencies that promulgate and enforce a diverse array of regulations. Other administrative agencies exist at the state and local levels. The result is an overwhelming amount of bureaucratic control. When we travel on an airline, for example, we are subject to the administrative rules developed by the Federal Aviation Administration. The food and drugs we consume are approved and regulated by the Food and Drug Administration (FDA). When we telephone others, this communication is regulated by the Federal Communications Commission. If we purchase a house, our actions are influenced by interest rates, which are indirectly related to the actions of the Federal Reserve.

> **administrative law** the body of laws, rules, orders, and regulations created by an administrative agency.

An interesting example of the high degree of governmental regulation and control is given by Vago (2006). Vago indicates that a couple may be awakened by the buzz of an electronic clock or perhaps by a clock radio. This signals the beginning of a highly regulated existence for them. The clock or radio that wakes them is run by electricity provided by a utility company, regulated by the Federal Energy Regulatory Commission and by the state utility agencies. They listen to the weather report generated by the National Weather Service, part of the Commerce Department. When they go to the bathroom, they use products, such as mouthwash and toothpaste, made by companies regulated by the FDA. The husband might lose his temper trying to open a bottle of aspirin with a childproof cap, required by the Consumer Product Safety Commission (CPSC). In the kitchen, the wife reaches for a box of cereal containing food processed by a firm subject to the regulations of the United States Department of Agriculture (USDA) and required to label its products under regulations of the Federal Trade Commission (FTC). When they get into their car to go to work, they are reminded by a buzzer to fasten their seat belts, compliments of the National Highway Traffic Safety Administration. They paid slightly more for their car than they wanted to, because it contains a catalytic converter and other devices stipulated by the Environmental Protection Agency (EPA) (Vago 2006, 123–124).

▶ Sociolegal Perspectives and the Law

Just as there are various types of law, there are also many perspectives about the interaction between society and law. The analysis of the interaction of law and society has its early American roots in the writings of Oliver Wendell Holmes Jr., Louis Brandeis, and Roscoe

Pound. These authorities were among the first to criticize classical jurisprudence. Classical jurisprudence was concerned with applying a strict interpretation and application of the law. This formal and mechanical method of jurisprudence did not permit the courts to effect changes in social policy. Holmes, Brandeis, and Pound believed that law should be active and dynamic and useful for changing the social order. The perspective on law proposed by these authorities is sociological jurisprudence.

Sociological Jurisprudence

sociological jurisprudence view that holds that a part of law should be devoted to making or shaping public policy and social rules.

Sociological jurisprudence indicates that a part of law should concern itself with making social or public policy. Today this legal agenda is called judicial activism. Oliver Wendell Holmes believed that law should be responsive to and incorporate changing social conditions, although the legislature should remain the primary method of social change. Holmes said that "for the rational study of the law the black letter man may be seen as the man of the present, but the man of the future is the man of statistics and the master of economics" (Holmes 1897, 457). This statement suggests that law and/or judges should acknowledge and utilize social science to further develop and answer legally relevant questions.

The first person to use social science in litigation was Louis Brandeis. Brandeis embraced sociological jurisprudence and utilized social science to win cases. He often incorporated social science results into briefs to the court to bolster his arguments. One noteworthy case was *Muller v. Oregon* (1908), which involved a dispute about the working hours of women. Two years earlier, the case of *Lochner v. New York* (1905) was decided by the U.S. Supreme Court. The Court declared a statute unconstitutional that limited working hours to 60 per week. Aware of this case and holding, Brandeis believed that he had to show that it was harmful for women to work more than 60 hours per week. To substantiate his claim, Brandeis wrote a brief that included statements arguing that women were deleteriously affected by long hours of work. Brandeis used a variety of sources from labor statistics and statements from international conferences about labor legislation as his scientific sources. Dr. Theodore Wely has added that women bear the following generation whose health is essentially influenced by that of the mothers, and the state has a vital interest in securing itself for future generations capable of living and maintaining it (Wely 1904).

Breckenridge supported this sentiment by suggesting that the assumption of control over the conditions under which industrial women are employed is one of the most significant features of legislative policy. In many advanced industrial countries, the state not only prescribes minimum standards of decency, safety, and health, but also specifies minimal limits for wage earners. The state also takes cognizance of several ways for distinguishing sex differences and sex relationships. Furthermore, the state sometimes takes cognizance of the peculiarly close relationship that exists between the health of its women citizens and the physical vigor of future generations. It has been declared a matter of public concern that no group of its women workers should be allowed to unfit themselves, by excessive hours of work, by standing, or by other physical strain, for the burden of motherhood, which each of them should be able to assume. He adds that the object of such control is the protection of the physical well-being of the community by setting a limit to the exploitation of the improvident, unworkmanlike, unorganized women who are yet to be mothers, actual or prospective, of the coming generation (Breckenridge 1906).

The U.S. Supreme Court was persuaded by this argument and held that the adverse effects of women working long hours were detrimental to the public interest. There is no doubt that the justices of the U.S. Supreme Court were influenced by the social science evidence provided by Brandeis in his brief. The Court reasoned in *Muller* that a woman's physical structure and the performance of maternal functions place her at a disadvantage in the struggle for subsistence is obvious. This is especially true when the burdens of motherhood are upon her. Even when they are not, by abundant testimony of the medical fraternity, continuance for a long time on her feet at work, repeating this from day to day, tends to have injurious effects on the body, and as healthy mothers are essential to vigorous offspring, the physical well-being of women becomes an object of public care in order to preserve the strength and vigor of the race (*Muller v. Oregon*, 1908).

Roscoe Pound elaborated on the purpose and goal of sociological jurisprudence in several of his essays. He recognized that law was not and could not be autonomous or influenced by social conditions. He wrote that the important part of our system is not the trial judge who dispenses justice to litigants, but rather the judge of the appellate court who uses the litigation as a means of developing the law (Pound 1912, 489). Pound developed five strategies by which sociolegal jurists could distinguish themselves from more traditional jurists. These strategies include the following:

1. They are looking more to the working of the law than to its abstract content.
2. They regard law as a social institution, which may be improved by intelligent human effort, and hold it their duty to discover the best means of furthering and directing such effort.
3. They stress upon the social purposes which law subserves rather than upon sanction.
4. They urge that legal precepts are to be regarded more as guides to results.
5. Their philosophical views are very diverse. (Pound 1912, 489–490)

These three legal scholars and practitioners represented a dramatic change in thinking about the law. They believed that classical jurisprudence and jurists should be the only ones to strictly apply existing law. These jurists believed that law and society were inextricably linked. One influenced the other. One was necessary for the other. Judges cognizant of or trained in sociological jurisprudence realized that one of the major functions of law was social change. Lawyers and jurists should apply law with the idea of fostering social change.

Legal Realism

Sociological jurisprudence provided the foundation for legal realism. This perspective is described in the early work of Karl Llewellyn (1931). Llewellyn had a broader agenda than his predecessors. He argued that law was dynamic and often inconsistent. Interestingly, the development of the National Reporter system published by West Publishing Company is believed to have contributed to this perspective. This is because the Reporter system disclosed that similar cases or existing legal precedents were actually applied or interpreted differently, depending upon the jurisdiction. Thus, it was that an appellate judge in California applied a particular legal precedent differently compared with how another appellate court judge in Texas applied the same legal precedent.

Karl Llewellyn also believed that the existing understanding of law was inadequate. He believed that law and society were constantly evolving. Realists also believed that law should be the means to a social end rather than an end in itself. Realists were distrustful of legal rules and the perspectives of rule formation. Rather, they were interested in determining the effects of law (Llewellyn 1931).

> **legal realism** views that law and society are constantly evolving and that law should be the means to a social end rather than an end in itself.

Critical Legal Studies

Critical legal studies is one of the most dynamic and controversial perspectives on law. This movement began with a group of junior faculty members and law students at Yale in the late 1960s. In 1977, the group organized itself into the Conference of Critical Legal

> **critical legal studies** movement recognizing that law is subjective rather than objective.

Studies, which presently has over 400 members and holds annual conferences that attract 1,000 or more participants (Vago 2006, 67).

The critical legal studies movement involves a thorough examination of the entire legal system. The theoretical underpinnings of critical legal studies are most often attributed to Roberto Unger. The critical legal studies movement had its origins in legal realism. Similarly, critical legal studies takes issue with formal rational law. Critical legal studies contends that we must recognize that the law is subjective rather than objective.

Critical legal scholars believe that law is not value-free. Essentially, these scholars believe that the law serves to preserve existing power relations in society. Law schools are structured to train students for hierarchy. In the classroom, students learn their social position during lectures. Law school teachers rely heavily on the Socratic method, whereby teachers ask students about different points of the law. The students, regardless of their responses, are always incorrect. The teacher relies on either lower or higher levels of abstraction to fit particular situations. Law schools justify this method because many law professors believe that it makes students think like lawyers. However, for many law school students, this process is a humiliating experience and serves to reinforce the hierarchy of law.

In order to remedy certain problems associated with acquiring a legal education, a radical restructuring of law school curricula and how law is taught is needed. In an ideal legal education, there would be few legal skills classes (e.g., learning legal rules and the categorization of cases), and the major focus in law school would be upon mastering social and political theory and an analysis of the existing social system (e.g., housing, welfare, and criminal justice).

Feminist Legal Theory

feminist legal studies views that women use a different type of logic than men when interpreting the law, favoring less litigation and more mediation.

Another perspective on the law has its origins in feminism. The diverse experiences of women and the law have evolved into various perspectives on the relationship between law and gender. The feminist's perspective of the law or feminist legal studies ranges from the radical to the pragmatic. Some feminists have examined how the law protects male interests. Some persons have argued that the law treats women as objects of men (Abrams 1995). Other feminists have examined how women have had an impact on the legal system. These investigations include research on the impact of women in law school and as attorneys (Chambers 1989) and as judges. The rationale for this view is that women reason differently from men, and therefore as lawyers and judges, women will use a different type of logic when applying the law. Women may be less adversarial and confrontational compared with men. This is quite possibly a positive result. The confrontational adversarial process has a winner and a loser. Women often express dissatisfaction with the win–lose nature of litigation because the real needs of the litigants are never addressed or accommodated. Rather, female lawyers might advocate a process involving less litigation and more mediation and fewer winner-take-all results (Menkel-Meadow 1986).

▶ Theoretical Perspectives of Criminal Court Decision-Making Practices

Decision-making practices of courtroom actors generally are viewed through two overarching theoretical perspectives. The first perspective posits that decisions are influenced primarily by the legally relevant factors in the case, such as the seriousness of the crime committed by the defendant and the defendant's prior criminal record. The idea that legally relevant factors are primary in the minds of prosecutors and judges when making decisions is referred to as formal rationality (Dixon 1995). This theoretical perspective purports that the formal legal rules guide outcomes in the criminal court system and extralegal factors, such as gender, race/ethnicity, and socioeconomic status of the defendant, will have no influence on court decisions. The second theoretical perspective posits that outcomes in criminal court decision-making practices are the product of influence from both legal and extralegal factors. Under this perspective, referred to as substantive rationality, courtroom actors may rely on stereotypes of dangerousness and risk of defendants that are linked to extralegal factors. Judges and prosecutors therefore make decisions using both legal and extralegal factors, such as gender, race, social class, or other social positions. The first theoretical perspective, formal rationality, would predict that a defendant's gender, race/ethnicity, or social class would not influence decisions by the courts. The second perspective would predict that a defendant's gender, race/ethnicity, and socioeconomic status would in some circumstances have an effect on decisions surrounding criminal court outcomes.

Courtroom outcomes and the decision-making processes of courtroom actors, however, are complex issues. At the outset, the court structure in the United States is somewhat confusing, and there is little uniformity among jurisdictions. The law and courts are very important institutions in society. They are the structures and the avenue through which social control is maintained and social change is achieved. Without the courts and rules of criminal procedure, the law could not function. These systems, however, are not perfect; there have been criticisms levied at all stages of legal processes and all members of the courtroom workgroup. Legal scholars and academics will continue to study and research the law, the courts, and their decision-making practices. The decisions that are made and the processes that are implemented will continue to be examined and scrutinized to ensure that procedural rules are adhered to, and due process rights are being fulfilled. This examination and scrutiny is important because a system of law and an organized court structure are essential to the democratic ideals of the U.S. society.

Summary

1. *Apply your knowledge of what the law is and the role that courts play in various facets of our daily lives.*

The law is a set of rules defining behavior for a particular place and at a particular time. The law can be perceived as either liberating or oppressive, preserving the *status quo*, or providing the means and opportunity to challenge the existing social order. Law has been used to both perpetuate and eliminate slavery, dominate and liberate women, and convict and acquit the innocent.

The courts play a critical role in the criminal justice system because both law enforcement and corrections rely on, or implement decisions from, the courts. In this sense, the courts are an important component to the functioning of the larger criminal justice system. Judges and prosecutors are also actors in the system who have a great deal of discretion. They are both very powerful actors in the U.S. criminal court system because of their wide-ranging discretion over liberty, and in some cases, life.

Courts have also been revered and criticized regarding the extent to which they make decisions that intrude on the lives of the citizenry. Courts have made decisions that have altered the status and role of many different groups in society. The law has operated directly and explicitly to prevent persons from attaining independence, and deprived them of formal legal remedies. The law has been used to redress inequalities through affirmative action, for example, which provides in part for fair and equitable hiring or promotion practices. Determining precisely how the law should enter society and the lives of citizens has proved to be elusive. Legislators, prosecutors, defense attorneys, judges, defendants, businesspersons, consumers, parents, students, priests, the wealthy, and the poor all have different perspectives about what the law is and how it should be applied.

2. *Compare and contrast the different functions of law, including social control, dispute resolution, and social change.*

Law has a variety of functions. Law is often used as a method of social control or to regulate our behavior. For instance, the law regulates whether or not females have the right to have an abortion, whether patients can use marijuana for medicinal purposes, and whether physicians can legally assist persons in ending their lives. When someone violates the law, the law is used as a method to punish them for their past behavior and to control their future behavior.

Another function of the law is dispute resolution. The law serves as a guide for resolving disputes. When there is a dispute, the law is often used to resolve that dispute. The law provides for rules of evidence and procedures that are employed to hear and process disputes. For example, the law resolves whether or not a person has violated a property law if their tree grows too far into a neighbor's yard; the law resolves whether or not a toy company has produced a faulty toy that has led to child injury and whether they are responsible to pay damages.

Another function of the law is social change. In the United States, the law is often used as an agent of social change. State legislatures are constantly passing laws to change the existing social order. For example, the legislature passes a law allowing narcotics users to sue their dealers, the legislators in various states amend their drinking and driving laws and lower the legal blood alcohol limit to .08, or the Supreme Court decides that the death penalty as administered is unconstitutional. Legislative action or law has changed how we perceive and react to various criminal offenses as a society.

3. *Understand the evolution of disputes and the formal resolution of them.*

Disputes occur frequently, and we can recognize that disputes follow particular patterns, and that a process for seeking legal remedies occurs only when several important factors converge. Some researchers have conceptualized the dispute process as consisting of various stages; for example, the evolution of disputes can be characterized by naming, blaming, and claiming. Naming involves identifying a party in a legal action, blaming is the stage where a victim singles out someone as a potential target for legal action, and claiming is filing of a formal grievance against the person or party responsible for victimization. Not surprisingly, most disputes do not result into formal lawsuits. Most injuries are never perceived, and if they are, it is difficult to identify a particular victimizer. Therefore, the courts are faced with and address only a small fraction of the disputes that evolve into formal complaints and where those involved seek legal remedies.

4. *Identify the difference between substantive law and procedural law.*

The law can be categorized as either substantive or procedural. Substantive laws are the laws on the books, the laws created by the legislature of federal and state governments and also by local authorities. Therefore, substantive law is what the law says. Procedural law, on the other hand, is the process of the law, how the law is applied. Procedural law is sometimes referred to as the law in action. It gives, for instance, officers guidelines on how to get a search warrant. It gives judges guidelines on evidence that is and is not admissible in court. It gives prosecutors and defense attorneys rules for selecting jurors for particular cases. Both substantive and procedural laws are typologies or classifications of the law that tell us what the laws are, as well as how they are to be implemented.

5. *Summarize the different types of law, including common law, civil law, and criminal and administrative laws.*

Four types of law were identified. Common law originated in England and was made by judges who traveled in circuits and dispensed justice according to the customs common to the region. For this reason, common laws vary in different jurisdictions. Although in recent years we have tried to make what violates law and the punishments for those violations more uniform, common law still exists. For example, in certain jurisdictions in the country, the punishment for prostitution may amount to what is thought of as a slap on the wrist, where a prostitute is basically arrested, required to pay a fine, and is released back to the street to again engage in prostitution. However, the punishment for a conviction of prostitution in another area of the country may involve aggressive prosecution of prostitutes to send a message and act as a deterrent to going back on the streets. It may depend on the prosecutor's agenda; it may depend on the sentiment from the community. How vigorously certain violations of law will be pursued depends on a number of things; the fact is that this is a form of common law that differs across jurisdictions.

Civil law is codified or written and documented. Civil law originated in ancient Roman law. Unlike common law, judges refer to the written law when deciding cases; these decisions then become law. Civil law is used for dispute resolution among private parties. The penalties are typically monetary, and are not crimes against the state. In civil law, there is also a different standard of proof to be held liable for your actions; it is by a preponderance of the evidence.

Criminal law is differentiated from other types of law in that the society as a whole is a victim, and the government brings charges against the accused when a criminal law is violated. Punishments under criminal law are more severe than those under civil law, and could include imprisonment. Those convicted have to be found guilty beyond a reasonable doubt as opposed to the preponderance of evidence standard in civil court.

Administrative law is the body of law, rules, orders, and regulations created by administrative agencies. Although we may not think about it too often, administrative law affects our lives almost daily. A number of regulatory agencies at both the federal and state levels exist and impose a lot of bureaucratic control on our lives. Every time you drive down the street, pick up prescriptions from the pharmacy, or take a flight to visit friends and relatives, there are various regulations that you, and others, are adhering to in order to ensure everyone's safety. When you drive your car, rules from the National Highway Traffic Safety Administration stipulate that you should fasten your seat belt and be sure your car has had a safety inspection. When you go to the pharmacy, rules from the FDA provide guidelines for how many pills to take and other drugs to avoid because of possible interaction effects. When you go to the airport, the Federal Aviation Administration mandates that certain items will not be allowed on aircraft. All in all, our daily lives are greatly affected by rules put forth by administrative agencies.

6. *Draw appropriate conclusions about the different sociolegal perspectives on law, such as sociological jurisprudence, legal realism, critical legal studies, and feminist legal theory.*

Another important aspect of law is how it is dynamic in that it interacts with society. Four perspectives were presented exploring this interaction. Sociological jurisprudence believes that law should be concerned with making social or public policy. Oliver Wendell Holmes and Roscoe Pound were avid proponents of this perspective and believed that the law cannot be uninfluenced by, and must be responsive to, existing social conditions. Legal realism believes that law should be the means to a social end. Karl Llewellyn believed that law and society were constantly evolving, and that we should be mindful of the effects of law. Critical legal studies is a rather controversial perspective in that it believes that the law is subjective, not objective, and therefore is not value-free. In other words, Roberto Unger and other proponents believed that the law was used as an instrument to preserve the existing power relations in society. Feminist legal theory purports that the law is used to protect male interests, or treats women as the objects of men. Feminist theorists believe that women apply a different logic to law, and that the law may better serve society if it was less adversarial and confrontational. Each of these offer different perspectives on the interaction between law and society.

Key Terms

administrative law *13*
beyond a reasonable doubt *12*
blaming *08*
civil law *12*
claiming *09*
common law *10*
conflict stage *09*
criminal law *12*
critical legal studies *15*

disputants *07*
dispute resolution *07*
dispute stage *09*
feminist legal studies *16*
grievance *09*
judicial activism *08*
law *04*
legal realism *15*
naming *08*

pre-conflict stage *09*
preponderance of the evidence *12*
procedural law *09*
social change *07*
social control *06*
sociological jurisprudence *14*
substantive law *09*

Critical Thinking Exercises

1. To date, numerous states have put a proposal for legalizing marijuana on the ballot before residents for a vote. Other states have decriminalized possession of marijuana in small amounts. As a public policy issue, do you think marijuana should be legalized? How much crime would be eliminated through the legalization of marijuana? What are some of the consequences of decriminalization or legalization for the

criminal justice system? Should the same decriminal-ization be applied to other substances, such as heroin and cocaine?

2. Many decisions from the court affect how persons in the criminal justice system perform their jobs. Oftentimes, court decisions have a broader impact on the lives of citizens, such as mandating that states abide by certain rules, or directing what types of policies certain entities and businesses can have in place. Recent Supreme Court decisions, for example, have required that all states must license and recognize same-sex marriages under the Four-teenth Amendment (*Obergefell v. Hodges*), and decided that the University of Texas' policy using race as a factor in admission decisions is permissi-ble under the Fourteenth Amendment's Equal Pro-tection Clause (*Fischer v. The University of Texas*). What do you think of the court having broad pow-ers to make decisions about what states must do and how entities such as universities can operate? Should states be able to decide what laws and rules and regulations they want to impose without fear of interference from the courts? Should universi-ties and other public institutions be able to form their own policies to conduct business? Or do you think that the courts should ensure uniformity of the law and policies across the states and other public institutions?

Case Study Decision-Making Exercise

You may not remember the name Jack Kevorkian, but he was a doctor who assisted people who wanted to end their lives. He was a longtime advocate for eutha-nasia, a practice of ending one's life when one has a terminal illness and is suffering from intense pain. If there is no hope for survival or a prolonged useful life, many patients in this condition want to end their pain and suffering in the most painless way possible. Kev-orkian supplied many terminally ill people with "sui-cide kits," and had to defend himself against various types of murder charges over the years. Many family members and the relatives of those who had terminated their lives with his assistance testified on his behalf. Living wills recorded on videotape from victims them-selves have supported Kevorkian's arguments that he was simply helping to alleviate the pain and suffering of terminally ill patients. Eventually, he was convicted of murder in 1999 in Michigan for his role in the assisted suicide of one victim. Subsequent to Kevorki-an's conviction, at least five states have passed some form of legislation allowing physician-assisted suicide in some form. What do you think? Do you believe that persons should be allowed to choose whether they live or die, if they are suffering from a terminally ill condi-tion and are suffering and in great pain? Should the courts play a role in determining whether individuals should be able to get assistance from doctors in termi-nating their lives? What do you think about the fact that this is legal or illegal varies by state? Should rules regarding something like this be uniform across the country? Is this a moral issue? How should this be resolved?

Concept Review Questions

1. What is law? What are two different types of law? Differentiate between each.
2. What was the significance of the *Dred Scott* case?
3. What roles do the courts play in the criminal justice system?
4. What are the three functions of law?
5. What is the significance of the view containing nam-ing, blaming, and claiming?
6. How does substantive law differ from procedural law? What do these different types of law govern? Explain.
7. What is common law? How do judges decide cases on the basis of common law?
8. What is meant by administrative law? Why is it important for social change?
9. What is sociological jurisprudence? How is sociolog-ical jurisprudence related to social change?
10. What is meant by legal realism? How does critical legal studies compare with legal realism?
11. How has feminism affected the development of law in the United States?

Suggested Readings

1. S. Barkan (2015). *Law and Society: An Introduction.* Routledge.
2. K. N. Llewellyn (2016). *The Common Law Tradition: Deciding Appeals* (Vol. 16). Quid Pro Books.
3. M. Arden (2015). *Common Law and Modern Society: Keeping Pace with Change.* Oxford University Press.
4. B. Leiter (2015). "Legal Realism and Legal Doctrine." *University of Pennsylvania Law Review*, University of Chicago, Public Law Working Paper No. 528. Available at SSRN: http://ssrn.com/abstract=2589327.
5. C. Sharp and M. Leiboff (eds.) (2015). *Cultural Legal Studies: Law's Popular Cultures and the Metamorphosis of Law.* Routledge.
6. M. D. Dubber (2014). "Critical Analysis of Law: Interdisciplinarity, Contextuality, and the Future of Legal Studies." *Critical Analysis of Law: An International & Interdisciplinary Law Review* 1:1.

2 The Structure of American Courts

LEARNING OBJECTIVES

As a result of reading this chapter, you will have accomplished the following objectives:

1 *Distinguish among the different ways to classify American courts, such as by jurisdiction, by its dual nature, and by type of court.*

2 *Recognize the different types of jurisdiction like subject matter, geographic, and hierarchical.*

3 *Explain how the United States has two court structures, a federal structure and a state structure.*

4 *Describe the difference between trial and appellate courts.*

5 *Compare and contrast the federal court structure, including, U.S. District Courts, U.S. Circuit Courts of Appeal, and the U.S. Supreme Court.*

6 *Summarize the state court structure, including courts of limited jurisdiction, courts of general jurisdiction, intermediate courts of appeal, and courts of last resort.*

Joe Garcia Espitia, who was charged in California with carjacking, rejected court-appointed counsel and elected to represent himself. As part of his case, he requested access to a law library while confined in jail prior to his trial, but these requests were denied. During his trial, he was allowed four hours of law library time just before closing arguments. He was found guilty and subsequently filed a federal *habeas corpus* motion declaring that his Sixth Amendment rights had been violated since he had been denied access to a law library. The district court rejected this appeal, but the court of appeals reversed stating that his Sixth Amendment rights were violated by denying him access to legal resources. The government appealed this appellate court decision and the U.S. Supreme Court decided to hear the case. In 2006, the U.S. Supreme Court reversed the court of appeals decision, holding that defendants do not have a clearly established right under federal law to access law libraries while they are in jail awaiting trial.

In another case, Jesse Montejo was arrested for murder and because he was indigent, he was given court-appointed counsel. Prior to meeting with his court-appointed attorney, however, Montejo gave his consent to be interrogated by police without his attorney present. The government used information from this interrogation against Montejo in court, and he was convicted. Montejo appealed that once he had been appointed an attorney, he could not be interrogated by police without that attorney. The Louisiana Supreme Court upheld the use of the interrogation evidence stating that Montejo consented to the interrogation and did not state that he wanted his counsel present. Montejo appealed to the Supreme Court and they upheld the Louisiana Supreme Court's decision stating that despite the fact that the government must ensure that defendants have waived their rights to counsel before interrogations take place, this does not mean that these interrogations cannot occur if a defendant has been appointed counsel but consents to interviews without them present.

How is it that in the above cases different courts made different decisions regarding the defendant or the case? How can one court say it is okay to deny access to legal resources such as a library or that it is okay to interrogate a defendant without the counsel being present and another court decide the opposite? Do different courts have jurisdiction over the same case, and can they over rule a previous court's decision? The structure of the U.S. court system is set up so that there is what is referred to as hierarchical jurisdiction. This means that certain courts have original jurisdiction to hear facts and try cases to determine guilt or innocence and other courts have appellate jurisdiction to determine whether or not an error was made, or whether the law was applied correctly by the lower court. Judges therefore at different courts utilize their understanding of constitutional and procedural laws to make these decisions. This process does not go on forever, most cases are not appealed, and those that are will eventually exhaust their right to appeal. The U.S. Supreme Court is the court of last resort for both the state and federal court systems, and although they hear very few cases, they have the final say in the cases that they do decide to hear.

▶ Introduction

The American court system is one of the most confusing systems in the world. In many countries, the court structure is a centralized system that is very uniform and easy to understand. For people from other parts of the world, the American public, and even students studying the American court system, it is difficult to understand the structure and operations of U.S. courts. There are 51 different court structures in the United States. Each state and the federal government have their own structure and process for resolving disputes and prosecuting criminals. Some states have indeterminate sentencing; others and the federal courts have determinate sentencing systems and sentencing guidelines. There are mandatory minimums, habitual offender statutes, and truth-in-sentencing laws in various jurisdictions that further complicate the U.S. system of courts and sentencing. Also, acquiring an awareness of only the state and federal court systems ignores other court systems, such as military tribunals, juvenile and family courts, probate courts, tribal courts, chancery courts, drug courts, and housing and land courts.

This chapter examines the structure of the American court system. It is beyond the scope of this book to list and describe all of the subtle differences of every type of court structure. Rather, this chapter will classify these court structures according to different jurisdictions and functions with the hope of providing students a better understanding of the American court system. This chapter will present three types of jurisdiction—geographic, subject matter, and hierarchical. The chapter also discusses the dual court system, meaning that in the United States, there is both a federal court structure and a state court structure. Finally, it will discuss the difference between trial courts and appellate courts, and the functions of each. The federal system is made up of U.S. District Courts, U.S. Circuit Courts of Appeal, and the U.S. Supreme Court. The state court system is characterized by courts of limited jurisdiction, courts of general jurisdiction, intermediate courts of appeal, and courts of last resort. We should not focus strictly on court names, however, since the meaning associated with a particular court name varies among counties and states. For example, it might be assumed that the Supreme Court is an appellate court of last resort at the state and federal levels. Most trial courts are called circuit courts or district courts. However, in New York, felony trials are within the purview of the Supreme Court. New York Supreme Courts are the functional equivalent of criminal courts in other states. They simply use the term "Supreme Court" for this type of court.

▶ Classifying America's Courts

One way of classifying American courts is by jurisdiction. Jurisdiction is the legal authority or power of a court to hear specific kinds of cases. Jurisdiction varies most often according to where the offense occurred, the seriousness of the offense, or whether the case is being heard for the first time or on appeal. There are three types of jurisdiction: (1) subject matter jurisdiction, (2) geographic jurisdiction, and (3) hierarchical jurisdiction.

Subject Matter Jurisdiction

Subject matter jurisdiction refers to the type of case the court has authority to hear. Usually, misdemeanors and preliminary hearings are processed or conducted by courts of limited jurisdiction. For example, if a person burglarizes a house and steals $499 worth of goods, the case typically will be heard by a court of limited jurisdiction (e.g., municipal court, city court, or county court). However, if the same person burglarizes the same house and steals $500 or more worth of goods, this case will likely be heard in a court of general jurisdiction (e.g., district court, circuit court, or superior court). Thus, the actual dollar value of property stolen determines whether the jurisdiction is limited or general. The greater the dollar value of property stolen, the more likely the case will be heard in a court of general jurisdiction. Courts of limited jurisdiction most often decide petty offenses where minor monetary sums are involved.

In many areas of the country, courts of limited jurisdiction are also responsible for processing the initial stages of felony cases. These courts usually issue warrants, conduct initial appearances, establish bail, and advise felony defendants of their rights and the charges they are facing, together with a date for a preliminary hearing to determine whether probable cause exists.

jurisdiction the power of a court to hear and determine a particular type of case.

subject matter jurisdiction the types of cases or crimes that a court has authority to hear.

limited jurisdiction court is restricted to handling certain types of cases such as probate matters or juvenile offenses.

general jurisdiction power of a court to hear a wide range of cases, both civil and criminal.

Geographic Jurisdiction

Geographic jurisdiction is determined by the political boundaries where the crime was committed. Geographic jurisdiction is the clearest type of jurisdiction to understand. A defendant's case will be heard by a court within the political boundary in which the offense occurred. If a crime is committed in a certain county, a county court will preside if there is a later trial. However, if the crime occurs in the city, then a city criminal court will preside. This, however, might also depend on the type of crime committed and which agency makes the arrest. In large cities, the sheriff's office and the city police department may both make arrests within the city limits that are within the county limits. There may also be federal agencies located in the city and county and the federal courts would also have geographic jurisdiction to hear a case where a federal crime was committed. Whether it is a county or state or federal offense might depend on the amount of money embezzled, and from which institution, or the amount of narcotics seized, for example. All three of these courts could hear the case as they would have jurisdiction but ultimately where the case is tried would depend on which agencies are involved. Often today local, state, and federal agencies work together in investigating certain types of crimes. If there is a lot of money taken or a large cache of drugs, it is likely that the federal courts would hear the case as the federal government has more resources and, in some cases, stiffer penalties. Thus, there are many geographic areas where court jurisdiction may be complex and overlapping compared with other jurisdictions.

There are other types of geographic jurisdiction besides the political boundaries of cities and counties. For instance, almost every Native American reservation and military base, fort, or installation is located within a particular state or territory. Thus, if someone commits a crime in Sequoia National Park in California, geography itself would seem to indicate that California would have jurisdiction. However, since Sequoia National Park is a federally protected area, the federal court has jurisdiction. Many offenses occurring in federally protected areas are heard by U.S. magistrates. Also, if a crime is committed by a military member on the premises of Lackland Air Force Base in Texas, it is not relevant that the crime has occurred within the geographic boundaries of Bexar County, Texas. Lackland Air Force Base is a federal military installation, and military police and courts will arrest, prosecute, and try criminal defendants. Texas state courts do not have jurisdiction in these cases, even though the land upon which the Air Base rests is centered within the geographical boundaries of Texas. Politically, the jurisdiction of Texas courts ends at the Air Force Base gates. To make this matter even more complex, if a crime is committed by a civilian on the Lackland Air Force Base, Federal District Court for the Western District of Texas would have jurisdiction over the case. In other words, the status of the offender (military or civilian) takes precedence over geographic jurisdiction.

Geographic jurisdiction may also be influenced by the perpetrator and victim (e.g., federal agent or federal property). For instance, in the case of *Morissette v. United States* (1952), Morissette, a civilian, was hunting deer one afternoon on a U.S. Army artillery range in Michigan. Although there were signs stating "Danger—Keep Out—Bombing Range," the area was known as good deer country and Morissette hunted there anyway. In the course of his hunting, he came across a number of spent copper bomb casings that appeared to be discarded. After a frustrating day of hunting, Morissette decided if he couldn't find a deer, he would offset some of his trip expenses by taking some of these casings and selling them for their copper value. He was arrested and charged with stealing U.S. government property. He was tried in federal district court and convicted, sentenced to imprisonment for two months, and fined $200. The U.S. Supreme Court reversed Morissette's conviction, holding that Morissette had no intention of committing a crime. Furthermore, he did not know that what he was doing was unlawful, and through his good

> **geographic jurisdiction** the power to hear particular kinds of cases depending upon the legally defined boundaries of cities, counties, or states.

character and openness in the taking of the casings, he demonstrated that his action was not deliberately criminal. It is significant here that Morissette's case was not heard in a military tribunal. This is because Morissette was a civilian and not subject to military law and sanctions. If the perpetrator had been a soldier in the U.S. Army, however, the soldier would have been tried by a military court for the criminal trespass offense.

Hierarchical Jurisdiction

Hierarchical jurisdiction is basically the difference between appellate and trial courts. Trial courts are often referred to as courts of fact, while appellate courts are referred to as courts of law. Trial courts are courts of fact because they are the forum where a judge or jury listens to the facts presented in the case and determines whether the defendant is guilty or not guilty. Trial courts are also responsible for sentencing the defendant. By contrast, appellate courts do not hear testimony or impose sentences. Appellate courts determine whether the law was applied correctly. For example, a trial court judge during the course of a trial may make many decisions regarding the admissibility of evidence and testimony. For each of these decisions, the judge relies on his or her understanding of constitutional and procedural laws. When a case is appealed, appellate court judges review whether trial court judges followed constitutional and procedural laws when they made their decisions. If the appellate court believes that the trial court followed these rules, the lower court's ruling will be upheld; if the trial court violated those rules, the lower court's ruling will be overturned and the case will be sent back down to the trial court for further action, such as a judge handing out a new sentence or a prosecutor deciding whether to retry the case.

▶ Federal Court Organization

Most courts in the United States trace their roots to the actions of colonists during the Constitutional Convention in the 1780s. Prior to the final vote on the Bill of Rights, convention delegates passed the Judiciary Act of 1789. Under the provisions of the Judiciary Act of 1789, three "tiers" of courts were created: (1) 13 federal district courts, each presided over by a district judge; (2) 3 higher-level circuit courts, each comprising two justices of the Supreme Court and one district judge; and (3) a Supreme Court, consisting of a chief justice and five associate justices.

The federal district courts were given jurisdiction in all civil and criminal cases. The circuit courts reviewed decisions of federal district courts, although they had some limited original jurisdiction. And finally, the Supreme Court was given jurisdiction that included the interpretation of federal legislation and balancing the interests between the state and the nation through the maintenance of the rights and duties of citizens. Figure 2-1 ■ shows the structure of the federal and state court systems.

The court system in the United States can be divided into two separate entities. One court system is at the federal level and consists of the U.S. Supreme Court, the U.S. Circuit Courts of Appeal, and the U.S. District Courts. The other court system is established through the authority of the states and consists of state and local courts. These court structures at the state and federal levels are referred to as a dual court system. In addition to adjudicating criminal cases, those in which a federal law violation has been alleged, the federal court system has the authority to hear cases identified by the Constitution. Article III, Section 2 of the Constitution identifies disputes that may be heard by federal courts. This includes cases in which the U.S. government or one of its officers is being sued. The Constitution also grants authority to the federal courts to hear cases, in the language of the Constitution, "Controversies between two or more states; between Citizens of

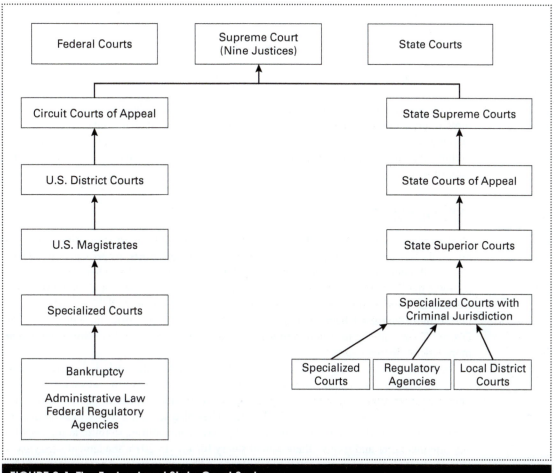

FIGURE 2-1 The Federal and State Court Systems

the same State claiming land under grants from other states." For example, one state might sue another state for importing hazardous waste. The case is heard at the federal level because the impartiality of the state courts in either state jurisdiction might be questioned.

The Constitution also extends federal court authority to hear cases involving counsels, ambassadors, and other public ministers. The federal courts are also authorized to hear cases involving laws enacted by Congress, treaties and laws related to maritime jurisdiction, and commerce on the high seas. Because of this authority, the federal courts often decide disputes involving interstate commerce. Congress has determined that some of these cases may also be heard by state courts, giving state and federal courts **concurrent jurisdiction**. An example is when a citizen from one state sues a citizen from another state. The case may be heard in the state courts or in a federal district court. However, the case will only be heard at the federal level if the amount of the dispute exceeds $75,000 (Title 28 U.S.C. §1332, 2007). Again, the amount of money involved in a dispute often determines which court will hear the case.

The federal courts therefore have a wide range of discretion and authority. Federal criminal courts decide whether someone has committed a crime and if so, what their punishment should be, and federal civil courts decide private disputes. Unbeknownst to many, the civil caseload actually comprises the majority of the federal court caseload.

dual court system a system consisting of a separate judicial structure for each state in addition to a national structure.

concurrent jurisdiction situation in which offender may be held accountable in several different jurisdictions simultaneously.

U.S. Magistrates

In 1968, Congress created the judicial office of federal magistrate. The magistrate's office was created to alleviate the workload of the U.S. District Court judges. In 1990, the position title was changed to magistrate judge. U.S. magistrate judges are appointed by the district judge and are assigned as either full-time or part-time magistrates depending on the caseload of the district court. Full-time magistrates are appointed to an eight-year term, whereas the terms of part-time magistrates are for four years.

Duties of the magistrate judge are similar to the duties of judges who serve in courts of limited jurisdiction at the state level. Magistrate judges hear disputes involving civil consent matters, misdemeanor trials, and the preliminary stages of felony cases, including preliminary hearing, pretrial motions, and conferences. In 2015, there were 536 full-time magistrate judges and 34 part-time magistrate judges.

U.S. magistrate judges judges who fulfill the pretrial judicial obligations of the federal courts.

U.S. District Courts

At the federal level, U.S. District Courts are courts of general jurisdiction. Most civil and criminal cases are tried and disposed of in the U.S. District Courts. Approximately 80 percent of all federal court cases are civil, while 20 percent are criminal. There are 94 district courts in the United States. Each state has at least one federal district court and these courts can also be found in the U.S. territories of Guam, Puerto Rico, the U.S. Virgin Islands, and the Northern Mariana Islands. Thirty-one states and the U.S. territories have only one U.S. District Court with the jurisdiction to hear federal cases. The remaining states have two or more federal district courts.

In 2015, there were 677 authorized federal judgeships in the 94 U.S. District Courts. As of the writing of this book, however, roughly 60 of these judgeships sat vacant awaiting Senate confirmation of individuals appointed by the president. Federal district judges are appointed by the president of the United States. They also serve life terms. Federal district judges who serve 10 or more years with good behavior are entitled to retire at their option anytime thereafter and receive their annual salary for life. In 2016, the annual salary for a U.S. District Court judge was roughly $200,000. Although judicial appointments are ideally made without regard to one's race, color, sex, religion, or national origin, these appointments are primarily political and reflect the interests and views of the president. The advice and consent of Congress is required for all such appointments. As such, in times when the political party of the sitting president and the political party that controls Congress are different, confirmations can be delayed despite the fact that well-qualified judges have been nominated for the federal judgeship that is vacant. As of the writing of this book, there were roughly 90 federal judicial vacancies with almost 60 of those positions having a nominee but due to a political gridlock in Congress, most are yet unconfirmed, including a nominee to fill a Supreme Court vacancy left by the death of Justice Antonin Scalia.

Criminal cases heard in federal district courts are commenced in the same way as cases are commenced in local and state courts. Federal law enforcement officers arrest suspects directly, or federal grand juries or federal prosecutors may issue indictments, presentments, or criminal informations against defendants. These defendants appear before magistrates where their bonds are established or where they are released on their own recognizance. Arraignment proceedings at the federal level are conducted in district courts by federal judges. Since arraignments include the entry of a plea by criminal defendants and the determination of a trial date, federal judges and their staffs can best determine an appropriate trial date because of the schedule of events on the federal court docket or calendar.

Again, federal judgeships are lifetime appointments. There is no mandatory retirement age, and federal district court judges may serve as long as they desire. This provision

U.S. District Courts the basic trial courts for federal civil and criminal actions.

TABLE 2-1 The 13 Judicial Circuits, Composition, and Number of Circuit Judges

Circuits	Composition	Number of circuit judges
District of Columbia	District of Columbia	11
First	Maine, Massachusetts, New Hampshire, Puerto Rico, Rhode Island	6
Second	Connecticut, New York, Vermont	13
Third	Delaware, New Jersey, Pennsylvania, Virgin Islands	14
Fourth	Maryland, North Carolina, South Carolina, Virginia, West Virginia	15
Fifth	Canal Zone, Louisiana, Mississippi, Texas	17
Sixth	Kentucky, Michigan, Ohio, Tennessee	16
Seventh	Illinois, Indiana, Wisconsin	11
Eighth	Arkansas, Iowa, Minnesota, Missouri, Nebraska, North Dakota, South Dakota	11
Ninth	Alaska, Arizona, California, Idaho, Montana, Nevada, Guam, Oregon, Washington, Hawaii	29
Tenth	Colorado, Kansas, New Mexico, Oklahoma, Utah, Wyoming	12
Eleventh	Alabama, Florida, Georgia	12
Federal	All Federal Judicial Districts	12
Total		179

Source: For more information, visit www.uscourts.gov and search for judgeships.

provides for an independent judiciary and allows judges to make decisions without the threat of being removed from office.

U.S. Circuit Courts of Appeal

In the early years of the United States, there were only three circuit courts of the United States without any permanent personnel. Two Supreme Court justices and a federal district judge comprised the transient judiciary of the circuit courts. These judges were called circuit riders. These judges were obligated to hold 28 courts per year. This created considerable hardship because transportation was poor and it was difficult to travel great distances. Furthermore, since federal district judges were a part of the original circuit judiciary, this placed them in the prejudicial position of reviewing their own decisions.

Over the next two centuries, numerous changes occurred in circuit court structure. Several reforms such as the Judiciary Act of 1891 or the Evarts Act were introduced to create what is the current scheme for federal appellate review. In 2009, there were 13 U.S. Circuit Courts of Appeal at the federal level (these include the District of Columbia and federal circuits) with 179 circuit court judges in practice. These are shown in Table 2-1 ■. These circuit court geographical boundaries are also shown in Figure 2-2 ■.

Typically, circuit courts hear cases with three-judge panels. In certain circuits, the volume of cases may be such that several three-judge panels may be convened simultaneously. These three-judge panels hear appeals from decisions in U.S. District Courts. On rare occasions, a case may be heard *en banc*. This is where the entire aggregate of judges in the circuit hears and decides the case appeal. Usually, appeals heard *en banc* involve important constitutional issues, and input from a larger number of judges is deemed important.

Like district court judges, appellate judges are appointed for life by the president and confirmed by the Senate. One of these judges is designated as the chief judge. Usually, the chief judge is the one with the greatest seniority and who is also under 65 years of age.

Evarts Act introduced in 1891 and sponsored by New Jersey lawyer William M. Evarts, this act created circuit courts of appeal to hear appeals emanating from the U.S. District Courts.

U.S. Circuit Courts of Appeal the federal circuit courts of appellate jurisdiction. There are 13 circuit courts of appeal zoned throughout the United States and its territories.

en banc "in the bench." Refers to a session of the court, usually an appellate court, where all of the judges assigned to the court participate.

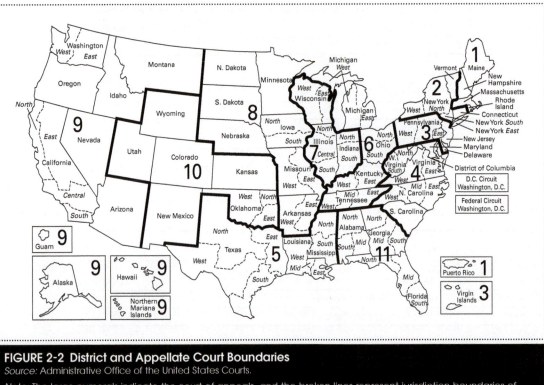

FIGURE 2-2 District and Appellate Court Boundaries

Source: Administrative Office of the United States Courts.

Note: The large numerals indicate the court of appeals, and the broken lines represent jurisdiction boundaries of district courts.

Chief judges perform additional duties apart from hearing cases, and their maximum term is seven years. In 2016, annual salary of circuit court judges on the U.S. Circuit Courts of Appeals was about $215,000.

Each of the circuit courts of appeal has appellate jurisdiction for all federal district courts in the particular circuit. For instance, the Eleventh Circuit Court of Appeals includes Alabama, Florida, and Georgia. These states are divided into several divisions, each containing one or more federal district courts. When a defendant wishes to appeal a decision of any federal district court within Alabama, Florida, or Georgia, the appeal is directed to the Eleventh Circuit Court of Appeals.

While all circuit courts of appeal have appellate jurisdiction from all final decisions from district courts, there are occasions where a direct review may be made by the U.S. Supreme Court. Panels of three circuit judges must convene at regular intervals to hear appeals from federal district courts. Of course, if a defendant disagrees with the decision of a circuit court, the U.S. Supreme Court is the court of last resort for appeals.

The U.S. Supreme Court

U.S. Supreme Court court of last resort; final and highest court that decides particular issues, usually issues with constitutional significance.

The court of last resort at the federal level is the **U.S. Supreme Court**. It is the only court specifically mentioned in Article III, Section 1 of the Constitution. The Constitution states that "the judicial power of the United States, shall be vested in one supreme court, and in such inferior courts as the Congress may from time to time ordain and establish." Like all of the other federal courts, U.S. Supreme Court justices hold their positions for life. They are nominated and appointed by the president, with Senate confirmation. The Supreme Court consists of eight associate justices and one chief justice. The chief justice has the additional responsibility of conducting conferences, supervising the federal judiciary, and assigning the task of writing various case opinions to a member of the judicial majority. Each of the associate justices is assigned to one of the appellate circuits for emergencies, such as death penalty appeals. In 2016, the annual salary of U.S. Supreme Court chief justice was just over $260,000 and for the associate justices it was almost $250,000.

The U.S. Supreme Court has both original jurisdiction and exclusive jurisdiction over (1) all actions or proceedings against ambassadors or public ministers of foreign states; and (2) all controversies between two or more states. Original jurisdiction means the court may recognize a case at its inception, hear that case, and try it without consultation with other courts or authorities. Exclusive jurisdiction means that no other court can decide certain kinds of cases except the court having exclusive jurisdiction. A juvenile court has exclusive jurisdiction over juvenile matters, for example. The adult criminal courts have no juvenile jurisdiction.

The Case of *Marbury v. Madison* (1803)

One of the most important decisions that established review powers for the U.S. Supreme Court was the case of *Marbury v. Madison* (1803). This case was a political conflict between the Federalists and anti-Federalists. Outgoing president John Adams made several new circuit court appointments and signed commissions for their appointment on his last day of office. However, Secretary of State James Madison withheld the processing of these commissions, anticipating a new president and a change in political party where party appointments could be made instead of the old administration appointees. This was an obvious attempt to create additional judicial appointments from party members favorable to the incoming president. One of these appointments was William Marbury, who petitioned the U.S. Supreme Court to force Secretary of State Madison to issue his new appointment. Chief Justice John Marshall ruled in Marbury's favor and issued a writ of *mandamus* to compel the Secretary of State to issue the commissions authorized by ex-president John Adams. Thus, the right of judicial review established the power of the U.S. Supreme Court to review and determine the constitutionality of acts of Congress and the executive branch.

The Supreme Court is the ultimate reviewing body regarding decisions made by lower appellate courts or state supreme courts. The Supreme Court is primarily an appellate court, since most of its time is devoted to reviewing decisions of lower courts. It is the final arbiter of lower court decisions unless Congress declares otherwise. Congress may change existing constitutional amendments or other acts. The U.S. Supreme Court meets for 36 weeks annually from the first Monday in October until the end of June (U.S. Code, Title 28, Sec. 5, 2007).

The U.S. Supreme Court is in session from the first Monday of October until the preceding day the next year. The year of the annual session is the year when the session is commenced. When the U.S. Supreme Court convenes in October 2016, all cases decided during that term are considered as cases decided during the 2016 term, even though a particular case might not be heard until May or June 2017.

Annually, the court receives about 7,000 appeals. Most appeals are disposed of when the U.S. Supreme Court decides not to hear the case because of the subject matter, or if it is not significant enough to merit court review. The decision to hear a case is made when the justices meet to review all cases. In order for all of the justices to hear a particular appeal, the case must pass a screening, which is known as the Rule of Four. This means that at least four of the nine justices must agree that the case has constitutional merit or national importance and that it should be heard by the entire court. If a case receives four or more votes from the justices, it is placed on the docket and scheduled to be heard. Only about 150 cases annually pass the Rule of Four and are placed on the docket for an opinion.

The primary method that cases reach the Court is through a petition known as a writ of certiorari. This is an order issued by the Supreme Court to the lower court to send the record for review. When the Court decides to hear a case, it is scheduled for written and

original jurisdiction first authority over a case or cause, as opposed to appellate jurisdiction.

exclusive jurisdiction specific jurisdiction over particular kinds of cases. Family court, for example, may have exclusive jurisdiction to hear child custody cases.

judicial review the authority of a court to limit the power of the executive and legislative branches of government by deciding whether their acts defy rights established by the state and federal constitutions.

Rule of Four U.S. Supreme Court rule whereby the Court grants *certiorari* only on the agreement of at least four justices.

writ of *certiorari* an order of a superior court requesting that the record of an inferior court (or administrative body) be brought forward for review or inspection. Literally, "to be more fully informed."

oral arguments by the opposing lawyers. The written arguments are filed with the Court and made available to the public. In some cases, other interested parties may file briefs for the Court to hear, on behalf of other parties. These types of filings are called *amicus curiae* briefs. *Amicus curiae* means "a friend of the court," and refers to a broad class of briefs that may be filed by one party on behalf of one or more other parties. For instance, an *amicus curiae* brief was filed on behalf of Gary Gilmore, a convicted murderer in Utah, by Amnesty International, an organization opposed to capital punishment. The brief was on behalf of Gilmore, who was scheduled to be executed. The brief sought relief in the form of a stay of Gilmore's execution, until the U.S. Supreme Court had time to hear and consider new arguments for why the death penalty should not be imposed in Gilmore's case. Although the brief was successful, in that it gave Gilmore several additional weeks, Gilmore did not wish to pursue further appeals. He declared that he wanted to die, and that the state should be allowed to execute him, despite the objections of Gilmore's family and Amnesty International. Gilmore was subsequently executed by a Utah firing squad.

Appearances by attorneys before the U.S. Supreme Court are highly regimented by prevailing protocol. The attorneys for the opposing sides are permitted 30 minutes each to present oral arguments. Green, yellow, and red lights similar to those that regulate automobile traffic flash for the different litigants. A green light means oral argument may proceed. A yellow light flashes when the 30-minute oral argument time limit is approaching. And a red light means that the oral argument terminates. During this time, justices are allowed to ask questions of the attorneys presenting the oral arguments. After oral arguments, the justices schedule a meeting, which is called a case conference. In this meeting, the justices take an initial position.

Traditionally, if the chief justice is in the majority, this justice assigns the writing of the majority opinion to one of the other majority justices. The senior justice for the minority or dissenting opinion assigns the writing of this opinion to one of the dissenting justices. The writing of the opinion may be quite complicated, especially when the justices on both sides have conflicting opinions about the case. For instance, not all of the majority justices may believe the case should be decided in a given way for the same reasons. Thus, each majority justice may write an independent opinion about why the justice voted a certain way. Accordingly, dissenting justices do not have to agree about why they dissent. Thus, several dissenting justices may write independent opinions about why they dissented. These opinions make for interesting reading for Supreme Court historians and others, since often the personal views of justices are made evident in their opinions.

When the topic of the opinion is controversial, such as a case involving abortion or the death penalty, each justice expresses different views about the issue. For example, in *Furman v. Georgia* (1972), all justices wrote separate opinions. In most cases, the opinion goes through several drafts before it is approved by the majority or dissenting justices, and before it is subsequently made available to the public. Unlike cases heard at the appellate level, the U.S. Supreme Court hears all cases *en banc*. All nine justices hear the case.

There are exceptions. Sometimes, a death or resignation from the U.S. Supreme Court may leave the court with seven or eight members temporarily, until a new justice or justices can be appointed. During the time interval when the Court does not have nine justices, it may still convene and hear and decide appeals. A majority of justices is still required, although a majority is more difficult to achieve. Eight justices may divide equally on a given issue, with a 4–4 vote. Such a vote results in no decision rendered about that particular appeal. Five or more justices are required to support any appeal. When a 4–4 vote occurs, the case is simply discarded and not scheduled for rehearing. The litigants may bring the case before the U.S. Supreme Court again, provided that they raise a different and meaningful issue as the basis for challenging a lower court decision. And the Rule of Four exists for all new case filings, regardless of whether a particular case has been previously heard. Four or more justices must agree to hear the case before it will be docketed.

► State Court Organization

Studying the American courts would be relatively easy if we didn't have to consider state court organization. But as we have seen, states such as Tennessee provide numerous different court structures and jurisdictions to create some complexity. And each state is different from the others in state court organization and function. Thus, we must add to the federal system the different court systems found in all 50 states. Figure 2-3 ■ shows the federal court system.

The organization and functions of the 50 different state court structures are diverse and complex. For example, Massachusetts has a supreme judicial court, appeals court, superior court, district court, probate/family court, juvenile court, housing court, municipal court, and land court. By contrast, South Dakota has only a two-tiered system with a circuit court and a supreme court. State courts often have overlapping and conflicting jurisdictions. The state courts are also very busy with variable caseloads. Millions of cases are filed and disposed of each year. In 2003, over 100 million disputes were heard by state courts (Schauffler, LaFountain, Kauder, and Strickland 2004). Most of these cases (about 40 percent) were traffic offenses. Caseloads in all five categories (criminal, civil, domestic relations, juvenile, and traffic) have continued to increase over the past several years (Schauffler et al. 2004). Figure 2-4 ■ shows a basic state court system. Not all states follow this particular diagram, with some states having separate criminal and civil appellate levels. But generally, this model is representative of most state court systems.

A more elaborate type of state court system is referred to as the traditional court model or the Texas model. This type of court system is illustrated in Figure 2-5 ■. It provides more extensive detail than the state court organization depicted in Figure 2-4 ■.

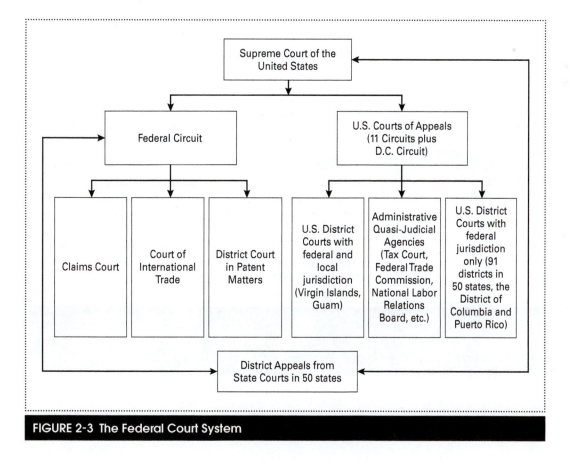

FIGURE 2-3 The Federal Court System

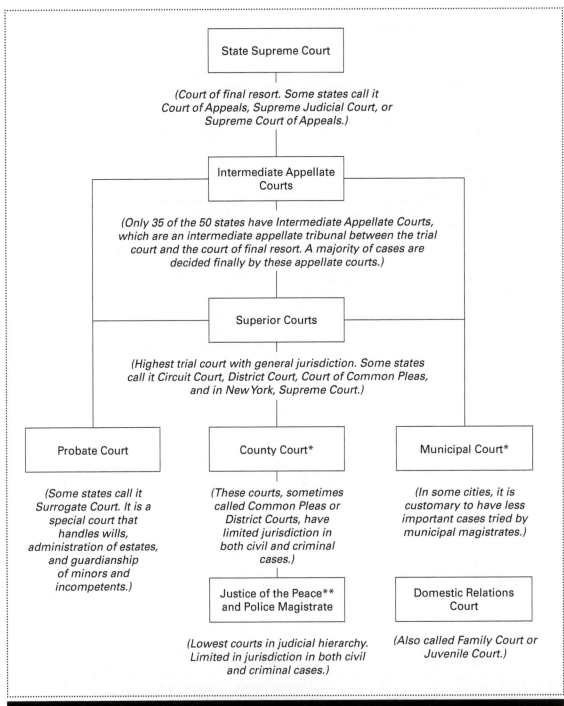

FIGURE 2-4 The State Judicial System

*Courts of special jurisdiction, such as probate, family, or juvenile courts, and the so-called inferior courts, such as courts of common pleas or municipal courts, may be separate courts or part of the trial court of general jurisdiction.

**Justices of the peace do not exist in all states. Where they do exist, their jurisdictions vary greatly from state to state.

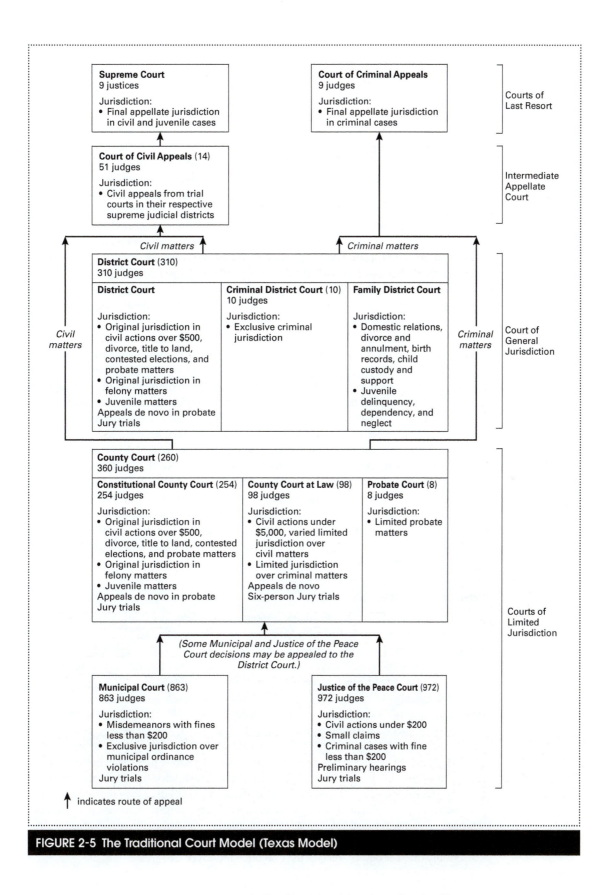

Supreme Court
9 justices

Jurisdiction:
- Final appellate jurisdiction in civil and juvenile cases

Court of Criminal Appeals
9 judges

Jurisdiction:
- Final appellate jurisdiction in criminal cases

Courts of Last Resort

Court of Civil Appeals (14)
51 judges

Jurisdiction:
- Civil appeals from trial courts in their respective supreme judicial districts

Intermediate Appellate Court

Civil matters   *Criminal matters*

District Court (310)
310 judges

District Court	**Criminal District Court** (10) 10 judges	**Family District Court**
Jurisdiction: - Original jurisdiction in civil actions over $500, divorce, title to land, contested elections, and probate matters - Original jurisdiction in felony matters - Juvenile matters Appeals de novo in probate Jury trials	Jurisdiction: - Exclusive criminal jurisdiction	Jurisdiction: - Domestic relations, divorce and annulment, birth records, child custody and support - Juvenile delinquency, dependency, and neglect

Civil matters   *Criminal matters*

Court of General Jurisdiction

County Court (260)
360 judges

Constitutional County Court (254) 254 judges	**County Court at Law** (98) 98 judges	**Probate Court** (8) 8 judges
Jurisdiction: - Original jurisdiction in civil actions over $500, divorce, title to land, contested elections, and probate matters - Original jurisdiction in felony matters - Juvenile matters Appeals de novo in probate Jury trials	Jurisdiction: - Civil actions under $5,000, varied limited jurisdiction over civil matters - Limited jurisdiction over criminal matters Appeals de novo Six-person Jury trials	Jurisdiction: - Limited probate matters

Courts of Limited Jurisdiction

(Some Municipal and Justice of the Peace Court decisions may be appealed to the District Court.)

Municipal Court (863)
863 judges

Jurisdiction:
- Misdemeanors with fines less than $200
- Exclusive jurisdiction over municipal ordinance violations
Jury trials

Justice of the Peace Court (972)
972 judges

Jurisdiction:
- Civil actions under $200
- Small claims
- Criminal cases with fine less than $200
Preliminary hearings
Jury trials

↑ indicates route of appeal

FIGURE 2-5 The Traditional Court Model (Texas Model)

Other types of court organizational systems have been proposed in past years. For instance, Ezra Pound advocated a simple model, consisting of a supreme court as the highest court, a major trial court, and a minor trial court. The American Bar Association has proposed its own simplified court organizational structure, modifying the Pound model by adding an intermediate appellate court. A later version of court organization devised by the American Bar Association envisioned a three-tiered system, with a supreme court at the top, an intermediate appellate court in the middle, and a trial court at the bottom.

Many jurisdictions do not require that judicial officers have a law degree. In fact, 36 states do not require that judges in a court of limited jurisdiction must be educated in the law. One reason is that many judges are elected rather than appointed or through some other form of merit selection. In short, these judges need to convince the electorate that they have the ability to serve rather than be legal practitioners with professional credentials. The lack of education and knowledge of the judicial process among many state court judges has caused a number of problems. Most of these courts are not courts of record, so it is difficult to monitor their activities formally. Because many elected judges do not know the limits of their authority or are unfamiliar with the processes of the judicial system, many states have established a legal training requirement for newly elected judges. Most of these judges are required to attend a legal training seminar sponsored by the state judicial conference or a committee or program sponsored by the Administrative Office of the U.S. Courts.

Despite provisions for the legal training of new judges in most jurisdictions, research about courts of limited jurisdiction has revealed that more than few inequities exist. Some of these injustices, such as judicial incompetence, have been highlighted in U.S. Supreme Court cases. For example, the U.S. Supreme Court was confronted with the matter of judicial competence in the case of *North v. Russell* (1976). Judge Russell worked in the coal mines of Kentucky after he dropped out of high school. Later, he was elected as a judge and presided over the case of Lonnie North, who had been accused of drunk driving. Judge Russell denied North's request for a jury trial, did not inform North of his right to counsel, and denied North's right to appeal the subsequent decision. Judge Russell listened only to the arresting officer's version of the incident and did not permit North testify on his own behalf and provide his version of events. Judge Russell sentenced Lonnie North to 30 days in jail when the statute provided a maximum sentence of a fine and no jail time. In this case, North's conviction was set aside by the U.S. Supreme Court and Judge Russell was criticized for his incompetence.

What Do You Think?

The U.S. Supreme Court decides many important cases annually. Most of these involve constitutional issues. Compared with Congress, the country's law-making body, the U.S. Supreme Court interprets the constitution and how the law should be applied. For example, some of their recent decisions have included a 9–0 decision overruling a small town in Arizona that had an ordinance placing different limits on political and ideological signage citing that the city ordinance violates the First Amendment, a 5–4 decision upholding the right of the state of Texas to reject issuing specialty license plates with the confederate flag on them, a 5–4 decision upholding the right under the Constitution of same-sex couples to marry, and a 9–0 decision stating that prison officials in Arkansas violated inmates' religious freedoms by not allowing them to grow beards. To some, these may not seem like important matters but to the various individuals citing constitutional rights violations they are very significant. What do you think about these SCOTUS decisions regarding same-sex marriage, town ordinances about religious signs, license plate preferences, and inmates who want to grow beards? Do you think these powers are within the scope of authority originally vested in the U.S. Supreme Court? Should the U.S. Supreme Court be subject to the scrutiny of other bodies, such as the executive branch or Congress?

State courts generally have a four-tiered court structure. These tiers are (1) courts of limited jurisdiction, (2) courts of general jurisdiction, (3) intermediate courts of appeal, and (4) courts of last resort.

Courts of Limited Jurisdiction

Courts of limited jurisdiction have the greatest variability among the states. These courts hear minor offenses such as violations of traffic laws, minor civil cases, and infractions. They also perform other administrative duties. Courts of limited jurisdiction comprise about 80 percent of the total number of state courts. They are the courts with the greatest caseloads in the nation. In 2009, of the roughly 106 million cases processed in state courts (including both criminal and civil cases), about 70 million, or 66 percent, were disposed of in courts of limited jurisdiction (LaFountain, Schauffler, Strickland, Gibson, and Mason 2011). On the average, they process over 50 percent of all cases brought before the state courts. The District of Columbia, Iowa, South Dakota, Idaho, and Illinois are the only states without courts of limited jurisdiction.

State courts of limited jurisdiction have many different names. Most of these courts are called municipal courts, county courts, city courts, or justice of the peace courts. Other courts are specialized courts of limited jurisdiction. Some of these courts might be called juvenile courts or family courts, probate courts, and courts of workers' compensation. Recent caseload estimates indicate that traffic cases between 1994 and 2003 in municipal courts comprised the largest percentage of incoming cases. These courts continue to be busy with heavy caseloads because of increases in all other types of cases, not just those involving traffic violations (Schauffler et al. 2004).

BOX 2-1

LEGAL ISSUES: TECHNOLOGY AND ACCESS TO THE FEDERAL JUDICIARY

Technological advances have affected all of us in some way. The federal judiciary is not immune to this trend. Since the 1990s, the federal court has made available to the public a number of resources to access information about the cases before the Court and the decisions reached by the Court. The service offered allows the public to obtain information about the actions of the Court without ever stepping foot inside the courthouse. Some of the services offered by the Court are as follows:

The U.S. Supreme Court Electronic Bulletin Board System

The U.S. Supreme Court Electronic Bulletin Board System (EBBS) service provides online access to the court docket, opinions, argument calendar, rules, and bar information forms. Additional information includes general and tour information and special notices.

Enzozo/Fotolia

The U.S. Supreme Court Clerk's Automated Response System

The U.S. Supreme Court Clerk's Automated Response System (CARS) provides callers with information

(continued)

about the status of cases by instructing callers to respond to telephone prompts.

Appellate Bulletin Board System

The Appellate Bulletin Board System (ABBS) is a source of information about judicial opinions offered to the public by federal circuit courts of appeal. These courts offer the public access to court decisions, argument calendars, case dockets, reports, notices, and press releases. Information can be downloaded and viewed online by computer users. Currently, there is a $.60 per minute fee for this service.

Public Access to Court Electronic Records

The Public Access to Court Electronic Records (PACER) is a service that allows users to dial into the bankruptcy court computer to access information about cases and decisions. Again there is a $.60 per minute charge. Users must first register with the PACER service center before they can use this service. Many district and circuit courts have established toll-free

numbers to users where additional costs of long-distance telephone calls are not incurred.

Party/Case Index

In 1977, the courts started a new service that would allow users to conduct searches of the bankruptcy court by party name or Social Security number. Searches can also be conducted to locate civil or criminal cases or cases beginning to be appealed. The search will retrieve the case filing date and filing location.

Electronic Filing and Attorney Docketing Service

The Electronic Filing and Attorney Docketing Service (EFADS) is another service that is being tested in selected district courts. This service allows attorneys to submit pleadings and other docket entries through the Internet. The case file and official docket can be viewed online or downloaded electronically.

Should all courts attempt to make access to information easier via various technological advances?

Courts of General Jurisdiction

Courts of general jurisdiction have jurisdiction over all major civil and criminal cases. These cases would include any felony or misdemeanor cases as well as criminal appeals from limited jurisdiction courts. These courts also differ from courts of limited jurisdiction because they are courts of record and general trial courts. They are courts of record because a record is made of all of the proceedings. Various methods are used to make records of these proceedings. Court reporters use tape recorders and several other devices to record whatever is said. With a few exceptions, courts of general jurisdiction are called circuit courts, district courts, superior courts, courts of common pleas, and supreme courts. A list of names of these courts for the different states is provided in Table 2-2 ■.

> **courts of record** any legal proceedings where a written record is kept of court matters and dialogue.

> **general trial courts** any one of several types of courts, either civil or criminal, with diverse jurisdiction to conduct jury trials and decide cases.

TABLE 2-2 Courts of General Jurisdiction for Each State*

Circuit court	Alabama, Arkansas, Florida, Hawaii, Illinois, Indiana,[a] Kentucky, Maryland, Michigan, Mississippi, Missouri, Oregon, South Carolina, South Dakota, Tennessee, Virginia, West Virginia, Wisconsin
Superior court	Alaska, Arizona, California, Connecticut, Delaware, District of Colombia, Georgia, Maine, Massachusetts, New Hampshire, New Jersey, North Carolina, Puerto Rico, Rhode Island, Vermont,[b] Washington
District court	Colorado, Idaho, Iowa, Kansas, Louisiana, Minnesota, Montana, Nebraska, Nevada, New Mexico, North Dakota, Oklahoma, Texas, Utah, Wyoming
Court of common pleas	Ohio, Pennsylvania
Supreme Court	New York[c]

*Compiled by authors.
[a]Indiana has both circuit courts and superior courts.
[b]Vermont has superior courts and district courts.
[c]New York also has county courts.

In 2004, state courts processed and sentenced over 1,079,000 adults for felony offenses. This figure does not include civil filings (Bureau of Justice Statistics 2005). Contrary to what is reported and portrayed by the media, criminal jury trials are relatively rare events. This is because over 90 percent of all criminals who are prosecuted are convicted in criminal courts through plea bargaining, where guilty pleas are entered in exchange for some form of leniency from prosecutors and judges. Thus, criminal trials are conducted only for about 10 percent of all criminal cases.

In recent years, the criminal courts have been processing cases more rapidly than in past years. For instance, in 1988, state courts processed 667,366 cases and the average case processing time from arrest to conviction was about seven months. In 1994, the courts processed 872,217 cases and the average time between arrest and conviction was six and a half months (Maguire and Pastore 2005). In 2000, the court processed 924,700 cases with a median time between arrest and sentencing of 5.1 months (Maguire and Pastore 2005). Many factors account for this decrease in processing time. One reason is that courts, faced with increasing caseloads, have learned and incorporated more efficient caseload management processes to reduce court delays. Or courts may realize the increased caseload and deliberately limit the number of delays and continuances that have been allowed in past years. The workload of the court is strongly associated with where the court is located. Typically, urban courts have more cases to process than rural courts. For example, Los Angeles, the busiest court system in the nation, processed 50,197 felony cases in 1994 (Maguire and Pastore 2005). This figure is greater than all of the felony cases processed in the entire federal system during that same year.

The demand for court services fluctuates greatly depending upon certain areas of the country. In 2003, for example, South Dakota processed only 26,384 cases in courts of general jurisdiction; this amounts to about 3,452 cases per 100,000 persons. In that same year, however, Wisconsin processed 248,960 cases in courts of general jurisdiction; this amounts to about 4,549 cases per 100,000 persons (Schauffler et al. 2004).

Judges in the courts of general jurisdiction usually have practiced law either as prosecutors or working in a law firm before becoming a judge. However, in Maine and Massachusetts, judges at this level are not required to have a law degree. The only requirement is that they are learned in the law (Rottman, Flango, Cantrell, Hansen, and LaFountain 2000). Most states require some combination of a law degree, being a member of the state bar for 5–10 years, and local and/or state residency requirements. Some states have age limitations for judges at this level. Usually, the minimum age is 25–30 years and the maximum age is 70–75 years. As of 2012, the median salary for judges in general jurisdiction trial courts was $132,500. Judges in Illinois' general courts were the highest paid in the nation with a salary of $180,802. The lowest-paid trial judges were in South Dakota with a salary of $110,377 (National Center for State Courts 2012).

Intermediate Courts of Appeal

Eleven states and the District of Columbia do not have intermediate courts of appeal. Most states have developed an intermediate court of appeal to review and screen the caseload on the state supreme court. These intermediate courts of appeal became necessary shortly after 1900. A few states such as Alabama, Tennessee, and Texas have separate appellate courts for civil and criminal cases. Most of the judges at this level are appointed by the governor after being selected by a nominating commission. Intermediate appellate court judges make slightly more than their colleagues in the general trial courts. The median salary in 2012 was $140,732; appellate court judges in California were paid the most at $204,599 and appellate court judges in Mississippi were paid the least making $105,050 (National Center for State Courts 2012).

Courts of Last Resort

The highest court structures at the state level are called courts of last resort. Usually, these are also called supreme courts. In states with an intermediate court of appeals, these courts have discretionary appellate review. This means that they decide which cases they will hear. By refusing to hear a case, they are allowing the decision of the lower court to stand. In states where there is no intermediate court of appeal, the state supreme court has no discretionary authority. Alabama, Oklahoma, and Texas are unique in this regard because they have two courts of last resort. One is designated to hear civil cases, while the other hears only criminal cases. Judges who preside in state supreme courts are usually selected by a nominating commission and appointed by the governor. In order to remain in their position, they must receive a majority vote in a retention election. The median salary for the state's highest court in 2012 was $146,915 for an associate justice and $152,500 for the chief justice; the highest-paid supreme court justices reside in California and make $218,237, while the lowest-paid justices of the highest state court are in South Dakota, where they receive annual salaries of $118,173 (National Center for State Courts 2012).

Summary

1. Distinguish among the different ways to classify American courts, such as by jurisdiction, by its dual nature, and by type of court.

The American court system is one of the most confusing in the world. Each state has its own court structure, and in many cases courts that perform the same functions are referred to by different names. Therefore, in order to understand the American court structure, we must understand how each court functions as well as the kind of matters they can hear. This is referred to as the court's jurisdiction. We can also compare these courts among the different states and the federal courts; with court systems at both the state and federal levels, this scenario is often referred to as the dual court system. Finally, we can also distinguish between courts by the type of cases they can hear and decide. For example, some courts are limited to certain types of cases, such as tax law violations, or can only hear minor cases, while others have much broader jurisdiction over all types of cases.

2. Recognize the different types of jurisdiction like subject matter, geographic, and hierarchical.

The best and easiest way to understand the American court structure is to classify these courts according to their particular jurisdiction. One of these is subject matter jurisdiction, which refers to the type of case a court can hear. Courts of limited jurisdiction are granted the legal authority to hear misdemeanor cases or the preliminary stages of felony cases. Courts of general jurisdiction are basically felony trial courts. They are also referred to as courts of fact.

Geography also defines the limits of a court's authority. A court's legal authority is limited by political boundaries. For example, a state court in Arizona does not have the legal authority to hear a criminal case from Nevada. Many municipalities have their own court systems, and their jurisdiction is limited to cases that occur within the city limits.

Appellate courts are called courts of law because they do not determine the facts of the case. Rather, they are charged with determining whether the law has been applied correctly. This is a classification known as hierarchical jurisdiction, basically that trial courts decide the case and appellate courts decide whether the law was applied correctly in a case.

3. Explain how the United States has two court structures, a federal structure and a state structure.

There are 51 different court structures in the United States. Each state and the federal government have their own structure and process for resolving disputes and prosecuting criminals. In other words, the United States has a dual court system, meaning that there is both a federal court structure and a state court structure. The federal system is made up of U.S. District Courts, U.S. Circuit Courts of Appeal, and the U.S. Supreme Court. The state court system is characterized by courts of limited jurisdiction, courts of general jurisdiction, intermediate courts of appeal, and courts of last resort. We cannot simply focus on court names, however, since the meaning associated with a particular court name varies among counties and states. The federal courts are also authorized to hear cases involving laws enacted by Congress. As such, the federal courts often decide disputes involving interstate commerce; however, some of these cases may also be heard in state courts, giving state and federal courts concurrent jurisdiction.

4. *Describe the difference between trial and appellate courts.*

Trial courts are often referred to as courts of fact, while appellate courts are referred to as courts of law. This is because the trial courts are where the facts of a case are heard and where based on these facts, a determination of whether the defendant is guilty or not guilty is made. Trial courts are also responsible for sentencing the defendant. By contrast, appellate courts do not hear testimony or impose sentences. The purpose of appellate courts is to determine if the law was applied correctly. In other words the appellate court makes sure that the legal and procedural rules were followed. When a case is appealed, appellate court judges review whether trial court judges followed constitutional and procedural laws when they made their decisions. If the appellate court believes that the trial court followed these rules, the lower court's ruling will be upheld, if the trial court violated those rules, the lower court's ruling will be overturned and the case will be sent back down to the trial court for further action such as a judge handing out a new sentence, or a prosecutor deciding whether to retry the case.

5. *Compare and contrast the federal court structure, including, U.S. District Courts, U.S. Circuit Courts of Appeal, and the U.S. Supreme Court.*

The basic trial courts in the federal system are the U.S. District Courts. Most civil and criminal cases of federal interest are tried and disposed of in these courts. There are 94 district courts in the United States. Federal district court judgeships are lifetime appointments and there is no mandatory retirement age.

The federal system also has 13 appellate jurisdictions or U.S. Circuit Courts of Appeal. These are the intermediate appellate courts at the federal level. Again these were created to alleviate the rising caseload of the Supreme Court. These courts then hear the appeals from the decisions made by the U.S. District Courts. Like their district court counterparts, judges in federal circuit courts of appeal are appointed for life by the president.

The U.S. Supreme Court is the court of last resort or the highest court in the land. Nine justices accept between 7,000 and 8,000 cases per year and write opinions in about 200 of them. Unlike trial courts, which have no control over what cases are presented to them, most

state courts of last resort and the U.S. Supreme Court decide which case appeals they will or will not hear. They do not, however, have the time to hear every case; rather, they marshal their time and use their discretion to hear the most important matters of the time, or matters that involve important federal questions.

6. *Summarize the state court structure, including courts of limited jurisdiction, courts of general jurisdiction, intermediate courts of appeal, and courts of last resort.*

The state court structure is a little more confusing. The state court structure is more difficult to understand because the functions and organization of the 50 different state court structures are diverse. The same or similar courts often have different names in different states, and state courts often have overlapping and conflicting jurisdictions. Many of the state jurisdictions do not require that judges have a law degree; 36 states do not even require education in the law for their limited jurisdiction court judgeships. One of the most likely reasons for this is that these judges are elected rather than appointed. Therefore, they need only convince the electorate that they can serve in the position well. This has caused a number of problems in the past regarding judicial incompetence and knowledge of the law.

The courts in most states have a four-tiered structure. The tiers include courts of limited jurisdiction, courts of general jurisdiction, intermediate courts of appeal, and courts of last resort, or state supreme courts. The courts of limited jurisdiction are the courts that are the least consistent among the states. These courts hear the most minor of offenses, minor civil cases, and traffic violations and also perform administrative duties. They are the courts with the highest caseloads in the country.

Courts of general jurisdiction hear all major civil and criminal cases. These courts are the general trial courts in the state system and are courts of record. Again, these courts have a fairly high caseload; however, contrary to popular media perceptions, more than 90 percent of these cases are disposed of through a plea bargain. A court's activity, however, varies in different areas of the country. The courts in large urban jurisdictions are obviously busier than those in rural areas. The judges in courts of general jurisdiction are usually more learned in the law than their limited jurisdiction judicial counterparts and have probably practiced law as either a prosecutor or a defense attorney.

The intermediate courts of appeal screen the caseload of the supreme court. Eleven states and the District of Columbia, however, do not have intermediate courts of appeal. States with high appellate caseloads probably have an intermediate court of appeal. Most of these judges, like their state supreme court counterparts, are appointed by the governor. These courts do not, however, have discretionary appellate review, which means that they have to hear all cases that have been properly filed.

Courts of last resort, also called state supreme courts, do have discretionary appellate review in the states that do not have intermediate courts of appeal. These judges are usually selected by a nominating commission, and then appointed by the governor.

Key Terms

amicus curiae 32
appellate courts 26
circuit courts 26
concurrent jurisdiction 27
courts of last resort 40
courts of record 28
dual court system 27
en banc 29
exclusive jurisdiction 31
Evarts Acts 29

federal district courts 26
general jurisdiction 24
general trial courts 38
geographic jurisdiction 25
hierarchical jurisdiction 26
judicial review 31
Judiciary Act of 1789 26
jurisdiction 24
limited jurisdiction 24
original jurisdiction 31

Rule of Four 31
subject matter jurisdiction 24
Supreme Court 26
trial courts 26
U.S. Circuit Courts of Appeal 29
U.S. District Courts 28
U.S. magistrates 28
U.S. Supreme Court 30
writ of *certiorari* 31

Critical Thinking Exercises

1. The U.S. Supreme Court receives about 7,000 appeals every year, the majority of which are disposed of when the U.S. Supreme Court decides not to hear the case because of the subject matter, or if it is not significant enough to merit court review. The decision to hear a case is made when the justices meet to review all cases. In order for all of the justices to hear a particular appeal, the case must pass a screening, which is known as the Rule of Four. This means that at least four of the nine justices must agree that the case has constitutional merit or national importance and that it should be heard by the entire court. If a case receives four or more votes from the justices, it is placed on the docket and scheduled to be heard. Annually, only about 100 or so cases pass the Rule of Four and are placed on the docket for an opinion. Should this rule be changed? Should the SCOTUS hear more cases considering that they receive almost 7,000 appeals every year? Perhaps a Rule of Two, or even if just one of the justices agrees that a case is important, the court should hear the arguments in the case. Should the highest court in the land weigh in to ensure justice is served in more cases than they currently do?

2. Attorney–client privilege affords defense counsel with considerable protection about the information that a defendant has shared with them. If you were an attorney and your client confessed to you that they were fully or partly involved in the crime, what would you do? Would you vigorously fight the prosecution's case, encourage your client to seek a fair plea bargain, or decide you don't really care what happens to the defendant and not put forth any effort in the case? Would this depend on the type of crime the defendant admitted to?

Case Study Decision-Making Exercise

Supreme Court Justice Antonin Scalia was found dead in his sleep on a ranch in Texas, in early 2016. Immediately, President Obama announced he would nominate someone to fill the vacancy. Senate Republicans, however, knowing that Obama was in his last year in office, vowed not to confirm anyone until a new president was elected.

This vacancy had an effect on the outcomes of several cases that were set to be decided by the court in its term. For example, in the case of *United States v. Texas*, the question was whether an executive action by President Obama toward immigration reform that would stop the deportation of unauthorized immigrants through his

Deferred Action of Parents of Americans (DAPA) program was constitutional. Having only eight justices on the court resulted in a 4–4 tie, which meant that the U.S. Court of Appeals decision to block the executive action would stand. In another case, *Friedrichs v. California Teachers Association*, a 4–4 vote was a win for organized labor because it meant that the Ninth Circuit Court of Appeals decision would be affirmed. The case involved a group of California teachers who argued that having to affirmatively opt out of the union each year or pay their fees for collective bargaining is a violation of their First Amendment rights. The U.S. Court of Appeals agreed with the district court that precedent allowed the teacher's union to engage in this practice, so those choosing not to join would have to opt out annually or pay the union dues. Without a ninth justice, the 4–4 tie affirmed the lower court's decision that favored the union. Should the rules be changed so that if there is a vacancy at the SCOTUS it must be filled in a timely manner so that there are no 4–4 tie decisions that an odd-numbered justice court was set up to avoid? Did these individuals waste their time appealing to the U.S. Supreme Court and did their cases get denied fair appellate review because the court had a vacancy and the Senate refused to confirm a new justice? Should the court stop making decisions on cases until the Senate ensures they are fully staffed?

Concept Review Questions

1. Differentiate between courts of limited and general jurisdiction.
2. What is meant by geographic jurisdiction? What is the power of courts with geographic jurisdiction?
3. Describe the U.S. magistrate and the duties of this particular type of court.
4. What is the basic trial court for the federal system?
5. When a defendant in a U.S. District Court case is found guilty of a crime, where is the appeal directed? What are the jurisdictional limits of the appellate court you have indicated?
6. What is the court of last resort? Why is it called the court of last resort?
7. What are courts of limited jurisdiction? What are some of the functions of courts of limited jurisdiction?
8. Describe intermediate courts of appeal. Are these courts the same in all states? Why or why not?
9. What is meant when a case is heard *en banc*?
10. What is the function of an *amicus curiae*?

Suggested Readings

1. N. Robinson (2013). "Structure matters: The impact of court structure on the Indian and U.S. Supreme Courts." *American Journal of Comparative Law*, **61:** 173–208.
2. R. G. McCloskey and S. Levinson (2016). *The American Supreme Court*. University of Chicago Press.
3. S. Goldman and C. M. Lamb (eds.) (2015). *Judicial Conflict and Consensus: Behavioral Studies of American Appellate Courts*. University Press of Kentucky.
4. J. H. Choper (2013). *Judicial Review and the National Political Process: A Functional Reconsideration of the Role of the Supreme Court*. Quid Pro Books.

3 The Prosecution

LEARNING OBJECTIVES

As a result of reading this chapter, you will have accomplished the following objectives:

1 *Understand the criminal court as an adversarial system seeking to determine the guilt or innocence of defendants charged with crimes.*

2 *Understand the many roles of prosecutors in pursuing cases against criminal suspects including that negotiating plea bargains is the most common method of obtaining a conviction.*

3 *Depict both exculpatory and inculpatory evidence that may be presented in criminal cases.*

4 *Describe the process of screening and prioritizing cases for criminal prosecutions.*

5 *Assess the potential for prosecutorial misconduct or discretionary abuses arising from the extensive powers of prosecutors.*

The prosecutor holds one of the most important attorney positions in the criminal justice system, and is one of the most powerful courtroom actors. Prosecutors have a great deal of discretion that comes with a great deal of responsibility; they decide who will be charged, what the charges will ultimately be, who they are going to enter into a plea bargain with, and what concessions will be made as part of a plea agreement. Because of this discretionary power, they are also held to very high standards. As part of its *Model Rules of Professional Conduct*, the American Bar Association (ABA) has put forth the special responsibilities that a prosecutor has as part of their decision-making practices in criminal cases. Some of these include (1) not filing a charge for which the prosecutor does not have probable cause, (2) disclosing all evidence to the defense and the court, even that which may negate the guilt of the accused, (3) ensuring that the accused is aware of their right to counsel and affording them an opportunity to get counsel, and (4) abstaining from statements or comments to the public that might condemn the accused in the public eye. Prosecutors have also been called the gatekeepers of the criminal justice system and make decisions that affect the lives of many persons, including those accused of crimes as well as victims, and the general public. In making a determination about whether or not to charge someone, prosecutors have to weigh the evidence that they have in a case against the seriousness of the offense as well as the likelihood of obtaining a conviction. In some cases, it may be easy to make a decision, in others it is not as black and white and prosecutors may decide to not pursue charges in a case where they have evidence that the accused has committed a crime, and likewise might pursue charges in a case where the evidence may not completely satisfy all the elements of the crime. Prosecutors are often judged by their conviction rates and scrutinized by the public to maintain community safety and ensure that justice is done in cases where an arrest is made for a crime, especially for more serious offenses. Given this scrutiny and pressure, how difficult or not would it be for you to follow some of the above-mentioned ABA rules? Also, in thinking about using tax payers' money wisely, could you pursue all cases where there has been an arrest? Most of the general public believes that those arrested should be prosecuted to the fullest extent of the law. What would you do in cases where you believe someone has committed a crime but there is little evidence, or vice versa where you have some doubts that the person arrested was the one who committed the offense?

▶ Introduction

Trial proceedings in criminal courts in the United States are exclusively adversarial proceedings. Adversarial proceedings mean that opposing sides present evidence and arguments favoring their position, inculpatory versus exculpatory evidence, either to a judge or to a jury, in order to convince them that a particular action should be taken. Depending upon the compelling arguments presented favoring these opposing positions, judges or juries are persuaded to find criminal defendants guilty or not guilty.

Persons charged with one or more crimes, defendants, are prosecuted by the government. The interests of defendants are represented by defense counsels, whose job is to convince judges or juries that insufficient evidence exists to conclude that the defendants are guilty of committing a crime. Criminal proceedings against defendants may be conducted at local, state, or federal level, and in each case, one or more prosecutors represent the government's interests in pursuing prosecutions.

This chapter begins with a description of the adversarial system of American courts, which is characterized by opposing sides in the search for the truth. In some respects, this adversarial system is like an athletic contest or sporting event, complete with rules of conduct and different strategies calculated to advantage one side or the other in winning the contest. The outcome of a criminal trial is far different from the outcome of an athletic event, however. One or more lives are at stake, and one's freedom within the community may be in jeopardy. Prosecutors present inculpatory evidence to judges and juries. Such evidence shows defendant's guilt. By contrast, defense counsels present exculpatory evidence that shows defendant's innocence. Usually, both sides have such evidence and present it to bolster their arguments for why judges or juries should decide in their favor. The conduct of any criminal case in court, as well as the introduction of both exculpatory and inculpatory evidence, is governed by rules of criminal procedure and evidence. Both state and local court systems have codified these procedures so that trials are uniformly conducted and everyone understands what is and is not permitted.

The next section describes the prosecutorial role. The roles of prosecutors at all levels—local, state, or federal—are very similar. One consistent feature of all prosecutors is that they have many duties and responsibilities. Prosecutors must screen cases for prosecution and decide whether to bring criminal charges against particular suspects. As the chapter-opening scenario suggests, prosecutors must prioritize the cases they prosecute and many factors affect their decision making, even financial and personnel resources influence these decisions. Not everyone who deserves to be prosecuted can be prosecuted; this is especially the case in smaller jurisdictions and in times when resources are limited. Prosecutors, therefore, use their discretion to make decisions about which cases to prosecute. Because of this discretion to prosecute or dismiss a case, many have commented that the prosecutor is the most important gatekeeper into the criminal justice system. U.S. Attorney General and Supreme Court Justice Robert H. Jackson once stated that "The prosecutor has more power over life, liberty, and reputation, than any other person in America." Beyond the power to screen cases for prosecution, prosecutors must devise effective strategies that they believe will enable them to obtain convictions against criminal defendants. In many cases, the inculpatory evidence against many suspects is overwhelming and the prosecutor's strategies are fairly simple and straightforward. Critics argue that because around 90 percent of cases are disposed of through some type of plea agreement, the system might be best characterized as negotiative rather than adversarial. The prosecutor often drafts a plea agreement wherein a defendant enters a guilty plea to one or more criminal charges in exchange for some form of concessions such as sentencing leniency. These plea deals are usually initiated by the prosecutor but must be approved by the judge. The types of plea bargains and the plea bargaining process are discussed in much greater detail in Chapter 8.

Although fewer than 10 percent of all criminal cases proceed to trial, this does not mean that there are few criminal trials. There are many thousands of criminal trials annually. In fact, the incidence of criminal trials is such that there are serious case backlogs in more than a few jurisdictions. Imagine the backlog, however, if everyone prosecuted exercised their right to have their day in court. Interestingly, because there are so many criminal trials to conduct and a limited time period within which to conduct them, this is a major reason why prosecutors must screen their cases and prioritize them for prosecution. It is simply not possible to prosecute everyone who deserves to be prosecuted for a crime. The screening process used by prosecutors to prioritize their cases will be examined and explained.

In larger cities where a much larger volume of criminal cases is generated, government prosecutors, sometimes known as state's attorneys, district attorneys, or U.S. attorneys, will have several assistant prosecutors to handle larger caseloads. Thus, the head prosecutor has the responsibility of assigning cases to various assistant state's attorneys or assistant district attorneys, or assistant U.S. attorneys, and these persons become responsible for prosecuting the cases they are assigned. Among the different responsibilities of prosecutors is interviewing witnesses and conducting depositions that will enable them to build compelling cases against criminal defendants. Prosecutors also work closely with law enforcement officers who have made arrests and/or collected important incriminating evidence. These persons will eventually testify in court or provide information about a defendant's guilt. These interactions between witnesses, law enforcement officers, and prosecutors will be described and explained.

All attorneys, regardless of whether they are prosecutors or defense counsels, are expected to abide by a code of ethics that prescribes a particular conduct that places these persons above reproach. However, more than a few attorneys have violated one or more of these ethical codes by engaging in prosecutorial misconduct. Like any type of misconduct in any profession, there are degrees of misconduct that may occur. Like misdemeanors and felonies, there are less serious and more serious forms of misconduct. Several types of prosecutorial misconduct are examined.

One type of misconduct is encouraging deceit from witnesses who testify against criminal defendants. Most prosecutors do not ask witnesses to lie under oath or commit perjury. But many prosecutors may encourage witnesses to slant their testimony in ways that help make criminal defendants look guilty. In many jurisdictions, prosecutors rehearse their witnesses prior to trial, reviewing the types of questions the prosecutors will ask as well as the kinds of questions defense attorneys might ask. Suggestions are given by prosecutors as to what witnesses might say or how they might respond. While rehearsing witnesses before trial is not unethical, it may raise questions about how such testimony might be interpreted by jurors. Some witnesses may exaggerate the significance of their testimony, and prosecutors may allow juries to draw their own conclusions about these exaggerated remarks. Of course, it is expected that good defense attorneys will clarify for jurors what certain witnesses say and how such information should be interpreted.

Another type of prosecutorial misconduct occurs behind closed doors in confidential grand jury proceedings. About half of all states use grand juries to determine whether sufficient evidence exists against particular defendants in order for the case to proceed to trial. Grand jury proceedings are one-sided affairs, where prosecutors present only evidence that they want grand jurors to see. Thus, prosecutors are in absolute control concerning the particular evidence a grand jury will see against a criminal suspect. If the prosecutor knows of any exculpatory evidence that favors the defendant, he/she may withhold such evidence from the grand jury. This is the prosecutor's decision. If the prosecutor has strong feelings about the case and wants the grand jury to indict the defendant, excluding exculpatory evidence from the grand jury will improve the prosecutor's chances of securing an indictment. Ultimately, the exculpatory evidence will come to light in court when the trial is conducted. In the meantime, however, the defendant, who may be innocent, remains charged with a crime through the indictment. Although indictments do not mean that indicted defendants are guilty of anything, many citizens interpret "being indicted" as tantamount to guilt anyway.

The process of prosecutorial bluffing will be described. Prosecutors may attempt to bluff their way through a case prior to trial, leading some defendants to believe that they have inculpatory evidence against them when they have no such evidence. Many guilty pleas have been entered by innocent defendants because of prosecutorial bluffing. If defendants believe that the jury will likely convict them of a crime and their sentence will be severe, these defendants may decide to accept a plea agreement offered by the prosecutor, which usually involves considerable leniency in punishment compared with what a judge may have imposed through a jury verdict of guilt. Several types of prosecutorial bluffing will be described, and the implications of prosecutorial bluffing for defendants will be indicated.

More serious forms of prosecutorial misconduct include deliberately withholding exculpatory evidence from defense counsels prior to trial. Another form of misconduct is pursuing a case against a criminal defendant where no basis exists for the criminal charges that have been filed. Sometimes prosecutors may file frivolous charges against defendants where such charges have little or no basis in truth. These malicious prosecutions against innocent defendants are clearly inexcusable, although proving malicious intent on the part of the prosecutor is often difficult.

Although it is not technically a form of misconduct, prosecutors almost always attempt to select jurors who are most likely to convict the defendant. Some prosecutors hire professional jury consultants to assist them in making such juror selections (Clark 2004b). Both prosecutors and defense counsels have several peremptory challenges and an unlimited number of challenges for cause, whereby they can strike any particular prospective juror from sitting on the jury. Defense counsels also attempt to select jurors who will react favorably toward their clients. Sometimes they hire jury consultants to assist them in juror selection. Since the jury selection process is not an exact science, it is questionable whether accurate forecasts can ever be made about how particular jurors will vote once the evidence from both sides has been presented. Another form of prosecutorial misconduct involves backdooring hearsay evidence. Prosecutors and defense counsel are both barred from making certain kinds of statements in front of jurors. But both sides may make occasional improper utterances or statements anyway, only to have the judge instruct the jury to disregard these statements. But once jurors have heard statements they shouldn't hear, it is difficult, if not impossible, for them to forget that they heard these statements. It is impossible to determine how much these improper statements influence juror opinions and voting during juror deliberations. Different types of backdooring hearsay will be described. The chapter concludes with an examination of the ethical norms and guidelines presently in place to regulate prosecutors and their conduct. Only during the last few decades have prosecutors been more carefully scrutinized by the legal profession and others, and some prosecutors have even had charges filed against them for misconduct. Prosecutorial codes of conduct and ethics will also be described.

▶ The Adversary System

adversary system legal system involving a contest between two opposing parties under a judge who is an impartial arbiter.

When a crime is committed, law enforcement officers frequently arrest a suspect who is believed to have committed the crime. Criminal suspects become defendants charged with one or more crimes. While all criminal defendants in the United States are entitled to the presumption of innocence before their guilt is established in court beyond a reasonable doubt, they are also entitled to counter the charges against them. Therefore, defendants are represented by defense counsels, whose job is to defend their clients against these criminal charges. Presumably, defense counsels who represent clients in court are more or less effective according to their training, expertise, and practical trial experience. The system of alleging criminal charges against defendants and defending them against such charges is known as the adversary system (Emmelman 2003). This adversarial system is not exclusively a U.S. creation. It is found and used frequently in other countries, such as Canada, England, Italy, and Australia (Ambos 2003).

prosecutor court official who commences civil and criminal proceedings against defendants. Represents state or government interest, prosecuting defendants on behalf of state or government.

The adversarial nature of the criminal court is evident by paying attention to the different roles of the prosecutor and defense attorney. The prosecutor's aim is to prove that the defendant committed a crime, and that the level of such proof should rise to beyond a reasonable doubt. The defense attorney contests any criminal allegations made against his/her client and seeks to dissuade the court or a jury from thinking that the defendant is guilty of a criminal offense.

defense attorney, counsel a lawyer who represents a client accused of a crime.

Recent high-profile white-collar prosecutions, for instance, have seen defense attorneys submitting testimony and evidence to the jury about client's lack of knowledge of accounting practices and other financial information. Prosecutors, on the other hand, usually provide memos and/or emails as evidence that an employee of the corporation did have knowledge of fraud and other criminal and regulatory violations. Evidence is presented to both sides in these adversarial proceedings to provide compelling arguments for and against guilt. Depending on the jury's interpretation of this evidence and their opinion about whether the defendant was aware of the criminal actions, corporate malfeasance for instance, persons are either found guilty or acquitted.

Comparing the criminal court to a game being played out from beginning to end is not new. The gamelike nature of the courtroom is reinforced by using court-relevant terminology, such as sides and prosecutorial or defense strategy. Prosecutors are on one side and use a particular strategy that they believe will enable them to win the game. For prosecutors, a win is a conviction against the accused. For the defense side, a win is the defendant's acquittal. Prosecutors and defense counsels are often labeled as players by different writers who seek to characterize courtroom procedures in certain ways. The law may not always be seen as a normative system where the most moral person wins, but rather where the more skillful player using the better strategy will win the game by defeating the other player (Black 1973; van Koppen and Penrod 2003).

The adversarial system of justice in the United States is rooted in the tradition of English jurisprudence dating back several centuries (Ambos 2003). In U.S. courts, the key players, prosecutors, defense attorneys, and judges are the courtroom workgroup (Hoskins, Ruth, and Ruback 2004). They are bound to observe standardized **rules of criminal procedure** as well as a well-defined **ethical code** (Birzer and Tannehill 2003; Boyle, Newman, and Schmidt 2003). Thus, there are specific rules governing the order in which a case is presented against a defendant and the response from defense counsel (DiCristina 2004). Besides following a predetermined pattern or protocol for presenting a case against and for a defendant, other rules exist that govern the nature and types of evidence and witnesses who may be called for either side. Each side attempts to manipulate the evidence presented in ways that enhance their respective arguments. **Witnesses** are examined and cross-examined by the different sides in an effort to bolster their arguments. Ideally, the side with the most persuasive and compelling argument, either against or for the accused, wins. Juries decide the facts in the case before them, and their deliberations most often favor either guilt or acquittal. On rare occasions, juries may not be able to reach an agreement as to which side, the prosecution or defense, has the more persuasive argument. In these instances, juries are deadlocked or hung, and mistrials are declared. Subsequently, the adversarial process begins anew with another trial. In each trial proceeding, it is expected that both sides will adhere to an accepted ethical code and conduct themselves accordingly.

Throughout the criminal trial, evidence is presented by both sides for its persuasive effect. Prosecutors usually present **inculpatory evidence**, or testimony or other forms of evidence that tend to show the guilt of the defendant. For instance, the defendant's fingerprints might have been found on the murder weapon, or eyewitnesses may have seen the defendant pull the trigger of the gun that killed the defendant. This evidence would be considered inculpatory, because it shows the guilt of the accused. By contrast, defense counsel introduces **exculpatory evidence**, or testimony or other forms of evidence that show the innocence of the defendant. For example, one or more persons may testify that the defendant was with them at the time the murder was committed. Credit card receipts or video surveillance from restaurants or shopping malls may indicate that the defendant was somewhere else when the crime occurred. Thus, alibis and other relevant information may show that the defendant couldn't have been the one who committed the crime when it occurred (Cossins 2003).

rules of criminal procedure rules legislatively established by which a criminal case is conducted. Law enforcement officers, prosecutors, and judges use rules of criminal procedure in discretionary actions against suspects and defendants.

ethical code canons of professional responsibility articulated by professional associations such as the American Bar Association.

witnesses persons who have relevant information about the commission of a crime that may incriminate or exonerate a defendant.

inculpatory evidence any information that places the defendant in an unfavorable light and increases the likelihood of his/her guilt.

exculpatory evidence any information that reflects favorably upon the accused and shows that they are innocent of the crimes with which they are charged.

▶ The Prosecution

Besides the judge who makes important rulings in criminal cases and oversees trial proceedings, the prosecutor has perhaps the most powerful position in the criminal justice system (Schoenfeld 2005). Prosecutors are either elected or appointed officials who pursue

district attorneys city, county, and state prosecutors who are charged with bringing offenders to justice and enforcing the laws of the state.

state's attorneys government prosecutors.

prosecuting attorneys see prosecutor.

county prosecutor district attorney at the county level.

U.S. attorney's office chief prosecuting body affiliated with each U.S. District Court in the federal court system.

U.S. attorney official responsible for the prosecution of crimes that violate the laws of the United States. Appointed by the president and assigned to a U.S. District Court jurisdiction.

attorney general senior U.S. prosecutor in each federal district court. A cabinet member who heads the Justice Department.

assistant U.S. attorneys (AUSAs) government prosecutors who are subordinates to the U.S. attorney who heads the prosecutor's office for each federal district.

criminal cases against those charged with crimes. Prosecutors are held to the same standards of ethical conduct as defense counsel (Connell 2004). Depending upon the jurisdiction, prosecutors are known by different names. They may be known as **district attorneys, state's attorneys, prosecuting attorneys,** or **county prosecutors.** In the federal system, each U.S. District Court has a **U.S. attorney's office.** The **U.S. attorney** in each federal district is appointed by the president of the United States with the advice and consent of Congress. The **attorney general** of the United States, also a presidential appointee, appoints one or more **assistant U.S. attorneys (AUSAs)** to serve in each of these district offices. The number of AUSAs varies from district to district, depending upon the civil and criminal caseload. For instance, the Southern District of New York has approximately 220 AUSAs, whereas the Western District of Texas has 129 AUSAs, and the District of Wyoming has only 18 AUSAs (U.S. Office of Personnel Management 2010).

The Roles of Prosecutors

The primary roles of all prosecutors in criminal courts are to represent the government's interests and pursue criminal charges against those alleged to have committed crimes. For state's attorneys or district attorneys, their roles are similar throughout the different U.S. jurisdictions. A summary of these roles is as follows:

1. To screen cases for prosecution
2. To determine the best strategy for prosecuting cases
3. To make case assignments to assistant district attorneys
4. To interview prospective witnesses against the accused
5. To work closely with law enforcement officers to determine the nature of inculpatory evidence against the accused

In the federal system, the U.S. attorney's offices in the various federal districts are charged with the following broad roles:

1. To prosecute all offenses against the United States
2. To prosecute or defend, for the government, all civil actions, suits, or proceedings in which the United States is concerned
3. To appear on behalf of the defendants in civil actions and suits or proceedings pending in the district against collectors or other officers of the revenue or customs for things they have done or for the recovery of any money exacted by or paid to them
4. To institute and prosecute proceedings for the collection of fines, penalties, and forfeitures incurred for violation of any revenue law
5. To report as the attorney general directs

Screening Cases

Screening cases means to assign priority to different cases on the basis of which ones are most deserving of prosecution. The screening function of prosecutors is very important as it relates to obtaining guilty pleas from criminal defendants. Most convictions are obtained through plea negotiations between prosecutors and defense counsel, where some form of leniency from the prosecution is extended in exchange for a defendant's guilty plea. Thus, prosecutors have broad discretionary powers concerning which cases to pursue and what types of offers to extend those charged with crimes as inducements for guilty pleas (Forst 2004).

Prosecutors have the power to determine the types of cases that will be prosecuted more vigorously than others. Domestic violence or child abuse cases may receive high priority in certain jurisdictions because of strong interest from community and/or religious leaders. Prosecutors and police officers can assist these leaders in the prevention and deterrence of domestic violence by vigorously prosecuting and seeking maximum penalties in domestic violence cases. Organized or gang-related crime may have high priority for prosecutors in certain large urban jurisdictions.

Prosecutors seek convictions, and prosecutorial effectiveness is often gauged by the number of convictions they obtain (Keller 2005). The greater the number of convictions, the more effective are the prosecutors. Therefore, it is in the prosecutor's interest to select cases for prosecution that are the easiest to prosecute and obtain a conviction. Where clear and convincing evidence exists against an accused, prosecutors are in a stronger position to succeed in obtaining a conviction. More than a few cases, however, have little incriminating evidence and are based purely on circumstantial evidence. A prosecutor's vigor, persistence, and demeanor are often sufficiently convincing for jurors in courtrooms (Rockwell and Hubbard 2004). Prosecutors must decide whether these cases are worth pursuing, where the conviction of the accused is less of a certainty compared with a case with considerable inculpatory evidence.

Determining Court Strategy

Prosecutors must devise their theory of how and why the crime was committed. They must attempt to link the defendant to the crime in such a way that the jury will be convinced beyond a reasonable doubt of the accused's guilt. There are many potential explanations for a defendant's conduct relative to the crime. It is not necessary that the prosecutor selects the true explanation, only a plausible one. The theory of the crime and its commission is often suggested by the nature and quality of the evidence against the defendant. For example, if one's spouse was violently killed and the surviving spouse stands to collect on a $1 million insurance policy, then this fact provides a motive for why the surviving spouse might have committed the murder. However, if there is another person with whom the surviving spouse has had an affair, then the motive for the murder may be love and not money. It is fairly easy to see how different spins can be given to any criminal scenario.

Assigning Cases

Prosecutors in most jurisdictions usually have assistant prosecutors who can handle some of the case workload (Champion 2005a). In fact, most large-city district attorney's offices are bureaucratized to the extent that there are various specialty areas for different types of legal cases. A general civil–criminal distinction exists, where some of the assistant district attorneys may be assigned civil cases, while other assistants are assigned criminal ones. Further subdivisions may be made, depending upon case volume. Criminal cases may be divided according to sex crimes, property crimes, and other logical divisions. Certain prosecutors acquire considerable expertise in selected legal areas, and this expertise enables them to prosecute certain cases involving their expertise more effectively than other prosecutors without this expertise. For instance, prosecutors with substantial experience with forensic evidence, such as DNA testing, may be more skillful at eliciting more compelling testimony from expert witnesses, and they may also do a better job of cross-examining defense experts on the same subject matter. Other prosecutors may have considerable experience and facility with child eyewitnesses. Each case poses certain types of problems for prosecutors, and thus, it is prudent for prosecutors to make strategic case assignments on the basis of which assistant district attorneys can do the best job of prosecuting under the circumstances.

Interviewing Witnesses

Prosecutors and their assistants must interview persons who have knowledge about the crime. Often, witnesses for both the prosecution and defense are deposed. A deposition is a sworn written record of oral testimony. Persons who are deposed are deponents. The purpose of a deposition is to have a written record of what one's testimony is as well as an indication of its relevance to the case. When witnesses testify in court later, their depositions can be used to refresh their recollections. Sometimes depositions can be used to impeach witnesses if they are lying or say things that are inconsistent with their earlier depositions (Carey 2001).

Information provided to prosecutors by witnesses can be interpreted in various ways. Witness interviews can help prosecutors to formulate their strategy for prosecuting a case. The state may use expert witnesses to verify whether a defendant is sane or insane, competent or incompetent. If certain defendants are sufficiently incompetent to stand trial, then prosecutors can use this information to seek their commitment indefinitely in a mental hospital (Bullock 2002).

Prosecutors can determine in which order they will present their witnesses against the accused later in court. Thus, they can use witnesses to build their case against defendants. In complex serious criminal cases, there will probably be numerous witnesses called by both sides. It is important, therefore, that some effort should be made to organize the witnesses into an orderly presentation that will create the most convincing case against the accused. Observations of actual criminal trials reveal such orderly presentations of witnesses for both sides.

Working Closely with Law Enforcement Officers

It is important for prosecutors to develop a working rapport with law enforcement officers. Law enforcement officers have direct crime scene experience and can testify about their conversations with the defendant. If a confession has been obtained, or if the defendant has provided police officers with incriminating information, this information can be developed in court to the defendant's disadvantage.

Law enforcement officers are subject to cross-examination by defense counsel. Experienced defense attorneys can seriously impair the state's case against a defendant by evoking responses from officers that show their ineptness. Prosecutors and their assistants can assist officers in learning how to give testimony that will minimize any weaknesses in the state's case.

Police officers also testify about the evidence they collected at the crime scene that incriminates the defendant. Their testimony is quite important in this respect, and it is vital that prosecutors have the trust of these officers when they are questioned under direct examination in court (Leo 1994). In federal district courts, AUSAs work closely with other agents from the FBI, DEA, Border Patrol, and other federal authorities in presenting evidence against those charged with federal crimes. These agents learn to permit AUSAs the latitude of presenting the case against the defendant in a particular way. Federal agents also learn to be adept at giving testimony in certain ways that will heighten the inculpatory or incriminating effect of it. It is up to the defense counsel, therefore, to attempt to get the agents to admit that other less incriminating interpretations might be drawn from the testimony given.

What Do You Think?

In some jurisdictions, a special prosecutor will be assigned where a police officer or officers are accused of criminal offenses, but in most jurisdictions, usually the same prosecutor who works daily with law enforcement has the power to decide whether or not to charge the police officers. Should jurisdictions have outside prosecutors take over when the police are accused of wrongdoing? Do you think that outside or special prosecutors would be better able to make an unbiased and fair decision than one who relies daily on police testimony to try cases and get convictions?

Changing the Venue for Trials

The venue is the jurisdiction where the case originates. If a crime is committed in San Antonio, Texas, the venue is San Antonio. A judge in San Antonio will most likely hear the case. The jury will be selected from Bexar County, where San Antonio is located. If the case is an especially high-profile one, either the defense or the prosecution may attempt to change the venue where the case is heard. This is because of the substantial publicity given to the case and the possibility that an impartial jury cannot be impaneled to hear it. Jurors in any criminal case are expected to hear all evidence impartially and to render an objective decision as to the guilt or innocence of a defendant. If pretrial publicity is adverse to defendants, defense counsels may make a motion to change the venue for hearing the case to another county. Prosecutors may oppose such motions.

But changes of venue, which are rarely granted, may also be initiated by prosecutors. If the crime occurs in a locality where the defendant is well known and liked by the community, it may be difficult to find an impartial jury that would convict the defendant, despite the compelling evidence favoring a conviction. In these cases, prosecutors may attempt to change the venue to a jurisdiction where the defendant is less well known. Thus, both prosecutors and defense counsels have a stake in determining the best location for where the ensuing trial will be held. Many circumstances, including pretrial publicity and media coverage, influence such decision making as well as which side will request a change in venue (Posey and Dahl 2002). Neither prosecutors nor defense counsels can mandate changes of venue for their cases, but they can make motions for such changes. They must present compelling arguments to judges for venue changes. Unless there are overwhelming circumstances suggesting that defendants would not receive a fair trial in the original venue, motions for changing the venue of the trial are typically not granted.

Obtaining Indictments or Filing Criminal Informations

In about half of all states, grand juries are convened to hear evidence against particular defendants. This evidence is presented by prosecutors in most circumstances, and based on the evidence presented, grand juries issue true bills or indictments. These true bills or indictments are merely declarations by grand juries that sufficient probable cause exists to believe that one or more crimes were committed and that the defendant may have committed the crime(s). Grand juries, therefore, do not decide one's guilt or innocence. Rather, prosecutors work to persuade grand juries to indict defendants so that their cases may proceed to trial (Schmid 2002).

For less serious offenses, such as misdemeanors, prosecutors may act on their own and file charges against criminal defendants by filing criminal informations or simply informations. Informations are similar to indictments, except that prosecutors initiate them on their own. Prosecutors believe that probable cause exists that a crime was committed and that a particular defendant committed the crime. Therefore, prosecutors can file an information against any criminal suspect. The result is the same as an indictment. The defendant will face a criminal trial where their guilt can be decided by the judge or jury.

Prosecutorial Misconduct

Whether prosecutors in various jurisdictions are elected or appointed, there are many pressures on them from different sources. First, there is the immediate pressure to win cases and obtain convictions against defendants. Second, there is pressure to make a weak case look like a strong case. This means that the evidence may have to be manipulated or collected in ways that are inconsistent with proper police procedure (White 2002).

Just like there are varying degrees of attorney competence, there are also varying degrees of prosecutorial misconduct (Schoenfeld 2005). Not all forms of misconduct have the same weight or importance. Some misconduct may be trivial, although the cumulative

venue area over which a judge exercises authority to act in an official capacity. Place where a trial is held.

true bills grand jury decisions that sufficient evidence exists that a crime has been committed and that a specific suspect committed it.

indictments charges or written accusations found and presented by a grand jury that a particular defendant probably committed a crime.

criminal informations; informations written accusations made by a public prosecutor against a person for some criminal offense, without an indictment.

effect of minor or trivial misconduct may arouse juror suspicions to the degree that a guilty verdict is subsequently rendered. Prosecutors may encourage experts to exaggerate their claims or evidence to enhance their case against a defendant; prosecutors may overwhelm grand juries with purely inculpatory evidence and deliberately exclude any exculpatory evidence; prosecutors may bluff with defendants and threaten or intimidate them; prosecutors may suppress certain types of exculpatory evidence from the defense; prosecutors may exclude prospective jurors who have views favorable to defendants; prosecutors may offer inadmissible evidence in court; and prosecutors may engage in malicious prosecutions. While it is presently unknown precisely how much prosecutorial misconduct occurs nationally, it has been reported by the Center for Public Integrity that since 1970, 20 percent of 11,452 appellate-reviewed cases where the defendants claimed prosecutorial misconduct were dismissed, reversed, or reduced from the original sentence partly or wholly because of prosecutorial misconduct (The Center for Public Integrity 2003; Weinberg, Gordon, and Williams 2005).

BOX 3-1

KEY CASES: LAW REGARDING PROSECUTORIAL MISCONDUCT

Buckley v. Fitzsimmons, 509 U.S. 259 (1993)

Buckley was charged with murder. Prosecutors made various statements surrounding the indictment of Buckley for the murder, including several untrue statements. Subsequently, the charges against Buckley were dropped, and he sued the prosecutors under Title 42 U.S.C. Section 1983, alleging that his civil rights had been violated by this prosecutorial misconduct. The prosecutors sought absolute immunity from this suit and the U.S. Supreme Court heard the case. The U.S. Supreme Court upheld Buckley's right to sue the prosecutor, who only enjoyed qualified immunity from such suits. Prosecutors are liable for statements they make publicly if such statements are false and they result in harm to defendants who are innocent of criminal wrongdoing.

Banks v. Dretke, ___U.S.___, 124 S.Ct. 1256 (2004)

Delma Banks was convicted of capital murder in the death of 16-year-old Richard Whitehead, which occurred in mid-April 1980. Banks was originally implicated in the murder by two associates, Jefferson and Farr, who were working with the county sheriff, Willie Huff, as informants. Unknown to Banks before and during the trial was the allegation that Jefferson and Farr were testifying against Banks in order to avoid drug charges, which were threatened by the sheriff and prosecutor. At the same time, a confidential informant,

Cook, also furnished the prosecution with incriminating circumstantial evidence against Banks. This information was also withheld from Banks pursuant to a motion for discovery. Although Banks had no prior criminal record, testimony from Farr and Jefferson provided the jury with innuendo that Banks had an unsavory and criminal past, which was untrue. Banks's efforts to impeach Farr and Jefferson were undermined because of his own witnesses, who were themselves impeached on cross-examination. Banks was sentenced to death and sought postconviction relief, alleging that the prosecution failed to disclose exculpatory evidence as required by *Brady v. Maryland* (1963), including the threats made to Farr and Jefferson as well as the confidential informant, Cook. In its answer, the state claimed that nothing had been kept secret from Banks and no deals had been made with government witnesses, including Cook. In 1993, Banks's postconviction claims were denied outright by an appellate court. Following this loss, Banks filed for *habeas corpus* relief in a U.S. District Court, which granted relief on Banks's death sentence. In 1999, Banks filed discovery and evidentiary hearing motions, both supported by affidavits sworn to by Farr and Jefferson that the prosecution had wrongly withheld crucial exculpatory and impeaching evidence. The federal court determined that the state, indeed, had failed to disclose Farr's informant status during the original discovery phase of Banks's trial. Therefore, a writ of *habeas corpus* was granted to Banks with respect to his death sentence, but not to his conviction. Banks petitioned the U.S. Supreme Court, who heard the case. The U.S. Supreme Court reiterated that under *Brady*, a prosecutorial misconduct claim must establish three things: (1) the evidence at issue must be favorable to the accused, either because it is exculpatory or because it is impeaching; (2) evidence must have been suppressed by the state, either willfully or inadvertently; and (3) prejudice must have ensued. In its response, the state contended that "it can lie and conceal and the prisoner still has the burden to discover the evidence." The U.S. Supreme Court ruled this assertion to be untenable and a violation of Banks's due process rights. Banks presented sufficient evidence to support his *Brady* claim and was thus entitled to a full evidentiary hearing and a certification of appealability.

Encouraging Deceit from Experts and Other Types of Witnesses

When prosecutors construct their case presentation, they arrange the testimony of various expert witnesses and others who have relevant evidence to present. Often, expert witnesses may be able to provide too much information in court, and prosecutors must work with them to ensure that only selected pieces of information are disclosed about the case (McKimmie et al. 2004). Thus, experts have their testimony shaped and tailored by prosecutors so that it fits more closely with the scenario of the crime and its commission as envisioned by the state. Therefore, much of the prosecutorial melodrama in court is carefully orchestrated in advance. If certain witnesses are considered weak and have little direct inculpatory information against the accused, they may be brought to the witness stand to testify early in the trial, so that the jury can forget about their weaknesses toward the end of the trial.

Seemingly innocent expert witness statements can appear very incriminating. The prosecutor may ask, "Was the blood found on the defendant's shirt consistent with the blood of the victim?" The expert witness says, "Yes, I can say definitely that there was such a consistency." The jury is transfixed by such riveting testimony. However, the defense breaks this bubble by asking the expert witness on cross-examination, "Can you say positively that the blood on the defendant's shirt is the victim's blood?" And the expert witness lowers his head and says, "No, I can't say positively that the blood found is that of the victim's. I can only say that it is consistent with the victim's blood." The defense probes further. "In what respect is the blood found consistent with the victim's blood?" The expert witness says, "It is Type O positive." And the defense asks, "And is it not so that the defendant also has Type O blood?" And the expert says, "Yes, that is true." And the defense asks, "And is it not possible that the blood on the defendant's shirt is the defendant's own blood from a cut on the defendant's arm?" And the expert witness says, "Yes, that is true."

While DNA matching is increasingly important to show precisely whose blood it is that is found at crime scenes, the fact remains that much contamination of blood can occur to make blood typing and identification somewhat unreliable. Furthermore, due to limited resources, DNA testing does not occur in all cases. This does not prevent prosecutors from using this evidence, regardless of its potential unreliability, to the disadvantage of the defendant.

Overwhelming Grand Juries

When grand juries are convened, prosecutors are interested in obtaining indictments against defendants. Grand juries consider evidence presented by the prosecutor and determine whether there is sufficient probable cause to believe that a crime was committed and that the defendant probably committed it. Grand juries do not determine the guilt or innocence of the accused. They merely determine whether probable cause exists and that a case should go forward to trial for a legal resolution.

Prosecutors are in a unique position relative to grand juries. Prosecutors direct which evidence and testimony will be presented to the grand jury. Thus, if a prosecutor has considerable evidence and numerous witnesses, he/she may decide to present only the most damaging evidence and the most incriminating testimony. Some witnesses interviewed by the prosecutor may actually provide an alibi for the defendant, showing that the defendant may not have been at the place where the crime was committed at the time when it occurred. Prosecutors exercise their discretion here and determine to present only the evidence and witnesses that show the defendant's guilt.

Since grand juries see only one side of the case against an accused person, they may think only the worst about that defendant. Indictments are issued, therefore, when grand juries are convinced that there is sufficient probable cause to believe that the defendant committed the crime. They are not permitted the luxury of a presentation by the defense counsel to rebut whatever was presented by the prosecutor.

Several attempts have been made by different court systems to monitor prosecutorial conduct before grand juries. For instance, in federal grand jury proceedings, tape recordings have been made and reviewed later by federal district court judges. Misconduct before the grand jury has been referred to as pre-indictment impropriety. However, recordings of grand jury proceedings can help to uncover any prosecutorial misconduct that is disclosed. Some of these federal judges have recommended that a full disclosure of grand jury proceedings be made available later to defense counsel and others. Presumably, these recommendations are intended to cause prosecutors to engage in more ethical conduct. It is doubtful that such recordings of grand jury proceedings and subsequent disclosures have curbed prosecutorial abuses of discretion in grand jury proceedings, however.

Prosecutorial Bluffing with Criminal Defendants: Threats or Intimidation?

prosecutorial bluffing attempt by prosecution to bluff the defendant into believing the case is stronger than it really is. Used to elicit a guilty plea from a defendant to avoid a trial where the proof of a defendant's guilt may be difficult to establish.

When criminal defendants are not represented by counsel or are represented by weak defense lawyers, and/or when the cases against criminal defendants are weak, prosecutors may engage in prosecutorial bluffing (White 2002). Prosecutorial bluffing means to threaten defendants with a lengthy list of charges, each of which carries serious penalties of fines and lengthy incarcerative terms. The intent of prosecutorial bluffing is to cause a defendant to enter a guilty plea to one of the more minor charges in exchange for prosecutorial leniency. For instance, if the defendant pleads guilty to one felony charge, the other five felony charges will be dropped. Or maybe the prosecutor will accept the defendant's guilty plea to a misdemeanor, in exchange for a sentence of probation and dropping more serious felony changes.

The Center for Public Integrity (2003) and other organizations have conducted various polls and surveys of prosecutorial misconduct in recent years with some fascinating results. For instance, it has been found that within the 2,341 jurisdictions in the United States, local prosecutors in most of these jurisdictions have stretched, bent, or broken the rules to win convictions since 1970. Individual judges and appellate court judges have cited numerous instances of prosecutorial misconduct as a major factor in dismissing many cases, reversing convictions, or reducing sentences in over 2,000 cases. Prosecutorial misconduct has been found to warrant reversals of jury verdicts in another 500 cases. In thousands more of these cases, judges have labeled prosecutorial behavior as inappropriate, but they have upheld convictions nevertheless under the doctrine of "harmless error." Misconduct by prosecutors has led to the convictions of many innocent individuals who were later exonerated. Even guilty defendants have had their convictions overturned and were released back out on the streets because of prosecutorial misconduct. Some prosecutors violate the rules more than others. More than a few are cited multiple times for misconduct. These prosecutors give recidivism a new meaning. Prosecutorial bluffing is not limited to criminal defendants. Prosecutors may also threaten or intimidate prospective witnesses.

Suppressing Evidence from the Defense

Prosecutors are able to view all evidence collected from the police and material witnesses in criminal cases. While some of this evidence may tend to show the guilt of the defendant, other evidence may show the defendant's innocence. If a prosecutor has such exculpatory evidence, he/she is obligated to disclose this evidence to the defense for its use. However, evidence suggests that much of the time, exculpatory evidence is deliberately suppressed by prosecutors, even in capital cases (Harmon 2000, 2001).

Excluding Prospective Jurors who are Favorable to Defendants

When prospective jurors are being questioned concerning their qualifications and beliefs or prejudices, both the prosecution and defense have an opportunity to challenge them. Particularly in high-profile trials involving well-known persons, a concerted attempt is made by both sides to configure the best jury most favorable to either side. While jury voting cannot be predicted by either side in advance, prosecutors and their associates attempt to select jurors who will be pro-prosecution in their views.

In a capital murder case, for instance, prospective jurors with strong feelings against the death penalty may be excluded because these prospective jurors believe that their own feelings might not permit them to impose the death penalty if they find the defendant is guilty of the capital crime. When prosecutors dismiss these jurors, they narrow the pool of prospective jurors who might be favorably disposed toward the defendant. Frequently, prospective jurors are dismissed by prosecutors since these jurors exhibit other views that are associated with anti-death penalty sentiments. Defense counsel can engage in similar behavior by excluding those who are in favor of capital punishment (Martin and Roberts 2005). Always the number of jurors who can be dismissed by either the prosecution or defense because of the juror's sentiments is limited. Despite these limitations, prosecutors can skillfully maneuver and create a jury composition that they believe is unfavorable to a defendant (Nadeau, Burek, and Williams 2005). Because of the diffuse grounds used to dismiss particular prospective jurors, it is not easy to determine when prosecutors are engaging in this type of misconduct.

Offering Inadmissible Evidence in Court

A prosecutorial tactic sometimes used in a weak criminal case is to backdoor hearsay evidence. **Backdooring hearsay evidence** means to mention or comment about evidence against the accused that is not admissible evidence. Perhaps the defendant, charged with trafficking in heroin, has been arrested five times in the past for heroin and cocaine possession. However, these arrests have resulted in case dismissals. Insufficient evidence existed to move forward with criminal prosecutions in each of these five arrest situations. In many jurisdictions, prosecutors may only introduce evidence about one's prior criminal convictions. It is not permissible for prosecutors to mention any arrests that never resulted in convictions. But the prosecutor might make a statement in court while questioning the defendant or a witness. "Were you with the defendant when he was arrested for cocaine and heroin possession on five different occasions during the last three years?" the prosecutor might ask. Before the witness can speak, an objection is made by the defense and the judge sustains the objection, admonishing the jury to disregard the prosecutor's question. But the damage has already been done. The question has been raised and heard by the jurors. They now know that the defendant has been arrested in the past for heroin and cocaine possession. More important, the jurors have no way of knowing that these arrests never resulted in prosecutions or convictions on the drug charges. Inadmissible evidence has been admitted through the back door, although the judge has declared that the jury should ignore it. Jurors cannot ignore whatever they have heard.

It is difficult for the court to determine whether the utterances of prosecutors are deliberate or willful, intentional or unintentional. Prosecutors may claim that they had no intention of violating court rules by mentioning inadmissible evidence, although they may have done so deliberately. Most courts interpret such utterances as harmless error.

> **backdooring hearsay evidence** action by prosecutor where prosecutor comments about or mentions information to the jury that is otherwise inadmissible in court.

Malicious Prosecutions

The pressure on prosecutors to obtain convictions may induce them to file charges against certain defendants who are innocent of any crime. When prosecutors bring charges against the accused with the full knowledge that the accused is innocent of the crimes alleged, this is a malicious prosecution.

Misconduct Risks and Sanctions

When prosecutors commit prosecutorial misconduct, particularly in the courtroom, there is always the chance that the misconduct will be detected and sanctioned in some way. Prejudicial commentary by the prosecutor will cause defense counsel to object. Judges will sustain these objections, but the harm has already been done. The jury has heard the prejudicial commentary, and despite an admonition from the judge to disregard such prejudicial commentary, the jury cannot forget about it entirely. For instance, a prosecutor may be barred from mentioning a defendant's sexual preferences in a murder trial occurring in a small religious community. However, the prosecutor may allude to a homosexual defendant's gay rights activism, even though this commentary has nothing to do with the case before the court. Defense counsel will object strenuously, and the judge will sustain this objection. But the jury cannot erase from their memories the prosecutor's statement about the defendant's gay rights activities. Jurors may assume that the defendant is gay, and this assumption may be sufficient to prejudice some of them. Because some of the jurors may dislike gays, they may punish the defendant by voting for his guilt, despite the fact that the defendant's guilt has not been established beyond a reasonable doubt. The prosecutor is successful, therefore, in prejudicing jurors against the defendant by alluding to one or more extralegal factors.

Ethical Norms

Prosecutors can get away with their courtroom misconduct largely because of an absence of ethical norms as standards against which to gauge their conduct. In case after case where prosecutorial misconduct is alleged, the U.S. Supreme Court has failed to articulate clear and consistent ethical norms to guide prosecutors.

Interestingly, juries are more inclined to consider inadmissible evidence favorable to defendants than inadmissible evidence unfavorable to defendants. Despite this factor of defense favoritism, prosecutors might be tempted to sway the jury by introducing highly prejudicial inadmissible evidence. By doing so, they risk jeopardizing any resulting conviction. However, the likelihood of having one's conviction overturned in these instances is extremely remote. The most significant reason for the continued presence of prosecutorial misconduct is the harmless error doctrine. Under this doctrine, an appellate court can affirm one's conviction despite the presence of serious prosecutorial misconduct during the trial. Thus, the desirability of the doctrine is undermined when the prosecutor is able to commit misconduct without fear of sanction (Carter 2001). The harmless error doctrine also can pertain to serious cases where the death penalty can be invoked.

Also, the standards currently used in ruling on motions for retrial based on false testimony fail to strike an acceptable balance between the right of the accused to a fair and impartial trial and the demand for efficient administration of the criminal justice system in court. Ideally, motions for retrial based on false testimony presented by prosecution witnesses should be governed by a standard drawn from newly discovered evidence and prosecutorial misconduct. The proper test for a new trial based on newly discovered evidence of false testimony is whether there is a significant chance that a jury with a knowledge of the false testimony would avoid convicting the defendant.

---

malicious prosecution prosecutorial action against someone without probable cause or reasonable suspicion.

prosecutorial misconduct any deliberate action that violates ethical codes or standards governing the role of prosecutors.

harmless error doctrine errors of a minor or trivial nature and not deemed sufficient to harm the rights of parties in a legal action. Cases are not reversed on the basis of harmless errors.

Summary

1. Understand the criminal court as an adversarial system seeking to determine the guilt or innocence of defendants charged with crimes.

The criminal court is an adversarial system. The adversaries are the prosecutor and defense counsel. These persons are regarded as sides in a form of competition to win. The general goal of the prosecutor is to convict those accused of crimes, while the goal of the defense counsel is to secure an acquittal for his/her client. Deciding which side is right is the judge or jury's role in a bench or jury trial proceeding. Both sides abide by rules, including state or federal rules of criminal procedure and rules of evidence. These rules regulate virtually all permissible conduct from the beginning of a prosecution to the end of it.

2. Understand the many roles of prosecutors in pursuing cases against criminal suspects including that negotiating plea bargains is the most common method of obtaining a conviction.

Depending upon the jurisdiction, the roles of prosecutors are relatively simple. All prosecutors function to screen which cases to prosecute and which ones not to prosecute. This means that they must prioritize their cases. Thus, prosecutors decide on their own or in groups whether to pursue particular cases. These decisions are often made according to how much evidence exists against particular defendants, the likelihood of winning the case and securing a conviction, the media visibility of the case, and case seriousness.

Prosecutors are responsible for devising the best strategies for winning cases. They must interview witnesses, including victims of crime and those who saw the crime occur. They must work closely with law enforcement officers who made arrests and conducted criminal investigations. They must also work with forensic teams who analyze evidence collected from crime scenes.

The lead prosecutors in any jurisdiction may also assign cases for prosecution to their assistant district attorneys or state's attorneys. At the federal level, U.S. attorneys assign different criminal cases to their group of assistant U.S. attorneys.

3. Depict both exculpatory and inculpatory evidence that may be presented in criminal cases.

Evidentiary matters are an important part of the adversary process; judges make decisions according to various rules that have been established to govern whether certain types of evidence are admissible by either the prosecutor or the defense or both. Evidence introduced by either side is either inculpatory or exculpatory. Inculpatory evidence shows the defendant's guilt, while exculpatory evidence shows defendant innocence.

4. Describe the process of screening and prioritizing cases for criminal prosecutions.

When a prosecutor screens cases, it simply means they are assigning priority to cases based on which are the most deserving of prosecution. This is a very important task because it also involves decisions about plea bargains. Most convictions are obtained through plea negotiations between prosecutors and defense counsel. Prosecutors also have to decide the types of cases that will be prosecuted more vigorously than others; child abuse or drinking and driving cases may receive high priority in certain jurisdictions because of problems with these offenses in the particular jurisdiction. In other jurisdictions, gangs may be a problem, and organized crime or gang-related crime may have high priority for prosecutors.

Prosecutors must also decide which cases are worth pursuing. There will be cases where the conviction of the accused is less of a certainty compared with a case with a considerable amount of inculpatory evidence. Prosecutors must also determine their strategy in court that includes coming up with a theory of how and why the crime was committed. They must attempt to link the defendant to the crime in such a way that the jury will be convinced beyond a reasonable doubt of the accused's guilt. The theory of the crime and its commission is often suggested by the nature and quality of the evidence against the defendant. In larger jurisdictions, prosecutors must also assign the caseload to other assistant prosecutors. Cases, for example, may be assigned according to the type of offense, such as sex crimes and property crimes. Particular prosecutors may have expertise or a lot of experience in certain types of cases that enables them to be more successful than others without this expertise and experience.

Prosecutors and their assistants must also interview persons who have knowledge about the crime. This is usually done via a deposition, where witnesses for both the prosecution and defense are deposed. The purpose of this is to have a written account of testimony so that when witnesses testify in court later, their depositions can be used to refresh their memories.

Next to the judge who presides over trials, the prosecutor, also known as the state's attorney, the district attorney, or the U.S. attorney or assistant U.S. attorney, is one of the most powerful members of the court. Prosecutors represent the state's or federal government's interests whenever one or more crimes are alleged against defendants. Prosecutors are often political appointees or elected persons, all of whom have law degrees or other equivalent entitlements that enable them to practice law. Prosecutors have an immense amount of power. In jurisdictions with grand jury systems, prosecutors attempt to secure indictments or charges against those accused of crimes. They make their cases before grand juries and present inculpatory evidence to them. These are largely one-sided proceedings, since defense counsels are not permitted to present exculpatory evidence in favor of their clients.

Prosecutors usually obtain over 90 percent of their convictions against criminal defendants through plea bargaining. While judges must approve all plea bargain agreements, they do not always detect when innocent defendants enter pleas of guilty to crimes they have not committed. Prosecutors must prioritize the cases they prosecute and many factors affect their decision making, even financial and personnel resources influence these decisions. Despite what the general public believes, not all persons who deserve to have charges filed against them can be prosecuted. Prosecutors, therefore, use their discretion to make decisions about which cases to prosecute based on the available evidence, the seriousness of the offense, and whether or not they believe they can obtain a conviction via a plea bargain or through a criminal trial.

5. *Assess the potential for prosecutorial misconduct or discretionary abuses arising from the extensive powers of prosecutors.*

As attorneys, all prosecutors are bound by codes of ethics, depending upon the professional organizations to which they belong. Most attorneys in the United States belong to the ABA, which has articulated ethical codes and standards over the years for its membership to follow. Canons of ethics include exhibiting integrity and competence, assisting the legal profession in various ways to bring distinction upon it, assisting in preventing the unauthorized practice of law, preserving confidence of clients and others, representing the government and/or clients competently, representing the government and/or clients zealously within the boundaries of the law, assisting in improving the legal system, and avoiding the appearance of impropriety.

Prosecutorial misconduct does not typify most prosecutors, although it exists throughout state and federal systems to an uncomfortable degree. Several forms of prosecutorial misconduct have been described. Prosecutors may coach their witnesses by encouraging them to relate what evidentiary information they have in ways that favor the prosecutor's argument that the defendant is guilty of a crime. In some instances, prosecutors may encourage defendants to commit perjury on the witness stand and say things about the defendant that are not true. This is subornation of perjury and a crime. Another form of prosecutorial misconduct is malicious prosecution. Malicious prosecution is the prosecution of someone who is innocent of the crime alleged, and this innocence is known or believed by the prosecutor. Nevertheless, the prosecutor moves forward against these defendants anyway.

Prosecutors may also engage in prosecutorial bluffing. Prosecutorial bluffing is intended to frighten criminal defendants and their defense counsels into thinking that prosecutors have more inculpatory evidence than they really have. Often, prosecutorial bluffing encourages defendants to enter into guilty pleas through plea bargain agreements, especially if defendants are offered light sentences of probation in exchange for guilty pleas to minor charges. Another form of prosecutorial misconduct is to deliberately withhold exculpatory evidence from defense counsels prior to or during trials. Under discovery rules, certain materials and evidence must be made available to defense counsels. These materials, known as Brady or Jencks materials after their respective U.S. Supreme Court cases that declared certain materials as discoverable, must be disclosed to defense counsels and are often crucial in showing the innocence of their clients. Finally, prosecutors may backdoor hearsay testimony before juries during trial proceedings. This is clearly an unethical and unwarranted practice, where prosecutors will ask questions of witnesses or make statements during their opening or closing arguments that violate either the rules of criminal procedure or the rules of evidence or both. These statements, which often tend to incriminate defendants or disclose past behaviors that are clearly inadmissible in court, often result in sustained objections from the opposing side, but the jury has heard these statements.

Key Terms

adversary system *48*

assistant U.S. attorneys (AUSAs) *50*

attorney general *50*

backdooring hearsay evidence *57*

county prosecutors *50*

criminal informations *53*

defense attorney *48*

deponents *52*

district attorneys *50*

ethical code *49*

exculpatory evidence *49*

harmless error doctrine *58*

inculpatory evidence *49*

indictments *53*

informations *53*

malicious prosecution *58*

prosecuting attorneys *50*

prosecutor *48*

prosecutorial bluffing *56*

prosecutorial misconduct *58*

rules of criminal procedure *49*

state's attorneys *50*

true bills *53*

U.S. attorney *50*

U.S. attorney's office *50*

venue *53*

witnesses *49*

Critical Thinking Exercises

1. Many forms of prosecutorial misconduct go unnoticed or unreported. Even when uncovered and reported, judges often uphold convictions under the harmless error doctrine. Should jurisdictions hold prosecutors more accountable to the ABA's Model Rules of Professional Conduct? What should happen to prosecutors who violate these rules? Should the criminal court system rethink the harmless error doctrine and make it easier for judges to overturn convictions where misconduct has been found, or make the sanctions greater for prosecutors where there has been serious prosecutorial misconduct?

2. About half of all states use grand juries to determine whether probable cause exists against defendants to proceed with prosecutorial charging. These grand jury proceedings are one-sided affairs where only the prosecutor gets to present evidence. Should grand juries be revised to include evidence from the defense counsel? If there is exculpatory evidence that favors the defendant in the case, should this information also be brought to the grand jury's attention? Do you see any problems with allowing defense testimony to a grand jury? What about the case where a defendant is not represented by counsel?

3. In the majority of jurisdictions, roughly 90 percent of convictions are obtained through a plea bargain. Plea bargaining benefits both sides in that prosecutors get better conviction rates and defendants get leniency in exchange for pleading guilty. However, there are criticisms of plea bargaining that is it too coercive and defense attorneys are too quick to give up their defendant's rights, that serious offenders escape serious punishments, and that it invalidates the Sixth Amendment right to a jury trial. Considering that we characterize our system as an adversarial system of justice, do you believe that more cases should go to trial to determine a defendant's guilt or innocence? Should our system hold prosecutors accountable to proving beyond a reasonable doubt the defendant's guilt to a judge or jury. If so, how do you think this would change the functions that the prosecution and defense perform under the current system?

Case Study Decision-Making Exercise

With an increasing number of persons being exonerated by advancements in DNA after serving many years in prison, critics are paying more attention to prosecutorial charging practices and the process by which wrongful convictions might occur. Some of the wrongful convictions have uncovered prosecutorial misconduct such as withholding evidence that showed the defendant's innocence. Even if wrongful convictions only occur in 1 percent of cases, with two million people in prison, this could mean that tens of thousands of innocent people are incarcerated for crimes they didn't commit. Many organizations, such as the Innocence Project, have started chapters in many states around the country to exonerate the innocents who have been wrongfully convicted, but what else could jurisdictions do to have more certainty that they have convicted the right person? Should states have special oversight committees that also screen cases for errors? Should states ensure that defense counsel do a better job of questioning prosecutorial evidence? The next chapter will focus on defense counsel and we will discuss how misconduct and neglect of their duties by the defense can also lead to wrongful convictions.

10 *Understand the relation between prosecutors and defense counsel and the discovery process.*

11 *Describe the various affirmative defenses attorneys may raise when representing persons charged with crimes.*

In the early part of 2016, the American Civil Liberties Union sued the state of Louisiana and the city of New Orleans for denying defendants their Sixth Amendment right to legal counsel as well as for underfunding their public defender system. Many other states, and Congress, have been criticized for not adequately funding indigent defense despite the fact that 50 years have passed since the Supreme Court's landmark ruling in *Gideon v. Wainwright* mandating that indigent defendants be entitled to an attorney if they cannot afford one. Despite increases in funding over the past couple of decades, numerous criticisms still plague the system for provision of counsel in the United States. One of the most oft cited quotes of indigent defense comes from a qualitative study of inmates in a Connecticut jail; when the interviewer asked the inmate whether he had a lawyer when he went to court, he replied, " No, I had a public defender" (Casper 1972). Besides the major criticism that indigent defense is extremely underfunded, there are also criticisms that caseloads are too high especially for public defenders, that attorneys are underpaid, and that because of this, they are too quick to bargain with the prosecution and encourage their client to enter a guilty plea. What do you think? Should legislators and the courts give more attention to our Sixth Amendment rights, perhaps the way that they do to other rights such as the First Amendment? Should states and the federal government appropriate more resources to indigent defense and public defense systems to uphold the Sixth Amendment right to counsel? Why do you think that the government and our criminal justice system have not fully fulfilled *Gideon's* promise?

▶ Introduction

The Sixth Amendment to the U.S. Constitution states that "In all criminal prosecutions, the accused shall enjoy the right to have the assistance of counsel for his defense." The Supreme Court in *Gideon v. Wainwright* recognized that the due process of defendants could not be guaranteed unless they had the assistance of counsel. Today, in both state and federal jurisdictions, all persons charged with crimes are entitled to counsel. Therefore, if a defendant is indigent, and cannot afford an attorney, one will be provided for him/her. This chapter examines the role of defense counsel in great detail. The first section describes one's right to counsel and how it is exercised. Indeed, many criminal defendants are indigent and cannot afford to hire counsel. In these cases of indigence, public defenders will be appointed by the court to furnish legal representation to defendants to ensure that their rights are observed. Some defendants wish to represent themselves and reject counsel appointed by the court. These persons proceed on a *pro se* basis, but they are warned by the court that self-representation is not a very good idea if they have no legal background. An old adage states that a defendant who represents himself/herself has a fool for a client.

The chapter next examines the attorney–client relationship and the confidentiality associated with it. Whatever conversations pass between an attorney and his/her client cannot be compelled for disclosure to the prosecutor and others. This confidentiality privilege is quite important in preserving the integrity of the criminal justice system, and it protects defendants against self-incrimination. Also examined in this section is the issue of ineffective assistance of counsel. Not all defense counsels are equally gifted in the ways of the law, and from time to time, some defense counsels will fail to act in ways that best represent their clients' interests. When this situation occurs, convicted offenders may challenge their convictions by alleging ineffective assistance of counsel. Subsequently, the U.S. Supreme Court has ruled decisively and determined the criteria used to evaluate whether or not a defense counsel is competent.

For the small percentage of cases that proceed to the trial phase of one's criminal processing, defense attorneys must present convincing cases to judges or juries, whether bench or jury trials are conducted (Zalman 2004). The standards for jury trials have been articulated by the U.S. Supreme Court and will be examined here. For example, in the case of petty offenses and for offenses where the maximum incarceration is six months or less, defendants are not entitled to a jury trial as a matter of right.

The chapter next examines the process whereby indigent defendants have attorneys appointed for them. Different states use one of several types of public defender systems. Some states use several systems simultaneously, but in different counties. These systems include the public defender system, the contract system, and the assigned counsel system. Each system is described, and the advantages and disadvantages of each system for indigent defendants are discussed. The general question of whether private attorneys or public defenders are more effective in representing clients will also be examined. There have been criticisms of indigent defense systems, and the chapter will provide an in-depth discussion of each of the types of systems. Finally, it will also explore why some argue that perhaps the public defender is able to secure more favorable outcomes for clients than a privately retained criminal defense attorney.

The various functions of defense counsels are also explained and discussed. These functions include faithfully representing clients, attacking vigorously the prosecutor's case against the defendant, counseling with defendants to determine the best defense strategy, negotiating with prosecutors in plea agreement proceedings to configure a plea most favorable for the defendant, vigorously cross-examining prosecution witnesses during trials to undermine their credibility or impeach their veracity, and using any and all legal means at their disposal to defeat the government's case against their defendant. From time to time, defense counsel may confront some ethical issues in their day-to-day duties. Like prosecutors, there are certain ethical guidelines within which defense counsel should conduct their duties and functions. Sometimes they overstep the boundaries between zealous advocacy and unethical behavior.

One important function of defense counsels is to interact with prosecutors and seek discovery of relevant evidentiary information. The discovery process is described as well as its significance for the trial outcome. Discovery has been influenced by several important U.S. Supreme Court cases, which will be described. Materials subject to discovery rules have been variously labeled as Brady materials or Jencks materials, after the major cases where high court rulings were rendered. Much of the discoverable evidence provided to defense counsels is important to the defense's case. Several types of evidence are distinguished and examined, including conclusive evidence, direct evidence, circumstantial evidence, and demonstrative evidence. Defense counsels must decide how and when to use different types of evidence they possess most effectively.

The chapter concludes with an examination about what several of the defense attorneys might use to explain away the conduct of their clients. These are mostly affirmative defenses, and they include automatism or insanity, intoxication, coercion or duress, necessity, alibi, entrapment, defense of property, ignorance or mistake, and self-defense. While this list of defenses is not exhaustive, most affirmative defenses used by defense counsels are presented here. Several examples of these defenses are also discussed.

► On Legal Ethics and Professional Responsibility

Lawyers have been the butt of more than a few jokes. For instance, there's the one that asks what do you throw to a drowning lawyer? The answer . . . his partner! There are several reasons for such jokes. First, some lawyers have engaged in disreputable or dishonest activities. When they have been caught, they often make headlines in their local newspapers. There are hundreds of disbarment proceedings against lawyers every year, where different forms of misconduct have been alleged. The U.S. Supreme Court has rejected most of their appeals for reconsideration. A second reason is that some lawyers have bad reputations for taking advantage of their clients and exploiting them. The public seems to reflect a general mistrust of lawyers as well. Public opinion polls have been taken regarding the honesty of lawyers and other professional persons. In 1997, for instance, lawyers were ranked nineteenth in honesty behind funeral directors, newspaper reporters, dentists, police, and real estate agents (Maguire and Pastore 2005).

In an effort to improve the image of lawyers throughout the United States, various professional associations and organizations have evolved codes of ethics or standards by which lawyers should conduct their behavior. For instance, the American Bar Association (ABA) first adopted its Canons of Professional Ethics at a meeting in Seattle, Washington, in 1908. Intended as a means of self-regulation, the Canons of Ethics are a part of the ABA Model Code of Professional Responsibility. Attorneys in all U.S. jurisdictions ideally are expected to adhere to this code on a voluntary basis. Whenever violations of this code occur or are alleged, disciplinary rules are invoked to sanction those who are believed to have engaged in unethical conduct. There are nine Canons of Ethics (Morgan 1983, 3), including

1. A lawyer should assist in maintaining the integrity and competence of the legal profession.
2. A lawyer should assist the legal profession in fulfilling its duty to make legal counsel available.
3. A lawyer should assist in preventing the unauthorized practice of law.
4. A lawyer should preserve the confidences and secrets of a client.
5. A lawyer should exercise independent professional judgment on behalf of a client.
6. A lawyer should represent a client competently.
7. A lawyer should represent a client zealously within the bounds of law.
8. A lawyer should assist in improving the legal system.
9. A lawyer should avoid even the appearance of professional impropriety.

Besides the ABA and its rules and Canons of Ethics, all states have state bar associations. These associations are powerful enough to require that all persons who practice law in these states must be approved by these bars in advance. Thus, attorneys who attend law school and graduate with a law degree must first pass one or more state bar examinations in order to qualify as practicing lawyers in those states.

Defense counsels are practicing lawyers and must pass state bar examinations in order to demonstrate their familiarity with local and state laws. Besides passing tests and taking other types of examinations, all lawyers are expected to adhere to codes of ethics and to conduct themselves in a way that will not compromise their integrity. Thus, it is expected that the ABA Canons of Ethics and the ABA Model Code of Professional Responsibility are applicable to virtually all practicing attorneys in the

Canons of Professional Ethics part of ABA Model Code of Professional Responsibility formulated in 1908 pertaining to representing clients, improving the legal system, avoiding the appearance of impropriety, and observing client confidences.

ABA Model Code of Professional Responsibility American Bar Association standards of behavior, which are voluntary and intended as self-regulating for lawyer conduct in the courtroom and between lawyers and clients.

state bar associations professional organizations of lawyers bound to observe the laws of the various states where they reside.

United States. Although not all attorneys in the United States belong to the ABA, the ethical and professional responsibility provisions promulgated by the ABA are generally and implicitly applicable to them anyway.

▶ The Right to Counsel

The Sixth Amendment says that all defendants shall have the right to a speedy trial by an impartial jury, the right to be informed of the nature of the charges against them, the right to confront their accusers in court, and the right to have assistance of counsel for their defense. Originally, this was interpreted to mean that if a defendant had an attorney, they could bring them to court. Eventually, the Supreme Court, through a series of rulings, rendered the Sixth Amendment's right to counsel clause as mandating provision of counsel to those who could not afford it. While the Sixth Amendment does not declare that counsel must be competent, the Supreme Court handed down a ruling in another case, *Strickland v. Washington*, which provided guidelines with which to gauge attorney effectiveness and competence.

The right to counsel as guaranteed under the Sixth Amendment was not applied to the states until 1963. For many decades, therefore, those accused of crimes were free to hire their own attorneys to represent them (Smith 2004). However, indigent defendants, defendants without the money or means to hire their own counsel, were often prosecuted, tried, and convicted without benefit of any defense counsel (Cunningham and Vigen 1999). Until the 1960s, indigent defendants in state courts were not entitled to a court-appointed attorney unless they were charged with a capital crime, such as murder. If indigents were charged with noncapital offenses, then they were unable to compel courts to furnish them with an attorney. Without an attorney to defend them, therefore, many indigents were convicted, whether or not they were guilty of the crime(s) alleged. In 1942, the U.S. Supreme Court condoned these state practices. In the case of *Betts v. Brady* (316 U.S. 455 [1942]), Betts, a robbery suspect, claimed that he was indigent and demanded a court-appointed attorney to defend him on the robbery charge. The court said that Betts could have access to appointed counsel only for rape or murder cases, and his request for an attorney was denied. In felony cases in which life or death was not an issue, the U.S. Supreme Court ruled that the states were not required to furnish counsel to indigent defendants in every case. It should be noted, however, that many states *did* provide counsel for indigent defendants during this period because it was required by the state legislatures.

> **indigent defendants** poor persons; anyone who cannot afford legal services or representation.

Extending the Right to Counsel to State Court Proceedings

In 1963, the U.S. Supreme Court reviewed and decided the case of *Gideon v. Wainwright* (372 U.S. 335 [1963]). Clarence Gideon broke into a Florida poolroom with the intent to commit larceny. This act was a felony in Florida. Gideon was indigent and asked for a lawyer to represent him. He was advised by the judge that counsel could only be appointed to indigents if they were charged with a capital crime. Since he was denied an attorney, Gideon represented himself. Subsequently, he was convicted and appealed. The U.S. Supreme Court overturned Gideon's conviction, holding that all indigent defendants are entitled to court-appointed counsel in any serious case. The Florida courts interpreted serious case to mean any felony. Thus, the *Gideon* case established that court-appointed counsel would be provided for any indigent defendant who was charged with a felony. The Supreme Court in *Gideon,* in essence, applied the Sixth Amendment right to counsel to the states.

Nine years later, the case of *Argersinger v. Hamlin* (407 U.S. 25 [1972]) was decided by the U.S. Supreme Court. This also occurred in Florida. Argersinger was an indigent charged with carrying a concealed weapon. This charge was a misdemeanor in Florida and punishable by a fine and six months' imprisonment. Argersinger claimed to be indigent and demanded that the court appoint counsel to represent him. Argersinger's request was denied, because, according to *Gideon*, only felony charges entitled indigent defendants to court-appointed counsel. Argersinger was convicted of the misdemeanor and sentenced to 90 days in jail. He appealed, and the U.S. Supreme Court overturned his misdemeanor conviction. Essentially, the U.S. Supreme Court said that anyone facing possible imprisonment is entitled to court-appointed counsel if they are indigent and cannot afford to hire private counsel.

Self-Representation

Under certain circumstances, defendants may wish to represent themselves in court and not use the services of a defense attorney (Sabelli and Leyton 2000). Any criminal defendant may elect to defend himself/herself and reject court-appointed counsel. When defendants engage in **self-representation**, they are said to be proceeding *pro se*, which means "on his or her own behalf" (Arrigo and Bardwell 2000). Defendants who defend themselves do not have to be trained lawyers, nor do they have to be skilled in criminal law or trial techniques. However, in most instances where persons have elected to represent themselves in court, judges have appointed lawyers to assist or advise them anyway, although the roles of these counsels are somewhat passive (Cunningham and Vigen 1999). Self-representation in criminal proceedings is not exclusively an American phenomenon. Other countries, such as England, permit defendants to represent themselves if they request to do so (Tague 1999).

Relatively few persons, however, defend themselves in court. An old adage says that one who represents himself/herself has a fool for a client. At one point in our history, however, indigent defendants were compelled to defend themselves. As you will see later in the case of *Gideon v. Wainwright* (1963) (see Box 4-2), Clarence Gideon was on trial in Florida for burglary. At the time of Gideon's trial, it was the law in Florida that indigent defendants were not entitled to court-appointed counsel unless they were charged with a capital offense. Gideon defended himself and was subsequently convicted. He appealed, contending that he was entitled to counsel and was denied counsel. The U.S. Supreme Court heard his appeal and overturned his conviction, holding that all indigent criminal defendants are entitled to court-appointed counsel in serious cases or felonies. Subsequently, court-appointed counsel was extended to any person charged with either a misdemeanor or felony (*Argersinger v. Hamlin*, 1972) (see Box 4-2).

Attorney–Client Privilege and Confidentiality

Other rules have evolved as well to cover the relation between attorneys and their clients (Canon 4). **Attorney–client confidentiality and privilege** is intended to protect clients from having their attorneys disclose incriminating details of their lives to others, such as prosecutors. If a defense attorney hears a confession from a client, the attorney is vested with considerable legal protection. Prosecutors cannot compel defense counsels to provide them with incriminating information about their clients. The attorney–client privilege is as inviolate as the relation between parishioners and their priests.

Attorney Competence and Effective Assistance of Counsel

Probably all attorneys think that they are competent. However, a troubling number of allegations are raised by convicted offenders who believe that their defense counsels are

self-representation;
pro se acting as one's own defense attorney in criminal proceedings. Representing oneself.

attorney–client confidentiality and privilege relation between a counsel and his/her client wherein any information exchanged between parties will not be disclosed to others, such as prosecutors.

BOX 4-1

KEY CASES: SELF-REPRESENTATION

Illinois v. Allen, 397 U.S. 337 (1970)

Allen was charged with robbery. He waived his right to counsel and elected to represent himself. During the jury selection and trial, he was abusive and argued constantly with the trial judge until eventually he was ordered removed from the courtroom. The trial was held anyway and he was convicted. Later, Allen appealed to the U.S. Supreme Court, arguing that his Sixth Amendment right had been violated because he was not present at his own trial when convicted. The U.S. Supreme Court upheld his conviction, saying that repeated warnings to Allen from the judge had had no effect on his conduct, which was so disruptive as to prevent the jurors from properly considering the evidence. Thus, there was nothing unconstitutional about the judge's removing Allen from the courtroom.

Faretta v. California, 422 U.S. 806 (1975)

Faretta, who was charged with grand theft, desired to represent himself. The judge ruled that he had no constitutional right to represent himself in the case and appointed a public defender to defend him. Faretta was convicted. He appealed, arguing that he had a right to represent himself. The U.S. Supreme Court overturned his conviction, holding that Faretta indeed had a right knowingly and intelligently to waive his right to counsel and represent himself in the criminal proceeding.

Thus, he had been denied his constitutional right to act as his own counsel.

Becker v. Montgomery, 532 U.S. 757 (2001)

Becker was an Ohio state prisoner who instituted a *pro se* civil rights action in federal court contesting the conditions of his confinement under Title 42 U.S.C. Section 1983. The federal district court dismissed the complaint because of Becker's failure to state a claim for relief. In a timely manner, within 30 days of the federal court action, Becker appealed, filing a *pro se* notice of appeal with the Sixth Circuit Court of Appeals. However, Becker failed to sign the appeal form. The form contained no requirement indicating that it should be signed. The Sixth Circuit dismissed Becker's appeal because it was unsigned. The Sixth Circuit further declared that Becker's notice of appeal was fatally defective and deemed this defect jurisdictional and therefore not curable outside the time allowed to file the notice of appeal. No court officer had earlier called Becker's attention to the need for a signature. Becker appealed to the U.S. Supreme Court. The Court reversed the Sixth Circuit, holding that when a party files a timely notice of appeal, the failure to sign the appeal does not require the court of appeals to dismiss the appeal. The Court stated further that imperfections in noticing an appeal should not be fatal where no genuine doubt exists about who is appealing, from what judgment, and to which appellate court.

WHAT DO YOU THINK?

Should the courts allow someone to proceed *pro se*, or represent themselves in court? Given that most persons, let alone those accused of crimes, are not learned in the law and criminal court procedures, should our justice system ensure that their due process rights are being afforded to them by requiring counsel in their defense? Why would our system allow someone who does not have a law degree or passed the bar exam to defend a case, even if it is their own?

---

incompetent and ineffective. There is considerable variation among lawyers regarding attorney competence; both defense counsel and prosecutors differ in quality and effectiveness. Attorneys of all types vary considerably according to their expertise, years on the job, personal and professional experience, and enthusiasm for defending or prosecuting. However, attorneys are tacitly expected to zealously perform their defense tasks, and in a competent manner (Canons 5, 6, and 7).

> **attorney competence** standards for determining whether clients are fairly and intelligently represented by their lawyers when they are charged with crimes.

BOX 4-2

KEY CASES: RIGHT TO ASSISTANCE OF COUNSEL

Betts v. Brady, 316 U.S. 455 (1942)

Betts claimed that he was indigent and thus demanded a court-appointed attorney to defend him on a robbery charge. The court said that Betts could have access to appointed counsel only for rape or murder cases, and denied his request. He appealed. The Supreme Court ruled that in felony cases in which life or death is not an issue, the states are not required to furnish counsel in every case; many states at this time, however, provide counsel because it is required by their own constitutions or by court rulings in state courts. This decision was overturned as the result of the ruling in *Gideon v. Wainwright* (1963), in which the U.S. Supreme Court concluded that in all felony cases, state or federal, indigent defendants are entitled to counsel.

White v. Maryland, 373 U.S. 59 (1963)

White, an indigent, was suspected of murder. At his arraignment, he entered a not-guilty plea, but later at a preliminary hearing, he pleaded guilty. He was not represented by counsel at the preliminary hearing, and his guilty plea was introduced later in the trial as evidence against him. He was convicted. White appealed, contending that the preliminary hearing was a critical stage requiring appointment of counsel to represent him. Thus, the guilty plea he entered should have been inadmissible in court later. The U.S. Supreme Court agreed with White and overturned his conviction, saying that preliminary hearings are critical stages in which indigent defendants must be represented by counsel.

Gideon v. Wainwright, 372 U.S. 335 (1963)

Gideon broke into a poolroom allegedly with the intent to commit larceny. This act was regarded as a felony in Florida. Gideon was indigent and asked for a lawyer to represent him. He was advised by the judge that counsel could only be appointed to persons if the offense involved the death penalty. Therefore, Gideon represented himself and was convicted. He appealed. The U.S. Supreme Court overturned his conviction, saying that all indigent defendants are entitled to court-appointed counsel in felony cases. (See *Argersinger v. Hamlin* [1972] for a narrowing of this provision to minor crimes or misdemeanor cases.)

Coleman v. Alabama, 399 U.S. 1 (1970)

Several defendants, including Coleman, were accused of assault with intent to commit murder. As indigents, they were denied counsel at their preliminary hearing, with the Alabama judge declaring that nothing that happened at the preliminary hearing would influence the trial later. Coleman was convicted, and he appealed. The U.S. Supreme Court ruled that preliminary hearings are critical stages. Because indigent defendants are entitled to counsel at critical stages, which Coleman had been denied, his conviction was overturned.

Argersinger v. Hamlin, 407 U.S. 25 (1972)

Argersinger was an indigent charged with carrying a concealed weapon. In Florida, this crime is a misdemeanor punishable by imprisonment of up to six months and a $1,000 fine. Argersinger was not allowed to have court-appointed counsel, as required for a *felony*, because his crime was not a felony (see *Gideon v. Wainwright* [1963]). He was convicted of the misdemeanor and sentenced to 90 days in jail. He appealed, and the U.S. Supreme Court overturned his misdemeanor conviction. The U.S. Supreme Court said that any indigent defendant is entitled to counsel for *any* offense involving imprisonment, regardless of the shortness of the length of incarceration. Thus, it extended the *Gideon* decision to include misdemeanor offenses, holding that no sentence involving the loss of liberty (incarceration) can be imposed where there has been a denial of counsel; defendants have a right to counsel when imprisonment might result.

Baldasar v. Illinois, 446 U.S. 222 (1980)

Baldasar was convicted in a theft of property not exceeding $150 in value. Although this offense was a misdemeanor, it was Baldasar's second offense, and therefore, it became a felony. He was sentenced to one to three years in prison. He appealed, claiming that he had not been represented by counsel at the time of his first conviction. Therefore, the enhanced penalty from the second conviction was not constitutional. The U.S. Supreme Court agreed with Baldasar and overturned his conviction, holding that no indigent criminal defendant shall be sentenced to a term of imprisonment unless the state has afforded him/her the right to assistance of counsel. Baldasar had requested but had been denied counsel in the trial for his original misdemeanor, which became a crucial step in enhancing the penalty resulting from his second conviction.

Ideally at least, attorneys are expected to do their best, whether they are prosecuting or defending someone on a criminal charge. Counsel competence is difficult to assess objectively. It is more frequently the case that the effectiveness and competence of counsel are assessed subjectively. It is precisely because of the diffuseness of the concepts of effectiveness and competence that more than few challenges are made by convicted offenders where the performance of their attorneys is called into question. These questions pertain to the ineffective assistance of counsel.

The leading case concerning attorney competence is *Strickland v. Washington* (466 U.S. 668 [1984]). Conduct in Strickland's case of whether ineffective assistance of counsel was rendered was measured according to the following standards: (1) Was the counsel's conduct such that it undermined the functioning of the adversarial process so much that a trial cannot be relied upon to render a just result? (2) Did the counsel's behavior fall below the objective standard of reasonableness? There must be a reasonable probability that, but for counsel's unprofessional errors, the result of the proceedings would be different.

Thus, *Strickland* established the standards of (1) whether counsel's behavior undermined the adversarial process to the degree that the trial outcome is unreliable; and (2) whether counsel's conduct was unreasonable to the degree that the jury verdict would have been different otherwise. This does not mean that all attorney conduct must be flawless and that every stone, large or small, has been overturned in all cases. Most attorneys make one or more mistakes and exercise bad judgment occasionally when defending a client. But many of these mistakes or instances of bad judgment are inconsequential and would not ordinarily affect the trial outcome. There is no obligation on the part of any attorney to raise every nonfrivolous issue in a criminal case (*Jones v. Barnes*, 463 U.S. 745 [1983]; *Murray v. Carrier*, 477 U.S. 478 [1986]) or use a particular defense to criminal conduct (*Knowles v. Mirzayance*, 556 U.S. 07-1315 [2009]).

Ineffective Assistance of Counsel

The U.S. Supreme Court has decided instances of **ineffective assistance of counsel** on occasion. For instance, in a recent death penalty case, *Rompilla v. Beard*, 125 S.Ct. 2456 (2005), the attorney for the defendant made no effort to present mitigating evidence in the case as to why Rompilla should not be sentenced to death, such as his troubled childhood, his alcoholism, and his mental illness. He was sentenced to death and appealed arguing that his counsel was ineffective. The state appellate court rejected the appeal, but the U.S. Supreme Court reversed the sentence citing the defense counsel's failure to examine the evidence at the sentencing phase of his capital murder trial fell below the level of reasonable performance and that this prejudiced him.

> **ineffective assistance of counsel** standard for determining whether client is defended in a competent way; guidelines for determining counsel's effectiveness articulated in case of Strickland v. Washington (1984).

Defendants should have a reasonable expectation, therefore, that the counsel representing them is competent and effective. But this expectation should not be that the defense counsel is necessarily the best defense available. The standard of reasonableness is very important, since there are varying degrees of counsel competence and effectiveness that are within the reasonable parameters articulated in *Strickland*. Furthermore, defendants may assume with some confidence that defense counsel will adhere to the ethical codes and manner of professional responsibility articulated by their state bar associations and other professional organizations established to regulate attorney quality and performance.

Recently, the Supreme Court decided in the case of *Vermont v. Brillon*, 556 U.S. _ (2009), that a defendant's Sixth Amendment right to a speedy trial was not violated because his public defender caused delays in his case. Justice Ginsburg, writing for the court, did, however, state that broader problems with a state's public defender system that may cause delays might be in violation of the Sixth Amendment's speedy trial clause.

BOX 4-3

KEY CASES: ATTORNEY INCOMPETENCE

Strickland v. Washington, 466 U.S. 668 (1984)

Conduct in Washington's case of whether ineffective assistance of counsel was rendered was measured according to the following standards: Was the counsel's conduct such that it undermined the functioning of the adversarial process so much that a trial could not be relied on to render a just result? Did the counsel's behavior fall below the objective standard of reasonableness? There must be a reasonable probability that, but for counsel's unprofessional errors, the result of the proceedings would have been different.

Rompilla v. Beard, 125 S.Ct. 2456 (2005)

Ronald Rompilla was convicted in a Pennsylvania court of first-degree murder and other offenses. During the penalty phase, the jury found several aggravating factors that were presented by the prosecution. Rompilla's family provided several mitigating factors. Rompilla's attorney relied upon these mitigating factors and made no effort to discover other mitigating evidence, such as Rompilla's troubled childhood, alcoholism, and mental illness. Rompilla was sentenced to death, therefore, and he appealed, arguing that his counsel was ineffective because he failed to make a reasonable effort to obtain and review evidence of both aggravation and mitigation. The state courts rejected Rompilla's appeals, and ultimately the U.S. Supreme Court heard his case. The U.S. Supreme Court reversed, holding that (1) defense counsel's failure to examine the file on Rompilla's prior convictions for rape and assault at the sentencing phase of his capital murder trial fell below the level of reasonable performance, and (2) such failure was prejudicial to Rompilla, warranting *habeas corpus* relief on grounds of ineffective assistance of counsel.

Lafler v. Cooper, 566 U.S. _ (2012)

Anthony Cooper was convicted of assault with intent to murder. He claimed ineffective assistance of counsel because his attorney advised him not to take a plea deal. The attorney believed that he would have no chance that the intent to murder would be dropped because Copper shot at the woman's head but then hit her in the buttocks and thigh. The Sixth Circuit Court of Appeals overturned his conviction because of the attorney's bad advice. The Michigan court appealed that decision and the Supreme Court heard the case in conjunction with *Missouri v. Frye* to determine whether the attorney's advice not to take a favorable plea constituted ineffective assistance of counsel. In its 5–4 decision, the court stated that the attorney's advice not to accept the plea was ineffective under *Strickland v. Washington* because both the defendant and the trial court would have accepted the plea in which case his sentence would have been less severe. The SCOTUS decision stated that the prosecutor should offer the plea again and if the defendant agrees to the plea, the court can determine the new sentence.

Missouri v. Frye, 566 U.S. _ (2012)

Galin Frye was facing charges of driving with a revoked license. The prosecution offered him two plea deals but Frye's attorney never apprised him of the offers. He subsequently pleaded guilty to a felony and was given a three-year prison sentence. Frye appealed on the grounds that he was not aware of the initial plea offers and a Missouri appellate court decided in his favor. The prosecution appealed the decision and the Supreme Court heard the case in conjunction with *Lafler v. Cooper* and determined that under the Sixth Amendment defense attorneys must let their clients know of any formal plea offers from the prosecution. The court furthered that there is no right of a defendant to a plea bargain from the prosecution; the majority of cases in both state and federal courts result in plea agreements. Thus, counsel is ineffective if they do not communicate these offers to their clients.

▶ The Right to a Trial by Jury

jury trial proceeding by which guilt or innocence of defendant is determined by jury instead of by the judge.

One of the most significant cases challenging the court's authority to grant or deny a defendant the right to a jury trial was *Duncan v. Louisiana* (391 U.S. 145 [1968]). Duncan was convicted in a bench trial of simple battery in a Louisiana court. The crime was a misdemeanor, punishable by a maximum prison term of two years and a fine of $300. However,

Duncan was sentenced to only 60 days and fined $150. He appealed, contending that he was denied his constitutional right to a jury trial under the Sixth Amendment. The U.S. Supreme Court agreed with Duncan, saying that any crime carrying a maximum punishment of two years is a serious crime, despite the fact that a jail sentence of only 60 days was imposed. Thus, for serious crimes, under the Sixth Amendment, Duncan was entitled to a jury trial as a matter of right.

Eventually, the standard was established whereby criminal defendants are entitled to a jury trial as a matter of right. The standard was set in the case of *Baldwin v. New York* (399 U.S. 66 [1970]). Baldwin was arrested and prosecuted for jostling or pickpocketing, a Class A misdemeanor punishable by a maximum term of imprisonment of one year in New York. Baldwin asked for a jury trial, but he was denied one. At the time, New York law defined jostling as a petty offense, one that did not require a jury trial. Baldwin was subsequently convicted and sentenced to 90 days in jail. He appealed. The U.S. Supreme Court heard Baldwin's appeal and declared that petty offenses carrying a one-year incarcerative term are *serious* in that jury trials must be provided if requested by defendants. Specifically, the wording of *Baldwin* gives substantial significance to the *months* of imprisonment that defines a serious crime. The U.S. Supreme Court said that a potential sentence in excess of six months of imprisonment is sufficiently severe by itself to take offense out of the category of petty as respects one's right to jury trial (at 1886, 1891). Therefore, the U.S. Supreme Court overturned Baldwin's conviction on these grounds. Presently, jury trials must be granted to any defendant where the possible punishment involves incarceration of beyond six months.

No Jury Trials for Defendants Charged with Petty Offenses

The U.S. Supreme Court has made clear its position about jury trials and when defendants are entitled to them. According to *Baldwin*, jury trials are available as a matter of right only to defendants charged with serious crimes, where their loss of liberty is beyond six months. Jury trials are not available as a matter of right in other nonserious cases. For instance, in *United States v. Nachtigal* (507 U.S. 1 [1993]), Nachtigal was convicted of drunk driving while operating a motor vehicle in a national park. When he appeared before the U.S. Magistrate, Nachtigal asked for a jury trial but was denied one. His offense carried a maximum incarcerative penalty of six months in jail, and thus it did not qualify for a jury trial. Nachtigal appealed his conviction on the Sixth Amendment grounds that he was denied a jury trial, but the U.S. Supreme Court upheld his conviction, saying that jury trials may not be granted in petty offense cases.

One exception to *Baldwin* is as follows. Sometimes, judges will conduct bench trials without juries when a defendant is charged with a serious crime. But these judges will advise the defendant in advance that if the defendant is found guilty, the incarcerative punishment will be six months or less. Judges must keep this promise. Thus, if a defendant is found guilty by the judge later, following court proceedings in a bench trial, then the judge cannot impose an incarcerative sentence longer than six months. If a judge were to violate his/her promise to a defendant and sentence him/her to a term of imprisonment of beyond six months, then the convicted offender would have solid grounds to have a higher court review the judge's action and overturn the conviction. Judicial promises made must be kept.

▶ The Defense

Defense counsels are attorneys who represent those individuals charged with crimes. Defense attorneys adhere to the ABA code of professional responsibility and are obligated to do all that is ethically possible to defend their clients. All criminal defendants are entitled to an attorney as a matter of right. Many defense counsels are retained privately by persons able to afford them. Yet other defense counsels are appointed by the courts in their jurisdictions to represent clients without money to hire their own attorneys (indigent defendants). Defense counsels who are hired by the state to represent indigent defendants are called public defenders (Maxwell, Dow, and Maxwell 2004).

Forms of Legal Aid for Indigents

By 1996, 82 percent of defendants in state courts in the 75 most populous counties and 66 percent of federal defendants were represented by court-appointed counsel (Harlow 2000). Court-appointed legal representation for indigent criminal defendants plays a critical role in the criminal justice system. A 2001 Bureau of Justice Statistics report reveals that state governments provided 90 percent or more of the funding for indigent defense in 21 states; in 1982, these states spent $251 million on indigent defense services, and by 1999, it had tripled to $662 million (DeFrances 2001). Table 4-1 ■ shows various types of public defender systems in the United States from a survey conducted in 1992. Not every state has the same type of public legal aid for indigent defendants (Smith and DeFrances 1996, 1). Each state is at liberty to establish its own particular form of legal aid services. According to a recent Bureau of Justice Statistics report (Langton and Farole 2010), almost all of the states (49) had public defender offices but in 22 states, these were state-run public defender programs, and in the other 27 states, the public defender offices were run at the county level. The report also reveals that there were approximately 15,000 attorneys comprising public defender offices around the country; in 2007, these public defender officers represented close to 5.6 million indigent defendants at a cost of approximately 2.3 billion dollars.

Thus, different states have evolved different indigent defense systems, and most states leave it up to the county on whether to use a public defender's office, an assigned counsel program, or a contract system. This may depend on the population and resources available to a county. For example, small counties would not have enough cases to warrant funding a public defender's office, and in other counties, the elected officials may not want to spend the taxpayer dollars necessary to fund a public defender program. The most common public defender system used in 28 percent of all U.S. counties is called simply the public defender system. This system is state and county funded and serves the needs of numerous persons unable to afford legal aid. The public defender system began in 1914 in Los Angeles, California (Klein and Spangenberg 1993). Public defenders are hired by the state and county to represent indigent clients who are in need of a defense. They draw salaries and are expected to mount the best defense possible, under the limited resources of

> **public defender system** means whereby attorneys are appointed by the court to represent indigent defendants.

TABLE 4-1 Indigent Defense Systems Used by Local Jurisdictions

Type of system	Percentage of type of counsel provided
Public defender program only	28
Assigned counsel system only	23
Assigned counsel and public defender	23
Contract attorney system only	8
Public defender and contract	8
Assigned counsel, public defender, and contract system	6
Assigned counsel and contract system	3
Other	1
Total	100

Source: Smith, Steven K., and Carol J. DeFrances (1996). *Indigent Defense,* Washington, DC: U.S. Department of Justice, 1996, 2.

their agencies. Quite often, their funds for legal defense are limited, and they do not enjoy investigative luxuries and other expenditures that might be available to privately acquired counsel by more affluent defendants.

Two other types of systems are known as the assigned counsel system and the contract system. The assigned counsel system, used in roughly 25 percent of all local jurisdictions, is used in cities and towns where there aren't many attorneys. Small towns and sparsely populated counties may not have a great many practicing lawyers. Local bar associations function as liaisons between association members and the courts to provide legal services for indigent clients on a voluntary basis. Ordinarily, the local bar association submits a list of attorneys' names to judges who select defense counsel to represent indigent defendants on a case-by-case basis. In most jurisdictions where assigned counsel systems are operative, assigned counsels are paid a fixed rate per day for compensation. Compensation may range from $50 to $125 per day for these attorneys, and thus, this is a small sum compared with what an attorney might charge a private client. Actually, these per diem rates are more like hourly rates charged by attorneys who are affiliated with small law firms. Some more experienced attorneys in large law firms may bill their clients at the rate of $500 per hour or more. About one quarter of all local jurisdictions use a combination of the assigned counsel and public defender systems (Weiss 2004).

Because the compensation for indigent client legal services is inadequate, those who furnish their legal services to indigent clients under such a system are not always enthusiastic about defending their clients. For many of these attorneys, they merely want to go through the motions of negotiating the best deals for their clients with prosecutors. They often encourage their clients, though innocent, to plead guilty to a lesser criminal charge in exchange for a short jail term or probation. They may persuade their clients to waive their right to a jury trial and opt for a quick plea bargain. The saying "You get what you pay for" is often applicable to attorneys who work as either public defenders or assigned counsel for indigents. In some jurisdictions, the lack of incentives (e.g., monetary remuneration for legal services) causes them to lack the motivation and zeal they should have, in view of the Canons of Ethics and professional responsibility codes they should abide by through the ABA and other state professional legal affiliates.

The contract system involves competitive bidding among different law firms in various jurisdictions for providing legal services to indigent clients. A law firm may submit a bid to represent indigent clients on the basis of a fixed amount of money per hour or per day. The state or county will accept the most attractive bid in order to hold down defense costs. Roughly 10 percent of all U.S. counties use the contract system to provide indigent defendants with counsel (Smith and DeFrances 1996). Another 10 percent or so use a combination of the contract and public defender systems, while another roughly 6 percent use various combinations of all three systems.

One drawback with the contract system is that the low bidders may not be the most competent counsel. A law firm may assign its new and least experienced lawyers to defend indigent clients charged with serious crimes. When the least trained attorneys are expected to defend indigent clients in serious and complex cases, they may not be qualified or have the necessary experience to perform an adequate defense job. This could lead to a higher number of claims of ineffective assistance of counsel alleged by convicted indigents.

Despite the flaws of these and other defense systems for indigents, the fact remains that all criminal defendants are entitled to counsel. The U.S. Supreme Court has never made explicit the exact nature of attorney competence other than what has previously been articulated in *Strickland v. Washington* (1984). In the *Strickland* case, the U.S. Supreme Court declared that an attorney's performance should be such that the adversarial process should not be undermined, or that but for the attorney's conduct, the trial verdict may have been different. The *reasonableness* of attorney conduct was stressed by the Court, although

assigned counsel system program wherein indigent clients charged with crimes may have defense attorneys appointed for them.

contract system providing counsel to indigent offenders by having an attorney under contract to the county to handle some or all of these types of cases.

it failed to give a precise definition to reasonableness. Therefore, the U.S. Supreme Court has left this determination up to individual state supreme courts and lower courts whenever allegations of attorney incompetence are lodged by convicted offenders.

Are Public Defenders as Effective as Privately Retained Counsel?

Under assigned counsel, public defender, and contract systems, states and the federal government set fixed hourly rates for remunerating attorneys who defend indigent clients. These hourly rates, which may be as low as $25, are well below the $250 to $500 hourly rates (or higher) charged by private counsel who are hired by more affluent defendants. Many public defenders who work in public defender's offices are fresh out of law school and are interested in acquiring courtroom experience. They are willing to work for lower pay in exchange for gaining this experience. Other public defenders and court-appointed counsel who work on an assigned counsel basis may be apathetic or hostile toward their clients and the general job of defending those accused of crimes. In many cases, criticisms are that public defenders will try to get through their overwhelming caseloads by encouraging their clients into plea agreements, not taking time to review the merits of the case.

This rapidity of case processing is particularly prevalent in those jurisdictions with contract systems. A primary consideration in contracting is economizing resources and expediting case processing for maximum efficiency. Such rapid resolution of criminal cases may deprive some defendants of an adequate defense and seriously jeopardize their chances of obtaining equality under the law (Maxwell et al. 2004).

At the federal level, the Federal Defender Services program exists, which provides legal counsel for those who cannot afford attorneys. In 1970, the Criminal Justice Act authorized the establishment of federal public defender offices for provision of defense counsel in the federal system; today, there are 81 federal public defender offices that serve 91 of the 94 federal district courts (Administrative Office of the United States Courts 2016). As the number of cases in the federal system has increased in the past two decades, so too has the cost to operate the federal public defender system. Salaried federal public defenders in these 81 offices represent roughly 60 percent of indigent federal defendants annually with another roughly 10,000 contracted panel attorneys representing the remaining 40 percent. As of January 2016, the hourly rate for compensating panel attorneys was $129 in noncapital cases and $183 in capital cases up to a case maximum that is also specified (Administrative Office of the United States Courts 2016).

In 2007, state programs spent a total of $830 million to represent indigent defendants (Langton and Farole 2010). However, not all states fully fund their indigent defense programs, some of them leave it up to the local county to foot the bill. The amount of money in total that is spent on indigent defense therefore is much higher than what states appropriate. As of 2008, total spending on indigent defense, including state, county, and federal funding, was over $5 billion (Stevens, Sheppard, Spangenberg, Wickman, and Gould 2010). Public defender programs accounted for about $2.3 billion of the costs for indigent defense (Langton and Farole 2010).

There is a substantial lack of communication, coordination, and cooperation among the various agencies providing indigent defense services. There is an insufficient number of staff in every category to handle the current caseload and a lack of early representation in the public defender's office. There is virtually no training for public defenders in the office, and little supervision. Salaries are low as well as the morale. Greater use of technology has enabled many jurisdictions to cut their operating costs while maintaining fairly high-quality attorney representation for indigents, however (Spangenberg et al. 1999).

Thus, the general question arises, are court-appointed counsel as effective compared with their privately retained counterparts? Some early research suggests that defense

▼

services for indigents in certain jurisdictions have been substandard, especially in homicide cases (Steelman and Conti 1987). More extensive continuing education requirements were recommended in order for many of these defense attorneys to improve their criminal law skills. More recent research suggests that inadequate compensation of attorneys for indigents in capital cases produces an increasing number of appeals from convicted offenders who allege ineffective assistance of counsel (Champion 2005a). Despite these criticisms, because 90 percent of cases are disposed of through some type of plea bargain, the public defender works closely with the prosecutor and judge to negotiate appropriate pleas. If a defendant is not contesting their guilt, some argue that because the system is characterized by negotiation among the courtroom workgroup, public defenders are as effective as privately retained attorneys at securing favorable outcomes for their indigent clients (Hartley, Miller, and Spohn 2010). In short, public defender's offices have been found to be equally effective at defending indigent clients, thus contradicting long-standing criticisms portraying indigent defenders as incompetent, ill-equipped, and poorly trained.

In sum, there is perhaps an element of truth in both views of public defender or assigned counsel systems. Particularly in larger urban jurisdictions, it is true that public defender's offices are often staffed with new attorneys, with little or no criminal trial experience, who have caseloads that are above the recommended number. This fact operates to their disadvantage when relating with prosecutors and configuring plea agreements beneficial to criminal defendants. But in assigned counsel and contract systems, there are also many seasoned attorneys with considerable criminal law experience. Presently, there is great diversity in quality concerning court-appointed legal representation for indigent criminal defendants. At least 80 percent or more of all criminal defendants continue to have court-appointed counsel, meaning they are too poor to afford an attorney.

Functions of the Defense

The functions of defense counsel are to (1) represent their clients faithfully, (2) attack the prosecution's case vigorously, (3) counsel with the defendant as to the best course of action in the case, (4) negotiate with prosecutors for a case resolution most favorable to their client, (5) vigorously cross-examine prosecution witnesses to attack and undermine their credibility in front of jurors, and (6) use all legal means to defeat the government's case.

Representing Clients Faithfully

It is expected that defense counsel will represent their clients faithfully. This means that they will take an active interest in the case rather than a detached passive interest. They will strive to collect relevant exculpatory evidence, interview crucial witnesses, and engage in proper trial preparations. They will consider the defendants' needs and give them every consideration. They will assume that their clients are innocent, even though incriminating evidence might exist to the contrary.

Attacking the Prosecution's Case Vigorously

Defense counsels are expected to attack the government's case in a vigorous manner. They should take steps to point out all aspects of the prosecutor's case that are weak or raise reasonable doubt about the defendant's guilt. They should be aggressive and promote their clients' interests to the best of their ability.

Counseling with Defendants Concerning the Best Course of Action in a Case

It is sometimes the case that defense counsel will be assigned cases where overwhelming direct and conclusive evidence exists about the defendant's guilt. In these types of cases, a vigorous defense should be implemented, designed to provide a plausible explanation for why the crime was committed. One part of the counseling process involves determining the client's view of the case and a disclosure of crime details. This shared information and subsequent defendant disclosures are confidential through attorney–client confidentiality and privilege. Whatever the defendant tells his/her attorney will remain private and confidential. If the defendant admits guilt to his/her attorney, the defense counsel must continue to represent the client with enthusiasm. Defense counsels are in crucial positions to understand the consequences of a trial. In some cases, it may be more prudent to work out deals for clients with prosecutors instead of proceeding with a trial. These bargains often involve some measure of leniency for their clients. The prosecutor may be amenable to reducing more serious charges to less serious ones in exchange for a defendant's guilty plea. If a counsel's client were to reject the bargain offered by the prosecutor and proceed with a trial, a conviction would almost guarantee an increase in the harshness or severity of the penalty imposed by the judge. Therefore, good defense counsels should explain all viable options to their clients and work out what is best for them through close collaboration. Good advice to a client might be to plead guilty to a lesser charge and accept a less severe punishment rather than take a chance in court where a conviction and more severe sentence are imminent.

Negotiating with Prosecutors for a Case Resolution Most Favorable to Clients

Prosecutors determine which charges should be filed against defendants. Defense counsels are expected to negotiate with prosecutors in an effort to reach a compromise with them favorable to their clients. Sometimes, defense counsels may request diversion for their clients, where their cases are temporarily removed from the criminal justice system. Under diversion, clients would be expected to be law-abiding, pay monthly maintenance fees, and perhaps pay restitution to victims or engage in community service. The result of a successful diversion might be that the prosecutor would drop all criminal charges against the defendant or downgrade the charges eventually filed from felonies to misdemeanors. Defense attorneys are key players in facilitating such negotiations between prosecutors and defendants.

Vigorously Cross-Examining Prosecution Witnesses and Undermining their Credibility

Good defense attorneys engage in vigorous cross-examinations of prosecution witnesses in an effort to undermine their credibility. Often, eyewitness testimony is damaging to defendants, and defense counsels can sometimes cause eyewitnesses to express doubt about what they observed. If defense counsels can encourage prosecution witnesses to admit to uncertainty about what was seen, this strategy can undermine the prosecution's case considerably (Bradfield and McQuiston 2004).

Using All Legal Means to Defeat the Government's Case

Within the limits of propriety and the code of ethics that binds together defense counsels throughout the United States, defense attorneys are encouraged to use any and all legal means at their disposal to defeat the government's case against their client. Some of the means may be considered unsavory, although they may be entirely legal. For instance, if a man is suspected of killing his wife and if there are older children or relatives who did not get along with the deceased, it is proper for the defense counsel to suggest to the jury that others might have been motivated to kill. Thus, certain relatives might be named as possible suspects, even though the defense attorney may not believe that they were involved in the woman's death. Rather, the intent of such a strategy is to plant a seed of doubt in the minds of jurors. Someone else may have committed the crime. Others may have had strong motives to kill besides the defendant. If sufficient doubt can be raised by deflecting possible guilt to others, then the jury may acquit the defendant later following their deliberations (Roberts, Gau, and Brody 2004).

One fact that operates to the disadvantage of defense counsels everywhere is that other types of attorneys do not hold criminal defense lawyers in particularly high regard. Defending criminals is viewed by more than a few citizens as an unsavory profession. Defending criminals means having to interact with them. For many attorneys, interacting with criminals is undesirable. Therefore, criminal defense counsels often engage in thankless tasks. They may even be viewed with disdain by their own criminal clients. If they win their cases, they are accused of "getting guilty defendants off" and escaping punishment. If they lose, their clients may appeal and allege that their defense counsels are incompetent or ineffective. Even criminal court judges regard defense counsels with a certain amount of contempt. Thus, for many criminal defense attorneys, considerable stress is generated.

Defense Misconduct

Much of the misconduct that occurs in court processes has been the result of prosecutorial actions or abuses of judicial discretion. However, misconduct is also committed by the defense counsel. While prosecutors are barred from mentioning or admitting into evidence certain types of incriminating information, defense counsels are likewise admonished to avoid saying anything that might prejudice the jury in favor of their client. With advances in science and technology, both sides can do much more with presentation of evidence; however, some of these techniques may not be sufficiently reliable for introduction as evidence in courtrooms (Cook, Arndt, and Lieberman 2004).

For instance, it is widely accepted that testimony about polygraph tests (lie detectors) is inadmissible. This is because lie detector results are unreliable and cannot be interpreted with the same degree of precision as fingerprint evidence or other tangible direct evidence. But suppose the defendant submitted to a lie detector test administered by the local police department. Further, assume that the defendant passed the lie detector test. The test results would be interpreted to mean that the defendant was telling the truth and that this fact might be considered exculpatory evidence. However, the prosecutor decides to move forward with the prosecution anyway, feeling that the polygraph test results were unreliable. What if the defense counsel asked a police officer who was testifying for the state, "My client took a lie detector test about this crime and passed, didn't he?" The prosecutor would object and the judge would sustain the objection. Just as prosecutors would be guilty of committing harmless errors by backdooring inadmissible evidence, the defense counsel would be equally guilty of backdooring another type of inadmissible evidence, such as the lie detector test results. The judge can order the jury to disregard the defense counsel's question, but can the jury ever forget the question/statement by the defense? No. This is just one example of defense misconduct.

Another type of defense misconduct occurs whenever the defense attorney knows that the defendant is guilty. The defendant has confessed his/her crime to the defense counsel, and it is expected that this confession will remain confidential. The privilege of confidentiality exists between an attorney and his/her client, and it is unethical for an attorney to violate this privilege. While the defense counsel is obligated to defend his/her client despite the confession, the defense counsel is prohibited from advising his/her client to take the stand and lie about the client's role in the crime. Advising one's client, or advising the client's witnesses, to lie is the subornation of perjury. Suborning perjury means to encourage someone to lie under oath. If a defense attorney were to suborn perjury, this would constitute defense misconduct. Further, it would be a crime.

> **lie detectors** apparatuses that record sensory responses. Designed to determine whether one is telling the truth during an interrogation. Also known as polygraphs. Results of tests are not admissible in court.

> **subornation of perjury** the crime of procuring someone to lie under oath.

▶ Interactions Between Prosecutors and Defense Attorneys

Most of us are quite familiar with courtroom drama. We see programs on television such as *Law and Order*. These shows focus on the courtroom as the major contact point between prosecutors and defense counsels. But these programs give us only one dimension of a much larger picture of interaction between the defense and the prosecution. Both prosecutors and defense attorneys are integral parts of the courtroom workgroup. Actually, their interactions with one another and other members of the courtroom workgroup are more frequent outside rather than inside the courtroom. For instance, defense attorneys who maintain good relations with various court officers can benefit by being assigned more cases. Defense attorneys, especially recent law graduates, need to earn a living. Being assigned more cases will enable these attorneys to earn more money to support themselves as well as help to establish their law practices. Defense attorneys with poor attitudes may lose out on various case assignments that are given to more compliant defense counsels despite the fact that in most jurisdictions these cases are supposed to be assigned as they come up to whoever is next on the list.

Defense attorneys consult frequently with prosecutors concerning defendants. Prosecutors work closely with the police and detectives who gather incriminating evidence of crimes, interviews with suspects, and conversations with various experts and eyewitnesses. Some of this information is made available to defense attorneys so that they may advise their clients concerning which course of action is best.

Although the interactions between defense counsels and prosecutors are often characterized as adversarial and antagonistic, the fact is that most of these persons have amicable relations with one another both on and off the job. Most prosecutors are known by defense counsels on a first-name basis, and sometimes even talk and joke with each other prior to the judge entering the courtroom. As such, their relationships are almost always friendly, even though once the formal proceedings begin in the courtroom, their respective demeanors might suggest otherwise.

Another consequence of close interactions between prosecutors and defense attorneys is that they both learn about each other's interests and objectives. They are able to assess each other's skills and strategies. Thus, some prosecutors know that they can expect a serious challenge from some defense attorneys who have been successful in garnering acquittals for their clients. This mutual understanding between prosecutors and defense attorneys facilitates the process of whether defendants will enter guilty pleas to certain charges in exchange for leniency.

Also, in certain respects, it is important for both prosecutors and defense counsels to maintain good relations with one another, since negotiations almost always have to take place in order for cases to proceed through the system. The wheels of justice turn more smoothly to the extent that relations between prosecutors and defense counsels are cordial and cooperative. However, some prosecutors resent having to share case information with defense attorneys, and some defense attorneys are openly antagonistic toward prosecutors. Information exchanges from both sides are slowed and hampered by formality. Under a cooperative scenario, for example, prosecutors would willingly share case information with defense attorneys since it is important for these attorneys to know what they are facing regarding inculpatory evidence against their clients. Under less cooperative conditions, defense counsels would be obligated to write detailed letters requesting case information to which they are entitled. Prosecutors might drag their feet and delay turning over case materials in a timely manner. Ultimately, however, both sides will exchange information in the process known as discovery.

If the defendant confessed to the crime, and if the confession was videotaped and transcribed, then the defense is entitled to see a copy of the videotape and have a transcription of it for use in the subsequent trial. Accordingly, if the defense has certain types of information, it is also discoverable by the prosecution. Thus, discovery involves an exchange between the prosecution and the defense of relevant information in the case. Both sides must allow each other to see certain types of information they plan to introduce as evidence at the subsequent trial.

▶ The Discovery Process

Discovery is the procedure or mechanism whereby the prosecution shares information with the defense attorney and the defendant. More than a few countries permit discovery of relevant evidence and materials related to crimes (Gubanski 2004). Specific types of information are made available to the defendant and his/her counsel before trial, including results of any tests conducted, psychiatric reports, transcripts, or tape-recorded statements made by the defendant. Also shared between prosecution and defense is the list of witnesses both sides plan to call to testify at the trial (Gubanski 2004). Increasingly, electronic data and the gathering, preserving, and reporting of it, sometimes referred to as E-discovery, is also becoming an important part of the criminal court procedures. Again, for clients with little to no resources, gathering and presenting these kinds of data are out of the question.

The premise upon which discovery is based is that all defendants are entitled to a fair and impartial trial. If the government with its immense resources were to restrict access to various test results and tangible evidence, even oral testimony and reports of experts, this restriction would jeopardize a defendant's right to a fair trial (Schmid 2002). Fundamental fairness is that the defense shall not be deprived of a fair trial. This means that the disclosure of certain types of evidence by the prosecution is mandatory (O'Sullivan 2001).

> **discovery** procedure where prosecution shares information with defense attorney and defendant. Also known as "Brady materials" after a specific court case.

BOX 4-4

KEY CASES: DISCOVERY

Campbell v. United States, 365 U.S. 85 (1961)

Campbell was charged with bank robbery. During the testimony of a government witness, it became known that a previous statement had been made by that witness. The defense sought to obtain that statement, but the court denied them access to it. The government also denied the *existence* of the statement, when, in fact, it actually existed. Campbell was convicted. He appealed, arguing that under the Jencks Act, he was entitled to discovery of the prior statement given by the government witness in order to impeach the witness. The U.S. Supreme Court overturned his conviction and held that under the Jencks Act, such information is discoverable and should be turned over to the defense by government attorneys. Thus, Campbell had been deprived of the right to a fair trial.

Kyles v. Whitley, 514 U.S. 419 (1995)

Kyles was accused in Louisiana of first-degree murder. During the trial, the prosecution failed to disclose to Kyles favorable and exculpatory evidence under discovery. For instance, eyewitness testimony and statements favorable to Kyles were withheld, as were statements made to police by an informant. A computer printout of all car license numbers at or near the murder scene, which did not include Kyles' car license number, was in the possession of the prosecution but was not made available to Kyles or his attorney when they demanded discovery. Kyles was convicted and sentenced to death. Appeals by Kyles to higher state courts resulted in affirmation of his original conviction and sentence. Then he sought relief by an appeal to the U.S. Supreme Court. The Court overturned Kyles' conviction, holding that the prosecution had violated Kyles' *Brady* rights (see *Brady v. Maryland* [1963]) to have relevant exculpatory information made available to him by the prosecution. The significance of this case is that it is the constitutional duty of prosecutors to disclose favorable evidence to defendants in criminal prosecutions.

(continued)

Bracy v. Gramley, 520 U.S. 899 (1997)

Bracy was tried, convicted, and sentenced to death in an Illinois court presided over by Judge Thomas J. Maloney. Maloney was subsequently convicted of taking bribes for fixing other murder cases in Operation Greylord, a federal sting operation intended to detect and prosecute judicial corruption. Bracy appealed his conviction and filed a *habeas corpus* action, arguing that Judge Maloney had a vested interest in Bracy's conviction in order to deflect suspicion that he was taking bribes in other cases. Further, Bracy alleged that Maloney had deliberately suppressed exculpatory evidence that may have mitigated Bracy's sentence. His *habeas corpus* appeals were denied and he appealed directly to the U.S. Supreme Court, where the case was heard. The U.S. Supreme Court reversed Bracy's conviction, holding that Bracy, who was convicted before a judge who was himself later convicted of taking bribes from defendants in criminal cases, showed "good cause" for discovery on his due process claim of actual judicial bias in his own case.

Strickler v. Greene, 527 U.S. 263 (1999)

Strickler was convicted of capital murder in Virginia and sentenced to death. During his trial, Strickler's attorney was permitted to examine prosecutors' files for exculpatory evidence. However, the prosecutor did not advise defense counsel that police files may have contained exculpatory information favorable to Strickler, which may have impeached the veracity of one of the witnesses against Strickler. Strickler filed a *habeas corpus* petition, alleging that the prosecutor had a duty to reveal police documents that may have impeached witnesses against him. Presently, there are three components of a true *Brady* violation: (1) the evidence at issue must be favorable to the accused, either because it is exculpatory or because it is impeaching; (2) the evidence must have been suppressed by the state, either willfully or inadvertently; and (3) prejudice must have ensued. The U.S. Supreme Court heard Strickler's case and decided that although the *Brady* rule had been violated in part, the materiality of the evidence would not have affected the trial outcome. The U.S. Supreme Court held that (1) undisclosed documents impeaching eyewitness testimony as to circumstances about the abduction of the victim were favorable to Strickler for purposes of *Brady*, and (2) Strickler reasonably relied on prosecution's open-file policy and established cause for procedural default in raising a *Brady* claim, but (3) Strickler could not show either materiality under *Brady* or prejudice that would excuse Strickler's procedural default.

Banks v. Dretke, 124 S.Ct. 1256 (2004)

Delma Banks was convicted of capital murder in the death of a 16-year-old. Banks was originally implicated in the murder by two associates, Jefferson and Farr, who were working with the county sheriff as informants. Unknown to Banks before and during the trial was the allegation that Jefferson and Farr were testifying against Banks in order to avoid drug charges, which were threatened by the sheriff and prosecutor. At the same time, a confidential informant also furnished the prosecution with incriminating circumstantial evidence against Banks. This information was also withheld from Banks pursuant to a motion for discovery. Although Banks had no prior criminal record, testimony from Farr and Jefferson provided the jury with innuendo that Banks had an unsavory and criminal past, which was untrue. Banks was sentenced to death and sought postconviction relief, alleging that the prosecution failed to disclose exculpatory evidence as required by *Brady v. Maryland* (1963), including the threats made to Farr and Jefferson as well as the confidential informant, Cook. In its answer, the state claimed that nothing had been kept secret from Banks and no deals had been made with government witnesses, including Cook. In 1993, Banks's postconviction claims were denied outright by an appellate court. He then filed for *habeas corpus* relief in a U.S. District Court, which granted relief on Banks's death sentence. In 1999, Banks filed discovery and evidentiary hearing motions, both supported by affidavits sworn to by Farr and Jefferson that the prosecution had wrongly withheld crucial exculpatory and impeaching evidence. The federal court determined that the state, indeed, had failed to disclose Farr's informant status during the original discovery phase of Banks's trial. Therefore, a writ of *habeas corpus* was granted to Banks with respect to his death sentence, but not to his conviction. Banks petitioned the U.S. Supreme Court, where the case was heard. The U.S. Supreme Court reiterated that under *Brady*, a prosecutorial misconduct claim must establish three things: (1) that the evidence at issue must be favorable to the accused, either because it is exculpatory or because it is impeaching; (2) that evidence must have been suppressed by the state, either willfully or inadvertently; and (3) that prejudice must have ensued. In its response, the state contended that "it can lie and conceal and the prisoner still has the burden to discover the evidence." The U.S. Supreme Court ruled this assertion to be untenable and a violation of Banks's due process rights. Banks presented sufficient evidence to support his *Brady* claim and was thus entitled to a full evidentiary hearing and a certification of appealability.

Illinois v. Fisher, 124 S.Ct. 1200 (2004)

Gregory Fisher was arrested for and charged with cocaine possession following a routine traffic stop by police officers in Chicago, Illinois, in September 1988. In October 1988, Fisher filed a motion for discovery, requesting all physical evidence seized by police officers when he was arrested. Prosecutors stated that all evidence would be made available to Fisher at a reasonable date and time upon request and a trial date was set for July 1989. When the trial date occurred, it was discovered that Fisher had fled the jurisdiction, ultimately residing in Tennessee for the next 11 years. An outstanding arrest warrant for Fisher was subsequently executed in September 1999, and Chicago authorities reinstated the 1988 cocaine charges. Fisher renewed his demand to have access to the original evidence seized, but the prosecutor stated that according to established procedures, the substance seized from him had been destroyed after several years of preservation. Fisher moved to have the charges against him dismissed, as the evidence against him no longer existed. The trial court denied his motion and Fisher was convicted by a jury for cocaine possession, based in large part upon police testimony and the admission of four laboratory tests that confirmed the substance seized at the time of Fisher's 1988 arrest was cocaine. Fisher was sentenced to one year in prison. Fisher appealed, alleging a violation of his right to due process, since the substance he was accused of possessing had been destroyed by police years earlier, and thus they had framed him for the crime. The appellate court reversed Fisher's conviction, holding that the due process clause required the dismissal of the original charge in the absence of incriminating evidence. The government appealed and the U.S. Supreme Court heard the case. The Supreme Court reversed the Illinois Appellate Court, holding that due process did not require dismissal of cocaine possession charges on the grounds that police, nearly 11 years after Fisher was charged, destroyed the cocaine seized. The Supreme Court held that unless a criminal defendant can show bad faith on the part of police, their failure to preserve potentially useful evidence does not constitute a denial of due process of law. Fisher failed to demonstrate bad faith on the part of police; thus, his claim of a violation of his due process rights was dismissed. There is nothing in the record to indicate that the alleged cocaine was destroyed in bad faith.

In several jurisdictions, defense counsel must make a motion for discovery, itemizing the testimony and other evidence it wants. If the defense does not ask for specific items in the possession of the government, the government is not obligated to volunteer them to the defense. This fact is underscored in the case of *Kimmelman v. Morrison* (477 U.S. 365 [1986]). In this case, Neil Morrison was convicted of rape in a bench trial in New Jersey. During the trial, a police officer testified about some evidence, a bedsheet found at the crime scene, which had been seized without a proper search warrant. The defense attorney objected and moved to suppress statements about the bedsheet. The judge, however, ruled that it was too late to register such an objection, that the proper time would have been during discovery, when the items seized and to be used as evidence against Morrison were disclosed to him. Following his conviction, Morrison filed a *habeas corpus* petition, alleging ineffective assistance of counsel relating to the bedsheet issue and the motion to suppress it. Because of the defense attorney's incompetence by not raising a motion at an earlier and more proper time, Morrison argued that he was deprived of the effective assistance of counsel, and this problem led to his conviction. An appellate court reversed his conviction on these grounds, and the state appealed to the U.S. Supreme Court. The U.S. Supreme Court heard the case and affirmed the lower appellate court, concluding that Morrison's counsel was ineffective due to his failure to conduct any pretrial discovery and determine what the state had planned to present as incriminating evidence. Further, the counsel clearly failed to make a timely motion to suppress such evidence. On these grounds, Morrison's conviction must be reversed.

It is beyond the scope of this book to list all types of discoverable information. One reason is that there is considerable interstate variation concerning what is or is not

> **habeas corpus petition** writ filed, usually by inmates, challenging the legitimacy and the nature of their confinement. Document commands authorities to show cause why an inmate should be confined in either a prison or jail.

discoverable material or statements. Confession statements are always discoverable in all jurisdictions. However, the statements of material witnesses may or may not be immediately discoverable. Usually, when lists of witnesses are exchanged by the prosecution and defense, each side seeks to interview the witnesses to be called. This is to avoid a trial by ambush, where a witness will give testimony unknown to the other side, and the testimony given will influence the trial outcome. Neither side wishes to be surprised by the other.

A leading case about discovery is *Brady v. Maryland* (373 U.S. 83 [1963]). Brady was convicted of murder and sentenced to death. He appealed on the grounds that he was denied access to various statements made by a confederate. Actually, Brady took the stand in his own defense and admitted to participating in the crime, but Brady declared that the confederate was the one who actually killed the victim. Various statements had been made to police and prosecution by the confederate. The prosecutor denied the defense access to these statements, alleging confidentiality. Following Brady's conviction, some of this evidence came to light and proved favorable and exculpatory to Brady. He sought an appeal, claiming that he was denied due process by having these important statements withheld during his trial. The U.S. Supreme Court agreed with Brady and overturned his murder conviction, saying that "suppression by prosecution of evidence favorable to an accused upon request violates due process where evidence is material either to guilt or to punishment, irrespective of good faith or bad faith of prosecution." Subsequently, both prosecutors and defense attorneys have referred to discoverable materials and evidence as **Brady materials**. When the prosecutor or defense counsel withholds certain discoverable information, this is called a **Brady violation**.

Actually, an earlier case involving a similar issue was *Jencks v. United States* (353 U.S. 651 [1957]). The *Jencks* case involved the withholding by prosecutors from the defense of prior inconsistent statements by a key government witness against Jencks. In the *Jencks* case, the U.S. Supreme Court ruled that the government must disclose such inconsistent statements to the defense prior to a criminal trial. In Brady's case, the U.S. Supreme Court overturned his conviction and held that according to ruling in the *Jencks* case, such information is discoverable and should be turned over to the defense by government attorneys. In a way similar to the case of *Brady v. Maryland* (1963), the *Jencks* case has led to discoverable evidence being called **Jencks materials**.

▶ Defense Attorneys and Defenses for Criminal Conduct

Who Bears the Burden of Proof in Criminal Prosecutions?

In any criminal prosecution, it is the responsibility of the state to prove beyond a reasonable doubt that the defendant committed the crime(s) charged. This means that prosecutors must prove beyond a reasonable doubt that (1) a crime was committed and (2) the defendant committed the crime. Thus, the prosecutor bears the **burden of proof** in asserting a criminal charge (Haynes 2000; Schmid 2002). This burden is meant by providing the jury with **evidence** of the crime.

The burden of proof standard, also known as the **evidentiary** standard, in all criminal cases does *not* mean that prosecutors must produce witnesses or victims who can furnish **conclusive evidence** of a defendant's guilt. Conclusive evidence might suffice if several persons watched a defendant commit the crime in plain view. Such evidence is so compelling and strong that it cannot be disputed or contradicted. For instance, a man might shoot his wife, killing her. Then he turns the gun on himself, intending to commit suicide. But somehow he survives the bullet wound and is subsequently tried for his wife's murder. He might have left a highly incriminating suicide note indicating the reasons for why he killed his wife. The suicide note is a type of derivative evidence, or written evidence. The weapon he used has his fingerprints on it, his hands have powder residue from firing the weapon, and he is found holding the weapon after his neighbors report the sound of gunshots to police. In this instance, the facts are generally not disputed. District attorneys sometimes prosecute cases with this sort of conclusive evidence (Fisher 1999).

Also, the burden of proof standard does *not* mean that prosecutors must produce any direct evidence of the crime. As in the case of conclusive evidence, direct evidence involves incriminating information such as fingerprints or eyewitness testimony (Prentice 2001). Rather, prosecutors may be able to convince a jury that a defendant is guilty of the crime based on circumstantial evidence alone. In one New York murder case, for example, a physician, Robert Bierenbaum, was suspected of killing his wife, Gail Katz Bierenbaum, in the summer of 1985. Prosecutors believed that he loaded her body aboard a rented airplane, flew out over the ocean, and dumped her body into the sea. No trace of his wife was ever found. Furthermore, police investigators never found any traces of Bierenbaum's wife's blood in Bierenbaum's automobile trunk or inside the airplane. If such evidence would have been found, this would have been demonstrative evidence or derivative evidence, since it is tangible and does not relate to eyewitness testimony. Neighbors reported that they often heard Bierenbaum arguing with his wife. On the day his wife disappeared, Bierenbaum was seen taking off from the airport and flying in the direction of the ocean in a rented airplane, although the police didn't know Bierenbaum had rented the airplane until a year had elapsed. The case was dormant for 15 years, because police didn't have sufficient evidence to charge Bierenbaum with a crime. Subsequently, a check of airport records showed that Bierenbaum had altered his flight log to show that his flight occurred on a different day and time. Also, on the day his wife disappeared, she had spoken with a friend that morning and said that she was leaving Bierenbaum and moving in with a new boyfriend. When the person called her back 40 minutes later, Bierenbaum answered the telephone and told the caller that his wife had just left and he didn't know when she was returning. All of these circumstances and corroboration didn't prove that Bierenbaum killed his wife. But prosecutors eventually decided to indict Bierenbaum for his wife's murder in December 1999. He was tried and convicted of murder in New York on October 24, 2000. Despite the fact that the case against Bierenbaum was entirely circumstantial, the jury drew inferences from all of this information and found him guilty of second-degree murder (Rogers, Cotliar, and Erwin 2000).

In another murder case, this time in Atlanta, Georgia, a man was accused of killing his wife and setting his own home on fire to cover up any incriminating evidence. He managed to crawl out of a second-story window of his home while it went up in flames. He told passersby that his wife was inside and had been overcome with smoke. He said that the fire seemed to come from the kitchen in a downstairs area, and that he and his wife were sleeping. He claimed that his wife was too overcome with smoke to assist in her own flight to safety, and that he was too weak to carry her to a window. Thus, he was only able to save himself. Again as in the New York murder, this man had taken out a large life insurance policy on his wife a few months earlier, and he had named himself as the primary beneficiary. It was also found that he was deeply in debt and that his business was failing. Prosecutors surmised that he killed his wife in an effort to save his company from bankruptcy by using the insurance money from her death. The case was purely circumstantial, but the jury was convinced that the man did, indeed, murder his wife and he was convicted of her murder.

Usually, prosecutors must convince a jury that the accused had the means, motive, and opportunity to commit the crime(s) alleged. Since many criminals perform their criminal acts in secret and do not brag about what they have done because they don't want to get caught and convicted, the prosecutor's burden is a somewhat difficult one. Judges will eventually instruct jurors about how they should regard the evidence presented during the trial, and how to weigh that evidence.

derivative evidence information obtained as the result of previously discovered evidence.

direct evidence evidence offered by an eyewitness who testifies to what was seen or heard.

circumstantial evidence material provided by a witness from which a jury must infer a fact.

demonstrative evidence material related to a crime that is apparent to the senses, in contrast to material presented by the testimony of other persons.

corroboration evidence that strengthens the evidence already given.

The defense is under no obligation to prove anything to the jury. It is not their place to prove their client's innocence. Rather, they may simply offer alternative explanations for how the crime may have occurred. Defense counsels often recommend that their clients should not testify. The fact that defendants do not often testify in their own criminal trials is greatly misunderstood by the public, even many defendants. One of the first things an innocent defendant wants to do is get up on the witness stand and proclaim his/her innocence to the jurors. But prosecutors have many clever ways of distracting and upsetting innocent defendants and twisting their own words to prosecutorial advantage. The defendant's demeanor and self-control are important factors that jurors can observe. On more than one occasion, prosecutors have disturbed defendants so much on the witness stand that they lose their tempers and act guilty, even though they are innocent. It is a fundamental right of defendants, therefore, to remain silent while the prosecution attempts to prove their guilt. This is due process, and all defendants are entitled to it. Some jurors might believe that if the defendant doesn't take the stand and testify, then this is some sort of guilt by omission. That is, if defendants do not declare their innocence on the witness stand, an inference may be drawn that they have something to hide. This is absolutely untrue. While all defendants have the right against self-incrimination, they also have the right to due process, which means in part that if they do not testify, this is *not* a form of incrimination. Ordinarily, judges read jury instructions to jurors and highlight this fact so that jurors must not and cannot consider a defendant's refusal to testify as evidence of their guilt. In fact, *no inferences may be drawn* by jurors about the defendant's guilt or innocence when the defendant does not testify.

However, defense attorneys are seldom content to allow the prosecutors' allegations to go unchallenged. A vigorous defense is expected from any competent defense attorney. But most frequently these defenses are designed to explain away the case prosecutors have crafted against the accused. As we have seen, defense attorneys may provide jurors with alternative explanations for why the crime occurred and who might have committed the crime. But when there is direct evidence that a defendant committed the crime, the defense must act aggressively here as well. Under these circumstances when criminal conduct is alleged, the defense attempts to counter the criminal charges with one or more defenses to criminal conduct. Defenses to criminal conduct also are called **affirmative defenses**.

> **affirmative defenses** responses to a criminal charge where the defendant bears the burden of proof which go beyond simple denial of facts. These defenses include automatism, intoxication, coercion or duress, necessity, alibi, entrapment, defense of property, ignorance or mistake, and self-defense (Fisher 1999).

Automatism and/or Insanity

The defense of **automatism** is that the defendant was incapable of formulating criminal intent because he/she blacked out or was acting unconsciously. For example, someone may sleepwalk and commit the crime of breaking or entering, entering the home of another when they think they are entering their own home. The *mens rea* or guilty mind is eliminated as a criminal element (Jordan and Meyers 2003).

> **automatism** a set of actions taken during a state of unconsciousness.

Insanity is occasionally raised in criminal cases. Insanity is defined in different ways among U.S. jurisdictions (Arpey 2003). Usually, it means acting under an irresistible impulse, an inability to conform one's conduct to the requirements of the law, a mental disease or defect, and not knowing the difference between right and wrong (Arpey 2003). If the defendant was not sane when the crime was committed, then the *mens rea* component of a crime can be overcome (Litwack 2003). Therefore, a crime is not committed.

Currently, most states and the federal government have adopted the guilty, but mentally ill plea, where it is no longer the burden of the prosecution to show that one is sane (Mulford et al. 2004). The insanity defense is used in other countries besides the United States. In England, for instance, insanity is used to indicate diminished capacity in criminal cases (Mitchell 2003).

Intoxication

Intoxication is often raised in criminal cases to show that the defendant was not fully capable when the crime was committed. However, intoxication rarely excuses criminal conduct. Intoxication may be used to show that certain elements of the crime may not be present (Brocke et al. 2004). For instance, in premeditated murder cases, the intoxication of the defendant may help the defense to show that the defendant was not capable of premeditating the crime. States differ in the weight given to intoxication as a way of negating criminal intent.

In Tennessee, for instance, Wayne Adkins was charged with and convicted of first-degree murder in the death of Junior Adams (*State v. Adkins*, 1983). Witnesses testifying about what they saw said that Adkins had consumed a case of beer shortly before the shooting and was drunk when he killed Adams. The jury recommended the death penalty nevertheless. The Tennessee State Supreme Court set aside the death penalty, however, and ruled that Adkins was not capable of premeditating the murder as the result of intoxication. This holding is not necessarily indicative of how other state supreme courts might rule on similar issues.

> **intoxication** the state of being incapable of performing certain tasks legally. Can be induced through consumption of alcoholic beverages, inhaling toxic fumes from petroleum products, or consumption of drug substances.

Coercion or Duress

When persons act under coercion or duress, they feel compelled to act in certain ways in order to avoid harm from others. In youth gang activities, for instance, the gang may pressure younger members of the gang to commit various crimes. The older gang members may intimidate younger gang members by threatening them with bodily harm. "We will beat you up, maybe even kill you, if you don't steal these things from the store," the gang might say to younger gang members. Thus, when the younger gang members commit theft and are caught, they may claim duress. They will allege that the gang made them do it or they would face retribution (Gilbertson 2005).

In another case involving duress, two female inmates held in a California minimum-security prison were charged with escape when they walked away from the prison. They fled the prison when they were threatened by other inmates with physical harm if they did not submit to sexual advances. Later, when the women were free of the prison and the circumstances that might have caused them physical harm, they surrendered themselves to local law enforcement authorities. They claimed duress resulting from the threats of lesbian inmates. They were convicted of escape in a lower California court, but an appellate court set their conviction aside, accepting their defense of duress as valid (*California v. Lovercamp*, 1974). This doesn't mean that prisoners are always entitled to flee from their prison confines if they feel threatened by other prisoners. Each case must be resolved on an individual basis. However, in this *California* case, duress was successfully used. Thus, if a defendant is made to perform conduct that is criminal, duress or coercion may be an affirmative defense to remove it from criminal conduct.

> **coercion** affirmative defense similar to duress, wherein defendants allege that they were made or forced to commit an illegal act.

> **duress** affirmative defense used by defendants to show lack of criminal intent, alleging force, psychological or physical, from others as stimulus for otherwise criminal conduct.

Necessity

In most cases of emergency, persons dial 911 but others take it upon themselves to drive themselves or the injured party to the hospital. If someone was severely injured, or perhaps their pregnant wife was in labor, they may race as fast as they can to the nearest hospital breaking the speed limit and other potential laws such as dangerous and reckless driving. It is likely that if stopped by the police in these instances, the police would transport the injured or pregnant woman to the hospital. However, if they were late charged with speeding or reckless driving, they could bring up the defense of necessity that might be accepted by the court because the person was trying to save his or another person's life.

> **necessity** a condition that compels someone to act because of perceived needs.

Alibi

Whenever a defendant claims an alibi, he/she intends to show that he/she was somewhere else when the crime was committed. Thus, if a crime is committed in St. Louis, Missouri, at 10:00 p.m. on a Monday night, and if the defendant can show that he/she was in New York City at 10:00 p.m. on that same Monday evening, the witnesses who testify on his/her behalf provide him/her with an alibi. The idea is that if someone can put themselves somewhere else other than where and when the crime took place, they have an alibi. Perhaps they were across town at a restaurant with friends. Depending upon the veracity or truthfulness of witnesses, an alibi defense is a strong defense to criminal conduct.

Entrapment

Entrapment occurs whenever a defendant is lulled into criminal conduct by another. Usually, the conduct is something that is extraordinary for the defendant, and not conduct that is normally a routine or practice (Gubanski 2004). Sometimes law enforcement officers seek to induce people to commit a crime so that they can make an arrest. Female officers pose as prostitutes in an effort to arrest those seeking to buy sex. Many prospective customers of prostitutes are thus snared in police stings. However, sometimes the police go out of their way to encourage others to violate the law. They may knock on motel doors until they find someone willing to invite the officer/prostitute in for sex. This aggressive policing often leads to charges of entrapment, where customer/defendants are lured into committing acts that are not ordinarily contemplated by them.

Defense of Property

Defense of property can sometimes be cited as an excuse for criminal conduct. If someone attempts to steal one's car, for example, a defendant is entitled to use reasonable force to deter criminals from committing this crime. Several states have adopted what are referred to as "No Duty to Retreat" or "Castle Doctrine" laws, which allow persons to defend their homes with deadly force. These laws allow homicide to be justifiable under certain circumstances such as when an intruder breaks into someone's residence with intent to steal property or is fleeing the residence with stolen property. Several states have recently expanded or changed their laws to allow deadly defense of one's home or the property therein. The law in Texas, for instance, has even been expanded to include the use of deadly force in defense of a neighbor's property. These laws vary by state and so it depends on where a person lives as to whether deadly force is an acceptable defense of property. The states without the "No Duty to Retreat" laws, however, might allow a defendant to engage in aggravated assault to discourage criminals from stealing his/her valuables or vehicle. Thus, more than a few persons have been acquitted of criminal charges, even murder, when they have been able to demonstrate that they were merely defending their property when they attacked their attackers.

Ignorance or Mistake

The old adage "ignorance is no excuse" is applicable here to a degree. If someone doesn't know what the law is regarding a certain type of conduct, this fact should reduce the seriousness of whatever they do. Persons who visit foreign countries, for instance, may not know what the laws of the foreign country are. They may unwittingly violate a criminal law by engaging in conduct that might be acceptable in their own country.

In certain cultures, for example, it is customary to perform an operation on all female children to remove their clitoris. This is a ritual that is condoned and socially and religiously approved. However, it is against the law in the United States for such a procedure to be performed. In California and other states, however, some persons have been prosecuted for performing these religious rituals. Thus, the courts have had to weigh the religious and cultural significance of these illegal rituals and their legality in other countries (Tonry 2004). In the United States, however, these rituals are considered illegal and are therefore prohibited.

Mistake or ignorance may be acceptable under other conditions. For example, Morissette was a hunter who routinely hunted on an army artillery range. It seems that this particular artillery range, although enclosed by a perimeter wire fence, was considered a good deer-hunting area by local hunters. Furthermore, a section of the army post wire fence perimeter had been cut away where private citizens could drive their trucks through and make it easier to hunt deer. One afternoon, Morissette drove his truck into the military artillery range and hunted deer. After a long unsuccessful afternoon of deer hunting, Morissette was about to leave when he spied a pile of copper artillery shell casings. Weeds had grown up around the pile of copper shell casings, and it appeared to Morissette that these casings, some of which were rusting away, had been abandoned. Thus, Morissette loaded the shell casings into his truck and sold them subsequently at a local flea market for their metal value. With the money, he went to a bar and treated his friends to several rounds of drinks. Nearby enlisted men from the military post overheard Morissette brag about the copper shell casings he had found and he was reported to police who arrested him for theft of military property. He was convicted, but he appealed, arguing that he didn't know that he was stealing government property when he took the copper shell casings. In this instance, the appellate court believed Morissette and overturned his conviction. However, this is a relatively rare instance where courts will accept ignorance or mistake as an excuse for otherwise criminal conduct.

> **mistake** affirmative defense that alleges an act was not criminal because the person charged did not know the act was a prohibited one.

Self-Defense

If someone commits a crime and raises the affirmative defense of self-defense, it must be shown that the conduct was justified because the defendant believed his/her life was in jeopardy (Hemenway 2004). Self-defense is often raised in homicide cases where one person kills another. If the facts are unclear, a murder charge may be filed against the defendant. Later in court, the defendant raises self-defense as the explanation for the conduct (Hollander 2004). The trial provides the factual forum, where witnesses and others testify about what happened. If the defendant believed that his/her life was in jeopardy and that the only course of action available was to kill the aggressor and eliminate the threat, then the jury will acquit the defendant of the murder charge. Self-defense is always a good defense to this type of criminal conduct if there is sufficient factual information to back up that particular defense (Kaufman 2004).

> **self-defense** affirmative defense in which defendants explain otherwise criminal conduct by showing necessity to defend themselves against aggressive victims.

Summary

1. Understand the legal ethics and responsibilities of defense counsels who represent criminal clients.

Most defense counsels are members of the American Bar Association (ABA), and many of them belong to local bar associations. These associations have established Canons of Professional Ethics. The ABA has evolved the Model Code of Professional Responsibility. Also, all defense counsels are under an obligation to avoid the appearance of impropriety. Attorneys who violate one or more of these ethical codes are subject to varying degrees of sanctions, including possible loss of membership and disbarment proceedings, depending upon the seriousness and nature of the ethical code violation.

2. Understand the Sixth Amendment and one's right to counsel regardless of whether the defendant is indigent.

In most serious criminal cases, defendants have the right to counsel. When persons are charged with crimes, they have counsel appointed (if indigent) or they hire their own counsel. Under certain circumstances, persons may act as their own counsel and represent themselves. This self-representation is called acting *pro se*. For indigent defendants who cannot afford counsel, each state and the federal government have established methods for assigning defense counsel to such defendants. Essentially, the U.S. Supreme Court through various rulings has stated that anyone facing possible imprisonment is entitled to court-appointed counsel if they are indigent and cannot afford to hire private counsel. The most common types of indigent defense systems include the public defender system, the assigned counsel system, and the contract system.

3. *Describe the process of self-representation or acting* pro se.

Under certain circumstances, defendants may wish to represent themselves in court, and under the law, defendants are allowed to act as their own attorney in criminal cases. This is not a unique practice to the United States as several other countries also allow defendants to represent themselves. Most persons learned in the law believe this is not a good idea as most defendants do not have any legal training or experience in criminal law or trial procedures. In most *pro se* cases, judges will still appoint an attorney to advise the defendant throughout the process.

4. *Understand the attorney–client privilege and the confidentiality associated with that relationship.*

There exists an attorney–client privilege between the defendant and his/her counsel, and prosecutors may not seek to violate this confidentiality by any means. Attorney–client privilege means that any information exchanged between a defense counsel and his/her client will not be disclosed to others, such as prosecutors. This also means that attorneys are protected from disclosing information about the clients they represent because of this privilege. In other words, if a defense attorney hears a confession from a client, the attorney is vested with considerable legal protection to not have to disclose the information. Prosecutors cannot compel defense counsels to provide them with incriminating information about their clients.

5. *Describe what is meant by ineffective assistance of counsel and learn the criteria used by courts to assess attorney competence.*

Some convicted offenders may challenge their convictions and allege ineffective assistance of counsel. The U.S. Supreme Court has articulated standards governing which conduct rises to the level of incompetence and which conduct does not. Under *Strickland v. Washington*

(1984), ineffective assistance of counsel occurs whenever counsel's behavior undermines the adversarial process to the extent that the trial outcome is unreliable, and/or if the counsel's conduct is unreasonable to the extent that the jury verdict would have been different otherwise. Both actions and inactions on the part of defense counsel may rise to the level of ineffective assistance of counsel. These counsels may say or do something to jeopardize one's case, or they may fail to do important tasks with the same result. Most defendants alleging ineffective assistance of counsel find that it is difficult to sustain such charges against their attorneys if convicted of a crime.

6. *Assess the circumstances under which defendants may request and receive a jury trial.*

The Sixth Amendment guarantees a right to a jury trial. The standards governing whether defendants are entitled to a jury trial, however, have been clarified by the U.S. Supreme Court. If defendants are in jeopardy of being incarcerated for a period of beyond six months, they are entitled to a jury trial with one exception. This exception is if the judge assures the defendant that he/she will not suffer loss of liberty of beyond six months if a bench trial is conducted and finds the defendant guilty.

7. *Understand the multidimensional role of defense counsels and the different functions they perform.*

Criminal defense attorneys perform various duties and have several important functions. Several of these duties and functions relate closely to the ethical codes of conduct or canons of professional responsibility of their professional organizations. Defense counsels must represent their clients faithfully and vigorously, within the boundaries of the law. They must attack the prosecution's case and do their best to show the innocence of their defendants.

In cases where there is overwhelming evidence of defendant's guilt, it is the defense counsel's responsibility to secure the minimum punishment for their clients through plea bargaining (Fisher 2000). This means that defense counsels must consult with prosecutors and agree on a plea and a punishment. Judges approve all plea agreements contemplated between the defense and the prosecution.

8. *Describe different types of public defender systems, including the assigned counsel system and the contract system.*

Under the public defender system, state- or county-funded public defender agencies are established and staffed with defense counsels who are assigned to indigent criminal cases. The assigned counsel system is used in about one-fourth of all states. Often the jurisdictions where the assigned counsel system is operative are sparsely populated and there are few attorneys. The local bar association rotates defense counsel duties among its membership, and the payment for one's services as defense counsel for indigents is modest. Under the contract system, different law firms in more urban jurisdictions will submit bids to the state or county specifying how much they will charge per client per day to represent indigents. County or state agencies will award contracts to these firms according to varying criteria, most often associated with the lowest cost to the government.

One commonality is that all forms of defense for indigents lack financial sources equivalent to those of private law firms that are retained by more affluent clients. Lacking financial resources greatly restricts public defenders from conducting their own thorough investigations, and thus, the generalization is frequently made that indigent representation by public defenders or assigned counsel is not as effective as representation by private counsel. The literature suggests that there is often a factual basis for this generalization, given the outcomes of many indigent criminal cases.

9. *Understand what is meant by defense misconduct and describe its various forms.*

Some defense counsels may engage in unethical or illegal practices when defending their clients. While it is permissible to coach clients who will testify in court on their own behalf, it is illegal to suggest to clients that they commit perjury on the witness stand. This is subornation of perjury, and if it is detected, defense counsels may be charged with a crime and prosecuted.

Also, like prosecutors, defense counsels are forbidden from making certain statements in court that are inadmissible and may prejudice the jury (Cook et al. 2004). For instance, it is improper for defense counsels to mention the results of lie detector or polygraph tests administered to their clients by law enforcement personnel, even if those results are exculpatory.

10. *Understand the relation between prosecutors and defense counsel and the discovery process.*

Defense attorneys must be responsible and seek discovery of any and all information about the crime and the defendant in the possession of prosecutors and police. Some of this information is not discoverable, but much of it is. Obtaining this information usually benefits criminal clients in different ways.

Materials subject to discovery include confessions, transcripts of interviews between police interrogators and the defendant, psychological test results, and other materials. These discoverable materials are called Brady materials or Jencks materials after the U.S. Supreme Court cases where such materials were declared discoverable.

Different types of evidence may be presented during a criminal trial. Evidence may be direct or circumstantial. Direct evidence is usually the most damaging, and it is either eyewitness testimony or incriminating fingerprint evidence (Schram, Koons-Witt, and Morash 2004). Circumstantial evidence is less compelling, but it is nevertheless important. In murder cases, for instance, bodies of victims are sometimes never discovered. Nevertheless, there may be substantial circumstantial evidence showing defendant's guilt. Evidence may also be corroborated by other persons. This assists prosecutors in building their cases against defendants (Matthews, Pease, and Pease 2001).

11. *Describe the various affirmative defenses attorneys may raise when representing persons charged with crimes.*

Defendants and their attorneys have available to them a variety of defenses to criminal conduct. These defenses are often known as affirmative defenses. One type of affirmative defense is automatism or insanity. The argument is that the defendant was incapable of formulating criminal intent or lacked the *mens rea* to understand what he/she was doing was wrong.

The insanity defense isn't used often, and when it is used, it is often not used successfully. Legislatures have modified the insanity defense standard so that today many jurisdictions allow defendants to plead guilty but mentally ill. This type of plea usually lessens the harshness of their punishment (McSherry 2004).

Other affirmative defenses include intoxication, coercion or duress, necessity, and alibi. Some defendants claim that they were intoxicated at the time the crime was committed. This is sometimes considered a mitigating circumstance, although most jurisdictions consider intoxication to be a voluntary condition and merely consider it as a minor contributing factor.

Coercion or duress means that the defendant was made to commit the crime by means of a threat. The defense of necessity means that the crime was committed because it was necessary to do so. Someone who breaks into a neighbor's home late at night to put out a fire may claim necessity later if charged with breaking and entering.

Alibi as a defense means that the defendant alleges he/she was elsewhere when the crime was committed. Usually, one or more persons will testify as to one's alibi if it is used as an affirmative defense.

Other affirmative defenses include entrapment, defense of property, ignorance or mistake, and self-defense. Entrapment occurs when someone is encouraged to break the law, usually by some law enforcement officer acting in an undercover capacity, and it is not customary for the defendant to engage in such criminal behavior.

Defense of property may be a defense if it can be shown that the defendant was merely defending his/her property from damage, intrusion, or theft by another. Some trespassers have been shot by home owners who later claim defense of property. In certain states, this affirmative defense is successful.

The defense of ignorance or mistake is sometimes used. While ignorance of the law may be claimed, it is usually insufficient to excuse a violation of the law. But sometimes defendants make an honest mistake and violate the law. On income tax returns, for instance, some persons may avoid criminal prosecution for income tax evasion if they are ignorant of the tax laws in some way or if they make a genuine mistake. This situation is almost always a judgment call by either the judge or jury.

Finally, some defendants allege that they were acting in self-defense. Self-defense is usually a good affirmative defense if it can be shown that the victim's behavior was menacing, potentially lethal, and could not be avoided. The use of one or more of these defenses is available to any defense attorney when representing a client in criminal court. In jury trials, juries must decide whether to believe the defendant when such defenses are alleged to account for his/her criminal conduct.

Key Terms

ABA Model Code of Professional Responsibility 66
affirmative defenses 86
alibi 88
assigned counsel system 75
attorney competence 69
attorney–client confidentiality and privilege 68
automatism 86
Brady materials 84
Brady violation 84
burden of proof 84
Canons of Professional Ethics 66
circumstantial evidence 85
coercion 87

conclusive evidence 84
contract system 75
corroboration 85
defense of property 88
demonstrative evidence 85
derivative evidence 85
direct evidence 85
discovery 81
duress 87
entrapment 88
evidence 84
evidentiary 84
habeas corpus petition 83
indigent defendants 67
ineffective assistance of counsel 71

intoxication 87
Jencks materials 84
jury trial 72
lie detectors 79
mistake 89
necessity 87
polygraph tests 79
pro se 68
public defender system 74
self-defense 89
self-representation 68
state bar associations 66
subornation of perjury 79

Critical Thinking Exercises

1. The discovery process is very important to the ability of the defendant and his/her attorney to mount an adequate defense to the prosecution's case. Do you think that the rules for discovery should be stricter? In other words, if the government believes it has evidence to convict someone of a crime, should the prosecution have to give all of this evidence to the defense instead of the defense having to make a motion for discovery? If it were the case that the prosecution had to turn over all evidence as a matter of right to the defendant, would it make it easier for the prosecution to convict, say through a plea bargain, or more difficult as the defense may be able to present a more informed case? Would it depend on the strength of the evidence that the government had?

2. Attorney–client privilege affords defense counsel with considerable protection about the information that a defendant has shared with them. If you were an attorney and your client confessed to you that they were fully or partly involved in the crime, what would you do? Would you vigorously fight the prosecution's case, encourage your client to seek a fair plea bargain, or decide you don't really care what happens to the defendant and not put forth any effort in the case? Would this depend on the type of crime the defendant admitted to?

Case Study Decision-Making Exercise

It has been over 50 years since the Supreme Court decision in *Gideon v. Wainwright* guaranteed assistance of counsel to those who cannot afford it and yet there are still criticisms that indigent defense is grossly underfunded. In fact, some states are actually reducing the amount of funding for indigent defense despite the fact that caseloads are increasing. What do you think, should states have to adequately fund defense in a way that is comparable to the amount they spend on prosecution? More money could reduce the caseloads of indigent defenders and allow them more time and effort on each case and therefore perhaps better representation. Do you think *Gideon's* promise is going unfulfilled even 50 years later? Does this lack of funding call into question the ability of the criminal justice system to provide fairness and equality under the law?

Concept Review Questions

1. What are five defenses to criminal conduct? Explain in each case how each might be used.
2. What is discovery and what are its purposes? What are the general rules governing discovery?
3. Under what circumstances are criminal defendants entitled to an attorney? Under what circumstances are defendants entitled to a jury trial? What are some leading legal cases having to do with the right to counsel?
4. What is meant by ineffective assistance of counsel? What are some leading cases where ineffectiveness of counsel is defined?
5. What are some major Canons of Ethics that are a part of the ABA Model Code of Professional Responsibility? Why are they important?
6. What is meant by the courtroom workgroup and who makes up its key components? Why is it important for defense attorneys to work closely with the courtroom workgroup?
7. What are several forms of provision of counsel for indigent defendants?
8. Are court-appointed counsels as effective as privately retained counsel when representing criminal defendants? Why or why not? Explain.
9. What is meant by defense misconduct? What are some different forms of defense misconduct?
10. What is meant by subornation of perjury?
11. What is meant by a Brady violation?
12. Who bears the burden of proof in criminal prosecutions? Under due process, what can be assumed about the guilt or innocence of the accused?

Suggested Readings

1. A. Hollander, M. Jacobsson, and S. Sjöström (2007). "Defender, Spokesperson, Therapist: Representing the True Interest of the Client in Therapeutic Law." *International Journal of Social Welfare* **16:**373–381.
2. B. H. Brummer (2009). "The Banality of Excessive Defender Workload: Managing the Systemic Obstruction of Justice." *St. Thomas Law Review* **22:**104–195.
3. Whitley Kaufman (2004). "Is There a 'Right' to Self-Defense?" *Criminal Justice Ethics* **23:**20–32.
4. D. E. Chemerinsky (2012). "Lessons from *Gideon*." *The Yale Law Journal* **122:**2676–2693.

WavebreakmediaMicro/Fotolia

5 Judges

LEARNING OBJECTIVES

As a result of reading this chapter, you will have accomplished the following objectives:

1 *Distinguish among the different kinds of judges and their roles in the criminal court system.*

2 *Recognize the qualifications a judge must have in order to sit on the bench.*

3 *Compare and contrast the different judicial selection methods and the advantages and disadvantages of each type of judicial selection method.*

4 *Analyze the different methods of judicial training.*

5 *Understand the different types of judicial misconduct and abuses of discretion.*

6 *Understand some of the current criticisms of judges and the ways in which judges can be removed from office.*

A judge in Indiana came under fire for a sentence of home confinement and probation. A 52-year-old man in Indiana who was convicted on six felony charges for drugging and sexually assaulting his wife was given a sentence of eight years of home confinement and two years on probation. He was also given a 12-year suspended sentence that requires no incarceration as long as he completes the term of home confinement and probation. Prosecutors wanted a sentence of 40 years in prison but with the home confinement sentence handed out by the judge, the defendant will serve no prison time and will be able to leave his house for work. He was also not required to get treatment. Under Indiana law, each of the charges could be punished by 6–20 years but there is also no minimum sentence required under the law. Most people would disagree with the sentence this judge handed out in this case; however, as long as judges adhere to legal statutes, they often have wide discretion in sentencing defendants. After the sentence, in which the judge told the wife she needed to forgive her husband, the wife responded that it felt like a punch in the gut. The two, now divorced, were married for 12 years. One critic of the sentence remarked that they will ensure that the judge does not get re-elected. Should judges have this much discretion to determine appropriate sentences? Just because the public may disagree with a particular sentence, does this mean a judge who has seen all of the evidence in the case is wrong to impose it?

Sources: Based on *The Los Angeles Times, Nation Now,* "Indiana judge assailed for light sentence in husband–wife rape case," May 20, 2014, *The Los Angeles Times, Nation Now,* "No prison time for Indiana man convicted of drugging, raping wife," May 19, 2014, and *The New York Daily News,* "Wife outraged when husband who drugged, raped her avoids jail time: 'I was told I needed to forgive my attacker'," May 20, 2014.

▶ Introduction

The public has several general conceptions about judges and their qualifications and what duties they perform in their judicial role. But some of these conceptions are misconceptions and depending on the type of judge, the job responsibilities often entail much more than making decisions about law and sentencing convicted defendants. There are many different kinds of judges with diverse amounts of judicial powers. For instance, we usually think of a judge as being an ultimate arbiter, a ruler over courtroom proceedings, and the person responsible for meting out punishments. Although a judge is all of these things, in addition, they are also courtroom administrators and docket managers. In some jurisdictions, especially where the judge is elected, there are no requirements for previous knowledge or experience, or education and training on all of the duties they will be required to perform.

This chapter examines judges, their duties, and their qualifications. There is great variation among judges in the United States in their backgrounds, the legal expertise they have, and how they became judges. Not all judges have the same degree of legal expertise, nor are all judges lawyers or possess law degrees. They differ greatly in their personalities and idiosyncrasies. They may have many prejudices and limitations in their abilities. Often, citizens in communities are interested in how certain persons became judges, and the general public from time to time wonders how they come to make decisions. Spohn (2009) states that there are often misconceptions of judges and their duties; sometimes they play a leading role in the criminal court system and at other times only a supportive role. This may depend on the type of judge they are (i.e., magistrate judge versus district court judge), what type of cases they are allowed to hear (i.e., criminal versus civil or felony versus misdemeanor), and whether they have the authority to make legal decisions in cases or have oversight over other courts (i.e., trial courts versus appellate courts).

Further, sometimes their decisions are not solely their own; in the sentencing process, for instance, a number of other courtroom actors are involved in the determination of the final sentence (Spohn 2009). For example, the legislature enacts legislation regarding minimum and maximum sentences allowable, the prosecutor decides which charges to file, which will ultimately affect what type of sentence will be handed out, a jury may be involved in conviction or acquittal, a probation officer may recommend a sentence to a judge through a presentence investigation report, and then the judge has the responsibility for deciding a sentence. In other words, some judges may have wide-ranging discretion to make decisions and others may be restricted by legal and administrative rules.

This chapter will describe the judicial selection process in different jurisdictions. Some judges are elected, others are appointed, and still others reach the bench through a merit selection process. This chapter will also discuss the advantages and disadvantages of each of these methods for judicial selection.

The next section of the chapter discusses judicial training. All judges are bound by certain rules that are integral to a court's efficiency and effectiveness. Judges sometimes, however, make decisions that are reversed by a higher court, or sometimes judges allow evidence that should have been inadmissible. The judge decides what is or is not relevant testimony. The judge uses these rules and these decisions to control the trials that come into the courtroom. Some judges are not learned in law; as such, there have been criticisms of some of their decisions, as well as blaming them for court delays. Most jurisdictions now have special training that most judges must go through to make them better able to manage their court caseload.

Because there is great variation in the quality of the judiciary throughout all U.S. jurisdictions, the nature of judicial appointments will be examined. In recent years, the judiciary has come under close scrutiny by various interests and agencies, and some evidence of judicial misconduct has surfaced. Sentiments beginning in the 1980s that judges were too lenient in sentencing have led many jurisdictions to fetter the discretion that some judges enjoy by implementing determinate sentencing and guideline sentencing structures. Sentencing goals, structures, and judicial discretion are further discussed in Chapters 9 and 10. Although the majority of judges are probably effective decision makers and abide by legal rules set forth, from time to time, some judges abuse their discretionary powers. As such, different types of judicial misconduct will be presented. Finally, selected criticisms of judges will be provided, together with an examination of several other relevant issues for judicial duties in the courtroom context.

judge a political officer who has been elected or appointed to preside over a court of law, whose position has been created by statute or by Constitution, and whose decisions in criminal and juvenile cases may only be reviewed by a judge, or a higher court.

judicial process the sequence of procedures designed to resolve disputes or conclude a criminal case.

▶ Judges and Their Qualifications

In any courtroom, the key figure is the judge. Judges make decisions that affect the lives of many people, including but not limited to defendants. All judges have certain rules to follow that are an integral feature of the judicial process. Sometimes judges make decisions that are reversed by higher courts. A judge may allow the introduction of incriminating evidence against a defendant, or the judge may decide to exclude such evidence. The judge, considering arguments from the prosecution and defense, decides what is or is not relevant testimony. The judge controls the conduct of all trials.

It is a common misconception among citizens that all judges are lawyers and have legal expertise. However, in numerous jurisdictions throughout the United States, many judges have no legal training and are not former lawyers. One implication is that in many jurisdictions, judicial selection is more a matter of politics than judicial expertise. The political nature of judicial selection has its roots in seventeenth-century England. Minimum age for appellate and trial court judges across the 50 states ranges from 18 to 35 years (Rottman and Strickland 2006, 29–32, 40–45). These minimum-age requirements, however, are somewhat deceptive since it might appear that an 18-year-old could become an appellate or trial court judge. States with these minimum-age provisions eliminate this possibility by also requiring their prospective judges to be members of the state bar association for a certain period of time, say 5 or 10 years. Thus, it is highly unlikely that any 18-year-old would ever hold a judicial post in these states where 18 years is the minimum age.

Only a couple of states list U.S. citizenship as a statutory requirement for persons to hold appellate or trial judge posts and residency requirements within the state vary considerably from 10 days to 10 years with a few states having no provisions for minimum residency times at all (Rottman and Strickland 2006). Other qualifications specified by some states include certain personal characteristics such as good moral character, sobriety of manners, integrity, wisdom, and sound legal knowledge. Thus, there is considerable variation among the states about the qualifications necessary to be seated as a judge.

The Politicalization of Judicial Selection

The politicalization of the judicial selection process cannot be overstated. When politics is the dominating factor in judicial appointments, one's qualifications for a judgeship are practically irrelevant. When a partisan election or a gubernatorial or a presidential appointment leads to one's becoming a judge, the result is often a judicial appointment that reflects party politics rather than one's professional qualities for deciding cases fairly. This doesn't mean that political judicial appointees are incapable of being fair in judging cases, but rather, they might be expected to adhere to a fixed political agenda associated with the party placing them in power (Pinello 1995).

Political influence also works to the detriment of women and minorities in judicial appointments. Bias has been present in more than a few systems whereby judges are appointed by politicians, and women and minorities are routinely excluded from judicial consideration. So despite the fact that the United States is more diverse than ever, the judiciary hasn't kept pace (Torres-Spelliscy, Chase, and Greenman 2010). This is especially true at the state level where the vast majority of judges are white males (Myers 2013). Several critics argue that political appointments of judges place too much power in the hands of the appointer, such as the governor or president (Tomasi and Velona 1987). Politically appointed judges have considerably lower levels of accountability, and weak sanctioning mechanisms are in place for their discipline or removal. Those who oppose elections of judges say that voter apathy and disinterest, political influence, and a general lack of information about candidates and their qualifications make this process meaningless. Current research is mixed on which of the systems of judicial selection is better at attaining a judiciary that is diverse with respect to gender and race/ethnicity; some studies have found that appointments lead to greater diversity, others show merit selection is the best way to increase diversity, others still have found that elections are best, especially for female candidates, and finally some studies reveal no relationship between diversity and the type of judicial selection system (Myers 2013).

President Jimmy Carter created nominating commissions for federal circuit courts and district courts. Under Carter's administration, judicial appointees were more likely to have professional experience, age and years at the bar, a legal education, and higher American Bar Association (ABA) ratings compared with subsequent Reagan appointees. Subsequently, President Reagan discontinued the nominating commission method of judicial appointments.

President Obama has appointed the highest number of females and minorities to the bench (Goldman, Slotnick, and Schiavoni 2013). Over 40 percent of his appointees have been female; he has also appointed a higher percentage of African Americans, Hispanics, and Asian Americans than any other president (Goldman et al. 2013; Sourcebook of Criminal Justice Statistics 2013).

Early research about the qualities of judicial applicants has shown that nominating commissions have identified the following criteria for their judicial selections: age, health, impartiality, integrity, judicial temperament, industry, professional skills, community contacts, social awareness, collegiality, writing ability, decisiveness, and speaking ability (Greenstein and Sampson 2004). However, no precise guidelines have been established to indicate how these qualities should be measured or assessed. The American Bar Association and its Standing Committee on the Federal Judiciary reviews presidential appointments to the bench and rates them according to their professional qualifications. Their rating includes well qualified, qualified, and not qualified; however, there is usually no review of the qualifications of judges at lower levels. Historically, there hasn't been much by way of guidelines regarding the qualities of judges and transparency was often lacking as well. In early England, for example, much secrecy was involved in the process of selecting judges (Pickles 1987). Judicial selection criteria were purposely diffuse and ambiguous so that only conservative types of persons could hold judicial posts. These persons were often manipulated by politically influential constituencies (Pickles 1987).

Today, in selected jurisdictions, model guidelines have been generated to assist judges in learning about courtroom protocol and the diverse functions of courtroom personnel. For instance, the National Center for State Courts in Williamsburg, Virginia, has produced a resource manual that is designed to enhance the performance of trial judges (Hewitt 1995). The manual includes a discussion of terminology interpretation, judicial training issues, and general court interpreter services.

Reforms relating to judicial selection are not new. Aggressive court reforms have been undertaken for many decades, as different waves of state and federal judges have manifested characteristics that suggest inexperience and ineffectiveness. Many formal recruitment and judicial selection systems have been proposed, but relatively few have come up with any conclusive data indicating the kinds of qualitative differences that might result from alternative selection systems. Interviews with judges themselves suggest mixed reactions to any type of selection system, whether it is through appointment or election (Johnson 2004).

State Judicial Selection Methods

Judges are either appointed or elected. Alfini (1981, 253) has identified five methods of judicial selection as basic variations on appointments or elections: (1) partisan election, (2) nonpartisan election, (3) gubernatorial appointment, (4) legislative appointment, and (5) selection through the merit plan.

Partisan Elections

partisan elections elections in which candidates endorsed by political parties are presented to the voters for selection.

Partisan elections of judges are the same as elections for other public offices. Democrats, Republicans, and others advance their own slate of candidates for various offices, including judicial vacancies. The public votes for their choice by secret ballot. Persons who win these elections become judges for a fixed term, such as four years. There are only six states that use partisan elections for selecting the highest appellate judges: Alabama, Illinois, Louisiana, Ohio, Pennsylvania, and Texas (American Judicature Society 2008a).

Nonpartisan Elections

nonpartisan elections voting process in which candidates who are not endorsed by political parties are presented to the voters for selection.

In nonpartisan elections, candidates are simply listed to fill judicial vacancies regardless of their political affiliation. Fifteen states used nonpartisan elections to fill the highest appellate court posts. These states included Arkansas, Georgia, Idaho, Kentucky, Michigan, Minnesota, Mississippi, Montana, Nevada, North Carolina, North Dakota, Oregon, Washington, West Virginia, and Wisconsin (American Judicature Society 2008a).

Problems with Partisan and Nonpartisan Elections of Judges

There are several problems with electing judges by popular vote. One criticism is whether either partisan or nonpartisan elections actually reflect the people's choices. Usually, some amount of private financing is behind each judicial candidate. The slate of candidates is generated by different political parties and special interest groups, regardless of whether elections are partisan or nonpartisan. Thus, those persons who are placed on the ballot may not be the persons most likely to represent the interests of the general public.

But despite the partisan nature of judicial voting, there is evidence to indicate that an attentive public is out there who makes informed selections of judges in their voting booths. Interestingly, investigations of voter knowledge of the judicial selection process show that while voters may not understand fully the nature of voting reforms, they are informed about the opinions and views of the respective judicial candidates (Pinello 1995).

By contrast, research has shown that depending upon the section of the country where judicial selections are made, there is significant partisanship in public voting but perhaps the most significant criticism of using elections for filling judicial vacancies is that the most popular judges may not be the most qualified judges. One's political influence may take precedence over one's competence to be a judge.

In the last four decades, there have been several recommendations for standardizing the qualifications, training, and selection of judges. One such recommendation is that judicial elections should be publicly financed and not dependent upon private contributions. A standard amount of money should be available to all judicial candidates for their election campaigns and no private contributions of any kind should be allowed. Further, filing fees should not be required of anyone seeking a judgeship (Beechen 1974). In some county elections, more affluent judges may spend considerably more of their own money on judicial campaigning compared with less affluent candidates. The relative difference in campaign money spent by the different candidates may create the potential for the appearance of improper influence. Further, those candidates of modest means are disadvantaged and may be deterred from seeking public office.

Subsequent studies of the judicial selection process through partisan elections have revealed that private contributions and frivolous candidate expenditures have raised more than a few questions about judicial ethics and fairness (Keil et al. 1994). Further, the bars of various states have disclosed that they have little influence on the nature of voting for one judicial candidate or another in terms of his/her comparative qualifications (Keil et al. 1994).

Some evidence, however, suggests that voters are more attentive to the judicial policy preferences and ideological inclinations of judges than researchers have predicted. Based on a random sample of 1,012 ballots cast in the November 1988, Marion County, Oregon, judicial race, which occurred simultaneously with the Bush–Dukakis presidential campaign, voters were very much aware of the political philosophies and personal ideologies of those competing for judicial vacancies. In nearby Washington State, a survey of voters in a 1986 judicial election indicated that voter knowledge about judicial candidates and their views was critical in their voting participation (Lovrich and Sheldon 1994). In other states such as California, however, voters in judicial elections did not appear to be as informed or educated about the issues involved in other judicial selections (Champion 2005b). The number of states using partisan election has decreased in recent years because of criticisms; however, other methods for judicial selection such as judicial appointments by executives are criticized as being equally flawed.

Appointments of Judges by Governors

Governors made the highest appellate judicial appointments in only three states: California, Maine, and New Jersey (American Judicature Society 2008a). Governors may or may not make use of state and local bar association recommendations for judgeships. Gubernatorial

judicial appointments selections of judges by political figures, such as governors or presidents.

appointments are not necessarily made on the basis of which judges are best qualified to serve. Rather, these judgeships are political appointments. Thus, major contributors to a governor's election campaign make recommendations to the governor for particular judgeships, and quite often, these recommendations result in particular judges being appointed (Pinello 1995).

In many other jurisdictions, persons campaign for judgeships much as candidates run for political offices. In fact, politics is the primary contributing factor that accounts for large numbers of nonlawyers in posts such as municipal judges, justices of the peace, and county court judges. There has been considerable debate about whether judges should be appointed or elected, although no judicial selection method has been found superior to others (Myers 2013). Some researchers have observed that gubernatorial judicial appointments in certain jurisdictions result in racial or gender bias in judicial decision making (Pinello 1995).

Legislative Appointments of Judges

Only two states (South Carolina and Virginia) use legislative appointment to select judges (American Bar Association 2008). Nominating committees advance a list of judicial candidates for legislative approval. Although legislative appointments of judges affect only a small portion of the judiciary, critics say that there are substantial impacts for judicial performance on the bench. Daniel Pinello (1995) has indicated that where judges have been selected by legislatures compared with those selected by partisan/nonpartisan elections or by gubernatorial appointments, their subsequent performance as judges has been characterized as acquiescent and inactive.

Legislative appointments also tend to be extremely political and reflect the political leanings of legislators who have been voted into office by the citizens of the state. Thus, a legislature controlled by Democrats might be disposed to appoint Democrat judges, while Republican-dominated legislatures would be expected to appoint Republican judges. There is a great propensity on the part of state legislators to appoint former legislators to judicial vacancies; in both South Carolina and Virginia, general assemblies of the legislature appoint judges (Edwards 2004). Although in South Carolina, the General Assembly appoints judges from a list submitted by the state Judicial Merit Selection Commission, this 10-member commission is made up of persons appointed by the Speaker of the House, the Chairman of the Senate Judiciary Committee, and the President pro tempore of the Senate (Edwards 2004). Dependent on the party of majority in the legislature, this commission that comes up with the list is likely not nonpartisan as their membership is appointed by some of the same persons who will be ultimately voting to appoint the judges as well. The question then becomes, does the legislature appoint the most qualified persons to vacant judgeships? Not if these appointments are based on former political ties to the legislature or other political offices within the state.

Problems with Politically Appointed Judges

Politically appointing judges raises several important issues. Some of these issues are the same as those raised in jurisdictions where partisan and nonpartisan elections are used to fill judicial vacancies. Are the most qualified persons selected for the judgeship? Some research shows that judicial outcomes do differ between judges who are elected and judges who are appointed (Besley and Payne 2003; Helland and Tabarrok 2002). Other studies conclude that judicial quality, rated on a scale from 0 to 100, differs between elected and appointed judges where quality scores are on average higher for those appointed (Sobel and Hall 2007). A study examining the decisions of judges for technical accuracy and legal justification, however, found no significant differences between elected or appointed judges (Dubois 1990).

Another issue is whether political appointments contribute to corruption among the judiciary. Judges, because of their powerful positions, may influence trial outcomes, dismiss cases, or find innocent defendants guilty or vice versa. They can also regulate the harshness of penalties imposed whenever a jury verdict of guilty is rendered. All states have judicial sanctioning boards. These are usually operated through state bar associations, and provisions exist for officially questioning judicial behavior.

Regardless of the method, arguments are that politics is heavily involved in both appointment and election of judges, especially where they are seated through partisan elections. Berkson, Caufield, and Reddick (2010) report that even in the early history of the country, concerns were that judges were elected and controlled by the political machinery. Studies comparing the qualities of judges elected versus those appointed show mixed results regarding the quality of judges placed on the bench. When accountability and independence are examined, results do not seem to differ significantly (Blankenship, Sparger, and Janikowski 1994).

Some jurisdictions are taking notice and attempting to hold governors more accountable for their judicial appointments when the result is either incompetent or corrupt judges (*Villanova Law Review* 1982). Several states have increasingly moved away from appointment as a method to seat judges as insufficient oversight has resulted in occasional selections of poor judges. Suggested alternative judicial selection methods include a gubernatorial appointment system whereby the records of prospective judicial appointees can be carefully scrutinized by the press and state bar associations. One method being increasingly utilized as a superior method for judicial selection is on the basis of merit.

Merit Selection of Judges

Throughout the nation's history, there has been debate about how judges should be selected (Berkson et al. 2010). Prior to 1933, no state had any type of merit selection plan for filling vacant judgeships. By far, the most popular methods of selecting judges involved partisan and nonpartisan elections. Other systems used included gubernatorial or legislative appointments. In the late 1800s, there was concern that politics was too powerful in the judicial selection process and many states modified their methods to select judges through nonpartisan elections (American Bar Association 2008). In the early 1930s, Albert Kales proposed a method for selecting judges based on merit; nominating commissions would put forth a list of qualified candidates for judicial vacancies from which the governor or legislators appoint someone. Its adoption, however, was slow. One reason for the slow adoption of merit systems for judicial appointments was the strong sentiment that the public should be involved in the process and that judges should be accountable to the people they serve (American Bar Association 2008). By the late 2000s, 33 states utilized some form of the Kales Plan or merit system for filling judicial vacancies.

> **merit selection** reform plan in which judges are nominated by a committee and appointed by the governor for a given period. When the term expires, the voters are asked to signify their approval or disapproval of the judge for a succeeding term. If judge is disapproved, the committee nominates a successor for the governor's appointment.

The Missouri Plan

A popular method of judicial selection adopted by several states is the Missouri Plan. The Missouri Plan was introduced in 1940 and is a method of judicial selection using the merit system for appointments to judgeships (President's Commission on Law Enforcement 1967, 66–67). The essential features of the Missouri Plan are as follows:

> **Kales Plan** the 1914 version of Missouri Plan, in which a committee of experts creates a list of qualified persons for judgeships and makes recommendations to governor.

1. A nominating committee consisting of lawyers and nonlawyers appointed by the governor and chaired by a judge.

2. A listing of qualified candidates who are nominated by the committee for each judicial vacancy.

3. Each judicial vacancy is filled by the governor by referring to the list of candidates nominated by the committee.

4. Any appointed judge seeking re-election will run only on the issue of whether or not he/she should be retained on the basis of merit.

> **Missouri Plan** method of selecting judges in which merit system for appointments is used. Believed to reduce political influence in the selection of judges.

The Missouri Plan is a version of the 1914 Kales Plan (Kales 1914). The Kales Plan has survived in various forms in several states over the years, and its influence on the Missouri Plan is evident. The Kales Plan requires a nonpartisan committee of lawyers, judges, and nonjudicial personnel to draft a list of the most qualified judicial candidates on the basis of their records and expertise. This list is then submitted to the governor to make judicial appointments. Judicial vacancies occur because of death, retirement, or removal because of incompetence, although the latter rarely happens. The idea behind the merit selection plan is that any choice a governor makes from the approved list would by definition be a good choice. Ideally, politics is removed from such gubernatorial appointments.

But some critics question whether *any* merit plan, including both the Kales and Missouri versions, can eliminate politics from judicial selection (Blankenship et al.1994). Many states use some form of a merit selection plan, and others have a combination of selection methods to form a hybrid system of sorts (Berkson et al. 2010). Whether or not politics can be removed from the process may depend on how the nominating committees are formed (i.e., if the governor selects the committee members, the committee may just be a political extension of his or her own ideologies), how individuals are vetted and put forth as qualified candidates, and accountability and method for retaining the judgeship. Some argue that it may be difficult to completely remove politics from the process and political control may actually just move behind closed doors (American Bar Association 2008). Despite this, other scholars argue that merit plans are useful for promoting greater accountability and fairness among judges (Scheb 1988).

One way of making the merit selection plan more palatable to the public is to ensure that the qualification procedures for judicial applicants should be made more rigorous (Dubois 1990). In effect, a thorough screening procedure should be operative as a standard against which to compare different judicial candidates. Thus, when the matter of selecting a judge to fill a judgeship arises, the public knows that all judicial nominees have been thoroughly screened and tested concerning their competency and abilities.

One troubling aspect of merit selection occurs in those states where governors have the power to appoint interim judges to fill unexpected vacancies. When a judge dies, becomes infirm, or is unable to perform his/her duties in midterm, governors in some states are allowed to make temporary judicial appointments without consulting any merit selection committee. Interim judges generally have an easier time as incumbents when it comes time to appoint or elect a new judge for a subsequent term.

At the federal level under President Jimmy Carter, Executive Order 11972 was issued, establishing the U.S. Circuit Judge Nominating Commission. This commission radically altered the method of selecting federal judges. Carter wanted to devise a system whereby judges would be appointed on the basis of their professional merit and potential for quality service on the bench. Further, he wanted to develop a mechanism that would allow him to place larger numbers of women and minorities in judgeships. One criticism of this method of judicial selection is that Carter may have undermined the merit system in favor of affirmative action considerations. During his presidency, Carter appointed 91 percent of the judges from his own Democratic Party. However, he dramatically increased the presence of women and minorities on the federal bench, with 14 percent being women and 22 percent being racial or ethnic minorities (Sourcebook of Criminal Justice Statistics 2013, Table 1.82). President Reagan, however, ended this federal Circuit Judge Nominating Commission with another executive order. Subsequently, only 8 percent of President Reagan's appointees were female and 7 percent were minorities; a similarly high percentage (91) was from his own Republican Party (Sourcebook of Criminal Justice Statistics 2013, Table 1.82).

Are Merit Systems for Judicial Selection Better than Election Methods?

The debate over which judge selection plan is best is largely dependent upon the assumption that it makes some kind of measurable difference which plan is used—that one plan

interim judge
temporary judge who is appointed following the death, resignation, or retirement of another judge, usually to complete the original judge's term; after the interim judge serves, a new judge is appointed or elected according to the rules of judicial selection in the particular jurisdiction.

incumbents political officers who are currently in power, but who are seeking to be re-elected or reappointed.

results in better-qualified judges. As stated earlier, research on this question yields mixed results. Some studies report a few differences among the various plans in terms of the quality of judges (Swain 1985). Others report better quality through appointment processes (Sobel and Hall 2007). Ultimately, the answer may depend on which qualities are being assessed. Some studies have examined expertise (Glick and Emmert 1987), others have looked at actual performance once on the bench (Choi, Gulati, and Posner 2010), and others still have analyzed judicial disciplinary rates as a measure of quality and effectiveness (Goldschmidt, Olson, and Ekman 2009).

For many decades, it has been assumed by the public that judicial selection systems that emphasize merit rather than political interests create greater judicial accountability and independence. Elections are perceived as popularity contests, often rigged to accommodate one vested interest group or another. Gubernatorial selection methods result in the appointment of political hacks as judges who cater to the interests of the governor and the governor's friends. Merit selection, it is argued, results in the most qualified persons performing judicial roles. However, several researchers have raised questions about whether any of these methods is better than the rest. Michael Blankenship, Jerry Sparger, and Richard Janikowski (1994) suggest that the election–merit selection dichotomy is more a myth than fact. They contend that appointive methods for selecting judges are no more effective than the elective process in placing qualified judges on the bench. They add that neither elections nor appointments of judicial candidates succeed in fulfilling the long-range philosophical expectations of judicial accountability and independence.

In one research study, however, judges seemed to favor merit plans over elections (Scheb 1988). In a national survey of 562 state appellate judges and their attitudes toward alternative judicial selection methods, the judges responded overwhelmingly that the merit plan was the more professional selection method over political appointment and partisan elections. Judges reported that merit selection plans tended to professionalize the courts. The researcher also concluded that judges selected under the merit system were far less likely to become involved in political causes or debates compared with those judges who were either gubernatorial appointees or elected (Scheb 1988).

The above legal issue raises questions about which of the methods of judicial selection is best at increasing the likelihood of obtaining a diverse judiciary. Research on this issue is mixed: some studies finding appointive systems increase diversity, others concluding that elections produce more minority and female judges, and others still finding no relationship between the method of selection and the diversity of the bench (Reddick et al. 2009). Although there is research that supports that merit selection is likely to produce more minority judges, and that elections are beneficial toward the selection of female judges (Reddick et al. 2009), the question of whether any one method, merit selection included, results in increased diversity on the bench is very complex (Myers 2013). A number of other factors, other than the selection method in and of itself, may play a role in the likelihood of female and minority candidates being selected. Reddick and colleagues (2009) also cite that the number of minority attorneys in the state predicts racial and ethnic diversity on the court, and that the region of the country might be a context in which more or less minority and female judges will be selected. Finally, it may depend on the jurisdiction of the court, trial versus appellate, and a combination of the method of selection and the above contextual factors.

In 1985, 1994, and most recently in 2008, the American Judicature Society published a report entitled Model Judicial Selection Provisions that set forth some best practices for selection, retention, and evaluation of judges (American Judicature Society 2008b). This report provides jurisdictions information on a number of topics, including establishing and implementing nominating commissions to appoint judges and establishing and implementing programs to evaluate judges for retention. Some of the recommendations include that jurisdictions establish rules of procedure for nominating commissions and that they also

BOX 5-1

LEGAL ISSUES: DIVERSITY ON THE BENCH

Most judges in the United States are white males, prompting some to contend that the "law is too pale and too male" (Judge Bruce M. Wright in Washington 1994). Issues of a diverse judiciary have also arisen regarding criticisms of judicial selection methods. Although diversity on both the state and federal bench has increased over time (Reddick, Nelson, and Caufield 2009; Sourcebook of Criminal Justice Statistics 2010), white males are overrepresented and every other demographic group is underrepresented when compared with their numbers in the population (Torres-Spelliscy et al. 2010). One of the arguments for a diverse judiciary includes that public confidence would be increased in the criminal justice system and in judicial decisions if we had a judiciary that is as diverse as the population (Brown 1998). Others contend that the criminal justice system is given more legitimacy, and has the appearance of impartiality (Hurwitz and Lanier 2008) when all races and ethnic backgrounds are represented on the bench. Finally, arguments for diversity include that if the goal is truly equal justice for all under the law, a diverse bench is necessary (Torres-Spelliscy et al. 2010).

In your opinion, are the above arguments valid? Is it important in an increasingly diverse society that judges and other officials also be diverse? Should judges be representative of the populations they serve?

Rawpixel.com/Fotolia

engage in training and education. The American Judicature Society also encourages diversity on the nominating commission that strengthens the recruitment of qualified judicial applicants. Finally, they also caution that commissions strive to achieve a balance between affording transparency of the judicial nomination process and setting provisions for protecting the privacy of potential applicants.

Federal Judicial Selection Methods

The Nature of U.S. Supreme Court Appointments

The president of the United States exerts direct influence on the nature of U.S. Supreme Court appointments and judicial appointments to lower federal courts. The president recommends persons for district, circuit, and supreme court judgeships, with the advice and consent of Congress. U.S. Supreme Court appointments have not necessarily depended upon previous judicial experience, however. From 1930 to 1967, there were 23 U.S. Supreme Court justices appointed. Of these, only seven had previous federal judge experience with all but one serving five or fewer years on the federal bench. And only 4 of these 23 appointments had experience as state judges. Only former justice Cardozo, appointed in 1932, had more than 8 years' experience, having served 18 years in state courts.

Today that is not the case; most persons appointed to the federal bench have previous occupational experience as either a judge or a prosecutor or defense attorney. For instance, over half of President Clinton, George W. Bush, and Obama's appointments have had previous judicial experience and just under half had experience as a prosecutor (Sourcebook of Criminal Justice Statistics 2010). It will be interesting to see if President-elect Donald J. Trump continues this trend, and whether confirmation by Congress will continue to be as contentious as it was for President Obama.

U.S. district court judgeships are appointments by the president of the United States, and subject to congressional approval. These are lifetime appointments. Because these judgeships are presidential appointments, they often reflect a president's vested interests. An examination of all of the appointees made by presidents since President George H. W. Bush in 1989 reveals that well over 80 percent of the time, the person being appointed is of the same party as the appointing president (Sourcebook of Criminal Justice Statistics 2010). Therefore, the judicial philosophy of the judge and its consistency with that of the president is probably a more important factor in appointments of federal judges rather than their qualifications.

American Bar Association ratings of the quality of federal judicial appointments within the same timeframe, however, reveal that most of the time the appointee is qualified. For instance, the ABA rated 57 percent of George H. W. Bush's appointees as exceptionally well qualified or well qualified and 42 percent of them as qualified; for President Clinton, President George W. Bush, and President Obama, 59, 70, and 75 percent, respectively, were rated as exceptionally well qualified or well qualified, and 40, 28, and 25 percent, respectively, were rated as qualified (Sourcebook of Criminal Justice Statistics 2010).

During the 1990s, two U.S. Supreme Court justices were appointed by President Bill Clinton, a Democrat. His most significant appointment was Ruth Bader Ginsburg in 1993. She was the first Democrat to serve on the U.S. Supreme Court in 26 years as well as the second woman appointed since Sandra Day O'Connor. Although there have been Jewish U.S. Supreme Court justices in past years, Justice Ginsburg's appointment marked another turning point in the composition of the U.S. Supreme Court. President Obama's first Supreme Court appointees included the first Hispanic woman on the Supreme Court, Justice Sonia Sotomayor, as well as another female Elena Kagan (the fourth female on the Supreme Court), who is Jewish, a woman, and from an academic background; she was the former dean of Harvard Law School.

Presidential appointments to the U.S. Supreme Court are also characterized according to whether the appointees are conservative, liberal, or moderate. U.S. Supreme Court justices under Republican administrations have tended to be very conservative or conservative, while justices appointed under Democratic administrations have tended to be moderate or liberal. These philosophical orientations have been very crucial in determining various social policies during the last 50 years. For instance, in the 1960s, the chief justice of the U.S. Supreme Court was Earl Warren, who had been appointed to the high court in 1953 by President Dwight Eisenhower. When Warren became chief justice, the Court became known as the "Warren Court." Under Warren's guidance, the U.S. Supreme Court made a number of rulings that regulated police tactics relative to custodial interrogations and searches and seizures. During Warren's tenure as chief justice, the U.S. Supreme Court seemed to be anti-police, since many of its rulings were viewed by critics as tying the hands of law enforcement officers when investigating crimes. The most notable rulings included *Mapp v. Ohio* (1961), which required police officers to have search warrants before conducting searches of one's premises, and *Miranda v. Arizona* (1966), which required police officers to advise suspects of their right to an attorney prior to being interrogated.

Later U.S. Supreme Courts issued rulings that created various exceptions to warrantless searches and effectively untied the hands of police. Under Warren E. Burger, the chief justice of the U.S. Supreme Court who was appointed by President Richard M. Nixon in 1969, the "Burger Court" established the "totality of circumstances" and "good faith" exceptions to the exclusionary rule, which permitted law enforcement officers considerable latitude when conducting warrantless searches of one's premises, person, and automobile. During the 1990s, the newly configured U.S. Supreme Court presided over by Chief Justice William H. Rehnquist, the "Rehnquist Court," has issued more conservative rulings relating to searches and seizures.

Thus far, Chief Justice John Roberts has followed in Rehnquist's footsteps; Roberts was once a clerk for Rehnquist, and Rehnquist's teaching has had an impact on his life and legal career. Despite a decision in which he sided with the four more liberal judges on the court to uphold Obamacare, it is likely that the Court will continue to steer to the right with Roberts at the helm. Thus, the influence of presidential appointments on the composition of the U.S. Supreme Court cannot be ignored. These appointments, which are highly political, are intended to increase the likelihood of particular social agendas being implemented. During any election year, a key factor governing one's decision to vote for one presidential candidate or another is what types of Supreme Court justices will be appointed and what will be the nature of their decision making in future years? Since these appointments are lifetime appointments, the long-term social policy implications can be far reaching.

Circuit Court Judgeships

Judges who serve in circuit courts of appeal are appointed by the president of the United States as well. Their nomination by the president must be approved by the advice and consent of Congress. The Senate Judiciary Committee hears arguments both for and against these presidential appointees and either approves or rejects them. Not all nominated judges are acceptable to the Senate Judiciary Committee. In 2014, there were 179 court of appeals judgeships throughout the nation; the 94 federal districts are divided into 12 regional circuits and the circuit court judges hear appeals from the district courts within their circuit. The decisions of judges in these circuit courts are binding on the lower district courts. They also hear appeals from administrative agencies at the federal level. The twelfth circuit is for the District of Columbia and the thirteenth circuit is a Court of Appeals for the Federal Circuit; this court has national jurisdiction pertaining to certain cases such as patents and trademarks as well as government contracts to name a few.

U.S. District Court Judges

There were 677 federal district judgeships in 2014. Federal district judges are also appointed by the president of the United States. They also serve life terms under Article III of the U.S. Constitution. The advice and consent of Congress is required for all such appointments. There are no other specific qualifications for assuming a federal judgeship. Vacancies are created when a federal judge retires, and new judgeships can be created for both the district courts and the court of appeals via legislation enacted by Congress. The Judicial Conference conducts a survey of the needs of courts every two years and presents its recommendations to Congress. A number of factors may go into whether Congress creates a new position in a particular district or circuit such as the number and types of cases per judge, and the number of senior judges in the district.

U.S. Magistrate Judges

U.S. magistrate judges are appointed by a majority vote of district court judges and have jurisdiction over petty federal crimes and other duties as assigned by each court. They serve terms of four or eight years, depending upon whether they are full-time or part-time magistrates. U.S. magistrate judges have various duties. Besides having jurisdiction over cases involving federal misdemeanors and petty offenses, these magistrates also issue search warrants and arrest warrants/summonses, hold detention hearings, review bail for arrestees, issue seizure warrants, and conduct preliminary examinations. These magistrates also have civil duties as well as criminal ones, although their criminal responsibilities outweigh their civil responsibilities. They hold pretrial conferences, rule on motions, conduct evidentiary hearings, and hear some prisoner litigation involving *habeas corpus* petitions and civil rights submissions. Much of their civil work relates to conducting pretrial conferences, ruling on motions, and screening prisoner litigation (Maguire and Pastore 2005, 79).

▶ Judicial Training

Theories of management and organizations have sometimes been applied in the judicial selection and training process. For instance, bureaucracy and its derivative bureaucratic theory emphasize centralization of authority in decision making, thus creating a degree of standardization in judicial selection. However, strict adherence to bureaucratic principles may not always result in selections of the most qualified judges in local jurisdictions. A departure from bureaucratic theory would be to decentralize the judicial selection process, to place greater decision-making power in the hands of local commissions for judicial appointments, with some authority given to state supreme courts to oversee the selection process. The legislative electoral process is one way of rationalizing and objectifying the selection process. This would enable local bar elements to recommend those most qualified for judgeships, while the legislature would make the best judicial selections with state supreme court approval.

> centralization limited distribution of power among a few top staff members of an organization.

In the late 1970s, a survey by the American Judicature Society disclosed that there was no uniformity or pattern of organization among different lower courts among state jurisdictions (Knab 1977). The qualifications for state judges were diverse and inconsistent from one jurisdiction to the next. Different standards existed for selecting judges, determining their qualifications to serve in judicial positions, compensation, and retirement or removal of judges.

Several recommendations have been made since then to improve the quality and accountability of judges in different jurisdictions. For instance, the U.S. Advisory Commission on Intergovernmental Relations (1971) suggested that a set of uniform rules should be established to govern the conduct of judges. Further, procedures for judicial retirement, removal, and discipline should be established with a high degree of uniformity. Finally, a term limit should be established to eliminate the possibility of certain judges serving for long periods. Mandatory retirement ages should be implemented. In order to upgrade and improve the quality of judicial selection, codes of judicial ethics ought to be established, together with explicit judicial compensation and qualification criteria.

There are, however, no standard objective criteria used to evaluate one's judicial qualifications. Most jurisdictions do not require judges to pass tests or engage in any sort of qualifying competition for these important posts. Those elected to judicial positions but who lack experience are often sent through training programs designed to teach basic judicial skills. These courses attempt to familiarize judges with the rules of criminal procedure and the rules of evidence in their particular jurisdictions. The question becomes whether these short courses on judge-making can bring an unlearned judge to the point where he/she possesses the competence and experience to make the best decisions in important criminal cases.

Research conducted by Thomas (2006) examined education and training for judges across jurisdictions in the United States and other countries around the world with respect to training delivery, training curriculum, and judicial evaluation. One of the main conclusions from the study is that because of more complex laws, larger caseloads, and shifts in the way judges are recruited, the need for judicial training is more critical today than ever before. Other interesting findings include that the focus of judicial training varies; the most common topics, however, include substantive law and legal skills (i.e., expert evidence, witnesses, writing opinions, and sentencing), ethics and social context of the law (i.e., race, gender, and age discrimination), and judicial skills (i.e., management skills and technology and the media).

Thomas (2006) also cites that the United States, Australia, and Canada provide training modules (some are online) to judges in order that judges can get a great deal of training on different topics in smaller, more manageable segments. This is more practical for judges as they sometimes do not have a lot of flexibility in their schedules. Finally, this report also lists major barriers to training and educating judges, one of which is time and funding issues. Online modules therefore might be the future as they decrease the cost and time that would be involved to take time off from the court schedule to travel to receive multi-day trainings.

▶ Judicial Misconduct and Abuses of Discretion

Most states have some form of judicial conduct and discipline commission in place to monitor and oversee judicial conduct. These commissions are usually responsible for investigating complaints of judicial misconduct and making decisions about appropriate sanctions such as admonishment, suspension, reprimand, and removal or retirement (Reddick n.d.). In most states, there are a number of ways that judges can be sanctioned. Some states give authority to disciplinary commissions to investigate, conduct hearings, and make sanctioning decisions that can be appealed to the state supreme court. In other states, the commission's decision is only a recommendation to the state supreme court and that body then makes a determination about sanctions. Most state constitutions also allow provisions for a judge to be impeached by a vote of the house of representatives of the legislature or be removed via recall election. In the latter case, a certain percentage of voters would be required to sign a petition in order to hold this type of election where voters would decide whether to remove or retain the judge. At the federal level, the only method by which a judge can be removed is through impeachment that involves both House of Representatives and Senate vote.

Forms of Judicial Misconduct

There are several forms of judicial misconduct. However, most misconduct relates to the performance of one's job as judge. A judge is a powerful person in the criminal court system because the judge manages courtroom processes and makes rulings that have immense influence over trial outcomes. The judge in most cases also makes the determination of an appropriate punishment.

Judges can Influence Trial Outcomes by Exhibiting Prejudice in Evidentiary Rulings

One of the most frequent types of judicial misconduct is to prejudice the court proceedings in such a way that the trial outcome is favorable to either one side or the other. Such behavior on a judge's part is difficult to detect, however. Simply ruling unfavorably against one side or the other may be explained by numerous frivolous motions filed by that side. Further, most judges can rationalize their conduct if pressed to do so.

Judges can Deliberately Aggravate or Mitigate One's Sentence Following Conviction

When offenders are convicted, judges can deliberately increase or decrease the severity of the sentence imposed. Again, it is difficult for court watchers to detect this form of misconduct whenever judicial intervention is the result of objective decision making or personal vindictiveness. Judges must consider a wide variety of factors when determining a sentence but the primary determinants should be seriousness of offense and prior criminal history.

Judges can Accept Bribes from Various Parties in Court Actions

Judges may also accept bribes where their rulings may be influential. Especially in bench trials where judges decide the outcomes of cases, it is easy to decide in favor of someone where a financial bribe has been received. Again, this form of misconduct is difficult to detect. It is not completely undetectable, however. In 2011, in Pennsylvania, for example, a judge was convicted for taking bribes from a builder of juvenile detention centers in exchange for sentencing juveniles to detention even though they were in most cases first-time offenders who had committed minor offenses. Subsequently, the Pennsylvania Supreme Court decided to overturn thousands of cases that the judge had presided over dating back to 2003 (Urbina 2009).

> **What Do You Think?**
>
> Should states make it easier to remove judges accused of wrongdoing? What if the judge has been elected by popular vote? Can you think of a better mechanism than is currently in place to investigate and sanction judicial wrongdoing?

► Other Issues with Judicial Behavior

Inexperience

Judicial effectiveness is often associated with one's experience as a judge. When inexperienced judges rule on motions from the prosecution or defense, these judges may not understand fully the rules of evidence and whether the motion should be granted or denied. Often, inexperienced judges make these decisions on the basis of their emotional sentiment during the trial. Whenever judges make mistakes of judgment in ruling on motions, these are errors. They vary in their importance. Many errors are harmless, meaning that the outcome of the trial would not have been affected if the judge had ruled differently. Other types of errors are harmful errors or reversible errors.

Harmful Errors

Harmful errors or reversible errors may result in judicial decisions being overturned by higher appellate courts. However, (1) not all errors are detected in a trial, (2) not all *guilty* verdicts are appealed, and (3) not all appeals are heard on their merits by higher courts. Appellate courts use their discretionary power to determine the number and types of cases they will rule on. It is assumed by all appellate courts that the original judgment or verdict rendered by a lower trial court was the correct one. Therefore, clear and convincing evidence must be presented by the defendant supporting a reversal of a verdict by the trial judge or jury. It is insufficient simply to prove that errors were committed. Even harmful errors are insufficient under certain conditions when attempting to overturn a judge's decision.

> **harmful errors** errors made by judges that may be prejudicial to a defendant's case. May lead to reversals of convictions against defendants and to new trials.

> **reversible errors** mistakes committed by judges during a trial that may result in reversal of convictions against defendants.

Court Delays and Clogged Court Calendars

Serious court delays are commonplace in most jurisdictions. A study of case processing in New York City, for instance, has revealed that a significant obstacle contributing to court delays is inadequate judicial training. Technology presently exists that facilitates case processing in many modern court systems. However, some New York City courtrooms are slow to acquire new technology. Further, courses offered for judges on case management training have relatively low enrollment. Realistic timetables are not adhered to, and more than a few judges inadvertently impede one's right to a speedy trial because of their inefficient case management practices (Correctional Association of New York 1993).

Other factors besides judicial inexperience contribute to case processing delays as well. In some cases, there are attorney appearance conflicts, witness unavailability, attorney unpreparedness, vacations, and illness-precipitated court appearances. Court delays in various jurisdictions are also due to a lack of resources and judicial support staff and equipment. Increasing judicial education through mandatory education programs is one means of facilitating case processing (Clark 2004a).

Disparate Sentencing

Judicial discretion in sentencing is often criticized in that judges make decisions primarily on extralegal factors rather than legal ones. Legal factors include one's prior record, seriousness of the current offense, age, and acceptance of responsibility. Extralegal factors refer to race or ethnicity, gender, socioeconomic status, and attitude (Champion 2005b). Sentencing disparities attributable to race, gender, socioeconomic status, and other extralegal factors have plagued judges for years (Champion 2005b). Attempts have been made by commissions and state legislatures to create greater sentencing consistency and bind judges to certain minimum and maximum sentencing standards.

Sentencing guidelines have been created in most jurisdictions to make uniform the punishments for various offenses. Some observers question whether structured sentencing guidelines will eliminate disparities in judicial decision making, however. Experiments on various types of sentencing reforms have evidenced some success in improving judicial fairness (Kramer and Ulmer 1996). Some studies, however, reveal that despite the fact that sentencing guidelines were designed to reduce unwarranted disparity in sentencing, minorities and the poor may continue to receive harsher treatment because guidelines can be manipulated, or circumvented altogether (Johnson, Ulmer, and Kramer 2008). Additionally, there is evidence of unwarranted disparity in departures from guidelines (Stith and Cabranes 1998; Tillyer and Hartley 2013); whites and females more often receive non-prison sentences and downward departures (Kramer and Ulmer 1996; Mustard 2001).

The recent Supreme Court case of *Blakely v. Washington* (2004) seriously called into question the constitutionality of the federal sentencing guidelines, as well as those of nearly a dozen states. Following *Blakely*, the case of *United States v. Booker* (2005) ruled that the Sixth Amendment necessitates that the federal sentencing guidelines be advisory in nature rather than mandatory. This now means that federal judges are to consult the guidelines when meting out sentences but can depart from them for various reasons. Subsequent cases decided by the Supreme Court (*Rita v. United States*, *Gall v. United States*, and *Kimbrough v. United States*) have given judges more discretion under the federal guidelines to impose sentences they deem appropriate. Currently, about 20 states have sentencing guideline structures that range from voluntary to mandatory with a number of states structures falling in between (Kauder and Ostrom 2008). Finally, it is difficult to determine whether extralegal factors were considered related to a judge's decision-making practices. Because we cannot get inside of the judge's head, researchers do not know for certain the various factors a judge may have used in arriving at what they believe is an appropriate sentence.

▶ Removing Judges from Office

Whenever corrupt or incompetent judges are identified, there are relatively few mechanisms available to remove them from office. In New York, judicial conduct is monitored by the Commission on Judicial Conduct. The commission receives or initiates complaints with respect to the conduct, qualifications, fitness to perform, or performance of official duties of any judge in New York State. After investigation and a hearing, the commission may admonish, censure, remove, or retire a judge. However, decisions made by the commission are directly appealable to the New York Court of Appeals.

The creation of independent commissions to oversee judicial misconduct is not new. The first state to implement a commission to deal with judicial misconduct was California. In 1960, California created a judicial conduct commission, which was charged with investigating complaints against judges. Comprised of attorneys, other judges, and politically prestigious others, these commission members function as a part of the California Supreme Court. They meet in secret and their findings are confidential. They investigate misconduct reports against various California state trial judges and make recommendations to the California Supreme Court. Their array of sanctions includes recommendations for private censure, removal from the bench, or retirement. The California Supreme Court has the final authority concerning recommendations made by the judicial conduct commission.

All states today have some type of judicial conduct commission. Critics contend that the United States has one of the poorest records for sanctioning the behaviors of bad judges. Compared with other nations, such as France, Italy, and England, judicial conduct organizations in the United States institute relatively few cases of judicial sanctioning (Volcansek, DeFranciscis, and Lafron 1996). One reason for this lack of commitment to sanction bad judges could be that these committees are often made up of former judges and the fact that American judges enjoy a great deal of judicial independence. There is relatively little accountability for some types of judicial misconduct. In some cases, however, bad judges can be removed through either impeachment or recall elections.

In order to provide some idea about the effectiveness of processing complaints that allege judicial misconduct, during the period of 1999, 12,068 misconduct complaints were received by various state judicial conduct organizations. In the various states, anywhere from 71 to 100 percent of these complaints were dismissed outright, while most of the remaining cases were informally disposed of with reprimands, short-term suspensions, and fines. Only 48 cases resulted in judges vacating their offices during the investigation, and only 11 judges were suspended as a final sanction (Maguire and Pastore 2005). Thus, the system is weighed heavily in favor of judges, even bad ones. The likelihood that a complaint against any given judge will be sustained is less than 5 percent. It is even more alarming that there are few provisions for issuing severe sanctions against the worst judges. Thus, while the existence of judicial conduct organizations is commendable, it is also clear that these organizations have relatively little power in administering judicial sanctions.

Impeachment

Impeachment means to allege wrongdoing against a judge or other public official before a legislative or judicial body vested with the authority to remove that judge or public official from office. In order for impeachment to be successful, the allegations must be well founded and upheld by compelling evidence against the accused. In many jurisdictions, the state supreme court is the sanctioning body that hears impeachment allegations against judges and has the power to act to either remove the judge or dismiss the allegations.

For instance, suppose a judge continually fails to safeguard the rights of indigents in criminal cases. A judge might require a defendant to plead without representation by court-appointed counsel. A judge may tell a jury that he believes a defendant is guilty. A judge might set a particularly high and arbitrary bail amount for someone who is not dangerous or likely to flee the jurisdiction. The judge may coerce defendants out of the appeal rights. These forms of disrespect for the law occur from time to time in U.S. courts. However, few mechanisms have existed to remove these persons from office.

In more recent years, procedures have been suggested to systematize the judicial sanctioning process. Certain rules have been promulgated by the Federal Judicial Center, such

judicial conduct commission investigative body created in California in 1960, comprised of other judges, attorneys, and prominent citizens; task was to investigate allegations of judicial misconduct, incompetence, and unfairness.

impeachment proceeding for the removal of a political officer, such as a governor, president, or judge.

confidentiality any privileged communication between a client and an attorney.

as rules governing how complaints are filed, the review of complaints by chief judges, the review of the chief judge's disposition of the complaint, an investigation and recommendation by a special committee, rules dealing with confidentiality, public availability of decisions rendered, disqualification, and withdrawal of complaints and petitions for review.

Recall Elections

recall election special election called to remove a politician or judge from his/her office.

Another mechanism is through a recall election. A petition is circulated by interested citizens or by a city council in response to one or more complaints against a judicial official. A special election is held, with alternative candidates presented to fill the judicial post. A popular vote results in the bad judge being removed from office. The election also results in the support of a new judge who replaces the bad one. Recall elections depend heavily on citizen involvement and concern.

One other option is for a bad judge to simply resign. For instance, in Lakewood, Washington, a suburb of Seattle, Lakewood municipal judge Ralph H. Baldwin admitted to drinking beer with a defense lawyer and the prosecutor while the jury deliberated the fate of a defendant facing drunk-driving charges. Even after the case was over and the jury had rendered a verdict of guilty, the judge invited the jury members into his chamber and served them alcoholic beverages. Some jurors were clearly offended by the judge's actions, and his conduct was immediately reported to the Lakewood City Council. The city council confronted Baldwin with the allegations and he admitted them, stating that "I want you to know that none of my words or actions on that evening arose from malice but rather from a misguided sense of congeniality and extremely poor judgment. To each of you, I extend my sincere apologies." Baldwin had only served for three months as municipal judge, a $65,000 a year job, when the incident occurred (Associated Press 1998, A2). Baldwin was not available for comment about his resignation when reporters attempted to contact him.

Summary

1. Distinguish among the different kinds of judges and their roles in the criminal court system.

In any court proceeding, the key official is the judge although, as we have seen, some of the judicial duties such as sentencing can be thought of as a collaborative process. The judge makes decisions about admissibility of evidence, whether or not bail will be set, courtroom administration, in some cases guilt or innocence, and finally punishment. Some of these decisions are more influential on case outcomes than others, and some judges are limited in the types of decisions they can make. There is also great variation among the legal expertise, roles, and decision-making powers of different types of judges. Some judges have a great deal of authority and power, and others do not have much discretion or play only a supportive role. This depends on the type of judge they are, and what type of cases they preside over. In some cases, judicial decisions might be the result of a collabo- ration of decision-making practices by other courtroom actors such as the prosecutor and defense attorney.

2. Recognize the qualifications a judge must have in order to sit on the bench.

Not all judges are lawyers or have the same degree of legal experience. In many cases, judges have no legal training and may not even have a law degree. This is because numerous jurisdictions throughout the United States elect judges and therefore the most popular, and not necessarily the most qualified, candidate may win a judicial seat. Qualifications for becoming a judge also vary greatly across the states. Some states have residency requirements, as well as education and legal requirements such as state bar association membership, and others do not. Most have minimum-age requirements, but all qualifications vary depending on the type of judicial position, say municipal, county, or state trial and appellate judgeships.

3. *Compare and contrast the different judicial selection methods and the advantages and disadvantages of each type of judicial selection method.*

At the local, state, and federal levels, judges are either elected or appointed. Among state courts, partisan and nonpartisan elections account for about two-thirds of all judicial positions. State governors and the U.S. president make other judicial appointments. The president selects U.S. District Court judges, U.S. Circuit Court appellate judges, and U.S. Supreme Court justices, subject to congressional approval. An increasingly popular judicial selection method is judicial appointments on the basis of merit. One of these merit plans is known as the Missouri Plan. Both partisan and nonpartisan elections are criticized that those on the ballot are not the most qualified, and that voter apathy makes the process meaningless. Gubernatorial and legislative appointments are criticized that the nominations are too political, and again, the best candidate is not being appointed.

Merit selection attempts to overcome these criticisms by requiring that a list be drafted of the most qualified judicial candidates based on their expertise or qualifications and then the governor can use this list to make appointments. Judges themselves, when surveyed, seem to favor merit selection over election as a more professional method. Research, however, has shown that really there are few differences in the type of judicial selection method used and the quality of judges on the bench. If you look at the characteristics of presidential appointees to district, appellate, and Supreme Court positions, they overwhelmingly come from the same political party as the president, indicating that the selection process is highly political.

4. *Analyze the different methods of judicial training.*

In order to ensure better judicial performance among those less skilled in the law, many judges are required to undergo judicial training. This training familiarizes judges with procedural and evidentiary law, and it socializes them concerning different motions that may be made by prosecutors or defense counsel, as well as how to rule on such motions. Many jurisdictions have also adopted procedures for judicial discipline, removal, and retirement. Some questions arise whether training can adequately provide the necessary skills that are important to the job, or make up for lack of experience. Despite extensive and continued training, it may still be difficult to evaluate judicial quality and effectiveness.

5. *Understand the different types of judicial misconduct and abuses of discretion.*

More than a few judges deliberately engage in various forms of misconduct, which may include influencing trial outcomes because of bribery, or deliberately aggravating or mitigating one's sentence upon conviction. Judges are supposed to be impartial and base their decisions with reference to the facts of the case and the law. Misconduct can be sometimes difficult to detect and we cannot know for certain whether judges made decisions using extralegal criteria, such as race/ethnicity, socioeconomic status, and/or gender. Justice is supposed to be blind but some research shows that extralegal factors can and do influence judicial decisions in some instances. Again, in some cases it is difficult to uncover whether the decision was objectively made or was based on some sort of bias.

6. *Understand some of the current criticisms of judges and the ways in which judges can be removed from office.*

There is great variation among judges concerning their judicial effectiveness and how their courts are administered or managed. There have been many criticisms of judges, not only on the basis of harmful errors; other criticisms have been levied that judges are the reason for court delays and clogged court calendars. This could be due to inefficient case management practices, where again proper training may help alleviate these issues, or factors out of their control like attorney time conflicts, unavailable witnesses, and attorney unpreparedness.

Appellate courts can usually more easily manage their caseloads. When appeals are filed by either side following a judgment, appellate courts assume that the original trial judge's decision was the correct one, regardless of whether it was correct or not. This presumption is quite difficult to overcome by appellants who must prove by a preponderance of the evidence that the ruling was wrong. Errors are cited by appellants, which may be harmless, harmful, or reversible. Harmless or harmful errors may be insufficient to change the original trial outcome. Reversible errors often result in convictions being set aside or simply overturned. Under these circumstances, prosecutors must decide whether to retry the case and expend scarce resources for a new trial.

For judges who engage in misconduct, it is difficult to recall them and have them removed from office. Various states have judicial conduct commissions to investigate complaints; most, however, are rejected. Hard evidence must be presented in order for particular judges to be sanctioned, and even harder evidence is necessary for judges to be removed from office. In some jurisdictions, judges may be removed from their positions through recall elections. Usually, in response to complaints about an elected official, a special election is held to fill the position. A popular vote will result in removal of the judge from office. Another strategy for removing judges from office is impeachment. Under the rules of impeachment, evidence of a judge's wrongful conduct must be presented to a legislative body. Usually, it is the state supreme court that oversees the impeachment proceedings. Again, a high standard of proof is required in order for particular charges of misconduct against judges to be sustained and to justify the type of sanction taken.

Key Terms

centralization *107*

confidentiality *112*

harmful errors *109*

impeachment *111*

incumbents *102*

interim judges *102*

judge *96*

judicial appointments *99*

judicial conduct commission *111*

judicial process *96*

Kales Plan *101*

merit selection *101*

Missouri Plan *101*

nonpartisan elections *98*

partisan elections *98*

recall election *112*

reversible errors *109*

Critical Thinking Exercises

1. Currently there are not any uniform qualifications across the country for judges in state courts. What kinds of qualifications do you think are important for a judge to possess, and why? Which do you think are important and a necessity, and which do you think could be taught through education and training?

2. There are criticisms that current methods to sanction judges who engage in misconduct are not utilized often enough and are not effective. For which types of misconduct do you believe there should be certainty of sanctions and what in your opinion would be the best method of implementing these? Does this depend on the type of misconduct?

3. What are your thoughts about a diverse judiciary? Provide arguments for or against having judges that resemble the population that they serve.

Case Study Decision-Making Exercise

It happened in Tennessee; a judge ruled that a couple could not name their newborn son "Messiah" because that name was reserved for only one person, Jesus Christ. The couple appealed and the judge's decision was overturned citing the Establishment Clause of the Constitution that government decisions cannot favor one religion over another. What do you think, should people have the right to name their children whatever they want? Besides the religious provisions of the Establishment Clause, could a judge make a ruling about a name with reference to the child's well-being and safety while growing up?

Concept Review Questions

1. Distinguish between partisan and nonpartisan elections of judges. Is one type of election better than the other? Why or why not?

2. In some states, judges are appointed by governors. What are some criticisms of gubernatorial appointees?

3. How are U.S. Supreme Court justices, U.S. Circuit Court judges, and U.S. District Court judges appointed? Who must approve these appointments?

4. What is a popular merit method for selecting judges? Why is it favored in various states?

5. Is the merit plan for judicial selection superior to legislative or gubernatorial appointment methods? Why or why not?
6. Differentiate between the Kales and the Missouri plans.

7. What sort of training do judges typically receive before becoming judges?
8. Identify four types of judicial misconduct.
9. What are two mechanisms for removing bad judges from the bench? Briefly describe each process.

Suggested Readings

1. L. P Moyer (2012). "The Role of Case Complexity in Judicial Decision Making." *Law & Policy* **34**:291–312.
2. R. E. Barkow (2012). "Sentencing Guidelines at the Crossroads of Politics and Expertise." *University of Pennsylvania Law Review* **160**:1599–1630.
3. C. Spohn (2009). *How Do Judges Decide? The Search for Fairness and Justice in Punishment*. Thousand Oaks, CA: Sage.
4. M. Klatt (2007). "Taking Rights Less Seriously. A Structural Analysis of Judicial Discretion." *Ratio Juris* **20**:506–529.

Roy Grogan/Fotolia

6 Juries

LEARNING OBJECTIVES

As a result of reading this chapter, you will have accomplished the following objectives:

1 *Summarize the history of juries as well as the development of the grand jury and the petit jury.*

2 *Apply your knowledge of the jury selection process to obtaining a fair and impartial jury, including a definition of what the* venire *is, as well as the purpose of the* voir dire.

3 *Give examples of the different ways in which jurors can be excluded, including challenges for cause and peremptory challenges.*

4 *Describe what jury consultants are, and illustrate the science behind jury selection.*

5 *Recognize jury sequestration and other methods of minimizing exposure of the jury to trial publicity.*

6 *Analyze the process of jury decision making and voting.*

7 *Understand some of the current controversies surrounding jury verdicts, including jury nullification.*

8 *Identify what constitutes jury or juror misconduct.*

In Louisiana, Mark L. Stephens was on trial for armed robbery and aggravated assault. It was alleged that Stephens had entered a convenience store late at night and pistol-whipped and robbed a clerk. The case was weak and was based primarily on the testimony of three eyewitnesses and the clerk who identified Stephens in a police lineup. Stephens had been released from prison on parole about six months prior to the robbery, where he had been serving a 10-year sentence for armed robbery and attempted murder. However, Stephens had two alibi witnesses who swore that he was with them all evening in a late-night poker game at the home of one of the witnesses. These witnesses were former offenders, and thus their credibility as witnesses was suspect. When the trial was over, the jury deliberated for four days without reaching a decision. On the fifth day, they returned to the courtroom and advised that 11 of them believed that Stephens was guilty, while the twelfth juror believed Stephens was innocent. The judge accepted the 11–1, nonunanimous jury decision and Stephens was convicted. The judge sentenced him to 20 years in prison.

In nearby Mississippi, Roland Abernathy was on trial for armed robbery and aggravated assault. Abernathy had allegedly robbed a convenience store late at night in Biloxi and had shot and wounded the store clerk, making off with over $300 in cash. No one other than the clerk was in the store at the time, and thus the clerk's testimony was the only clear evidence against Abernathy, who had a prior record for three armed robberies. Like Stephens, Abernathy had two alibi witnesses who placed him over 100 miles away from Biloxi at the time of the robbery, claiming that he was drinking with friends at a bar until the early morning hours. The jury heard all of the testimony and when the case was concluded, they deliberated for over five days, failing to reach a verdict. They returned to court on the sixth day and advised the judge that they were not unanimous in reaching a verdict. Of the 12 jurors, 11 voted for guilty, while one juror voted for not guilty. The 11–1 vote was questioned by the judge, who asked the jurors if they believed that further deliberation would be helpful in arriving at a unanimous verdict. The jurors said that they were "hopelessly deadlocked" and would "never reach agreement." Therefore, the judge declared a mistrial.

Why was Stephens convicted of armed robbery in Louisiana in an 11–1 jury decision, while Abernathy was not convicted by the same 11–1 jury vote in Mississippi? Do jury verdicts have to be unanimous? Under state law, which has been upheld by the U.S. Supreme Court, nonunanimous jury verdicts are constitutional in Louisiana. Under state law in Mississippi, however, jury verdicts must be unanimous. Should unanimity of jury verdicts be uniform across the United States?

▶ Introduction

Many persons assume that the right to a jury trial has always been an important part of most societies. However, history suggests that using juries to make judgments in disputes is relatively rare. In ancient times, disputes or conflicts were resolved through direct interpersonal violence. The disputants engaged in some form of physical confrontation (e.g., duel or battle), and the winner of the confrontation was also the winner of the dispute. Jurors like judges are supposed to be impartial and hear the facts of the case, and base a decision of guilt or innocence on those facts only.

The next part of the chapter will discuss the history of the jury and relate anecdotes on the development of the grand and petit juries. Being selected for jury duty is an involved process that begins with a list of potential jurors called a *venire*; potential jurors are asked questions relating to their appropriateness to serve; if they answer in the affirmative, they will be asked to further proceed with a process called a *voir dire*. The process is to ensure the appropriateness of persons to sit on a jury but also to ensure a defendant's right to a "speedy and public trial, by an impartial jury in the state and district wherein the crime shall have been committed" (Sixth Amendment). This means trial by a fair jury composed of an adequate cross section of the community. Constructing an adequate cross section of one's peers who are impartial can sometimes be difficult, and there have been many defendants who have appealed their cases based upon a violation of their Sixth Amendment rights. There have been calls that jurors have been removed for no other reason than their gender or their skin color. The Supreme Court has made several rulings relating to the process of jury selection. These decisions will be detailed in this chapter. A number of these have been related to the use of peremptory challenges. These challenges are used by prosecution and defense to remove a juror for no particular reason; these challenges, however, are limited. Another method to remove a juror is a challenge for cause. The prosecution and defense are not limited in the number of these challenges they can request. This type of challenge removes the juror for a particular reason—the person is biased in some way or does not meet the requirements to serve.

The role of the jury has been constantly challenged and revised. A number of cases in the last few decades have caused more than a few critics to question the integrity of the jury system, and have spurred calls for reform. It seems that we are constantly confronted with cases where we believe the defendant is guilty only to have the jury announce a verdict of not guilty and the defendant is freed. Often, we are outraged by reports of juries awarding multimillion dollar damages to plaintiffs where the allegations against defendants have been questionable. It is the idea of excessive jury verdicts, and even calls for jury nullification of the law, that has led to calls for reform. Many legal scholars argue that juries should be replaced with panels of experts who would be more likely to see the merits of a case, understand the law, and not be swayed by emotion (Adler 1995). In fact, we have a system now that is quite the opposite, where experts in the law, law enforcement, professors of law, and members of the medical community are readily excused from sitting on a jury.

▶ The History of Juries

The jury system in America has not had a direct, linear evolution. The ancient Greeks were the first to rely on certain persons in their community to pass judgment in a variety of cases. At one point, the entire population of Athens was required to hear appeals from the magistrates. Thus, it is not surprising that this process became difficult to administer. This process was subsequently replaced with a procedure designed to select jury members drawn from a cross section of the community to work with the magistrate and render decisions in criminal cases. This new jury was called a dicastery.

The ancient Romans also relied on an early form of the jury. In 190 B.C., for instance, magistrates could assemble a jury for certain criminal acts, including forgery, counterfeiting, and embezzlement. The jury was comprised of 35–75 people who decided the guilt of the accused. No provisions for appeals of verdicts were made.

In earlier times, common-law juries had a dual function. They had the responsibility of investigating crimes and conducting trials of accused persons. However, subsequent to the Norman invasion, these two responsibilities were divided into separate functioning units. The grand jury was created to investigate and report crimes, while the petit jury was used to determine a defendant's guilt or innocence. Today, these different jury systems continue to perform the same functions.

▶ The Development of the Grand Jury

The earliest forms of the grand jury can be traced back to Germanic tribal law and Anglo-Saxon dooms. The earliest version of the grand jury had its origins in the Assize of Clarendon in 1166. An assize is essentially an order by the king and is binding throughout the kingdom. On this occasion, King Henry II ordered that 12 of every 100 family heads be placed under oath and report offenses or known criminals to the authorities. The most commonly reported offenses were robberies, murders, and theft. This practice was very similar to our contemporary neighborhood watch programs.

    In colonial times, since judges traveled in circuits and were only scheduled to visit certain cities or towns every few months, members of the grand jury were responsible for gathering information about known criminal activity and present their information to the authorities whenever they were in town. Most often, when judges heard the cases presented to them by the grand jury, they ordered the defendant banished from the community. In essence, all trials during these early years were bench trials. The judge decided the guilt or innocence of defendants and determined the nature of the punishment. The petit jury or trial jury as we know it did not descend directly from the grand jury. Rather, it gradually replaced trials by ordeal.

> **grand jury** investigative body whose numbers vary among states. Duties include determining probable cause regarding commission of a crime and returning formal charges against suspects.

▶ The Development of the Petit Jury

In medieval England, trials by ordeal were used to determine a defendant's guilt or innocence. The prevailing practice was to have the process blessed by a priest. The belief was that because the proceeding was endorsed by the church and ultimately God, it was also just. The trial participants believed that if a defendant was innocent, God would intervene and protect them from harm. For example, the trial by hot water required that defendants place their hands into a pot of boiling water and remove a rock placed at the bottom. Once the accused placed their hands into the water and removed the rock, their hands were wrapped in bandages. After a specified time, the bandages were removed and if the hands were burned, the defendants were believed to be guilty because God did not intervene and protect the accused from harm. This practice went unchallenged for centuries.

    During the Fourth Lateran Council in 1215, the church withdrew its support for the trial by ordeal. This meant that priests would no longer be present to bless the trial. Without the benefit of blessings from priests and the presence of the church, it was also believed that God would not intervene on behalf of innocent defendants. The trial by ordeal was gradually replaced by the petit jury or trial jury. Initially, those accused of crimes were reluctant to accept a jury trial because if they were found guilty, they would lose their property and their descendants would lose their inheritance. The same fate would not befall those who opted for the bench trial. Consequently, the initial structure of the jury trial had an additional penalty that was not included in the bench trial.

    Another significant event occurred in 1215. King John was forced to sign the Magna Carta. This document provided the foundations for the provisions of due process and the right to a jury trial of one's peers. Clause 39 of the Magna Carta that established this concept reads in part, "No Freeman is to be arrested, or imprisoned, or disseized, or outlawed, or exiled, or in any other way ruined, nor will we go against him or send against him, except by the lawful judgment of his peers or by the law of the land" (The Magna Carta Project 2016).

    Originally, these rights were extended only to freemen or nobility. This meant that most people were still denied justice and the due process of law. The rights of a jury trial and due process were addressed in the Statute of Westminster of 1275. The relevant portions of this statute mandated that "no City, Borough, nor town nor any maybe amerced [fined or punished arbitrarily] without reasonable cause, and according to the Quality of

> **petit jury** the trier of fact in a criminal case. The jury of one's peers called to hear the evidence and decide the defendant's guilt or innocence. Varies in size among states.

his Trespass, that is to say, every Freeman saving his Freehold, a Merchant saving his Merchandise, a Villain saving his Gaynage [his rights in agricultural land, his tools and the product thereof] and that by his or their peers" (McCart 1964, 6).

During this same time period, there were no lawyers to act as advocates. To address this deficiency, Parliament authorized 40 men to practice law throughout England. This number was believed adequate to fulfill the needs of the entire country. The trial jury during this period differed in one significant respect from the jury system in America today. The medieval jury was expected to have some knowledge of the case. It was believed that jurors' knowledge of the case would assist them in determining the guilt or innocence of the accused. Today, our notions of an impartial jury have been used to exclude those who have knowledge of the case. Historically, jurors were considered qualified if they were familiar with the facts of the case. Now jurors are considered more qualified if they have little or no knowledge of the facts of the case.

▶ The Jury Selection Process

Venire

In medieval England, jurors were selected by the king and only from the wealthy landowners. Throughout history those who were allowed to serve on juries were few in number. The selection of the *venire* or the venireman list of those qualified to serve as jurors has changed dramatically over time. For example, during most of American history, women were excluded from jury service. Some of the most prominent legal scholars of the eighteenth century argued that women should not be allowed to serve on juries. For example, it was believed that women should be excluded from jury service because of the defect of sex. This defect made it impossible for women to engage in intelligent decision making required for jury service. This perspective also existed in the United States. Women were excluded from jury service until 1919, when Utah became the first state to allow women to serve as jurors. The national sentiment against women as prospective jurors changed dramatically after the passage of the Nineteenth Amendment that gave women the right to vote. When the Nineteenth Amendment was passed, most states allowed women to serve on juries. However, in many jurisdictions, women were not automatically included in the *venire*. As recently as 1966, three states did not permit women to serve on juries. In many other jurisdictions, women had to go to the courthouse and ask to be included in the list of potential jurors. This process was known as affirmative registration. In 1966, the U.S. Supreme Court upheld the practice of excluding women from the jury pool when it reasoned, "The legislature has a right to exclude women so they may contribute their services as mothers, wives, homemakers, and also to protect them . . . from the filth, obscenity, and noxious atmosphere . . . of the courtroom" (*Hoyt v. Florida*, 1961:57). It wasn't until 1975 in the case of *Taylor v. Louisiana* that the U.S. Supreme Court changed its mind and ruled that the affirmative registration process was unconstitutional.

Currently, most jurisdictions use voter registration lists to obtain prospective jurors for the jury pool. Once persons have been drawn from the list, the court sends them a short questionnaire summoning them for jury service and asking then to complete a short questionnaire to determine if they are qualified for jury service. The short questionnaire includes questions that might automatically exclude them from jury service. The standard questions include but are not limited to the following:

1. Are you a U.S. citizen?

2. Are you at least 18 years old?

3. Do you have any mental or physical disability?

4. Have you ever been convicted of a felony?

venire, venireman list, veniremen list of prospective jurors made up from registered voters, vehicle driver's licenses, tax assessors' records. Persons must reside within the particular jurisdiction where the jury trial is held. Persons who are potential jurors in a given jurisdiction.

affirmative registration action on the part of women to actively seek to be included on juries that were formerly comprised exclusively of men.

Answering "yes" or "no" to any of these questions may be sufficient grounds to exclude certain persons from the jury pool. If these persons pass the initial screening, they are sent a letter advising them to appear for jury service at the courthouse on a particular date and time.

Some persons have argued that relying solely on voter registration lists systematically excludes segments of the population. Levin (1988) has estimated that voter registration lists could exclude upward of 60 percent of the population. Who does this process exclude? The poor, undereducated, minorities, and women are less likely to register to vote than men, more educated persons, and nonminorities. Most defendants in the criminal court share most of the same characteristics as those who are excluded from jury service. Ultimately, voter registration lists are ineffective for obtaining a cross section of the community. Levin suggests that states must draw upon voter registration lists, tax rolls, public utility records, driver's license records, and the telephone directory to make better prospective juror selections from those groups that are typically bypassed whenever states rely on voter registration lists. In particular, the undereducated, poor, and minorities will most likely drive a car, have a telephone, and use electricity. Relying on these records will increase the representativeness of those who are called to jury service.

Voir Dire

We have the expectation that jurors should be unbiased or impartial when they hear the facts of a case. The process of determining a person's appropriateness or worthiness to serve as a juror is called *voir dire*. *Voir dire* is the opportunity to learn about the existing prejudices of prospective jurors. *Voir dire* means to "speak the truth." *Voir dire* is the crucial process through which attorneys attempt to uncover prospective juror biases that might prevent certain jurors from providing defendants with a fair and impartial trial. Some persons have argued that while *voir dire* has frequently been called jury selection, this term really is inappropriate. This is because we don't actually select those who sit on a jury as much as we eliminate those who are unsuitable.

voir dire "to speak the truth." Interrogation process whereby prospective jurors are questioned by either the judge or by the prosecution or defense attorneys to determine their biases and prejudices.

The *voir dire* process is described as follows. During *voir dire*, the trial judge and/or attorneys may ask questions of prospective jurors to determine their qualifications for jury service, their knowledge of the defendant and the case, and attitudes toward issues or individuals on the case that bias their views of the trial evidence. For example, questions may be wide ranging or more specifically related to the case, depending on what the trial judge allows.

Despite the purpose of the *voir dire* process to remove prospective jurors with biases, many persons have argued that the process actually achieves the opposite result. Both prosecutors and defense attorneys attempt to select jurors who might be sympathetic to their particular position. If one side is successful in soliciting crucial information during *voir dire*, they can use this information to remove unsympathetic jurors and increase jury bias either against or in favor of the defendant. Typically, prosecutors seek prospective jurors who are middle-aged, white, and middle class. It is believed that these persons are more likely to be supportive of the prosecution. However, defense counsels seek to remove prospective jurors with extreme views.

▶ The Elimination of Jurors

Challenges for Cause

During the *voir dire* process, the trial judge and attorneys attempt to uncover any biases that might hinder prospective jurors from serving in an impartial manner. There are two methods used to eliminate biased jurors or those considered undesirable by either side for whatever reason. One type of challenge is known as a **challenge for cause** (also a strike for cause). The other type of challenge is called a peremptory challenge. Prospective jurors may be challenged for cause and removed from the jury if they do not meet certain state mandatory requirements (e.g., being underage or not being a U.S. citizen), as well as for a specific bias (e.g., being related by blood or marriage to the accused), or for a nonspecific bias (e.g., expressing prejudice toward the defendant). Either the judge or the attorney may ask these questions. However, when the defense or prosecution wants to have a juror removed through the use of a challenge for cause, they must provide the judge with a compelling reason for doing so. When challenges for cause are used to strike certain prospective jurors, the judge is the final arbiter of whether the juror stays or goes.

For instance, a prominent black Tennessee defense attorney from Nashville, Avon Williams, was noted for his ability to dismiss prospective white jurors for cause whenever he represented black defendants. He would ask these prospective jurors if they were prejudiced toward blacks. Most would answer "No." Then Williams would ask them where they lived and if they belonged to any country clubs. Many of these white jurors lived in all-white neighborhoods, and some belonged to country clubs. He would then ask if these country clubs barred or admitted blacks. These white prospective jurors would become agitated and say that their country clubs and neighborhoods did not include blacks. Williams would then ask the judge to strike these white prospective jurors for cause. The judge usually granted Williams's request, based on the nature of his *voir dire* questioning.

Peremptory Challenges

The second method for removing prospective jurors is by using a **peremptory challenge**. Unlike challenges for cause, peremptory challenges do not require any explanations from attorneys for either side. Both prosecutors and defense counsel are given a limited number of these peremptory challenges. The number of peremptory challenges varies according to the seriousness of the case. In the most serious cases or cases with a significant amount of pretrial publicity, attorneys are given a larger number of challenges. Attorneys involved in less serious cases have fewer peremptory challenges. For instance, in most misdemeanors and less serious felony cases, each side is given six peremptory challenges. For more serious cases such as murder trials, each side is given a dozen or more peremptory challenges. In some jurisdictions, as many as 20 peremptory challenges may be given to each side for their use in striking prospective jurors they don't like, for whatever reason.

How do prosecutors and defense counsels know which prospective jurors to remove? During the *voir dire* process, attorneys usually ask members of the jury pool about their occupation, their attitudes toward law enforcement, and their general perceptions about the offense. For example, it is not uncommon for a defense attorney in a drunk-driving case to ask prospective jurors if it is a crime to drink and drive. Some of the members of the jury pool will say that drinking and driving is a crime. Some defense counsels will use this opportunity to educate the jury pool that drinking and driving is not a crime, and that it only rises to the level of a criminal offense when someone becomes legally intoxicated and drives a vehicle. Attorneys for both sides also use the information gathered from the *voir dire* together with juror demographics (e.g., age, gender, and race) to develop a profile of how prospective jurors with similar characteristics feel about certain issues that might arise during the trial.

Social scientists have discovered that often demographic characteristics are quite important and influence one's perceptions and attitudes. For example, Winston and

BOX 6-1

KEY CASES: PEREMPTORY CHALLENGES AND THE *BATSON* DOCTRINE

Batson v. Kentucky, 476 U.S. 79, 106 S.Ct. 1712 (1986)

In Kentucky, a black man, Batson, was convicted by an all-white jury of second-degree burglary. The prosecutor had used all of his peremptory challenges to exclude the few black prospective jurors from the jury pool. Ordinarily, peremptory challenges may be used to strike particular jurors without the prosecutor having to provide a reason for doing so. In this case, the use of peremptory challenges was rather transparent, and Batson appealed. In a landmark case, the U.S. Supreme Court decided that peremptory challenges may not be used for a racially discriminatory purpose. Thus, creating an all-white jury by deliberately eliminating all prospective black candidates was discriminatory. The U.S. Supreme Court ruled in favor of Batson.

Griffith v. Kentucky, 479 U.S. 314, 107 S.Ct. 708 (1987)

Griffith, a black man, was arrested for conspiracy to distribute marijuana. During his 1982 trial in Jefferson County, the prosecutor used four out of five peremptory challenges to strike from jury duty four out of five prospective black jurors. Griffith was convicted. He later appealed, saying that the prosecutor had violated his right to due process by striking from jury duty most of the black candidates. He said the case of *Batson v. Kentucky* (1986) should be retroactively applied to his case. The U.S. Supreme Court overturned his conviction, holding that the *Batson* case, prohibiting prosecutors from using their peremptory challenges to give racial bias to a jury pool, should be retroactively applied where a showing exists that such conduct has occurred. Thus, Griffith's case qualified for a retroactive application of *Batson*. The U.S. Supreme Court held that a new rule for the conduct of criminal prosecutions is to be applied retroactively to all cases, state or federal, pending on direct review or not yet final, with no exception for cases in which the new rule constitutes a "clear break" with the past.

Powers v. Ohio, 499 U.S. 400, 111 S.Ct. 1364 (1991)

Powers was charged with murder, aggravated murder, and attempted aggravated murder, all with firearm specifications (calling for mandatory minimum sentences). A white man, he objected to the government's use of peremptory challenges to strike seven black prospective jurors from the jury. Subsequently, Powers was convicted. He appealed, alleging that his Fourteenth Amendment right had been violated under the Equal Protection Clause because of the alleged discriminatory use of peremptory challenges. The matter of excluding prospective black jurors by the use of peremptory challenges had already been decided in *Batson v. Kentucky* (1986), in which it was declared unconstitutional to use peremptory challenges to achieve a racially pure jury. In the *Batson* case, however, the defendant was black, and government prejudice was obvious in the use of these peremptory challenges. In the *Powers* case, the defendant was white, and prospective black jurors had been excluded. The U.S. Supreme Court heard Powers' appeal and overturned his conviction on the same grounds as *Batson*, holding that criminal defendants may object to race-based exclusions of jurors effected through peremptory challenges whether or not defendants and excluded jurors share the same race.

Hernandez v. New York, 500 U.S. 352, 111 S.Ct. 1859 (1991)

Hernandez was convicted of various crimes. During the selection of his jury, the prosecutor used several peremptory challenges to strike from potential jury duty four Latinos. Following his conviction, Hernandez filed an appeal, alleging that the prosecutor had deliberately deprived him of a fair trial by eliminating persons like Hernandez. The argument was similar to the one made in *Batson v. Kentucky* (1986), in which it was held that peremptory challenges cannot be used to create racially pure juries or to strike off members of a particular race. At the time, objections had been raised by defense counsel, but the prosecutor cited various valid reasons for using these challenges. The U.S. Supreme Court upheld his conviction, holding that an acceptable race-neutral explanation had been provided by the prosecutor for striking the Latino jurors in that case. No evidence to the contrary had been presented.

(continued)

Georgia v. McCollum, 505 U.S. 42, 112 S.Ct. 2348 (1992)

McCollum was indicted on charges of aggravated assault and simple battery. During jury selection, his attorney used his peremptory challenges to strike certain prospective jurors from jury duty because of their race. McCollum was acquitted. The state challenged the use of these peremptory challenges, arguing that they had created a biased jury as in *Batson v. Kentucky* (1986), in which the prosecutor used peremptory challenges for racial-bias purposes. The U.S. Supreme Court agreed with the state and rejected the defendant's attorney's use of peremptory challenges for racial purposes. Thus, according to *Batson* and *McCollum*, neither prosecutors nor defense attorneys may deliberately use their peremptory challenges to excuse jurors on the basis of their race.

Purkett v. Elem, 514 U.S. 765, 115 S.Ct. 1769 (1995)

Elem, a black man, was accused of second-degree robbery. During the selection of jurors, the prosecutor used one of his peremptory challenges to strike from the jury pool a prospective black juror. Elem appealed, alleging that this use of a peremptory challenge was in violation of a policy set forth in *Batson v. Kentucky* (1986) prohibiting the use of peremptory challenges for racial purposes. The U.S. Supreme Court heard Elem's *habeas corpus* petition and argument. It upheld Elem's conviction when it determined that the prosecutor had used the peremptory challenge in a racially neutral fashion. The reason given for striking this black prospective juror was that the man had long, unkempt hair and a mustache and beard. The U.S. Supreme Court accepted this explanation as being race-neutral. It held that opponents of peremptory challenges must carry the burden of proving that purposeful discrimination has occurred. The explanation given by those exercising their peremptory challenges need not be persuasive or even plausible; rather, these explanations are considered only in determining whether opponents have carried their burden of proof by showing that the peremptory strikes were discriminatory. In this case, the peremptory challenge was satisfactorily explained and Elem's conviction was upheld.

Miller-El v. Dretke, _U.S. _, 125 S.Ct. 2317 (2005)

Thomas Miller-El, a black man, and Kennard Flowers robbed a Dallas, Texas Holiday Inn in November 1985. During the robbery they bound and gagged two employees and then shot each twice in the back, killing one and seriously injuring the other. Subsequently, Miller-El was charged with capital murder. His trial lasted five weeks. At the beginning of Miller-El's trial during jury selection, 108 persons were selected as the *venire*. Of these, there were 20 blacks. Subsequently, 19 out of 20 blacks were rejected as jurors. Three were dismissed for cause; six were dismissed by parties' agreement; and 10 were struck by the prosecutor through the use of peremptory challenges. Miller-El objected to these strikes but his objections were overruled. Miller-El was convicted and sentenced to death. He filed numerous appeals over the years on different grounds. His most recent appeal was a *habeas corpus* action alleging that the prosecutor engaged in purposeful discrimination by striking 10 out of 11 black venirepersons. A U.S. District Court denied the petition and this decision was affirmed by the Fifth Circuit Court of Appeals. Miller-El appealed to the U.S. Supreme Court, where the case was heard. The U.S. Supreme Court reversed and remanded, holding that the Texas court's factual findings as to the nature of the state's race-neutral explanations for its use of peremptory challenges to excuse 10 of 11 black venirepersons were shown to be wrong by clear and convincing evidence. Based on the totality of relevant facts in Miller-El's case, discriminatory jury selection had been demonstrated. The prosecutors used peremptory challenges to exclude 91 percent of the eligible black *venire* panelists, a disparity unlikely to have been produced by happenstance.

Johnson v. California, U.S._, 125 S.Ct. 2410 (2005)

Jay Johnson, a black man, was convicted of second-degree murder in the death of a 19-month-old white child. During jury selection, several prospective jurors were excused for cause. The prosecutor used three peremptory challenges to strike all of the prospective black jurors, thus leaving Johnson to be tried by an all-white jury. These peremptory challenges were opposed by Johnson, but the judge rejected his arguments. The prosecutor failed to explain why he had excused these black prospective jurors, but the judge declared that he (the judge) had reviewed the record and was convinced that the prosecutor's strikes could be justified by race-neutral reasons. Johnson appealed through the California courts, alleging that the exclusion of blacks from the jury deprived him of a fair trial. An appellate court set aside Johnson's conviction but the California Supreme Court reinstated it, acknowledging that although the exclusion of all three black prospective jurors looked suspicious, the court deferred to the judge's ruling and explanation. Johnson therefore appealed to the U.S. Supreme Court, where the case was heard. The U.S. Supreme Court reversed Johnson's conviction, holding that California's standard is an inappropriate yardstick to measure the sufficiency of a *prima facie* case of purposeful discrimination in jury selection. The facts that the trial judge said that the case was close and the California Supreme Court said that it was suspicious that all three black prospective jurors were removed were sufficient bases for a *prima facie* case of discrimination in Johnson's case.

Rice v. Collins, _ U.S. _, 126 S.Ct. 969 (2006)

Steven Collins, an African American, was convicted of cocaine possession, in violation of California's three-strike rule that would subject him to a harsher sentence. Collins sought postconviction relief on *habeas corpus* grounds, in particular objecting to the peremptory challenge of an African American prospective juror on allegedly race-based grounds. The prosecutor defended his exclusion of the juror as race-neutral, contending (1) she was young and might be too tolerant of drug offenders; (2) she was single and lacked community ties; and (3) she had rolled her eyes when asked certain questions by the court. On appeal, the California Supreme Court upheld Collins's conviction, but the Ninth Circuit Court of Appeals set aside Collins's conviction on the grounds of an unreasonable factual determination by the prosecutor. The government appealed and the U.S. Supreme Court heard the case. The U.S. Supreme Court reversed the Ninth Circuit, reinstating Collins's conviction, holding that the Ninth Circuit's grounds for reversal were themselves based on a set of debatable inferences about prosecutorial conduct in jury selection.

Winston (1980) found that jurors who were opposed to the death penalty were usually under 45 years of age, had a high school education, were employed, and did not watch the news on television. However, those favoring the death penalty tended to be males age 60 and older who had less than a high school education, were unemployed or retired, and watched the news on television. If either the prosecution or defense wishes to strike particular prospective jurors, they may simply excuse them by using a peremptory challenge.

Several serious allegations are made about prosecutors who systematically remove minorities from juries where the criminal defendants are also minorities. Some persons have alleged that this has occurred even in the most high-profile cases. For example, Suggs and Sales (1981) describe how prosecutors have used most of their peremptory challenges to remove most blacks from the jury panel where a black defendant is on trial for a serious offense. Defense attorneys have also been accused of using peremptory challenges to remove certain types of persons who they believe would be unsympathetic to their position.

For many decades, the use of peremptory challenges was inviolate. But in 1986, the U.S. Supreme Court decided to review the issue of using peremptory challenges to systematically remove black jurors in the case of *Batson v. Kentucky*. The U.S. Supreme Court found that the peremptory challenges used by the prosecutor were race-based and therefore unconstitutional. In 1991, the Court applied the equal-protection argument to defense counsels (*Georgia v. McCollum*) and in civil cases such as *Edmonson v. Leesville Concrete Co.* (1991). In 2000, the Court in *United States v. Martinez-Salazar* ruled that the use of a peremptory challenge to exclude a juror based solely on their gender, race, or ethnic group is unconstitutional. Lastly, the Third Circuit Court of Appeals in 2003 in the case of *Rico v. Leftridge-Byrd* applied the ruling in *Batson* to Italian American members of the jury because they had been excluded due to their Italian last names.

BOX 6-2

LEGAL ISSUES: PURPOSEFUL DISCRIMINATION IN JURY SELECTION 30 YEARS POST *BATSON*

Timothy Foster was an 18-year-old black man in 1986 when he was charged with the murder of an elderly white woman. During jury selection, the prosecution struck all four of the black jurors who were qualified using peremptory challenges. The defense counsel objected to those strikes but the court held that the prosecutions rational for excluding them were sufficient. Foster was convicted of the murder by an all-white jury and was sentenced to death. Foster filed a post-judgment discovery motion for the prosecutions jury selection notes but the court denied the request. Two decades later, Foster filed a *habeas corpus* petition on a Batson Doctrine violation because he had

Aerogondo/Fotolia

obtained the prosecution's jury selection notes through the Georgia Open Records Act. The court denied his *habeas corpus* petition and the Supreme Court of Georgia affirmed, the Supreme Court of the United States, however, granted *certiorari* and in a 7–1 decision determined that sufficient evidence existed to establish a Batson Doctrine violation of purposeful discrimination. Chief Roberts in the opinion of the court stated that although the prosecutor had provided a list of reasons the black jurors had been excluded, the jury selection notes showed that the prosecutor had written "definitely no" by the names of the five black jurors, which is evidence that the jurors were never seriously considered to be on the jury. The opinion furthered that the notes continually highlighted race, and the reasons given for striking the black jurors were not applied to prospective white jurors who were chosen to sit on the jury.

What do you think? Should the original trial and state appellate courts over two decades earlier have come to the same conclusion as the Supreme Court did in 2016? Do you think this kind of purposeful discrimination still occurs today in jury selection 30 years after the *Batson* decision? What methods do you think the courts could adopt to ensure race-neutral jury selection processes?

▶ Jury Consultants and Scientific Jury Selection

scientific jury selection applying the scientific method to select jurors who it is believed will render favorable decisions for or against defendants.

F. Lee Bailey and Melvin Belli have been credited as being the first defense attorneys to hire experts to assist them in the jury selection process. However, it wasn't until the Berrigan brothers' trial that scientific jury selection became an important trial tactic. Daniel and Philip Berrigan were Catholic priests who had been charged with conspiracy to kidnap then-secretary of state Henry Kissinger, raid draft boards, and bomb tunnels in Washington, D.C. Jay Schulman, a social scientist who sympathized with the defendants, decided to use his skill in social research methods to assist the defendants. He wanted to determine how several demographic characteristics (e.g., age, political philosophy, and gender) influenced prospective jurors' perceptions of the issues surrounding the case and their attitudes toward the defendants. He and his colleagues conducted a telephone interview of 840 randomly selected registered voters. These interviews were followed by personal interviews of 262 people. During the face-to-face interviews, the respondents were asked questions in the following areas (Wanamaker 1978, 348): (1) media preferences (choice of newspapers, magazines, radio, and television stations); (2) knowledge of the defendants and their case (the defendants' names were embedded with the names of other people in the news and respondents were asked if they had heard of the person and what they had heard about them); (3) their opinion of the greatest American in the past 10 or 15 years (seeking to gauge respondent's values); (4) trust of the government (three questions were asked relating to the government's decisions and attempts to do what is right); (5) personal characteristics (ages and activities of respondents children, religious attitudes and commitment, leisure activities, and organizational memberships); (6) attitudes that were potentially related to the trial (the interviewers sought the extent of agreement with eight statements concerning issues, such as right to private property, support for the government, police use of force, and the like); and (7) scale of acceptable antiwar activities.

Using the results of this survey, the researchers were able to determine that conservatives with higher education and who received their news from metropolitan news sources held opinions that were unfavorable to the defendants. Surprisingly, the researchers found that religious affiliation was an important factor that the defense counsel should consider. Protestant denominations such as Methodists, Presbyterians, and Episcopalians were more likely to condemn the defendants for their actions. The research revealed that from the defendants' perspective, the most favorable type of juror was a female Democrat with no religious preference and employed as a white-collar professional or possibly a skilled blue-collar job (Wanamaker 1978, 349). It is impossible to determine if the information collected was useful in selecting a sympathetic jury for these defendants, but the jury in the actual case voted 10–2 to acquit the defendants. Had the jury voted to convict them, then the scientific jury selection process engaged in by Schulman and his colleagues would probably have never received much attention. But since the outcome of the trial favored the defendants, the legal community took special notice, and scientific jury selection subsequently became an important component in the jury selection process.

The process of scientific jury selection has evolved into an entirely new professional enterprise. In some of the most high-profile criminal cases, where defendants have the resources to spend, jury consultants have been used to assist both prosecutors and defense counsels in their selection of jury members. For example, in the O. J. Simpson criminal trial, the defense team hired Jo-Ellan Dimitrius from Trial Logistics, while the prosecution hired Don Vinson from DecisionQuest to aid in jury selection. Dimitrius and Vinson conducted extensive surveys and relayed this information to their clients during trial strategy sessions. It is interesting to note that Dimitrius assisted during the entire trial. However, Vinson was dismissed by the prosecution after two court appearances (Lafferty 1994).

Jury consultation has become a big business. This year the American Society of Trial Consultants will celebrate their twenty-fifth anniversary. Despite this rapid growth, much skepticism exists about the quality of scientific jury selection. Litigation Sciences boast a 95 percent success rate, although these success rates may not be attributable to scientific techniques.

Most of the jury consultants were hired in high-profile cases or political trials. In these cases, the defense attorneys are often in the best position to prepare their cases such that acquittal of their clients is more a matter of good lawyering rather than a matter of the advice received from professional jury consultants. Some persons have equated scientific jury selection with jury tampering, and they suggest that the integrity of the jury is undermined or compromised (Enriquez and Clark 2005).

▶ Jury Size

Anyone unfamiliar with the court process and who is charged with a felony may be surprised to see only six people sitting as jurors to decide their guilt or innocence. Doesn't the Constitution guarantee them the right to a 12-member jury? What effect will smaller jury sizes have on jury deliberations? Are smaller juries more likely to convict defendants rather than larger juries? These are just some of the questions defendants have raised about smaller jury sizes. These same questions have been asked and researched by legal scholars.

For instance, what is the special significance associated with the number "12"? Why is this number given such importance in our common-law legal history? Are 12 jurors better able to understand the evidence and reach a decision? The reason the number "12" is so deeply ingrained in our perception of the trial process has nothing to do with any scientific or legalistic reasoning. Rather, it has everything to do with historical tradition. Throughout most of the last several centuries, juries were comprised of 12 members.

Several legal scholars have studied the origins of the 12-member jury. Despite their intensive investigative efforts, there is still no definitive conclusion as to the origin of the number "12." Some scholars have traced the 12-member jury to ancient Greek mythology, while others have found antecedents of the 12-member jury in biblical writings (McConville and Mirsky 2005). The most direct lineage of the 12-member jury in America is traced to the Constitution of Clarendon, the Assize of Clarendon, and the Magna Carta.

The Constitution of Clarendon was signed by King Henry II in 1164. This constitution provided that the sheriff was to administer an oath to 12 men of the neighborhood that they would declare the truth and render verdicts in cases brought to them. The Assize of Clarendon was a court created by Henry II to give litigants a legal option to resolve a dispute rather than resolve it in the traditional manner, which was often a duel to the death. If a disputant chose the court rather than the duel, the court would issue a writ to the king to have 4 knights from the region select 12 jurors. The litigants were allowed to challenge the knights' decisions. This process continued until 12 acceptable jurors were selected. Finally, the Magna Carta, signed by King John, established the constitutional importance of the jury. The right to a 12-member jury remained essentially the same for almost 800 years. This tradition was changed by the U.S. Supreme Court in *Williams v. Florida* (1970).

At the time Johnny Williams was charged with robbery, Florida permitted 6-member juries to hear all noncapital criminal cases. Williams argued that his case should be heard by a 12-member jury. His motion was denied and he was tried and convicted by a 6-person jury. He was ultimately sentenced to life in prison. He appealed his conviction on the grounds that the Sixth Amendment guaranteed him a right to a 12-member jury. The U.S. Supreme Court held that the Sixth Amendment does not require a 12-person jury. The U.S. Supreme Court majority reasoned that the 12-member jury is a historical accident and unnecessary for the proper functioning of a jury. Justice White said that the essential feature of the jury obviously lies in the interposition between the accused and his accuser of the commonsense judgment of a group of laymen, and in the community participation and shared responsibility that results for the group's determination of guilt or innocence. The performance of this role is not a function of the particular number of the body that makes up the jury (*Williams v. Florida*, 1970).

With authority from the U.S. Supreme Court, many states began to challenge other aspects of the Sixth Amendment. For instance, the use of nonunanimous verdicts was upheld by the U.S. Supreme Court in *Apodaca v. Oregon* (1972) and *Johnson v. Louisiana* (1972) (see Box 6-3).

In the *Apodaca* case, the U.S. Supreme Court upheld the Oregon statute that allowed a 10–2 vote for either conviction or acquittal. In Louisiana, the law allowed jury verdicts with a 9–3 vote. The U.S. Supreme Court also accepted this practice as not violating the Sixth Amendment or the Fourteenth Amendment. One year later in *Colgrove v. Battin* (1973), the Court ruled that 6-member juries were acceptable in civil cases. In the majority opinion, the Court cited social science evidence they believed indicated that there was no substantial difference between 12-member and 6-member juries. The *Colgrove* court cited four studies they believed provided "convincing empirical evidence of the correctness of the *Williams* conclusion that there is no discernable difference between the results reached by the two different-sized juries" (*Colgrove v. Battin*,

BOX 6-3

KEY CASES: JURY VOTING AND UNANIMITY

Johnson v. Louisiana, 406 U.S. 356, 92 S.Ct. 1620 (1972)

Johnson was arrested without a warrant at his home based on a photographic identification by a robbery victim. He was later subjected to a lineup, where he was identified again. Johnson was represented by counsel. He was subjected to trial by jury for the robbery offense and convicted in a jury vote of 9–3. Johnson appealed, contending that the jury verdict should be unanimous. The U.S. Supreme Court affirmed his conviction, saying, in effect, that states have the right to determine whether conviction requires unanimity of jury votes or only a majority vote. The U.S. Supreme Court concluded by saying that the verdicts rendered by 9 out of 12 jurors are not automatically invalidated by the disagreement of the dissenting three. Johnson was not deprived of due process or a fair trial because of the 9–3 vote. This U.S. Supreme Court decision applies to states only and does not affect federal juries, who must be unanimous in their verdicts. Federal criminal jury sizes of 12 may be reduced to 11 under special conditions with judicial approval; either size must be unanimous.

Apodaca v. Oregon, 406 U.S. 404, 92 S.Ct. 1628 (1972)

Apodaca and others were found guilty of various serious crimes by less than unanimous jury verdicts. Oregon has a statute mandating a conviction or acquittal on the basis of a 10–2 vote, or what is referred to by the Oregon legislature as a 10-of-12 vote. In Apodaca's case, the vote favoring conviction was 11–1. Apodaca challenged this vote as not being unanimous, and the U.S. Supreme Court heard the case contemporaneously with the case of *Johnson v. Louisiana* (1972) on an identical issue. In Apodaca's case, the U.S. Supreme Court upheld the constitutionality of the Oregon jury voting provision, declaring that votes of these kinds do not violate one's right to due process under either the Sixth or the Fourteenth Amendment. The significance of this case is that less than unanimous jury votes among the states are constitutional and do not violate one's right to due process.

Early v. Packer, 537 U.S. 3, 123 S.Ct. 362 (2002)

William Packer was found guilty in a California court of second-degree murder, two counts of attempted murder, two counts of robbery, two counts of assault with a deadly weapon, and one count of assault with a firearm. He was acquitted on ten other counts. The jury had a difficult time in deliberating some issues, with one juror in particular claiming illness, indecisiveness, and fatigue. At various points during jury deliberations, the trial judge requested information from the jury foreman about the status of jury voting, and he questioned the particular female juror at some length. The judge repeated various instructions to the jury as to their deliberations, including that they should follow the law, determine whether or not the elements of the offense were present, and find unanimously whether Packer was guilty or not guilty of each of those offenses. Subsequently, the jury rendered its verdicts as noted above and Packer appealed, filing a *habeas corpus* petition. The petition alleged that the trial judge coerced the female juror into agreeing with the majority of other jurors in reaching their guilty verdicts on the above counts. Thus, he claimed, he was denied his due process right to a fair and impartial jury. The Ninth Circuit Court of Appeals granted Packer's petition and reversed his convictions. California appealed and the U.S. Supreme Court heard the case. The U.S. Supreme Court reinstated Packer's convictions, holding that the trial judge's remarks and instructions to jurors were not coercive, nor were they unreasonable or contrary to established federal law. Thus, it is not unconstitutional for a trial judge to urge a jury to continue deliberating as long as the judge does not attempt to coerce a particular type of jury verdict. In this instance, all of the judge's remarks clearly admonished jurors to follow and apply the law objectively and to make their decisions about Packer's guilt or innocence consistent with that objectivity.

1973:47). With the *Colgrove* decision, the Court seemed to give states the license to decrease their jury sizes. Georgia attempted this. A Georgia statute was passed allowing convictions based on deliberations by 5-member juries. This practice was challenged in *Ballew v. Georgia* (1978). Ballew was a theater manager in Atlanta who was charged with violating a Georgia ordinance prohibiting the distribution of obscene material by showing a pornographic and sexually explicit movie starring Marilyn Chambers, *Behind the Green Door*. Ballew appealed his conviction by a 5-member jury contending that it violated his Sixth and Fourteenth Amendment rights. Ballew's conviction was set aside after the U.S. Supreme Court declared that 5-member juries are too small to constitute a representative cross section of the community. Thus, the minimum jury size was established as six.

In all previous U.S. Supreme Court decisions, the justices were reluctant to specify a minimum jury size. But with the *Williams* decision, the Court was faced with a potentially serious dilemma. Again relying on social science, the U.S. Supreme Court argued that their conclusion rested on the assumption there was no difference between 12- and 6-member juries. The Court believed that the deliberative ability, representativeness, verdict reliability, likelihood of conviction, and the minority ability to resist majority pressure were not hindered by decreasing jury size. However, the Court's reading of the literature was seriously flawed. Most of the studies they relied upon evidenced several empirical flaws or limitations. Additionally, where studies were cited that had credibility and were empirically sound, the U.S. Supreme Court misinterpreted some of the results. The U.S. Supreme Court cited a study conducted by Asch (1966) that examined the minority's ability to resist group pressure. Asch found that when the minority position has an ally, it is better able to resist pressure from the majority position. In the context of jury deliberations, this means that in a jury vote of 10–2, the minority jury voters are better able to withstand group pressure more than minority jury voters where the jury vote is 5–1. However, the Court erred in its interpretation and understanding of the social research and concluded that there was no functional difference between the two juries. In any case, a 5–1 jury vote is unconstitutional, inasmuch as all 6-member jury voting must be unanimous.

▶ Jury Sequestration

jury sequestration the process of isolating a jury from the public during a trial; the objective is to minimize the influence of media publicity and exposure, which might otherwise influence juror opinions about the guilt or innocence of the defendant.

Historically, **jury sequestration** has been used to isolate jurors from the potential biasing influences of the press and community sentiment. Preventing outside information from reaching jurors allows jurors to be influenced only by the information and evidence presented to them at trial, the instructions of judges, and their fellow jurors. While jury sequestration has many critics, some persons have discovered that sequestration may have some positive effects. Apart from the obvious benefit of not having jurors influenced by outside forces, sequestration, on many occasions, has fostered a group bonding process among the jurors. Following trials, jurors have often referred to themselves as becoming a family who plan to see each other after the trial. Thus, the emotional connection developed as a result of sequestration may have a positive effect on deliberations. Researchers have learned that group communication is enhanced when individuals have formed an interpersonal connection among themselves. Therefore, jurors who have developed relationships with one another are more willing to listen to each other and discuss their differences. When this event occurs, sequestration has enhanced the deliberative process. While these are a few of the positive effects of jury sequestration, these are far outnumbered by criticisms of it.

During sequestration, if the jury develops intergroup rivalries among and animosity toward each other, the deliberative process suffers. People are more likely to gravitate toward people like themselves. This highlights the differences between group members and they begin to resent one other. Alliances are formed between certain jurors, and they form coalitions that become fairly powerful during jury deliberations. Sequestration also puts pressure on jurors who disagree with the majority. The jurors in the minority position see themselves as prolonging the sequestration. If they would only capitulate and agree with the majority, they could all go home and get back to their lives. Jury sequestration is also expensive.

In the O. J. Simpson criminal trial, the jury was sequestered for 266 days at a cost to the taxpayers of almost $1 million. Cost was one of the primary reasons the New York courts system eliminated its practice of mandatory sequestration. The cost savings by eliminating mandatory sequestration in criminal trials were almost $4 million each year. Sequestration may also be a primary reason people are trying to get out of jury service. For many jurors, being confined to a hotel and treated like a prisoner in a potentially hostile environment may be one reason why many persons who are called for jury service refuse to answer their calls for such service.

▶ Jury Decision Making and Voting

Considerable research has examined jury decision making and voting behavior. For instance, it has been found that women approach jury duty differently, perceive things differently, and often vote differently from men (Fischer 1997). Not only do gender differences influence decision making, but also the type of occupation, ethnicity, and socioeconomic status exert a profound influence on how people perceive things and process large amounts of evidence and other important information.

It has been found that several important trial and victim factors influence jury voting behavior. Factors associated with guilty verdicts are physical evidence, a defendant's prior criminal record, and victim attractiveness. Male jurors seem more likely to vote not guilty when the victim puts up some resistance against the offender. Guilty verdicts are also more likely when jurors have had prior jury service. Not guilty verdicts have been associated with offenders being employed, offenders being attractive, and where there has been some degree of victim facilitation (e.g., the victim allows a stranger to take him/her home from a bar). Jurors who have a tendency to blame the victim are also more likely to vote not guilty (Enriquez and Clark 2005).

Another factor is whether jurors are verdict driven or evidence driven. Research indicates that once juries reach the jury room, they commence the decision-making process by following one of two patterns or methods (Champion 2005b). The first pattern is called an evidence-driven jury. In evidence-driven cases, juries come together and begin discussing how to proceed. Most jurors or at least a vocal few decide that they should review the evidence as a group before they can contemplate a verdict. With this method, all the evidence is discussed, not simply the evidence individual jurors believe is relevant. However, a verdict-driven jury believes that discussing the evidence before a vote is unnecessary. Why debate the evidence when all jurors might vote the same way without a review of the evidence? Using this method, the jury votes first to see how many jurors favor guilt or acquittal. When discussed, evidence is used to support one position or another. Verdict-driven deliberations often take less time than evidence-driven deliberations since there is little or no time taken to review the evidence before jury votes are cast.

Some research shows that the jury deliberation process may not have much impact on the final verdict. In Kalven and Ziesel's (1966) classic study of the jury system, they compared the initial jury vote to the final verdict. They revealed that in the vast majority of cases, the first vote was most often the same as the final verdict. For example, on a 12-person jury, if seven of the jurors initially voted not guilty, the subsequent verdict tended to be not guilty. However, if the majority of jurors voted guilty, the final verdict would almost always be guilty. Only on rare occasions does the minority succeed in convincing the

evidence-driven jury jury that decides to consider all evidence presented as relevant rather than selected evidence based on juror interest or preferences.

verdict-driven jury jury that decides guilt or innocence first without considering adequately the relevant evidence in the case; jurors are polled initially to see to what extent they agree or disagree among themselves; if most or all of the jurors vote the same way, then they conclude their deliberations without further consideration of the evidence.

majority to change their vote. Kalven and Ziesel have said that the real decision is often made before the deliberation begins. The deliberation process might well be likened to what the developer does for an exposed film: a picture is developed, but the outcome is predetermined (1966, 488–489).

▶ Jury Verdicts

The media always seem willing to report about how the justice system has failed in one respect or another to convict guilty defendants. This most often occurs when we perceive that an obviously guilty person is found not guilty or the jury delivers an excessive damage award to a plaintiff in a civil case. Armed with this anecdotal evidence, more than a few critics have called for reforming the jury system. When we advocate changing the jury system, we have to make two assumptions. First, we have to assume that the jury made a mistake. Second, we have to assume that there is a better alternative. In most cases, advocates for jury reform believe that juries composed of laypersons from the community are often not able to understand or comprehend the complex information presented at trial. This has also been referred to as the complexity exception. Stephen Adler has argued that if a judge doesn't think the jury will understand a particular civil case, he can decide it without a jury (Adler 1995, 143). Adler argues that jury reform should include a return to the blue-ribbon jury. During the 1960s and 1970s, blue-ribbon juries were comprised from members of the best-educated or socially placed members of society because it was believed a jury should be composed of such persons. In fact, most persons who serve on juries today would not have been placed on these blue-ribbon juries in past years. In fact, the reverse of the blue-ribbon jury is often practiced in many jurisdictions. New York's judicial rules allow for the automatic exemption of lawyers, doctors, clergy, dentists, optometrists, psychologists, podiatrists, registered and practical nurses, embalmers, police officers, correctional officers, firefighters, sole business owners, and many other professional groups.

In many instances, if we agree with the idea that juries cannot understand the information presented to them and therefore are unable to arrive at a competent verdict, who will replace them? Most critics would shift the responsibility for determining guilt or innocence to the judges themselves. Are juries unable to understand the material presented to them? In an effort to answer this question, Kalven and Ziesel (1966) investigated how juries arrived at verdicts and how these jury verdicts differed from judicial decisions about the same cases. Kalven and Ziesel gathered data from 3,576 trials. In order to compare the differences between judges and juries, the researchers asked that judges say how they would have ruled in the particular case. The research showed that the verdicts of judges and juries were essentially the same in 78 percent of the cases. Conversely, judges and juries disagreed on the outcome in 22 percent of the cases. The data indicate that the largest disagreement came where judges said they would have convicted the defendant and the juries said they would acquit the defendant. In essence, judges were more likely to convict than juries. Thus, juries seem to be more lenient than judges in decision making about criminal defendants.

Those critical of the jury system might argue that juries are not more lenient, but rather, the differences in judge and jury case outcomes can be attributed to jury incompetence. They would argue that juries disagreed with judges and acquitted defendants when they should have convicted them, largely because the jurors did not understand the law and the evidence presented to them at trial. In order to address this criticism, Kalven and Ziesel (1966) had the judges rate whether the evidence was difficult or easy to comprehend. If jury incompetence was the reason for the differences, we might expect a higher rate of disagreement in those cases where the judge indicated that the evidence was too difficult to understand. However, the results indicate that judges and juries disagreed equally in both complex and simple cases.

blue-ribbon jury
a jury considered by either side, prosecution or defense, to be ideal because of its perceived likelihood of rendering a verdict favorable to that side; jurors often are selected because of their higher educational level and intellectual skills.

LEGAL ISSUES: PLAIN ENGLISH FOR JURY INSTRUCTIONS?

For many jurors legal jargon can be difficult to understand and even intimidating. Difficult to understand language can also be problematic in ensuring correct application of the law. Numerous states across the country have implemented reforms to simplify jury instructions with clearer and easy to understand language. The idea is that this will facilitate better comprehension of the duties of jurors in applying the law and lead to better informed verdicts. Research using mock jury subjects reveals that when instructions are in plain English, the rates of comprehension are greater (Randall & Graf, 2014). The judicial counsel of California spent eight years rewriting some of its jury instructions doing away with old and rarely used terms, for example, "willfully false" is now "lied," and "innocent misrecollection" is now "honestly forgot"

(Murphy, 2005). Because some research has shown that the average juror may only comprehend half of a judge's instructions (Elwork, Sales, & Alfini, 1982), recent recommendations for instructions to juries include the use of short, simple sentences, concrete instead of abstract words, and avoidance of legal jargon and uncommon words (Torrensen, 2016). Do you think that simpler instructions in more plain English will better enable jurors to understand instructions given to them, thereby facilitating less complex decision making? Should all states consider revising some of their complex legalese to help jurors understand? Does this decrease the seriousness of a court trial, or diminish the authority of the legal system? Does the goal of more informed jurors and verdicts outweigh the need of courts to appear serious and authoritarian?

Sources: Elwork, Amiram, Bruce Sales, and James Alfini (1982). *Making Jury Instructions Understandable.* Michie Company.

Murphy, Dean E. (2005). The New Language for Jurors in California: Plain English. *New York Times*, August 28:A12.

Randall, Janet, and Lucas Graf (2014). *Linguistics meets "legalese": Syntax, semantics, and jury instruction reform.* Paper presented at the Linguistics Society of America Annual Meeting, Minneapolis, MN.

Torrensen, Nancy (2016). *Pattern Criminal Jury Instructions for the District Court of the First Circuit.* Available online at: www.med.uscourts.gov/pdf/crpjilinks.pdf.

► Jury Nullification

Jury nullification is the refusal of juries to apply the law when they believe following the letter of the law would be a miscarriage of justice. In a criminal trial, the jury is the finder of fact and has the absolute authority to acquit the defendant regardless of the evidence. The jury is also our protection from the oppressive powers of the state. The constitutional protection against double jeopardy makes the jury's acquittal irreversible and the prosecution has no right to appeal the jury verdict. One exception is if there has been jury tampering or some other irregularity that has caused the jury to disregard the evidence against the accused. In a system designed with checks and balances to control state power, the jury system provides ordinary citizens with more power than our highest elected and appointed government officials.

> **jury nullification**
> jury refuses to accept the validity of evidence at trial and acquits or convicts for a lesser offense.

Although we have observed jury nullification in some recent spectacular cases (e.g., Marion Barry, Lorena Bobbit, and John DeLorean), it is not something that is particularly unique to our time. Juries have nullified the law or, more accurately, the actions of the state, for as long as juries have functioned in American and English courts. Jury nullification was common in England during the Bloody Code of the eighteenth and nineteenth centuries. The Bloody Code prescribed over 200 offenses that were punishable by death, including such minor offenses as stealing bread and pickpocketing. Because of the severity of the punishment relative to the offense, juries were reluctant to find defendants guilty of these offenses. The authority of the jury to engage in the practice of nullification was not challenged in England until 1670 in the *Bushell* case, and later in America in the *John Peter Zenger* case.

In 1670, William Penn and William Mead were being tried at the Old Bailey, the Central Criminal Court of England. Penn, subsequently the founder of the Colony of Pennsylvania and a leading proponent of correctional reform, was a Quaker like Mead, and the authorities saw both of them as radicals and extremists. Consequently, they were banned from preaching in the streets. However, this was their only forum because the authorities had barred them from their churches. On one occasion while they were preaching in the street, they were arrested and charged with unlawful assembly. Their fate ultimately rested in the hands of the jurors selected to hear the case. The witnesses included those who testified that Penn and Mead had preached on Gracechurch Street.

At the conclusion of the testimony, the jury was instructed to retire to the jury room and reach a verdict. When they returned with a verdict of not guilty, they were instructed to return to the jury room and deliberate until they reached a correct verdict. When they returned a second time, they found Penn guilty of speaking at Gracechurch Street but refused to convict him on unlawful assembly charges. The court reacted to this verdict by threatening Edward Bushell, who was identified as the leader of the jury revolt. They were sent back to deliberate once again, and when they returned, they announced that they had again found Penn guilty of speaking at Gracechurch Street, although they persisted and did not find him guilty of unlawful assembly. Additionally, they declared Mead innocent of any wrongdoing. The court was in turmoil. The court announced that Bushell and the rest of the jury would not be dismissed until they reached a verdict acceptable to the court. The judge ordered them locked up without "meat, drink, fire, and tobacco" until they reached an acceptable verdict. Facing this demand, the jury retired to deliberate and returned with an acquittal for Penn. They were ordered to go back and deliberate again, but this time they refused. The judge was outraged. Bushell and the rest of the jurors were fined 40 marks each and sent to jail until they could pay the fine. The jurors filed a *habeas corpus* appeal requesting their release from prison. The appellate court ordered that they be released and declared that the jury had the right to render a verdict according to its belief about the fairness of the law and not act consistent with what the court deemed appropriate.

▶ Jury and Juror Misconduct

juror misconduct
any impropriety by a juror; acceptance of illegal gratuities in exchange for a favorable vote for or against the defendant; not paying attention during the trial; reading newspaper accounts, listening or watching newscasters voice their opinions about the case, and then relating this information to other jurors in attempt to persuade them one way or another for or against the defendant.

Juror misconduct falls into two categories. The first is engaging in delinquency or lying to avoid jury service. The second is engaging in improper or prohibited behavior while serving as a juror. The first type of behavior is perceived as misconduct largely by those who believe that jury service is a civic duty and that all U.S. citizens are obligated to serve on juries when called to do so. Juror misconduct prior to trials most often involves jurors who lie to avoid jury service. Another problem involves jurors who lie and fail to disclose important information during *voir dire* so that they can remain on the jury. Those who are called to jury service often want to avoid it because of certain hardships jury service would pose. While jurors are compensated for their service, serving on a jury is still regarded by many persons as a financial hardship.

The types of financial hardships for jurors today are quite different from the financial burden on jurors in the 1700s. Jurors were usually compensated 1–2 dollars per day. However, many jurors had to travel long distances on foot or horseback to the courthouse. Because they could not return home each day, they had to pay for food and lodging. Often, these expenses were considerably more than the amount of the compensation received from the court for their jury service. Today, jurors continue to have the hardship of traveling to the courthouse, although in most instances, they are able to return to their homes each evening. In past centuries, judges routinely refused to feed jurors while they were deliberating in order to starve out a verdict. This is another hazard that contemporary jurors do not endure. The reasons for avoiding jury service have changed over time, although some persons still consider serving on a jury to be a hardship and that jury service is an activity to be avoided.

Another form of juror misconduct is lying. Most often, jurors lie to avoid jury duty. In the early 1900s in Cleveland, for example, residents from the wealthiest neighborhoods claimed illnesses more often than those from poorer neighborhoods. Still other persons would fabricate stories about how they were related to defendants in criminal cases simply to be dismissed as jurors. It was later revealed that they had no particular relationship with the accused and that their lies were ruses to avoid jury service (Stalmaster 1931, 74).

Engaging in inappropriate or prohibited behavior while serving as a juror, however, is the most serious form of juror misconduct. While juror misconduct has always plagued the jury system, it is more of a problem today than in the past. Over time, the definition of misconduct has not changed substantially, although what is different today is that jurors of the past had fewer opportunities to engage in inappropriate behavior. For instance, in past decades, it was not uncommon for a felony trial to have only one or two witnesses, and the trial lasted only a few hours. During this time, jurors were closely watched by the bailiff who prevented any misconduct from occurring. Today, trials are much longer and jurors have more unsupervised time. This provides jurors with more opportunities to be exposed to external influences and bribes from a defendant's friends, visiting the crime scene, discussing the evidence and the case prior to final deliberations, drinking alcohol, and reading, listening to, or watching prohibited media.

What are the implications of juror misconduct? For jurors themselves, they are most often held in contempt and are ordered to pay a fine or serve a short jail term. In rare instances, they are charged with criminal behavior by the prosecutor. Interestingly, jurors most often charged with misconduct by the prosecutor were members of juries where the result was an acquittal or a mistrial. One of the most common forms of juror misconduct is drinking alcohol during the trial or deliberations. Judges have been reluctant to declare a mistrial when they learn that jurors have been drinking. However, most judges consider drinking during deliberations more serious than drinking during the trial (Stacey and Dayton 1988). In short, it appears that judges believe that jurors must have a clearer head when deliberating the evidence than when hearing the evidence.

Jurors who engage in misconduct are rarely punished. One of the primary reasons for this is that jurors are short-term actors in the criminal justice process. Jurors who engage in misconduct are punished after the trial, so their fellow jurors are unaware of any punishment. Similarly, new jurors are entering the system everyday. They would typically not have any knowledge of prior punishment of deviant jurors. Therefore, when judges do punish jurors, it has little or no potential deterrent value. Thus, new jurors who elect to engage in misconduct have no knowledge of prior punishments imposed on other jurors. When jurors engage in misconduct, there is always the possibility that the judge will declare a mistrial. In fact, some defendants prefer mistrials, since the likelihood of a successive prosecution is minimized. One way to minimize the adverse effects of juror misconduct is the use of alternative jurors. Judges can replace offending jurors and continue with the trial.

Summary

1. Summarize the history of juries as well as the development of the grand jury and the petit jury.

The role of the jury in the common-law legal system has changed over time. Initially, juries were used very little as disputes were settled using other methods. The ancient Greeks were premiere in using persons from the community to decide on cases, at one time using the entire city of Athens to hear appeals from magistrates. The ancient Romans also used what would be an early form of the jury.

In early England, common-law juries both investigated crimes and decided the trials of accused. Eventually, it was decided that two separate units were needed for these tasks and the grand and petit juries were born. The grand jury's sole purpose was to investigate and report on crimes, whereas the petit jury was charged with determining the guilt or innocence of the accused. Over time, juries were granted more power and autonomy, and they have become an essential component of the American court process. Juries today are made up of cross sections of the community in which the crime has occurred. Indeed, juries are an integral part of our court system; as stated in the Sixth Amendment, the accused enjoys the right to a public trial by an impartial jury.

2. *Apply your knowledge of the jury selection process to obtaining a fair and impartial jury, including a definition of what the* venire *is, as well as the purpose of the* voir dire.

Most attorneys would agree that one of the most important stages in the criminal court process is the selection of the jury. It is during the jury selection process (*voir dire*) that lawyers decide who will hear the case. Both sides in the adversarial process attempt to select jurors who will be impartial. It starts with a list of potential jurors called the *venire*. Traditionally, in medieval England, the king would choose wealthy landowners to sit as jurors. Obviously this limited the number of persons eligible to become jurors.

Historically, in the United States, females were excluded from jury service as well. This has changed over time so that today persons chosen to form the *venire* are chosen from voter registration lists in an attempt to draw from a cross section of the community. Once names have been taken from this list of potential jurors, the court will send them a summons to appear for jury service. Questions relating to their citizenship status, their age, whether they suffer from any physical or mental disabilities, and also whether they have been convicted of a felony are asked to ensure they are qualified. Those who pass this initial screening are sent another letter asking them to again appear for jury service. This starts a process known as the *voir dire*. This stage further determines the appropriateness of the person to serve as a juror.

Voir dire literally means to speak the truth, and it is an opportunity for the prosecution and the defense to learn about any prejudices the potential jurors may have. This determination by both sides of impartiality is necessary to ensure a fair trial for the defendant. Although this has been referred to as jury selection, it is really the opposite where it eliminates those who are not appropriate to serve for jury duty. Some, however, argue that this process is really about the prosecution and defense determining which jurors will be sympathetic with their side. Jurors, who lawyers believe will not be sympathetic to their position, are removed.

3. *Give examples of the different ways in which jurors can be excluded, including challenges for cause and peremptory challenges.*

Two methods for removing potential jurors from the jury pool include challenges for cause and peremptory challenges. Challenges for cause are used to excuse a person from jury duty for a specific reason. They may be used to eliminate a potential juror because the person does not meet the requirements to serve (underage), has a specific bias (related or an acquaintance of the accused), or has a nonspecific bias (having prejudice toward crimes or criminals). In order to use this type of challenge, the attorney has to provide a convincing reason to the judge for the removal of the juror.

Peremptory challenges, unlike challenges for cause, do not require an explanation for the removal of a potential juror. Both sides are given a limited number of these types of challenges depending on the seriousness, or extent of pretrial publicity, of a case. In less serious cases, attorneys may receive six of these types of challenges, whereas in murder and other serious felony cases, attorneys may be given 12 or more. Attorneys can gauge the attitude of a potential juror toward crime, criminals, and even law enforcement officials by asking them certain questions. Attorneys may even have a particular profile of jurors who share certain characteristics that will be more likely to be sympathetic to their position. They can then use this information and their peremptory challenges to eliminate those persons who do not fit this profile.

4. *Describe what jury consultants are, and illustrate the science behind jury selection.*

Jury Consultants are behavioral scientists or experts who assist the prosecution or defense in jury selection processes to attempt to select a jury that will be sympathetic to their side. Some questions arise whether or not the use of research and the scientific method can actually assist in these processes. In other words, is it possible to scientifically select a jury that will help your case? Others question the use of scientific jury selection on ethical grounds that it is jury tampering and that it undermines or compromises the jury's integrity. Nonetheless, it has become big business, with associations boasting memberships in the hundreds, and success rates of 95 percent. There are, however, some who are skeptical about whether this success rate can be attributed to scientific techniques. It should also be noted that the Supreme Court has handed down several decisions regarding the jury selection process, specifically regarding where the pool of potential jurors comes from, the reasons for which a juror can be excluded from sitting on a jury, and jury size.

5. *Recognize jury sequestration and other methods of minimizing exposure of the jury to trial publicity.*

Jury sequestration is a method to isolate jurors from biases and influences from the media and the community. This is an attempt to prevent them from being subject to outside information that could possibly damage their impartiality. There have been other advantages to sequestration as well. Some believe it fosters a bonding process that better enables the jurors to come to a decision in deliberations. These advocates say that group communication is enhanced with sequestration because the jurors have formed an interpersonal connection with one another. There have, however, been critics who point out that in the same ways that sequestration can foster bonding processes, it can also foster rivalries and animosities to be formed, which would hinder coming to a decision during deliberations.

6. *Analyze the process of jury decision making and voting.*

Although jury deliberations are protected from the public, there have been some studies on how juries make decisions. After the case is given to the jury for deliberations, they usually engage in one of two methods of reaching a decision about the guilt or innocence of the defendant. The first method is the evidence-driven jury where all evidence is examined and discussed before a jury vote is taken. The second form of decision making is the verdict-driven jury. In this scenario, the jury first conducts a vote and then, if needed, the evidence is examined and discussed. However, if all jurors agree on the verdict, their deliberations are concluded.

7. *Understand some of the current controversies surrounding jury verdicts, including jury nullification.*

From time to time we hear stories of the justice system failing to convict guilty defendants; this often occurs when in a high-profile case, the public perceives an obviously guilty person has been found not guilty by a jury. Those critical of the jury system might argue that juries are too lenient or even that juries are incompetent to hear complicated testimony. They would argue that judges are in a better position to make determinations of guilt or innocence based on law and evidence that is presented at trial. Most research, however, reveals that the verdicts of judges and juries would essentially be the same 80 percent of the

time. In the other 20 percent or so of cases, juries acquit when judges would have convicted. Although we don't know the reasons for this difference in the 20 percent of cases, juries are very powerful in our adversarial system to determine guilt or innocence and their decision stands.

For example, jury nullification is the when a jury returns a verdict contrary to the evidence presented in the case. More often than not this is where the jury finds a defendant not guilty although the evidence strongly shows the defendant's guilt. The refusal of juries to apply the law is in their purview because the jury is the finder of fact and has the absolute authority to acquit the defendant regardless of the evidence. The constitutional protection against double jeopardy makes the jury's acquittal irreversible. This often occurs where a jury believes that following the letter of the law would be a miscarriage of justice. The right to a jury trial is also seen as protection from an oppressive government and a check and balance on state power.

8. *Identify what constitutes jury or juror misconduct.*

Finally, juror misconduct can be minor (lying to avoid jury service) or serious (engaging in improper conduct while serving on a jury), but is an ever-present concern, especially since today's trials are much longer, increasing the opportunity for engaging in inappropriate behavior. Engaging in inappropriate or prohibited behavior while serving as a juror, however, is the most serious form of juror misconduct. While juror misconduct has always plagued the jury system, it is more of a problem today than in the past. In the past, felony trials may only have a couple of witnesses and trials were over in half a day. Today, trials are much longer and jurors have more unsupervised time. This provides jurors with more opportunities to be exposed to external influences and bribes, or to discuss evidence and the case prior to final deliberations, and especially listening to, or watching prohibited media, and conducting online research about the case. Because juror punishment is rare and usually only involves a fine or a short time in jail, it still occurs from time to time. Another reason is that jurors are short-term actors in the criminal justice process, so their fellow jurors and future jurors are unaware of any punishment.

Key Terms

affirmative registration *120*	juror misconduct *134*	scientific jury selection *126*
blue-ribbon jury *132*	jury nullification *133*	*venire 120*
challenge for cause *122*	jury sequestration *130*	venireman list *120*
evidence-driven jury *131*	peremptory challenge *122*	verdict-driven jury *131*
grand jury *119*	petit jury *119*	*voir dire 121*

Critical Thinking Exercises

1. The job of jury consultants is to assist both defense and prosecuting attorneys in figuring out the types of people who will be most likely inclined to find in favor or against particular defendants. Several jury consultant firms have bragged that they have a nearly perfect batting average in picking juries favorable to defendants. However, the job of being a jury consultant is becoming increasingly difficult. This is primarily because of media coverage, particularly in high-profile trials. When allowed by judges, jury-consulting firms can develop questionnaires that seek to draw out potential biases among jurors through a blend of psychology and educated guesswork, but their work to shape a favorable jury panel for a particular defendant is limited. What do you think? Can prospective jurors' behaviors be predicted with precision?

2. Are juries pro-police? Numerous tragic events have recently occurred where unarmed African American men have lost their lives at the hands of the police. From Ferguson, Missouri to Baltimore, Maryland, despite public outcry, prosecutors have been unable to prosecute and convict some of the officers involved in the incidents. Do juries give police the benefit of the doubt because of the job that they are tasked with, even if it appears that they may have crossed boundaries related to excessive use of force? Amid allegations of pro-police officer bias, there have been numerous incidents around the United States to undermine public confidence in police officers. Even though these officers may have been bad apples, and the majority of officers on the force do not exhibit these behaviors, officers are more often than not acquitted. Do you think juries are pro-police, or is it just more difficult to find them guilty because of the nature of their job? How can juries be selected in ways that minimize their possible bias and unfair attitudes?

Case Study Decision-Making Exercise

In the case of *Miller-El v. Cockrell* (2003), Thomas Miller-El, his wife Dorothy, and Kenneth Flowers robbed a Holiday Inn in Dallas, Texas, in 1985. They bound and gagged two employees and then shot them. One employee died, but the other recovered and was able to identify Miller-El and his associates as his assailants. Subsequently, Miller-El was indicted and tried for capital murder in a Dallas criminal court in 1986. During jury selection, the prosecutor used his peremptory challenges to exclude 10 of the 11 African American prospective jurors, thus creating a largely white jury. Following the jury selection, Miller-El moved to strike the jury on the grounds that the prosecution had violated the Equal Protection Clause of the Fourteenth Amendment by excluding African Americans through the use of peremptory challenges. Miller-El's motion was denied. Upon his subsequent conviction for murder, Miller-El was sentenced to death. He began a lengthy series of appeals, contending that blacks had been systematically excluded from the jury. During his appeals, the case of *Batson v. Kentucky* (1986) was decided and established a three-part process for evaluating claims that a prosecutor used peremptory challenges in violation of the Equal Protection Clause. Both Texas appellate court and the federal Fifth Circuit Court of Appeals denied Miller-El's petitions, citing that insufficient evidence existed to show bias on the part of the prosecutor. The U.S. Supreme Court heard the case and disagreed. The U.S. Supreme Court overturned the circuit court, holding that Miller-El was entitled to appeal the issue of biased jury selection in his original trial. Do you think that the make-up of the jury would matter in crimes as heinous as these? Do you think that the Supreme Court despite the nature of the crimes was making a statement about the jury selection process and how prosecutors select juries to make it clear that no matter the crime, the process of selecting a jury must be without prejudice to uphold the Sixth Amendment right to a fair trial by an impartial jury? Why do you think that prosecutors despite the heinous nature of the crime and substantial evidence against the defendants would still attempt to thwart the rules of jury selection and systematically remove jurors that are the same race as the defendant?

Concept Review Questions

1. Describe the history and development of the grand jury.
2. How has jury size changed over time?
3. What is jury nullification? Do you agree or disagree that juries should have this power?
4. Describe the difference between evidence-driven juries and verdict-driven juries.
5. Should defendants be allowed to spend money to hire scientific jury consultants? If so, does this give them an unfair advantage?
6. What is *voir dire*?
7. What is the relevant case law that has shaped our current constitutional requirement on jury size?
8. What are some of the types of hardships cited by contemporary prospective jurors to avoid jury duty?
9. What are several different forms of juror misconduct?

Suggested Readings

1. J. J. Tomkovicz (2012). "Twenty-Five Years of Batson: An Introduction to Equal Protection Regulation of Peremptory Jury Challenges." *Iowa Law Review* **97:** 1393–1969.
2. D. Hale (2016). *The Jury in America.* University Press of Kansas.
3. John Clark (2000). "The Social Psychology of Jury Nullification." *Law and Psychology Review* **24:**39–57.
4. A. R. Nance (2014). "Social Media Selection: How Jury Consultants Can Use Social Media to Build a More Favorable Jury." *Law and Psychology Review* **39:**267.
5. E. Finch and V. E. Munro (2005). "Juror Stereotypes and Blame Attribution in Rape Cases Involving Intoxicants." *British Journal of Criminology* **45:**25–38.
6. Harry Kalven Jr. and Hans Zeisel (1966). *The American Jury.* Little, Brown and Company.

misdemeanors, felonies, or both. The use of the term *alleged* is critical because guilt is only established through a trial proceeding or plea bargaining. The chapter opens by discussing arrests and the booking process. Arrested persons are ordinarily taken to local lockups or jails, where they are processed and held. Early in a defendant's processing, he/she will have an initial appearance before a judicial official or magistrate. The initial appearance is important because it is usually during such a proceeding that the matter of bail is raised and settled.

Bail is a surety that guarantees a defendant's subsequent appearance in court for further proceedings, including a criminal trial. The right to bail is examined and discussed. Not everyone is entitled to bail as a matter of right. Normally, persons who are likely to flee the jurisdiction or pose a significant danger or risk to others are denied bail. For others, bail is largely discretionary with the judicial official. Many persons are released on their own recognizance, or ROR, and the reasons for such a release are described. Bail bonds and the bonding process are described in some detail. The Bail Reform Act of 1984 is defined and discussed, and its implications for criminal defendants are described. Several bail experiments have been conducted in different jurisdictions, and the results of some of these studies will be presented and evaluated. Whenever persons placed on bail do not appear for additional criminal proceedings later, bounty hunters or fugitive recovery agents are sent after them. The practice of using bounty hunters is examined, and several examples of bounty hunter activities are discussed.

Although, as described in previous chapters, the trial process is rare (most cases are processed through some type of plea agreement), there are many different types of trial systems. A trial could involve a judge (bench trial) or a jury of one's peers (jury trial). A jury trial begins with the selection of a 12-member jury. A bench trial is simply a trial by judge, and is usually conducted for defendants charged with petty offenses. In this type of trial, the defendant waives his/her right to a jury trial and the judge hears the evidence, and then decides on the case according to the rules of law. Those persons who are charged with felonies are guaranteed the right to a jury trial. In these cases, the jury will hear the case and decide guilt or innocence based on the facts presented, and then the judge would be responsible for handing out a sentence, if one was mandated. In many jurisdictions, voter registration lists are used to select persons from the community for possible jury service. These persons form the pool from which the jurors will be selected. The jury selection process is important in order to ensure the defendant a fair trial. That process will further be presented in this chapter.

Several constitutional amendments pertain to jury trials and one's right to a trial. The Sixth Amendment guarantees all persons the right to a trial by jury. The Seventh Amendment provides that the right of trial by jury shall be preserved. And finally, the Fourteenth Amendment provides that no state shall make or enforce any law that deprives citizens of their right to due process or of enjoying all privileges or immunities as citizens.

The chapter begins by examining one's right to a speedy trial. The idea of a speedy trial varies among the states and the federal government. Several important speedy trial cases will be presented. According to the federal government, a speedy trial occurs within a 100-day timeline. Probably the longest speedy trial period is in New Mexico, which sets forth a 180-day timeline for a trial. Some states have speedy trial provisions of 90 days. These different definitions of speedy trials will be examined.

Next, bench and jury trials will be distinguished. The process of selecting jurors is described in detail, commencing with the creation of a list of prospective jurors called a *venire* and following through with a screening process known as *voir dire*. Once jury members have been selected and the trial commences, judges still serve the function of observing rules of criminal procedure. These rules govern the conduct of trial proceedings. Other rules, such as rules of evidence, govern the nature of evidence that may be introduced or excluded.

Trial proceedings are also accompanied by several pretrial motions. Such motions will be described and explained. Both the prosecution and defense present opening statements. The government presents its case against the defendant, followed by the defense's case. Witnesses

▼

from both sides are called in these adversarial proceedings. Witnesses could include eyewitnesses, who give an interpretation of the events as they saw them and provide the degree to which the defendant may or may not have been involved, or expert witnesses, who are used by both sides to interpret the meaning of certain types of evidence. Witnesses are cross-examined by each side to determine their veracity and credibility. When the trial is concluded, the prosecution and defense present summations or closing arguments and the jury deliberates. Juries either reach unanimous verdicts or judgments or fail to agree. The process of jury deliberation and voting will be described. Both the federal government and the states have different criteria that govern jury deliberations and voting, either for a defendant's guilt or acquittal. These different scenarios will be described. The chapter concludes with an examination of the aftermath of jury deliberations and verdicts, as well as the judge's role in sentencing.

▶ Arrest and Booking

Arrest

An arrest means taking offenders into custody. Usually, arrests of criminal suspects are made by police officers.

Arrested persons are referred to as arrestees. Arrests of suspects may be made directly by police officers who observe law violations. Depending upon whether a misdemeanor or felony is alleged, officers must have at least reasonable suspicion to stop and detain for investigation anyone suspected of committing a felony. If subsequent developments provide the officers with probable cause to believe that the suspects they have detained probably committed the alleged offense, the officers can arrest the suspect(s) and take them to jail for further processing and identification. If a misdemeanor is committed and is not directly observed by the officer, the officer may stop suspects and make inquiries. But without reasonable suspicion to inquire further, officers are not empowered to arrest possible misdemeanants if the officers lack probable cause (Beger 2003; Stalans et al. 2004).

In a felony case, for instance, officers in a cruiser sitting on the shoulder of Highway 55 may receive a report that a convenience store was just robbed by two men wielding shotguns. The men were described as a white male wearing a red cap and a Hispanic male wearing a green cap. The men were last seen driving east on Highway 55 in a black 1966 Chevrolet van. Just then a black 1966 Chevrolet van driven by a white man in a red cap goes by. The officers give chase and eventually stop the van. The officers cautiously approach and order the suspects to exit from the van. When the suspects are out of the van, the officers observe that the passenger is Hispanic and is wearing a green cap. The officers shine their flashlights into the van's interior and see some money bags on the back seat. These similarities are overwhelming, and thus the officers arrest the two men on suspicion of robbing the convenience store. While these officers didn't see the actual robbery, the descriptions of the fleeing suspects, their vehicle, and the money bags in the van have provided the officers with probable cause to make the arrests.

Booking

Once persons have been arrested, they are usually booked. Booking is an administrative procedure obtaining personal background information about arrestees for law enforcement officers (Palermo 2004). Booking includes compiling a file for defendants, including their name, address, telephone number, age, place of work, any relatives, and other personal data. The extensiveness of the booking procedure varies among jurisdictions. Most jurisdictions now have a digital booking procedure, utilizing digital photographing and fingerprinting of criminal suspects. Some jurisdictions also screen for any mental health or

arrest taking persons into custody and restraining them until they can be brought before court to answer the charges against them.

arrestees persons who have been arrested by police for suspicion of committing a crime.

misdemeanor crime punishable by fines and/or imprisonment, usually in a city or county jail, for periods of less than one year.

felony crime punishable by incarceration, usually in a state or federal prison, for periods of one year or longer.

probable cause reasonable belief that a crime has been committed and that a particular person committed it.

reasonable suspicion warranted suspicion (short of probable cause) that a person may be engaged in criminal conduct.

booking process of making written report of arrest, including name and address of arrested persons, the alleged crimes, arresting officers, place and time of arrest, physical description of suspect, photographs, sometimes called "mug shots," and fingerprints.

substance abuse problems. Today, many persons with mental health and substance abuse issues are winding up in the justice system, and many jurisdictions flag these persons for treatment and diversion rather than incarceration depending on the crime committed. Sometimes, arrestees are merely detained for several hours and released on personal or commercial bond (Sacks and Pearson 2003). They are usually required to appear in court later to face charges. For example, those arrested for drunk driving may be held temporarily in a local jail overnight. When they are sober in the morning, they are released but must appear before a judge to face DWI charges later. A growing number of jurisdictions are also videotaping the entire booking process for individual offenders, in the event that irregular or improper actions are exhibited by jail or police officers as offenders are booked (Schulman 2005). Booking is also a phase of pretrial services. One reason for videotaping this phase is to ensure that discrimination does not occur based on racial, ethnic, gender, or socioeconomic factors (Lobo-Antunes 2004).

▶ Initial Appearance

initial appearance
formal proceeding during which the judge advises the defendant of the charges, including a recitation of the defendant's rights and a bail decision.

The **initial appearance** of a defendant before a magistrate is a formal proceeding during which a magistrate or other judicial official advises the defendant of the charges. An initial appearance follows the booking process. The magistrate determines from a reading of the charges whether or not they are petty offenses. Petty or minor offenses vary in interpretation among states. Indicators of petty offenses are usually small fines (less than $500) and short sentences (six months or less) associated with the criminal offense. More serious offenses involve larger fines and longer sentences, usually one year or longer in duration (Champion 2005b).

Crime seriousness has been critical in determining whether or not defendants have a right to a jury trial. For instance, the case of *Duncan v. Louisiana* (1968) involved a 19-year-old man who was convicted and sentenced to serve 60 days in jail and pay a $150 fine for simple battery. Duncan requested a jury trial but was denied one. Louisiana claimed that Duncan's crime was a petty offense and thus the offense did not entitle him to a jury trial. The U.S. Supreme Court disagreed. The high court observed that Louisiana's law pertaining to battery, although a misdemeanor or petty offense, carried a two-year maximum sentence and a $300 fine. The U.S. Supreme Court observed that most states define petty offenses as punishable for terms less than one year, and in some jurisdictions, the maximum sentence is no more than six months and a $50 fine. Without defining precisely, the meaning of a petty offense, the U.S. Supreme Court said that "We need not . . . settle in this case the exact location of the line between petty offenses and serious crimes. It is sufficient for our purposes to hold that a crime punishable by two years in prison is . . . a serious crime and not a petty offense." Duncan's conviction was overturned.

The Sixth Amendment says that all persons in criminal prosecutions are entitled to the right to a speedy and public trial, by an impartial jury of the state. But this amendment is interpreted differently depending upon the jurisdiction where the petty offenses are committed. Some jurisdictions discourage jury trials to resolve petty offense charges. In a New Jersey case, a defendant was indicted by a federal grand jury on federal misdemeanor charges, and the prosecutor for the government expressed strongly the opinion that the man ought to waive his jury trial rights. The man refused, and so the prosecutor brought new felony charges against the man in retaliation. In this case, the court dismissed all charges against the man as the fair remedy, and the prosecutor was criticized for his misconduct (*United States v. Lippi*, 1977).

When any crime is alleged, it is important for defendants to be advised of the specific charges against them (Nunn 2003). They should also be advised of their rights under the circumstances (Vaughn, Topalli, and Pierre 2004). When persons are arrested by police, their initial appearance before a magistrate, therefore, is a formal proceeding where defendants are advised of the charges against them. At that time, the magistrate advises the defendants of their rights, and bail is considered. This is also the occasion where magistrates determine the date for a preliminary examination or a preliminary hearing to establish whether probable cause exists to move forward toward a trial. Between the time of defendants' initial appearance and the preliminary hearing or examination, defendants can hire defense counsel to represent them (Nunn 2003). If a defendant is indigent, then an attorney will be appointed by the court to represent him or her. Before we examine preliminary examinations or hearings, the bail process will be described.

▶ The Right to Bail

Bail has its roots in New England in the 1690s. Early English common law applicable during that period encompassed many of the guarantees later included in the Bill of Rights, including the right against unreasonable searches and seizures, double jeopardy, compulsory self-incrimination, grand jury indictment, trial by jury, and the right to bail (Hermida 2005; Kuckes 2004). Bail is not unique to the United States. Other countries, such as Australia, have done much to establish bail provisions for criminal defendants and conditions under which bail is granted (Demuth 2003).

Following one's arrest, a decision is made about whether the defendant will be brought to trial. If a trial is imminent because of case seriousness, most defendants can obtain their temporary release from jail. Many arrestees may not have to post bail, in that they are eligible for release on their own recognizance (ROR). If they have strong community ties and it is unlikely that they will flee from the jurisdiction, they may be freed on their own recognizance (ROR) by the magistrate or judicial officer (Harris and Dagadakis 2004).

> **bail** surety provided by defendants or others to guarantee their subsequent appearance in court to face criminal charges; is denied when suspects are considered dangerous or likely to flee.

> **release on their own recognizance (ROR)** arrangement where defendants are able to be set free temporarily to await a later trial without having to post a bail bond.

BOX 7-1

KEY CASES: THE RIGHT TO BAIL

Schilb v. Kuebel, 404 U.S. 357 (1971)

In a case in Illinois in which a defendant was ultimately acquitted, 1 percent of the bail amount was forfeited to the bail bond company, which by Illinois law is permitted to make a small amount of money as a commission for posting bail for criminal suspects. Schilb and others filed a class-action suit against the bail bond company as being discriminatory and unconstitutional in its procedures. They further challenged the release-on-own-recognizance scheme as discriminatory. The U.S. Supreme Court upheld the Illinois bail law, saying that its fee of 1 percent of bail was not excessive and that there had been no discrimination between the poor and the rich; in short, the Illinois law did not violate any constitutional amendment.

Stack v. Boyle, 342 U.S. 1 (1951)

Stack was charged with conspiracy to commit a crime, and bail was set at $50,000. She protested, saying that the bail was excessive and that no hearing was ever held to determine how much bail should be set. The U.S.

Supreme Court agreed with Stack and remanded the case back to the district court, where a hearing could be held on the bail issue. The Court held that bail had not been fixed by proper methods in this case. It did not try to determine or define "proper methods," however.

United States v. Salerno, 481 U.S. 739 (1987)

Salerno and others were arrested for several serious crimes and held without bail as dangerous under the Bail Reform Act of 1984. Salerno was convicted and sentenced to 100 years in prison. He appealed, being among the first to challenge the constitutionality of the new Bail Reform Act and its provision that specifies that dangerous persons may be detained prior to trial until such time as their case may be decided. He objected that the new act violated the Eighth Amendment provision against "cruel and unusual" punishment. The Supreme Court upheld the constitutionality of pretrial detention and declared that it did not violate the defendant's rights under the Eighth Amendment if a specific defendant was found to be dangerous.

---

bail bond a written guarantee, often accompanied by money or other securities, that the person charged with an offense will remain within the court's jurisdiction to face trial at a time in the future.

cash bail bond situation where defendants obtain release by paying in cash the full amount, which is recoverable after the required court appearances are made.

bail bond companies any organization established for the purpose of posting bail for criminal suspects.

bail bondsperson, bail bondsman person who is in the business of posting bail for criminal suspects. Usually charges a percentage of whatever bail has been set.

When the character of the defendant is unknown, or if the offenses alleged are quite serious (e.g., aggravated assault, rape, and armed robbery), the magistrate will often set bail or specify a **bail bond**. Bail is a surety to procure the release of those under arrest, to assure that they will appear to face charges in court at a later date. A bail bond is a written guarantee, often accompanied by money or other securities, so the person charged with an offense will remain in the court's jurisdiction to face trial at a time in the future (Demuth 2003).

Motorists may be required to post a **cash bail bond** for minor traffic violations such as speeding or reckless driving. These cash bonds guarantee the motorist's appearance in court later to face charges of violating traffic laws. If the motorist fails to appear, the cash bond is forfeited. The bond set is often the exact amount of the fine for violating the traffic law anyway.

When arrestees do not have the money to post their bail, they may use **bail bond companies**. These companies are usually located near jails. For a fee, they provide the service of posting bail for various offenders. **Bail bondsmen or bondspersons** appear at the jail and post bond for defendants. Defendants are usually required to pay the bonding company a fee for this service, which is 10 percent of the bail bond set by the magistrate. For instance, if the bond set by the magistrate for a particular offense is $25,000, the bonding company may post this bond for the defendant if the defendant is considered a good risk, and if the defendant or an associate of the defendant pays the bonding company a nonrefundable fee of $2,500. If a defendant is unable to pay the fee and no one will pay it for him/her, the defendant must remain in jail until trial is held.

▶ Bail Bondsmen and Bonding Companies

Bail bondsmen are persons who either own or work for bonding companies. Bonding companies are authorized to post bail for various criminal suspects up to a fixed amount. Bonding companies usually have property investments and other capital that they use as a type of insurance with a city or county government. For example, a bonding company may be authorized by a city to post bonds of up to $5 million for various persons charged with crimes. The bonding company owner may have stocks, securities, property, and other assets that he/she has assigned to the city or county as collateral. Thus, the city or county is protected from a potential loss of revenue if the bonding company guarantees the bond amount for the release of a defendant. If the defendant fails to appear later in court, the bonding company forfeits the bond it has posted unless it can produce the defendant later.

If the bonding company is authorized to write bonds of up to $5 million, once this ceiling has been reached, the bonding company can no longer write bonds for defendants. Bonding companies are released from their obligations to cities or counties once defendants have been convicted or acquitted of crimes, or the bail bonds are canceled. Bonding companies profit from the 10 percent nonrefundable fees they collect from persons who want to be released from jail before their trials are held. In most jurisdictions, there are several bonding companies that can provide bail for various arrestees.

▶ Competing Goals of Bail

excessive bail any bail amount that so grossly exceeds the proportionality of the seriousness of the offense so as to be prohibited by the Eighth Amendment.

Under the Eighth Amendment, citizens are advised that **excessive bail** shall not be required, nor excessive fines imposed. Some citizens believe that regardless of the offense alleged, bail will be set and defendants will be permitted to remain free until the date of trial. This is not true. Depending upon the circumstances of a particular criminal offense and the evidence obtained, some defendants may have a very high bail, while others may not be granted bail at all. They will be required to remain in jail until trial.

The Eighth Amendment provision against excessive bail means that bail shall not be excessive in those cases where it is proper to grant bail (*United States v. Giangrosso*, 1985). The right to bail is not an absolute one under the Eighth Amendment (*United States v. Bilanzich*, 1985; *United States v. Provenzano*, 1985). In some cases, suspects are detained for trial without bail (*United States v. Acevedo-Ramos*, 1984), while in others defendants are subject to detention if they are unable to pay high bail ranging from $25,000 to $1 million (*United States v. Szott*, 1985; *United States v. Jessup*, 1985). If a murder suspect is caught in the act or is a habitual offender, bail will probably be denied. This is because it is probable that such defendants will attempt to flee the jurisdiction to avoid prosecution, or may be a danger to the community. States vary in permitting judges the discretion for making this decision.

Whether or not bail is granted is not exclusively determined by whether a crime is violent (Harris and Dagadakis 2004). More than a few defendants who are charged with nonviolent crimes are denied bail. Magistrates consider the totality of circumstances in setting bail on a case-by-case basis. A former bank president was denied bail in a case alleging fraudulent manipulation and theft of depositors' funds. While the former bank president had substantial community ties and property interests to protect, he also had a recently acquired passport and travel visas to several foreign countries where he also maintained property and business interests. In addition, $50 million in bank funds were missing as the result of a federal audit. The magistrate considered the bank president to be a risk if granted bail. There was a strong likelihood that the bank president would flee the jurisdiction and live on the embezzled $50 million in some remote location.

> **totality of circumstances** applied to bail decision making, where the entire set of circumstances is considered for persons considered bail-eligible.

Bail provisions of the U.S. Constitution have been challenged by the American Civil Liberties Union and other civil rights organizations. Their efforts as well as the efforts of a variety of special interest groups have prompted a number of bail reforms over the years. Some of the reasons given for such bail reforms have included the facts that (1) bail is inherently discriminatory against the poor or indigent defendants; (2) those who are unable to post a bail bond and must remain in jail cannot adequately prepare a defense or correspond effectively with their attorneys; (3) there is considerable variation from one jurisdiction to the next and from one case to the next within the same jurisdiction for establishing a bail bond for similar offenses; (4) withholding bail or prescribing prohibitively high bail offends our sense of one's presumption of innocence until guilt is proven in court; and (5) those who pose no risk to the community may suffer loss of job or other benefits from detention as the result of bail. It would seem, therefore, that to deny a defendant bail would be contrary to the presumption of innocence, which is an integral part of due process. Nevertheless, the right to bail is not absolute (Harris and Dagadakis 2004).

Race, gender, and socioeconomic status have been among the variables examined to determine their differential impact on bail decision making. These are extralegal variables and should have absolutely no bearing on whether a defendant is granted bail. However, minorities seem to be at a definite disadvantage in the criminal justice system regarding bail decision making. Racial or gender differences seem to make a difference to judges when making pretrial release and/or bail decisions about particular defendants. For instance, female defendants are granted more lenient pretrial release terms compared with men in many jurisdictions (Jordan 2004a).

Katz and Spohn (1995) investigated whether these data might show a pattern of discrimination in bail decision making according to race or gender. A sample of 8,414 defendants was divided according to race and gender. Because of missing information, the sample consisted of 6,625 records for black defendants and 1,005 for white defendants. A small percent of the sample were females. These researchers asked whether it made any difference in the bail decision, as well as the amount of bail, whether defendants were black or white or male or female. When taking offense and prior record into account, race made no difference on the bail decision. However, gender did make a difference. For different types of offenses, female defendants faced significantly lower bail compared with their male counterparts. Regarding pretrial release decision making, however, white defendants were more likely to be released before trial compared with black defendants. Further, females tended to be granted pretrial release more than males. These findings are inclusive, but they suggest that while race and gender may help to explain bail and pretrial release decisions, these variables may not be as important in influencing these pretrial release and bail decisions as was previously thought by other investigators. Other researchers have found similar inconsistencies in bail decision making and race and gender variables (Gallinetti, Redpath, and Sloth-Nielsen 2004).

The bail reform movement assumes that bail is inherently discriminatory. The **Bail Reform Act** was passed in 1966 and provided that the purpose of this act is to revise the practices relating to bail to assure that all persons, regardless of their financial status, shall not needlessly be detained pending their appearance to answer charges. More recently, the **Bail Reform Act of 1984** was passed that vested magistrates and judicial officers with greater autonomy in bail-setting and releasing persons on their own recognizance (Champion 2005b). Presently, bail is available only to those entitled to bail. These are usually persons who do not pose a threat to themselves or others and/or do not pose escape risks. There is nothing inherently unconstitutional about keeping persons jailed prior to their trials, however, under various forms of pretrial detention (*United States v. Salerno*, 1987). Sometimes, pretrial detention of suspects is abused and lawmakers should keep its use within reasonable limits. One reason for this belief is that it is often difficult to forecast accurately who will or will not be dangerous or good candidates for bail (Champion 2007).

Several states have passed **sexual predator laws**, which are targeted at violent sex offenders (Levenson 2004). Washington State, for instance, passed a Sexual Predator Act in 1990 aimed at those likely to engage in future acts of sexual violence. However, the act was soundly criticized because of its failure to cite realistic predictive criteria that would identify which sex offenders would actually commit future dangerous sexual acts following some type of sex therapy or treatment. Although such laws have drawn criticisms from various civil rights groups, the U.S. Supreme Court upheld the constitutionality of such laws in 1998.

Interestingly, Nebraska passed a sexual predator law concerning a sex offender's right to bail in 1978, 20 years before the U.S. Supreme Court upheld the constitutionality of the Washington State Sexual Predator Act. In 1978, Nebraska amended its constitution to require the denial of bail to defendants charged with forcible sex offenses when the proof is evident and the presumption of guilt is great. Other jurisdictions, such as Texas and California, have enacted similar provisions (Champion 2005b).

▶ Other Forms of Pretrial Release

The 1984 Bail Reform Act was innovative in that it contained provisions for judicial officers to release defendants subject to certain conditions, such as (1) complying with a curfew; (2) reporting on a regular basis to a designated law enforcement agency; (3) abiding by specific restrictions on one's personal associations, place of abode, and travel; (4) maintaining or commencing an educational program; and (5) maintaining employment or actively seeking employment if currently unemployed.

Before the Bail Reform Act of 1984 was passed, experiments were conducted to determine the effectiveness of ROR. A National Bail Study was conducted in 20 jurisdictions in the United States (Thomas 1976, 1977) between 1962 and 1971. There was a significant

Bail Reform Act original act passed in 1966 to assure that bail practices would be revised to ensure that all persons, regardless of their financial status, shall not needlessly be detained to answer criminal charges.

Bail Reform Act of 1984 revision of original 1966 Bail Reform Act where changes in bail practices were implemented to assure that all persons, regardless of their financial status, shall not needlessly be detained to answer criminal charges; gave judges and magistrates greater autonomy to decide conditions under which bail would be granted or denied.

sexual predator laws somewhat ambiguous laws enacted in various states to identify and control previously convicted sex offenders; may include listing such persons in public announcements or bulletins, or some other form of community notification.

drop in both felony and misdemeanor defendants who were detained in jails during those years, and there was an accompanying increase in the numbers of defendants who were released on their own recognizance (ROR). More judges seemed to be relying on ROR for the pretrial release of defendants, and thus, this meant more limited use of cash bonds, a primary criticism of bail opponents.

Between January 1981 and March 1982, an experiment was conducted concerning bail guidelines in the Philadelphia Municipal Court. This was called the Philadelphia Experiment (Goldkamp and Gottfredson 1984). Twenty-two judges were selected for experimentation. One objective of the study was to create visible guidelines for judges to follow in using ROR in lieu of bail in pretrial release decisions. When bail was established, median bail figures for judges not following prescribed guidelines was $2,000 whereas the median bail figure was $1,500 for those judges adhering to the guidelines provided.

Although the findings were inconsistent regarding the use of ROR, the researchers said that the experiment yielded significant improvements in the equity of bail decisions for defendants generally. The study also encouraged greater use of supervised or conditional release programs as outlined within the Bail Reform Act of 1984. As the Philadelphia Experiment suggested, this alternative would provide some degree of relief for jail over-crowding at the very least.

Subsequently, the New York City Department of Correction discharged 611 jail inmates in November 1983 (Gerwitz 1987). Of these, 75 percent were released on bail, while 25 percent were released on their own recognizance. Only four ROR defendants were charged with felonies, while about 75 percent of the bail defendants were similarly charged. Forty percent of the released defendants failed to appear for at least one pretrial hearing. ROR defendants were far more likely than bail-release defendants to fail to appear in court later. Over a third of the ROR defendants were rearrested prior to trial. Failure to appear means that persons scheduled for trial and are temporarily released on bail or ROR do not show up in court on their scheduled trial dates. Although obligating defendants to post bail does not necessarily guarantee their subsequent court appearances, it does result in fewer failures to appear compared with those released on ROR.

▶ Bounty Hunters

It is advantageous for bonding companies if the defendant can post property assets as collateral for the bonding fee. Thus, if a defendant leaves the jurisdiction before trial and jumps bond, the bonding company forfeits the bond it has posted with the court, but it is entitled to seize the defendant's tangible assets or property to cover the cost of the forfeited bond. Defendants may bypass bonding companies altogether by pledging their own real property assets to the court as bond in lieu of confinement. Courts are permitted to accept other types of assets, such as bank deposits, securities, or valuable personal property. When defendants must post their own property as bail, there is a greater likelihood that they will appear later in court compared with those defendants who have bail posted for them by bonding companies. The bail options available to defendants vary among jurisdictions (Dabney, Collins, and Topalli 2004).

When bonding companies provide bond for defendants, they do so on the assumption that bailees will reappear later in court to face the criminal charges against them. Bonding companies avoid furnishing bail to those likely to jump bail and leave the jurisdiction to avoid a subsequent criminal prosecution. Jumping bail means to leave the jurisdiction while on bail to avoid prosecution. However, a certain number of defendants leave the jurisdiction and fail to appear later in court. When this happens, the bonding company forfeits its bond to the city or county court. The more bail jumpers a bonding company has, the less bonding funds it has available to use for other defendants. Sizeable profits are

Philadelphia Experiment study conducted involving setting bail guidelines in Philadelphia, Pennsylvania, during 1981–1982 and the use of release on one's own recognizance (ROR); experiment led to greater equity in bail decision making for persons of different socioeconomic statuses.

failure to appear when defendants fail to present themselves for trial or some other formal proceeding, such as arraignment or a preliminary hearing/examination.

jumping bail act by defendant of leaving jurisdiction where trial is to be held. Attempt by defendant to avoid prosecution on criminal charges.

lost, at least temporarily, whenever someone jumps bail. For this reason, many bonding companies post bounties or monetary incentives to employ bounty hunters to track bail jumpers down for a fee and bring them to court. These persons are more recently known as fugitive recovery agents and bail recovery agents (Dabney et al. 2004). Unfortunately, we have been unable to devise foolproof mechanisms for predicting which defendants will jump bail and which ones won't jump bail. However, some prediction models work better than others.

In recent years, there have been several incidents involving acts of irresponsibility of bail bondsmen and bounty hunters. Specifically, the wrong persons have been targeted as bail jumpers. As a result, several innocent victims have suffered either serious injuries or deaths as the result of a bounty hunter's actions. Despite these inappropriate and indiscriminate actions by bounty hunters, bondsmen continue to enjoy a broad range of procedural safeguards in surety arrests under both federal and state statutes.

▶ Preliminary Hearings

Following an initial appearance and a bail hearing, defendants are entitled to a preliminary hearing. Preliminary examinations or preliminary hearings are held after defendants have been arrested and have had their initial appearance before a magistrate. Preliminary hearings are conducted by the magistrate or judicial official to determine whether defendants charged with a crime should be held for trial. It is an opportunity for magistrates to determine if probable cause exists that a crime has been committed and the person charged committed it. The preliminary hearing is the first screening of charges against defendants.

The preliminary hearing does not establish the defendant's guilt or innocence at a trial. The government is required to present evidence or proof that (1) a crime has been committed and (2) the defendant committed the crime. If the government fails to present a convincing case to the magistrate, the charges against the defendant will be dismissed.

This option by the magistrate does not preclude the possibility that the prosecutor will take the case to the grand jury for their consideration. In those jurisdictions with grand juries, this is sometimes done. However, if the magistrate believes the case presented by the prosecutor is weak, grand juries probably will not issue indictments either. But there is an important difference in the two strategies. In preliminary hearings, defendants have the right to present facts and evidence supporting their innocence of the crimes alleged. Defendants may even cross-examine witnesses and bring in witnesses supportive of their own position. Again, this is an opportunity for magistrates to determine probable cause that a crime has been committed and the defendant committed it.

In a grand jury proceeding, however, prosecutors present only the government's side of the matter. If magistrates determine that the accused should be released for lack of probable cause, subsequent grand juries may issue indictments or presentments against defendants. In some jurisdictions, preliminary hearings are used instead of grand juries for the purpose of establishing probable cause. Defendants have the right to retain counsel, to be fully informed of the complaint against them, and of the general circumstances under which they may secure pretrial release. If the defendant cannot afford counsel, an attorney will be appointed to consult with and represent the defendant.

When the defendant appears before a magistrate, the magistrate will determine whether the defendant wishes to waive the preliminary hearing. With the exception of certain petty offenses, which may be tried by the magistrate directly, the defendant may either (1) waive the right to a preliminary hearing or (2) not waive the right to a preliminary hearing.

The Defendant Waives the Right to Preliminary Hearing

If the defendant waives his/her right to a preliminary hearing, the magistrate or judicial official will bind over the defendant to the grand jury. In those states without grand jury systems, prosecutors may file informations or criminal informations against defendants. Criminal informations are charges against defendants filed directly by prosecutors. The result of filing criminal informations against a defendant is a subsequent arraignment before a trial judge, one who will usually preside if a trial is forthcoming.

The Defendant Does Not Waive the Right to Preliminary Hearing

If the defendant does not waive the right to a preliminary hearing, then the preliminary hearing is held. The magistrate will determine whether probable cause exists or does not exist. If probable cause does not exist, in the opinion of the magistrate, the defendant is discharged. However, if probable cause exists, again in the opinion of the magistrate, then the defendant will face arraignment on the criminal charges.

Grand Jury Action

Grand juries are bodies of citizens convened to hear criminal charges against suspects. The grand jury will hear evidence from the prosecutor against the defendant and issue either a true bill or a no bill. If a no bill is issued, the defendant is discharged and the criminal charges are dismissed. If a true bill is issued, defendants face arraignment on the charges against them. About half of all states have grand jury systems.

Sometimes grand juries will be convened for special purposes. These may be investigative grand juries. Perhaps there is a car theft ring operating in several states. Grand juries are convened to hear evidence in these cases. On the basis of evidence collected and examined, these grand juries may issue presentments, which are the same thing as indictments. The difference is that presentments are not issued as the result of a request from a prosecutor. Rather, the grand jury, on its own, decides that probable cause exists that one or more persons have committed a crime and submit their own true bill. Thus, indictments are the result of requests from prosecutors to charge defendants with one or more crimes, while presentments are independent grand jury actions leading to the same result, but without prosecutor intervention. Prosecutors ordinarily present these charges before grand juries. Federal grand juries consist of 24 persons, while different states have variable numbers of grand jury members.

The result of a charge coming from the grand jury alleging certain criminal offenses on the part of defendants through indictment or presentment brings those defendants to the arraignment stage of the justice process. Thus, the arraignment stage is reached through (1) a finding of probable cause in a preliminary hearing (possibly resulting from criminal information filed by the prosecutor) or (2) an indictment or presentment from grand jury action.

Arraignments

At the federal level and for many state and local jurisdictions, an arraignment is the official proceeding where defendants are informed of the formal criminal charges against them and they enter a plea of (1) guilty, (2) not guilty, or (3) *nolo contendere.* An alternative set of pleas in the state of Kentucky includes (1) not guilty, (2) guilty, and (3) guilty, but mentally ill. Pleas of *nolo contendere* in Kentucky are prohibited, for instance.

informations written accusations made by a public prosecutor against a person for some criminal offense, without an indictment. Usually restricted to minor crimes or misdemeanors. Sometimes called criminal informations.

grand jury investigative bodies whose numbers vary among states. Duties include determining probable cause regarding commission of a crime and returning formal charges against suspects.

true bills grand jury decisions that sufficient evidence exists that a crime has been committed and that a specific suspect committed it.

no bill, or no true bill grand jury decision that insufficient evidence exists to establish probable cause that a crime was committed and a specific person committed it.

presentment an accusation, initiated by the grand jury on its own authority, from jurors' own knowledge or observation, which functions as an instruction for the preparation of an indictment.

indictments charges or written accusations found and presented by a grand jury that a particular defendant probably committed a crime.

arraignment official proceeding in which defendant is formally confronted by criminal charges and enters a plea; trial date is established.

If the arraignment stems from grand jury action rather than a preliminary hearing, a copy of the indictment or presentment is given to defendants. In many arraignments, indictments or presentments are read to defendants by either magistrates or clerks of the court.

Guilty Pleas

A guilty plea is the equivalent of a confession of guilt in open court. While the procedures vary among jurisdictions, judges usually are expected to inquire of defendants if their plea is voluntary and if they understand the nature of the charge or charges, the mandatory minimum penalty under the law, the possible maximum penalty under the law, and that they are still entitled to an attorney if they have not obtained one. Furthermore, the judge will likely also inquire whether the plea of guilty has been obtained through threats or coercion from anyone, if the defendant understands that the plea can be withdrawn and a plea of not guilty entered, if the defendant understands that they are entitled to a trial if desired, if the defendant understands that they have the right to confront witnesses against them and cross-examine them, as well as that they have the right not to incriminate themselves, and whether there is a factual basis for that plea. In short, the judge usually extends every opportunity to defendants to exercise all possible constitutional rights to which they are entitled.

Not Guilty Pleas

not guilty a defendant's formal contesting of any wrongdoing in court to charges contained in a complaint, information, or indictment.

A plea of not guilty obligates the judge to fix a date for trial. The judge also determines whether bail will be continued, if the defendant is currently out of jail on bail. Or the judge may permit defendants to continue ROR if that is their current pretrial release status. Any number of options are available to the judge at this stage. The primary decision reached in an arraignment proceeding after a plea of *not guilty* has been entered is the establishment of a trial date, however.

Nolo Contendere Pleas

A plea of *nolo contendere* is considered the legal equivalent of a guilty plea. Technically, it is not a plea of guilty, but rather, a plea of no contest. The defendant is not contesting the facts as presented by the prosecution. However, the defendant may take issue with the legality or constitutionality of the law allegedly violated. For instance, the defendant may say, "Yes, your honor, I do not question the facts presented by the prosecution that I possessed two ounces of marijuana, but I also do not believe that the law prohibiting marijuana possession is constitutionally valid."

Sometimes, businesspersons enter pleas of *nolo contendere*. Even though these pleas are treated as the equivalent to guilty pleas in criminal proceedings, they are not considered admissions of guilt in possible future civil proceedings. If a businessman is charged with a criminal offense alleging fraud in the construction of a large building, a plea of *nolo contendere* or "no contest" will result in criminal penalties being invoked. The plea will be treated as though the businessman had actually pled guilty. However, if the building collapses and some persons are injured or killed as a result, they may sue the businessman for damages in a civil action later, but they are prevented from using the *nolo contendere* plea as evidence of an admission of guilt on fraud charges against the businessman. In the case of a guilty plea to the same fraud charges, the businessman could have the plea of guilty used against him in the subsequent civil action as evidence not only of his guilt in the fraud scheme, but also of his negligence. Therefore, a *nolo contendere* plea is sometimes a strategic option for a person wishing to avoid civil liability connected with criminal activities, traffic accidents, or some other law infraction where civil liability may be incurred.

Using a "worst case" scenario, if a defendant enters a not guilty plea, then the arraignment, usually conducted by the trial judge, will accomplish three objectives. As we have seen, arraignments involve entering a plea. They also involve a finalized listing of charges against the defendant. A third objective is to set a trial date. In sum, arraignments are for the purpose of (1) setting forth all charges against a defendant, (2) entering a plea, and (3) setting a trial date. This third feature is significant inasmuch as the trial judge presiding is usually the judge who will eventually hear the case. He/she knows the court docket and schedules the defendant's trial within a relatively short period of time following the arraignment.

▶ Trial Process and Procedures

The Speedy Trial

Many options are available to defendants from the time they are arrested to the time they are arraigned and a trial date is set. In fact, there are many contingencies available to defendants even during the trial and after the conclusion of it.

A plea of not guilty by a defendant will obligate the presiding judge to set a trial date and eventually conduct a trial. Normally, this is the case unless some alternative plea is entered, or the prosecution elects to drop charges against the defendant, or if an agreement can be reached between the defendant and prosecutor whereby a formal trial can be avoided. This last contingency is usually referred to as a plea bargain agreement.

Federal courts are bound by law to observe the Speedy Trial Act of 1974 and its subsequent 1979 and 1984 amendments. The purposes of the Speedy Trial Act are (1) to clarify the rights of defendants, (2) to ensure that (alleged) criminals are brought to justice promptly, and (3) to give effect to a citizen's Sixth Amendment right to a speedy trial (*Klopfer v. North Carolina*, 1967).

According to the provisions of this act, suspects must be charged with a criminal offense within 30 days following their arrest or receipt of a summons. Then the trial should commence not less than 30 days or more than 70 days from the suspect's initial appearance. A 100-day federal provision exists, which is spread out as follows: 30 days from arrest to initial appearance; 10 days from initial appearance to an arraignment; and 60 days from the date of an arraignment to trial.

> **Speedy Trial Act of 1974 (amended 1979, 1984)** compliance with Sixth Amendment provision for a citizen to be brought to trial without undue delay of 30–70 days from date of formal specification of charges, usually in arraignment proceeding.

The leading case relating to a speedy trial is *Klopfer v. North Carolina* (1967). In Klopfer's case, he was charged with criminal trespass. Klopfer eventually went to court and his case resulted in a mistrial. Klopfer then tried to find out if the government intended to prosecute him again for the same crime, but government officials declined to make a commitment. Instead, they formally entered upon the court record a "*nolle prosequi* with leave," which meant that while they were permitting the defendant to be discharged, they were allowing themselves an opportunity to retry Klopfer at a later, unspecified date. This case eventually came before the U.S. Supreme Court, where it was declared that the government violated Klopfer's Sixth and Fourteenth Amendment rights, and that it was unconstitutional to indefinitely postpone his trial without providing an adequate reason. The Supreme Court cited some of the reasons for its decision to endorse a speedy trial provision, which included the facts that (1) witness testimony would be more credible through an early trial; (2) the defendant's pretrial anxiety would be minimized; and (3) the defendant's ability to defend himself/herself and the fairness of the trial would not be jeopardized through extensive, adverse pretrial publicity.

Notwithstanding certain delays for a variety of reasons attributable to the defense, prosecution, or both, the Speedy Trial Act of 1974 provides the following:

1. In a case where a plea of "not guilty" is entered, the trial shall commence within 70 days from the date when an information or indictment has been made public or from the date of the defendant's arraignment, whichever date last occurs.

2. Unless the defendant consents in writing to the contrary, the trial shall not commence less than 30 days from the date on which the defendant first appears through counsel or expressly waives counsel and elects to proceed *pro se* (on his own).

These provisions not only make it possible for a criminal defendant to enjoy the right to a speedy trial, but also eliminate delays otherwise caused by crowded court dockets (*United States v. Nance*, 1982). Some courts have been notorious for their slowness in conducting trial proceedings. Federal judges have considerable power in deciding what evidence to admit and what evidence to exclude, for example. One judge may permit lengthy tape recordings of conversations between an FBI agent and a defendant. These recordings may consume many hours. In another district court, however, the judge may deny the admission of such tape recordings and insist that such materials be presented through more direct and brief testimony from witnesses. With the provisions of the Speedy Trial Act in force, all federal judges are obligated to comply with these provisions in spite of the "general congestion of the court's calendar" (Title 18 U.S.C. Sec. 3161 (h)(8)(C), 2007). Certainly one consequence of this provision is a more rapid trial proceeding.

BOX 7-2

KEY CASES: SPEEDY TRIALS

Dickey v. Florida 398 U.S. 30 (1970)

Dickey was charged with various crimes in 1968 for crimes allegedly committed in 1960. He made motions to have an immediate trial in several different court appearances, but for various reasons, his trial was delayed until 1968. Between 1960 and 1968, some witnesses died, while others became unavailable for various reasons. Also, some relevant police records were destroyed or misplaced. Following his conviction, he appealed, arguing that his speedy trial rights had been violated. The U.S. Supreme Court overturned his conviction, saying that prompt inquiry is a fundamental right, and the charging authority has a duty to provide a prompt trial to ensure the availability of records, recollection of witnesses, and availability of testimony.

Barker v. Wingo 407 U.S. 514 (1972)

Barker and another person were alleged to have shot an elderly couple in July 1958. They were arrested later and a grand jury indicted them in September 1958. Kentucky prosecutors sought 16 continuances to prolong the trial of Barker. Barker's companion, Manning, was subjected to five different trials, where a hung jury was found except in the fifth trial, where Manning was convicted. Then, Barker's trial was scheduled. During these five trials, Barker made no attempt to protest or to encourage a trial on his own behalf. After scheduling and postponing Barker's trial for various reasons, his

trial was finally held in October 1963, when he was convicted. He appealed, alleging a violation of his right to a speedy trial. The U.S. Supreme Court heard the case and declared that since, from every apparent factor, Barker did not want a speedy trial, he was not entitled to one. The case significance is that if you want a speedy trial, you must assert your privilege to have one. Defendants must assert their desire to have a speedy trial in order for the speedy trial provision to be invoked and for amendment rights to be enforceable. In Barker's case, the U.S. Supreme Court said that Barker was not deprived of his due process right to a speedy trial, largely because the defendant did not desire one (at 2195).

Strunk v. United States 412 U.S. 434 (1973)

Strunk was arrested for a crime and eventually tried 10 months later. He was convicted and appealed, arguing that the ten-month delay was a violation of his speedy trial rights. The U.S. Supreme Court heard the case and noted several considerations in determining whether speedy trial rights of suspects have been violated. These considerations are (1) whether there are overcrowded court dockets and understaffed prosecutor's offices; (2) whether there is substantial emotional distress caused to defendants because of long delays; and (3) whether an accused is released pending a trial and whether there is little or no immediate interest in having a trial.

(continued)

▼

Dillingham v. United States 423 U.S. 64, 96 S. Ct. 303 (1975)

Dillingham was arrested for a crime. After a 22-month interval, an indictment was issued against Dillingham, and 12 months after that, Dillingham was brought to trial. Dillingham was convicted and appealed, arguing that the 22-month interval between his arrest and indictment violated his speedy trial rights under the Sixth Amendment. His conviction was overturned and the U.S. Supreme Court declared that invocation of the speedy trial provision thus need not await indictment, information, or other formal charge. Thus, the delay was unreasonable between arrest, indictment, and trial to satisfy Dillingham's speedy trial rights under the Sixth Amendment.

Doggett v. United States 505 U.S. 647, 112 S. Ct. 2686 (1992)

Doggett was convicted of conspiracy to distribute cocaine in a U.S. District Court. Because of various delays, mostly caused by the government, Doggett's trial was not held for $8^1/2$ years. He appealed his conviction, contending that the $8^1/2$-year delay before his case was tried violated his speedy trial rights under the Sixth Amendment. The U.S. Supreme Court overturned Doggett's conviction, concluding that an $8^1/2$-year delay in one's trial, largely because of government causes, violates the Sixth Amendment rights of the accused.

Fex v. Michigan 507 U.S. 403, 113 S.Ct. 1085 (1993)

Fex, a prisoner in Indiana, was brought to trial in Michigan 196 days following his trial request to Michigan officials and 177 days after the request was received by Michigan prosecutors. Fex was convicted and appealed, alleging that the 180-day speedy trial time period was violated, inasmuch as his trial commenced 196 days after his own request was submitted to Michigan to have a trial. The U.S. Supreme Court heard Fex's appeal and upheld his conviction, noting the detainer warrant phraseology that the statutory 180-day period did not begin until the Michigan prosecutor received his request. The U.S. Supreme Court said that if the warden in Indiana delayed the forwarding of a prisoner's request for a speedy trial, it merely postponed the starting of the 180-day clock. Thus, the receipt of such a notice from a prisoner under a detainer warrant in another state by the state prosecutors triggers the 180-day clock to determine whether one's speedy trial rights are being observed.

The not less than 30 or more than 70 days provision of the Speedy Trial Act applies to the period between one's initial appearance and trial. Ordinarily, there is a 10-day interval between the initial appearance of a defendant and the defendant's arraignment. A federal trial date should be set within 60 days following one's arraignment. The time interval is designed to permit a defendant, together with defense counsel, adequate time to prepare a defense and to spare the defendant any undue delay in coming to trial. If the defendant wishes to consent to an earlier trial date, however, it is the defendant's right to do so under the act.

Many factors affect the 70-day requirement, however. Defendants may discharge one attorney and appoint another. New attorneys will need sufficient time to examine the case and prepare for a defense of their clients (*United States v. Darby*, 1984). The defendant may be ill (*United States v. Savoca*, 1984), or an important witness for either the prosecution or defense must be called and requires additional time to arrive (*United States v. Strong*, 1985). The judge may even request a psychiatric examination of a defendant if, in the judge's opinion, there is reason to believe the defendant is not competent to stand trial (*United States v. Howell*, 1983; *United States v. Crosby*, 1983).

Many local and state jurisdictions follow the federal provisions set forth in the Speedy Trial Act, although they are not bound to do so. For example, North Carolina has a 90-day limit from the time of arrest or arraignment to trial, while New Mexico has a 180-day limit. The "speedy trial" provision of the Sixth Amendment is construed differently from one jurisdiction to the next. Federal courts are bound by the Speedy Trial Act provisions, however.

▼

▶ Bench Trials and Jury Trials Contrasted

While the jury system first appeared in the United States in 1607 under a charter granted to the Virginia Company in Jamestown by James I, jury trials existed as early as the eleventh century in England. A criminal trial is an adversarial proceeding within a particular jurisdiction, where a judicial examination and determination of issues can be made and where a criminal defendant's guilt or innocence can be decided impartially by either a judge or jury (Black 1990, 52). There were about 924,900 persons convicted of felonies in state courts in 2000, criminal trials accounted for only 5 percent of these, and the remaining 95 percent were guilty pleas (Maguire and Pastore 2005).

In U.S. District Courts, there were 83,530 criminal cases concluded in 2003 (Maguire and Pastore 2005, 426). Federal district judges dismissed 7,957 of these cases (9.5 percent), while less than 1 percent of the defendants were acquitted either by the judge or the jury. There were 74,850 defendants convicted, or about 89 percent. Of these, 96.3 percent (72,110) entered guilty pleas through plea bargaining or by pleading nolo contendere or "no contest." In federal criminal trials for the 3,463 defendants whose cases actually went to trial and were not plea bargained, federal juries found 2,413 of these defendants guilty, while judges found 327 defendants guilty. Thus, nearly 80 percent of those who went to trial were convicted.

In both state and federal courts, therefore, trials are comparatively infrequent, inasmuch as plea bargaining is used most of the time to secure convictions. But in approximately 10 percent of all criminal cases, there are trials conducted. These are either (1) bench trials or (2) jury trials.

Bench Trials

A bench trial, also known as a trial by the court or trial by the judge, is conducted either where petty offenses are involved and a jury is not permitted or in cases where defendants waive their right to a jury trial. A judge presides, hears the evidence, and then decides the case, relying on rational principles of law.

Several popular television shows depict bench trials. Television programs such as *Judge Judy* and *Judge Joe Brown* are examples of bench trials. In cases heard by these courts, litigants or parties to the lawsuits have waived their right to a jury trial and have permitted the judge to decide their cases. In criminal courts, defendants often waive their right to a jury trial and permit the judge to decide their cases based on the evidence introduced.

One explanation for waiving one's right to a jury trial is that juries are sometimes more likely to convict persons for felonies than judges. If the crimes alleged are especially heinous or involve emotionally charged issues, defendants will often opt for a bench trial instead of a jury trial, because juries might be more persuaded by emotional appeals and arguments from prosecutors rather than the cold, hard facts of the case. In the early 1990s, for example, the Reverend Moon, known for his indoctrination of children known as "Moonies," was on trial for income tax evasion. Because of the sensationalism associated with his religion and the impact he had on thousands of teenage followers, his defense attorney requested a bench trial, where the judge would decide his guilt or innocence (Wettstein 1992). Other cases involving child abuse in cults have also been decided by judges rather than juries, reflecting the defense counsel's belief that judges can be more impartial when evaluating the factual evidence (Wettstein 1992). Research has also revealed that judges are more likely to impose shorter sentences as the result of a bench trial as opposed to a jury trial, although many other investigations do not support this view (Champion 2005b).

From a purely practical standpoint, bench trials are more efficient than jury trials. If the process of jury selection does not occur, judges can hear evidence and decide a case in less time, since jury deliberations are avoided. For instance, in New York City, a **Misdemeanor Trial Law** was enacted and took effect in 1985. The purpose of this law was to make it possible to reduce the incarcerative punishments for certain types of misdemeanors to six months or less, meaning that jury trials for defendants charged with these misdemeanor offenses could be avoided (Dynia 1987, 1990). Case backlogs were expedited and overall case processing time greatly decreased. Interestingly, sentencing patterns among judges remained the same both before and after the new law went into effect.

There are several criticisms of bench trials. When judges determine one's guilt or innocence, they may be influenced by extralegal factors, such as one's race, class, ethnicity, and/or gender. Judges are also influenced in their decision making by their own personal feelings about the types of charged offenses. For example, some judges impose more severe sentences upon convicted offenders who commit specific types of heinous offenses, such as child sexual abuse, compared with sentences they might impose for rape, aggravated assault, and murder convictions (Champion 2005b).

When judges decide cases on their own, their susceptibility to corruption is increased. Some judges become susceptible to bribery by influential defendants. In recent years, more than a few judges at the state and federal levels have been charged with corruption and accepting bribes to render decisions favorable to their constituency. **Bribery** is the giving or offering of anything to someone in a position of trust to induce that person to act dishonestly. In 2011, a juvenile court judge in Pennsylvania was convicted and sentenced to 28 years in prison for taking $1 million in bribes from juvenile detention centers in return for sending juveniles in his court to those detention facilities. The Pennsylvania Supreme Court overturned about 4,000 juvenile cases that the judge had presided over in a five-year period citing that he had violated the juvenile's constitutional rights. In 1987, the FBI investigated 105 Pennsylvania judges because of allegations of judicial misconduct. The results of these FBI investigations led the Pennsylvania Supreme Court to temporarily suspend 15 of these judges for bribery. In another FBI investigation, Operation Greylord, a sting operation was conducted against several corrupt judges. Operation Greylord was commenced in 1978 in Cook County, Illinois. FBI agents tapped judges' telephones, recorded conversations, and initiated bogus bribery attempts to induce judges into acting dishonestly in deciding cases. Operation Greylord was successful over the next several years in obtaining convictions against over 60 judges for various criminal misconduct charges, including bribery (Bensinger 1988). Recommendations made by the American Bar Association following Operation Greylord included adopting new ethical requirements for judges and attorneys and the implementation of procedural safeguards to monitor judicial discretion.

Despite this misconduct by a few judges, the following briefly summarizes the major advantages of bench trials:

1. Case processing is expedited.

2. Cases are usually decided on the merits of the case rather than on emotionally charged appeals in the case of heinous offenses.

3. Appearances of defendants may be undesirable to jurors, but judges can usually be dissuaded from considering such extralegal factors.

4. In complex cases, judges are often in a better position to evaluate the sufficiency of evidence against the accused and make fairer judgments.

5. Judges are less persuaded by media attention given to high-profile cases where juries might be unduly influenced against defendants.

6. Bench trials are usually cheaper than jury trials, since they don't take as long to complete and require less defense attorney time.

Misdemeanor Trial Law action by New York City passed in 1985 permitting low-level misdemeanor cases involving incarceration of six months or less to be disposed of by bench trials rather than jury trials; a time-saving strategy for more rapid criminal case processing.

bribery crime of offering, giving, requesting, soliciting, receiving something of value to influence a decision of a public official.

Some of the major disadvantages of bench trials are as follows:

1. Judges may impose more severe punishments on certain defendants, depending upon the crimes they have committed.

2. Judges are more susceptible to corruption when left to their own decision making.

3. Defendants waive their right to a jury trial, where the defendant's situation, appearance, and emotional appeal may work to the defendant's benefit.

Jury Trials

Persons charged with felonies are guaranteed the right to a jury trial in the United States. This guarantee also applies to the states. The landmark case of *Duncan v. Louisiana* (1968) has specified an objective criterion that restricts the right to a jury trial only to those offenses other than petty crimes where the possible punishment of imprisonment of more than six months can be imposed. Other cases such as *Baldwin v. New York* (1970) and *Blanton v. City of North Las Vegas, Nev.* (1989) have upheld this standard.

In the last few decades, the number of trials by jury has increased for both major crimes and the lesser offenses or misdemeanors (Maguire and Pastore 2005). While trials by jury are increasing compared with their frequency in previous years, the trend is that criminal convictions are obtained increasingly through plea bargaining. And in at least one major city, the number of jury trials conducted for all felony arrests has dropped to about 2 percent (Vidmar 2000).

BOX 7-3

KEY CASES: RIGHT TO JURY TRIALS

Duncan v. Louisiana 391 U.S. 145 (1968)

States must provide jury trials for defendants charged with serious offenses. Duncan was convicted in a bench trial of simple battery in a Louisiana court. The crime was punishable as a misdemeanor, with two years' imprisonment and a fine of $300. In Duncan's case, he was sentenced to only 60 days and a fine of $150. He appealed, saying that he demanded a jury trial and none was provided for him. The U.S. Supreme Court agreed with Duncan, saying that a crime with a potential punishment of two years is a *serious crime*, despite the sentence of 60 days imposed. Thus, for serious crimes, under the Sixth Amendment, Duncan is entitled to a jury trial.

Baldwin v. New York 399 U.S. 66 (1970)

Baldwin was arrested and prosecuted for "jostling" (pickpocketing), a Class A misdemeanor punishable by a maximum term of imprisonment of one year in New York. New York law prescribed at the time that this was a petty offense and one not entitling a defendant to a

jury trial. Baldwin asked for and was denied a jury trial. The U.S. Supreme Court heard Baldwin's appeal and declared that petty offenses carrying a one-year incarcerative term are *serious* in that jury trials are required if requested. Specifically, the wording of Baldwin attaches great significance to the months of imprisonment constituting *serious* time. The U.S. Supreme Court said that a potential sentence in excess of six months' imprisonment is sufficiently severe by itself to take offense out of category of "petty" as respects right to jury trial (at 1886, 1891). The U.S. Supreme Court overturned Baldwin's conviction and sent the case back to the lower court for a jury trial for Baldwin.

Blanton v. City of North Las Vegas 489 U.S. 538 (1989)

Melvin Blanton was charged with DUI (driving under the influence). Blanton requested but was denied a jury trial by the North Las Vegas, Nevada Municipal Court. In Nevada, the maximum sentence for a DUI conviction

(continued)

was six months in jail, while the maximum fine was $1,000. Blanton's driver license was suspended for 90 days and he was ordered to pay court costs and perform 48 hours of community service while dressed in attire identifying him as convicted of a DUI offense. Blanton appealed, contending that he was entitled to a jury trial because the offense, he alleged, was "serious" and not "petty." The U.S. Supreme Court considered his appeal and upheld his DUI bench trial conviction, saying that the most relevant criteria for determining the seriousness of an offense is the severity of the maximum authorized penalty fixed by the legislature. Thus, any offense carrying a maximum prison term of six months or less, as does Nevada's DUI law, is presumed to be petty unless it can be shown that any additional statutory penalties are so severe that they might distinguish the offense as "serious." A further proclamation by the U.S. Supreme Court was that the $1,000 fine did not approach an earlier standard of $5,000 established by Congress in its 1982 definition of "petty" offense, Title 18 U.S.C. Section 1. Thus, the *Blanton* case clearly affirms the earlier holding in *Baldwin* that a defendant is entitled to a jury trial only if the possible incarceration is beyond six months.

▶ The Trial Process

Trial procedures vary greatly among jurisdictions, although the federal district court format is followed most frequently by judges in state and local trial courts. Figure 7-1 ■ shows a diagram of a typical trial from the indictment stage through the judge's instructions to jury members.

> **trial** an adversarial proceeding within a particular jurisdiction, in which a judicial examination and determination of issues can be made, and in which a criminal defendant's guilt or innocence can be decided impartially by either a judge or jury.

Pretrial Motions

Before the start of court proceedings, attorneys for the government or the defense may make pretrial motions. Pretrial motions are motions *in limine*, and one purpose of such motions is to avoid potentially serious or embarrassing situations that may occur later

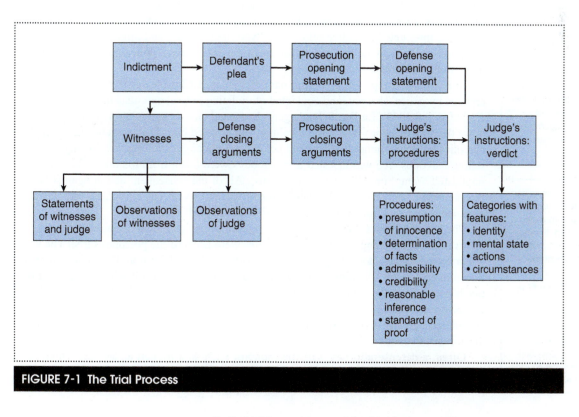

FIGURE 7-1 The Trial Process

motions *in limine* a pretrial motion, generally to obtain judicial approval to admit certain items into evidence that might otherwise be considered prejudicial or inflammatory.

motion to suppress an action before the court to cause testimony or tangible evidence from being introduced either for or against the accused.

exclusionary rule rule providing that where evidence has been obtained in violation of the privileges guaranteed by the U.S. Constitution, such evidence may be excluded at the trial.

fruits of the poisonous tree doctrine a U.S. Supreme Court decision in Wong Sun v. United States (1963) holding that evidence that is spawned or directly derived from an illegal search or an illegal interrogation is generally inadmissible against a defendant because of its original taint.

motions oral or written requests to a judge asking the court to make a specific ruling, finding, decision, or order. May be presented at any appropriate point from an arrest until the end of a trial.

motion to dismiss an action before the court requesting that the judge refuse to hear a suit.

during trial, such as the attempt by either side to introduce evidence that may be considered prejudicial, inflammatory, or irrelevant. In a brutal murder case, for example, it may be considered inflammatory for the prosecution to introduce photographs of a dismembered body or a mutilated corpse. The jury may be emotionally persuaded to interpret the photographs as conclusive evidence that the defendant committed the crime. Or the photographs may enhance sentencing severity, if additional and overwhelming evidence exists of the defendant's guilt.

In some instances, a defense attorney will make a motion to suppress certain evidence from being introduced because it was illegally seized by police at the time the defendant was arrested (Bell 1983). This is known as the exclusionary rule, and it provides that where evidence has been obtained in violation of the privileges guaranteed to citizens by the U.S. Constitution, the evidence must be excluded at the trial (Black 1990, 564). Generally, any evidence seized by law enforcement officers as the result of an illegal search would be considered inadmissible in court later. Such evidence would fall within the exclusionary rule, and it would be excluded as evidence against the accused. The leading case in the adoption of the exclusionary rule is *Mapp v. Ohio* (1961). This case involved an illegal search of Ms. Dollree Mapp's premises by police officers in Cleveland, Ohio. Police were searching for a suspect in a bombing incident and believed he was hiding in Mapp's home. They entered her home without a warrant and proceeded to search it. They found nothing incriminating, but in their search, they discovered crude pencil sketches in an old trunk in Ms. Mapp's basement. They considered these drawings as obscene, and they charged Ms. Mapp with violating a Cleveland obscenity ordinance. She was subsequently convicted of possessing obscene materials.

Later, the U.S. Supreme Court overturned Ms. Mapp's conviction because of the illegal search, and they declared that the seizure of the "evidence" by police was unlawful and therefore inadmissible against Mapp. Without the evidence, there was no case against Mapp. The U.S. Supreme Court took that particular opportunity to chide the police officers who conducted the illegal search of Mapp's premises. They warned police officers that in future cases, such misconduct would not be tolerated. Thus, the exclusionary rule was subsequently interpreted by police officers as "tying their hands" and limiting their investigative powers, although the real reason for the rule was to prevent police misconduct relating to warrantless searches.

In another leading case involving narcotics sales, a Chinese suspect, Wong Sun, was arrested by police, charged, and convicted of violating federal narcotics laws (*Wong Sun v. United States*, 1963). Earlier, federal agents had acted on a tip and without a warrant, broke down the door of James Wah Toy's dwelling, and arrested him. They searched his home for narcotics but found none. But Toy told police later under questioning that Johnny Yee was selling narcotics. Yee was arrested and narcotics were taken from his home. Yee, in turn, implicated Wong Sun, who was also arrested. All of the subsequent action against Wong Sun stemmed from an original unlawful search of James Wah Toy's premises and illegally obtained statements from Toy when immediately arrested.

The U.S. Supreme Court overturned Wong Sun's conviction and declared that the statements implicating Wong Sun in narcotics sales were fruits of the poisonous tree. The fruits of the poisonous tree doctrine provides that evidence derived from an illegal search or an illegal interrogation is inadmissible against a defendant because it has been tainted. If the tree is poison, then the fruit from the tree will also be poison. Similarly, if a search is illegal and evidence is seized, then the "fruits" of that search or the seized evidence will also be considered illegally seized. Such illegally seized evidence will be excluded later against the accused in court.

Often, a defense attorney will file motions, such as a motion to dismiss, which is a motion attacking the prosecutor's evidence as insufficient or to signify the absence of a key prosecution witness upon which a conviction depends. Such pretrial motions are ordinarily conducted outside of the presence of the jury. The judge rules on these motions and the trial proceeds. A summary of some of the more frequently used pretrial motions is presented below.

1. **Motion for dismissal of charges** (motion seeking to dismiss the case against an accused based on the failure of the prosecution to state a sufficient case to be prosecuted; alleges critical weaknesses in prosecution's case).

2. **Motion for discovery** (motion to obtain and examine certain documents and evidence collected by the prosecution and the list of the witnesses to be called).

3. **Motion for a bill of particulars** (motion to require the prosecutor to furnish a written statement of charges, outlining the crime(s) alleged, the time and place of crime, and other information).

4. **Motion for continuance** (motion seeks to delay trial proceedings, usually in order to interview additional witnesses and collect additional evidence).

5. **Motion for severance** (if more than one defendant is charged in a conspiracy or crime where several defendants are involved, attorneys for each client may wish to separate the cases so that each defendant can be tried independently in order to avoid any conflict of interest, where one defendant may incriminate other defendants).

6. **Motion for suppression of evidence** (motion seeks to exclude incriminating evidence against the accused, such as any evidence illegally seized from one's premises in violation of Fourth Amendment provisions against unreasonable searches and seizures; in the Denver, Colorado, federal trial of Timothy McVeigh and Terry Nichols, charged with the bombing of the Oklahoma City, Oklahoma, federal building in 1995, for example, several incriminating statements made by Nichols and a receipt for bomb materials with McVeigh's fingerprint on it were the subject of a motion to suppress by their defense attorney).

7. **Motion for determination of competency** (motion seeks to question whether the defendant is competent or sufficiently sane to stand trial; an examination by a psychiatrist might be requested before the trial proceeds).

8. **Motion for a change of venue** (the trial of Timothy McVeigh for the bombing of the Murrah Federal Building in Oklahoma City in 1995 was moved from Oklahoma City to Denver, Colorado, where it was believed that a more impartial jury could be selected, which would be less prejudiced toward McVeigh compared with an Oklahoma jury).

9. **Motion for intention to provide alibi** (motion seeks to demonstrate that the defendant did not commit the offense alleged since the defendant was elsewhere when the crime was committed).

10. **Motion for summary judgment** (motion requesting the judge to order a judgment for the defendant based on the insufficiency of evidence presented by the prosecution to sustain a conviction).

Opening Arguments

Unless both the prosecution and defense attorneys agree to waive their opening statements, the prosecutor makes an opening statement to the jury. Usually, this statement includes the state's theory about the case and why the defendant is guilty. Often, prosecutors will tell the jury what they intend to prove and attempt to persuade them to consider the importance of certain kinds of evidence to be presented later. This outline or summary of the nature of the case is to advise the jury of the facts to be relied upon and the issues involved (Black 1990, 1091).

The defense attorney is also permitted to make an opening statement. The defense is given considerable latitude by the court in addressing the jury. Basically, the defense's statement is intended to undermine the state's case against the defendant and to indicate that in the final analysis, the accused should be acquitted of all charges.

The State Presents Its Case

The prosecution begins its case by calling witnesses and presenting evidence that a crime has been committed and that the defendant committed it. Each witness is sworn in by a court officer. Being sworn in means that a witness is obliged under the law to be truthful in all subsequent testimony given. This stage is termed direct examination. Direct examination is the question–answer exchange between the prosecutor and the prosecutor's witnesses, or between the defense and the defense's witnesses.

The defense has the right to challenge any question asked to a witness by the prosecution on direct examination. Usually, defense attorneys raise objections to certain questions. Or they may object to an answer given by a witness. The presiding judge rules on such objections and either sustains or grants them or overrules or denies them. The same option is available to defense attorneys whenever evidence is introduced by the prosecution. Objections by either side may be raised at any time, and the judge sustains or overrules these objections. When the defense presents witnesses, prosecutors may also raise objections for the same purposes. Sometimes, following an adverse ruling on an objection by the prosecution or defense, the prosecutor or defense counsel will say the word, "exception." The judge will usually say, "Exception noted." This use of "exception" is outmoded in contemporary courtrooms, although some older attorneys continue to use this term. This is because whenever a motion is denied or sustained, this ends further dialogue about the motion. More than anything else, the term is intended to annoy the judge because it is entirely unnecessary. In essence, it is an insulting remark and is intended by either side to chide the judge for whatever ruling is made about the particular motion.

The Federal Rules of Evidence contain explicit guidelines for judges and attorneys to follow regarding which types of evidence are admissible and which evidence is inadmissible (Saltzburg and Redden 1994). These are very elaborate and technical rules. If they are not followed by any of the major participants in the trial proceeding, such rule violations could be the basis for overturning a "guilty" verdict on appeal to a higher court. The prosecution is also entitled to appeal a "not guilty" verdict on similar grounds. If certain evidentiary rules were violated, the verdict in favor of the defendant could be reversed on appeal. This scenario actually occurred in the cases of Stacey Koon and Laurence Powell, Los Angeles police officers who were convicted in a federal district court in the Rodney King beating. The federal judge was especially lenient in sentencing Koon and Powell, and the U.S. Attorney's Office appealed the lenient sentences to the Ninth Circuit Court of Appeals. The Ninth Circuit overruled the federal judge. Later, attorneys for Koon and Powell appealed the Ninth Circuit ruling to the U.S. Supreme Court, which rendered a mixed opinion in the matter. The point is that either side may appeal a judge's rulings or particular conduct to a higher court.

The Right of Cross-Examination

After the prosecution has questioned a witness, the defense has the right to ask that same witness questions. This is known as cross-examination. The right to cross-examine witnesses is not only a constitutional right, but it also illustrates the adversarial nature of the trial system. The defense attorney attempts to impeach the credibility of the prosecutor's witnesses or to undermine their veracity or truthfulness to the jury (Graham 1985). Sometimes, defense attorneys can use prosecution witnesses to their own advantage and elicit statements from them that are favorable to the defendant.

direct examination questioning by attorney of one's own (prosecution or defense) witness during a trial.

witnesses persons who have relevant information about the commission of a crime; persons who have seen or heard inculpatory or exculpatory evidence that may incriminate or exonerate a defendant.

objections actions by either the prosecutor or defense requesting that certain questions not be asked of witnesses or that certain evidence should or should not be admitted.

Federal Rules of Evidence official rules governing the introduction of certain types of evidence in U.S. District Courts.

cross-examination questioning of one side's witnesses by the other side's attorney, either the prosecution or defense.

Once testimony has been given by a witness from either side, that witness may be cross-examined by the opposition. Once such cross-examination has been completed, additional questioning of the witness may be done by the side who called the witness initially. This questioning is called re-direct examination. The purpose of re-direct examination is to clarify certain issues that may be confusing to juries, or to cause the witness to elaborate on points the other side may have introduced, which appear to be incriminating. In contrast with the direct examination, the lawyer conducting the cross-examination is allowed to proceed in a leading fashion. Typically, the lawyer during cross-examination will use short, clear statements that cannot reasonably be denied and that ultimately support the lawyer's version of events. Questions during cross-examination do not seek to disclose new information. Rather, this is an opportunity for the attorney to direct the testimony in support of the position of the questioning party.

re-direct examination
questioning of a witness following the adversary's questioning under cross-examination.

For instance, a witness may testify on behalf of the defense in a case where the defendant, Mr. X, a noted sports figure, claimed to have cut his hand *after* a murder had been committed in Denver, Colorado, where the unknown assailant had been injured on the hand. Some blood at the crime scene does not appear to be the victim's blood. In fact, investigators suspect that the blood is from the perpetrator, probably from a cut sustained to his hand from a knife wound during the murder. However, the time interval is such that the defendant claims to have cut his hand on the day following the murder when the unknown assailant's injuries occurred. It is claimed by the defendant, for instance, that he boarded an airplane on the evening of the terrible murder. Investigators have fixed the time of death of the deceased at about 10:00 p.m. At 11:30 p.m., it is known that the defendant boards an airplane and flies to New York. As a passenger on the airline, the defendant sits next to another passenger. The passenger and the defendant converse. The following day, the defendant is notified of the murder and is suspected of it. He flies back to Denver on another airline. He has a cut on his hand. The defendant claims that when he learned of the death of the victim the following day, he smashed his hand down on a table in his hotel room while holding a glass. The glass shattered and the pieces cut his fingers. While on the return flight to Denver, the defendant sits next to another passenger and they converse throughout the trip.

On the witness stand, the passenger who sat next to Mr. X on the first flight is called as a witness for the defendant. The witness is called to confirm that Mr. X did not have a cut hand or fingers later in the evening, after the murder had occurred. The witness is asked some questions by the defense counsel on direct examination.

DEFENSE:	"Did you sit next to Mr. X on Flight 161 to New York on the evening of February 26th?"
WITNESS:	"Yes."
DEFENSE:	"Did you have a conversation with Mr. X during this flight?"
WITNESS:	"Yes."
DEFENSE:	"Did you notice whether there were any cuts on Mr. X's hands while you were talking with him?"
WITNESS:	"I didn't see any cuts on Mr. X's hands."
DEFENSE:	"Did you know Mr. X by reputation when you were sitting next to him?"
WITNESS:	"Yes, I did."
DEFENSE:	"Did you make any special requests of Mr. X?"
WITNESS:	"Yes, I asked him to autograph a pad of paper in my pocket."
DEFENSE:	"You asked Mr. X for his autograph?"
WITNESS:	"Yes, I did."

DEFENSE:	"Did he sign something for you?"
WITNESS:	"Yes, he signed the paper pad."
DEFENSE:	"Where exactly did he sign this pad, you know, did he sign it while holding it in his lap or did he write on some surface?"
WITNESS:	"He wrote his autograph on the pull-out tray in front of my seat. He leaned over and signed my paper pad on my pull-out tray."
DEFENSE:	"The pull-out tray on *your* seat. OK. And therefore, this gave you a good opportunity to look closely at his hands?"
WITNESS:	"Yes, it did."
DEFENSE:	"And you didn't see or notice any cuts on his hands or fingers?"
WITNESS:	"No, I didn't."
DEFENSE:	"And the overhead lights were on when he gave you his autograph?"
WITNESS:	"Yes, the lights were on."
DEFENSE:	"And you had a clear view of *both* of his hands?"
WITNESS:	"Yes, he used one hand to hold the pad and the other to sign his name."

[The prosecutor takes over and cross-examines the witness.]

PROSECUTION:	"Sir, could Mr. X have been sitting in such a way so as to hide his hands from you?"
WITNESS:	"I don't think so. We talked a lot that evening, and he was quite animated, using his hands."
PROSECUTION:	"But you cannot say for certain that there were *no* cuts on his hands when you were talking with him?"
WITNESS:	"No, I can't say for certain."
PROSECUTION:	"And so if there *were* cuts, it is possible that you just didn't happen to see them that evening."
WITNESS:	"That's right. I didn't see any cuts when he gave me his autograph, but maybe I just didn't notice them."

[The defense *re-directs*]

DEFENSE:	"Well, you say that you can't say for sure that there were no cuts on Mr. X's hands. Is that right?"
WITNESS:	"Yes, that's right."
DEFENSE:	"But suppose there was a deep gash, or perhaps even several deep gashes on Mr. X's hands? If such gashes were there, they would probably be bloody. Perhaps you would notice, for instance, if Mr. X was wearing some sort of covering to protect such cuts if they were there?"
WITNESS:	"I didn't see any bandages."
DEFENSE:	"But if there was a deep cut, and if it had been made a short time before Mr. X boarded the plane, then you would probably have noticed that, wouldn't you?"
WITNESS:	"Sure, I probably would have noticed that. We were sitting side-by-side in adjacent seats. Lights were on overhead, and I could see both of his hands."
DEFENSE:	"And you saw no cuts?"

WITNESS:	"No, I saw no cuts on his hands. I think I would have seen them if there had been cuts there."
DEFENSE:	"Was there any blood on the paper pad where he signed his autograph?"
WITNESS:	"No. There was no blood on the paper pad. Just his autograph."

Now, suppose we have the second witness on the stand, the one who sat next to Mr. X on his return flight from New York back to Denver. The next witness, also called by the defense, is asked the following questions.

DEFENSE:	"Were you a passenger on Flight 215 from New York to Denver on the day of February 27th?"
WITNESS:	"Yes, I was."
DEFENSE:	"And who did you sit next to while on the airplane, if anyone?"
WITNESS:	"I sat next to Mr. X."
DEFENSE:	"Did you have a conversation with Mr. X while you flew from New York to Denver?"
WITNESS:	"Yes, we talked with one another."
DEFENSE:	"Did you notice Mr. X's hands while you were talking to him?"
WITNESS:	"Yes, I did."
DEFENSE:	"Was there anything unusual or extraordinary about them that you recall?"
WITNESS:	"Yes, there was a big bandage on one of his fingers on his right hand. It looked like it was seeping with blood."
DEFENSE:	"You say the wound was seeping with blood?"
WITNESS:	"That's the way it looked to me."
DEFENSE:	"Did Mr. X tell you how he received that wound?"
WITNESS:	"Yes, he said he cut it on a glass in his hotel room."
DEFENSE:	"Did he say *when* he cut his hand?"
WITNESS:	"Yes. He said he cut it this morning, after he received an upsetting telephone call."

The prosecution cross-examines the second witness:

PROSECUTION:	"When you saw this wound, you don't know precisely *when* the wound was made, do you?"
WITNESS:	"Mr. X says it happened that morning, a few hours before the flight to Denver."
PROSECUTION:	"Yes, but you don't really know for sure *when* that cut was made, do you?"
WITNESS:	"No, I don't."
PROSECUTION:	"It could have been the night before, couldn't it, maybe even around 10:00 p.m. at night?"
WITNESS:	"I suppose so."
PROSECUTION:	"So you really don't know *when* the cut was made, and that it could perhaps have been made the night before, is that right?"
WITNESS:	"That's right."

The defense re-directs:

DEFENSE: "Did you actually *see* the cut on Mr. X's hand or just the bandage covering it?"

WITNESS: "I saw the cut. He changed the bandage once, just before we landed."

DEFENSE: "When you saw the cut, how did it look to you?"

WITNESS: "What do you mean?"

DEFENSE: "Did it look like an old cut or a new one?"

WITNESS: "It looked like a cut that was made fairly recently."

DEFENSE: "If a cut like the one you saw had been made the night before you actually saw it, would it still be bleeding like that, as you have described?"

WITNESS: "I don't think so. It probably would have healed some. I don't know."

DEFENSE: "And so you are saying that the cut looked entirely consistent with Mr. X's explanation that he had just cut his hand on some glass in his hotel room, is that it?"

WITNESS: "Yes, that's it."

As can be seen from the above exchange, each side, the defense and prosecution, attempts to use these two witnesses in ways that work to each side's particular advantage. The prosecution wants the jury to think that the cut occurred when Mr. X, believed to be the murderer, used a knife to kill the victim. The defense wants to show that there were no hand or finger cuts when Mr. X left Denver late on the evening of the murder, but that a cut *was* there when Mr. X was seen by others the following day. If it can be established that Mr. X's hand cut occurred the day following the murder, then it couldn't have been made when the murder was committed. The prosecution wants the jury to believe that the cut occurred during the murder, not afterward. Both the defense and prosecution are permitted to engage in re-direct examinations and re-cross-examinations of each witness until they feel that they have adequately made their respective points. They are shaping and forming versions of events that make a case for or against Mr. X. We might even consider re-direct and re-cross-examinations as refinements of witness testimony, to know for sure what the witness saw or did not see. The jury listens and decides which version seems most believable.

> **re-cross-examination** opposing counsel further examines an opposing witness who has already testified.

While some persons consider re-cross-examination prolonging an otherwise long trial, each side is entitled to re-cross-examine witnesses and recall witnesses to the stand for further questioning. This tactic is particularly important whenever new evidence is revealed from other witnesses. Judges may abbreviate extensive cross-examinations and re-cross-examinations if they believe that attorneys are merely covering previous information disclosed in earlier testimony.

Impeaching witnesses means to call into question the truthfulness or credibility of a witness. If either the prosecutor or defense attorney can demonstrate that a particular witness may be lying or is otherwise unreliable, then that witness's testimony is called into question. Jury members may not believe such witnesses and the evidentiary information they provide for or against defendants. Of course, defendants themselves are subject to impeachment if they testify.

There are several ways defense attorneys can impeach a witness. Attorneys can obtain inconsistent testimony from the witness or can get the witness to admit confusion over certain facts recalled. Or attorneys can introduce evidence of the untruthfulness of the witness based on previous information acquired through investigative sources. Perhaps a witness previously has been fired from a company because of embezzlement. Embezzlement is one form of dishonesty, and an inference may be made by jurors that if witnesses were dishonest in their employment, they may not be telling the truth on the witness stand even though they may be telling the truth in the present case. Of course, when the defense presents its witnesses, the prosecution has the same cross-examination rights and can make similar attempts to impeach the credibility of the witnesses called on the defendant's behalf.

Eyewitnesses and Expert Witnesses

There are many instances in criminal law where expert testimony is solicited (Penrod, Fulero, and Cutler 1995). Experts can testify and identify blood samples, firearms, and ballistics reports; comment on a defendant's state of mind or sanity; and provide opinions about any number of other pieces of evidence that would link the defendant to the crime. By the same token, defense attorneys can introduce expert testimony of their own to rebut or counter the testimony of the prosecution's experts.

Expert witnesses are used by either side to interpret the meaningfulness of evidence presented by either the prosecution or defense (Ross, Read, and Toglia 1994). Expert witnesses have extensive training and experience in matters of fact that may be introduced as evidence in a trial. Their opinions are given more weight than those of laypersons who do not have such training and experience. Complex issues or topics are clarified for jurors whenever expert testimony is presented (Penrod et al. 1995).

Being an expert witness involves certain hazards or risks, however. Some expert witnesses have reported that they were harassed by defendants or their attorneys outside of the courtroom. Particularly in the case of forensic psychiatrists who might testify as to a defendant's sanity or criminal motives, some expert witnesses have reported actually being physically assaulted or threatened with harm (Read, Yuille, and Tollestrup 1992). A majority of cases involving harassment involved criminal cases or where the insanity defense was raised.

Eyewitnesses are also of significant value to both prosecutors and defense attorneys (Davies et al. 1995). They can provide opinions and interpretations of events they actually experienced, and they can provide accounts of the defendant's involvement in the crime alleged. But some researchers have explored the impact of eyewitness testimony on jury verdicts and have suggested strongly that any such testimony should be corroborated with additional supportive evidence in order to be more fully reliable (Champion 2005b).

There has been some criticism and suspicion about the credibility and reliability of eyewitness testimony. Despite these doubts, countless hundreds of persons every year are convicted on little more than the testimony of witnesses. This has become a problem for courts that they have yet to resolve in spite of research showing that juries overrate the reliability of witnesses (Loftus 1996).

A major problem faced by prosecutors is obtaining the cooperation of victims or witnesses to testify in court as to pertinent information they might have about a particular case. The courtroom is a frightful experience for many persons, and the thought of enduring questioning on the witness stand is not a desirable one. In an effort to allay fears of victim–witnesses, various victim–witness assistance programs have been initiated, particularly by prosecutors and courts in various jurisdictions.

Victim–witness assistance programs are services that are intended to explain court procedures to various witnesses and to notify them of court dates. Additionally, such programs permit victim–witnesses to feel more comfortable with the criminal justice system generally. One particularly important function performed by such programs is to assist witnesses in providing better and clearer evidence in criminal prosecutions, with the result that a greater number of convictions will be forthcoming where their testimony has been given (Finn and Lee 1985).

One area that has received much attention in recent years is the reliability of the testimony of child witnesses, especially in cases alleging child sexual abuse (Dent and Flin

expert witnesses witnesses who have expertise or special knowledge in a relevant field pertaining to the case at trial. Witnesses who are qualified under the Federal Rules of Evidence to offer an opinion about the authenticity or accuracy of reports, who have special knowledge relevant to the proceeding.

eyewitnesses persons who testify in court as to what they saw when the crime was committed.

victim–witness assistance programs plans available to prospective witnesses to explain court procedures and inform them of court dates, and to assist witnesses in providing better testimony in court.

▼

1992; McGough 1994). The scientific study of child witnesses by psychologists in the United States began during the early 1900s, and some researchers have concluded that children are the most dangerous witnesses of all (McGough 1994). One reason for this view is that a child's memory of an especially traumatic event such as a rape or homicide is often distorted, and that their recall or true impression of what actually occurred is flawed in one respect or another (Dent and Flin 1992; Mason 1991).

A large number of child victims of sexual abuse are under age 12, and nearly a third are under age 6 (McGough 1994). By 1994, half of all states had adopted special hearsay exceptions when children are giving testimony about being abused, however. Of primary concern to the judge and other participants in the courtroom scene is the ability of children to distinguish between real and imagined events (Davies et al. 1995; Whitcomb et al. 1994).

In addition to the obvious trauma of being asked about emotionally disturbing events such as sexual molestation, the parents of sexually abused children are often reluctant to allow their children to testify in court. Some persons have suggested that children be permitted to testify in an isolated location away from the actual courtroom, and that their testimony should be monitored through closed-circuit television (Whitcomb et al. 1994). Under the Sixth Amendment, however, defendants are entitled to a face-to-face confrontation with their accusers (Ceci and Bruck 1995; Zaragoza 1995). Thus, at least for the present, it would seem that the utilization of closed-circuit television in cases such as child sexual abuse will need to be assessed further by the U.S. Supreme Court before it is approved on a national scale.

At the conclusion of the state's case against the defendant, the defense attorney may make a motion for a **directed verdict of acquittal**. A directed verdict of acquittal requests the judge to dismiss the case against the defendant because the prosecution has not proved the defendant's guilt beyond a reasonable doubt. Thus, the defense believes that their client has not been proved guilty and should be freed. No evidence exists to indicate the frequency with which such a verdict is requested, but such a motion is probably made often in many criminal cases. One reason is that it doesn't cost the defense anything to make such a motion. And on occasion, the motion may be granted. In most instances, if the case is being tried by a jury, the presiding judge is reluctant to grant such a motion. The jury is charged with the responsibility of determining one's guilt or innocence. Judges may grant such a motion, however, if they believe that the state has failed to present a compelling case of the defendant's guilt. If the case is a high-profile one, the judge is even less likely to grant such a motion.

The Defense and Summation

The defense attorney presents all relevant evidence and calls all witnesses who have relevant testimony favorable to the defendant. The prosecutor may object to the introduction of certain witnesses or to any kind of evidence the defense intends to introduce. Defendants may or may not choose to testify on their own behalf. Their right not to testify is guaranteed under the Fifth Amendment of the U.S. Constitution, and no defendants may be compelled to give testimony against themselves. Evidence from defendants themselves may be self-incriminating, and the Fifth Amendment provides for the right against self-incrimination. Of course, if a defendant does not testify, the jury may believe that the defendant has something to hide. It is difficult to make the jury understand that defendants are merely exercising their right not to testify under the Fifth Amendment, and that no inferences should be made by jurors if the defendant elects not to testify on his or her own behalf. It is the responsibility of the state, the prosecution, to prove the case against the defendant beyond a reasonable doubt. The defendant is entitled to a presumption of innocence until guilt is established according to the "beyond a reasonable doubt" standard. The judge is charged with the responsibility of instructing the jury in this regard and acquainting them with the Fifth Amendment protections extended to defendants under the law.

directed verdict of acquittal order by court declaring that the prosecution has failed to produce sufficient evidence to show defendant guilty beyond a reasonable doubt.

Some persons erroneously claim that if a jury finds a defendant not guilty and votes for acquittal, it doesn't necessarily mean that the defendant is innocent. Thus, the status of being found "not guilty" is not the equivalent of the status of being acquitted of criminal charges. But this erroneous belief undermines the fundamental principles of the U.S. Constitution and the rights it conveys to all citizens, regardless of how guilty they may appear to the public or media. Therefore, if we presume correctly that a defendant is innocent until proved guilty in a court of law, beyond a reasonable doubt, then an acquittal causes the presumption of innocence to remain unchanged. The presumption of innocence continues as a part of our right to due process throughout a trial and its conclusion, unless a guilty verdict is declared by the jury.

Interestingly, two books talk about jurors getting it wrong but one discusses wrongfully convicting the innocent, the other about wrongfully acquitting the guilty. A work by Ron Huff, Arye Rattner, and Edward Sagarin, *Convicted but Innocent: Wrongful Conviction and Public Policy*, and another work, *Guilty: The Collapse of Criminal Justice*, by Harold J. Rothwax, both address fundamentally different views of jury voting. Jury decisions may result in convictions of innocent persons, while jury decisions may result in acquittals of guilty persons. Rothwax, a former judge, suggests that current laws and procedures handicap the police and prosecutors from apprehending and convicting criminals, and preventing the courts from resolving the primary question of whether the accused committed the crime. He explores various drastic changes in the laws so that the ends of justice might be served more effectively, through more frequent convictions and fewer reversals of convictions on technical grounds. The work by Huff and his colleagues examines various wrongful convictions, where innocent persons were convicted anyway, despite the fact that they were innocent. Presently, we acknowledge that our legal system is flawed, and it is likely that it will always be flawed.

Various interesting scenarios have been portrayed by motion pictures, where a guilty offender is convicted of murder but later his conviction is overturned because evidence is found implicating another offender of the murder. The other offender has murdered several persons, and so it is believed that he is fully capable of murdering one more person. The fact is that the second murderer has entered into an agreement with the first murderer. The agreement is that the second murderer wants his parents killed, and the first murderer (who really is a murderer) agrees to kill the second murderer's parents if the first murderer is freed. Therefore, a plot unfolds where evidence is suddenly discovered that leads to freeing the first murderer. While this convoluted plot seems peculiar, it is no more silly than imagining scenarios where guilty suspects are acquitted and innocent suspects are convicted. In many murder cases, only the real murderers know for sure. While these two books offer criticisms of the criminal justice system that allows for such events to occur, there is no foolproof way of preventing their occurrence, no matter what reforms are implemented.

Can Prosecutors Criticize Defendants for Not Testifying on Their Own Behalf?

The prosecution is forbidden from mentioning a defendant's refusal to testify to the jury (*Griffin v. California*, 1965). For instance, if the prosecutor were to say, "Ladies and gentlemen of the jury, if this defendant were innocent, he would get up here on the stand and say so," this statement would be improper, and the judge would order the statement stricken from the record. In fact, such an utterance by the prosecutor may cause the judge to declare a mistrial. Both prosecutors and defense attorneys alike are bound by legal ethics to comply with court rules when presenting a case or representing a client in the courtroom. But occasionally, some attorneys engage in unethical conduct, either deliberately or inadvertently. Sometimes, such conduct will result in the judge declaring a mistrial, and the case will have to proceed from the beginning in front of a new jury.

Ordinarily, judges will give the jury instructions when it is ready to deliberate and decide the case. These instructions include statements about the rights of the accused and whether any inferences, either positive or negative, may be drawn from an accused's right not to testify on his or her own behalf. The jury is instructed not to consider the fact that a defendant chose not to testify on his own behalf. One reason for this admonition is to remind the jury that it is the prosecutor's burden to show, beyond a reasonable doubt, that the accused is guilty of the crime(s) alleged. It is not the responsibility of the accused to prove himself *innocent* to the jury. While these admonitions may seem self-evident, more than a few jurors have been influenced by the refusal of defendants to testify. We cannot possibly know what impact this refusal to testify will have on jury decision making.

Each side is permitted a summation at the conclusion of all evidence presented. Ordinarily, defense attorneys present the final oral argument on behalf of their client. This argument is followed by the closing argument of the prosecuting attorney. Sometimes, with court consent, prosecutors may present a portion of their closing argument, followed by the closing argument of the defense, followed by the remainder of the prosecutor's closing argument. In short, the prosecutor gets in the final remarks to the jury. There is a very good reason for this order of summation. Since the burden of proving guilt beyond a reasonable doubt is so difficult, prosecutors are given the last word. It is assumed that if these prosecutorial remarks are the last words heard by the jury, besides the instructions they receive from presiding judges, then their subsequent deliberations will be tainted initially by these prosecutorial remarks. During jury deliberations, however, a critical examination of all evidence introduced will lead the jury to one conclusion or the other. If the prosecutor has failed to carry the burden of proof in the case, the jury will vote to acquit the defendant.

▶ Jury Deliberations

After the prosecution and defense have presented their final arguments, the judge instructs the jury on the procedures it must follow in reaching a verdict, and the jury retires to the jury room to consider the evidence and arrive at a verdict. The judge's instructions to the jury often include a recitation of the charges against the defendant, a listing of the elements of the crime the prosecution must prove beyond a reasonable doubt, and a charge for jurors to carefully weigh and consider the evidence and testimony of witnesses.

Again, depending upon whether the case is in federal district court or in a state jurisdiction, the jury must either be unanimous or comply with the particular state rules governing jury verdicts. It will be recalled that federal juries must be unanimous. If a jury of 12 persons fails to agree, a mistrial will be declared by the federal judge. And if one jury member becomes ill, an 11-member federal jury, with court approval, is acceptable and must render a unanimous verdict as well. In states such as Louisiana and Oregon, the particular state rules governing jury verdicts have approved 9–3 or 10–2 majority votes in order for verdicts of guilty to be rendered. In 6-person juries, the jury must reach a unanimous decision, according to the U.S. Supreme Court (*Burch v. Louisiana*, 1979).

Jury deliberations and the decision-making process of arriving at particular verdicts have also been targeted for study by social scientists in recent years (Kerr 1994; Kerr and MacCoun 1985). The primary difficulty confronting those interested in studying jury deliberation processes is that such deliberations are conducted in secret. Some investigators have participated as actual jury members in their respective jurisdictions. And the insight gained through such experiences has been instrumental in preparing defense attorneys more adequately in presenting convincing cases to juries on behalf of their clients.

Jury deliberations have often been the subject of feature films and novels. The 1957 drama *Twelve Angry Men*, starring Henry Fonda, epitomized the emotion and anger of jurors in a murder case. In that film, Fonda was the lone juror voting "not guilty" against the other 11 "guilty" votes. The remainder of the film described the jury's attempt to convince Fonda that he was wrong. As it turned out, Fonda convinced the other jurors that *they* were wrong, and the defendant was acquitted. And in a 1996 novel by author/lawyer John Grisham, *The Runaway Jury*, a detailed depiction of jury deliberations is presented, with an incredible amount of interplay among jurors and the ease with which jurors' opinions are changed by particularly dominant jury members.

Jury deliberations such as those occurring in *Twelve Angry Men* are not uncommon. Jurors who differ as to their estimation of the value of particular evidence attempt to persuade the other jurors to side with them. At the outset, jurors may take an informal ballot or vote to see where they stand for conviction or acquittal. More often than not, this initial ballot influences significantly the final verdict by presenting to all jury members the disposition or determination of the majority of jurors favoring guilt or acquittal.

Group pressure is often responsible for changing minority factions in a jury to aligning themselves with the majority opinion. And in jurisdictions where the majority-rule option is in effect, such as Oregon and Louisiana, agreement among jurors is achieved more rapidly than in those states where unanimity of opinion is required. Figure 7-2 ■ shows the jury deliberation task.

When deliberations commence, juries may or may not establish a deliberation agenda. But ordinarily, discussions take place concerning the relevance and importance of particular pieces of evidence and witness testimony. If there is an initial vote and the jury is in disagreement as to the verdict, deliberations continue until a verdict is reached. If the jury simply cannot agree on a verdict, or if the required majority cannot be obtained in those jurisdictions providing for a majority vote for conviction, the judge will likely declare a mistrial.

Must Juries Agree on a Verdict?

In federal district courts, juries consist of 12 persons. The judge may or may not permit the selection of alternate jurors. Alternate jurors are used in the event that one or more of the regular jurors become ill during the proceedings. Also, during jury deliberations, if a juror cannot continue to serve, Title 18 U.S.C. Rule 23 (2006) provides that "if the court finds it

> **alternate jurors** jurors who have been selected to replace any of the regular jurors who may become ill and cannot attend the full trial proceeding; these jurors have been vested with the same tasks as regular jurors who will hear and decide cases.

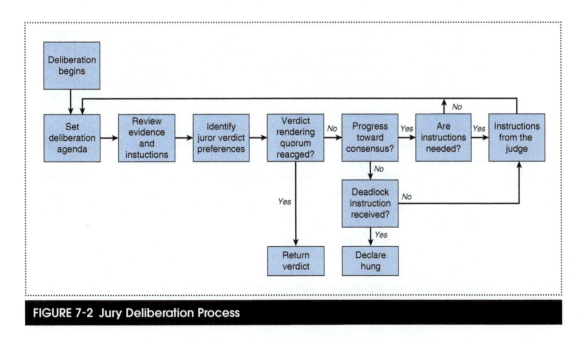

FIGURE 7-2 Jury Deliberation Process

necessary to excuse a juror for just cause after the jury has retired to consider its verdict, in the discretion of the court a valid verdict may be returned by the remaining 11 jurors" (Title 18 U.S.C., 2006). In federal courts, whether a 12- or 11-member jury hears a case, the decision reached for either guilt or acquittal must be unanimous. If one or more jurors disagree and persist in their disagreement with the other jurors, the judge declares a hung jury and a mistrial is declared. Mistrials are erroneous, invalid, or nugatory trials (Black 1990, 1002). This means that the entire case will have to be heard again before a new jury later. Mistrials also occur during the trial, especially if irregularities or errors occur to jeopardize a defendant's fair trial rights. Sometimes, inadmissible evidence may be admitted erroneously. A witness may make an utterance which may tend to substantial jury bias. Whenever such trial irregularities and other errors occur, the judge ordinarily grants a motion by either side for a mistrial (Hodge 1986; Institute for Court Management 1983).

In state courts and at the local level, however, the federal rule for jury agreement or unanimity does not always apply. Under existing U.S. Supreme Court guidelines, state juries may vary in size from a minimum of 6 to 12 persons. Actually, the U.S. Supreme Court has established the minimum number of jury members at six in the case of *Williams v. Florida* (1970). However, no such precedent has been established for upper limits of jury sizes. Thus, it is conceivable that a defendant may request a jury consisting of more than 12 persons, such as 25 or 50 jurors. But this would be very unusual. It would also pose severe logistical problems for courtrooms, where it would be difficult to find sufficient seating for all of these jurors. Furthermore, there would be considerable difficulty for all of these jurors to reach agreement about the guilt or innocence of criminal defendants.

Six-member juries must be unanimous in their verdict (*Burch v. Louisiana*, 1979). However, if juries consist of 12 persons, a majority verdict may be acceptable in certain states, unless unanimity is required under state or local laws. For instance, in the cases of *Apodaca v. Oregon* (1972) and *Johnson v. Louisiana* (1972), the respective defendants were convicted by a majority of jurors, but there was no unanimity of agreement. In most states, however, unanimous verdicts are required by statute.

An example of a legitimate nonunanimous verdict is the case of *Johnson v. Louisiana* (1972). In the *Johnson* case, Frank Johnson was arrested, tried, and convicted of armed robbery in 1968. The 12-person jury convicted him by a 9–3 vote (the absolute minimum majority required under Louisiana law). In another case, unanimity of jury voting was not required either. This was the case of *Apodaca v. Oregon* (1972). In Apodaca's case, Robert Apodaca and several other defendants were convicted of assault with a deadly weapon. Apodaca was convicted by an 11–1 jury vote. In Oregon, the minimum vote required by a jury for conviction is 10–2. Their respective appeals were heard by the U.S. Supreme Court. The U.S. Supreme Court upheld both of their convictions and underscored the right of states to utilize the rule of a majority vote in their jury trials. Also some states, such as Tennessee, where the Tennessee State Legislature has copied the Federal Rules of Criminal Procedure, require their 12-member juries to be unanimous in their voting. There are some exceptions to nonunanimous jury voting, however. In capital cases where the death penalty may be imposed, the jury vote for conviction must always be unanimous.

Judges will frequently poll jurors once they have rendered their verdict. **Polling jurors** simply refers to asking each juror to state in open court whether the verdict is a true reflection of his/her feelings and how he/she voted. It is unlikely that a jury will vote to acquit a defendant, where a particular juror will say to the judge that he or she did not agree with that vote. In those cases where juries must be unanimous in their decision to convict or acquit defendants, such an event is especially important. In situations such as in *Louisiana* or *Oregon* where unanimous votes are not needed, polling individual jury members identifies the specific vote breakdown. However, in the event that one or more jurors disagree with the majority in a state or federal court where the jury vote must be unanimous, judges will send the juries back to deliberate more extensively, until unanimity of voting is

polling jurors a direct method of asking jurors to state whether they have voted in a particular way.

reached. Otherwise, if the jury deliberates for an unusually long period and cannot agree on a verdict, a mistrial will be declared and a new trial may be scheduled. Scheduling a new trial is up to the prosecutor. Mistrials are sometimes based on unclear or insufficient evidence. If prosecutors believe that the issues to be resolved in particular criminal cases are so controversial that no jury will likely agree in the future, then no further prosecution against the defendant will be conducted.

During the 1980s and 1990s, increasing interest has been expressed in jury deliberations and the factual accounts of what transpires in jury rooms (Kerr 1994). Juries have become increasingly scrutinized bodies. Individual jury members have exploited their jury membership to their advantage for profit. This phenomenon is not peculiar to the United States. Other countries, such as Australia and Great Britain, have found that jurors in particularly high-profile cases have focused on the profit motive as a primary reason for their jury involvement (Findlay and Duff 1988).

In particularly sensational trials, jury members' opinions about jury deliberations are increasingly marketable products. Several jurors in the murder trial of O. J. Simpson were excused as jurors when it was learned by the judge that the jurors were planning to write books about their experience and actually negotiating with publishers for book contracts. One former juror had been keeping a journal about his experiences as a juror. Keeping such a journal of trial events was forbidden and regarded as juror misconduct. Another juror, a former airline attendant, was excused for a different reason. It was learned that she had been approached by representatives of *Playboy* magazine and had agreed to pose nude for a large sum of money when the trial was completed. Thus, she was exploiting her role as a juror in the high-profile trial. While posing nude for a men's magazine is not against the law, it raises serious questions about the juror's original motives for becoming a juror.

Whenever jurors in any trial consider the potential profits stemming from their roles as jurors, this raises doubts about their veracity or truthfulness when the *voir dire* was originally conducted. If they have hidden agendas, such as writing a book about their experiences, no laws prohibit subsequent expressions of their opinions and views. But it is juror misconduct to keep journals about their jury involvement and observations. If the prosecution or defense learns about such activities or behaviors, then these revelations become grounds to bar these jurors from further jury service.

In one New York City trial, for instance, a highly publicized event occurred in the Howard Beach community. The case involved a racial attack. During the trial, several jurors contacted the media in an attempt to sell their story and give their account of jury deliberations. Some news reporters believed that such conduct by jurors was acceptable and within the boundaries of free speech. The court and prosecution took a different view by condemning those jurors who sought to profit from their experiences as jurors. The jurors were excused (Kleinig 1989).

What if persons seek to become jurors for the purpose of advancing some political view or social cause? Ideally, juries are comprised of persons who will render fair decisions and consider and weigh all factual information presented by both sides during the trial. But if some jurors are sidetracked with collateral issues not directly relevant to the trial proceedings, this may impair their ability to render fair judgments about what they have seen and heard.

▶ The Verdict and Its Aftermath

After deliberating, the jury returns to the courtroom and delivers its **verdict** to either the judge or an officer of the court. The defendant rises and faces the jury, while either the jury foreman or the judge reads the verdict aloud. If the verdict is "not guilty," the defendant

verdict decision by judge or jury concerning the guilt or innocence of a defendant.

is released. In some cases, acquitted defendants may be rearrested for other crimes that have occurred. Ordinarily, an acquittal effectively removes the defendant from the criminal justice system.

In the event that a "guilty" verdict is rendered by the jury, the defendant has the right to appeal the verdict. The defense attorney may again request the judge to issue a directed verdict of acquittal despite the jury's decision. The judge may, indeed, exercise this option. However, if the judge sets aside the jury verdict and declares the defendant acquitted, the prosecution may appeal that decision to a higher court.

If the judge does not grant the defense attorney's request, the defendant is sentenced. The appeals process may take many years. In all of the U.S. Supreme Court cases presented in this and previous chapters, the interval of time between the offense, the conviction, and the U.S. Supreme Court decision has been several years. Before a case gets before the U.S. Supreme Court, however, it must be reviewed by higher courts within the particular state jurisdiction where the original judgment was entered against the defendant. This appeals process consumes much time as well. Cases presented before the U.S. Supreme Court usually involve constitutional issues. Were a defendant's constitutional rights violated at any stage of the criminal proceeding? Were there procedural errors committed by different court participants, such as the judge, such that the original conviction might be set aside and a new trial ordered?

BOX 7-4

LEGAL ISSUES: WRONGFUL CONVICTIONS

A man from California, spent over 20 years in prison for the murder of his girlfriend's 3-year old son. After many years and appeals, the case was reopened because it was discovered that as the man maintained, the boy had fallen and hit his head; he also had an undiagnosed blood disorder and a doctor at the hospital treated him with the drug Mannitol which exacerbated the bleeding and swelling leading to his death (McNamara 2006). The man's conviction was overturned and he was freed. The State Compensation Board in California awarded the man $750,000, about $100 per day that he spent in prison (McNamara 2006).

A man in Arizona who regularly played darts at a local Phoenix bar where a bartender was murdered was called in for questioning and asked to give an impression of his teeth as the homicide victim had been bitten several times. The man was eventually convicted in 1992 based on testimony from a forensic pathologist who said the teeth impression matched the bite marks on the victim's body (DeFalco 2005). Ten years later in 2002, new DNA tests showed a match with another man already in the FBI database for another offense; that man was charged and the other man was freed and his

Carlos Yudica/Fotolia

conviction expunged (DeFalco 2005). The man subsequently sued the City of Phoenix who eventually agreed to pay him $3 million for his wrongful conviction.

How much liability should cities, counties, states, or the federal government absorb for wrongful convictions? Should states set amounts that wrongfully convicted persons can recover from their governments following the discovery of new evidence showing their innocence? Should it be based on the amount of time they served for a crime they didn't commit? What do you think?

Sources: McNamara, Melissa (2006). "$750K for Man Wrongfully Jailed," *The Associated Press*, January 20, 2006. Available online at: http://www.cbsnews.com/news/750k-for-man-wrongfully-jailed/

DeFalco, Beth (2005). "City Approves $3 Million Settlement for Wrongfully Convicted Man," *The Associated Press*, September 28, 2005. Available online at: http://ccadp.proboards.com/thread/1935

Summary

1. *Understand the arrest and booking process, and the initial appearance.*

The criminal justice process commences with the commission of a crime. The crime is investigated, and in a proportion of the cases, one or more perpetrators are arrested. An arrest means to take someone into custody. Types of crimes for which persons are arrested include misdemeanors and felonies. Misdemeanors, or minor crimes, are distinguished by the fact that they are punishable by less than one year in a jail or prison, and a possible fine. A felony, or major crime, is punishable by confinement in a jail or prison for one year or longer, and a fine may also be assessed contemporaneous with one's incarceration. Persons are arrested based on probable cause that a crime was committed and the person arrested probably committed it. Subsequently, a trial will decide whether the defendant is innocent or guilty of the crime(s) alleged.

Following an arrest, arrestees are booked, usually at a local jail or police station. Booking is a process whereby law enforcement officers collect detailed information about one's identity, formal criminal record if any, and other relevant information. Those charged with serious offenses are subject to an initial appearance before a magistrate or other judicial official. The purpose of an initial appearance is to advise the defendant of the charges against him/her and determine whether bail should be granted.

2. *Describe the bail-granting process and the conditions under which bail may be granted.*

Bail is a surety, sometimes known as a bail bond, which is usually posted for less serious offenses and permits defendants' freedom in the community until they can be tried for the crime(s) alleged. Bail is not an entitlement to everyone. Under the Eighth Amendment, excessive bail is prohibited, but this does not mean that all persons are eligible for bail. Those denied bail are usually deemed likely to flee the jurisdiction to avoid prosecution, or they pose a serious risk to the community if released temporarily pending trial. Bail bondspersons usually are available to post bail for persons granted it.

3. *Summarize the Bail Reform Act of 1984 and its implications for clients released on bail.*

For many persons, bail is not necessary, and such persons may be released on their own recognizance (ROR). Under the Bail Reform Act of 1984, greater autonomy was given to magistrates and other judicial officials to determine the amount of bail or whether bail should be required to guarantee one's appearance in court later. Several bail experiments have been conducted over the years with many of these studies showing that persons released on their own recognizance subsequently appear in court. The Philadelphia Experiment was designed to determine bail fairness, and although the results were inconclusive, the equity of bail decision making was greatly improved in Philadelphia and other jurisdictions. ROR is increasingly used instead of cash bonds or other forms of sureties. A totality of circumstances test is usually used to determine which persons should be granted bail and which ones should not be granted it.

4. *Identify the role of fugitive recovery agents or bounty hunters who track down those who fail to appear or abscond from the jurisdiction to avoid prosecution.*

When some persons fail to appear in court to face the criminal charges against them or jump bail, fugitive recovery agents or bounty hunters usually are hired to track them down. Bonding companies in various cities usually have a fixed amount of money they may use for posting one's bond, and if someone flees, the bond is forfeited. Bonding companies cannot afford to lose these bonds and thus resort to bounty hunters to recover their funds.

5. *Explain the necessity for a speedy trial for a defendant.*

A trial proceeding provides defendants with the opportunity to confront and cross-examine their accusers and to offer exculpatory evidence favoring a verdict of "not guilty." A trial is an adversarial proceeding, where the prosecution attempts to establish a defendant's guilt and the defense attempts to ensure the defendants' rights are not violated. Federal courts are bound by law to observe the Speedy Trial Act of 1974 and its 1979 and 1984 amendments. According to the provisions of this act, suspects must be charged with a criminal offense within 30 days following their arrest or receipt of a summons. The trial should then commence not less than 30 days or more than 70 days from the suspect's initial appearance. The idea of a speedy trial varies among the states and the federal government. Probably the longest speedy trial period is in New Mexico, which sets forth a 180-day timeline for a trial. Some states have speedy trial provisions of 90 days.

6. Compare and contrast bench trials and jury trials.

Trial procedures vary from one jurisdiction to the next. A bench trial could be held where the judge oversees the proceedings and is responsible for hearing the facts of the case and making a judgment based on those facts. Bench trials are usually used for less serious and petty offenses in which the defendant has waived his/her right to a jury trial. Some advantages of a bench trial include the following: case processing is expedited, judges are less likely than juries to consider extralegal factors, judges are usually in a better position to decide the sufficiency of evidence in more complex cases, judges are less persuaded by media attention, and bench trials are usually cheaper than jury trials. Disadvantages, however, include that judges may impose more severe punishments on certain defendants, and defendants waive their right to a jury trial where maybe their appearance, emotional appeal, and situation could have worked to their benefit in front of a jury.

Defendants charged with felonies are guaranteed the right to a trial by jury. This guarantee also applies to the states; the case of *Duncan v. Louisiana* specified the right to trial by jury for those charged with offenses other than petty crimes for which the possible punishment imposed could be six months of imprisonment. Where a jury trial is conducted, the number of jurors ranges from 6 to 12. At the federal level, a jury verdict must be unanimous. At the state and local levels, however, a unanimous verdict may or may not be required, depending upon the prevailing laws.

7. Understand the trial process from indictment through to the judges' instructions to the jury.

The trial process is varied in the different jurisdictions of the United States. There are many stages that characterize the trial process beginning with the indictment of a defendant through to the judge's instructions to the jury members. Some of these stages include a defendant's plea, the prosecution's opening statement, the defense opening statement, presenting evidence and testimony from witnesses from both sides, cross-examination by both sides, defense closing arguments, prosecution closing arguments, and judge's instructions to the jury regarding various procedures such as the standard of proof required.

8. Recognize the different pretrial motions, including motion to suppress, motion for dismissal of charges, motion for discovery, motion for continuance, motion for change of venue, and others.

There are also a number of motions that may be made, and either granted or denied. Pretrial motions are used to ensure that there are no surprises at trial. For instance, a motion to suppress is used in an attempt to exclude certain evidence from being introduced at trial, evidence that the defense believes has been obtained illegally. The exclusionary rule provides that evidence obtained in violation of certain privileges U.S. citizens enjoy must be excluded at trial. A motion to dismiss may be filed by the defense attorney, stating that he/she does not believe the prosecutor has sufficient evidence to proceed with a trial. A motion for discovery is usually made by the defense, which will enable them to obtain and examine evidence collected by the prosecution as well as the witnesses they plan to call to testify. A motion for continuance is usually made to allow delay of the trial for the purposes of collecting more evidence or interviewing additional witnesses. A motion for determination of competency is made to question if the defendant is competent or sufficiently sane to stand trial. A motion for change of venue is a request to hold the trial elsewhere in the belief that in the current jurisdiction the ability of the defendant to have a fair trial would be difficult. These and many other motions are usually made before a trial begins in order to ensure that the defendant is given a fair trial by an impartial jury.

9. Describe and illustrate what opening arguments are for, how the state presents its case, and the right to cross-examination and re-cross-examination.

During the actual trial process itself many procedures are also followed. Each side is permitted to address the jury with an opening statement. Both the prosecution and the defense will make opening arguments where each side will give a preview of what they are going to prove or disprove throughout the trial. The prosecution will usually present their theory of the events and why the defendant is in fact guilty. The defense will try to undermine the state's case saying that the prosecution doesn't have enough evidence to prove the elements of the crime, and that when all is said and done, the jury will see that the defendant should be acquitted. Following opening statements, the prosecution will present its case by presenting evidence and bringing in witnesses that prove a crime has been committed and that the defendant is the one who committed it.

There are Federal Rules of Evidence that judges and the attorneys must follow regarding which types of evidence are admissible or inadmissible. Judges are responsible for determining the relevance of objections and evidence. The defense also has the right to question the prosecution's witnesses; this is known as cross-examination. This is where the defense will attempt to show that the witness is not a credible one. Once cross-examination is finished, the prosecution can then ask additional questions of their witness; this is called re-direct examination. As the trial progresses and new evidence surfaces, prior witnesses can be called to the stand again; this is known as re-cross-examination.

10. *Explain the role of eyewitnesses and expert testimony.*

Both sides usually call to the stand eyewitnesses and expert witnesses to give various testimony. Expert witnesses are used to give meaning to the evidence that is presented. Usually, expert witnesses will have extensive training and experience in particular matters. This gives their testimony more influence than the testimony of laypersons. Eyewitnesses can also be of value to both the prosecution and defense. These witnesses provide opinions or interpretations of the events that transpired, and can account for the involvement or lack of involvement of the defendant in the crimes alleged.

11. *Describe and illustrate the process of defense presentation of its case and summation, including closing arguments.*

After the prosecution has rested, the defense then presents its case, revealing evidence and witness testimony favorable to the defendant. The process continues until both sides are satisfied that the evidence before the jury has been adequately presented. The final procedure involves a summation by both sides. This time the defense presents its closing arguments first, and the prosecution has the last word to show that it has proven, beyond a reasonable doubt, that the defendant is in fact guilty of the crimes he/she has been charged with.

12. *Analyze jury deliberations, whether or not a jury must agree on a verdict, and the jury verdict and its aftermath.*

After summations, the judge will instruct the jury on the procedures to be followed in deliberations. The jury system first emerged in the United Stated around 1607; however, they existed in England as early as the eleventh century. Juries are made up of persons from a cross section of the community or region in which the crime has occurred. The selection of jury members involves questioning them concerning their possible biases or prejudices in the case before the court; whether biases are specific (knowing the defendant) or general (having certain ideas about crime and criminal

offenders), a potential juror with either should be excluded from duty so that an impartial jury can be formed. Both prosecution and defense attorneys attempt to select jurors favorable to their particular interests. Jurors are excluded from jury duty for reasons of illness or their occupations, or if they do not meet requirements, and both prosecution and defense attorneys may challenge any juror for cause. Jurors may also be excluded by means of peremptory challenges, as the prosecutor and defense attorney attempt to construct the most favorable jury for their particular position. These peremptory challenges may not be used for purposes of discrimination, however.

The science of jury selection is popular. Many attorneys turn to consulting firms that specialize in the selection of jury members. However, the results of studies investigating particular jury member characteristics and their decision-making inclinations have been inconsistent and disappointing. No one has been able to predict with 100 percent certainty how particular jury members will vote in a given trial. Questions of ethics about scientifically selecting a jury have also been raised.

Jury deliberations are conducted following the presentation of witnesses and evidence from both the prosecution and defense, and a verdict is determined. Jury deliberations are done in secret, meaning that no one other than jury members is allowed in this process. Jurors may attempt to persuade each other to side with their decision. Research has shown that group pressure can cause those in the minority decision to align themselves with the majority. Depending on whether the case is a federal, state, or other trial, the verdict must either be unanimous or in compliance with the jurisdiction's rules regarding verdicts. Federal juries must be unanimous. If the jury cannot agree on a verdict as local, state, or federal law requires, the presiding judge will declare a mistrial. This will require a new trial before a new jury. If a jury finds the defendant guilty of the crime alleged, the judge will sentence the convicted offender, either at the conclusion of the trial or in a separate subsequent proceeding.

After deliberations, the jury returns to the courtroom to give its verdict. The defendant must rise and face the jury, and the foreperson or the judge will read the verdict aloud. If a verdict of guilty is found, the defendant may appeal; appeals can take several years before they are exhausted depending on the seriousness and nature of the appeal. If found guilty, the judge is responsible for handing out a punishment to the defendant. Usually the defendant is remanded to custody and the sentence will be given at a sentencing hearing on a subsequent date.

Key Terms

Critical Thinking Exercises

1. What is the difference between a "bench trial" and a "jury trial?" Having learned about both of these types of trials, is there any evidence to indicate that a defendant is better off having a bench trial as opposed to a jury trial? If you were charged with an offense which would you choose, and why? What might be some reasons you would want to have a jury of your peers hear the evidence against you? Do you think that under the Sixth Amendment, all those accused of a crime should have the right to a jury trial?

2. On the basis of some of the research conducted about jury size, is a 12-member jury more representative of community interests compared with a 6-person jury? What are some differences between these jury sizes other than the number of jurors? Do you think that all juries should be comprised of 12 members? What do you think about whether juries should have to be unanimous in their decisions?

Case Study Decision-Making Exercise

The Speedy Trial Act ensures that (alleged) criminals are brought to justice promptly. It sets out provisions for the number of days within which a suspect must be charged, the time frame within which the initial appearance should take place, and how long before a trial should begin.

In the case of *Klopfer v. North Carolina* (1967), the defendant was charged with criminal trespass and his case resulted in a mistrial. Instead of retrying the case, the government stated in the court record a motion of "*nolle prosequi* with leave," not specifying whether, or when they intended to make a decision about prosecuting the case. Klopfer appealed this decision, and the U.S. Supreme Court eventually weighed in stating that it was unconstitutional to indefinitely postpone Klopfer's trial without providing an adequate reason for doing so. In other words,

this type of delay violated the Sixth Amendment and would jeopardize the credibility of witness testimony, and the fairness of the trial due to perhaps extensive pretrial publicity. What are your thoughts about the time frame within which the government should prosecute someone they believe has violated the law? Is it unconstitutional to delay and not decide whether a defendant will be prosecuted again after a mistrial? Why do you think the Supreme Court decided with the defendant in this case? Would not knowing what the prosecution is going to do harm a person's ability to put the case past them and move on with their life, especially where the jury couldn't decide guilt or innocence in a previous trial? Should the government be able to retry someone after they have already failed to prove guilt beyond a reasonable doubt in one trial?

Concept Review Questions

1. What are sexual predator laws? What is their significance regarding whether someone is granted bail?
2. Who is a bail bondsman? Is a bail bondsman also a bounty hunter? Distinguish between each.
3. What is a bail bond? How can persons obtain bail?
4. Is everyone entitled to bail? Under what circumstances might one not be entitled to bail?
5. Describe the process of arrest, booking, and an initial appearance.
6. What is a preliminary examination or hearing?
7. What does it mean to release someone on his/her own recognizance?
8. How are failure-to-appear rates affected by whether one is granted bail or is released on his/her own recognizance?
9. What are the competing goals of bail?
10. What were some important provisions of the Bail Reform Act of 1984 in terms of how citizens were treated when arrested?
11. What is a pretrial motion? What is it called? What are some examples of pretrial motions?
12. What is a trial? What are some of the functions of a trial proceeding?
13. Does a criminal defendant have to have a jury trial if he/she is charged with murder? Can the defendant

waive his/her right to a jury trial? What constitutional amendment pertains to jury trials?
14. Identify three functions of juries. Which U.S. Supreme Court decision pertained to setting lower limits for jury sizes? What was the limit established?
15. In a particular criminal case before a 6-person jury, the jury brought back a verdict of guilty, but the vote was 5–1. Evaluate this verdict in view of what you have learned about jury size and unanimity of agreement among jurors.
16. What are five "maxims" believed by many attorneys about juror characteristics and accompanying juror attitudes?
17. What is meant by the "fruits of the poisonous tree"? What does it have to do with evidence? Explain briefly.
18. What is the exclusionary rule?
19. How reliable is the testimony of a child witness? Cite some research that has investigated the competency of child witnesses.
20. What is the purpose of a victim–witness assistance program?
21. Who usually gets the last word and closing argument in a criminal case before a jury?

Judge Rejects Plea Bargain Agreement

In the fall of 2001, a young man in Laredo, Texas, was shot and seriously wounded. He was hit in his upper leg following an argument with another man. A subsequent investigation by police and a search of the shooter's residence revealed a sawed-off shotgun, a 9mm handgun, and several other weapons. The man was arrested and charged with two counts of aggravated assault with a deadly weapon. The man's attorney met with the prosecutor and worked out a plea bargain in which the shooter would serve two years in prison. The judge in the case, however, in examining the plea agreement rejected it. The judge said he would not accept the agreement because there were various aggravating circumstances involved in the case and, therefore, the deal was too lenient. The judge ordered the attorneys to come up with a more reasonable plea agreement.

Do judges have the power to reject plea bargains wherein the state and defendant have entered into an agreement for leniency in exchange for his guilty plea? Some people criticize plea bargain agreements as being too lenient on offenders. Plea bargaining, however, is a necessary part of the criminal court system due to its ability to keep the wheels of justice moving.

▶ Introduction

It is difficult to imagine an efficient criminal justice system operating without plea bargaining. This chapter explores plea bargaining in great detail. Plea bargaining is a preconviction agreement or negotiated guilty plea between the government and defendant wherein the government offers some form of leniency, usually a lighter sentence, in exchange for a guilty plea to lesser charges. Thus, through plea bargaining, the state benefits because it avoids a protracted and expensive trial. The defendant benefits in that a sentence is accepted, which is often much shorter and less severe than a sentence that may have been imposed had the case proceeded to trial and the person had been convicted. All plea bargain agreements are subject to judicial approval.

The chapter opens with an examination of plea bargaining generally and the issue of why defendants should enter into plea bargain agreements. A brief history of plea bargaining in the United States is presented. Plea bargaining is not unique to the United States and occurs with some frequency in many other countries. Over 90 percent of all criminal cases are concluded annually through plea bargaining of some kind. This section examines the conditions under which plea bargaining may occur and when it may occur, which is at any time from the point when one is arrested through the jury deliberation process. The coercive aspects of plea bargaining are examined. Also discussed is the matter of promises made by prosecutors to induce defendants to enter guilty pleas. Under all circumstances, these promises from prosecutors must be honored; otherwise, plea agreements are invalidated.

The next section examines several types of plea bargaining. Implicit plea bargaining is examined, where it is generally understood by both prosecutors and defense counsels alike what the going rate is for a particular crime charged. Usually, agreements are reached between these opposing parties about the type of plea the defendant will enter and the punishment recommended. Another type of plea bargaining is charge reduction bargaining. Where many charges have been filed against criminal defendants, prosecutors may agree to drop most charges if defendants plead guilty to one or more of the lesser charges. A third type of plea bargaining is judicial plea bargaining, where the judge recommends a sentence

going rate local view of the appropriate sentence or punishment for a particular offense, the defendant's prior record, and other factors; used in implicit plea bargaining.

to a defendant in exchange for a plea of guilty. The fourth type of plea bargaining is sentence recommendation bargaining. Under this type of plea bargaining, the prosecutor recommends a specific sentence to the defendant in exchange for a guilty plea. The weaknesses and strengths of each of these types of plea bargaining are examined.

The chapter next examines a wide array of arguments favoring plea bargaining as well as a lengthy list of arguments opposing it. Arguments in favor of plea bargaining include that it results in fewer trials and trial delays, more convictions are obtained, expensive trials are avoided, and defendants can anticipate some form of leniency in sentencing. Opponents of plea bargaining claim that plea bargaining violates one's right against self-incrimination, since one must admit guilt in order to receive a more lenient sentence or sentence recommendation. Other arguments include that judges lose control over cases that are plea bargained; defendants may be ignorant of the rights they are waiving when entering into plea agreements; guilty pleas may be rejected by the court; habitual offender statutes may be circumvented; some persons may receive more lenient sentences when their crimes deserve harsher penalties; some heinous aspects of crimes are not disclosed through plea agreements; plea agreements may appear to be too routine and rubber-stamped; the potential exists for gender bias in plea bargaining; the jury process may be invalidated; sentencing reforms may be hampered; negotiated guilty pleas are too bureaucratized; and lawyers may be vested with too much authority in the plea bargaining process. In some jurisdictions, plea bargaining has been banned. Despite the ban on plea bargaining, it still exists even in jurisdictions that have banned it. Some of the reasons for banning plea bargaining are listed and discussed.

The chapter finally examines the important role of judges in the plea bargaining process. Judges must determine whether defendants wish to waive their right to a trial. They must also determine if there is a factual basis for the guilty plea. More than a few instances have occurred where defendants have been bullied into guilty pleas by aggressive prosecutors where no evidence of defendant guilt exists. Under these circumstances, judges have rejected such plea agreements and acquitted defendants, despite the fact that they entered guilty pleas to various crimes. Also, judges may or may not participate in the plea bargaining process. North Carolina is a state that allows judges to sit in while plea bargaining occurs between prosecutors, defendants, and their attorneys. In most jurisdictions, however, judicial participation in this process is banned. Furthermore, in some jurisdictions where sentencing guidelines have been established, plea bargaining may pose problems for enforcing these guidelines. Thus, different forms of sentencing may affect the plea bargaining process in a variety of ways (Wooldredge and Griffin 2004).

▶ Plea Bargaining: Negotiated Guilty Pleas

Why Should Any Defendant Plea Bargain?

Ideally, defendants who wish to enter guilty pleas to criminal charges know that they are guilty. There is substantial evidence against them. They have the right to compel the state to try them in a court of law. All criminals have a right to their day in court. However, in cases where one's guilt is not seriously contested, trials are perfunctory rituals with almost absolutely predictable results.

Unfortunately for criminal defendants, trial convictions usually result in more stringent applications of sanctions (Champion 2005a). Judges tend to deal more harshly with convicted offenders who have insisted on trials despite the existence of substantial evidence of their guilt beyond a reasonable doubt. However, pretrial agreements where guilty pleas are entered often result in less severe sanctions or sentences. Early research on the differences in sentences imposed through plea bargaining or trial has highlighted a pattern of judicial sentencing behavior. In more than a few jurisdictions, judges have advised defendants of the sentences they plan to impose (Cummingham 2005). Judges further advise that if the plea bargain is rejected and the case proceeds to trial, convicted offenders are likely to incur a harsher sentence. Thus, those who contest their guilt compared with those who plead guilty are subjected to established practices whereby judges sentence them more harshly (Kirschner and Galperin 2001). The harsher sentence is imposed as a punishment for burdening the state with the responsibility of proving one is guilty beyond a reasonable doubt.

Plea bargaining usually results in reduced charges for criminal defendants. In some instances, criminal charges may be dropped altogether in exchange for valuable information about a crime. For instance, a man was engaged to a school teacher in a northeastern state during the 1980s. The woman broke off the engagement. Enraged, the man killed the woman and buried her body off an old logging trail about ten miles from her home. The woman's disappearance was quickly noticed, although there was no evidence of foul play. The man was the key suspect in the case, but the prosecutor was helpless. There was no direct or circumstantial evidence of his culpability or anything to suggest that he had harmed her. The man subsequently moved to a western state where he found work and started a new life for himself. After over a decade of searching for the missing woman, the prosecutor contacted the man during the 1990s and said that if the man told him where the body could be found, no charges would be brought against him for the crime. The man entered into an agreement with the prosecutor to disclose details about how the woman came to be missing. The man said that he had killed her in a jealous rage when she had spurned him. And then he carefully concealed the body in a large shower curtain and buried the woman on the logging trail. He led police and the prosecutor to the exact spot where the woman was buried. Her body was recovered and she was given a proper burial by her family members. The man was not prosecuted for this murder and returned to his state to resume his life. The prosecutor was soundly criticized by the public and media for this agreement not to prosecute the man, but the prosecutor stated that unless he had made that agreement, the woman's body never would have been recovered. At least her family had the peace of mind of knowing what had happened.

In less dramatic cases played out in courtrooms throughout the United States, prosecutors and defense counsel attempt to arrive at the most favorable sentences for state interests and for defendant's interests. Depending upon whether offenses alleged are felonies or misdemeanors, negotiations between prosecutors and defense counsel are geared to arrive at an appropriate term of years or months for defendants who wish to enter guilty pleas. The prosecution seeks to maximize these years or months, while the defense seeks to minimize them (Tappan 2005).

For instance, suppose a defendant is charged with burglary and conversion of stolen property. The burglary and conversion of stolen property statutes provide a $5,000 fine and up to five years in prison on each charge. A worst case scenario would result in a jury trial and convictions on both charges, a $10,000 fine, and consecutive sentences of the maximum five years each for a total of 10 years. Seeking to avoid both the fine and a 10-year term of imprisonment, the defendant may enter into a plea bargain agreement and plead guilty to one of the charges, such as the burglary. The prosecutor will drop the conversion of stolen property charge and recommend waiver of the $10,000 in fines. The prosecutor may suggest a two- or three-year prison term in exchange for a guilty plea to burglary. While the defendant wishes to avoid prison entirely, he is faced with either accepting the two- or three-year sentence or taking his chances in court. There is a strong likelihood that he would be convicted of both offenses. Further, the judge would likely impose a harsher sentence, such as five or more years. Therefore, a powerful incentive exists for defendants to enter guilty pleas rather than face potentially harsher punishments in courts if they are subsequently convicted.

Fines attached to criminal statutes are rarely imposed by judges. One reason for not imposing fines is the state's inability to collect fines from convicted offenders, who are most frequently unemployed and indigent. Crime may be their only livelihood. When offenders are apprehended, convicted, and incarcerated, they have no means whereby to earn money to pay off fines imposed earlier by judges. An offender's inability to pay fines cannot be used to lengthen his/her sentence. However, if certain defendants have assets, including property, automobiles, or expensive possessions, these items of value may be subject to seizure under asset forfeiture. An embezzler might have purchased property and other material possessions with money stolen from a business. One way of restoring the business's money is to seize the offender's assets and liquidate them. The proceeds from such liquidations are given to the business from which the money was stolen.

In typical property offense cases, however, convicted offenders may be drug or alcohol dependent. Their drug or alcohol habits may cause them to steal and obtain money to purchase more drugs or alcohol. Gambling addiction may drive offenders to steal another's property and convert it to money to satisfy their gambling addiction. Thus, many offenders have no assets and are deeply in debt when arrested by police. Because there are no assets to seize, the government can impose fines of any amount with little or no expectation of ever recovering even a fraction of the fines imposed.

Why Should Prosecutors Bargain with Criminals?

Are prosecutors obligated to collaborate with defense counsels and work out negotiated guilty pleas for each defendant? No. The U.S. Supreme Court has declared that prosecutors are under no obligation to enter into plea bargain agreements with any criminal defendant (*United States v. Benchimol*, 1985). Plea bargain agreements are sought by both prosecutors and defense counsels. It is to a prosecutor's advantage to resolve criminal cases without formal trial proceedings. Trials involve considerable preparation and state expense. There is no guarantee that juries will convict guilty defendants, regardless of how much evidence exists against them. Plea bargains avoid trials and the often difficult burden of proving defendant's guilt beyond a reasonable doubt. Most successfully concluded plea agreements result in convictions. Prosecutors are driven to convict defendants by one means or another. By far, the cheapest and easiest convictions obtained by prosecutors are through plea bargain agreements (Thompson 2005).

The effectiveness of prosecutors is most often evaluated in terms of their record of successful prosecutions. Successful prosecutions are those resulting in convictions. Thus, more the convictions, more the prosecutor's effectiveness. If some prosecutors have political aspirations, aspire to judgeships, or seek promotions within their own district attorney's offices, their conviction records are direct evidence of their effectiveness as prosecutors (O'Sullivan 2001). Their reputations are enhanced and their careers are furthered to the extent that they are effective at whatever they do (Schram, Koons-Witt, and Morash 2004). It is in the prosecutor's best interests to seek quick convictions through plea bargaining.

Thus, plea bargaining has subsequently emerged as a powerful political tool. It has become an increasingly visible and integral part of the criminal justice process. Within the criminal justice system, plea bargaining has shifted a great deal of power to prosecutors who have become the ultimate decision makers about a defendant's life chances (Boari and Fiorentini 2001; Rose-Ackerman 2002). Prosecutors now perform pivotal roles as they decide which cases should be prosecuted and which cases should be dropped. Prosecutors contemplate particular sentences for defendants charged with various crimes.

It is also important to understand that in most plea bargaining and the hearings that follow, ordinarily, judges see only what prosecutors decide to reveal against criminal defendants. Judges may be unaware that other charges against specific defendants were not included in the plea agreement but simply ignored or dropped by the prosecutor in order to elicit a guilty plea. This is not the fault of judges. Usually, there are so many plea agreements submitted to judges for their approval that most judges don't have the time to study each agreement in detail. Furthermore, many judges view plea bargaining as a fundamental feature of the criminal justice process, and they cooperate with prosecutors by approving plea agreements that are seen as a reasonable trade-off between crime control and due process (U.S. Sentencing Commission 2003). There are some important exceptions, however.

In an Alabama case, James Smith entered a guilty plea and was convicted of first-degree burglary and rape. Earlier, a grand jury had indicted Smith for burglary, rape, sodomy, and assault. In exchange for a 30-year sentence, Smith entered a guilty plea to the burglary and rape charges, provided that the prosecutor dropped the sodomy charge. When the judge approved the plea agreement, he sentenced Smith to two concurrent 30-year sentences. However, a procedural technicality raised later by Smith resulted in a higher court vacating his original 30-year sentences. Subsequently, Smith went to trial on all four charges and was convicted by a jury. This time, the same judge sentenced Smith to life imprisonment on the burglary and sodomy convictions, and 150 years on the rape conviction. The judge explained the different sentences because he had not been fully aware of the circumstances under which these terrible crimes had occurred. The trial disclosed all of these details. Smith appealed unsuccessfully to the U.S. Supreme Court, contending that the judge was deliberately being vindictive with the imposition of these enhanced sentences. Rejecting his appeal, the U.S. Supreme Court said that in cases that go to trial, greater and more detailed information is available to sentencing judges compared with the information contained in a plea bargain agreement. This additional information justifies the court's harsher sentencing decision (*Alabama v. Smith*, 1989).

Ultimately, however, the decision to charge any particular defendant with specific crimes lies with the district attorney's office. Whether prosecutors interact with private counsel or public defenders, these persons wield considerable power in deciding how rigorously certain cases are pursued. Prosecutors have the greatest amount of power in cases where multiple offenses have been committed by a defendant. If a gun was used during the commission of a robbery, for example, prosecutors can decide whether or not to include this charge in a subsequent indictment or information. Usually, plea bargaining will result in some reduction in the number of charges filed. If prosecutors can be persuaded by defense counsel to leave out the fact that a weapon was used during the commission of a felony and charge simple robbery instead of armed robbery, the result will likely be a guilty plea to the lesser charge. This is because when weapons are used during felonies, they often involve mandatory incarcerative penalties. For example, some states have a "one with a gun gets you two" statutes, meaning that an automatic addition of two years of **flat time** is added to a convicted offender's sentence where a weapon was used during the commission of a felony. It is to the defendant's advantage if the prosecutor decides not to file a weapons-related charge. Thus, this fact becomes a bargaining chip for the prosecutor and can be used strategically to elicit guilty pleas more easily from defendants who have committed weapons-related offenses (Cunningham 2005).

Another factor that affects the prosecutor's decision making about which cases to pursue vigorously is case pressure. In jurisdictions where the volume of cases processed is high, prosecutors may elect to **nolle prosequi** or decline to prosecute marginal cases that might have been pursued earlier for a guilty plea. Prosecutorial options under these conditions might include reducing more charges against defendants, recommending lighter sentences, or demanding more severe sentences after a trial.

How Long Has Plea Bargaining Been Used in the United States?

Historians have investigated the use of plea bargaining in the United States. Evidence suggests that plea bargaining occurred in the various states during the period following the Declaration of Independence in 1776. A study of plea bargaining in New York during the period 1800–1865 shows a pattern of plea bargaining usage that escalated during the

flat time actual amount of time required to be served by a convicted offender while incarcerated.

nolle prosequi an entry made by the prosecutor on the record in a case and announced in court to indicate that the specified charges will not be prosecuted. In effect, the charges are thereby dismissed.

second half of the nineteenth century (McConville and Mirsky 2005). The use of plea bargaining accompanied the rise in importance of district attorney's offices, the presence of elected judges, the judicialization of magistrates, the reorganization of the police, the marginalization of juries, and politicization of crime.

During the 1800s, plea bargaining was simply referred to as a guilty plea. No formal classification of guilty pleas existed. In the early part of the nineteenth century, jury trials were proscribed for almost all criminal offenses. State reliance on jury trials was strong. However, by the mid to late-1800s, the growth of attorney organizations and increasing professionalization of police work modified greatly the art of criminal investigations. At the same time, court dockets became overcrowded and the glut of jury trials worsened. Thus, guilty pleas with one or more prosecutorial concessions gained in popularity as an alternative to formal courtroom trial procedure.

The professionalization of police meant that larger numbers of minor prosecutions were shifted to municipal and police courts, such as those in Boston during the period 1814–1850 (Ferdinand 1992). Data analyzed from over 30,000 cases from the Boston Police Court during the early to mid-1800s showed that between 1814 and 1850, the caseload for police courts doubled. During the same time interval, the municipal court docket load increased by over 1,000 percent. Plea bargaining in Boston became increasingly commonplace as a means of resolving most cases. At the same time, court officers became more professional and formal courtroom procedures grew more intricate (Ferdinand 1992). It was in just such a milieu that the modern criminal court was born. Today's criminal

> **guilty plea** a defendant's formal affirmation of guilt in court to charges contained in a complaint, information, or indictment claiming that they committed the offenses listed.

BOX 8-1

LEGAL ISSUES: PLEA BARGAINING RESULTING IN GREATER PUNISHMENT?

Over 90 percent of all criminal convictions are obtained through plea bargaining, even in jurisdictions where it has been banned. Police and court professionalization, along with increasingly crowded court dockets lessened the popularity of ensuring jury trials for all those accused of crimes (Ferdinand, 1992). In most plea-bargained cases, defendants enter guilty pleas to reduce charges in order to avoid more serious penalties. This strategy almost always works to the benefit of both prosecutors and defendants. In some ways, plea bargaining is an outgrowth of industrialization and has reduced substantially the courtroom workload.

Plea bargaining in the United States is successful and widely used because it may actually assist prosecutors to impose greater punishment. For example, a district attorney who has 100 cases a year and a budget of $100,000 has only $1,000 to spend investigating and prosecuting each case (Olin, 2002). It is likely, therefore, that many of these cases could not be tried due to time and financial constraints. But if the prosecutor can get 90 of the 100 defendants to enter guilty pleas and avoid expensive investigations and trials, he or she can then utilize office resources on the other 10 percent, still have a conviction rate that will be above 90 percent (Olin, 2002). Pleas agreements are the cheapest and easiest way to obtain convictions (Thompson 2005).

Viewed from the defendant's perspective, plea bargaining makes a lot of sense. In the federal system, the conviction rate of criminal cases that go to trial is over 90 percent, depending on the nature of the offense. If there is a 90 percent chance of being convicted and receiving a severe sentence, most defendants will enter into plea bargains with U.S. attorneys to obtain less severe sentences from judges (United States Sentencing Commission, 2003).

Sources: Olin, Dirk (2002). "The Way we Live Now: 9-29-02:Crash Course; Plea Bargain," *The New York Times Magazine*, September 29, 2002. Available online at: http://www.nytimes.com/2002/09/29/magazine/the-way-we-live-now-9-29-02-crash-course-plea-bargain.html.

U.S. Sentencing Commission (2003). *Downward Departures from the Federal Sentencing Guidelines.* Washington, DC: U.S. Sentencing Commission.

courts are high-volume and multipurpose. The sheer numbers of cases crowding these court dockets made plea bargaining especially appealing, since valuable court time could be saved by out-of-court bargaining between prosecutors and defense attorneys.

The growth of formal legal education was apparent during this same period. More persons were acquiring formal legal training from newly established law schools, and the numbers of lawyers invading criminal courts to represent growing numbers of clients meant more protracted litigation. A relief valve was plea bargaining. A more educated lawyer contingent made plea bargaining more attractive to criminals as well as to judges, since criminals could bargain their way to lesser penalties without formal trial proceedings (Blackwell 2004). The trend toward greater use of plea bargaining continued into the 1900s. Since the 1960s, plea bargaining has escalated in use to the extent that over 90 percent of all criminal convictions are secured through plea negotiations. Because of the great savings in case processing time, most courts today are able to function with only moderate delays. It is difficult to contemplate what our courts would be like today if plea bargaining was banned outright.

Is Plea Bargaining Unique to the United States?

No. Many countries use some form of plea bargaining as a means of speeding up criminal case processing. Plea bargaining is used frequently in Australia, Canada (Kellough and Wortley 2002), France (Ma 2002), Germany (Ma 2002), Israel (Ajzenstadt and Steinberg 2001; Herzog 2003), Italy (Boari and Fiorentini 2001), and the United Kingdom (Ma 2002). Citizen discontent with plea bargaining in these countries is about the same as it is in the United States. In Canada, for example, a survey of 1,049 citizens revealed that most disapproved of plea bargaining. One primary complaint was that plea bargaining appeared to result in insufficient penalties for criminals. However, these citizen respondents also indicated that if judges were to take a more proactive role in the plea bargaining process to ensure fairness to victims and the punishment process generally, then they would be inclined to be supportive of it (Goodman and Porter 2002). And in Germany, plea bargaining has been evaluated by prosecutors, judges, and defense counsels. They vary in their opinions toward plea bargaining depending upon the various costs and benefits of plea bargaining versus trial (Ma 2002).

How Much Plea Bargaining Is There Today?

In order to understand both the need for and use of plea bargaining, we must first appreciate the magnitude of federal and state litigation and rapid growth of criminal cases. In the federal system, for example, there were 44,144 criminal prosecutions in U.S. District Courts in 1982. This figure had risen to 64,000 in 1994. There were approximately 49,000 convictions in federal courts in 1994 and this number continued to rise reaching a peak of a little over 86,000 in 2011 and has declined to roughly 75,000 in 2014 (U.S. Sentencing Commission 2015). Roughly 90 percent of all federal criminal convictions are obtained through plea bargaining and without an expensive and lengthy trial. In state courts, there were over 500,000 prosecutions in 1982, and by 1994, there were 1.2 million prosecutions in state courts, resulting in 872,217 convictions (Champion 2005b). By 2009, there were almost 4 million criminal case filings in courts of general jurisdiction across the states; if cases in single-tiered courts and courts of limited jurisdiction are included, the number of cases rises to just over 21 million (LaFountain, Schauffler, Strickland, Gibson, and Mason 2011). As is obvious by these statistics, the country's criminal courts are overwhelmed with trying to keep up with the increased caseloads.

The rate of plea bargaining has remained fairly constant during the period 1970–2005 (U.S. Department of Justice 2005). In the 1970s, at least 90 percent of all convictions were obtained through plea bargaining. Today, it is more than 95 percent in some jurisdictions and at the federal level. Even with 90 percent of all guilty pleas in either state or federal courts resulting from plea bargaining, the trial court delays in the criminal justice system today are notorious. High-profile cases consume several months of court time before they are resolved, but less celebrated cases also consume large amounts of court time. Most cases were low-profile and received little media attention (Maguire and Pastore 2005). Despite this inattention, these trials are sufficiently drawn out to underscore the necessity for plea bargaining. Without it, federal and state courts would probably come to a grinding halt. Or at the very least, case backlogs would be such that most scheduled criminal cases could not be heard for at least one or more years. In view of a defendant's right to a speedy trial, these courts would be hard-pressed to comply with this important constitutional provision.

Do All Jurisdictions Use Plea Bargaining?

No. Most jurisdictions use it. In some jurisdictions, plea bargaining has been banned in some forms. The most visible jurisdiction prohibiting plea bargaining is Alaska (Champion 2005b). The ban against plea bargaining was announced by the Alaska Judicial Council in 1975. Routine sentence agreements between prosecutors and defense attorneys were virtually eliminated after the ban and have not returned. Presently, most defendants are sentenced by a judge at an open hearing, with participation by the prosecutor, defense, and a presentence reporter. Thus, the responsibility for sentencing rests primarily with the judge. In 2013, Alaska reiterated its ban on plea bargaining, especially in violent offense cases. The Attorney General of Alaska announced that prosecutors no longer have the discretion to negotiate sentence lengths as part of pleas agreements. Prosecutors can still bargain with defendants to drop or reduce charges but sentence length decisions will be left entirely up to judges.

Some jurisdictions, such as Bronx County, New York, have sought to limit plea bargaining to specific phases of criminal processing. Whether a defendant has been indicted is significant here. A pre-indictment period is the time before criminal defendants are formally indicted for specific offenses. A post-indictment period occurs following their indictment. Once indictments have been issued in Bronx County, plea bargaining has been discouraged under a new policy. At the same time, pre-indictment plea bargaining has been openly encouraged.

In El Paso, Texas, a felony plea bargaining ban was implemented in 1975 (Holmes et al. 1992). Researchers investigated the effects of this ban on case processing and dispositions. While the conviction rate was generally unaffected, much greater numbers of cases went to trial. As a result, there was a gradual decrease in the disposition rate. Thus, it was concluded that the plea bargaining ban in El Paso adversely impacted the ability of district courts to move felony case dockets along efficiently.

Later in 1981, the Superior Court of Merrimack County, New Hampshire, banned plea bargaining in response to criticisms of the practice and the perceived decline in public confidence in the judicial system's ability to effectively administer criminal sanctions. Unexpectedly, the quality of indictments against criminal defendants in Merrimack County did not improve. Actual sentence lengths imposed for various criminal offenses have remained unaffected by the ban. Court backlogs were increasing when researchers conducted a two-year follow-up and ban assessment (Champion 2005a).

When Can Plea Bargaining Occur?

In most jurisdictions unless otherwise prohibited by policy or legislative statements, plea bargaining can occur at virtually any stage of a criminal proceeding prior to a finding of guilt. While most plea bargaining occurs before a trial is conducted, plea bargain negotiations may transpire throughout a trial. In some cases, plea bargains have been struck while a case is in progress or while a jury is deliberating.

Interrupting a criminal trial with a plea bargain has about the same effect of refusing to plea bargain in the pretrial and pre-indictment periods. Considerable expense has been incurred by the state in the defendant's prosecution. Judges are unhappy with events such as these. However, the prosecution bears some of the responsibility by entering into these late plea bargaining negotiations. Perhaps prosecutors believe that there might be a chance that the jury will acquit, and thus, a plea bargain is attractive since it would guarantee a conviction. Where plea bargains are struck this late, it is likely that neither side is willing to gamble on the jury outcome in view of the different types of evidence presented.

Is Plea Bargaining Coercive?

There is no question that plea bargaining is coercive. Almost no offender wants to admit guilt to any wrongdoing. Therefore, when an offer is made by the prosecutor to plead guilty to reduced charges or face prosecution on more serious charges, most defendants find this choice coercive. Even judges think plea bargaining is coercive (Champion 2005a). At the same time, however, judges concede that plea bargaining is a suitable trade-off between due process and crime control. Further, plea bargaining makes life much easier for these judges, prosecutors, defense counsel, and criminals.

The U.S. Supreme Court has ruled in several important cases where coercion relating to plea bargaining has been alleged.

BOX 8-2

KEY CASES: IS PLEA BARGAINING COERCIVE?

McMann v. Richardson 397 U.S. 759 (1970)

In this case, the defendant entered a guilty plea knowingly and voluntarily to murder. He was sentenced to 30 years in prison as the result of the plea bargain agreement. Later, he appealed, contending that his guilty plea had been coerced by the prosecutor. The U.S. Supreme Court heard his argument and ruled that no evidence existed to show that his guilty plea was coerced. Therefore, merely alleging that you were coerced into a plea agreement is insufficient to succeed on an appeal and have one's conviction overturned.

North Carolina v. Alford 400 U.S. 25 (1970)

In this case, Alford was indicted for first-degree murder and faced the death penalty if convicted. Alford maintained his innocence and that he had murdered no one. Subsequently, he was permitted to enter a *nolo contendere* plea to second-degree murder in exchange for a 30-year sentence that the judge imposed. *Nolo contendere* pleas are treated the same as guilty pleas, although they technically do not involve admissions of guilt by defendants. Rather, defendants enter such pleas and merely acknowledge the facts as set forth in indictments without actually admitting their guilt.

Later, Alford contested the 30-year sentence, arguing that he was coerced into pleading guilty in order to avoid the death penalty, which may have resulted from a subsequent jury verdict. The U.S. Supreme Court was unsympathetic and held that when an accused, such as Alford, enters a plea voluntarily, the accused knowingly and understandingly consents to the imposition of a prison sentence even though he/she is unwilling to admit participation in the crime, or even if his/her guilty plea contains a protestation of innocence, when, as here, he/she intelligently concludes that his/her interests require a guilty plea and the record strongly evidences his/her guilt. Put more simply, plea bargaining is not considered coercive when a defendant chooses a lengthy prison sentence in order to escape the possible imposition of the death penalty (Foley 2003).

Brady v. United States 397 U.S. 742 (1970)

Brady was a codefendant in a case involving kidnapping. The offense carried the maximum penalty of death. Brady initially pleaded not guilty to the kidnapping charge. However, Brady's codefendant decided to plead guilty to a lesser charge in exchange for his testimony against Brady in a later trial. Brady changed his

(continued)

mind and pleaded guilty to the kidnapping charge in exchange for a 50-year sentence that was subsequently commuted to 30 years. However, Brady brooded about the lengthy prison term and eventually filed an appeal, alleging that his guilty plea had been coerced. The U.S. Supreme Court heard Brady's appeal and upheld his conviction. The Court held that a plea of guilty is not invalid merely because it is entered to avoid the possibility of the death penalty. The U.S. Supreme Court further noted that although Brady's plea of guilty may well have been motivated in part by a desire to avoid a possible death penalty, we are convinced that his plea was voluntary and intelligently made and we have no reason to doubt that his solemn admission of guilt was truthful.

Bordenkircher v. Hayes 434 U.S. 357 (1978)

Paul Hayes was a career criminal, who was arrested for check forgery in Fayette County, Kentucky. The possible punishment for check forgery was a prison sentence of 2–10 years. Hayes had several prior felony convictions, and thus, he was eligible to be prosecuted under Kentucky's habitual offender statute. Under this statute, Hayes faced a sentence of life imprisonment. The prosecutor offered Hayes a plea bargain, which included a guilty plea to a bad check charge in exchange for a three-year sentence in prison. Hayes rejected the plea bargain and proceeded to trial. Hayes was prosecuted on the forgery charge as well as a habitual offender under the habitual offender statute. He was convicted and sentenced to life imprisonment. Later he appealed to the U.S. Supreme Court and claimed that the prosecutor had attempted to coerce him into pleading guilty to one crime while threatening to prosecute him for another crime. The U.S. Supreme Court concluded that Hayes had not been coerced. If prosecutors have grounds for filing particular criminal charges, then their threats to file such charges if defendants don't plead guilty to lesser charges are not considered coercive. In sum, prosecutors may use additional charges against defendants as leverage to elicit guilty pleas to lesser charges whenever there is probable cause to believe that the additional crimes have been committed by the defendant. There must be a factual basis underlying any criminal charge.

If Promises Are Made by Prosecutors to Obtain Guilty Pleas from Defendants, Are Prosecutors Obligated to Fulfill These Promises?

Yes. If a prosecutor promises to recommend leniency or a specific sentence in a plea agreement, then the prosecutor is bound to observe that promise if it is used to elicit a guilty plea. A prosecutor cannot promise a specific form of leniency merely to elicit a guilty plea from a defendant. Prosecutors must follow through on their promises.

In the case of *Santobello v. New York* (1971), Santobello was charged with two felony counts and pleaded guilty to a lesser-included offense following a prosecutor's promise *not* to make a sentence recommendation at the plea bargain hearing. However, the plea bargain hearing did not occur for several months. When the proceeding was conducted, a new prosecutor had replaced the earlier one. The new prosecutor, unaware of the earlier prosecutor's promise to Santobello, recommended the maximum sentence under the law, which was imposed by the judge. Santobello appealed, arguing that his guilty plea resulted from a promise by the former prosecutor not to recommend a particular sentence. While the judge himself said that he was unaffected by the new prosecutor's statement to maximize Santobello's sentence, the U.S. Supreme Court saw things differently. Santobello's conviction and sentence were overturned, since a promise had been made to Santobello as a means of inducing him to plead guilty. The U.S. Supreme Court held that the second prosecutor was honor-bound to observe the earlier prosecutor's promise. Santobello was allowed to withdraw his guilty plea. A prosecutor may not make promises to defendants to obtain guilty pleas from them, unless the prosecutor fully intends to keep the promises.

This same idea works both ways. If a prosecutor offers a reduced sentence to a defendant in exchange for that defendant's testimony against another defendant, then the defendant must fulfill his/her promise to testify or the plea bargain and sentence imposed are withdrawn. In the case of *Ricketts v. Adamson* (1987), Adamson was one of several codefendants charged with first-degree murder. Before his conviction, however, Adamson entered into a plea agreement with prosecutors to testify against his codefendants. In exchange for his testimony against other codefendants in separate trials later, Adamson was permitted to plead guilty to second-degree murder and receive a prison term instead of the death penalty. Adamson was convicted of second-degree murder. Later, when the trials of his codefendants were scheduled, Adamson refused to testify, breaking his earlier promise to prosecutors. The prosecutors appealed Adamson's conviction and sentence and the Arizona Supreme Court overturned the conviction. New first-degree murder charges were filed against Adamson and he was later convicted of this offense, which carried the maximum penalty. Adamson appealed to the U.S. Supreme Court, alleging that his right against double jeopardy had been violated with the new trial following his earlier conviction. The U.S. Supreme Court upheld his second conviction saying that his breach of the original plea agreement removed the double jeopardy bar that otherwise would prevail, assuming that under state law, second-degree murder is a lesser-included offense of first-degree murder. Therefore, even criminal defendants are obligated to keep their promises in order to make the plea agreement enforceable.

BOX 8-3

LEGAL ISSUES: WHY DO DEFENDANTS TAKE A PLEA DEAL?

23-year-old Patsy Jarrett, a North Carolina resident, drove to New York with a friend for a summer vacation. Three years later, police showed up at her door and she learned that sometime during their New York stay, her friend had robbed a gas station and murdered the attendant. The evidence against Jarrett's friend was strong. The only evidence against Jarrett was that an elderly witness said he saw a car at the time of the crime with someone inside. The man did not know, however, whether the person was a man or a woman. To avoid a trial, prosecutors offered Jarrett a plea bargain: if she would plead guilty to the robbery, they would drop the murder charge and give her a 5- to 15-year prison sentence. Jarrett said, "I told my attorney I can't do this." Her attorney said, "Well, my hands are tied. They want to drop the murder charge against you if you plead guilty to the robbery." And Jarrett said, "But I haven't robbed anybody." Convinced that the jury would believe her, Jarrett refused the plea bargain and went to trial. She was subsequently convicted and sentenced to 25 years to life. Jarrett commented after the trial and sentence, "I believed in the American system of justice. I believed that, you know, just tell the truth and the judge and jury will hear you and nothing will happen to you. But I was wrong." Interestingly, 12 years into her prison sentence, Jarrett's case was reversed, but the state appealed the reversal. The state offered her another plea bargain: admit to committing the crimes, and she would be sentenced to time served and released. Jarrett steadfastly maintained her innocence and

refused the plea bargain. Her conviction and sentence were reinstated and she has now spent over 30 years in prison for crimes she claims she never committed.

Charles Gampero, Jr., 20, was arrested and charged with second-degree murder. Gampero insisted that he was innocent of the crime. He admitted to having a fight with the victim outside of a bowling alley on the night the victim died, but he claimed that the victim was very much alive when he left him. There were numerous unanswered questions about the case. The victim's family, for instance, had told police that the victim had been the target of harassment and vandalism by unknown parties during several weeks before his death. Gampero believed that a jury would acquit him if the case went to trial. During the process of jury selection, however, the judge advised Gampero that if the case went to trial and Gampero were found guilty, the punishment would be a sentence of 25 years to life. But if Gampero pleaded guilty to a lesser charge, then the judge would impose a sentence of only 7–21 years instead. The judge told Gampero's parents point blank, "I will give your son 25 years to life, so you better take the plea, or if you don't take the plea, he's getting it." Charles Gampero, Sr., Gampero's father, encouraged his son to take the plea, believing that his son would only serve seven years. Gampero, Sr., said, "We took the plea agreement, thinking that my son would be home by the time he's 27. It didn't work out."

Erma Faye Stewart was arrested in a major drug sweep based on information provided by a police

(continued)

informant who was later deemed not credible. Stewart, 30, maintained her innocence, but her court-appointed attorney didn't want to hear it. "He was like, pushing me to plead guilty and take probation. He wasn't on my side at all." After spending 25 nights in a crowded jail, Stewart finally agreed to follow her attorney's advice and plead guilty. "Even though I wasn't guilty," she said, "I was willing to plead guilty because I had to get home to my kids. My son was sick." When she accepted the plea bargain and a 10-year probation, Stewart was freed. What she didn't know was that under the terms of her probation, she would be required to pay a monthly fee to the probation department. Her felony conviction also meant that the single mother was banned from the federal food stamps program. Within three years of falling behind in her probation payments, Stewart was evicted from her home. Steve Bright, a defense attorney and law professor with the Southern Center for Human Rights, says of plea bargaining that "One reason a lot of people plead guilty is because they're told that they can go home that day, because they will get probation. What they usually don't take into account is that they are being set up to fail."

How can the criminal justice system do a better job of ensuring that persons entering into plea agreements are in fact guilty of the alleged crimes? Should there be greater scrutiny of plea agreements by the courts? Are both prosecutors and defense attorneys to blame for trying to dispose of cases too quickly? What is the judges' responsibility in the plea bargaining process?

Source: Adapted from "The Plea," *Frontline*, June 17, 2005.

▶ Types of Plea Bargaining

There are four types of plea bargaining. These include (1) implicit plea bargaining, (2) charge reduction bargaining, (3) judicial plea bargaining, and (4) sentence recommendation bargaining. These types of plea bargaining are ordinarily distinguished according to which party initiates the bargaining. In three types of plea bargaining discussed below, either judges or prosecutors initiate plea negotiations with the defense counsels and their clients. A fourth type of plea bargaining actually occurs through a mutual understanding among parties of what charges will result and what penalties will be expected in exchange for guilty pleas entered (Champion 2005a).

Implicit Plea Bargaining

Implicit plea bargaining is an understanding between defense counsel and the prosecutor that a guilty plea will be entered to a specific offense, which carries a conventional punishment. The expected and contemplated punishment is usually somewhat less than the maximum sentence that could be imposed. The key word in this definition is *understanding*. Much hinges upon what sentences have been imposed for similar offenses in the past, depending upon the jurisdiction. Those who have entered guilty pleas to burglary charges in the past have sustained penalties ranging from straight probation to 48-month prison terms. There are also jurisdictional variations among cities and counties involving identical crimes, even within the same states (Myers and Reid 1995).

In view of one's prior record, age, mental state, and a host of other factors, defense attorneys are generally in a position to know the going rate for specific offenses. For first offenders, the going rate for burglary may be 18 months in prison. Depending upon the circumstances of the burglary (e.g., whether there were victim injuries and the amount of property loss/damage), a defendant may receive probation for a specified period, such as two or three years. In the case of chronic offenders who have multiple convictions for burglary and other crimes, courts are inclined to impose more severe sentences. Maximum sentences may be contemplated. Further, because the defendant is a habitual offender, there is an additional charge that could be filed by prosecutors. Most states have habitual offender statutes, meaning that for habitual offenders, a conviction on a habitual offender charge would lead to life imprisonment or life without parole.

> **implicit plea bargaining** occurs when defendant pleads guilty with the expectation of receiving a more lenient sentence.

Thus, when defense attorneys consult with their clients, they acquire an intimate familiarity with the defendant's prior record and other background factors. Defense counsels have a fairly good idea of what they can expect from the prosecutor's office regarding a plea bargain for their clients. Knowledge of the going rate for specific offenses enables these defense counsels to advise their clients accordingly and to let them know what they can likely expect from the prosecutor and court.

The practice of implicit plea bargaining begins when a defense counsel advises his/her client that if the client enters a guilty plea to a specific charge, the result will probably be a particular sentence. The defendant is induced to plead guilty based upon the expertise of the defense attorney and his/her familiarity with the legal system. Offers to enter guilty pleas in exchange for particular punishments are attractive to prosecutors, since obtaining guilty pleas relieves them of having to prove the case against the defendant later in court. Because of the defense counsel's knowledge and agreeability of prosecutors, most plea agreement negotiations are completed rather quickly.

Exceptions are high-profile cases or cases that are particularly offensive, such as child sexual abuse, mutilation or torture, or some type of perversion. However, in some types of cases, court policy may dictate that no plea bargains will be struck with certain types of offenders. This is precisely the kind of plea bargaining that Alaska has recently stated that prosecutors cannot engage in because the sentence is strictly the purview of the judge. Other jurisdictions may decide that they will not plea bargain with drug dealers or DUI defendants over a certain BAC level. Thus, the emphasis of a strong law-and-order stance is taken by the courts and prosecutors with these types of bans on plea bargaining. Drug dealers would become aware that if they were arrested, their plea bargaining chances were nonexistent. However, while prosecutors were not permitted to plea bargain drug cases, it did not prevent judges from dispensing with such cases quickly, often without trial. In these instances, judges would dismiss more troublesome cases or make their own sentence recommendations to conclude cases. In short, one form of plea bargaining may be replaced with another, as the responsibility for initiating bargains shifted from prosecutors to judges (McConville and Mirsky 2005).

An example of implicit plea bargaining is illustrated below. The characteristics of two criminals, Joe Jones and Phil Smith, both charged with burglary and larceny are listed below. Each has broken into homes and stolen jewelry and other valuables assessed at $2,000.

	Joe Jones	Phil Smith
Age	25	24
Education	9th grade	completed high school
Family stability	stable	stable
Marital status	single, never married	divorced, two children
Prior record	three felony convictions for larceny, fraud	none
Employment	unemployed	employed as day laborer
Drug use	yes	no
Alcohol use	yes	yes

This information is often derived from arrest reports and booking documents. It is known both to the defense counsel and the prosecutor. Jones has a more serious criminal record compared with Smith. The most important factor weighing against Jones is his prior record, consisting of three prior felony convictions for larceny and fraud. The most important factor weighing in favor of Smith is his lack of a criminal record. In other respects, compared with Smith, Jones has less education, has less of a chance for holding a steady job, and is involved with both drugs and alcohol. The going rate for Jones in the present case may be five to seven years in prison. The prosecutor may threaten to bring habitual offender charges against him, and these charges would be easily substantiated. In Smith's case, the going rate might be probation or a short jail sentence. The facts that Smith is a first-offender, is employed, has two children from a prior marriage, and has a high school education make him an ideal candidate for some form of probation or leniency.

One point made by this comparison is that the going rate varies depending upon an offender's prior record and general background. The same crime committed is punished differently because of the difference in criminal histories for two otherwise similar offenders. Another feature of implicit plea bargaining is that no specific agreement or bargain is reached between the defendant and prosecutor. Guilty pleas are entered in the hope that leniency will be extended by both the prosecutor and the judge. In most situations, some form of leniency issues from judges in exchange for guilty pleas. However, there are no rules that obligate judges or prosecutors to extend leniency to anyone who enters a plea of guilty to any crime. Judges remind defendants of this very fact before the guilty plea is accepted (Pohlman 1995).

Charge Reduction Bargaining

Charge reduction bargaining or **charge bargaining** is an offer from the prosecutor to minimize the number and seriousness of charges against defendants in exchange for their pleas of guilty to lesser charges. When crimes are perpetrated, often there are multiple offenses arising from the original crime. For instance, Joe Jones and Phil Smith steal a car; enter a convenience store and rob it at gunpoint with automatic weapons; wound two customers who attempt to intervene; shoot and kill the convenience store clerk who attempts to telephone police; elude police who chase them through four counties; cause extensive damage to multiple vehicles during the hot pursuit; engage in a shootout with police and wound several innocent bystanders; and severely wound a police officer before they are subdued and taken into custody. The list of charges against Jones and Smith include murder, attempted murder, armed robbery, menacing, eluding police, firing upon law enforcement officers, resisting arrest, hit-and-run, aggravated assault on the police and bystanders, vehicular theft, and possession of illegal automatic weapons.

Charge reduction bargaining would involve the prosecutor, who would probably suggest a guilty plea to second-degree murder and armed robbery. The punishment sought would be life imprisonment. Without the plea bargain offer, the prosecutor would file all of these charges against these defendants. The death penalty would probably be sought as well. The result might well mean the imposition of the death penalty or consecutive life imprisonment terms. The offer to reduce the charges and the recommended punishment might sound attractive to Jones and Smith. After all, they avoid the death penalty and are parole-eligible. But plea bargaining of this sort is not always one-sided (Worden 1995). Negotiations include counter offers from defense counsels. Thus, charge reduction bargaining and several other forms of plea bargaining are considered episodic, occurring over time and involving multiple defense counsel/prosecutor encounters. Further affecting the use of charge reduction bargaining is the bureaucratization of courts in different jurisdictions. The greater the sheer volume of cases in particular jurisdictions, the greater the use of charge reduction bargaining as a technique to facilitate case processing and move more cases through the system more rapidly (Champion 2005b).

In another case, this time involving two real defendants, two young men were under police surveillance and suspected of dealing drugs. They happened to be members of a nationally recognized football team in a southern state and were quite popular. The city police, county detectives, and state bureau of criminal investigation were involved in a coordinated effort to investigate them and determine the extent of their alleged drug dealing. An informant, another football player, agreed to plant a bug in the telephone of their

> **charge reduction bargaining, charge bargaining** negotiation process between prosecutors and defense attorneys involving dismissal of one or more charges against defendants in exchange for a guilty plea to remaining charges, or in which the prosecutor downgrades the charges in return for a plea of guilty.

apartment. Other listening devices were planted throughout the apartment at the order of the local criminal court. Subsequently, the young men were videotaped and telephonically recorded engaging in at least 28 transactions. Each of these 28 transactions involved Class X felonies, which meant life-without-parole sentences on each count or charge. This is because the quantity of drugs (many kilos of cocaine, heroin, and marijuana) was substantial and qualified their crimes as Class X, the most serious felony category in the state.

The young men were eventually arrested. The most prominent criminal defense attorneys were hired for them by the football team's booster club and other private supporters. With this formidable defense and the local popularity of these football players, the prosecution knew that despite their clear-cut evidence of criminal conduct and seized drugs, there was a possibility that these men would either be acquitted later or be convicted of some downgraded charge. Thus, the prosecutor approached their attorneys with the following deal: have your clients plead guilty to simple possession of a controlled substance (cocaine), and get six months' jail time (with time off during days and weekends to play football), and do an additional two years on probation with 400 hours of community service. The plea agreement was concluded quickly and the young men were sentenced to six-month jail terms. Each was permitted to leave during the day for football practice and required to report back to the jail during evening hours at 9:00 p.m. Weekends were spent playing football with the rest of the team.

Many citizens in the community were upset by the excessive leniency extended to these football players by the court. It was believed that their status and popularity as football players overshadowed their otherwise criminal conduct, which under other circumstances would have qualified them for 28 consecutive terms of life without parole. But the prosecutor defended his action by arguing that a jury may have thrown out the case against these defendants, despite the mountain of evidence that had been compiled, the incriminating drug deals videotaped and telephonically recorded, and numerous statements of informants and undercover agents. The final irony of this case is that *both* players failed to comply even with the simplest of conditions associated with their jail terms. They failed to observe their 9:00 p.m. curfew on at least three occasions and the judge invited them back to his courtroom where four-year prison terms were imposed. The football players eventually were sent to the state penitentiary.

Cases such as this have been cited to underscore the ethics of plea bargaining and the morality of prosecutorial discretion in reflecting public interest in honest law enforcement (Connell 2004). Cases in which prosecutorial discretion is flagrantly abused, such as the football player scenario above, do little to foster public perceptions of prosecutorial integrity. In fact, such prosecutorial indiscretions have functioned as platforms for plea bargaining and sentencing reforms in most states (Wilmot and Spohn 2004). Also, plea bargaining may be unethical and counterproductive relative to the courts manifest goals of retribution, deterrence, incapacitation, and rehabilitation.

Judicial Plea Bargaining

judicial plea bargaining recommended sentence by judge who offers a specific sentence and/or fine in exchange for a guilty plea.

Judicial plea bargaining occurs when judges make offers of sentences to defendants in open court in exchange for their guilty pleas. One of the most frequent uses of judicial plea bargaining involves petty offenses, such as public order offenses like public intoxication or disturbing the peace. Persons arrested for being drunk and disorderly appear before judges in the morning following their arrest. Very often, they are eager to leave the courtroom and get on about their business. The judge knows that the criminal punishment for their conduct is not especially severe.

In New Orleans, for instance, judges must face thousands of intoxicated arrestees every Mardi Gras. Bourbon Street and the French Quarter generate large numbers of targets inviting arrest by police for public intoxication. While their crime is not especially serious, they may do themselves harm by being out on city streets in their condition. Thus, the drunk tanks of local jails fill rapidly and empty the following morning. Judges bring in 20 or more persons charged with public intoxication and inform them as a group as to the punishment contemplated. They are usually given fines and suspended sentences. Many courts accept credit cards in lieu of cash payments. The proceedings are concluded quickly, as justice is rapidly dispensed through judicial plea bargaining. Anyone wishing to contest the matter can remain jailed and stand trial later, where the outcome will likely be the same (McDonald 1985).

Judicial plea bargaining is the functional equivalent of a bench trial, but without much of the formality of prosecutorial involvement. In many cases, defense attorneys are not involved. Historically, bench trials such as those described above frequently involve a defendant's waiver of the right to a jury trial. However, defendants who waive this right are rewarded, while those who demand a jury trial are punished (Cohen 2004). Known as the jury waiver system, this method of concluding cases is far less restrictive of one's Sixth Amendment rights than plea bargaining *per se*.

> **jury waiver system** occurs when defendants waive their constitutional right to a jury trial and enter into a plea bargain agreement with the prosecutor.

But the frequency with which judicial plea bargaining occurs has certain adverse consequences for defendants. Decisions to plead guilty are encouraged, and the circumstances under which judges offer specific sentences to defendants, even fines, are somewhat coercive and threatening. Many defendants do not take the time to consider their options and frivolously enter guilty pleas, even if there is the possibility that they are innocent. Being rushed into a guilty plea, therefore, compromises due process to an extent. This is especially true regarding indigent defendants. In New York, for instance, data were obtained from 236 indigent defendants involved in 150 felony cases (McConville and Mirsky 2005). Assignment of counsel to these indigent defendants included showing defendants that they will receive more severe penalties if they fail to plead guilty. Then these defendants are given exactly 15 seconds to accept or reject the pleas and sentences offered by these judges. Almost all defendants acceded to the judge's request for them to plead guilty to the recommended charge and accept the proposed sentences (McConville and Mirsky 2005).

One unfortunate consequence is that once a guilty plea has been entered, even to a minor charge, it cannot ordinarily be withdrawn later. If it is withdrawn successfully later, there is little to prevent prosecutors from using the initial plea of guilty to their advantage in the courtroom later if the case proceeds to trial. Thus, defendants lose in several different ways no matter what their decision might be.

Judicial plea bargaining also results whenever power is removed from prosecutors to strike deals or plea bargains with defendants. If charge reduction or sentence recommendation bargaining is minimized or prohibited, then the responsibility for deciding punishments and negotiating with defendants shifts to judges. When judges are given this additional responsibility, they become concession givers, roles previously performed by prosecutors. More than a few judges get bogged down in their docket loads when dealing with defense counsel who seek reassurances for their clients that probation or some minimal jail time will be imposed. Judges who are not prepared to grant probation in certain cases tend to develop docket problems.

> **concession givers** judges who make plea agreement offers to criminal defendants, wherein the defendants will plead guilty to a criminal charge in exchange for judicial leniency in sentencing.

Sentence Recommendation Bargaining

The fourth type of plea bargaining is sentence recommendation bargaining. Sentence recommendation bargaining occurs when the prosecutor proposes a specific sentence in exchange for the defendant's guilty plea. In one respect, sentence recommendation bargaining is an overt articulation of implicit plea bargaining. A prosecutor informs the defense counsel representing a client as to the contemplated sentence in exchange for a guilty plea. In a take-it-or-leave-it fashion, the defense counsel relays the information to the client, who decides whether the proposed punishment is worth the guilty plea. It usually is.

> **sentence recommendation bargaining** negotiation in which the prosecutor proposes a sentence in exchange for a guilty plea.

Sentence recommendation bargaining is not entirely discretionary with the prosecutor. In fact, judges must approve all plea bargain agreements in all jurisdictions (Worden 1995). Therefore, if the prosecutor proposes a punishment that will later be rejected by the judge, it is viewed as a waste of court time, and the prosecutor will be chastised accordingly. Thus, prosecutors must be knowledgeable about what the court will or will not accept. This means that all actors (e.g., prosecutor, defense counsel, and judge) must have a general understanding of the going rate for any crime, given contextual factors and defendant backgrounds, including their criminal histories.

Sentence recommendation bargaining is often finely tuned, depending upon a prosecutor's experience with the system and relationship with the judge. There is a clear relation between a judge's beliefs about the leniency and coerciveness of plea bargaining and the trade-off between crime control and due process, and their own willingness to cooperate with a prosecutor who attempts plea negotiations with defendants (Worden 1995). In the mid-1990s, however, efforts were underway in several jurisdictions to overhaul the architecture of plea bargaining to remove its extralegal properties. Various forms of sentencing classification have been proposed as guidelines in plea negotiations. Of course, this raises the informal nature of plea bargaining to a much more formal and predictable level. Thus, the clear intent of plea bargaining reformers is to structure plea bargaining and eliminate the often protracted interplay between prosecutors and defense attorneys. In many respects, the reform envisioned would be similar to guidelines-based sentencing schemes such as those used in Minnesota, Washington, 20 other state jurisdictions, as well as the federal court. Offense-specific charts would be consulted, where one's crimes would be cross-tabulated with one's criminal history. Where the points intersect would define a range of months or years that would determine the latitude of the plea bargainers. Jurisdictions such as Massachusetts have been experimenting with sentencing commissions vested with such powers over plea bargaining and certain sentencing issues (Champion 2005a).

One troubling feature of sentence recommendation bargaining and other plea bargaining forms is gender disparity (Auerhahn 2004). Gender disparity occurs when one gender receives preferential treatment or consideration in plea negotiations and sentencing. Gender disparity studies indicate that females with no prior records are more likely than similar males to receive charge reductions and less severe sentence recommendations from prosecutors (Champion 2005a). The typicality hypothesis proposes that women are treated with chivalry in criminal processing, but only when their charges are consistent with stereotypes of female offenders. Selective chivalry suggests that decision makers extend chivalry disproportionately toward white females. Finally, differential discretion suggests that disparity is most likely in informal charge reduction bargaining than in the final sentencing process and sentencing hearing (Champion 2005a). A research study examining the records of almost 10,000 felony theft cases and over 18,000 felony assault cases, and controlling for prior record found that females were more likely than their male counterparts to receive charge reductions and have a greater chance of probation. Such chivalry has been described in other jurisdictions as well, as evidence of gender bias and preferential treatment by courts (Williams, Craig-Moreland, and Cauble 2004).

We have also seen how indigents seem to receive unfair treatment during plea bargaining, especially when they are assigned public defenders who are usually courtroom novices (Weiss 2004). Not only are they assigned less-competent counsel, they also are rushed into accepting reduced sentences from prosecutors and judges in exchange for their guilty pleas. The coerciveness for indigents is that they almost always face the prospect of harsher penalties from a jury trial on more serious charges. Plea bargaining is the symbolic poster child for socioeconomic unfairness in the criminal justice system. The phrase "you get what you pay for" has special significance here.

Unfortunately, there is no easy way to eliminate socioeconomic status as a relevant extralegal variable in the complex plea bargaining equation. This is one reason plea

typicality hypothesis view that judges give women greater consideration than men during sentencing, but only when their criminal charges are consistent with stereotypes of female offenders.

selective chivalry view that judges tend to favor white females in their sentencing decisions compared with females of other races or ethnicities or males.

differential discretion view that sentencing disparities are more likely to occur during informal charge reduction bargaining than in the final sentencing process following trial and the sentencing hearing.

bargaining was banned in Alaska several times in the last 30 years. However, simply banning something does not mean it does not occur informally. In fact, plea bargaining did not disappear in Alaska following these bans, and it is alive and well in some forms. Prosecutors and defense counsel have simply modified their strategies for circumventing the Alaska plea bargaining ban (Champion 2005b).

But because plea bargaining occurs at the front end of the criminal justice system and affects virtually every stage following it, the potential for disparities attributable to almost any variable must be carefully monitored (Ball 2005). While the bureaucratic apparatus is in place to ensure strict compliance with sentences imposed through plea bargains, there is a glaring absence of controls to protect against the unwarranted intrusion of social status variables in any particular plea negotiation.

▶ The Pros and Cons of Plea Bargaining

Plea bargaining has its proponents and opponents (Herzog 2004). Below is an extensive list of reasons why plea bargaining is both popular and unpopular with the public and justice experts.

Arguments for Plea Bargaining

1. Reducing the Uncertainties of Criminal Trials

There are several arguments favoring the use of plea bargaining in the United States. Plea bargaining reduces the uncertainties and risks inherent in a trial for willing participants (Herzog 2004). This means that offenders who decide to plead guilty to one or more criminal charges know with some degree of certainty the nature and extent of their punishment, including about how much time they will serve, either on probation or in jail, and any other conditions contemplated by the prosecutor and approved by the judge. If the case were to go to trial and the defendant were convicted, it is more difficult to predict with certainty what the judge will impose. Case processing time is more rapid through plea bargaining (Greenstein 1994). If cases are plea bargained, case processing time is much faster than if the case were to go to a lengthy trial.

2. Fewer Trials and Trial Delays

Plea bargaining also means fewer trials and trial delays. Prosecutors do not have to prove critical elements in state's cases against defendants. Trials obligate prosecutors to present arguments to the jury about the defendant's guilt beyond a reasonable doubt. Juries may not be easily convinced. This does not relieve prosecutors from proving one's guilt, however. In any plea agreement, the prosecutor must lay out for the judge in writing what evidence would have been presented to show the defendant's guilt beyond a reasonable doubt if the case had gone to trial. This is called the **factual basis for the plea**. This evidence is often minimal, but it may be sufficient to convince most judges of the soundness of the prosecutor's case against the defendant. It should not be assumed literally that prosecutors do not have to prove anything against the accused in a plea bargain agreement. The prosecutor is obligated to furnish the judge who oversees the plea agreement with sufficient evidence that would have been introduced to show the defendant's guilt, if the case had gone to trial. Some plea bargain agreements have been rejected by judges because of insufficient evidence presented by prosecutors.

3. Plea Bargaining Means More Convictions

Plea bargaining results in larger numbers of convictions. Usually, the concessions arising from plea bargaining are sufficient to induce most defendants to plead guilty. Ninety percent or more of all convictions are obtained through plea bargaining. Without plea

> **factual basis for the plea** evidence presented to the judge by the prosecutor that would have been used if a plea-bargained case had gone to trial; evidence of one's guilt beyond a reasonable doubt to substantiate a plea bargain agreement.

home confinement housing of offenders in their own homes with or without electronic monitoring devices. Sometimes an intermediate punishment involving the use of offender residences for mandatory incarceration during evening hours after a curfew and on weekends. Also called "house arrest."

electronic monitoring the use of electronic devices (usually anklets or wristlets) which emit electronic signals to monitor offenders, probationers, and parolees. The purpose of their use is to monitor an offender's whereabouts.

intensive supervised probation varies from standard probation and includes more face-to-face visits between probation officers and probationers under community supervision.

negotiated guilty pleas pleas of guilty entered in exchange for some form of sentencing leniency during plea bargaining.

United States Sentencing Guidelines rules implemented by federal courts in 1987 obligating federal judges to impose presumptive sentences on all convicted offenders. Guidelines are based upon offense seriousness and offender criminal history.

bargaining, trials would determine one's guilt or innocence. With juries deciding many cases, it is likely that there would be fewer convictions, even under conditions where evidence against the accused is strong. There are fewer jail backlogs and less jail and prison overcrowding as the result of plea bargaining. This is because the use of probation and nonincarcerative alternative sentencing options (e.g., home confinement, electronic monitoring, and intensive supervised probation) are seriously considered and often imposed as enticements to elicit guilty pleas (Erez and Ibarra 2004).

Plea bargaining involves negotiated guilty pleas. Because these guilty pleas are negotiated, they are often better than trials in terms of the deals arranged for guilty defendants. Again, trials are often unpredictable in outcome. And if a defendant is found guilty through a trial, then the punishment is often harsher than if the case had been concluded through plea bargaining. Plea bargaining avoids potential jury bias and emotional influence of adverse evidence. More rational sentencing decision making through bargaining is achieved and the factual circumstances of terrible crimes, such as murder or aggravated rape, are less emotionally charged (Fearn 2004). Juries may be persuaded to find someone guilty of a serious crime because of sympathy generated by the prosecutor for the victim and the victim's survivors (Enriquez and Clark 2005). Emotional persuasion is often strong and overrides sound, cold deliberations that are expected of jurors when both sides have presented their case (Fryling 2005).

Offenders convicted through plea bargaining often avoid the taint of a formal criminal prosecution. They do not spend much time in court, except to participate in the plea agreement hearing. Little fanfare accompanies such hearings, which are not attended by many persons. As opposed to trials, plea agreement hearings are not usually announced to the public. Most plea agreement hearings, although open to the public, are held only with the judge, court reporter and other court officers, the prosecutor, defense counsel, and defendant. Thus, the specter of a lengthy courtroom drama is avoided. Judicial discretion is more limited because of the conditions and concessions outlined in plea agreements (Champion 2005a). Judges reserve the right to reject plea agreements if they feel that plea agreements are too lenient. However, judicial rejection of plea agreements is rare. Most plea agreements are rubber-stamped by most judges in most jurisdictions.

4. Plea Bargaining and Anticipated Leniency

Plea agreements may also soften the impact of sentencing guidelines in states that have them (Barrile and Slone 2005). Guidelines schemes tend to be excessively rigid. Prosecutors may downgrade the seriousness of one's offense or write the plea agreement in such a way so as to subvert the intended impact of guidelines to systematize the sentencing process and create greater uniformity in sentencing (U.S. Sentencing Commission 2003). However, each case is developed and rests on its own merits. Each plea bargain agreement is slightly different from others, even in the same jurisdictions. Their uniqueness is about as varied as personality systems.

5. Reducing the Costs of Trials

Regarding its cost-effectiveness, plea bargaining is far less expensive than jury trials (Champion 2005b). In jury trials, witnesses must be subpoenaed. Experts must be obtained. Evidence must be examined in greater detail for use in court. The valuable time of judges, court officers, and other key participants is expensive. Thus, from a pure economic standpoint, plea bargaining is a cheap way of getting a guilty plea. In the federal system, for instance, the U.S. Sentencing Guidelines have severely limited the use of plea bargaining with extremely lenient sentences to less than 20 percent (U.S. Sentencing Commission 2003). Under the pre-guidelines indeterminate sentencing followed by the U.S. District Courts, probation was granted to convicted offenders about 60 percent of the time. Under the United States Sentencing Guidelines, which went into effect in October 1987, the use of probation as a sentence in federal courts decreased to about 12 percent. In fact, the U.S. Sentencing Guidelines table provides for probation in only the least serious misdemeanor or felony cases. U.S. probation officers are obligated to file more complete reports under the federal sentencing guidelines. The additional mandatory information to be included negates any attempt by federal prosecutors to leave out details that would intensify one's offense seriousness (Barrile and Slone 2005). Under previous indeterminate sentencing, prosecutors could leave out details, such as the use of a weapon during the commission of the crime, in an attempt to negotiate a more lenient sentence for a federal defendant in exchange for a guilty plea. The fact that federal judges used probation 60 percent of the time under pre-guidelines sentencing is strong evidence that presentence investigation reports were often modified to give judges the impression that they were sentencing defendants who were less serious offenders.

Arguments Against Plea Bargaining

1. The Self-Incriminating Nature of Plea Bargaining

There is considerable opposition to the use of plea bargaining in negotiating guilty pleas. One argument is that defendants who plea bargain give up their constitutional right to a jury trial. Further, they give up the right to cross-examine their accusers. They also relinquish their right against self-incrimination. However, the greater leniency extended to defendants in exchange for giving up these rights is sufficient to justify their waivers of jury trials and insistence of observance of their constitutional rights to full due process. Many convicted offenders are thankful for plea bargaining, since a jury trial would almost certainly have involved harsher punishment for them. As a consequence, there are fewer trials with plea bargaining, and thus, fewer forums are convened where defendants can present the full body of exculpatory evidence showing their innocence (Holmes et al. 1992). More than few experts are bothered by this fact. Their belief is that jury trials mean that all facts will be heard and that the fairest decision will be rendered by the jury hearing all of the evidence.

self-incrimination the act of exposing oneself to prosecution by answering questions that may demonstrate involvement in illegal behavior. Coerced self-incrimination is not allowed under the Fifth Amendment.

2. The Loss of Judicial Control

Plea bargaining may signify a loss of judicial control of courtrooms, giving lawyers free reign to divert jurors from the facts with theories that portray their clients as supposed victims of an unfair criminal justice system (Champion 2005a). Most defendants are more than willing to ride through this loss of judicial control with a relatively lenient plea agreement, however. If a defendant is convicted through a trial, the punishment is almost invariably harsher than whatever had been contemplated in a plea bargain. Once a defendant has entered a guilty plea and a sentence has been imposed by the judge, it is difficult to withdraw the guilty plea. Despite the predictability of plea bargaining, there is always an elusive element. This is judicial privilege, which means that judges may accept or reject one or more plea bargain agreement terms and substitute more or less punitive sentences. Thus, although clients have been reassured by their counsel and the prosecutor that entering a plea of guilty to a specific charge will likely result in one type of sentence, another type of sentence may actually be imposed by the judge. Again, judges are not obligated to follow precisely every condition noted in plea agreements.

judicial privilege power of judges to change plea bargain agreements and substitute their own punishments; the power to override prosecutors and defense counsel concerning the agreed upon terms of plea agreements.

3. Defendant Ignorance and Plea Bargaining

Ignorance or mistake often leads to guilty pleas. Therefore, the plea agreement process may lack sufficient guarantees to ensure proper application of the law and sentencing options. Many defendants are ignorant of the law. Those with some knowledge of the law may lack the foresight to appreciate and understand the seriousness of the guilty plea they enter. Criminal convictions are serious and often result in a loss of one's job. Or naive defendants may enter into plea agreements with prosecutors not knowing that they have the right to litigate fully any charges against them. Their own attorneys often fail to apprise them of their various legal options. Relevant defense evidence is not presented. Opponents of plea bargaining single out this particular factor as most damaging to defendants. If the accused enters a guilty plea, crucial evidence that may have resulted in an acquittal if the case had gone to trial instead is often overlooked or deliberately ignored. Thus, opponents of plea bargaining argue, the true extent of one's case cannot be known unless it is subjected to a trial proceeding. But many defendants enter into plea agreements hoping that some of the evidence against them will never be heard. They see plea bargaining as a way of slipping through the system with minimal damage. Plea bargains often offer more benefits to the accused than would be forthcoming at a trial, where circumstances could be much worse.

4. Rejections of Guilty Pleas and Judicial Payback

Judges are more likely to be more severe with defendants who reject initial plea bargain agreements. Thus, one danger of plea bargaining is that if an offer to a defendant is made to plead guilty in exchange for what the prosecutor (and judge) believe is a reasonable punishment, refusal to accept that agreement and force the case to trial will sometimes disturb the judge. Upon conviction, the judge may exact some revenge by extending one's sentence by one or more years. Judicial intervention is minimized such that the ineffective-assistance-of-counsel issue cannot be adequately explored. When plea agreements are negotiated, there is little, if any, opportunity to ascertain whether one's defense counsel is representing the best interests of the client. Is defense counsel competent? With so many cases being plea bargained, and in fairly standard ways, there is no clear opportunity to evaluate defense competence.

The judge becomes an advocate intent on inducing a defendant to plead guilty, when due process presumes one innocent until proven guilty beyond a reasonable doubt. This particular factor is another sore point with plea bargaining opponents. They do not want judges to engage in a form of bribery by dangling attractive lenient sentences before defendants who would face much worse if they went to trial on the same charges. When plea bargaining is allowed, judges wield a great deal of power in the offers they make through judicial plea bargaining. There is a hint of coercion in plea bargaining, particularly implicit plea bargaining, where threats of greater punishments are implied if guilty pleas are not entered to less serious charges, which may cause some persons to plead guilty to crimes they did not commit. Thus, some innocent people may accept criminal convictions in order to avoid harmful or fatal punishments. Usually, these are cases where innocent defendants are swept into the criminal justice system through suspicious circumstances. Persons who cannot account for their whereabouts when crimes have occurred or appear to be involved may find themselves in the unenviable position of facing harsh punishments if convicted. Death rows throughout the United States have set free occasional convicts who were subsequently determined to be innocent through newly discovered evidence or confessions from the real perpetrators.

5. Circumventing Habitual Offender Statutes

habitual offender statutes statutes that generally provide life imprisonment as a mandatory sentence for chronic offenders who have been convicted of three or more serious felonies within a specific time period.

three-strikes-and-you're-out policies a crime prevention and control strategy that proposes to incarcerate those offenders who commit and are convicted of three or more serious or violent offenses; usual penalty is life imprisonment or the life-without-parole option.

Plea bargaining may circumvent **habitual offender statutes** or **three-strikes-and-you're-out policies**, where mandatory penalties are contemplated. The danger of plea bargaining here is that chronic or persistent offenders with multiple felony convictions can avoid mandatory punishments an unlimited number of times through plea bargaining. The purpose of mandatory penalties is to remove chronic and persistent offenders from society by incarcerating them either for life or substantial terms of years. Such punishments are thwarted through plea bargaining, however. Because of plea bargaining, therefore, there is an inconsistent application of mandatory penalties among jurisdictions (Vincent and Hofer 1994). Habitual

▼

offender statutes are frequently used as leverage for inducing guilty pleas from defendants. There is no apparent intent on the part of prosecutors to enforce such habitual offender statutes, however. Circumvention of sentencing guidelines is encouraged by plea bargaining (Stemen, Wilson, and Rengifo 2004). Sentencing guidelines are designed to establish fairness in sentencing. Whenever these guidelines are bypassed through plea bargaining, fairness is unevenly applied for those who do not plead guilty but rather, go to trial.

6. Sentencing Reductions for Those Undeserving of Sentencing Reductions

Sentences for many serious offenders are reduced when such sentences shouldn't be reduced (Kramer and Johnson 2004). Sex offenders and child sexual abusers find themselves given sentences that are often far too lenient, given the seriousness of their offending. Often, critical case information may be buried or overlooked in an attempt to get a plea bargain negotiated. Therefore, some very serious offenders may get lighter sentences, when in fact their punishments should be more severe. At the same time, such offenders may avoid helpful counseling and therapy that otherwise might occur through traditional trial convictions (Alexander 2004). Plea bargaining may reduce the sheer volume of criminal prosecutions. There is no reliable evidence, however, that the absolute number of prosecutions is abbreviated because of plea bargaining. We must remember that plea bargaining results from a prosecution. Thus, a decision by a prosecutor to prosecute someone for a crime sets the stage for offers and counteroffers from defense counsels and prosecutors, as plea bargain agreements are negotiated.

7. Concealing Heinous Aspects of Crimes Through Plea Bargaining

Prosecutors and others may be able to conceal more serious aspects of a crime from the sentencing judge by withholding certain information from a plea agreement. Some professionals object to this circumstance as ethically wrong. Justice somehow seems politicized by this process (Champion 2005b). Defense lawyers who have cultivated amicable relations with prosecutors over the years are more seasoned and better prepared to negotiate desirable plea bargains for their clients. New lawyers performing public defender functions are at a disadvantage, since they are often unaware of how the system works in a particular jurisdiction. Where who you know gets you a better deal in the plea agreement process, this is a fairly clear indication that plea bargaining has been politicized.

8. Rubber-Stamping Plea Agreements

Judges tend to rubber-stamp plea bargain agreements without doing their jobs effectively. Judges are supposed to determine whether a factual basis exists for a defendant's plea of guilty. Judges must also determine whether guilty pleas are voluntary. Do defendants wish to relinquish critical constitutional rights, such as giving up the right to cross-examine accusers or give evidence on one's own behalf? Because of the glut of court cases in many jurisdictions today, judges are often relieved to merely approve agreements where guilty pleas have been entered. They often are lax when performing their oversight functions. Since plea agreements often result in more lenient treatment for offenders, they tend to acquire a cynical view of the criminal justice system. They may take subsequent chances by committing new crimes, expecting leniency in the future because it had been extended in the past. They are not wrong in their appraisal of the criminal justice system, nor are they wrong in anticipating further leniency from prosecutors.

9. The Potential for Gender Bias in Plea Bargaining

It is claimed that women tend to benefit to a far greater degree from plea bargaining than men. Women tend to be granted probation more often than men, given the similarity of their prior records, instant offenses, and other salient factors. Because of this less than even-handed application of justice, therefore, the goals of deterrence, incapacitation, and

▼

rehabilitation are either undermined or defeated. Another form of discrimination in the use of plea bargaining applies to the poor and those in the lower socioeconomic statuses (McConville and Mirsky 2005). Courts are deluged with thousands of indigent defendants, often drawn into the criminal justice system through police sweeps in drug-infested sections of cities. Much street crime is perpetrated by those who are unemployed. Youthful offenders are drawn into the criminal justice system as well, especially minority youths (Champion 2007). Less affluent defendants are less likely to avail themselves of jury trials, where private counsels are most effective.

10. Plea Bargaining Invalidates the Jury Process

Some critics say that plea bargaining invalidates the jury system (McConville and Mirsky 2005). By bypassing a jury trial, defendants are dealt with more swiftly and without the benefit of jury trials. However, it is incumbent upon judges to advise defendants of their right to a trial by jury and whether they wish to voluntarily relinquish that right. In more than a few instances, it is disadvantageous to criminal defendants to air their cases before juries, since the details and circumstances of their crimes may offend more sensitive jurors. This, in turn, could lead to more serious criminal convictions with accompanying and commensurate sentencing consequences. Thus, for some offenders at least, jury trials are not desired and for good reason (Enriquez 2005). Plea bargaining encourages more proactive policing and arrests of indigents (McConville and Mirsky 2005). According to this line of thinking, police officers are interested in making increasing numbers of arrests that will result in convictions. Street people, indigents, drug users, and youthful offenders who loiter or act suspiciously are often arrested and charged with assorted offenses. Police officers know that there is a strong likelihood that many of those arrested will be offered plea bargains resulting in probation or charge reductions. Convictions result in greater approval of the actions of law enforcement officers, and thus a self-reinforcing cycle is set in motion with predictable consequences.

11. Hampers Efforts to Reform Sentencing

Sentencing reforms are hampered through plea bargaining. If 90 percent or more of all convictions are obtained through plea bargaining, it is more difficult for reformists to convince legislatures of the necessity for sentencing reform. The existence of going rates and other traditional plea bargaining features has become institutionalized nationally. There is no dramatic need to reform a system that seems to be accepted by criminals, prosecutors, defense counsels, and judges. However, plea bargaining is blamed for some amount of sentencing disparity (Park 2005). One obvious disparity resulting from plea bargaining is the difference in sentencing severity between plea-bargained cases and convictions resulting from trials. Another type of disparity occurs that is more difficult to detect. Different attorneys continually network with various assistant state's attorneys or district attorneys to work out agreements for their diverse clientele. All plea bargains are individualized; therefore, there is an inherent inequality that exists.

Only judges monitor plea agreements, and little effort is made by these judges to ensure that sentencing uniformity occurs according to the salient factors that should influence sentencing decisions (e.g., prior record or criminal history, instant offense, victim injuries, and other aggravating or mitigating factors) (Johnson 2004). Without any consistent monitoring mechanisms to govern plea bargaining in any particular jurisdiction, sentencing disparity must be assumed to occur. We do not know how much sentencing disparity exists resulting from plea bargaining.

12. Racial Discrimination and Plea Bargaining

More people of color are discriminated against through plea bargaining. This means that much racial and ethnic discrimination occurs (Clark 2004a). Racial and ethnic discrimination also exists at other stages of criminal justice processing, including imprisonment

(Spohn and Keller 2005). Street crimes are given greater attention by police officers, and proactive policing discussed above targets street people most often. These persons are frequently ethnic and racial minorities. These persons, frequently indigent, must accept defense counsels who often lack the experience and expertise of seasoned private attorneys retained by more affluent criminal clients. Efforts are currently being made to upgrade legal services for indigents. But such efforts are sporadic and unevenly applied among jurisdictions. Also, there is no one to monitor the actions of prosecutors. Thus, a serious accountability problem exists. Who should oversee the credibility and quality of case screening and prioritizing? Prosecutors in many jurisdictions have virtually unbridled authority to drop or pursue a case, adjust charges, and make recommendations (Connell 2004). In short, prosecutors have too much decision-making power in charging decisions. Also, shifting greater decision-making power to prosecutors reduces justice system accountability as case decision making is shifted toward the front of system. Rights activists are concerned that due process protections for the accused are jeopardized and that victim participation is minimized under widespread plea bargaining.

13. The Bureaucratization of Negotiated Guilty Pleas

The perfunctory nature of plea bargaining has certain bureaucratic characteristics. If there is greater reliance on bureaucratization, then there is less individualized attention given to more important cases (Ferdinand 1992). The existing administrative structures of some jurisdictions, such as Pennsylvania, are frequently relied upon by prosecutors so as to ensure consistency in plea bargaining practices. A positive consequence of bureaucratization in plea bargaining is that extralegal factors, such as race, social class, and gender, are less important in negotiating guilty pleas. In coconspirator cases, it is more difficult for innocent defendants to separate themselves from guilty defendants (Champion 2005a). If the guilty defendant enters into a plea agreement with prosecutors and agrees to testify against an innocent party named as a coconspirator, the innocent coconspirator is tainted. Thus, if the case comes to trial for the codefendant who does not plead guilty, such circumstances work to the disadvantage of the innocent party.

> **coconspirator**
> another party besides the defendant who is alleged to have committed the same crime in concert with the defendant.

14. Lawyers Are Vested with too Much Authority in Plea Bargaining

Some critics say that plea bargaining gives too much authority to lawyers. There is little or no weight given to juries. Essentially, this is a complaint that jurors are in a better position to determine guilt or innocence and evaluate evidence in contrast to a prosecutor–defense attorney plea agreement where all pertinent facts about the crime may not be disclosed and weighed properly. Plea bargaining is so pervasive that many defense attorneys have become complacent about it. If defense counsel must defend indigents, these attorneys are not paid at rates equivalent to private counsel. Thus, the financial incentives do not exist to work hard for indigent clients. Particularly where indigents are involved, defense counsels are often quick to conclude a case with a plea bargain (Champion 2005a). If cases do go to trial, there are questions about the competence of defense counsel required to represent indigents. Are they enthusiastic enough to present the best defense, or do they go through the motions of defending clients, taking the easiest path that will conclude proceedings?

▶ Why Is Plea Bargaining Banned in Some Jurisdictions?

Plea bargaining has been banned in various U.S. jurisdictions, most notably in Alaska. When Alaska announced that it was banning plea bargaining on a statewide basis in 1975, other jurisdictions were apprehensive. Would such a ban mean a glut of trials involving petty offenders? Would the wheels of Alaskan justice come to a grinding halt as more cases were processed without informal plea agreements worked out in advance?

It is important to note that although plea bargaining in Alaska was officially banned, it did not disappear. What occurred is that plea bargaining gave prosecutors considerably greater charging powers. With greater power over charging decision making, prosecutors in Alaska were more careful to screen those cases destined for trials. One result was that there was actually a reduction in the number of criminal prosecutions, as many cases that once were plea bargained were simply dropped. A more significant consequence of the Alaska plea bargaining ban was to create greater charge bargaining. Prosecutors were vested with considerably more authority to decide which charges should be brought against defendants. Subsequent bans of various types of plea bargaining were renewed in Alaska more recently as well as in other jurisdictions, such as New Hampshire. Their implementation has revealed similar patterns, a substantial increase in charge bargaining (Herzog 2004).

At the core of plea bargaining bans is the unfairness inherent in sentencing bargaining. Most plea agreements contemplate a particular punishment. Much of the punishment meted out through plea bargaining is more lenient than traditional punishments associated with trial convictions. Thus, the leniency of plea bargaining concerning sentences received by convicted offenders, often serious offenders, has been objectionable to more than a few citizens and lawmakers.

Reasons for Banning Plea Bargaining

1. Where plea bargaining has been banned, a greater amount of charge reduction bargaining occurs. This has shifted much of the decision-making power to prosecutors and away from judges. Some experts view this shift unfavorably.

2. Under a plea bargaining ban, there is greater likelihood of incarceration. This means that jail and prison overcrowding could be exacerbated by an absence of plea bargaining. On the one hand, those who favor strong get-tough anticrime measures will applaud the elimination of plea bargaining. On the other hand, jail and prison officials may not be pleased with the overcrowding that will likely result.

3. Under a plea bargaining ban, cases are more carefully screened by prosecutors. Thus, only the more serious cases for which strong evidence exists will move forward to criminal trials.

4. Selective bans against bargaining with certain offenses targeted (e.g., no deals with dope pushers) appear to work in selected jurisdictions. Thus, when offense-specific plea bargaining restrictions are implemented, prosecutors are prohibited from accepting reduced-charge guilty pleas from drug dealers. This doesn't necessarily mean that convicted drug dealers will be treated harshly, however. Current sentencing policies in certain jurisdictions are intended to incarcerate more offenders who commit certain types of offenses, such as drug dealing, for longer periods of time (Champion 2005b).

5. Even if plea bargaining is banned, judges and others find ways to get around it (Spohn 2004). It is virtually impossible to eliminate plea bargaining. Informal negotiations will always occur, no matter how stringent the controls or plea bargaining restrictions.

▶ Judicial Instructions for Accepting Guilty Pleas and Rights Waivers

In most jurisdictions, judges are obligated to determine the factual bases for guilty pleas, encourage frank discussion of the facts of the case, and facilitate further consideration of sentencing alternatives. In federal district courts, for example, judges must observe all of the

Federal Rules of Criminal Procedure relating to plea bargaining (Ulmer and Burchfield 2004). Specifically, this is 18 U.S.C. Rule 11 (U.S. Code, 2001). Rule 11 outlines with considerable precision whatever judges must do in the process of approving plea agreements. Under Rule 11, federal judges must make sure that defendants who enter guilty pleas to criminal charges understand the following:

1. The nature of the charge(s) to which the plea is offered.

2. The maximum possible penalty provided by law.

3. The mandatory minimum penalty as provided by law.

4. The effect of any special supervised release term and any special provisions for compensating victims.

5. That a defendant who does not have an attorney has a right to one; and if the defendant cannot afford an attorney, one will be appointed at state expense.

6. That the defendant has the right to plead not guilty and to withdraw a guilty plea at any time.

7. That the defendant has the right to a trial by jury and the right to the assistance of counsel at the trial.

8. That the defendant has the right to confront and cross-examine prosecution witnesses.

9. That the defendant has the right not to incriminate himself or herself.

10. That if the plea of guilty or *nolo contendere* is accepted, there will be no further trial of any kind; therefore, the plea is a waiver of the right to a trial.

11. That there is a factual basis for the plea.

12. That the plea is voluntarily given and that it is not the result of force, threats, or coercion apart from a plea agreement.

13. That the judge may accept or reject the plea agreement.

14. That the plea is accurate.

15. If the plea is the result of prior discussions between prosecutors and defendants or their attorney.

Items 11, 12, 13, and 14 are of great significance to defendants. These items are to determine whether the guilty plea entered by a defendant is voluntary. There must be a factual basis for the plea, the judge may accept or reject the plea agreement, and the plea agreement is an accurate summarization of the facts. These provisions seemingly protect defendants from overzealous prosecutors who threaten long sentences and drawn-out prosecutions if guilty pleas are not entered and suggested sentences are not accepted. This is the ideal scenario. It does not always happen this way in the real world.

Federal judges have no special litany for determining these and other facts about a defendant's guilty plea and the nature and terms of the plea agreement. The spirit of the law is that federal judges must ascertain these facts, in open court, by orally addressing the defendant. Each judge uses his or her own style for covering these important items. Thus, Rule 11 provides general guidelines for judges to follow. Past challenges from defendants about whether judges asked them about these items in precise ways have been unsuccessful. That is, federal judges are not compelled by Rule 11 to recite these questions precisely in the context of the rule.

If a federal judge is not satisfied with the evidence proffered by a U.S. attorney or his/her assistant, then the judge is not bound to accept the plea agreement. Judges can throw out charges against defendants if the evidence against them does not or would not support a subsequent conviction if the case proceeded to trial. A case in Tennessee provides a good example.

A man from Chattanooga, Tennessee, was charged with several felonies relating to copyright infringement governing the use of 16mm films and their possession by private film collectors. He had collected feature films as a hobby, but the Motion Picture Association of America (MPAA) and the Film Security Office under the direction of President Jack Valenti instituted a series of legal actions against private collectors to prevent them from trafficking in these motion pictures. The government's theory, at the urging of the MPAA, was that no motion picture had ever been sold to private individuals; therefore, all motion picture 16mm prints in the hands of film collectors must be stolen or obtained in nefarious ways. While there are several flaws in the government's theory about the critical elements of criminal copyright infringement, suffice it to say that the Chattanooga film collector was innocent of any criminal wrongdoing. He had purchased most of his 16mm prints of these motion pictures from film rental companies or from film reclamation services. Thus, he had legal title to these pictures. At the time, film collecting was regarded by the MPAA as jeopardizing the profits of major motion picture film companies. In reality, the number of motion picture collectors was small and the sum of their monetary profits from dealing in motion pictures was trivial. Subsequently, these motion pictures have been made available in DVD format, and any private citizen may now own just about any motion picture sold in this format.

In Chattanooga, Tennessee, however, the defendant was a fairly high-volume trader of motion pictures at the time. While he probably profited from motion picture film trades and sales, he never intended to defraud film companies of any revenue that they might obtain through film rentals or leases. In any event, the assistant U.S. attorney (AUSA) for the federal district court in Chattanooga brought several criminal copyright infringement charges against the film collector. The defendant was in his early fifties and had a heart condition. He was employed only on a part-time basis and supported himself from a portion of the revenue he realized from his film collecting.

The AUSA in Chattanooga approached the defendant with an offer—plead guilty to a **federal misdemeanor** and the AUSA would recommend a three-year probationary term. The defendant, who was assigned a court-appointed attorney, declined any offer to plead guilty to any criminal charge relating to his film-collecting hobby. However, a persuasive public defender pointed out to the defendant that a three-year probationary term wasn't bad compared with the 30 years and $200,000 fine associated with felony convictions on the criminal copyright infringement charges. Reluctantly, the defendant agreed to plead guilty.

On the day of the plea agreement hearing, however, the defendant stood before the federal district court judge and answered the different questions faithfully. When it came to the matter of whether the defendant wanted to plead guilty to this crime, even a federal misdemeanor, the defendant balked. "I never committed any crime, judge," he said. With a frustrated expression on his face, the judge asked the defendant's attorney if he wanted to confer with his client before proceeding. The defense counsel had a lengthy discussion with his client who later went back into court before the judge and entered the guilty plea. Here is where things get interesting.

The judge next asked the AUSA what evidence would have been submitted to show that the criminal elements existed and could have been proved beyond a reasonable doubt. The AUSA said that the evidence was summarized as a part of the plea agreement. The judge asked, "Is that all you have against this man?" The AUSA said, "Yes, your honor." At that point, the judge faced the defendant and said, "You are hereby freed, as I am dismissing all criminal charges against you." Then he turned to the AUSA and chastised him for bringing such a poorly prepared case before him. It was clear to the judge that the defendant had been cajoled into pleading guilty for fear of a harsher prosecution.

> **federal misdemeanor**
> any federal crime where the maximum punishment is less than one year in prison or jail.

Unfortunately, for many federal and state criminal defendants, not all judges are as judicious and meticulous in examining federal or state plea agreements and their contents (Johnson 2004). A majority of federal and state court judges "rubber-stamp" these plea agreements, since the court is backlogged with many serious cases to be plea bargained. Many judges give plea agreements only a cursory glance and overview before holding plea agreement hearings. Thus, often their actions relating to accepting plea agreements are perfunctory.

Can Judges Participate in Plea Negotiations Between Prosecutors and Defense Counsel?

Yes and No. At the federal level, district court judges are prohibited from participating in plea agreement negotiations between defense counsels and prosecutors. The policy about judicial participation in plea bargaining negotiations varies among the states. However, most states follow the federal government and prohibit judicial involvement in these negotiations. The primary reason is that where judges are involved in these discussions, it places them in the position of configuring an agreement that they will most certainly approve later. This type of influence is considered unethical and inappropriate in most jurisdictions.

Only a few states, such as North Carolina, permit state court judges to participate in plea negotiations. Thus, defense counsels and prosecutors can confer with judges about what judges will accept or reject as plea agreement terms. Some opponents of judicial participation in plea bargain negotiations rightly note that the adversarial nature of the justice system is substantially removed through judicial intervention of any kind (Worden 1995).

Should Judges Be Excluded from Plea Bargaining Negotiations Between Prosecutors and Defense Counsels?

Some researchers believe that judges should be an integral part of the plea bargaining process. Judges can give both parties a clearer idea of what the sentence will be, the specific parameters of plea negotiations, and various correctional options. Essentially, judges can tell prosecutors and defense attorneys, "This is the deal I will accept. Don't bring me anything more lenient than that."

Sometimes judicial concern focuses more on particular offenses, such as those involving drugs. Political sentiment and the judiciary in one jurisdiction, a county in the Midwest, established a policy of "no deals with drug pushers" (Church 1976). In that Midwest jurisdiction, reduced-charge plea bargaining for drug cases was all but eliminated, but trial rates soared. Court dockets were incredibly crowded. Judges were hard-pressed to resolve their court cases quickly. Interestingly, judges became concession givers, a role abandoned in drug cases by the district attorney. Defense counsel shifted their attention to judges and negotiating with them instead of prosecutors. If defense counsel could not obtain probation for their clients charged with various drug offenses, then they would insist on a full-fledged trial, a time-consuming proceeding. Judges were compelled to make concessions, usually by granting probation or short jail terms for a majority of charged drug offenders.

Judicial participation in plea negotiations is sometimes suspect because of the implication that the defendant is guilty. Traditionally and consistent with due process, judges are supposed to assume a stance of neutrality and consider all defendants innocent until their guilt is proven in court beyond a reasonable doubt. Suppose a judge says that he/she will approve a particular guilty plea from Defendant X. Later Defendant X withdraws his guilty plea and goes to trial before the same judge. Can that judge continue to remain neutral and impartial in rulings on motions and other matters during Defendant X's trial? It seems somewhat contradictory for a judge to be an advocate during plea bargaining who encourages the defendant to admit his guilt, and then turn around in the defendant's trial and judge him fairly if he decides to reject the plea bargain agreement.

▶ Sentencing Systems and Plea Bargaining

Plea bargaining has been modified in different jurisdictions depending upon the sentencing scheme adopted (Herzog 2004). One purpose of sentencing reform is to reduce sentencing disparities among judges, which are attributable to extralegal factors, such as one's race, age, ethnicity, gender, or socioeconomic status. Sentencing guidelines have been created in most jurisdictions to create sentencing uniformity, although no sentencing guideline scheme has completely eliminated the influence of extralegal factors in sentencing offenders (McManimon 2005b).

Sentencing Guidelines and Restrictions on Plea Bargaining

In federal courts, the U.S. Sentencing Guidelines have operated to limit the negotiating parameters of prosecutors and defense counsel (Levine 2005). Prior to the establishment of U.S. Sentencing Guidelines, federal prosecutors could tailor their plea agreements in ways that would maximize a defendant's acceptance of the plea agreement terms and encourage more guilty pleas. If a firearm was used in the commission of a robbery, for instance, the prosecutor could leave that fact out of the plea agreement. This omission would enable prosecutors to downgrade more serious felonies to less serious ones and offer defendants more lenient (and acceptable) punishments. Probation was used about 60 percent of the time in most federally plea-bargained cases prior to the establishment of sentencing guidelines.

When the federal sentencing guidelines were established, new rules were instituted requiring U.S. probation officers to include all relevant legal variables in **presentence investigation reports (PSIs)**. Prosecutors were prohibited from omitting these relevant variables. Thus, if a federal defendant used a firearm during the commission of a felony (e.g., robbing a U.S. post office), this fact had to be reported and noted in subsequent plea agreements. Further, the use of probation under the new federal sentencing guidelines (October 1987) dramatically decreased to about 12 percent of all plea-bargained cases. Guidelines tables now exist that restrict the use of probation to only a limited number of minor federal offenses (Ulmer and Burchfield 2004). If federal defendants are recidivists, then the chances for probation as a sentence are eliminated. Thus, federal prosecutors have lost an important plea bargaining chip in the game of negotiating plea agreements with those charged with federal crimes. Furthermore, under new federal and state sentencing guidelines, penalties for specific types of offenses, such as drug trafficking, have greatly increased (Inciardi et al. 2004).

If a particular offense carries with it a mandatory term, this means that judges must impose a specific sentence as required by law. Their hands are effectively tied. However, under **indeterminate sentencing** or **determinate sentencing** schemes, in absence of any guidelines or other restrictions, judges and prosecutors may operate more or less freely in configuring plea bargain agreements with various defendants. There is considerable jurisdictional variation in this regard. In many jurisdictions without definite guidelines in place for offender sentencing, judges' sentencing practices are often influenced more by their work circumstances, their close relationships with courtroom prosecutors, and an absence of competing recommendations from probation (Worden 1995).

presentence investigation reports, presentence reports (PSIs) reports filed by probation or parole officer appointed by the court containing background information, socioeconomic data, and demographic data relative to defendant. Facts in the case are included. Used to influence the sentence imposed by the judge and by the parole board considering an inmate for early release.

indeterminate sentencing sentencing scheme in which a period is set by judges between the earliest date for a parole decision and the latest date for completion of the sentence.

determinate sentencing sanctioning scheme in which court sentences offender to incarceration for fixed period, and which must be served in full and without parole intervention, less any good time earned in prison.

Summary

1. Define what plea bargaining is and the conditions under which it is applied.

Over 90 percent of all criminal convictions, both felonies and misdemeanors, are obtained through plea bargaining. Plea bargains or plea bargain agreements are preconviction agreements wherein defendants enter guilty pleas in exchange for some form of sentencing leniency from prosecutors and judges. It is difficult to imagine how the criminal justice system would operate smoothly without plea bargaining, inasmuch as criminal court dockets are notoriously clogged even with plea bargaining eliminating over 90 percent of all criminal trials.

Several advantages for criminal defendants are that plea bargaining generally results in a lesser punishment than one that might have been imposed had the case gone to trial. Plea bargaining thus results in shorter sentences, greater use of probation, and generally greater freedoms for defendants. Prosecutors are advantaged by plea bargaining, since they are spared having to prove their cases against criminal defendants in court beyond a reasonable doubt. The sheer volume of criminal cases is reduced. Prosecutors generate much higher conviction rates and improve their chances of re-election in those areas where their positions are contested by popular vote. Generally, plea bargaining works well for prosecutors who have weak cases and for defendants where evidence against them is strong. Under plea bargain agreements, some of the more serious aspects of one's crime(s) may never be disclosed, since the plea agreement may stipulate such omissions. Plea bargaining has been used to resolve criminal cases for several centuries. Furthermore, plea bargaining exists in many other countries. It is not a uniquely American phenomenon.

Not all state jurisdictions condone plea bargaining in the United States. In Alaska, for instance, plea bargaining has been banned. However, informal forms of plea bargaining continue to exist in Alaska despite the ban. Plea bargaining may occur at almost any stage in offender processing. Plea bargaining is typically attempted before a case comes to trial, in an effort to spare the state the expense of a lengthy trial. If plea bargaining efforts are not successful, plea bargaining may nevertheless occur during a trial as evidence is disclosed against the defendant, and even during jury deliberations. Some persons have labeled plea bargaining as coercive, since prosecutors sometimes overcharge defendants and then offer lenient sentencing options if defendants enter guilty pleas to lesser offenses. Generally, if there is a basis for one or more charges against a defendant, then plea bargaining is not coercive. It only becomes coercive if prosecutors engage in malicious prosecutions or pursue charges against criminal suspects where insufficient evidence exists to convict them. Whenever prosecutors make promises to defendants in order to induce guilty pleas from them, these promises must be kept. Otherwise, plea bargain agreements are invalidated. Judges oversee and approve all plea agreements between prosecutors, defendants, and defense counsels.

2. Distinguish among different forms of plea bargaining, including implicit plea bargaining, charge reduction bargaining, sentence recommendation bargaining, and judicial plea bargaining.

Four major types of plea bargaining have been identified. These include implicit plea bargaining, charge reduction plea bargaining, judicial plea bargaining, and sentence recommendation plea bargaining. Implicit plea bargaining is a subtle form of plea bargaining where both prosecutors and defense counsels are familiar with going rates for particular types of offenses. Negotiated guilty pleas generally are close to these going rates associated with particular offenses. An understanding is reached between prosecutors and defense attorneys and a plea agreement is configured that both sides can live with, with judicial approval.

Charge reduction bargaining arises when prosecutors stack multiple charges against defendants. Subsequently, prosecutors offer to drop one or more of the serious charges in exchange for a guilty plea, usually to a lesser charge. Defendants see charge reduction bargaining as beneficial since they will not be prosecuted for other offenses they may have committed. Judicial plea bargaining occurs whenever judges offer defendants a particular sentence in exchange for a guilty plea. Often this type of plea bargaining occurs in misdemeanor cases, where judges may offer defendants fines in exchange for guilty pleas.

Sentence recommendation plea bargaining is initiated by prosecutors. Prosecutors make a recommended sentence known to defense counsels who advise their clients whether to accept it. The pros and cons of the sentence are evaluated, and defendants enter guilty pleas if the offered sentence recommendation is acceptable. Although prosecutors generally initiate sentence recommendation plea bargaining, judicial approval is necessary. Thus, some knowledge about what judges will or will not approve is quite useful when configuring sentences to recommend.

3. *Compare and contrast the advantages and disadvantages of plea bargaining both for the criminal justice system and criminal defendants.*

There are several arguments for and against plea bargaining. Arguments in favor of it include that the uncertainty is removed from the outcome of a criminal trial if one were held. It is difficult to anticipate what juries will decide, even if defendants are innocent of the charges against them (Gants 2005). More than a few innocent defendants have been convicted of crimes they have never committed. Also, plea bargaining reduces the sheer number of trials conducted and the delays such trials would cause. Plea bargaining also guarantees more convictions for prosecutors. Plea bargaining generally reduces the harshness of sentences and reduces the costs of criminal trials, since they are essentially avoided.

Arguments against plea bargaining, some of which are used by Alaska where it is banned, include that plea bargaining is self-incriminating. Defendants must admit to crimes they may or may not have committed in order to secure lenient treatment from prosecutors. In this respect, at least, plea bargaining has a coercive dimension. Although judges must approve all plea agreements, some degree of judicial control is relinquished as the interaction between the prosecution and defense becomes more important. Sometimes defendants are ignorant of the full implications of pleading guilty to certain charges. They literally relinquish all of their constitutional rights to a jury trial, to cross-examinations of witnesses against them, and they cannot give statements or testimony on their own behalf. Other rights are also waived voluntarily. In some instances, plea bargains are rejected by judges inasmuch as prosecutors have failed to provide sufficient evidence to support guilty pleas entered by less sophisticated defendants.

Another criticism is that plea bargaining circumvents habitual offender statutes that most often carry mandatory penalties. Habitual offender statutes are designed to remove chronic and dangerous offenders from the streets, but plea bargaining often bypasses these mandatory penalties that would result in an offender's incarceration. Also, some heinous aspects of one's crime are not disclosed in plea agreements approved by judges. Thus, some offenders may escape harsher sanctions simply because judges are not aware of the full extent of their crimes and the harm they have caused victims. Plea agreements are often rubber-stamped with little or no effort by judges to ascertain whether a factual basis exists for the plea. Although judges must determine from defendants the voluntariness of their pleas and give close attention to the plea agreements they sign, there are simply too many plea agreements in many jurisdictions for judges to do a proper job in this respect.

Plea bargaining is said to invalidate the jury process, since trials are almost always avoided. But since greater leniency is extended to offenders through plea bargaining compared with what the penalty would be if the case were tried before a jury, most criminal defendants are satisfied with the results of plea agreements and their punishments. Plea bargaining also hampers attempts to reform different types of sentencing systems. If sentencing systems are designed to provide certainty of sentencing as a deterrent, these efforts are more than offset by plea bargaining, which undermines such efforts.

Another criticism of plea bargaining is that it may result in gender and/or racial bias in its application. Often, indigent defendants who cannot afford more competent counsel are pressured into accepting plea agreements without fully understanding their consequences. Guilty pleas are also bureaucratized and streamlined, as both prosecutors and defense counsels seek quick solutions to otherwise lengthy trial proceedings. The matter of power in the hands of lawyers is also a criticism of plea bargaining. Some persons question whether attorneys should have such powers to determine one's fate.

4. *Analyze why plea bargaining has been banned in various U.S. jurisdictions in the past and the reasons for this action.*

In jurisdictions where plea bargaining has been banned, such as Alaska, authorities have cited several reasons for such a ban. These include that there is a greater likelihood that just deserts and justice will be served and that offenders will have to suffer some loss of liberty through incarceration. At the same time, however, others say that more charge reduction bargaining occurs where greater decision-making power shifts from the judge to prosecutors and attorneys (Connell 2004). In some jurisdictions, selective bans on plea bargaining have targeted particular offenses, such as capital murder or aggravated rape. Ultimately, however, even where plea bargaining has been banned outright, various courtroom actors have found ways to defeat the ban. In short, it is impossible to completely eradicate plea bargaining in any jurisdiction.

5. *Identify judicial actions when approving plea bargain agreements, including the information required by judges before they can accept guilty pleas from criminal defendants.*

All plea agreements are supervised and approved by judges. In most jurisdictions, judges are prohibited from participating in plea agreement proceedings and exerting undue influence on this process by declaring what they will or will not approve. Judges are obligated in all jurisdictions to determine the voluntariness of one's plea, whether one wishes to waive the right against self-incrimination, the right to cross-examine one's accuser, and other important due process rights. One of the more important functions of judges in overseeing the plea agreement process is to determine whether a factual basis for the guilty plea has been exhibited. It is incumbent upon prosecutors to demonstrate for judges what evidence would have been presented to show defendant's guilt had the case gone to trial. Absent such incriminating evidence, the plea agreement fails, and more than few plea agreements have been rejected by judges and cases against defendants have been dismissed for lack of evidence.

6. *Apply your knowledge of the different sentencing systems used by judges in various jurisdictions at both the state and federal levels, and how these sentencing schemes relate to plea bargaining.*

Dependent on the type of sentencing structure set up in a particular jurisdiction, plea bargaining may be somewhat modified. For example, sentencing guidelines have been established in over 20 states in attempts to create more uniformity in sentencing. In the federal system, the U.S. Sentencing Guidelines have operated since 1987 and are in some cases a hindrance to plea bargaining. Prior to the implementation of the guidelines, federal prosecutors could tailor their plea agreements in ways that would induce a defendant to accept. Probation was used about 60 percent of the time in federally plea-bargained cases prior to the establishment of sentencing guidelines. When the guidelines went into effect, however, U.S. probation officers were mandated to include all relevant legal variables in their presentence investigation reports which precluded prosecutors from omitting these from the plea. Thus, if a gun was used in the commission of a felony, it had to be noted in the plea agreements. Probation under the new federal sentencing guidelines diminished to be used in only about 10 percent of all plea bargains. On the other hand, under indeterminate or determinate sentencing structures, judges and prosecutors may operate more or less freely in entering into plea agreements with defendants.

Key Terms

charge bargaining *195*
charge reduction bargaining *195*
coconspirator *205*
concession givers *197*
determinate sentencing *210*
differential discretion *198*
electronic monitoring *200*
factual basis for the plea *199*
federal misdemeanor *208*
Federal Rules of Criminal
  Procedure *207*
flat time *186*

going rate *182*
guilty plea *187*
habitual offender statutes *202*
home confinement *200*
implicit plea bargaining *193*
indeterminate sentencing *210*
intensive supervised probation *200*
judicial plea bargaining *196*
judicial privilege *201*
jury waiver system *197*
negotiated guilty pleas *200*
nolle prosequi 186

presentence investigation reports
  (PSIs) *210*
selective chivalry *198*
self-incrimination *201*
sentence recommendation
  bargaining *197*
three-strikes-and-you're-out
  policies *202*
typicality hypothesis *198*
United States Sentencing
  Guidelines *200*

Critical Thinking Exercises

1. Some jurisdictions have banned certain forms of plea bargaining as a response to some very lenient sentences handed out to what were perceived to be serious crimes. Having learned the pros and cons of plea bargaining, do you think plea bargaining should be banned? Why or why not? What might be the consequences of effectively banning plea bargaining? Would prosecutors have to do a more thorough job of proving the guilt of those accused of crimes? Would offenders get punishments more proportionate to their crimes? Would the court system grind to a halt because of backlogs of cases? Is plea bargaining a necessary evil to keep cases moving through the system?

2. What is the nature of judicial participation in plea bargaining for individual states and the federal government? Do you think that judges should play a more active role in the plea bargaining process? Should the prosecution and defense counsel have to disclose more to judges prior to getting approval for a plea agreement? Do you think judges would want more control over plea agreements, or that they are happy to simply approve if both parties agree because they also usually have large caseloads?

Case Study Decision-Making Exercise

In Ohio, in the case of *Bradshaw v. Stumpf* 545 U.S. 175 (2005), Stumpf was involved in a robbery and aggravated murder with another accomplice. Stumpf admitted to shooting one individual but maintained that his accomplice had shot the other victim who died. He eventually pled guilty and was sentenced to death for the murder. In the trial of his accomplice, however, the state provided evidence that the accomplice admitted to the shooting death. Stumpf filed an appeal to remove his plea based on the evidence presented at his accomplice's trial. The Ohio court denied his appeal, as did a federal district court but the Sixth Circuit Court of Appeals reversed the decision. The Supreme Court heard the case and had to decide whether Stumpf's conviction was valid because the prosecution used evidence that was inconsistent in the trials of him and his accomplice. In a 9–0 decision, the court decided that Stumpf's plea was valid because his attorney had explained to him the charges and entered into the plea agreement knowingly. The court did opine, however, that the death sentence may be in error because of the prosecutor's conduct in the trials. They remanded the case back to the Sixth Circuit to make that determination. What are your thoughts about plea bargaining where there are multiple defendants? Should the government have to determine who is responsible for which offenses before they enter into plea agreements, or can they use different facts in different cases in attempts to elicit plea bargains? Was it okay for the prosecution to pin the murder on Stumpf and get him to enter a plea even though he maintained he did not shoot the victim, and then use his accomplice's confession to the murder in the accomplice's case? Should Stumpf's attorney have advised him to not accept the plea if he believed that Stumpf did not shoot the victim? Should the court of appeals have required the prosecution and defense to renegotiate considering the evidence presented?

Concept Review Questions

1. What is plea bargaining? Why is it controversial?
2. Name four types of plea bargaining and differentiate between each. Which one do you prefer and why?
3. What is meant by the going rate?
4. Briefly outline the history of plea bargaining in the United States.
5. In some jurisdictions, such as Alaska, plea bargaining has been banned. Does plea bargaining still go on in Alaska, even though it has been banned?
6. What is the significance of Federal Rule of Criminal Procedure 11 as it relates to plea bargaining?
7. What specific rights are waived by defendants who enter into plea bargain agreements?
8. How does the type of sentencing scheme influence plea bargaining?

Suggested Readings

1. G. Nicholas Herman (2012). *Plea Bargaining*. Juris Publishing, Inc.
2. B. L. Kutateladze, N. R. Andiloro, and B. D. Johnson (2016). "Opening Pandora's Box: How Does Defendant Race Influence Plea Bargaining?" *Justice Quarterly* **33**:398–426.
3. S. Herzog (2004). "Plea Bargaining Practices: Less Covert, More Public Support?" *Crime and Delinquency* **50**:590–614.
4. S. Bushway, A. D. Redlich, and R. J. Norris (2014). "An Explicit Test of Plea Bargaining in the 'Shadow of the Trial.'" *Criminology* **52**:723–754.
5. B. L. Kutateladze, V. Z. Lawson, and N. R. Andiloro (2015). "Does Evidence Really Matter? An Exploratory Analysis of the Role of Evidence in Plea Bargaining in Felony Drug Cases." *Law and Human Behavior* **39**:431.
6. P. Marcus, C. A. Brook, B. Fiannaca, D. J. Harvey, J. McEwan, and R. Pomerance (2016). "A Comparative Look at Plea Bargaining in Australia, Canada, England, New Zealand, and the United States." *William & Mary Law Review* **57**:1145–1224.

world blind, most persons when asked why those who have committed crimes should be punished will reply with some notion of retribution as justification for punishment such as that they deserve it.

The other four philosophies that will be discussed are perhaps more in line with Gandhi's sentiments about punishment. Incapacitation, rehabilitation, restoration, and deterrence are all based on utilitarian justifications for punishment, which focus on promoting good (Hospers 1977). In the strictest sense, the utilitarian philosophy believes that if there is no benefit from punishing someone, the punishment should not occur. In a more practical interpretation, for today's legal system, utilitarian justifications for punishment argue that the goal of punishment should be to prevent crime in the future. Although retributive and utilitarian punishment philosophies are seen as opposites regarding the purpose of punishment, they have both been utilized as reasoning for criminal sanctions at differing times in the United States. Haist (2009, 793) notes that the debate over which philosophy is most appropriate to justify punishing those convicted of law violation "has evolved over hundreds of years and will probably continue to advance over the next hundred years." As such public debate over the purposes and justification of punishment may not be settled, but lawmakers and criminal justice system officials must choose which they are going to give more authority to in order to come up with appropriate sanctions for offenses as these dueling philosophies may suggest very different punishments for the same or similar crimes (Tuckness 2010).

Incapacitation

The primary aim of punishment under this philosophy is to incapacitate those convicted of crimes, particularly those who are persistent or chronic offenders. Career criminals who make their living from crime are frequently targeted by the criminal justice system to receive the harshest penalties. Special statutes have been written to make it possible to mete out stringent penalties for chronic recidivists or chronic offenders. It is believed by many state legislatures that if persistent felony offenders and chronic recidivists are removed from society for prolonged periods through longer sentences, then they cannot commit new crimes against society while confined in prison. Thus, the system takes these offenders out of the population for a period of years. Incapacitation achieves the goal of preventing crime in the future because the individual offender will be locked up and therefore unable to commit further offenses or victimize others. If such offenders are allowed to remain in their communities through some form of probation, then probation departments maintain surveillance over these clients by monitoring their whereabouts in different ways. Home confinement and electronic monitoring systems are used, together with regular face-to-face visits with probation officers. These forms of managing convicted offenders in their communities don't prevent them from committing new crimes in any absolute sense, but for many of these offenders, there exists some degree of crime prevention depending on the nature of these management methods.

Unfortunately, research has shown that our ability to predict who will reoffend is very poor. In other words, we do not know for certain which offenders will reoffend and therefore which offenders need to be incapacitated. Incarcerating offenders also costs states and counties a great deal of tax dollars. The United States, in the past three decades, has used incapacitation a great deal as a punishment for those who have violated the law. As the costs of incarceration have continued to increase, however, several states are rethinking the philosophy of incapacitation, especially for offenders who have not committed violent offenses. According to a report from the Vera Institute of Justice, states' corrections expenditures have nearly quadrupled in the last 20 years (Henrichson and Delaney 2012).

The loss of tax revenue that followed the housing bubble and the downturn in the U.S. economy around 2008 forced many states and especially small jurisdictions around the

career criminals those offenders who make their living through crime. Usually, offenses occur over the lifetime of the offender.

chronic recidivists persons who continue to commit new crimes after being convicted of former offenses.

persistent felony offenders habitual offenders who commit felonies with a high recidivism rate.

incapacitation, isolation philosophy of corrections espousing loss of freedom proportional to seriousness of offense. Belief that the function of punishment is to separate offenders from other society members and prevent them from committing additional criminal acts.

country to rethink their heavy reliance on incarceration and experiment with alternatives while at the same time still attempting to achieve crime prevention. At the close of 2012, for instance, the United States' adult prison population was 6,937,600; this, however, was down about 50,000 inmates from the previous year and the fourth year in a row that the prison population had declined (Glaze and Herberman 2013). These alternatives, however, require some ability to predict or select those who are a low risk to reoffend and divert them away from prison or jail and into some type of community-based correctional program. Some of these alternative types of programs including diversion and specialty courts will be discussed in further detail in Chapter 13. Other states such as California, because of years of tougher sentencing laws, are now being forced by federal courts to reduce their prison population as some facilities had double the number of inmates they were designed to house. Incarceration is a very costly endeavor and some states are feeling the pain of their overuse of it as a sentencing option. Henrichson and Delaney (2012) conducted a survey of state incarceration costs and issued a report citing the costs an average of $31,286 per year to house an inmate (roughly $85 a day) but this cost ranges from a low of roughly $14,000 per year in Kentucky to a high of roughly $60,000 a year in New York.

What Do You Think?

The Vera Institute of Justice study discussed in this chapter estimated that the average cost to incarcerate an inmate is roughly $30,000 per year. Let's say a state has on average, 100,000 inmates incarcerated in prisons on any given day. That works out to $3 billion dollars per year of taxpayer's money to incarcerate the state's offenders. In times where funding for police, fireman, and education has been cut, should states attempt to use better methods of determining who truly is a danger to the community and therefore who needs to be incarcerated? Do you think there are some offenders who could be better supervised in the community at a much lower cost? Should judges be forced to incarcerate only the most dangerous offenders?

Rehabilitation

Another intended function of punishment is rehabilitation. Rehabilitation is focused on preventing crime in the future by correcting the offender's behaviors, attitudes, or thought processes. A high degree of cynicism is prevalent among society, however, concerning just how well corrections in any form actually rehabilitates convicted offenders. Some experts believe that rehabilitation never occurs, while others believe that for many offenders, particularly those incarcerated in prisons, rehabilitative programs have been successful in enabling them to turn their lives around and become law-abiding citizens when they are eventually released back into society.

Rehabilitation is also sometimes referred to as the medical or treatment model because it aims to "cure" the offender (Spohn 2009). Critics, however, believe that rehabilitation can only work for those who want to reform. Further, rehabilitation assumes that we know the causes of the offender's bad behavior and can therefore subject him/her to the best cure. Judges often may not know the exact reasons why the defendant engaged in the wrongful behavior or there could be a number of explanations involved that resulted in the criminal offending. Most persons would probably agree that judges often do not have the time or necessary information to play pathologist at sentencing.

Rehabilitation, however, is present in some form or another in conjunction with other punishment philosophies such as incapacitation. Indeed, most prisons include various vocational/technical/educational programs for offenders who wish to take advantage of

rehabilitation, rehabilitative ideal correcting criminal behavior through educational and other means, usually associated with prisons.

these rehabilitative services. Individual and group counseling and other forms of social and psychological assistance are also provided to inmates. Some jails and prisons have rules and regulations requiring inmates to participate in certain programs, whether or not they wish to participate. Literacy programs have been established in many jurisdictions where it is expected that illiterate inmates who are serving long prison terms must learn how to read and write as one condition for their early release. Some authorities question whether voluntary or mandatory participation in any particular prison program is directly responsible for one's rehabilitation over time. A recently released report from the Bureau of Justice Statistics, for example, found that just over two-thirds (68 percent) of prisoners released in 2005 from prison in 30 states were rearrested within three years, and 77 percent were rearrested within five years of release; roughly 37 percent of these were rearrested in the first six months (Durose, Cooper, and Snyder 2014). Critics argue that statistics like these reveal that corrections does not correct behavior for most individuals and beg the question of whether incarceration is an effective method of preventing future offenses.

Finally, most jurisdictions include treatment or education as a condition of probation. Offenders convicted of drug or drinking and driving offenses may be required to attend treatment classes such as Alcoholics Anonymous and Narcotics Anonymous, or some type of victim impact training sessions. Those who have committed assault or domestic violence offenses might have anger management and family therapy sessions as a condition of their probationary sentence. Other types of offenders may be required to obtain their GED, or attend vocational or employment training. Finally, those offenders who are high risk, high need, especially if they have drug abuse issues or other co-occurring mental health issues may be sentenced to inpatient or outpatient rehabilitation programs in lieu of incarcerative sentences. Usually, the offender would have to successfully complete the treatment of rehab program or risk being resentenced to jail or prison.

Restoration

Restoration takes a more holistic approach to punishment and prevention of crime in the future. Restorative justice ideals aim at repairing the harm that occurred as a result of the criminal act and focus on including the victim and/or larger community along with the offender in the punishment equation (Braithwaite 1998). Restoration believes that if the true aim is justice and promoting good in the future, then all parties must be involved in the punishment process. Restoration or those who advocate restorative justice believe that in order to prevent crime in the future, all persons affected by the crime, not just the offender, must be involved in restoring the balance back to relationships, communities, and society (Spohn 2009). Stated another way, if it takes a village to raise a criminal, it also takes the village to reform, restore, or rebuild the lives affected.

For example, perhaps community service or restitution to the victim of the crime better serves justice than simply having the judge place an offender on probation or send them to jail. Often victims may feel a better sense of justice if they are allowed to participate in determining an appropriate punishment or relaying to the offender how the crime has impacted them. Other victims may benefit from receiving monetary reparation for the harm or injury they suffered. The use of restorative processes in the criminal justice system has increased in the last decade. Obviously, restoration may be better suited for certain types of crime; for especially violent crimes such as homicide, it may be difficult to restore the lives of people affected by the harm or injury. Most programs are geared toward first-time and nonviolent offenders but there are some programs in place for serious offenders as well (Urban, Markway, and Crockett 2011). Victim-offender mediation model and Victim Offender Dialogue programs have been established to connect the families of victims with the offender who committed the offense (Umbreit 2001). In 2009, for instance, 24 states had VOD programs for offenses such as homicide, rape, and domestic abuse (Urban et al.

victim–offender mediation model meeting between criminal and person suffering loss or injury from criminal whereby third-party arbiter, such as a judge, attorney, or other neutral party decides what is best for all parties. All parties must agree to decision of third-party arbiter.

2011). These programs are usually initiated by the victim or victim's family and are initiated years after the commission of the crime, sometimes as much as 8 or 10 years after (Borton 2008). These mediations or dialogues involve the victim, the offender, and a facilitator and have many purposes such as allowing the victim to ask the offender questions about why they did what they did, and being able to forgive the offender (Umbreit and Vos 2000). Often the offender wants an opportunity to apologize and be forgiven as well.

Deterrence

Sentencing is also symbolic, both to convicted offenders and to those who are contemplating committing crimes. When judges impose sentences, there is a tacit expectation that others will consider the harshness of these sentences and refrain from crime because of their fear of punishment. Thus, punishment and sentencing are designed as forms of crime prevention and/or deterrence. One direct intention of handing out harsher penalties for offenders is to set examples and deter others from crime. The death penalty is regarded by some persons as an effective deterrent for those who are contemplating capital offenses. No one wants to be executed. Theoretically, if the death penalty is the punishment for murder, then fewer murders will be committed. This view, however, has been challenged by experts frequently, and most criminal justicians agree that the death penalty does not necessarily deter some persons from killing others (Robinson and Darley 2004). Deterrence theory requires that punishments be swift, certain, and severe in order for them to have a deterrent effect (Bernard, Snipes, and Gerould 2009). Although punishments for certain crimes may be severe, the swiftness and certainty of them are called into question. Even clearance rates for violent offenses nationally are only about 50 percent (U.S. Department of Justice 2013); in other words, even for serious crimes, the chances of being caught and punished are not certain.

Nevertheless, in an ideal world, sentencing is supposed to act as a deterrent and prevent others from committing crime. Largely because of this aim, the sentencing systems of all jurisdictions throughout the United States have been changed to maximize sentencing effectiveness. As we will see in the next section, sentencing reform has yielded several important types of sentencing schemes to further the aim of crime deterrence and prevention. Unfortunately, all forms of sentencing have generated criticism from experts and the general public, with little agreement as to which sentencing scheme is best (Champion 2005b).

Deterrence also assumes that criminals are rational and that they weigh the costs and benefits of committing crimes. When the benefits outweigh the costs, they will commit the crime; detection, prosecution, and punishment therefore are important costs in this equation. Deterrence advocates state that the punishments must outweigh the costs of committing crime in order to deter. Obviously, there are critics who would argue that a lot of criminals are not rational when they commit a crime such as assault or murder; these are often crimes of passion or happen because the offender was under the influence of drugs or alcohol at the time of the offense. Further, it might be hard for some persons to imagine criminals conducting a cost–benefit analysis in their heads before deciding whether or not to violate the law; although we may be able to agree that criminals might contemplate odds of getting caught, it is doubtful that they are thinking about the possible punishments for their behaviors.

▶ Reintegration

Related to utilitarian ideals of punishment and the prevention of future crime is the notion of reintegration. Reintegration involves assisting criminals to become readjusted into neighborhoods and communities. This aim is most often associated with nonincarcerative

crime prevention any overt activity conducted by individuals or groups to deter persons from committing crimes. May include "target hardening" by making businesses and residences more difficult to burglarize; neighborhood watch programs, in which neighborhood residents monitor streets during evening hours for suspicious persons or automobiles and equipping homes and businesses with devices to detect crime.

deterrence, general or specific actions that are designed to prevent crime before it occurs by threatening severe criminal penalties or sanctions. May include safety measures to discourage potential lawbreakers such as elaborate security systems, electronic monitoring, and greater police officer visibility.

reintegration punishment philosophy that promotes programs that lead offenders back into their communities. Reintegrative programs include furloughs, work release, and halfway houses.

sentences, including all forms of probation, but many states have begun programs that are focused on helping those who have been incarcerated to readjust to life outside of prison. When judges sentence offenders to probation, there are usually several conditions of probation attached.

These conditions might include mandatory participation in counseling programs, job placement services, restitution programs, and other activities that assist offenders in finding employment and becoming self-sufficient, all these geared toward making it less likely that an offender will return to crime. Particularly for first offenders, community correctional programs are quite helpful in enabling them to remain in society. They may retain contact with their families and receive their social support. Further, these offenders will not have to be exposed to the criminogenic influence of incarceration. For those who are incarcerated, this process may be even more difficult. Adjusting to life outside of the strict routine of prison can often be too difficult for those recently released. Compounding this difficult readjustment is the stigma that society places on those who have been locked up; it may be very difficult to obtain a job or find living arrangements because of some requirements to disclose any criminal convictions on job applications or apartment and housing leases as well as background checks conducted by some employers. Because recidivism rates and the costs of incarcerating repeat offenders are so high, most jurisdictions have, or are seriously discussing the adoption of reintegration programs that can facilitate adjustment of released offenders back into society. Most legislative officials are now realizing the need for reintegration programs to prevent the public from being revictimized in the future as well as to curb the increasingly high costs of incarceration.

▶ Forms of Sentencing

Federal and state judges tend to believe that the toughest part of their jobs is imposing punishments on convicted offenders. There are so many types of offenders with varied backgrounds and criminal histories that the act of sentencing them is one of the most stressful and complex decisions made by these judges (Aas 2004). Assisting judges in their sentencing decision making are various legislatively enacted sentencing schemes. These sentencing schemes provide a rational structure within which to make sentencing decisions. There are generally four main types of sentencing schemes used by various jurisdictions throughout the United States. These are (1) indeterminate sentencing, (2) determinate sentencing, (3) presumptive or guidelines-based sentencing, and (4) mandatory sentencing.

Indeterminate Sentencing

Indeterminate sentencing is a sentence imposed by the judge that includes a minimum term of years and/or months and a maximum term, where the offender's early release from prison is determined by a parole board. Thus, the maximum term may or may not be served by any particular offender, depending upon their institutional behavior and other factors (Stemen 2004).

Indeterminate sentencing has its roots in early correctional history from the 1850s and 1860s. Influenced by penal reforms in Ireland, Scotland, and England, the United States was inclined to experiment with indeterminate sentencing as a means of providing incentives for inmates to behave well while confined. Provided that their institutional conduct was acceptable, once inmates had served the minimum portion of their sentences as imposed by judges, they would become eligible for parole or early release or serving their full terms. Parole boards would decide whether to grant early release to these parole-eligible inmates. Their institutional conduct would be examined, together with the circumstances and seriousness of their conviction offenses, and the parole board would either

parole board, paroling authority body of persons either appointed by governors or others or elected, which determines whether those currently incarcerated in prisons should be granted parole or early release.

grant or deny their parole. Those denied parole on one occasion may apply for it on subsequent occasions, usually at regular intervals such as once a year or every two years. Most paroling authorities in the United States today continue to make such decisions.

Indeterminate sentencing, however, has been criticized for its potential for discrimination on the basis of race, gender, and/or socioeconomic status (Champion 2005b). Both judges and parole boards have been accused of respectively abusing their sentencing and early-release discretionary authority by making decisions on factors other than legal ones. Some believe that parole boards release prisoners too soon (Burke 2003). Others cite that extralegal factors such as race, ethnicity, and gender, or socioeconomic statuses affect these decisions (Kerbs, Jones, and Jolley 2009). Although the seriousness of the offense and the offender's criminal history are primary determinants of these decisions, some research shows that the make-up of the parole board itself and the personal characteristics of the parole board members may also influence decisions (Lindsey and Miller 2011). Those with private counsel often are treated more leniently in sentencing compared with indigent convicted offenders who are represented by public defenders or court appointed counsel (Weiss 2004). Since these factors should not be considered as significant in such decision making, substantial efforts have been made by different interests to reform state and federal sentencing policies and practices. Criticisms were that parole boards in practice were biased and inconsistent (Petersilia 2003). Today many states and the federal government have abolished parole in favor of what they believe to be more equitable sentencing schemes. One noticeable shift among many states has been from indeterminate sentencing to determinate sentencing (Champion 2005b). Most states that still use parole boards to determine early release, however, use risk prediction scales to aid them in their decisions and to lessen the likelihood of extralegal factors being influential (Lindsey and Miller 2011).

> **extralegal factors** any element of a nonlegal nature. In determining whether law enforcement officers, or prosecutors and judges are influenced by particular factors when encountering persons on the street or defendants in court, extralegal factors are those that are not legally relevant to case processing decisions such as race, ethnicity, and sex.

Determinate Sentencing

Determinate sentencing is a sentence imposed by the judge involving a fixed minimum term and a fixed maximum term, but where one's early release from prison is determined by the accumulation of good-time credit, which is deducted from one's maximum term. Good time or good-time credit is a fixed number of days inmates may accumulate based upon the amount of time they serve. A substantial number of states provide that offenders may accumulate up to 30 days for every 30 days they serve. Thus, if an inmate serves one year, he/she may accumulate one year of good-time credit. This credit is deducted from the maximum sentence originally imposed by the judge. It is conceivable, therefore, that inmates sentenced to 10 years under a determinate sentencing system may serve only five years, with the accumulated good time deducted from their maximum 10-year sentences.

> **Good time, good-time credit** an amount of time deducted from the period of incarceration of a convicted offender, calculated as so many days per month on the basis of good behavior while incarcerated. Introduced in early 1800s by British penal authorities, including Alexander Maconochie and Sir Walter Crofton.

Determinate sentencing is believed by its proponents to correct the potential for discrimination according to extralegal factors by judges and parole boards. With determinate sentencing, inmates can calculate their own approximate early-release dates. Thus, there is greater release certainty with determinate sentencing compared with indeterminate sentencing. But inmates may jeopardize their good-time credit by misbehaving while confined. They may receive write-ups from correctional officers for fighting or possessing illegal contraband or drugs. Violations of other institutional rules will result in good time being revoked or cancelled.

Determinate sentencing has received mixed criticisms. Several states, such as Delaware, Colorado, Iowa, Minnesota, and Washington, have used determinate sentencing to replace indeterminate sentencing. Some of these states, including Minnesota and Washington, have opted to implement guidelines-based sentencing after experimenting with determinate sentencing for several years. Despite the promise of significant reform in curing previous ills of discrimination in sentencing, determinate sentencing has not been as successful in this regard as originally projected.

Presumptive or Guidelines-Based Sentencing

Presumptive sentencing or guidelines-based sentencing is the establishment of fixed punishments for each criminal offense, graduated according to offense severity and one's criminal history. Punishments for different offenses are ranged according to months. Punishment range midpoints are the presumptive number of months imposed according to a fixed table. Minnesota was one of the first states to implement sentencing guidelines (DeLone and Wilmot 2004; Kramer and Johnson 2004). Subsequently, many other states established their own guidelines, such as Florida, California, and North Carolina (Crow 2004). To date, over 20 states have adopted some form of sentencing guideline structure to aid judges in their decisions (Kauder and Ostrom 2008). The guidelines usually take the form of a grid where a recommended sentence range is given based on legally relevant factors that can be considered at sentencing. The federal government established sentencing guidelines, following the extensive work of the United States Sentencing Commission. The U.S. Sentencing Commission originated as the result of the Comprehensive Crime Control Act of 1984 and promulgated punishment guidelines for all federal crimes. These guidelines were implemented in 1987. Federal parole was abolished in 1992 and replaced with supervised release.

An example of guidelines-based or presumptive sentencing is the U.S. Sentencing Guidelines. These guidelines are shown in Table 9-1 ■. Across the top of the table are Criminal History categories. These range from I, where offenders have little or no criminal history, to VI, which reflects persons who have the most extensive and serious criminal histories. Down the left-hand side of the table are offense levels ranging from 1 to 43. There is an offense seriousness level for every federal crime. The more serious the crime, the larger the offense seriousness score. In the body of the table, where the criminal history and offense seriousness scores intersect, are ranges of months. These are guidelines used by judges when sentencing offenders.

Although these sentencing grids vary across the different states and at the federal level, judges must remain within these month ranges in most cases. The midpoint in each month range is considered the presumptive sentence judges must impose, unless certain factors dictate otherwise. For instance, if the month range is 40–50, the presumptive number of months is 45. If the range is 3–40 months, then 35 would be the presumptive number of months. Judges may move upward or downward within each range, depending upon whether there are aggravating or mitigating circumstances.

TABLE 9-1 U.S. Sentencing Guidelines Grid (Sentence in Months)

	Offense level	Criminal history category (Criminal history points)					
		I (0 or 1)	II (2 or 3)	III (4, 5, 6)	IV (7, 8, 9)	V (10, 11, 12)	VI (13 or more)
Zone A	1	0–6	0–6	0–6	0–6	0–6	0–6
	2	0–6	0–6	0–6	0–6	0–6	1–7
	3	0–6	0–6	0–6	0–6	2–8	3–9
	4	0–6	0–6	0–6	2–8	4–10	6–12
	5	0–6	0–6	1–7	4–10	6–12	9–15
	6	0–6	1–7	2–8	6–12	9–15	12–18
	7	0–6	2–8	4–10	8–14	12–18	15–21
	8	0–6	4–10	6–12	10–16	15–21	18–24
	9	4–10	6–12	8–14	12–18	18–24	21–27

TABLE 9-1 *(continued)*

	Offense level	Criminal history category (Criminal history points)					
		I (0 or 1)	II (2 or 3)	III (4, 5, 6)	IV (7, 8, 9)	V (10, 11, 12)	VI (13 or more)
Zone B	10	6–12	8–14	10–16	15–21	21–27	24–30
	11	8–14	10–16	12–18	18–24	24–30	27–33
	12	10–16	12–18	15–21	21–27	27–33	30–37
Zone C	13	12–18	15–21	18–24	24–30	30–37	33–41
	14	15–21	18–24	21–27	27–33	33–41	37–46
	15	18–24	21–27	24–30	30–37	37–46	41–51
	16	21–27	24–30	27–33	33–41	41–51	46–57
	17	24–30	27–33	30–37	37–46	46–57	51–63
	18	27–33	30–37	33–41	41–51	51–63	57–71
	19	30–37	33–41	37–46	46–57	57–71	63–78
	20	33–41	37–46	41–51	51–63	63–78	70–87
	21	37–46	41–51	46–57	57–71	70–87	77–96
	22	41–51	46–57	51–63	63–78	77–96	84–105
	23	46–57	51–63	57–71	70–87	84–105	92–115
	24	51–63	57–71	63–78	77–96	92–115	100–125
	25	57–71	63–78	70–87	84–105	100–125	110–137
	26	63–78	70–87	78–97	92–115	110–137	120–150
	27	70–87	78–97	87–108	100–125	120–150	130–162
Zone D	28	78–97	87–108	97–121	110–137	130–162	140–175
	29	87–108	97–121	108–135	121–151	140–175	151–188
	30	97–121	108–135	121–151	135–168	151–188	168–210
	31	108–135	121–151	135–168	151–188	168–210	188–235
	32	121–151	135–168	151–188	168–210	188–235	210–262
	33	135–168	151–188	168–210	188–235	210–262	235–293
	34	151–188	168–210	188–235	210–262	235–293	262–327
	35	168–210	188–235	210–262	235–293	262–327	292–365
	36	188–235	210–262	235–293	262–327	292–365	324–405
	37	210–262	235–293	262–327	292–365	324–405	360–life
	38	235–293	262–327	292–365	324–405	360–life	360–life
	39	262–327	292–365	324–405	360–life	360–life	360–life
	40	292–365	324–405	360–life	360–life	360–life	360–life
	41	324–405	360–life	360–life	360–life	360–life	360–life
	42	360–life	360–life	360–life	360–life	360–life	360–life
	43	life	life	life	life	life	Life

Source: U.S. Sentencing Commission. U.S. Sentencing Guidelines, Washington, DC: U.S. Government Printing Office, 2013.

Sweeping reforms to state sentencing structures have occurred in the last three decades. State politicians believed that judges were to blame for lenient sentences and disparity according to extralegal factors and, therefore, promulgated new legislation to change the methods by which convicted offenders were sentenced. The federal government passed the Sentencing Reform Act of 1984 that led to the creation of the U.S. Sentencing Commission and a revision of the entire federal criminal code. According to Kauder and Ostrom (2008), although there is some debate about whether some states are actively using sentencing guidelines, about 21 states have adopted presumptive sentencing or guidelines-based schemes.

About half of these adopted what have been characterized as voluntary (meaning judges are not required by law to follow them) guidelines, while the others have mandatory sentencing guidelines. Presumptive sentencing was considered one of the most promising sentencing reforms because of its potential for minimizing sentencing disparities according to extralegal factors, minimizing incarceration rates, and reducing prison overcrowding.

Perhaps the most immediate impact of newly implemented presumptive sentencing guidelines is the reduction of sentencing disparities, where similar offenders receive widely divergent sentences (Davis-Frenzel and Spohn 2004). Minnesota, for example, experienced a decline in sentencing disparity in the year following the implementation of guidelines. A 60 percent reduction in sentencing inequality for the length-of-time-in-prison decision was also observed. Likewise, studies revealed that disparities in sentencing had declined in Pennsylvania, Washington, and Oregon (Spohn 2009). At the federal level, sentences are more punitive, more uniform, and the guidelines have reduced some but not all disparity. There is still disparity in sentencing of similar cases between judges and disparity in sentences imposed across the 94 federal districts (Spohn 2005; Spohn 2009). Ulmer (2005), and Johnson, Ulmer, and Kramer (2008) found inter-district variation regarding departures from the guidelines. Hartley (2008) likewise found similar inter-district variation in the sentences given to narcotics offenders in four federal districts in the southwestern United States. The findings from these studies call into question the idea that adopting sentencing guidelines will necessarily result in increased uniformity and amelioration of disparity.

Part of the issue may be that judges may impose sentences outside of the recommended range if they believe there are circumstances to justify such departures (Ulmer 2004).

BOX 9-1

KEY CASES: REGARDING SENTENCING GUIDELINES

Blakely v. Washington 542 U.S. 296 (2004)

In this case, the U.S. Supreme Court invalidated Blakely's 90-month sentence, holding that because the facts supporting Blakely's exceptional sentence were neither admitted in the plea agreement nor found by a jury, the sentence violated his Sixth Amendment right to a trial by jury.

United States v. Booker 543 U.S. 220 (2005)

Similar to the Blakely case, the U.S. Supreme Court held that the federal sentencing guidelines are subject to Sixth Amendment jury trial requirements, and that if a judge authorizes a punishment on the finding of a fact, that fact must be found by a jury beyond a reasonable doubt.

Kimbrough v. United States 552 U.S. 85 (2007)

The *Kimbrough* case has to do with the mandatory minimum trigger ratio between powder and crack cocaine. The U.S. Supreme Court ruled that because *Booker* made the guidelines advisory, a judge could reasonably depart from the presumptive sentence. This case set precedent for the idea that the district courts can deviate from the 100:1 crack-to-powder cocaine

sentencing minimum ratio. Congress has since passed legislation reducing disparity between crack and powder cocaine sentencing from 100:1 to 18:1.

Gall v. United States 552 U.S. 38 (2007)

The U.S. Supreme Court decided that if a judge gives a below-guideline sentence, a court of appeal should only reverse if it is deemed that the judge abused his or her discretion.

Rita v. United States 551 U.S. _ (2007)

The U.S. Supreme Court ruled that judges have considerable discretion to impose sentences and that within guideline sentences should be seen as reasonable. This, however, may not be the case dependent on the facts and circumstances and should be determined on a case by case basis.

Alleyne v. United States 570 U.S. _ (2013)

The U.S. Supreme Court held that the facts used in imposing a mandatory minimum sentence also must be found as facts beyond a reasonable doubt by a jury.

Several recent Supreme Court decisions have also altered the presumptiveness of the current federal sentencing guideline structure. In the case of *United States v. Booker* (2005), for instance, the Supreme Court stated that the guidelines were no longer mandatory, only advisory. What this means is that judges still must consider the guidelines in a decision about an appropriate sentence for a given defendant; however, they are no longer required to apply the presumptive guideline sentence. Judges, therefore, now have more discretion to mete out what they believe is an appropriate sentence.

Mandatory Sentencing

Mandatory sentencing is the obligatory imposition of a specified period of years and/or months for specific types of offenses. Judges are bound to impose a mandatory sentence for certain types of conviction offenses. For instance, Michigan has a mandatory penalty of two years for using a gun during the commission of a felony and under federal law there are over 60 mandatory minimums that cover over 100 offenses (Tonry 1996). The use-a-gun-and-go-to-prison law in Michigan is added to whatever sentence is imposed by the judge when offenders are convicted. The intent of mandatory minimum laws is to deter criminals from using weapons or engaging in other serious criminal behaviors.

The most important feature of mandatory sentencing is the obligation it places on judges to impose consistent sentences for a variety of convicted offenders, regardless of other factors in the case. Under these mandatory sentencing provisions, judges must impose specific sentences as authorized by their state legislatures. However, even mandatory sentencing policies may be circumvented. Prosecutors may choose to ignore those aspects of one's crime that carry mandatory penalties. Larger numbers of plea bargains are obtained if certain facts about one's crime are ignored. Armed robbery may be downgraded to simple robbery, for instance. Thus, sentencing judges may never see the full set of circumstances involving the crime committed. If crimes with mandatory penalties are not included in the charges, or the plea bargain agreement, the judge cannot impose the minimum.

Such a scenario occurs too frequently throughout the United States, according to some critics. Many law-and-order proponents advocate greater truth in sentencing. If someone uses a gun when committing a crime, then this fact ought to be made known to the court. Further, if the convicted offender is a recidivist with prior felony convictions, this information ought to be made known to the court. All states have habitual offender statutes that apply to persistent or habitual offenders with lengthy criminal records. Some of these persons are in jeopardy of being given a life-without-parole sentence as a mandatory sentence for their conviction as habitual offenders.

mandatory sentencing, mandatory sentence sentencing where court is required to impose an incarcerative sentence of a specified length, without the option for probation, suspended sentence, or immediate parole eligibility.

habitual offenders persons who have been convicted of two or more felonies and may be sentenced under the habitual offender statute for an aggravated or longer prison term.

life-without-parole sentence penalty imposed as maximum punishment in states that do not have death penalty; provides for permanent incarceration of offenders in prisons, without parole eligibility; early release may be attained through accumulation of good-time credits.

▶ Habitual Offender Statutes and Truth-in-Sentencing Laws

Habitual Offender Statutes

Chronic, persistent, and violent felony offenders pose the greatest risk to the public. These criminals commit new crimes frequently, and these crimes often result in serious victim injuries and/or deaths. There is also a broad class of chronic and persistent felony offenders who commit property crimes, such as larceny, vehicular theft, and burglary. All types of chronic recidivists have been targeted in recent decades for special and harsher treatment by the criminal justice system. Since the 1970s, virtually every jurisdiction throughout the United States has evolved habitual offender statutes (Champion 2005b). In some jurisdictions, these laws are called persistent offender statutes. Habitual offender or persistent offender statutes are laws that proscribe life sentences for those who are convicted of three or more felonies.

The intent of habitual offender statutes is to incapacitate those who persist in committing crimes. If these high-rate offenders are removed from society, then some crime prevention or crime control occurs. The primary problem is that there may be so many persistent and chronic felony offenders that there isn't enough prison space to house them for extended terms. Furthermore, more than a few inmates convicted as habitual offenders have filed lawsuits challenging their lengthy prison sentences compared with the nonserious nature of their conviction offenses. These are usually *habeas corpus* actions, where relief is sought in the form of sentence reductions (Fletcher 2004). Also, some experts do not consider these statutes as particularly beneficial as deterrents or methods of crime control (Crow and Johnson 2008; Freedman 2001; Hack 2003; Kovandzic 2001).

Who Are Habitual Offenders?

A key problem confronted by all jurisdictions with habitual offender statutes is defining who are habitual offenders? Do habitual offenders include all types of offenders, or is the definition limited to those committing only the most serious and violent types of felonies? This problem seems universal in nature. England, for instance, has been vexed by the problem of habitual offender legislation and its inability to provide precise guidance about who qualify as habitual offenders. Are habitual offenders only violent criminals who pose an immediate threat to society, or are they also the bumbling petty thieves and property offenders?

Florida has attempted to refine the habitual offender definition by establishing a limited number of categories and a guideline matrix (Champion 2005b). Thus, not every Florida felon with numerous convictions qualifies as habitual offender. Further, Florida law provides for gradations in offense seriousness and whether certain convicted offenders will be classified as habitual offenders.

A subsequent study of the application of Florida's habitual offender statute has generated an offender database consisting of 25,806 persons eligible for habitualization. Interestingly, only 18 percent or 4,783 persons from this database were actually prosecuted and convicted as habitual offenders (Florida Joint Legislative Management Committee 1992). This finding is consistent with the earlier work of Hunzeker (1985), who found that although every state has habitual offender statutes, relatively few inmates are serving sentences as habitual offenders. In fact, eight states have reported that 2–3 percent of the inmates were serving terms as habitual offenders. Nine states reported that less than 1 percent of their inmate populations were serving terms as habitual offenders.

Which raises the question of whether or not we truly need these laws in place? If legislators pass these laws by arguing these offenders are problematic and responsible for a large number of offenses, why are so few of them actually serving sentences under these laws? The consensus is that while all states have habitual offender statutes, most states do not enforce these habitual offender statutes with any consistency (Champion 2005b). These statutes can also be circumvented or manipulated by prosecutors if they are used as mechanisms of coercion to elicit guilty pleas from persistent offenders (Austin, Clark, Hardyman, and Henry 1999). There are a few states, however, that have the opposite problem. California for instance, passed three-strikes laws and charged many offenders under it who were not serious violent offenders.

Narrowing the Habitual Offender Definition: Three-Strikes-and-You'Re-Out!

In recent years, the federal government and various states have enacted provisions to punish more serious felons with harsh punishments if they are convicted of three or more felonies. Such legislation is termed three-strikes-and-you're-out. Essentially, offenders convicted of three serious felonies are out in that they are sentenced to life terms in prison. The get-tough movement and general public seem supportive of legislation aimed at incapacitating persistent felony offenders (Ueckert 2005).

California's three-strikes legislation mandates that felons found guilty of a third serious crime must be locked up for 25 years to life. However, the problem was that these so called strikes could be imposed on offenders who had committed felonies that were not necessarily violent. In California, over 30 percent of persons convicted on a second strike, and just under 20 percent convicted on a third strike were drug offenders (convicted most often on possession charges), and another one-third were convicted of burglary (Austin and Irwin 2001). Because there hasn't been large scale evaluation of these laws, it is difficult to assess their overall impact on sentencing (Spohn 2009). These types of statutes vary across the states and so some have more of an impact on sentence length and prison populations than others but generally they have had little impact on their intended effect (Austin and Irwin 2001). California, however, may be the exception because of the types of offenses that would count as second and third strikes under the California statute. The states' prison population increased fairly dramatically because low level, nonviolent offenders convicted of drug possession and property crime were sentenced under the three-strikes law.

BOX 9-2

LEGAL ISSUES: THREE-STRIKES LAWS AND PRISON OVERCROWDING IN CALIFORNIA

The long-term effects of three-strikes legislation on California's correctional population have recently been realized. Most of California's prisons are operating at 150 percent of maximum capacity and some are housing twice as many inmates as they were designed for. With the economic downturn and housing crisis, California did not have the financial resources or sufficient prison space to accommodate all of these offenders, despite the fact that it has one of the nation's most vigorous prison construction programs (Stephenson-Lang 2005). In 2010, under federal court order, the California legislature along with Governor Schwarzenegger was devising plans to release upwards of 60,000 inmates. These plans, however, were not effective enough on reducing the states' prison population. In February of 2014, a panel of federal judges refused to vacate the earlier federal order but granted California a two-year extension to reduce prison overcrowding (Miley 2014). California has roughly 120,000 prisoners even though its institutions are only supposed to house about 80,000; the three-judge panel ordered the state to reduce its population to 137 percent of capacity by February of 2016 (Miley 2014). That would mean the California prison population would need to be

Prazis/Fotolia

roughly 110,000 within the next two years. This means California needs to reduce their population by another 10,000 inmates. This might mean releasing many more prisoners earlier than expected keeping in mind that new convicted offenders are sentenced to prison each day. Clearly, states looking to pass increasingly tough habitual offender statutes will want to look to the California experience and the annual costs incurred in housing these offenders because of implementation of these types of laws.

A Felony Is a Felony Is a Felony ...

Some attempt has been made by California and other states to limit the types of offenses that qualify under the habitual offender statute and three-strikes legislation. Distinctions have been made between those who commit **violent felonies** (rape, murder, aggravated assault, and armed robbery), **serious felonies** (robbery and drug dealing), and **felony property offending** (larceny/theft, vehicular theft, and burglary). In theory, at least, the most serious persistent felons will be given 25 years to life, while less serious felons will receive shorter sentences. But few states, including California, have found the three-strikes legislation to be effective in reducing violent crime (Ueckert 2005).

Use-a-Gun-and-Go-to-Prison Statutes

Not all mandatory penalties involve life imprisonment or life without parole. Some mandatory penalties are intended to downgrade the seriousness of violent crimes whenever they are committed. One way of discouraging some violent offenders from using firearms when committing their crimes is to provide mandatory sentences of incarceration whenever firearms are used (Lightfoot and Umbreit 2004). Other types of mandatory penalties are associated with crimes such as repeat-offense driving-while-intoxicated cases.

Michigan has enacted a mandatory penalty for using a firearm during the commission of a felony. This penalty is a **flat term**, a two-year sentence that must be served following whatever other sentence is imposed. Thus, if someone is convicted of armed robbery, a sentence of 10–20 years might be imposed for the armed robbery charge, and then a separate sentence of two years will be added on to the original sentence. This second sentence must be served in its entirety. If the offender is parole-eligible after serving 15 years of the 10- to 20-year sentence, then the two-year sentence commences. No time off for good behavior will be extended to those serving these mandatory sentences. California enacted such a law over a decade before Michigan (Champion 2005b). Presently, most states have such mandatory sentencing provisions for firearms usage whenever felonies are committed.

Many of these mandatory sentences are primarily symbolic, in that they show the public that the legislature and other politicians are concerned about public safety and citizen fear of crime (Spohn 2009). Frequently, mandatory penalties are circumvented by defense counsel, prosecutors, and judges through plea bargaining, where the violations incurring mandatory penalties are carefully omitted from any reports or written documents. Many presentence investigation reports may have absent all of the information surrounding the offense. If judges don't know whether particular defendants used a firearm when a felony was committed, then they cannot be compelled to impose mandatory penalties, even in Michigan. However, more than few jurisdictions have made it increasingly difficult for these mandatory sentencing provisions to be circumvented. The federal sentencing guidelines and changed roles of U.S. probation officers have greatly restricted the degree to which certain aspects of one's crime can be ignored (Champion 2005b).

Truth in Sentencing

The federal Violent Crime Control and Law Enforcement Act of 1994 provided monies to states that changed their sentencing provisions and adopt harsher sanctions known as truth-in-sentencing statutes. **Truth-in-sentencing laws** were a response to the reality that the actual time an offender serves is prison is always shorter than the time the judge sentenced them to serve. For instance, according to a Bureau of Justice Report, violent offenders released in 1996 served an average of 45 months before being released despite the fact that the average sentence handed out to them was 85 months (Ditton and Wilson 1999). Under truth in sentencing, however, violent offenders admitted to prison in 1996 would serve an average of 88 months in prison, almost double the current time serve for those released in 1996

(Ditton and Wilson 1999). Truth-in-sentencing statutes, therefore, also contribute to prison overcrowding as the average time served is now considerably higher.

According the Bureau of Justice, almost 30 states have adopted the 85 percent minimum time served standard, requiring that all convicted offenders would have to serve at least 85 percent of their maximum sentences before becoming parole-eligible (Ditton and Wilson 1999). A few other states like Texas and Nebraska have adopted a 50 percent of sentence standard, and still a few other states like Idaho, Nevada, and New Hampshire have adopted a 100 percent of the minimum requirement (Ditton and Wilson 1999). Politicians wanting to look like they are tough on crime and outcry from the public about the fact that inmates in many states have been serving only fractions of their actual sentences have led to reforms such as these.

While truth-in-sentencing laws have been enacted and the public's feelings have been assuaged to a degree, corrections officials have struggled to find more space for those offenders spending longer terms in prison. The direct result of truth in sentencing has been enormous prison population growth. Prison overcrowding is now a characteristic of all U.S. prisons. A significant contributing factor has been the **Crime Bill of 1994**. President Bill Clinton promoted this bill to provide for greater numbers of police officers on city streets as a means of preventing crime. Another provision of this bill was to maximize offender sentences so that convicted persons must serve between 80 and 90 percent of the maximum sentences before being granted early release or parole.

Originally, the intent of truth-in-sentencing provisions was to make sure that inmates would serve a large portion of their prison terms (McManimon 2005a). While this event has occurred in those jurisdictions where it has been mandated by state legislatures, other problems have been created. For instance, in 1994, before the Federal Crime Bill, North Dakota was one of six states without an overcrowding problem. The state prison in Bismarck could house about 650 inmates. Shortly after enacting truth-in-sentencing laws, however, the North Dakota Penitentiary in Bismarck quickly became overcrowded and a new prison facility had to be built in Jamestown. In 1998, North Dakota officials were planning two additional tiers in the Jamestown prison facility as dramatic increases in the inmate population were projected.

Thus, taxpayers in many states across the country are now faced with paying the bills or at least defraying the costs of new prison construction and housing record numbers of inmates. While the public may want tougher laws such as truth in sentencing, requiring longer prison terms for inmates, they may not want to pay the dollar cost of new prison construction in order for this policy to remain in place. Most states now have major prison overcrowding problems and state budgets that are too tight to continue building new prison facilities.

Finally, another consequence of prisoners serving a larger portion, or all, of their sentence is that they may be released outright without any further supervision. According to a report by the Pew Charitable Trusts (2014, 1), "Between 1990 and 2012, the number of inmates who maxed out their sentences in prison grew by 119 percent, from fewer than 50,000 to more than 100,000." The report also cites that today one in five inmates max out their sentence; the percentage of prisoners maxing out their sentence differs by state but the rates increased in 23 states. Florida was one of the first states to implement truth in sentencing and accounts for the highest number of prisoners maxing out. According to the statistics, Florida releases roughly 12,000 inmates without supervision, about 32 percent of those released; in 2012, the max-out rate had increased to 64 percent, resulting in more than 21,000 inmates leaving prison with no monitoring or support (Pew Charitable Trusts 2014, 3). One of the consequences of truth-in-sentencing laws then is that they may actually increase the likelihood of rearrest rather than acting as a deterrent as it was originally intended. Recent research reveals that shorter prison sentences with supervision in the community after release reduces the likelihood of recidivism (Pew Charitable Trusts 2014).

Crime Bill of 1994 legislation supported by President Bill Clinton designed to increase crime prevention measures and put more police officers on city streets; also established truth-in-sentencing laws to maximize the amount of time inmates must serve in relation to their maximum sentences.

In an earlier survey in 2012, Pew found that the majority of voters (67 percent regarding violent offenders and 69 percent regarding nonviolent offenders) preferred that inmates be released early with mandatory supervision rather than be held in prison until they completed their sentence which would mean no supervision upon release (Pew Charitable Trusts 2012). On their face, certain sentencing reforms sound like a good idea concerning deterrence and protection of the public, however, often neither legislators nor the general public think about the long-term consequences of their implementation, either financially or related to crime prevention and public safety.

Things may be shifting, however, as jurisdictions consider alternatives to incarceration for certain types of offenders. According to a Bureau of Justice Statistics report, for the first time since 1972, the U.S. prison population declined in 2010. Also, for the first time since BJS began collecting this data in 1977, the number of persons being released from prison exceeded the number of persons entering prison (Guerino, Harrison, and Sabol 2011). According to this report, half of the states reported a decrease in prison population with California seeing the largest decline (remember that California is under federal mandate to reduce their prison population), at just over 6,000 inmates. The authors of this report attribute the decline to a decrease in prison admissions as release rates and time served by prisoners was relatively stable (Guerino et al. 2011).

Summary

1. *Understand the goals of sentencing, including the punishment philosophies of retribution, deterrence, incapacitation, rehabilitation, and restoration.*

Although sentences for similar offenders may vary across the states and in the federal criminal justice system, goals and functions of sentencing are more or less universal. The goals of punishment include retribution, incapacitation, rehabilitation, restoration, and deterrence. Retribution focuses on the harm done and what the offender deserves for inflicting that harm. Although the notion of *lex talionis* and an eye for an eye are not applied in reality today, proportionality, or that the punishment should fit the crime, is a major goal of sentencing today.

Incapacitation as a goal of sentencing seeks to remove offenders from society, at least temporarily, so such offenders cannot commit new crimes against citizens. Prisons and jails in many jurisdictions have been increasingly used to warehouse offenders, to remove them from public view, and to place them in circumstances where they pose no threats to others. This is a form of crime control, since incapacitated persons are not in a position to reoffend.

Although rehabilitation is a sentencing goal, many persons believe that no type of sentencing or punishment is truly rehabilitative. Although vocational, technical, educational, and other useful programs are offered to persons convicted of crimes and incarcerated or placed under community supervision of some form, high recidivism rates among offenders suggest that only about a third of all convicted persons actually benefit from these programs. For those with addictions or who suffer from psychological problems, individual or group counseling and other treatment programs and therapies exist to assist them. But the benefits of these programs are limited to a small proportion of those willing to utilize these resources effectively. Thus, cynicism often characterizes the public view toward rehabilitation as a correctional goal.

Restoration seeks to repair the harm that was done and is a more holistic approach to justice by including the offender, the victim, and the larger community in decisions about appropriate punishments. Restorative justice therefore seeks to restore relationships or return things to the way they were before the crime occurred, hopefully preventing future criminal events from occurring again. In some serious violent cases, however, the victim and offender may agree to participate in victim–offender mediation or dialogue programs. These programs bring victims or victims' families together with the perpetrator of the crime, usually a number of years after the offense, so that a dialogue can take place related to the reasons for the offense and perhaps even for the victim to forgive the offender for what they have done. This may seem a bit scary to many people but many victims state that after a period of time part of the healing process is to forgive the offender for what they have done. After much time thinking about their crime, many offenders also want to apologize for their behaviors.

2. *Recognize reintegration as another function post sentencing which attempts to assist with prevention of future offending.*

Reintegration is also important to prevent future offending. Reintegration programs seek to maintain a convicted person's connection with his/her communities, families, and work. Probation is used as a punishment to foster reintegration, and parole permits incarcerated persons to be released short of serving their full sentences in order to live law-abiding lives through the assistance of parole officers and others. Many jurisdictions are also coupling reintegration with incarceration where an offender may be released early via a program that can help them reintegrate back into society by gaining employment or reconnecting with family, and therefore, hopefully having a lower likelihood of recidivating.

3. *Compare and contrast different forms of sentencing, including indeterminate, determinate, guidelines-based or presumptive, and mandatory sentencing and their implications for criminal defendants.*

Several types of sentencing are being used as methods for determining appropriate punishments for offenders. All of these sentencing schemes have been criticized for different reasons, largely because they seem ineffective at accomplishing their various goals and functions. No sentencing system seems to work perfectly in any jurisdiction, and thus considerable experimentation with different sentencing variations has been observed. Four basic types of sentencing schemes have been described. These include indeterminate sentencing, determinate sentencing, presumptive or guidelines-based sentencing, and mandatory sentencing.

Indeterminate sentencing has been used for over two centuries. This sentencing form specifies a minimum and maximum sentence, with one's early release from incarceration being determined by a paroling authority or equivalent body. Determinate sentencing is similar to indeterminate sentencing, but early releases of inmates are governed by an accumulation of good-time credits, or days off one's maximum sentence for so many days served. A shift from indeterminate to determinate sentencing occurred during the 1970s. It was believed that parole board discretion was not entirely objective. But removing discretionary power over one's early release has raised concerns among citizens and legislators that some inmates may be released automatically when it is believed that they should remain incarcerated for longer periods. There are no easy solutions to these particular sentencing conflicts and problems (Levine 2005).

Presumptive or guidelines-based sentencing has been used for several decades, by both the federal government and different states. Each crime is given a seriousness score, and one's criminal history or prior record and other factors are combined to determine an approximate range of months to be served. The middle number of months of any specified range is the presumptive sentence, and aggravating or mitigating factors can increase or decrease the number of months of incarceration imposed within the recommended range. The U.S. Supreme Court in 2005 declared that the federal sentencing guidelines which were established in 1987 are merely recommended sentencing ranges judges must reference, making them now only advisory in nature.

The intended function of sentencing guidelines is to create greater fairness in sentencing, where extralegal factors such as gender, socioeconomic status, race, and/or ethnicity are not serious considerations in determining a sentence. The implementation of sentencing guidelines was originally intended to limit or remove sentencing disparities among different judges according to these and other extralegal variables. However, despite the establishment of guidelines, sentencing disparities continue to exist in all jurisdictions.

Mandatory sentences are punishments of specified period of years and/or months for specific types of offenses. Judges are bound to impose a mandatory sentence for certain types of offenses which means that the offenders must serve that time, without any time deducted from their sentences for good behavior, however significant that behavior may be.

4. *Explain habitual offender or chronic offender statutes such as three-strikes laws and their use in different jurisdictions.*

Habitual offender statutes or chronic offender provisions seek to impose mandatory sentences on offenders who have been convicted of three or more felonies. California's three-strikes-and-you're-out law was intended to impose life sentences on persistent dangerous felons. It is believed that these mandatory penalties associated with the use of firearms during the commission of a felony will deter potential criminals from committing offenses with firearms. The effectiveness of these sentencing measures has been questioned, since deaths of persons from firearms use during crimes have not diminished significantly since such mandatory sentencing laws have gone into effect. Critics argue that these laws are easily manipulated and circumvented by prosecutors, defense attorneys, and judges to get defendants to enter into plea agreements.

5. *Describe truth-in-sentencing provisions and how such provisions have evolved.*

Many states have truth-in-sentencing provisions, where legislatures have acted to provide that convicted persons should serve most of their sentences instead of smaller portions of them. These laws evolved because of the fact that many offenders were only serving half of their sentences because of good-time credit. Violations of federal criminal laws now require that convicted federal offenders must serve at least 85 percent of their sentences before becoming eligible for early release. Many states have emulated the federal government by passing similar legislation. However, truth-in-sentencing laws have done little to deter violent crime, and in many jurisdictions, truth-in-sentencing laws have been ignored due to prison overcrowding, or by utilizing other alternative sentencing options (Champion 2005a).

Key Terms

career criminals *220*
chronic recidivists *220*
Crime Bill of 1994 *233*
crime prevention *223*
deterrence *223*
extralegal factors *225*
felony property offending *232*
flat term *232*
good time *225*
good-time credit *225*
guidelines-based sentencing *226*

habitual offenders *229*
incapacitation *220*
life-without-parole sentence *229*
mandatory sentence *229*
mandatory sentencing *229*
parole board *224*
persistent felony offenders *220*
persistent offender
 statutes *230*
presumptive sentencing *226*
punishment *219*

rehabilitation *221*
reintegration *223*
sentencing guidelines *226*
serious felonies *232*
three-strikes-and-you're-out *231*
truth-in-sentencing laws *232*
United States Sentencing
 Commission *226*
victim–offender mediation
 model *222*
violent felonies *232*

Critical Thinking Exercises

1. Which philosophies of punishment do you think should be the foundation for sentencing in the United States? In your opinion, can punishments achieve more than one of these goals of philosophies?
2. There are criticisms that all of the legislated sentencing reforms such as sentencing guidelines, mandatory minimums, habitual offender statutes, and truth in sentencing have caused incarceration rates to skyrocket and have led to current prison overcrowding in many states. Does the country really need all of these laws or should we trust judges to make appropriate sentencing decisions based on the seriousness of the offense, the offender's criminal record, and their dangerousness and risk for reoffense? If states were to give judges wide-ranging discretion to fashion a sentence, what could be a response or remedy for a judge who hands out a particularly lenient or harsh sentence given the offense, or appears to be using factors that are not legally relevant to determine a sentence?
3. What are your thoughts about sentencing guidelines where the offense seriousness and prior criminal record essentially determine the range of punishment that the judge can hand out? Should a judge be able to depart from this presumptive range for any circumstances?

Case Study Decision-Making Exercise

Many states' prisons are currently overcrowded (some are at 200 percent of the capacity they were built to house), and some states are under federal mandate to reduce their prison populations. Many have cited the cause of this overcrowding to be tougher sentencing laws and over legislation of habitual offender and mandatory minimum statutes. What do you think? Should legislators have to conduct analyses of how prison populations might be affected with new laws or changes in punishment for certain offenses as well as what the estimated costs to taxpayers might be? Do you think that these laws deter future offenders from engaging in certain criminal acts? Does the citizenry have a right to know, in addition to what certain get-tough laws are designed to do, how many offenders might be charged under the new laws based on previous arrest and conviction statistics?

Concept Review Questions

1. What are four general functions or aims of sentencing?
2. How does indeterminate sentencing differ from determinate sentencing?
3. What constraints are imposed on judges by presumptive or guidelines-based and mandatory sentencing schemes?
4. What is a habitual offender statute? Do most states have such statutes? Are these statutes used frequently by these states? Why or why not? Explain.
5. What is a use-a-gun-and-go-to-prison statute?
6. What is meant by truth in sentencing? How is truth in sentencing achieved?

Suggested Readings

1. J. Austin and J. Irwin (2001). *It's About Time: America's Imprisonment Binge* (3rd ed). Belmont, CA: Wadsworth.
2. M. S. Crow and K. A. Johnson (2008). "Race, Ethnicity, and Habitual Offender Sentencing." *Criminal Justice Policy Review* **19**:63–83.
3. M. Tonry (ed.) (2011). *Why Punish? How Much? A Reader on Punishment*. New York, NY: Oxford University Press.
4. M. Tonry (ed.) (2011). *Retributivism Has a Past: Has it a Future?* New York, NY: Oxford University Press.
5. J. T. Ulmer, J. Eisenstein, and B. D. Johnson (2010). "Trial Penalties in Federal Sentencing: Extra-Guidelines Factors and District Variation." *Justice Quarterly* **27**: 560–592.

Andrea Izzotti/Fotolia

10 Judicial Sentencing Options, Sentencing Disparities, and Appeals

LEARNING OBJECTIVES

As a result of reading this chapter, you will have accomplished the following objectives:

1 *Understand the options that judges have at sentencing and that these vary by type of crime and jurisdiction.*

2 *Summarize the death penalty and bifurcated trials, including the functions of such trial proceedings.*

3 *Describe the sentencing hearing and its various functions.*

4 *Describe presentence investigation reports, their contents and components, preparation, and usefulness in the sentencing process. Also, apply your knowledge of victim impact statements and the usefulness of such statements in the sentencing process.*

5 *Explain what sentencing disparities are and how factors such as race/ethnicity, gender, socioeconomic status, and age affect one's sentence.*

6 *Explain the appeals process, who initiates appeals, and various bases for appeals.*

According to a 2013 Bureau of Justice Statistics report, the make-up of felony defendants in the 75 largest urban counties in the United States has changed somewhat in the last two decades. The average age of defendants increased from 27 to 32 years from 1990 to 2009 and a larger percentage in 2009 (27 percent) were over 40 years compared with 1990 (10 percent). This also meant that the prison population was older; about 34 percent of state prisoners were over 40 years in 2009 compared to only 9 percent in 1990. The number of female felony defendants also increased slightly from 14 percent to 17 percent over that same time period. In 2009, 45 percent of defendants were black, 30 percent were white, and 24 percent were Hispanic. Drug offenders accounted for the largest percentage of defendants (33 percent), followed by property offenders (29 percent) and violent offenders (25 percent). What do you think about these statistics? Are judges solely to blame for the differences in demographic make-up of our prison populations? What will be the result of older offenders comprising an increasing share of those being charged with felonies?

Source: Reaves, Brian A. (2013). "Felony Defendants in Large Urban Counties, 2009 – Statistical Tables." Washington, DC: U.S. Department of Justice, Bureau of Justice Statistics.

▶ Introduction

For most serious crimes, incarceration is an option that judges have when deciding an appropriate sentence. Other options may include probation or some other alternative type of punishment; for those convicted of a capital crime, the **death penalty** is also a punishment option that can be invoked. In the United States, the most often used punishments are incarceration and probation. Critics have long argued that a just system of sentencing would allow for other options for the sentencing judge, especially those in between prison and probation or what are referred to as intermediate punishments (Morris and Tonry 1990). A discussion of both shock probation and split sentencing is also given. Most convicted felony offenders receive some incarceration time as part of their sentence, whereas convicted misdemeanants most often receive probation with certain conditions attached.

> **death penalty**
> imposition of death as a punishment for the most serious capital crimes.

A great deal of research has been conducted regarding judicial sentencing decisions and what factors judges consider when meting out appropriate punishments. As justice is supposed to be blind, most of this research focuses on examining whether extralegal factors (race/ethnicity, gender, age, and socioeconomic status) play a role in the decision-making practices of judges. Some of the results of this research are discussed.

A sentencing hearing is held following one's conviction. This hearing is to examine various aggravating and mitigating circumstances that exacerbate one's punishment or lessen it. Usually, victims or their relatives speak out against convicted offenders during these hearings, while offenders' relatives and close friends speak out on their behalf. Judges ultimately decide the punishment, which often is codified according to the seriousness of the offense.

The next section examines presentence investigation reports (PSIs), or documents that are usually prepared by probation officers. These reports contain a vast amount of information about the crime one has committed, his/her version of events, the police report, a victim impact statement (VIS), and the background of the defendant. Judges use PSIs in their sentencing decisions, although it is unknown how much credence such reports receive. These reports are also used later in parole decision making when parole boards are considering certain inmates for early release. The format and contents of PSIs are described and discussed. Other sentencing options are included and described, such as shock probation and split sentencing. Their implications for offenders are presented.

In death penalty cases, the U.S. Supreme Court has declared that such proceedings should be conducted in the form of bifurcated trials, where the trials consist of two stages. The first stage is to determine the guilt or innocence of the defendant. If the defendant is guilty, then the jury reconvenes and determines the sentence to be imposed. This sentence may be death or life imprisonment or several other sentencing options.

All convictions may be appealed. The next section of this chapter examines the appeal process. Several important bases for appeals are described. These include *habeas corpus* petitions, which challenge the length, nature, and fact of confinement. Another basis for appeals may be through a tort claim. Finally, inmates may appeal on the basis that their civil rights were violated in some way. This civil rights litigation is through the Fourteenth Amendment and is called a Section 1983 action, since it is found in Title 42, Section 1983, of the U.S. Code. Each of these bases for appeal is described and examples are provided illustrating their use by inmates.

Appealing a case to higher courts is also described. The U.S. Supreme Court may be petitioned through a writ of *certiorari*, and the appeals process is rather lengthy. It may be several years from the time an appeal is filed before it is eventually heard by the high court. Many cases are not heard at all and are dismissed because they lack merit or are frivolous. The appeals process is discussed and several implications for convicted offenders are indicated.

▶ Judicial Options at Sentencing

Incarceration

Because many jurisdictions have enacted increasingly tougher laws in the last three decades, including adopting determinate, guidelines-based, or mandatory sentencing schemes, for certain types of offenders and for certain criminal offenses, incarceration is not an option; it is a requirement (Spohn 2009). In other words, in many jurisdictions, especially for serious and repeat offenders, judges do not have any discretion to decide between prison and probation; the offender must be sent to prison. In some cases, where presumptive guidelines are in place, the judge may have little say in the length of the sentence as well. For less serious cases and jurisdictions that still practice indeterminate sentencing, however, judges have fairly wide discretion to tailor a sentence that they deem appropriate; they have the option to send the offender to prison or give them probation. Sometimes this may depend on whether the convicted offender pleads guilty through some sort of plea agreement; in others, it is left to the judge to decide and may depend on their previous criminal history.

As stated earlier, judges often exercise their right to incarcerate offenders. In fact, the United States has one of the highest incarceration rates in the world. The United States has 5 percent of the world's population, yet we house 25 percent of the world's prisoners (Liptak 2008; Shelden 2010). Table 10–1 ■ displays the percentage of felony defendants in the 75 largest counties in the country sentenced to prison or jail (incarceration) and probation (nonincarceration) in 2009. As can be seen, for all offenses together about one-quarter of defendants receive probation and the other three-quarters were incarcerated; 36 percent were sent to prison and 37 percent were sent to jail. Obviously, incarceration rates increase where the crimes are more serious; for instance, no murderers received probation, 98 percent were sent to prison, and 2 percent were sent to jail. From this table, it can be seen that even for property, drug, and public order offenses, roughly three-quarters are sentenced to jail or prison. At the very bottom of the table you can see that for misdemeanor offenses, a little over half receive a sentence of incarceration, although the majority (53 percent) are sent to jail. This table reveals that in large urban counties across the country, judges utilize incarceration in the majority of cases.

TABLE 10–1 Sentences Received by Convicted Defendants in the 75 Largest Counties, by Most Serious Conviction Offense, 2009

| Most serious conviction offense | Total | Percent of convicted defendants sentenced to— | | | | | |
| | | Incarceration | | | Nonincarceration | | |
		Total	Prison	Jail	Total	Probation	Other
All offenses	100%	73	36%	37%	27%	25%	3%
All felonies	100%	75%	42%	33%	25%	24%	1%
Violent offenses	100%	83%	57%	27%	17%	16%	1%
Murder	100%	1oo	98	2	0	0	0
Rape	100%	89	84	5	11	8	3
Robbery	100%	89	71	18	11	10	1
Assault	100%	81	47	34	19	18	1
Other violent	100%	78	47	31	22	21	1
Property offenses	100%	75%	42%	33%	25%	25%	1%
Burglary	100%	79	53	26	21	20	1
Larceny/theft	100%	72	40	32	28	27	0
Motor vehicle theft	100%	77	46	31	23	21	2
Forgery	100%	64	29	34	36	36	0
Fraud	100%	71	33	38	29	29	0
Other property	100%	78	32	46	22	21	1
Drug offenses	100%	71%	34%	37%	29%	28%	1%
Trafficking	100%	80	45	35	20	19	1
Other drug	100%	64	26	39	36	35	1
Public-order offenses	100%	79%	46%	34%	21%	20%	1%
Weapons	100%	80	53	28	20	19	
Driving-related	100%	83	44	39	17	16	1
Other public-order	100%	75	42	33	25	24	1
Misdemeanors	100%	56%	3%	53%	44%	31%	13%

Note: Data on type of sentence were available for 94.6% of convicted defendants. Sentences to incarceration that were wholly suspended were included under probation. Fifteen percent of prison sentences and 57% of jail sentences included a probation term. Sentences to incarceration or probation may include a fine, restitution, community service treatment or other court-ordered conditions. Other sentences may include fines, community service, restitution, and treatment Total for all felonies includes 17 cases that could not be classified into 1 of the 4 major offense categories. Detail may not sum to total due to rounding.

Source: Reaves, Brian A. (2013). "Felony Defendants in Large Urban Counties, 2009 – Statistical Tables, Table 24." Washington, DC: U.S. Department of Justice, Bureau of Justice Statistics.

With the inception of mandatory minimum statutes and truth-in-sentencing laws, inmates are also spending longer periods of time incarcerated. Table 10–2 ■ displays the mean and median sentence lengths for those convicted of a felony by type of offense in the 75 largest counties in the country.

As can be seen in the table, the average sentence length for all offenses is around 50 months but is much higher for violent offenses (90 months) and slightly lower for property (40 months), drug (40 months), and public order offenses (31 months). This table also displays the percentage of convicted defendants receiving a maximum sentence; for instance, 70 percent of those convicted of murder receive 10 years or more, another 20 percent get life sentences. For property, drug, and public order offenses, the highest percentage of offenders receive 1–24 months or a two-year maximum. Although incarceration rates

TABLE 10-2 Length of Prison Sentence Received by Defendants Convicted of a Felony in the 75 Largest Counties, by Most Serious Conviction Offense, 2009

Most serious felony conviction offense	Number of defendants	Number of months		Percent receiving a maximum sentence length in months of—					
		Mean	Median	1–24	25–48	49–72	73–120	120 or more*	Life
All offenses	10,769	52 mo	30 mo	48%	24%	13%	8%	8%	—
Violent offenses	2,707	91 mo	48 mo	28%	24%	13%	15%	19%	—
Murder	111	373	360	0	0	8	2	70	20
Rape	115	142	120	6	19	9	24	42	0
Robbery	1,038	90	60	22	23	15	20	20	0
Assault	898	62	36	33	32	13	11	12	0
Other violent	546	75	36	40	20	11	14	15	0
Property offenses	3,236	40 mo	24 mo	52%	23%	14%	7%	3%	—
Burglary	1,191	52	36	42	25	16	11	6	—
Larceny/theft	901	31	24	61	21	13	5	1	0
Motor vehicle theft	329	34	24	61	20	10	7	2	0
Forgery	194	32	24	53	27	17	1	1	0
Fraud	256	47	36	44	29	15	5	7	0
Other property	365	29	24	61	21	17	1	0	0
Drug offenses	3,022	40 mo	24 mo	53%	25%	13%	5%	5%	0%
Trafficking	1,748	49	36	42	29	16	7	6	0
Other drug	1,275	29	18	68	19	8	1	3	0
Public-order offenses	1,799	31 mo	24 mo	62%	23%	10%		2%	0%
Weapons	564	38	24	52	28	11	4	4	0
Driving-related	609	31	23	65	18	12	2	3	0
Other public-order	626	26	18	68	22	8	2	—	0

Note: Data on length of prison sentence were available for over 98.1 % of all cases in which a defendant received a prison sentence. Fifteen percent of prison sentences included a probation term and 14% included a fine. Total for all offenses includes 5 cases that could not be classified into 1 of the 4 major offense categories. Detail may not sum to total due to rounding.

-Less than 0.5%.

*Excludes life sentences.

Source: Reaves, Brian A. (2013). "Felony Defendants in Large Urban Counties, 2009 – Statistical Tables, Table 24." Washington, DC: U.S. Department of Justice, Bureau of Justice Statistics.

have gone up in the last decade, numerous states and counties are experimenting with alternatives to incarceration, especially for those defendants who have committed nonviolent offenses, in order to keep the costs of punishment down as well as to help curb recidivism rates (rehabilitate and reintegrate offenders). These alternatives to traditional case processing will be discussed further in Chapter 13.

Probation

In Table 10–1, we learned that roughly 25 percent of all offenders receive probationary sentences meaning that they are not required to spend time in prison or jail. Probation allows offenders to remain in the community and keep ties with family, employers, and perhaps even educational institutions. Although they are not subject to the rigorous structure and interaction with other convicted offenders that occurs in prison, probationers are still under the control of the criminal justice system and are thus required to comply with certain conditions. Table 10–3 ■ displays the conditions of probation most often received by offense type for the 75 largest counties in the United States. These conditions range from fines and treatment to community service and restitution and vary by offense type. For

▼

TABLE 10-3 Condition of Probation Sentence Received Most Often by Convicted Defendants in the 75 Largest Counties, by Most Serious Conviction Offense, 2009

Most serious conviction offense	Number of defendants	Percent whose sentence to probation included—			
		Fine	Treatment	Community service	Restitution
All offenses	7,454	28%	27%	23%	20%
All felonies	5,887	28	29	22	21
Violent offenses	712	26	29	27	22
Property offenses	1,916	19	18	23	37
Drug offenses	2,492	36	45	21	7
Public-order offenses	760	27	16	22	26
Misdemeanors	1,567	27	13	26	14

Note: Total for felonies includes 7 cases that could not be classified into 1 of the 4 felony offense categories. A defendant may have received more than one type of probation condition. Not all defendants sentenced to probation received probation conditions. Detail may not sum to total due to rounding.

Source: Reaves, Brian A. (2013). "Felony Defendants in Large Urban Counties, 2009 – Statistical Tables, Table 28." Washington, DC: U.S. Department of Justice, Bureau of Justice Statistics.

instance, 45 percent of drug offenders have a condition to attend treatment versus 18 percent of property offenders. On the other hand, 37 percent of property offenders were required to provide restitution versus only 6 percent of drug offenders. Perhaps you think that a larger percentage of drug offenders should have to attend treatment or a larger percentage of property offenders should be required to provide restitution. This may depend on the type of drug or property crime and whether or not the offender has an addiction, or who the victim of the property crime was.

Regardless of the conditions attached to a sentence of probation, all probationers are required to obey the law (not reoffend) and maintain contact through face-to-face visits with their probation officer; these may be monthly, weekly, or as frequent as several times per week. If those on probation fail to comply with these conditions, their probation may be revoked and they would have to reappear before a judge who would decide whether to continue them on probation or revoke their probation and send them to either jail or prison (Spohn 2009).

A 2009 Bureau of Justice Statistics report reveals that in 2008, there were nearly 4.3 million persons on probation in the United States (Glaze and Bonczar 2009). The report also shows that in 2008, about 17 percent of probationers were incarcerated due to revocation of probation; another 8 percent had absconded or could not be located. Similar to incarceration rates, 30 states plus District of Columbia reported increases in their probation populations while 20 other states and the federal system reported declines. These incarceration and probation statistics reveal that the number of persons under some type of criminal justice supervision continues to increase annually. Sometimes, judges will sentence certain offenders to both incarceration and probation hoping that this will be a greater deterrent effect to reoffending.

Shock Probation and Split Sentencing

Where judges are permitted great latitude in their sentencing discretion, they are inclined to impose probation for many first offenders convicted of minor offenses or less serious felonies. Offenders sentenced to some form of probation are assigned by the judge to a probation department or some community corrections agency where their behavior will be supervised for a period of time (Champion 2005b).

One type of sentence designed to shock or scare convicted offenders, particularly those who have never served time in a prison or jail, is shock probation, shock incarceration, or

shock probation/ incarceration/parole sentencing offenders to prison or jail for a brief period, primarily to give them a taste or "shock" of prison or jail life, and then releasing them into the custody of a probation or parole officer through a resentencing project.

shock parole. Shock probation and shock parole refer to planned sentences whereby judges order offenders imprisoned for statutory incarceration periods related to their conviction offenses. However, after 30, 60, 90, or 120 days of incarceration, these offenders are taken out of jail or prison and resentenced to probation or parole (Champion 2007). Ohio introduced shock probation for the first time in 1965. Since then, shock probation has spread to almost every U.S. jurisdiction.

The intent of shock probation is to literally shock or frighten convicted offenders through the incarceration experience (Champion 2005b). No one wants to be imprisoned. For those who have never been confined for either short or long terms, the experience of being behind bars for one or more months is sufficiently traumatic to deter them from further criminal activity. Early evidence suggests that the recidivism rates among shock probationers are relatively low compared with other probationers who have not been imprisoned for short periods (Vito 1984).

> **split sentencing**
> procedure whereby a judge imposes a sentence of incarceration for a fixed period, followed by a probationary period of a fixed duration. Similar to shock probation.

In several jurisdictions, judges may engage in **split sentencing**. Split sentencing, also known as mixed sentencing or intermittent sentencing, and jail as a condition of probation, are combination sentences imposed by judges, a portion of which includes incarceration and a portion of which includes probation. If an offender has committed more than one offense, then the judge may impose a separate sentence for each offense. One sentence may be one year in jail, while the other sentence for the second offense may be probation. Thus, this mixed sentence means that the offender will spend some time in jail as well as on probation.

Intermittent sentences involve offenders who are sentenced to partial confinement. These offenders may be sentenced to a jail on weekends, but they may be permitted freedom during the week to work at a job and support themselves and their families. Jail as a condition of probation is where the judge orders the offender to serve a specified term of months in a jail before being placed on probation (Vito 1984). The intent of these split sentencing options is to dramatize the seriousness of the offender's crime. Serving some time in jail or prison will make the point that crime is bad and should be avoided. Otherwise, imprisonment will result. This simplistic view underscores the fact that many shock probationers take this experience to heart and never reoffend. The effectiveness of shock probation varies among jurisdictions. Generally, however, shock probationers tend to have lower rates of recidivism compared with other types of offenders (Champion 2005b).

The Death Penalty and Bifurcated Trials

The most serious sentence criminal courts can impose is the death penalty. The death penalty is reserved only for those who have committed capital crimes, primarily murder. In recent years, the death penalty has been approved for use in cases where certain federal offenders have been convicted of large-scale drug dealing. Currently, 32 states have statutes authorizing the death penalty; however, many of these states haven't actually carried out a death sentence in many years.

The death penalty is controversial. However, according to a Gallup poll conducted in October 2013, 60 percent of all U.S. citizens support its use as a suitable punishment for those convicted of murder; 35 percent were opposed and 5 percent had no opinion (Gallup 2014). The percentage of those surveyed who support the death penalty, however, has been slowly declining in recent years. Also, despite the percentage who are in favor of the death penalty, Gallup found that only 52 percent believe that it is applied fairly, another 40 percent responded that they believe it is applied unfairly, and 8 percent had no opinion; in another poll conducted in 2011, Gallup found that a majority of people also do not think that the death penalty acts as a deterrent to homicide (64 percent responded that it is not a deterrent, 32 percent believed that it is a deterrent, and 4 percent had no opinion) (Gallup 2014).

Interestingly, in another survey they conducted in 2009, 59 percent of persons reported that they believed that an innocent person has been executed in the last five years; Gallup

▼

surveys also show weaker support for the use of the death penalty (49 percent) when subjects are given the option of choosing life without parole as an alternative for those convicted of murder (Gallup 2014). Recently three states, New Mexico in 2009, Connecticut in 2012, and Maryland in 2013, have abolished the death penalty. There have also been numerous exonerations of death row inmates, mostly due to DNA evidence, and thus many states have restricted the instances when a death sentence can be sought.

As a more humane method of execution, most states now use legal injection as their primary method to carry out sentences of death. Some states, however, still have other options in addition to the primary method of lethal injection: eight states still have electrocution as an option, three states (Arizona, Missouri, and Wyoming) have the gas chamber, three states have hanging (Delaware, New Hampshire, and Washington), and two states have firing squad (Utah and Oklahoma) (Death Penalty Information Center 2014). The number of death sentences handed out annually, however, has dropped in the last decade from 152 in 2003 to only 80 in 2013, and the number of executions has also dropped from 98 in 1999 to 65 in 2003 and to only 39 in 2013 (Death Penalty Information Center 2014).

What Do You Think?

Are you in favor of the death penalty? Do you think it is a deterrent to homicide? If given the option of life without parole for those convicted of murder, do you think that the public would be less likely to be in favor of the death penalty? What do your classmates think? Further, regarding method of execution, do you think lethal injection is humane? Can you think of any other methods that might be more suited for carrying out a sentence of death?

bifurcated trial
tribunal in capital cases where jury is asked to make two decisions. First decision is to determine guilt or innocence of defendant; if guilty, jury meets to decide punishment, which may include the death penalty.

Bifurcated Trials

A bifurcated trial is a two-stage proceeding wherein the first stage consists of the main trial, where one's guilt or innocence is established; if an offender is found guilty of the crime,

---

BOX 10-1

LEGAL ISSUES: LETHAL INJECTION

According to the Death Penalty Information Center (2014), the federal government and current states that authorize the death penalty use lethal injection as their primary method to carry out executions. States vary, however, in the number and types of drugs that are used. Some states use a three-drug protocol; others use only two and even one drug. In 2007, all states halted executions because of a Supreme Court case challenging the lethal injection drug protocol (*Baze v. Rhees*). After the Supreme Court ruled that lethal injection did not constitute cruel and unusual punishment, many states resumed executions using it. In 2014, however, a botched execution in Oklahoma using a three-drug protocol has reignited the use of lethal injection as a humane method of execution. Another death row inmate's execution scheduled for the same day was immediately stayed and executions in Oklahoma were

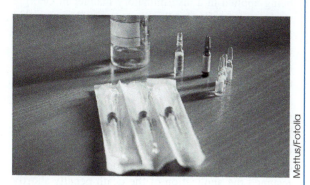
Mettus/Fotolia

put on hold until an investigation into the reasons for the failure of the protocol could be completed. It is likely that the Supreme Court may decide to weigh in again on the constitutionality of what has become the main method of execution in the United States, the lethal injection.

the jury meets in a second stage to consider the punishment and whether the death penalty should be imposed. Aggravating and mitigating factors are weighed by juries, and the death penalty will be recommended to the judge in those instances where the aggravating factors outweigh the mitigating ones (Kremling 2004).

Bifurcated trials are presently commonplace in those states with death penalty provisions. Bifurcated trials permit juries to consider both aggravating and mitigating circumstances (Gants 2005; Levine and Petitt 2005). It is believed that the nature of bifurcated trials overcomes the criticisms of those who believe that the death penalty is applied in a discriminatory manner. A sentence of death is not automatic just because a defendant has been found guilty; this should limit it being administered in an arbitrary or capricious manner, or according to the defendant's race or ethnicity.

Another feature of bifurcated trials is that death penalties can no longer be automatically applied. It used to be the case on some felony murders or when police officers were killed during a crime that those convicted of such crimes would automatically be sentenced to death. The *Gregg* case was significant in causing these automatic death penalty statutes to be declared unconstitutional. The 1980 case of *Woodson v. North Carolina* held that automatic death penalties were unconstitutional anyway, even though the essence of this holding was conveyed in *Gregg* four years earlier. The main reason is that automatic death penalties do not permit juries to weigh any possible aggravating or mitigating circumstances.

BOX 10-2

KEY CASES: DEATH PENALTY

Furman v. Georgia 408 U.S. 238 (1972)

In 1972, the constitutionality of the death penalty in Georgia was challenged. Disproportionately, large numbers of blacks were being executed compared with whites, often in cases involving rape or assault. In 1972, the U.S. Supreme Court declared in *Furman v. Georgia* that the death penalty as it was currently being applied in a discriminatory manner in Georgia was unconstitutional. All states temporarily suspended the death penalty until more information could be obtained from the U.S. Supreme Court about the procedural appropriateness of the death penalty and its application.

Gregg v. Georgia 428 U.S. 153 (1976)

In 1976, the U.S. Supreme Court held in *Gregg v. Georgia* that the revised procedural application of the death penalty in Georgia was constitutional. States resumed the application of the death penalty shortly thereafter. Gary Gillmore, a Utah murderer, was executed by firing squad in 1979 and was the first person executed after the U.S. Supreme Court approved of Georgia's new method for imposing death penalties on those convicted of capital crimes (Merlo and Benekos 2004). The U.S. Supreme Court approved Georgia's

legislative revision of the death penalty statute that called for a bifurcated trial in all capital cases.

Roper v. Simmons 543 U.S. 551 (2005)

In this case, the U.S. Supreme Court ruled that execution of minors constituted cruel and unusual punishment and therefore violated the Eighth Amendment. In a 5–4 opinion, the justices cited that many state legislatures around the country were against a juvenile death penalty, standards of decency toward punishment of minors had evolved, and there was international consensus around the world against execution of juveniles as rationale for their opinion. Imposing the death penalty on minors (those under 18 years at the time of their crime) is not banned.

Baze v. Rhees 553 U.S. _ (2008)

This case challenged Kentucky's four-drug protocol for carrying out executions as cruel and unusual under the Eighth Amendment. The U.S. Supreme court in a 7–2 decision decided that this four-drug protocol was not a violation of the Eighth Amendment but the court left open the possibility that states could violate the cruel and unusual punishment clause with the lethal injection if better methods were found.

▼

▶ The Sentencing Hearing

When offenders are convicted, they are sentenced by a judge to a term of years, either on probation or in jail or prison. In most felony cases, before offenders are sentenced, they must have a sentencing hearing. A sentencing hearing is a proceeding where evidence and testimony is presented both for and against the offender. The hearing furnishes the sentencing judge with additional information about the offender, the crime, and the victims. This information could be oral and in person or in some cases, letters can be written on behalf of the defendant and/or victim. In the context of this additional information, judges can make an informed decision about an appropriate sentence to impose.

Weighing the Aggravating and Mitigating Circumstances

The sentencing hearing is also important because it permits the judge to consider aggravating circumstances and mitigating circumstances. Aggravating circumstances are those factors that tend to intensify the severity of the punishment. Aggravating factors include whether the crime involved death or serious bodily injury, whether the offender was out on bail or on probation at the time the crime was committed, whether the offender has a prior criminal record, whether there was more than one victim, whether the offender was the leader in the commission of the offense involving two or more offenders, whether the victim was treated with extreme cruelty by the offender, and whether a dangerous weapon was used by the offender when committing the crime (Fryling 2005).

Mitigating circumstances are those that tend to lessen the severity of punishment. Mitigating circumstances include whether the offender was cooperative with police and gave information about others who may have been involved in the crime, whether the offender did not cause serious bodily injury or death to a victim, whether the offender acted under duress or extreme provocation, whether there was any possible justification for the crime, whether the offender was mentally incapacitated or was suffering from some mental illness, whether the offender made restitution to the victim, whether the offender had no previous criminal record, or whether the offender committed the crime to provide necessities for himself/herself or his/her family.

Judges consider these aggravating and mitigating circumstances, and it is determined whether the aggravating circumstances outweigh the mitigating ones. If this is the case, then judges can mete out harsher sentences. However, if the mitigating circumstances outweigh the aggravating ones, then judges can be more lenient with offenders in their sentencing decision (Fryling 2005).

When the jury or judge finds the defendant guilty, a sentence is not imposed immediately. Sentencing hearings are usually scheduled four to six weeks following the trial. Within the context of due process, defendants are presumed innocent of any crime until they are proven guilty beyond a reasonable doubt in court. When this event occurs, most judges wish to gather additional information about the convicted offender, the circumstances surrounding the commission of the crime, and the impact of the crime upon the victim(s). Probation officers are most frequently assigned the task of researching the background of each convicted offender in an effort to furnish judges with a fairly complete package of information. This information is compiled in a PSI. A probation officer needs time to gather all relevant information, and thus, this explains the lapse of time between conviction and sentencing. Probation officers interview the offender's employer, relatives, friends, church and school officials, and victims. The offender's criminal history is described as well. All of this information is summarized in the PSI and submitted to the judge. Defendants are also given the opportunity to describe their involvement in the crime and to take responsibility for what they did.

sentencing hearing optional hearing held in many jurisdictions in which defendants and victims can hear contents of presentence investigation reports prepared by probation officers. Defendants and/or victims may respond to the report orally, in writing, or both. This hearing precedes the sentence imposed by the judge.

aggravating circumstances events about crime that may intensify the severity of punishment, including bodily injury, death of victim, or the brutality of the act.

mitigating circumstances factors about a crime that may lessen the severity of sentence imposed by the judge. Cooperating with police to apprehend others involved, youthfulness or old age of defendant, mental instability, and having no prior record are considered mitigating circumstances.

probation officer professional who supervises probationers.

▶ The Presentence Investigation Report (PSI): Contents and Functions

A PSI is a written summary of information obtained by probation officers concerning an investigation of the convicted offender's background and other relevant evidence about the nature of the crime's commission and implications of the crime for all relevant parties, including victims.

Most PSIs compile considerable background information on the defendant often called a narrative so that the judge has adequate background information when it comes to making decisions about appropriate sentences. This report includes a number of things, including information about the convicted defendant and his or her family such as marital status and dependents, current living situation, including how long the defendant has lived at the address provided as well as education and employment information such as occupation and income, employer and gross monthly income, education, military service record, if any, type of discharge, and general physical condition. Obviously, information about the offense and prior criminal record are also included such as offense seriousness, date of offense and arresting agency, days in custody following arrest, codefendants if any, and information about the victim. A defendant's version of crime (offender's sentencing memorandum) and the investigating officer's version of crime, including other information such as the defendant's reputation, attitude, leisure-time activities, and associates is also included. Finally, comments by probation officer about sentencing alternatives, treatment proposals, community service, mandatory attachments, and the victim impact statement also comprise the PSI report. As part of the information listed above, probation officers sometimes locate school officials and associates of the offender and interview them. Likewise, victims and their families are interviewed.

It is important to note that both the sentencing hearing testimony and the contents of the PSI are considered by the judge. None of this information binds the judge to a particular sentence. At the federal level, prior to the *Booker* case, federal judges were required to sentence within the range recommended in the PSI; now this is only an advisory sentence recommendation. Judges, therefore, may give reference to the sentence recommended in the PSI, but can also consider any additional relevant information before imposing the actual sentence.

The sentencing hearing gives defendants a chance to speak on their own behalf, to apologize, and to accept responsibility for what they have done. Because defendants are not required to testify in their own criminal trials, they may not have had the chance to tell their side of the story until the PSI. Acceptance of responsibility for one's crimes is considered important as the first step toward rehabilitation (Champion 2005b). Sometimes judges are persuaded to be more lenient in cases where convicted offenders admit the wrongfulness of their actions and express genuine regret for what happened. However, additional testimony from victims may persuade the judge to deal more harshly with offenders when it is learned how much the lives of others were adversely affected by the offender's crime (Champion 2005b).

Functions of PSIs

The functions of PSIs are to (1) provide information for offender sentencing, (2) aid probation officers in determining the most appropriate treatment or rehabilitative programs for offenders in need of assistance, (3) assist prisons and jails in their efforts to classify offenders effectively, and (4) furnish parole boards with important offender background data to assist them in determining an offender's early release. Probation officers attempt to solicit the most accurate information about the offender and victims. The contents of

---

narrative a portion of a presentence investigation report prepared by a probation officer or private agency, which provides a description of offense and offender. Culminates in and justifies a recommendation for a specific sentence to be imposed on the offender by judges.

acceptance of responsibility a genuine admission or acknowledgment of wrongdoing. In federal presentence investigation reports, for example, convicted offenders may write an explanation and apology for the crime(s) they committed. A provision that may be considered in deciding whether leniency should be extended to offenders during the sentencing phase of their processing.

PSIs are disclosed not only to judges, but to prosecutors and defense counsel as well. This is to ensure that they are accurate reports. Disclosures of the contents of PSIs are usually mandated by legislative provisions for both the states and federal government. Two important components of PSIs are the offender's sentencing memorandum and VISs (Champion 2005b).

The Offender's Sentencing Memorandum

A defendant's sentencing memorandum is a document prepared by the convicted offender that describes the crime, why it was committed, and the attitudes and feelings of the offender concerning his/her involvement. The memorandum also provides an opportunity for the offender to accept responsibility for the crime.

> **defendant's sentencing memorandum** version of events leading to conviction offense in the words of the convicted offender. The memorandum may be submitted together with victim impact statement.

In recent years, the phrase *acceptance of responsibility* has become an increasingly important part of the sentencing process. The U.S. Sentencing Commission provided that acceptance of responsibility would enable sentencing judges to possibly mitigate one's sentence. Various states have added acceptance of responsibility to their sentencing provisions. Thus, offenders who make full admissions regarding their crimes and apologize for these crimes in open court during the sentencing hearing may incur some leniency from judges.

It is insufficient to merely declare, "Your honor, I'm sorry for what I've done and I accept responsibility for my actions." Much depends on the circumstances and sincerity of the person making such an admission. Many convicted offenders learn to act contrite and make false statements about their acceptance of responsibility. Judicial discretion is accorded great weight here. If the judge is convinced that the offender has truly accepted responsibility for the crime, then the judge may decide to mitigate the harshness of the penalties imposed. Defense counsels are often also key players in the sentencing hearing process. They have one final opportunity to summarize the facts as they see them and to make a case for judicial leniency toward their client.

Victim Impact Statements and Victim Input

Another important part of the sentence mosaic is the victim impact statement (VIS). VISs are oral and/or written testimony concerning how the victims and their close relatives were affected by the offender's crime. The nature of victim impact is very important, since judges can learn much more than what was originally disclosed about the crime during the trial. Most jurisdictions in the United States permit victims and their relatives to provide written and/or oral evidence of how the offender's crime has affected them. All states allow some type of victim impact information for use at a sentencing hearing. These may be either written or oral, and a majority of states require that this information be in the PSI (National Center for Victims of Crime 1996).

> **victim impact statement** information or version of events filed voluntarily by the victim of a crime, appended to the pre-sentence investigation report as a supplement for judicial consideration in sentencing the offender. Describes injuries to victims resulting from convicted offender's actions.

The inclusion of VISs in sentencing hearings is not new. Many states have provided for victim involvement in the sentencing process in past years. Between 1980 and well into the 1990s, victim involvement in sentencing decisions has dramatically increased (Phillips 1997). In 1987, the admissibility of VISs was prohibited by the U.S. Supreme Court in the case of *Booth v. Maryland*. However, by 1992, the U.S. Supreme Court changed its position to allow VISs in most criminal proceedings, including sentencing hearings (*Payne v. Tennessee* 1991).

VISs have additional uses beyond providing the judge with information at sentencing. There is evidence that victim participation in sentencing has a cathartic effect for them. This means that victims and their families who participate in the sentencing hearing tend to be more satisfied with the sentences imposed by judges. It has been suggested that victim participation may not directly influence judicial sentencing decisions, but victims or their relatives may feel as though their input *was* somehow influential nevertheless.

Victim input may also be allowed in jurisdictions that have a more restorative justice orientation where all parties are involved in determining an appropriate outcome for the criminal act.

They also may be seen as a fair manner in which to impose a sentence where all parties involved have a voice and in doing so, may assist in the recovery of crime victims as well as helping to educate offenders about the consequences of their actions (Cassell 2009). Further into an offender's processing and imprisonment, VISs may be relied upon by parole boards in determining whether any particular offender should be granted early release. Any written VISs are maintained in an offender's file and used by parole board members whenever an inmate's early-release eligibility occurs. Further, some victims may participate in parole hearings and give additional oral testimony about why the offender should be denied parole (Myers et al. 2004). However, not all victims present oral testimony against their victimizers. In some cases, victims will speak in favor of the offender's early release during parole hearings. While these cases are exceptional, they do occur with some frequency (Booth 2004).

▶ Imposing the Sentence

When sentences are imposed by judges, they are guided by information provided in PSIs, the offender's sentencing memorandum, probation officer recommendations, VISs, and their own interpretation and consideration of the offender and the crime's seriousness. Depending upon the sentencing scheme used in each jurisdiction, judges may be bound to sentence offenders in a consistent way. That is, there may be mandatory minimums in place for certain offenses, habitual offender statutes, or presumptive guidelines which must be adhered to. But judges are usually given some latitude under almost every type of sentencing scheme (Fryling 2005). This is what is referred to as judicial discretion. The more discretion judges have, the more leeway they have to fashion a sentence they see fit perhaps in line with their own philosophy or experience. Wide-ranging discretion sometimes opens the door to disparities in sentencing and even discrimination.

Judges may rely on what is referred to as a "going rate" or previous sentences in similar cases in the jurisdiction (Spohn 2009); this may be in an attempt to be fair and impartial when meting out a specific sentence (Austin et al. 1995). However, special consideration may be given to one's age in the case of elderly offenders. Likewise, if an offender is mentally ill, or in some other way impaired, judges may take these impairments into account when determining a sentence and on a case by case basis. Judicial sentencing decisions may be challenged, but appellate courts are inclined to assume that the original sentence imposed was the right one. It is difficult to overcome such a presumption on appeal.

▶ Sentencing Disparities

Sentencing Disparities According to Race/Ethnicity, Gender, and Socioeconomic Status

Disparity in sentencing refers to differences in incarceration rates or sentence lengths. For instance, in 2010, males had an incarceration rate that was 14 times that of females; the male imprisonment rate was 943 per 100,000 U.S. residents and for females, it was 67 per 100, 000 U.S. residents (Guerino, Harrison, and Sabol 2011). These statistics reveal a clear sex disparity in sentencing; however, some disparities are warranted, others are not. Usually, disparities based on extralegal factors, such as race/ethnicity, sex, and age, are unwarranted because the law does not allow judges to consider demographic characteristics under the law. Does the above statistic mean that judges discriminate against men? Not necessarily, there may be legitimate reasons why there are more men in prison than women. For instance, men often commit more serious offenses for which incarceration is more often warranted. Unwarranted sentencing disparities occur when judges impose different sentences on offenders charged with similar crimes and who have similar backgrounds (McManimon 2005b).

The sex disparity in incarceration rates between males and females likely reflects the larger male involvement in criminal activity, so arguments could be made that this disparity is warranted. There is, however, also research revealing that females are less likely than males to be incarcerated by judges all else being equal. What this means is that even where males and females have committed similar offenses and have similar criminal backgrounds, judges may be less likely to send females to prison than males. Similarly, blacks and Hispanic defendants may receive harsher sentences compared with white defendants when the same kinds of offenses are involved. Older offenders may receive less harsh sentences from judges compared with younger offenders even when they have committed the same crimes and have similar backgrounds (McManimon 2005b; Roy 2004).

Promoters of sentencing reforms have been quick to point out these sorts of deficiencies in our sentencing system. We have already discussed the many reforms to sentencing that have been implemented at the state and federal levels in attempts to decrease some of the discretion that judges have at sentencing. Such changes are usually accompanied by reductions in sentencing disparities attributable to racial, ethnic, gender, or socioeconomic qualities. Sentencing practices under determinate or guidelines-based structures are generally more uniform; however, several research studies have revealed that extralegal disparities are still present in some contexts.

Race and Ethnicity

Different jurisdictions report variations in sentencing attributable to race. Numerous empirical studies have found that race does play a role in sentencing decisions; more recent research has also revealed that ethnicity is also a predictor at the sentencing stage where ethnic minorities (Hispanics) are singled out for harsher treatment. Some critics contend that race and ethnicity are especially relevant in homicide cases and capital murder prosecutions where both the race of the offender and the race of the victim factor in the decision-making processes of prosecutors and judges (Walker, Spohn, and Delone 2000). For example, in an investigation of sentencing disparities among 685 white and black women in Alabama during the period 1929–1985, whites who killed blacks were the most likely to have light sentences (of one to five years) compared with blacks who killed whites (Hanke 1995). Besides stereotypes by criminal justice system officials, some have argued that racial and ethnic minorities are less likely to cooperate with criminal justice system officials or that there may be language barriers that hinder plea bargaining opportunities (Mirande 1987).

In a study of 755 defendants in Tucson, Arizona, and El Paso, Texas, Hispanic defendants did not receive sentences that were different from their white counterparts; however, in El Paso, Hispanic defendants were more likely to be convicted at trial and consistently received more severe sentences. Interviews with district attorneys and other officials in both cities indicated that the disparities may be partly attributable to differing language difficulties in the two jurisdictions, differing mechanisms for providing attorneys to indigent defendants, and differences between established Hispanic Americans and less well established Mexican American citizens and Mexican nationals (LaFree 1985). Again, we see race and ethnicity may interact with geography or place to produce divergent outcomes for racial and ethnic minorities.

Despite the increasing attention given to sentencing disparities and the sentencing reforms established to correct such disparate sentences, there is considerable evidence to indicate that racial and ethnic sentencing disparities still exist and are not diminishing (Van Zyl Smit and Ashworth 2004). Blacks are overrepresented at virtually every processing stage in the criminal justice system, and they are increasingly included in incarcerated populations. Hispanics are the fastest growing group of federal prison inmates due to the increasing focus on federal narcotics and immigration offenses (U.S. Sentencing Commission 2010). Table 10–4 ■ displays prison incarceration rates by race, ethnicity, and gender from 2000 to 2010. As can be seen in the table, for both males and females incarceration rates for blacks and Hispanics are much larger than those for whites.

Some scholars report that such disproportionate representation of blacks and Hispanics is due to greater offending rates (Blumstein 1982) and lengthier prior criminal histories (Tonry 1996). Others claim, however, that the disproportionate representation of blacks and other minorities in the criminal justice system can be attributed to poverty and unemployment (Spohn 2000). It has been recommended, for instance, that greater use of special circumstances should be exercised by judges when sentencing minority offenders. With more honest sentencing policies, less disproportionate sentencing should occur that is attributable to race or ethnicity (Williams and Holcomb 2004).

Many researchers have also found that race and ethnicity interact with other variables such as sex and age to produce the harshest sentences for young black and Hispanic males (Doerner and Demuth 2010; Steffensmeier and Demuth 2000; Steffensmeier, Ulmer, and Kramer 1998). Table 10–5 ■ displays prison incarceration rates by race, ethnicity, and gender for various age groups. As shown in the table, the highest incarceration rates are for young black and Hispanic males (ages 30–34 and 25–29). For females although the disparities aren't as great, there are similarly highest for young black and Hispanics.

TABLE 10-4 Incarceration Rates by Gender and Race/Ethnicity, 2000–2010

	Male				Female			
Year	Total[a]	White[b]	Black[b]	Hispanic	Total[a]	White[b]	Black[b]	Hispanic
2000	904	449	3,457	1,220	59	34	205	60
2001	896	462	3,535	1,177	58	36	199	61
2002	912	450	3,437	1,176	61	35	191	80
2003	915	465	3,405	1,231	62	38	185	84
2004	926	463	3,218	1,220	64	42	170	75
2005	929	471	3,145	1,244	65	45	156	76
2006	943	487	3,042	1,261	68	43	148	81
2007	955	481	3,138	1,259	69	50	150	79
2008	952	487	3,161	1,200	68	50	149	75
2009	949	487	3,119	1,193	67	50	142	74
2010[c]	943	459	3,074	1,258	67	47	133	77

Note: Counts based on prisoners with a sentence of more than 1 year Rates are per 100,000 U.S. residents as of January 1 in each reference population group- All estimates include persons under age 18. See *Methodology* for estimation method.

[a] includes American Indians, Alaska Natives, Asians, Native Hawaiians, other Pacific islanders, and persons identifying as two or more races.

[b] Exdudes persons of Hispanic or Latino origin.

[c] Data source used to estimate race and Hispanic origin changed in 2010. Use caution when comparing to prior years. See *Methodology* for estimation method.

Source: Guerino, Paul, Paige M. Harrison, and William J. Sabol (2011). "*Prisoners in 2010*, Appendix Table 14." Washington, DC: U.S. Department of Justice, Bureau of Justice Statistics.

▼

TABLE 10-5 Incarceration Rates by Gender and Race/Ethnicity for Various Age Groups

Age	Male				Female			
	Total[a]	White[b]	Black[b]	Hispanic	Total[a]	White[b]	Black[b]	Hispanic
Total[c]	943	459	3,074	1,258	67	47	133	77
18–19	462	149	1,555	563	20	11	40	31
20–24	1,511	638	4,618	1,908	102	72	182	122
25–29	2,098	980	6,349	2,707	168	125	299	202
30–34	2,261	1,061	7,299	2,808	175	136	309	189
35–39	2,014	995	6,600	2,486	158	124	289	153
40–44	1,752	916	5,637	2,146	147	106	290	156
45–49	1,489	788	4,751	1,901	115	81	238	117
50–54	1,051	552	3,441	1,495	68	45	150	88
55–59	650	347	2,239	1,031	34	22	76	55
60–64	391	233	1,262	679	17	12	33	29
65 or older	143	95	418	294	4	3	7	3

Note: Data source used to estimate race and Hispanic origin changed in 2010 and data source for age distributions was enhanced between 2009 and 2010. Use caution when comparing to prior years. Counts based on prisoners with a sentence of more than 1 year. See *Methodology* for estimation method.
[a] includes American Indians, Alaska Natives, Asians, Native Hawalfans, other Pacific Islanders, and persons identifying two or more races.
[b] excludes persons of Hispanic or Latino origin.
[c] includes persons under age 18.
Source: Guerino, Paul, Paige M. Harrison, and William J. Sabol (2011). "*Prisoners in 2010*, Appendix Table 15." Washington, DC: U.S. Department of Justice, Bureau of Justice Statistics.

Gender

Do women tend to receive more lenient sentences compared with men? Recall above that male incarceration rates are 14 times that of females. Research also concludes that males are more likely to be incarcerated than females and also receive longer sentences (Doerner and Demuth 2014; Starr 2012). Some studies show that judges may be inclined to be more lenient with female offenders even where they have committed crimes similar to males. If judges do use sex as a criterion in making sentencing decisions, this would be considered discrimination. If sex disparities disappear, however, once the seriousness of offense and prior criminal record are taken into account, this would not be discrimination but warranted disparity. This sex disparity would be warranted because there are increased chances of going to prison and for longer periods due to offense seriousness and the presence of priors. Some scholars have further argued that females may be treated more leniently than males because they are the primary caregivers of children or because they are seen as less blameworthy and culpable, and less likely to recidivate (Daly 1989; Stacy and Spohn 2006; Steffensmeier, Kramer, and Steifel 1993).

A recent meta-analysis, a study of studies, looked at 140 studies between 1991 and 2011 and found that although gender disparity appears to have declined over this time period, the effect of gender on sentencing is strong (Bontrager, Barrick, and Stupi 2013). Finally, some studies conclude that the effect of sex on decision-making practices may depend on the stage in the criminal justice process and the type of offense (Rodriguez, Curry, and Lee 2006). Zingraff and Thompson (1984), for instance, found that females were treated more leniently at the incarceration decision only. Steffensmeier et al. (1993)

▼

examined sex differences in Pennsylvania from 1985 to 1987 and found sex effects may also depend on offense seriousness; female defendants received longer sentences than males for minor offenses but shorter sentences than males for serious offenses. Other research shows that the gender effect may vary if other factors are considered (Freiburger 2011; Spohn 1999).

Daly and Bordt (1995) conducted an extensive statistical review of sentencing disparity literature to determine whether "sex effects" favoring women over men in sentencing exist. Over half of the 50 studies surveyed indicated that gender effects favoring women over men existed. One explanation for gender differentiation is the chivalry hypothesis, which is that decision makers or judges tend to treat female offenders with chivalry during sentencing, and further that judges will be inclined to dispense selective chivalry toward white females compared with other females or minorities of either gender (Kakar 2004).

Chivalry, however, may also depend on other factors. Tillyer, Hartley, and Ward (2013), for instance, report that the gender effect on sentencing is probably more complex. They looked at the effect of a defendant's criminal history on gender and chivalry for narcotics offenders and their results revealed that judges gave shorter sentences to females with lower criminal history scores but females with longer criminal histories were actually given more severe sentences than similar males. These authors conclude that preferential treatment of women with lower criminal histories may reflect a belief by judges that they do not deserve a strict punishment or that they might be less to blame for the offense and less likely to reoffend.

Socioeconomic Status

One's socioeconomic status plays a significant part in explaining sentencing disparities. Research evidencing sentencing disparities attributable to one's socioeconomic status is considerable. Empirical studies have shown that poor minorities are disproportionately represented in the criminal justice system and are more likely to be prosecuted for crimes that are subject to mandatory minimums (Caulkins, Jonathan, Rydell, Schwabe, and Chiesa 1998; Mauer 1999; Ogletree 2004; Tonry 1995). Specifically, research has shown that persons in poverty (Gustafson 2009), or who are from the lowest social strata (Chiricos and Bales 1991), or who are unemployed (Spohn and Holleran 2000) receive harsher punishments.

For example, studies of sentencing patterns in southeastern states have shown that there is an inverse relation between one's socioeconomic status and sentence length (D'Allessio and Stolzenberg 1993). When 2,760 convicted offenders were examined, those of lower socioeconomic status drew longer sentences than those of higher socioeconomic statuses. Thus, it was concluded that this extralegal factor was significant in explaining differential sentence lengths of offenders, controlling for one's criminal history and conviction offense (D'Allessio and Stolzenberg 1993). Other research has supported the idea that those with lower socioeconomic status are disenfranchised by the criminal justice system. However, the influence of socioeconomic status may adversely affect certain persons of higher socioeconomic statuses as well. A survey of white-collar offenders sentenced in seven U.S. District Courts showed that they tended to receive imprisonment more often compared with comparable offenders of lower statuses, and furthermore, the sentences imposed on white-collar offenders were longer (Weisburd, Waring, and Wheeler 1990). The general consensus seems to be that lower socioeconomic status offenders will tend to receive harsher and longer sentences compared with offenders of higher socioeconomic statuses, although there are always exceptions. Bernie Madoff's 150-year sentence for securities fraud is an example of this exception.

sentencing disparity inconsistency in sentencing of convicted offenders, in which those committing similar crimes under similar circumstances are given widely disparate sentences by the same judge. Usually based on gender, race, ethnic, or socioeconomic factors.

▶ Appeals of Sentences

The Purposes of an Appeal

Once defendants have been convicted of crimes, they are entitled to at least one appeal to a higher court. The primary purpose of an appeal is to correct a wrong that may have been committed during the criminal court process. These wrongs may be mistakes by police, the prosecution, or the court. Errors may have occurred that influence the trial outcome. Appeals are intended to correct these mistakes and errors.

A secondary purpose of an appeal is to render judgment about one or more issues that will influence future cases. Thus, when an appellate court hears a case from a lower trial court, the appellate court's decision becomes a precedent for subsequent similar cases. This is the doctrine of *stare decisis*, meaning that once a higher court has ruled a particular way on a particular issue, lower courts are bound to make rulings consistent with higher court holdings whenever similar cases are heard.

However, trial court judges have some discretion in deciding whether certain subsequent cases resemble previous cases where appellate courts have ruled. Thus, trial court judges may decide that although a subsequent case is similar in various respects to previous cases already decided by higher courts, there may be sufficient differences in the cases so that trial judges decide that the higher court rulings do not apply. In this case, judges would decide not to follow precedent.

> **appeal** any request by the defense or prosecution directed to a higher court to contest a decision or judgment by a lower court.

> **stare decisis** legal precedent. Principle whereby lower courts issue rulings consistent with those of higher courts, where the same types of cases and facts are at issue. The principle of leaving undisturbed a settled point of law or particular precedent.

Appeals of Sentences

Due to Supreme Court decisions in the *Furman* and *Gregg v. Georgia* cases, all sentences of death are automatically appealed. The appellate process for any case, capital or otherwise, begins by filing an appeal with the most immediate appellate court above the trial court level. When offenders are convicted in federal district courts, for instance, their appeals are directed to one of 13 different circuit courts of appeal.

In capital cases originating in state courts, state remedies must be pursued on appeal before the federal system is accessed. For instance, a person convicted of murder in Tennessee and sentenced to death must direct his/her appeal first to the court of criminal appeals. If there is an unfavorable ruling by that appellate court, then the offender can direct an appeal to the Tennessee Supreme Court. If the ruling by this court is unfavorable for the offender, then a direct appeal may be made to the U.S. Supreme Court for relief. Depending on the type of offense, not all convicted persons will be able to continue to appeal their cases to a higher level.

Appellants and Appellees

Appellants are persons who initiate appeals. Appellees are those who won in the trial court and make arguments against reversing the decision of the lower court. Those convicted of capital crimes and sentenced to death are appellants. In most instances, the state is the appellee. Cases are given names to fit the two parties. Thus, we have *Furman v. Georgia* and *Gregg v. Georgia*. In each of these cases, the appellant is mentioned first and the appellee second. There are many grounds on which to base appeals (Unnever and Cullen 2004). Further, appeals in most death penalty cases can drag out over a period of 10–15 years before the appellants are eventually executed (Harmon 2004). In some cases, appellants might never be executed; many states that have the death penalty option have not actually carried out a death sentence in decades.

> **appellants** persons who initiate an appeal.

> **appellees** parties who prevailed in lower court and who argue on appeal against reversing the lower court's decision.

habeas corpus

petition writ filed, usually by inmates, challenging the legitimacy of their confinement and the nature of their confinement. Document commands authorities to show cause why an inmate should be confined in either a prison or jail. Also includes challenges of the nature of confinement.

conditions of

confinement the nature of jail or prison incarceration; refers to heat and humidity, cleanliness of one's cell and surroundings, and general treatment; often is basis for legal action filed as *habeas corpus* petitions.

solitary confinement a sentencing philosophy seeking to remove the offender from other offenders when confined by placing prisoner in a cell with no communication with others. Also known as isolation, which originated in the Walnut Street Jail in Philadelphia, Pennsylvania in the late 1700s.

mistrial a trial that cannot stand, is invalid. Judges may call a mistrial for reasons such as errors on the part of prosecutors or defense counsel, the death of a juror or counsel, or a hung jury.

Bases for Appeals

Appeals may be directed to appellate courts on diverse grounds. Appellants may raise questions before appellate courts about the grounds on which they were originally arrested or processed. They may challenge the admissibility of certain evidence used in court to convict them. They may claim incompetence or ineffective assistance of counsel (Albonetti and Barron 2004). They also may challenge the sentence imposed by the judge. Almost every one of these challenges about what happened at different points in the processing of criminal defendants can be included within the scope of a *habeas corpus* petition. *Habeas corpus* means literally produce the body. A *habeas corpus* petition challenges three things: (1) the fact of confinement, (2) the length of confinement, and/or (3) the nature of confinement.

The fact of confinement involves every event that led to the present circumstances of the appellant (Belbot et al. 2004). If the appellant is on death row resulting from a capital offense conviction, then any aspect of the justice process leading to the offender's placement on death row is a potential *habeas corpus* target (Westervelt and Cook 2004). The length of confinement has been challenged numerous times by prisoners who feel that their sentences are too long and disproportionately harsh in relation to the crimes they have committed. The conditions of confinement of jails or prisons are frequent grounds for *habeas corpus* relief. Prisoners who are ordered confined in jails rather than prisons for long periods may object to the lack of facilities and amenities in jails that would ordinarily be found in prisons. Some prisoners also seek *habeas corpus* relief due to use of solitary confinement or isolation.

Other appeals involve the offender/petitioner alleging that the sentencing judge acted inappropriately by making prejudicial remarks in front of the jury. Inmates will also file *habeas corpus* petitions where they believe prosecutors acted in bad faith or engaged in improper conduct, such as suppressing exculpatory evidence. Sometimes cases result in a mistrial because of this and defendants are retried. Another reason for seeking *habeas corpus* relief is for ineffective assistance of counsel. If convicted offenders believe that they were not properly represented by counsel since they were convicted, they may allege that their counsel was ineffective. Most of these types of petitions, however, are denied by the U.S. Supreme Court.

Additional reasons for *habeas corpus* actions include failure of the court to provide counsel to the offender or to determine whether a guilty plea was indeed voluntary (*Carter v. People of State of Illinois*, 1946); failure of one's counsel to inform the offender of possible sentence enhancements because a firearm was used during the commission of a felony (*Custis v. United States*, 1994); that the search by police was conducted without a warrant where the circumstances required the issuance of one before the search would be lawful (*Gerstein v. Pugh*, 1975); and that exposure to cyanide gas is a cruel and unusual punishment (*Gomez v. United States District Court*, 1992).

Over the years, inmates have frequently abused the writ of *habeas corpus* by submitting numerous petitions with frivolous claims. The U.S. Supreme Court has limited such filings in recent years so that inmates and others cannot continue to abuse such petitions. Currently, the use of *habeas corpus* has been limited so that inmates must set forth all arguable issues encompassed by *habeas corpus* and not use a separate *habeas corpus* action per issue (*Delo v. Stokes*, 1990). Furthermore, state prisoners must first exhaust all of their state appellate remedies before seeking relief directly from the U.S. Supreme Court (*Duckworth v. Serrano*, 454 U.S. 1 [1981]). The significance of this case is that any petitioner who has been convicted of a state crime must first exhaust all state remedies before attempting to file petitions in federal courts. This is considered a landmark case because it obligates prisoners to direct their *habeas corpus* petitions first to state courts, before they pursue federal remedies.

New technological developments concerning identification of suspects through DNA testing or DNA fingerprinting and other forensic achievements have caused more than a few inmates to be released from prison after they have been determined to be innocent of the crimes for which they were originally convicted (Warden 2004). In order to obtain their release from prison or get new trials, inmates must file *habeas corpus* petitions. But the courts have been reluctant to cause old cases to be reopened, except under the most compelling of circumstances. This is consistent with the general policy change by the U.S. Supreme Court to make it more difficult in recent years for inmates to pursue *habeas corpus* writs without limit (Federman 2004).

Both the number of *habeas corpus* petitions filed by prisoners and the proportion of prisoners filing *habeas corpus* actions are declining steadily. Even in capital cases, *habeas corpus* appeals have declined. This is because of the greater restrictions imposed on such appeals by the U.S. Supreme Court and Congress. This trend is also being observed at the state level (Atherton 2004).

Writs of *Certiorari*

A writ of *certiorari* is issued by a higher court directing a lower court to prepare the record of a case and send it to the higher court for review. It is also a means of accessing the U.S. Supreme Court in order for a case to be heard. Writs of *certiorari*, especially from those on death row, must contain compelling arguments in order for the U.S. Supreme Court to grant them. Most writs of *certiorari* from those sentenced to death are denied. Of those petitions that are heard by the U.S. Supreme Court, only a handful, result in the death penalty being overturned. Usually, the U.S. Supreme Court will order a new trial if a particularly strong argument is presented showing a flagrant constitutional rights violation.

Initiating Appeals

Appeals are launched by appellants, or those who lose in the trial court. Most frequently, appellants are convicted offenders. They must first file a notice of appeal. A notice of appeal is a written statement of the appellant's intent to file an appeal with a higher court. Such notices are required within a fixed period of time following an offender's conviction.

A copy of the court record or complete transcript of proceedings is forwarded to the appellate court for review. Also, a brief is filed with the appellate court, outlining the principal arguments for the appeal. These arguments may pertain to particular judicial rulings, which are believed to be incorrect. Appellants are required to list the issues that are the substance of the appeal. If the appellant believes that 30 mistakes were committed by the trial judge, or if the prosecutor was believed to have made prejudicial remarks to the jury where such remarks are prohibited, or if the police did not advise the offender of his *Miranda* rights when arrested, all of these mistakes or errors should be listed in the brief or legal argument. These errors or mistakes are considered appealable issues. An offender's first appeal should contain all of these issues, since it is unlikely that courts will consider further appeals concerning omitted issues.

Appellees, or those who succeed in the trial court (usually the prosecution), may file briefs as well, noting why they believe there were no procedural irregularities or errors committed by different actors in the system. Thus, the groundwork is provided for argument later before the appellate court. Most states and the federal government have criminal appellate courts, where offenders direct their appeals. These appellate courts frequently consist of three-judge panels that will hear the legal arguments and decide whether the trial court was in error. Rulings by appellate courts that overturn a lower trial court are rare, however. One reason is that appellate courts assume that whatever transpired during the offender's trial was correct, and that the criminal conviction was valid. This is a difficult presumption for appellants to overcome. They must often present overwhelming evidence of prosecutorial misconduct or judicial indiscretion in order to convince an appellate court

warrant a written order directing a suspect's arrest and issued by an official with the authority to issue the warrant. Commands suspect to be arrested and brought before the nearest magistrate.

DNA fingerprinting Deoxyribonucleic acid (DNA) is an essential component of all living matter, which carries hereditary patterning. Suspects can be detected according to their unique DNA patterning, as each person has a different DNA pattern. Similar to fingerprint identification in which no two persons have identical fingerprints.

writ of *certiorari* an order of a superior court requesting that the record of an inferior court (or administrative body) be brought forward for review or inspection. Literally, "to be more fully informed."

death row arrangement of prison cells where inmates who have been sentenced to death are housed.

notice of appeal filing a formal document with the court advising the court that the sentence is to be appealed to a higher court or appellate court.

oral argument verbal presentation made to an appellate court by the prosecution or the defense in order to persuade the court to affirm, reverse, or modify a lower court decision.

reversed and remanded decision by the appellate court to set aside or overturn the verdict of a lower trial court with instructions to the trial court to rehear the case with suggested modifications.

affirm to uphold the opinion or decision of a lower trial court; usually an action by an appellate court.

dissenting opinion any judicial opinion disavowing or attacking the decision of a collegial court.

to reverse or set aside their conviction. And if a conviction is reversed, this decision does not absolve the offender of any criminal liability. A new trial may be ordered, or a sentencing decision may be modified to be consistent with a higher court ruling.

Presenting the case for the appellant is the defense attorney in most criminal cases, while the district attorney or state prosecutor (the U.S. attorney or assistant U.S. attorney in federal courts) will give the government's position in the matter to be argued. This dispute process is oral argument. Once the appellate court has heard the oral argument from both sides and has consulted the trial transcript, it will render an opinion. An opinion is a written decision about the issue(s) argued, and a holding as to which side, the appellant or appellee, prevails. If the appellate court holds in favor of the appellant, and if the appellant is a convicted offender, then the case is reversed and remanded back to the trial court with instructions for modifying the original decision. Whenever the ruling favors the government, the appellate court is said to affirm the holding or judgment against the appellant/offender. When the case against the offender is affirmed by an appellate court, the offender may direct an appeal to the next higher appellate court. In state courts, this higher appellate court is the state supreme court or court of last resort within the state judicial system. If the state supreme court affirms the conviction, the offender may direct an appeal to the U.S. Supreme Court.

In some opinions by appellate courts, not all of the appellate judges agree about the decision rendered. The minority view is sometimes summarized in a dissenting opinion. Legal historians value dissenting opinions, because they believe that appellate court policy change can be predicted over time. This is especially true if those rendering dissenting opinions are younger judges on appellate panels. However, the fact is that these minority or dissenting opinions have no impact on the appeal outcome. The majority opinion, however, is the governing opinion in the case and is the more important one. Appellate judges who write the majority opinion also outline the legal rationale for their opinion.

The Discretionary Powers of Appellate Courts

Appellate courts may or may not decide to hear appeals from lower courts. Their powers in this regard are discretionary. They may choose which cases to review as well as decide which cases not to review. Usually, only a small proportion of cases are reviewed by appellate courts at the state and federal levels annually. Thus, just because a convicted defendant files an appeal does not necessarily mean that the case will be heard. For instance, the U.S. Supreme Court receives thousands of appeals from convicted offenders annually. However, only a small fraction, 100 or so cases, are heard each year where written opinions are provided. Most appeals from convicted offenders are denied. The U.S. Supreme Court is also a discretionary body, where they use their discretion to regulate their caseload, and thus, the cases they will ultimately hear are carefully chosen and usually involve a constitutional issue or an important federal question.

Furthermore, the Rule of Four applies, where at least four or more justices must agree to hear the case. And even if the U.S. Supreme Court consents to hear a case, the sheer volume of scheduled cases may be such that the case may not be heard. This is because the U.S. Supreme Court's time is quite limited. More than a few scheduled cases are not heard each year, because the Court has run out of time. And, these cases are not carried over to the next term of the Court. Rather, appellants must refile their appeals with the Court the following term.

Appeals by Indigents

Indigent defendants who are sentenced to death are entitled to counsel on their first nondiscretionary appeals (Harmon 2001). However, more than a few inmates on death rows have filed numerous subsequent appeals, almost always at taxpayer expense, where public defenders have been appointed to assist them. However, as we have seen, the U.S. Supreme Court has recently limited the number of appeals indigents may file as well as their right to publicly appointed counsel each and every time they launch a new appeal.

Wrongful Convictions and Pardons

The American criminal justice system is not perfect. While no conclusive data are available to dispute the matter one way or another, more than a few innocent persons are sometimes convicted of serious crimes (Gould 2004). This is not a phenomenon that is unique to the United States (Denov and Campbell 2005). There are many reasons for wrongful convictions (Burrow 2004). Sometimes there is extensive circumstantial evidence that implicates the defendant and makes him/her appear to be guilty (Burnett 2005). A defendant may have the motive, means, and opportunity to commit particular crimes, and may be unable to account for his/her whereabouts when the crime was committed. Sometimes the simple fact of not being able to explain satisfactorily where you were at a particular time, coupled with other incriminating factors, may make you appear guilty in the eyes of jurors who hear and decide the case.

> **wrongful convictions** adjudications of guilt by either a judge or jury and where the convicted offender is actually innocent of the charges alleged.

Some aggressive prosecutors may threaten or intimidate certain defendants with the possibility of charging them with crimes that carry stringent penalties, such as long sentences of incarceration, and even the death penalty. While it is wrong and unethical to engage in such prosecutorial misconduct, some prosecutors threaten certain defendants with very serious charges in order to get them to plead guilty to a lesser-included offense. A gray area exists within which prosecutors have great latitude in their charging decisions. Most skillful prosecutors can present only incriminating or inculpatory information to grand juries about criminal suspects and withhold exculpatory information that might exonerate the suspect. Indictments can almost always be obtained, depending upon the prosecutor's intentions (Leo 2005).

> **circumstantial evidence** material provided by a witness from which a jury must infer a fact.

But as we have seen, indictments do not mean someone is guilty of a crime. Rather, indictments are simply findings by grand juries that probable cause exists to believe that a crime was committed and a particular suspect named by the prosecutor may have committed the crime. These one-sided proceedings, where defendants and their attorneys are barred from presenting their side or giving exculpatory evidence, frequently overwhelm those indicted for various crimes. Most citizens who read a newspaper article reading, "Federal Grand Jury Indicts James Jones for Six Counts of Burglary," or "The Craig County Grand Jury Indicts Elmer Gantry for Sexual Assault" likely conclude that James Jones or Elmer Gantry are probably guilty of these crimes based on the powerful innuendo of an indictment. But proving the facts alleged in an indictment in court beyond a reasonable doubt may be difficult, particularly if these cases lack direct evidence against particular suspects or are at best circumstantial.

For many suspects, their cases never come to trial. The plea bargaining process circumvents most trials in over 90 percent of all criminal cases. After being overwhelmed by very serious charges, defendants and their attorneys may be approached by prosecutors who wish to save the government the time and expense of a protracted trial. A compromise is offered, such as a lesser charge. If the defendant pleads guilty to a lesser charge, then probation may be offered instead of jail or prison time that might be imposed if a jury trial were held and the suspect were convicted. Many defense attorneys urge their clients to accept these "generous" offers from prosecutors, especially if these clients have prior criminal records or appear guilty because of the circumstantial evidence the state has compiled. Thus, many defendants relinquish their Sixth Amendment right to a jury trial as well as other important constitutional rights in an effort to avoid potentially serious punishments if a trial were held and they were convicted.

Then there are cases where innocent defendants go to trial anyway and are convicted, simply because they look guilty to the jury and the state has overwhelmed the jury with extensive circumstantial evidence. These innocent convicted persons spend a great deal of time seeking appeals of their cases by higher courts. But these innocent persons must overcome a powerful presumption that the trial court was correct when the case was originally decided. This is an extremely difficult presumption to overcome, especially if there is little or no hard evidence to substantiate one's claim of innocence.

In recent years, there has been greater media attention focused upon very serious cases, particularly death penalty cases, where technology has advanced to the point of conclusively demonstrating one's innocence (Davis 2005). Evidence in most serious criminal cases is carefully preserved for many years following the crime in anticipation of the appeals that will follow. During the 1990s, DNA typing was increasingly used as evidence against suspects (*Technology Review 2005*). But its use also led authorities to exclude certain persons as suspects. By 2005, many of those serving lengthy prison sentences or who were on death rows throughout the United States were demanding re-examinations of blood evidence that was originally used to convict them (Burnett 2005). Law enforcement agencies and correctional institutions are increasingly collecting blood specimens from suspects or convicted offenders and typing these specimens according to unique DNA patterns. The Supreme Court in 2013, in the case of *Maryland v. King*, upheld the practice of allowing police to take a DNA swab of those arrested for serious crimes. The court's rationale was that this is similar to taking fingerprints as part of a routine booking procedure and therefore police do not require a warrant as this does not violate the Fourth Amendment protection against unreasonable search and seizure.

Often, a confrontation of the actual perpetrator with DNA evidence may elicit a confession. While prosecutors are reluctant to admitting their mistakes, appellate courts have been persuaded with such DNA evidence and wrongful convictions have been overturned (Boller 2005). According to the Innocence Project, to date there have been 316 exonerations due to DNA in 36 states, 249 of these have been since 2000 and 18 of these were on death row (Innocence Project 2014a).

Finally, the president of the United States or a state governor may pardon certain persons who have been found to be wrongfully convicted of crimes. Pardons are unconditional releases from prison. Pardons are intended to overcome a governmental mistake or right certain wrongs. Pardons are not used extensively, but when used, they frequently have

BOX 10-3

LEGAL ISSUES: COMPENSATION FOR WRONGFUL CONVICTION

In the last 25 years, there have been over 300 exonerations of convicted persons serving time; over 260 of these have been found innocent through DNA testing and 138 were serving time for capital offenses, some on death row (Norris 2012). The federal government has recommended that compensation be $50,000 a year for each year spent in prison but only five states currently meet this standard (Innocence Project 2014b). Some states have flat amounts, some states have maximum payouts, and others allow support in the form of tuition for education; all however, have criteria that need to be met in order to qualify (Innocence Project 2014b). In New Hampshire, for instance, the maximum compensation is $20,000 no matter how much time the person spent in prison. Florida statute, on the other hand, allows $50,000 per year spent in prison with a maximum of $2 million along with 120 hours of tuition at a community college or state university but the person cannot have any prior felony convictions (Innocence Project 2014b). Montana does not compensate with any money, only assistance with education whereas Texas statute allows for $80,000 per year of wrongful imprisonment with no upper maximum (Innocence Project 2014b). Should states provide compensation to innocent persons who were wrongly convicted? What do you think is an adequate compensation package? Should the federal government require the states to adopt their recommendation of $50,000 per year of wrongful incarceration?

▼

the weight of restoring a person's citizen status that he/she had prior to being convicted of a crime. Persons may be pardoned from death row if they are subsequently found to be innocent of the crimes for which they were originally convicted.

The government may or may not compensate such persons for the time they were incarcerated until pardoned. According to the Innocence Project (2014b), only 27 states compensated those wrongfully convicted; however, of those exonerated by DNA, only 60 percent have received some type of compensation. The amount of compensation and the criteria for eligibility also varies across these 27 states (Innocence Project 2014a).

Summary

1. *Understand the options that judges have at sentencing and that these vary by type of crime and jurisdiction.*

The options available to judges at sentencing usually include incarceration or probation. Capital crimes also have the option of a sentence of death. In the United States, incarceration is almost always an option available to judges, especially where the crime is a felony. Probation is also used widely, especially where the crime is a misdemeanor. Critics argue that a just system of sentencing should make available more options to judges in between prison and probation; these are referred to as intermediate sanctions.

2. *Summarize the death penalty and bifurcated trials, including the functions of such trial proceedings.*

The death penalty is a special punishment that has evolved its own court protocol over the years. It is incumbent upon criminal courts today to provide bifurcated trials for those facing the death penalty as a possible punishment for capital murder and other crimes, such as terrorist acts or large-scale drug trafficking. A bifurcated trial is a two-part proceeding. The first part is the trial phase, where guilt or innocence of the defendant is determined. If the jury finds the defendant guilty, it must deliberate in a second stage or phase to determine and recommend a punishment, either death, life without the possibility of parole, or life imprisonment. All death sentences are automatically appealed. Most appeals of these sentences are unsuccessful.

3. *Describe the sentencing hearing and its various functions.*

Persons who are convicted of serious crimes are subjected to sentencing hearings. These are proceedings where both sides may present evidence and witnesses favoring harsher or more lenient punishments. Aggravating and mitigating circumstances are presented by the prosecutor and defense counsel, respectively, in an effort to influence the judge in his/her sentencing decision making. Usually, a presentence investigation report is issued that assists the judge in determining an appropriate sentence in the case.

4. *Describe presentence investigation reports, their contents and components, preparation, and usefulness in the sentencing process. Also, apply your knowledge of victim impact statements and the usefulness of such statements in the sentencing process.*

Relevant to sentencing hearings is the presentence investigation report (PSI), which is often prepared by a probation officer. PSIs contain a depiction of the crime committed, the police report, the offender's version of events, background information about the offender, psychiatric reports, a VIS, and other vital information useful to judges and others in making decisions about offenders. Offenders have an opportunity to accept responsibility in such reports in an effort to create a favorable impression on judges and secure some leniency in the sentences imposed.

Some offenders are given shock probation or split sentences. They may be placed in prison or jail for up to 120 days and then brought back before the court to be resentenced to probation. It is believed that the shock of incarceration for some persons at least is sufficiently traumatic to discourage them from committing new crimes. Split sentences involve mixed sentences of probation and confinement, usually in a jail, for short time intervals. Several split sentencing variations have been described. Victim impact statements (VISs) are a part of the restorative justice philosophy in that victims and others are asked to give statements about how they were affected by the crime either in writing or orally at the sentencing hearing.

5. *Explain what sentencing disparities are and how factors such as race/ethnicity, gender, socioeconomic status, and age affect one's sentence.*

Even though judges may have information at the sentencing hearing regarding the seriousness of the crime and the defendant's prior criminal record, other factors such as the race/ethnicity, sex, or socioeconomic status of the defendant may affect the sentencing outcome. Because these are legally irrelevant criteria, when a judge bases a sentence even partially due to one of these so-called extralegal factors, it leads to disparities in sentencing. If these disparities according to extralegal factors cannot be explained away by some legally relevant criteria, this is discrimination in sentencing. Some states have adopted presumptive sentencing structures to attempt to limit judicial discretion, and therefore, ameliorate some of the extralegal disparity in sentencing. Some studies show that these disparities have been ameliorated somewhat, but that for certain types of offenses disparity and discrimination still occur in sentencing.

6. *Explain the appeals process, who initiates appeals, and various bases for appeals.*

The appeals process for any criminal conviction is a lengthy and tedious process. If an offender is convicted, one or more appeals may be launched to the next higher court above the trial court. States have their own court hierarchy, and convicted offenders are expected to follow it when filing appeals. Sometimes offenders may file appeals in federal district courts, under certain circumstances. Ordinarily, state prisoners must exhaust all of their state court appeals remedies before approaching federal courts with their appeals.

The bases for appeals vary, although several types of appeals have been described. Convicted persons may file *habeas corpus* petitions, wherein they challenge the fact, length, and nature of their confinement. Generally, most appeals from convicted offenders are unsuccessful. A small portion of appeals each year is heard by the U.S. Supreme Court, especially where issues of constitutional significance are involved. U.S. Supreme Court appeals are initiated by writs of *certiorari*.

Key Terms

acceptance of responsibility *248*
affirm *258*
aggravating circumstances *247*
appeal *255*
appellants *255*
appellees *255*
bifurcated trial *245*
circumstantial evidence *259*
conditions of confinement *256*
death penalty *239*
death row *257*
defendant's sentencing
   memorandum *249*

dissenting opinion *258*
DNA fingerprinting *256*
habeas corpus petition *256*
isolation *256*
mistrial *256*
mitigating circumstances *247*
narrative *248*
notice of appeal *257*
oral argument *258*
probation officer *247*
reversed and remanded *258*
sentencing disparity *254*
sentencing hearing *247*

shock incarceration *243*
shock parole *244*
shock probation *243*
solitary confinement *256*
split sentencing *244*
stare decisis *255*
victim impact statement *249*
warrant *256*
writ of *certiorari* *257*
wrongful convictions *259*

Critical Thinking Exercises

1. The United States has used incarceration a great deal to punish those convicted of crimes. This has led us to have one of the highest incarceration rates in the world at an ever increasing expense to taxpayers. In your opinion, should we be reserving jail and prison only for the most serious offenders? Are there certain offenders for which other alternatives might be an adequate and less expensive option?

2. Do you think that judges should pay more attention to victim impact statements and the defendant's

▼

sentencing memorandum when determining appropriate punishments? What are some of the problems with these two parts of a sentencing hearing? Could this lead to harsher or more lenient sentences than if the judge just used the type of offense and criminal history to determine sentence?

3. What is your opinion of the current appeals process? Do you think there are too many appeals, or do you think that it is too difficult for an offender to get redress if there has been an error or mistake in the criminal justice process?

Case Study Decision-Making Exercise

Currently, 32 states authorize the death penalty; this is down in recent years due to states such as New Mexico, Connecticut, and Maryland who have abolished it. Of those 32 states, however, there are a few who have not executed anyone in at least 10 years. Colorado, Nebraska, and Oregon, for instance, haven't had an execution since 1997, and other states such as Kansas and New Hampshire last executed someone prior to 1976. Further, other states such as California with 741 persons on death row, actually carry out executions rarely. What is the purpose of having statutes authorizing the death penalty if it is not actually used, or is used very rarely? If a state isn't planning on executing an individual, should they remain on death row? Should these sentences be commuted to life in prison?

Concept Review Questions

1. What is a *habeas corpus* petition? What are three types of issues challenged by such petitions?
2. What is a writ of *certiorari*? Under what circumstances might this type of writ be used?
3. What are some trends regarding the use of *habeas corpus* petitions by jail and prison inmates? What factors seem to account for such trends?
4. What is a sentencing hearing? What are the major functions of such hearings?
5. What is a presentence investigation report? Who prepares it and how is it used to determine an offender's punishment?
6. What is a bifurcated trial? Under what circumstances is it used? What are two significant cases relating to bifurcated trials?
7. What are victim impact statements? Where are such statements found and what purposes do they serve in the sentencing process?
8. Why is the appeals process for death sentences so lengthy?
9. Why might disparity in sentencing occur? What does recent research reveal about disparities according to extralegal factors such as race/ethnicity and gender?

Suggested Readings

1. R. D. Hartley and R. Tillyer (2012). "Defending the Homeland: Judicial Sentencing Practices for Federal Immigration Offenses." *Justice Quarterly* **29**:76–104.
2. J. K. Doerner and S. Demuth (2010). "The Independent and Joint Effects of Race/Ethnicity, Gender, and Age on Sentencing Outcomes in U.S. Federal Courts." *Justice Quarterly* **27**(1):1–27.
3. C. Spohn (2000). "Thirty Years of Sentencing Reform: The Quest for a Racially Neutral Sentencing Process." In *Policies, Processes, and Decisions of the Criminal Justice System: Criminal Justice, 2000* (Vol. 3). Washington, DC: U.S. Department of Justice.
4. C. S. Yang (2013). "Free at Last? Judicial Discretion and Racial Disparities in Federal Sentencing." *Research Paper*, (661). University of Chicago, Coase-Sandor Institute for Law & Economics.
5. H. Bedau (ed.) (1998). *The Death Penalty in America: Current Controversies*. New York, NY: Oxford University Press.

Lisa F. Young/Fotolia

11   The Juvenile Justice System
Juvenile Rights and Case Processing

LEARNING OBJECTIVES

As the result of reading this chapter, you will have accomplished the following objectives:

1 *Distinguish among the basic components of the juvenile justice system and explain how juveniles are processed differently from adult offenders.*

2 *Compare and contrast the differences between delinquents and status offenders and the reasons for making such distinctions.*

3 *Understand the jurisdiction of juvenile courts and the influence of* parens patriae *on court actions.*

4 *Summarize the history of the juvenile court.*

5 *Apply your knowledge of influence of due process upon juvenile offender processing to examine the legal rights of juveniles.*

Each year roughly 50,000 cases of truancy are petitioned to the juvenile court system. Although the truancy rate is higher for males than females, the number of truancy cases from 1995 to 2007 more than doubled for both males and females, and has since declined about 25 percent; the highest truancy rates are for those of ages 15 and 16 years (Puzzanchera, Adams, and Hockenberry 2012). Obviously, schools are the greatest source of referrals to the juvenile court for truancy but they have also increasingly been the source of referral for other behaviors through school resource officers. Some argue that the reason for this increase in referrals was the passage of the Gun-Free Schools Act in 1994. This act mandated the adoption of zero tolerance policies for weapons in schools and a vast number of schools in the country decided at the same time to implement zero tolerance for other behavioral violations involving alcohol, tobacco, drugs, and violence (Hirschfield 2008). Zero tolerance policies basically shifted discretion regarding the discipline of students from teachers to administrative authorities at the school. Critics argue that this has increased both the expulsion and truancy rates but also created a second phenomenon referred to as the school-to-prison pipeline. Research has shown that students who are dealt with more formally by schools are more likely to drop out and less likely to graduate, which in turn makes it more likely that they will engage in further delinquent and criminal acts. State legislators are also starting to realize that an increased number of students have dropped out of school and ended up in the system, and thus, have recently debated the merits of zero tolerance policies and the increased costs associated with them. Educational administrators and schools in turn are examining new strategies to reverse the school-to-prison pipeline trend (Gonsoulin, Zablocki, and Leone 2012). What do you think? Have schools become more like mini criminal justice systems than educational institutions? Are schools using the juvenile justice system as a way to rid themselves of their problem students? Are there better ways to keep our schools safe and also keep students from dropping out and therefore slow this flow of students into the juvenile or criminal justice system?

▶ Introduction

This chapter examines the juvenile justice system, which is in some ways the analog of the criminal justice system for youthful offenders. Many adults who are processed by the criminal justice system began their criminal offending in their early years as juveniles. Some argue that most persons actually commit some form of delinquent act in their adolescent years and then desist as they get older and become adults (Piquero, Brezina, and Turner 2005), while others persist in committing criminal acts into their adult years. This chapter begins with an overview of the juvenile justice system. It discusses the distinction between juvenile delinquents and status offenders, which is important because juvenile delinquents are those who have committed or are alleged to have committed offenses that would be crimes if adults committed them. By contrast, status offenders commit acts that would not be crimes if adults committed them.

For many decades, the juvenile justice system has not differentiated between these types of offenders, despite the fact that delinquents commit considerably more serious offenses than status offenders and pose greater risks to society. This chapter describes the establishment of the Juvenile Justice and Delinquency Prevention Act of 1974 that contributed much to changing how status offenders are presently treated. In subsequent years, most juvenile courts have divested themselves of their jurisdiction over status offenders, preferring to focus their resources on more serious delinquent offenders. Although more recently, schools are referring students with behavior problems such as truancy to formal courts for processing which has raised criticisms about the consequences of this for young adults later on. An increasing number of school-aged kids are involved in the juvenile justice system because of their behaviors in school. Some studies have shown that students who are dealt with more formally are also less likely to graduate and more likely to engage in further delinquent and criminal acts. This is referred to as the school-to-prison pipeline (Hirschfield 2008) and many are starting to rethink zero tolerance programs and come up with strategies to reverse this trend (Gonsoulin et al. 2012).

Next, the chapter focuses upon the jurisdiction of the juvenile court. Jurisdiction refers to the power of courts to hear particular kinds of cases. A brief history of the juvenile court is presented, and several important contrasts between juvenile and criminal courts are illustrated. The juvenile justice process begins with a referral, which may be made by a parent, guardian, school official, police officer, or neighbor. In 2011, close to 1.5 million juveniles were arrested, this is down 11 percent from the previous year and 31 percent since 2002 (Puzzanchera 2013). The process of screening juveniles, or intake, is described. Beyond intake, juvenile court prosecutors perform chores relating to juveniles that are quite similar to the tasks performed by criminal court prosecutors. They must decide which cases to pursue and which ones not to pursue. A little over half of the juveniles petitioned appear before juvenile court judges (Puzzanchera and Robson 2014), where there cases are then adjudicated.

The next section discusses the legal rights of juveniles, and several important U.S. Supreme Court cases involving juvenile rights are presented. Their implications for juvenile court treatment are discussed. Several rights conveyed to juveniles by the U.S. Supreme Court include the right to an attorney, the right to a notice of charges, the right to cross-examine one's accuser, the right to give testimony on one's own behalf, the right against self-incrimination, and the right to the beyond a reasonable doubt standard where one's liberty is in jeopardy.

Also, juveniles have the right against double jeopardy, which may occur when a juvenile is adjudicated delinquent by the juvenile court and a criminal court subsequently finds him/her guilty of the same charge. This is considered double jeopardy and is thus unconstitutional. Juveniles do not have the right to a jury trial, however, unless provided for by state statutes or by judicial decree. Most juvenile court judges do not allow jury trials for juveniles, inasmuch as this procedure would delay juvenile court processing of youthful offenders considerably.

▶ # Delinquency, Juvenile Delinquents, and Status Offenders

Juvenile Delinquents

Juveniles

juvenile court jurisdiction power of juvenile courts to hear cases involving persons under the legal age of adulthood.

juveniles persons who have not as yet achieved their eighteenth birthday or the age of majority.

juvenile court a term for any court with original jurisdiction over persons statutorily defined as juveniles and alleged to be delinquents, status offenders, or dependents.

Juvenile court jurisdiction is dependent upon established legislative definitions of who juveniles are and the offenses they commit. There is considerable variation among the states as to which juvenile offenders are within the purview of juvenile courts. The federal government has no juvenile court. Rather, federal cases involving juveniles infrequently are heard in federal district courts, but adjudicated juveniles are housed in state or local facilities if the sentences involve incarceration. Ordinarily, upper and lower age limits are prescribed. However, these age limits are far from being uniform among jurisdictions. The common-law standard sets the minimum age of juveniles at seven, although no state is obligated to recognize this common-law definition. In fact, some states have no lower age limits that would otherwise function to limit juvenile court jurisdiction meaning that a child of any age could be subject to the jurisdiction of the juvenile justice system. Most of the states and the federal government use age 18 as the minimum age for criminal court jurisdiction (Champion 2007).

In most jurisdictions, youths under the age of seven are often placed in the care of community agencies, such as departments of human services and social welfare. These children frequently have little or no responsible parental supervision or control. In many cases, the parents themselves may have psychological problems or suffer from alcohol or drug dependencies. Youths from such families may be abused and/or neglected, and in need of supervision and other forms of care or treatment. Under common law, in those states where common law applies, children under the age of seven are presumed incapable of formulating criminal intent. If a six-year-old child kills someone, for instance, deliberately or accidentally, he/she will likely be treated rather than punished.

Juvenile Delinquency

Juvenile delinquency is the violation of a criminal law of the United States by a person prior to his eighteenth birthday, which would have been a crime if committed by an adult (18 U.S.C. Sec. 5031, 1997). Generally, juvenile delinquency is the violation of any state or local law or ordinance by anyone who has not yet become an adult. Any act committed by a juvenile that would be a crime if an adult committed it is a delinquent act. A juvenile delinquent is anyone who has committed juvenile delinquency.

Status Offenders

Status offenders commit offenses that would not be crimes if adults committed them. Typical status offenses are runaway behavior, truancy, and curfew violation. Adults may run away from home, be truant from their classes, and stay out late at night without violating the law. However, juveniles are required to observe these laws that pertain specifically to them (Urban 2005).

Runaways

According to the National Center for Juvenile Justice, in 2009, 16,000 runaway cases were processed by juvenile courts which was a 22 percent decrease from 1995 (Puzzanchera et al. 2012). Runaways consist of those youths who leave their homes, without permission or their parents' knowledge, and who remain away from home for prolonged periods ranging from several days to several years. Many runaways are eventually picked up by police in different jurisdictions and returned to their homes. Others return of their own free will and choice.

Truants and Curfew Violators

Truants are juveniles who do not attend school and do not have either school or parental permission to be absent. Curfew violators are juveniles who are out after specified evening hours when they are prohibited from loitering or not being in the company of a parent or guardian. The number of truancy cases heard by juvenile courts doubled from 1995 to 2007, and then declined about 25 percent by 2009; in 2009, there were roughly 50,000 truancy cases processed by juvenile courts (Puzzanchera et al. 2012). Similarly, youths processed for curfew violation in the United States increased from 1995 to 2000 and then declined by 33 percent to 13,500 cases by 2009 (Puzzanchera et al. 2012).

Juvenile and Criminal Court Interest in Status Offenders

Juvenile courts are interested in status offenders who habitually appear before juvenile court judges. Repeated juvenile court appearances may be symptomatic of subsequent

---

juvenile delinquency the violation of criminal laws by juveniles. Any illegal behavior or activity committed by persons who are within a particular age range; subjects them to the jurisdiction of a juvenile court or its equivalent.

juvenile delinquent any minor who commits an offense that would be a crime if committed by an adult.

status offenders juveniles who have committed an offense that would not be considered a crime if committed by an adult (e.g., a curfew violation would not be a criminal action if committed by an adult, but such an act is a status offense if engaged in by a juvenile).

runaways juveniles who abscond from their homes or residences without parental permission; often these youths seek a free life in another city away from parental control; a type of status offender.

truants juveniles who absent themselves from school during school hours and without excuse of parental or school consent; a type of status offender.

curfew violators persons under the legal age of adulthood who roam city streets beyond times when they are supposed to be in their homes; a type of status offender.

stigmatize the process of labeling someone as a delinquent or a criminal on the basis of their exhibited behavior.

divestiture of jurisdiction juvenile court relinquishment of control over certain types of juveniles, such as status offenders.

deinstitutionalization of status offenders (DSO) movement to remove nondelinquent juveniles from secure facilities by eliminating status offenses from the delinquency category and removing juveniles from or precluding their confinement in juvenile correction facilities. Process of removing status offenses from jurisdiction of juvenile court.

deinstitutionalization providing programs in community-based settings instead of institutional ones.

Juvenile Justice and Delinquency Prevention Act of 1974 (JJDPA) act passed by Congress in 1974 and amended numerous times, including 1984, encouraging states to deal differently with their juvenile offenders. Promotes community-based treatment programs and discourages incarceration of juveniles in detention centers, industrial schools, or reform schools.

adult criminality. The chronicity of juvenile offending seems to be influenced by the amount of contact youths have with juvenile courts. Greater contact with juvenile courts is believed by some experts to stigmatize juveniles and cause them either to be labeled or acquire stigmas as delinquents or deviants. Therefore, diversion of certain types of juvenile offenders from the juvenile justice system has been advocated and recommended to minimize stigmatization (McLean, Cocozza, and Skowyra 2004).

One way of removing status offenders from juvenile courts and their stigmatizing effects is to deprive juvenile court judges of jurisdiction over status offenders (Blackmore, Brown, and Krisberg 1988). Another way of minimizing status offender stigmatization is to remove them from custodial institutions where they are housed for various terms, such as industrial schools. These methods are known as divestiture of jurisdiction and deinstitutionalization of status offenders (DSO) or simply deinstitutionalization.

Under divestiture, juvenile courts cannot detain, petition, adjudicate, or place youths on probation or in institutions for committing *any* status offense. In lieu of juvenile court intervention, various community agencies and social services are used to care for and place status offenders. There is a prevalent belief that institutionalizing status offenders in juvenile industrial schools (e.g., prisons for juveniles) will harden them, thus increasing their likelihood of committing future, more serious offenses. Because of this idea, in the late 1960s, a movement began to remove status offenders from juvenile penal institutions such as industrial schools. In 1974, the U.S. Congress passed enabling legislation to accomplish this objective on a national basis.

The Juvenile Justice and Delinquency Prevention Act of 1974 (JJDPA) (and modified in 1984) was established in response to a national concern about growing juvenile delinquency and youth crime. This act authorized the establishment of the Office of Juvenile Justice and Delinquency Prevention (OJJDP), which has been extremely helpful and influential in matters of disseminating information about juvenile offending and prevention and as a general data source. The JJDPA provides for a state relations and assistance division. This division addresses directly the matter of removing juveniles, especially status offenders, from secure institutions (facilities similar to adult prisons), jails, and lockups. The second division, Research and Program Development, examines how juvenile courts process juvenile offenders.

The JJDPA has also been modified extensively since its inception in 1974. Congress modified the act in 1977 by declaring that the juveniles should be separated by both sight and sound from adult offenders in detention and correctional facilities. Also in 1977, states were given five years to comply with the DSO mandate. Congress prohibited states in 1980 from detaining juveniles in jails and lockups. Congress also directed that states should examine their secure confinement policies relating to minority juveniles and to determine reasons and justification for the disproportionately high rate of minority confinement (Mukoro 2005). In 1992, Congress directed that any participating state would have up to 25 percent of its formula grant money withheld to the extent that the state was not in compliance with each of the JJDPA mandates. States must comply with four requirements of the JJDPA in order to receive funding; deinstitutionalization of status offenders, housing juveniles separate from adults in secure facilities, removing juveniles from adult jails, and reducing disproportionate minority contact with the juvenile justice system (Office of Juvenile Justice and Delinquency Prevention 2014). In 2012, six states had funding reductions for noncompliance (Office of Juvenile Justice and Delinquency Prevention 2014). Thus, it is clear that state compliance with these provisions of the JJDPA is mandated and achieved by providing grants-in-aid to various jurisdictions wishing to improve their juvenile justice systems and facilities (Rodriguez 2004).

▶ The Jurisdiction of Juvenile Courts

The Age Jurisdiction of Juvenile Courts

Upper age limits for juveniles have been established in all U.S. jurisdictions (either under 16, under 17, or under 18 years of age). However, presently there is no uniformity concerning applicable lower age limits. Because of this, technically some juvenile courts would have jurisdiction over a five-year-old who commits murder. However, no juvenile court will adjudicate a five-year-old delinquent and place the child in secure confinement. The type of jurisdictional control over such children by juvenile courts is more care and treatment oriented. This treatment and care may include placement of children or infants in foster homes or under the supervision of community service or human welfare agencies that can meet their needs.

Neglected, unmanageable, abused, or other children in need of supervision (CHINS) are placed in the custody of these various agencies, at the discretion of juvenile judges. Generally, juvenile courts have broad discretionary powers over most persons under the age of 18 years.

The Treatment and Punishment Functions of Juvenile Courts

Not all juveniles who appear before juvenile court judges are delinquents. Many youths in juvenile court have not violated any criminal laws (Feld 2003). Rather, their status as juveniles means that they are within juvenile court control. Several circumstances make these youths susceptible to juvenile court jurisdiction. One circumstance may simply be that the quality of their parental supervision, if any, is not adequate in the court's eyes. Other circumstances may be that they run away from home, are truant from school, or loiter on certain city streets during evening hours. Runaways, truants, or loiterers are considered status offenders, since their actions would not be criminal ones if committed by adults.

Physically, psychologically, or sexually abused children are also within the jurisdictional control of juvenile courts. Many of these juvenile courts are instead called family courts. The majority of youthful offenders who appear before juvenile courts, however, are juvenile delinquents. Juvenile courts, therefore, have broad discretionary powers over all types of juveniles. Much of this state authority originated under the early English doctrine of *parens patriae*.

Parens Patriae

Parens patriae originated with the king of England during the twelfth century. It literally means the father of the country. Applied to juvenile matters, *parens patriae* means that the king is in charge of, makes decisions about, or has responsibility for all matters involving juvenile conduct. Within the scope of early English common law, parental authority was primary in the early upbringing of children. However, as children advanced to age seven and beyond, they acquired some measure of responsibility for their own actions. Accountability to parents was shifted gradually to accountability to the state, whenever youths seven years of age or older violated the law. In the name of the king, chancellors in various districts adjudicated matters involving juveniles and the offenses they committed. Juveniles had no legal rights or standing in any court. They were the sole responsibility of the king or his agents. Their future often depended largely upon decisions made by chancellors. In effect, children were wards of the court, and the court was vested with the responsibility to safeguard their welfare.

Since children could become wards of the court and subject to their control, a key concern for many chancellors was for the future welfare of these children. The welfare interests

Office of Juvenile Justice and Delinquency Prevention (OJJDP) established by Congress under the Juvenile Justice and Delinquency Prevention Act of 1974; designed to remove status offenders from jurisdiction of juvenile courts and dispose of their cases less formally.

children in need of supervision (CHINS) typically unruly or incorrigible children who cannot be supervised well by their parents. Also includes children from homes where parents are seldom present. State agencies exist to find housing for such children.

parens patriae "parent of the country." Refers to doctrine that the state oversees the welfare of youth, originally established by the king of England and administered through chancellors.

of chancellors and their actions led to numerous rehabilitative and/or treatment measures. Some of these measures included placement of children in foster homes or their assignment to various work tasks for local merchants. Parental influence in these child placement decisions was minimal.

Modern Applications of *Parens Patriae*

Parens patriae is pervasive in all juvenile court jurisdictions, despite the fact that most states have increased the number of juveniles being treated as adults. Waivers still only account for about 1 percent of all juvenile cases petitioned to the juvenile court (Puzzanchera and Robson 2014). The pervasiveness of this doctrine is exhibited by the wide range of dispositional options available to juvenile court judges and others involved in earlier stages of offender processing in the juvenile justice system. Most of these dispositional options are either nominal or conditional, meaning that the confinement of any juvenile for most offenses is regarded as a last resort. See Figure 11-1 later in this chapter for statistics on petitions, waivers, and dispositions.

The strong treatment or rehabilitative orientation inherent in *parens patriae* is not acceptable to some juvenile justice experts. Consistent with a growing trend in the criminal justice system toward just deserts and justice, a similar trend is being observed throughout the juvenile justice system (Lawrence and Hesse 2010). This get-tough movement is geared toward providing law violators with swifter, harsher, and more certain justice and punishment than the previously dominant rehabilitative philosophy of American courts. The juvenile courts, however, still by and large, place only a small percentage of overall juveniles referred to them into custody.

The get-tough movement is not the only reason the influence of the *parens patriae* doctrine has changed. The increase in rights of juveniles has also had an impact of the court's doctrine. Since the mid-1960s, juveniles have acquired greater constitutional rights commensurate with those enjoyed by adults in criminal courts. Some professionals believe that as juveniles are vested with greater numbers of constitutional rights, a gradual transformation of the juvenile court is occurring toward one of greater **criminalization** (Feld 2000, 2001). Interestingly, as juveniles obtain a greater range of constitutional rights, they become more immune to the influence of *parens patriae*. Quite simply, juvenile courts are gradually losing some of their jurisdiction over juveniles. Despite these greater due process rights in juvenile cases, the court processing of juveniles and adults is still very different.

> **What Do You Think?**
>
> Should the juvenile court still apply the English doctrine of *parens patriae*, meaning that the court should have a rehabilitative ideal? Has affording juveniles more due process rights limited juvenile court judge's ability to informally deal with a juvenile and use their discretion to rehabilitate first and punish as a last resort?

> **criminalization**
> transformation of civil proceedings into criminal proceedings; the juvenile court has undergone a transformation toward greater criminalization as juveniles have acquired almost the same number of legal rights as adults.

▶ Juvenile Court History

A Brief History of Juvenile Courts in the United States

Juvenile courts are primarily an American creation. The first juvenile court was established in Illinois in 1899 under the **Illinois Juvenile Court Act**. This does not mean that other states were unconcerned about juveniles at the time, or that other events had not occurred pertaining to youths, their conduct, and their welfare. In fact, numerous agencies and organizations had been established earlier in other jurisdictions, particularly during the latter half of the 1800s.

> **Illinois Juvenile Court Act** legislation establishing first juvenile court in United States in 1899.

Reformatories and the Child Savers

The first public reformatory for juveniles was the New York House of Refuge. It was established in New York City in 1825 by the Society for the Prevention of Pauperism (Champion 2005b). This house of refuge had several goals relating to juveniles, including providing food, clothing, and lodging for all poor, abused, or orphaned youths. However, the Society for the Prevention of Pauperism was comprised, in part, of many benefactors, philanthropists, and religionists, and these individuals sought to instill within the youths they serviced a commitment to hard work, strict discipline, and intensive study. These houses were established in various parts of New York and staffed largely by volunteers who knew little or nothing about individual counseling, group therapy techniques, or other useful interventions that might assist youths in surviving city hazards. Because the organization of these houses was decentralized, there were few, if any, external controls that could regulate the quality of care provided.

While houses of refuge operated to provide services for misplaced youths, other random efforts led to the creation of child-saving programs. Child savers referred to no one in particular, because anyone who wished to be of assistance in helping children and intervening in their lives for constructive purposes could define themselves as child savers. No one knows what child-saving meant, but many persons were involved in providing food, shelter, and other forms of care for needy children. Jane Addams established and operated Hull House in Chicago, Illinois, in 1889. This was a settlement home used largely by children from immigrant families in the Chicago area. Many adults worked long hours, and many youths were otherwise unsupervised and wandered about their neighborhoods looking for something to do. Using money from various charities and philanthropists, Addams supplied many children with creative activities to alleviate their boredom and monotony. Addams integrated these activities with moral, ethical, and religious teachings. In her own way, she was hoping to deter these youths from lives of crime with her constructive activities and teaching.

Truancy Statutes

Truancy laws were passed by the Massachusetts state legislature in 1852, where the first compulsory school attendance statutes were established. By 1918, all jurisdictions had truancy statutes. Juveniles who did not attend school were subject to being taken into custody. State homes were used to place such youths, where it could be demonstrated that they had little, if any, adult supervision at home. Today, truancy cases comprise a large share of the status offenses that are referred to the juvenile court.

Juvenile Court Uniformity and Specialized Juvenile Courts

Much variation exists among juvenile court organization and operation in the United States (Champion 2009). In fact, great variations in juvenile court operations and functions are found within the same state. Some jurisdictions have courts that adjudicate juvenile offenders as well as decide child custody. Thus, while it is true that all jurisdictions presently have juvenile courts, these courts are not always called juvenile courts and there is not much uniformity among them.

Most early juvenile court proceedings were different from criminal court proceedings. These proceedings often involved a juvenile charged with some offense; a petitioner claiming the juvenile should be declared delinquent, or dependent, or neglected; and a judge who would decide things. Juveniles had no rights, no attorneys, and were not permitted to call witnesses or testify on their own behalf. Juvenile court judges made decisions about juveniles according to what the judges believed to be in the best interests of the children. Thus, much individualized justice was dispensed by juvenile court judges.

Juvenile Court Proceedings—Bureaucracy and Criminalization

Early juvenile court proceedings were closed to the general public in order to protect the identities of the youthful accused. Mere allegations, together with uncorroborated

reformatory detention facility designed to change criminal behavior or reform it.

Society for the Prevention of Pauperism philanthropic society that established first public reformatory in New York in 1825, the New York House of Refuge.

child savers groups who promoted rights of minors during the nineteenth century and helped create a separate juvenile court. Their motives have been questioned by modern writers who see their efforts as a form of social control and class conflict.

statements and pronouncements from probation officers and others, were sufficient for juvenile court judges to declare any juvenile either delinquent or not delinquent. Penalties imposed ranged from verbal reprimands and warnings to incarceration in a state reform school or industrial school.

Generally, juvenile courts are viewed as due process courts rather than traditional courts (Feld 2003). Due process juvenile courts involve more formal case dispositions, a greater rate of intake dismissals, and greater importance attached to offense characteristics and seriousness. Traditional courts are characterized as less formal, with greater use made of secure confinement. Both defense and prosecuting attorneys play more important roles in due process juvenile courts compared with traditional ones (Guevara and Herz 2004). Greater procedural formality in the juvenile justice system has been observed relating to the appointment of public defenders for juvenile indigents. Formerly, a defense counsel for a juvenile often was the juvenile's probation officer or a social caseworker with a vested interest in the case. It is not entirely clear how these officers and workers were able to separate their law enforcement and defense functions to avoid allegations of conflicts of interest. Little public interest was exhibited in the quality of defense of juvenile cases.

In recent years, juvenile court proceedings have become increasingly formalized (Champion 2009). Further, public access to these proceedings in most jurisdictions is increasing. Thus, the presence of defense counsel, an adversarial scenario, a trial-like atmosphere where witnesses testify for and against juvenile defendants, and adherence to Rules of Procedure for Juvenile Courts are clear indicators of greater formalization, bureaucratization, and criminalization. Also with greater formalization, less disparity in dispositional decision making has occurred relating to one's gender, ethnic identity, or race (Charish 2004; Rosay and Myrstol 2004).

▶ The Juvenile Justice Process

Referrals, Intake, and Petitions

Many juvenile encounters with the juvenile justice system are prompted by referrals from police officers (Champion 2009). Referrals are notifications made to juvenile court authorities that a juvenile requires the court's attention. A referral may be made by anyone, such as concerned parents, school principals, teachers, neighbors, and others but most are made by law enforcement officers. Some researchers have suggested that disparities in juvenile offender processing begin at this stage and continue throughout the entire juvenile justice system, where factors such as race, ethnicity, gender, and socioeconomic status intervene to affect juveniles in different ways (Ketchum and Embrick 2004). Arrest and being taken into custody is the first of major processing points that involves the exercise of discretion from various actors in the juvenile justice system.

Intake varies in formality among jurisdictions (Worling 1995). Intake is a screening procedure conducted by a court officer or a probation officer, where one or several courses of action are recommended. Some jurisdictions conduct intake hearings, where comments and opinions are solicited from significant others such as the police, parents, neighbors, or victims. These proceedings are important, regardless of their degree of formality.

An intake officer is either a court-appointed official who hears complaints against juveniles and attempts early resolutions of them, or more often a juvenile probation officer who performs intake as a special assignment. In many small jurisdictions, juvenile probation officers may perform diverse functions, including intake screenings, enforcement of truancy statutes, and juvenile placements. Intake officers consider youths' attitudes, demeanor, age, offense seriousness, and a host of other factors. If the offenses alleged are serious, what evidence exists against the offender? Should the offender be referred to certain

due process courts juvenile courts where the emphasis is upon punishment and offender control rather than individualized treatments and assistance.

referral any citation of a juvenile to juvenile court by a law enforcement officer, interested citizen, family member, or school official; usually based upon law violations, delinquency, or unruly conduct.

intake review of a case by a court (juvenile or criminal) official. Screening of cases includes weeding out weak cases. In juvenile cases, intake involves the reception of a juvenile against whom complaints have been made. Decision to proceed or dismiss the case is made at this stage.

intake officer officer who conducts screening of juveniles. Dispositions include release to parents pending further juvenile court action, dismissal of charges against juvenile, detention, treatment by some community agency.

community social service agencies, receive psychological counseling, receive vocational counseling and guidance, acquire educational or technical training and skills, be issued a verbal reprimand, be placed on some type of diversionary status, or be returned to parental custody? Interviews with parents and neighbors may be conducted as a part of an intake officer's information gathering. In most jurisdictions, intake normally results in one of five actions: 1) dismissal of the case, with or without a verbal or written reprimand, 2) remand the juvenile to the custody of their parents, 3) remand juvenile to the custody of their parents with provisions for, or referrals to, counseling or other services, 4) divert juvenile to alternative dispute resolution program, or 5) refer juvenile to juvenile prosecutor for further action and possibly filing of delinquency petition.

A petition is a legal document filed by interested parties alleging that a juvenile is delinquent, a status offender, or in need of adult supervision. The petition requests that the juvenile court decide whether the allegations are true and determine an appropriate penalty or disposition. According to recent statistics from OJJDP, just over half of the 1,368,200 juveniles that were referred to the court in 2010 had a formal petition filed against them (Puzzanchera and Robson 2014). Of the 737,200 juveniles who had formal petitions filed against them, 40 percent resulted in the juvenile not being adjudicated as a delinquent; about 60 percent of those juveniles had their cases dismissed by a juvenile judge (Puzzanchera and Robson 2014).

Juvenile Court Prosecutors and Decision Making

Like their criminal court counterparts, juvenile court prosecutors have broad discretionary powers. They may dismiss cases against certain juveniles. They may screen cases by diverting some of the most serious ones to criminal court through waiver, transfer, or certification. A prosecutorial waiver is used for this purpose. Other perhaps less serious cases are diverted out of the juvenile justice system for informal processing (Feld 2000). Prosecutors may also file petitions or act on the petitions filed by others. These documents assert that juveniles fall within the categories of dependent or neglected, status offender, or delinquent, and the reasons for such assertions are usually provided (Champion 2009). Filing a petition formally places the juvenile before the juvenile court judge in many jurisdictions.

Figure 11-1 ■ displays the case flow for 1,000 typical delinquency cases as well as for all of the delinquency cases (1,368,200) in 2010. As can be seen, just a little over half (54 percent) of the cases referred to the court actually result in petitions. Of those juveniles petitioned, about 60 percent eventually are adjudicated as delinquent. The majority of juvenile delinquents (61 percent) are given a probationary disposition by juvenile court judges. About one-quarter are placed in custody and another 13 percent receive some other type of nominal sanction.

Just because a juvenile is not found delinquent, however, does not mean that the court will not decide to impose a sanction. Although 60 percent of the cases where the juvenile was not adjudicated as a delinquent are dismissed, one-quarter still receive a probationary disposition and another 14 percent receive some other sanction from the court.

For the just under half of cases that are referred to the court but not petitioned, about 42 percent are dismissed, 24 percent still receive a sanction of probation, and another 33 percent receive some other sanction. Overall then, of the almost 1.4 million cases referred to the court in 2010, roughly 450,000 were dismissed and another roughly 430,000 were actually found to be delinquent. Regardless of whether their case was petitioned, or whether they were adjudicated delinquent, roughly 490,000 of the juveniles referred were placed on probation, about 310,000 were given some other sanction, and only 112,000 were placed in custody. Clearly, *parens patriae* is present in the juvenile courts today in that very few juveniles are placed in custody and most are placed on probation or given some other nominal sanction in line with the rehabilitative ideals of the juvenile justice system. Finally, despite the fact that waiver of juvenile cases to adult court has increased recently, it still only amounts to about 1 percent of the total cases that were petitioned to the juvenile court.

petition a document filed in juvenile court alleging that a juvenile is a delinquent, a status offender, or a dependent and asking that the court assume jurisdiction over the juvenile or that the juvenile be transferred to a criminal court to be prosecuted as an adult.

prosecutorial waiver authority of prosecutors in juvenile cases to have those cases transferred to the jurisdiction of criminal court.

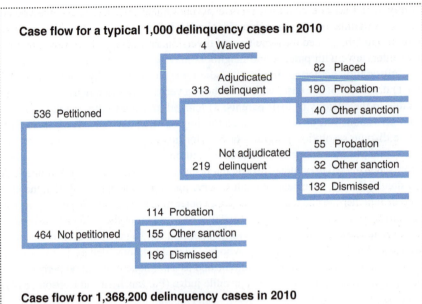

Case flow for a typical 1,000 delinquency cases in 2010

```
                                4  Waived

                                           82  Placed
                          Adjudicated
                      313 delinquent      190  Probation

                                           40  Other sanction

536  Petitioned
                                           55  Probation
                          Not adjudicated
                      219 delinquent       32  Other sanction

                                          132  Dismissed


                      114  Probation

464  Not petitioned   155  Other sanction

                      196  Dismissed
```

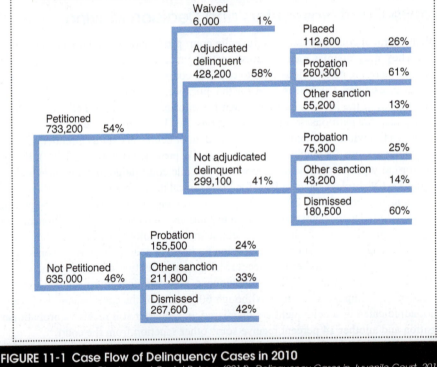

Case flow for 1,368,200 delinquency cases in 2010

```
                    Waived
                    6,000        1%        Placed
                                           112,600          26%
                    Adjudicated
                    delinquent             Probation
                    428,200     58%        260,300          61%

                                           Other sanction
                                           55,200           13%

Petitioned                                 Probation
733,200    54%                             75,300           25%

                    Not adjudicated        Other sanction
                    delinquent             43,200           14%
                    299,100     41%
                                           Dismissed
                                           180,500          60%


                    Probation
                    155,500       24%

Not Petitioned      Other sanction
635,000    46%      211,800       33%

                    Dismissed
                    267,600       42%
```

FIGURE 11-1 Case Flow of Delinquency Cases in 2010
Source: Puzzanchera, Charles, and Crystal Robson (2014). *Delinquency Cases in Juvenile Court, 2010.*
Washington, DC: U.S. Department of Justice, Office of Juvenile Justice and Delinquency Prevention.

▶ Juvenile Rights and Standards of Proof

During the mid-1960s and for the next 30 years, significant achievements were made in the area of juvenile rights. Although the *parens patriae* philosophy continues to be somewhat influential in juvenile proceedings, the U.S. Supreme Court has vested youths with certain constitutional rights. These rights do not encompass all of the rights extended to adults who are charged with crimes. But those rights conveyed to juveniles thus far have had far-reaching implications for how juveniles are processed. Box 11-1 outlines several landmark cases involving juvenile rights.

KEY CASES: JUVENILE DUE PROCESS RIGHTS

Kent v. United States **383 U.S. 541 (1966)**

Morris A. Kent, a juvenile was taken into custody and questioned by police in connection with robbery and rape of a woman. Kent admitted to the offense in addition to other housebreakings, robberies, and rapes. The case was summarily waived to criminal court by the juvenile court judge without a hearing on the waiver, which Kent's attorney had demanded. Kent was later found guilty of six counts of housebreaking by a federal jury, although the jury found him not guilty by reason of insanity on the rape charge. On appeal, the U.S. Supreme Court reversed Kent's conviction holding that his rights to due process and to the effective assistance of counsel were violated when he was denied a formal hearing on the waiver and his attorney's motions were ignored. Because of the *Kent* decision, waiver hearings are now considered critical stages requiring an attorney's advice and presence.

In Re Gault **387 U.S. 1 (1967)**

In re Gault (1967) is perhaps the most significant of all juvenile rights cases. It is certainly the most ambitious in terms of the rights sought by Gault. The U.S. Supreme Court granted the following rights for all juveniles as the result of the *Gault* decision: (1) the right to a notice of charges, (2) the right to counsel, (3) the right to confront and cross-examine witnesses, and (4) the right to invoke the privilege against self-incrimination.

The facts are that Gerald Francis Gault, a 15-year-old, was detained as a result of a complaint of lewd and indecent remarks filed by a neighbor. Gault was picked up while his mother and father were at work and held at a children's detention home. Gault's parents proceeded to the home and were advised that a petition had been filed against Gault and a hearing was scheduled in juvenile court the following day. No factual basis was provided for the petition, and Gault's parents were not provided with a copy of it in advance of the hearing. When the hearing was held, only Gault, his mother and older brother, probation officers Flagg and Henderson, and the juvenile court judge were present.

The original complainant, Mrs. Cook, was not there. No one was sworn at the hearing, no transcript was made of it, and no memorandum of the substance of the proceedings was prepared. The testimony consisted largely of allegations by Officer Flagg about Gault's behavior and prior juvenile record. Gault was adjudicated delinquent by the judge and ordered to serve a six-year term in the Arizona State Industrial School (a juvenile prison). After exhausting their appeals in Arizona state courts, the Gaults appealed to the U.S. Supreme Court. Needless to say, the Court was appalled that Gault's case had been handled in such a cavalier and unconstitutional manner. They reversed the Arizona Supreme Court, holding that Gault did, indeed, have the right to an attorney, the right to confront his accuser (Mrs. Cook) and to cross-examine her, the right against self-incrimination, and the right to have notice of the charges filed against him. Perhaps, Justice Black summed up the current juvenile court situation in the United States when he said, "This holding strikes a well-nigh fatal blow to much that is *unique* [emphasis mine] about the juvenile courts in this Nation."

In Re Winship **(1970)**

Winship established an important precedent in juvenile courts relating to the standard of proof used in established defendant guilt. The facts are that Samuel Winship was a

(continued)

12-year-old charged with larceny in New York City. He purportedly entered a locker and stole $112 from a woman's pocketbook. While the juvenile court judge in the case acknowledged that the proof to be presented by the prosecution might be insufficient to establish the guilt of Winship beyond a reasonable doubt, he did adjudicate Winship delinquent and ordered him placed in a training school for 18 months. The U.S. Supreme Court heard Winship's case and reversed the New York Family Court ruling stating that the stronger standard of proof of beyond a reasonable doubt is necessary for both adults and juveniles when establishing guilt.

McKeiver v. Pennsylvania 403 U.S. 528 (1971)

The *McKeiver v. Pennsylvania* case is important because the U.S. Supreme Court held that juveniles are not entitled to a jury trial as a matter of right. The facts are that in May 1968, Joseph McKeiver, age 16, was charged with robbery, larceny, and receiving stolen goods. While he was represented by counsel at his adjudicatory hearing and requested a trial by jury, the judge denied his request. McKeiver was adjudicated delinquent. On appeal to the U.S. Supreme Court, McKeiver's adjudication was upheld. The U.S. Supreme Court said that it is the juvenile court judge's decision whether to grant jury trials to juveniles.

Breed v. Jones 421 U.S. 519 (1975)

This case raised the significant constitutional issue of double jeopardy. The U.S. Supreme Court concluded that after a juvenile has been adjudicated as delinquent on specific charges, those same charges may not be alleged against those juveniles subsequently in criminal courts through transfers or waivers. Juveniles cannot be adjudicated on a given charge in juvenile court and then sent to criminal court to face conviction on the same charge.

Schall v. Martin 467 U.S. 253 (1984)

In this case, the U.S. Supreme Court issued juveniles a minor setback regarding the state's right to hold them in preventive detention pending a subsequent adjudication. The Court said that the preventive detention of juveniles by states is constitutional, if judges perceive these youths to pose a danger to the community or an otherwise serious risk if released short of an adjudicatory hearing. This decision was significant, in part, because many experts advocated the separation of juveniles and adults in jails, those facilities most often used for preventive detention. Also, the preventive detention of adults was not ordinarily practiced at that time. [Since then, the preventive detention of adults who are deemed to pose societal risks has been upheld by the U.S. Supreme Court (*United States v. Salerno*, 1987).]

The above cases are landmark in the granting of certain due process rights to juveniles in the administration of justice. Table 11-1 ■ summarizes some of the major rights available to juveniles today and compares these rights with selected rights enjoyed by adults in criminal proceedings.

TABLE 11-1 Comparison of Juvenile and Adult Rights[a]

Right	Adults	Juveniles
"Beyond a reasonable doubt" standard used in court	Yes	Yes
Right against double jeopardy	Yes	Yes
Right to assistance of counsel	Yes	Yes
Right to notice of charges	Yes	Yes
Right to a transcript of court proceedings	Yes	No
Right against self-incrimination	Yes	Yes
Right to trial by jury	Yes	No, in most states
Right to defense counsel in court proceedings	Yes	No
Right to bail	Yes	No, with exceptions
Right to cross-examine witnesses	Yes	Yes
Right to a speedy trial	Yes	No
Right to *habeas corpus* relief in correctional settings	Yes	No
Right to hearing for parole or probation revocation	Yes	No
Bifurcated trial, death penalty cases	Yes	Yes

▼

TABLE 11-1 (*continued*)

Right	Adults	Juveniles
Fingerprinting, photographing at booking	Yes	No, with exceptions
Right to appeal	Yes	Limited
Right to court-appointed attorney if indigent	Yes	No, with exceptions
Transcript required of criminal/delinquency trial proceedings	Yes	No, with exceptions
Pretrial detention permitted	Yes	Yes
Public access to trials	Yes	Limited
Conviction/adjudication results in criminal record	Yes	No

[a]Compiled by the authors.

BOX 11-2

LEGAL ISSUES: JURY TRIALS FOR JUVENILES

The right to a jury trial does not extend to all juveniles in the United States. In fact, the majority of states (31) do not allow a juvenile the right to a jury trial under any circumstances in juvenile court (Szymanski 2008). Nine other states (Alaska, Massachusetts, Michigan, Montana, New Mexico, Oklahoma, Texas, West Virginia, and Wyoming) allow jury trials; 11 other states also allow jury trials in limited circumstances. All states have implemented mandatory waivers of juveniles to criminal court for certain offenses and most have lowered the age at which juveniles can be transferred to adult court where they would be afforded the right to a jury trial under the Sixth Amendment. What do you think? Should the right to a jury trial for a juvenile depend on which state you are from? Should the statutes be more uniform across the states regarding the instances when this right is afforded to a juvenile? Would you vote for the 31 states to allow juveniles the right to a jury trial or would you revoke this right in the other 20 states?

▶ Variations in Criminal and Juvenile Court Processing

Due to the fact that juveniles do not enjoy all of the due process rights afforded to adults, some of the major differences between juvenile and criminal courts are outlined in the following paragraphs. First, juvenile court proceedings are civil proceedings exclusively designed for juveniles, whereas criminal court proceedings are designed to try adults charged with crimes. The civil–criminal distinction is important because a civil adjudication of a case does not result in a criminal record. Similarly, juvenile court proceeding are characterized by informality, whereas criminal proceedings are formal. Juvenile court judges frequently address juveniles directly and casually. Formal criminal or evidentiary procedures are not followed rigorously, and hearsay from various sources is considered together with factual evidence.

In 31 states, juveniles are not entitled to a trial by jury; in nine states the right to jury trials for juveniles is allowed, and in the 11 other states juveniles can be provided with jury trials under special circumstances, such as where they are subject to be sent to an adult prison, or for certain serious and repeat offenders (Szymanski 2008). All criminal courts are courts of record, whereas transcripts of most juvenile proceedings are made only if the judge allows it. However, some juvenile court judges may have the resources and/or interest to provide for such transcriptions, particularly if serious offenses against certain juveniles have been alleged.

The standard of proof used for determining one's guilt in criminal proceedings is beyond a reasonable doubt. This same standard is applicable in juvenile courts where violations of criminal laws are alleged and incarceration in a juvenile facility is a possible punishment. However, the less rigorous civil standard of preponderance of evidence is used in most other juvenile court matters where one's loss of liberty is not at issue. Finally, criminal courts have the full range of penalties, including death and life-without-parole options. Juvenile courts cannot impose sentences of death (*Roper v. Simmons*) or life without parole (*Miller v. Alabama*).

Summary

1. Distinguish among the basic components of the juvenile justice system and explain how juveniles are processed differently from adult offenders.

The juvenile justice system is a civil entity that parallels closely the criminal justice system, particularly in how juveniles are processed. Juvenile courts have jurisdiction over all juveniles who commit delinquency, or acts that would be crimes if adults committed them. Juveniles are any persons who have not reached the age of their majority or adulthood.

Some similarities and differences between juvenile courts and criminal courts have been described. As previously noted, juvenile courts are civil, while criminal courts process adults who are charged with committing felonies and misdemeanors. The consequences of a conviction in criminal court result in a criminal record, whereas civil consequences from juvenile court adjudications are largely noncriminal and are expunged from one's record upon attaining adulthood. All criminal courts are courts of record and juvenile courts are not.

Both types of courts are adversarial, and both use the "beyond a reasonable doubt" standard of proof. Juvenile courts use this standard only when a juvenile is in jeopardy of losing his/her liberty or may be confined for any period of time. Criminal courts have a broader range of punishments, including life without the possibility of parole and the death penalty, which are beyond the scope of a juvenile court's jurisdiction. In most states, jury trials for juveniles are not permitted except with judicial approval. Juvenile court proceedings are generally less formal compared with those of criminal courts, although in recent years, this difference has rapidly diminished.

2. Compare and contrast the differences between delinquents and status offenders and the reasons for making such distinctions.

Juvenile delinquents are distinguished from status offenders, who commit acts that would not be crimes if adults committed them. Status offenders may be runaways, truants, curfew violators, or those who engage in underage drinking. In more than a few jurisdictions, social welfare agencies and human services have gradually been granted jurisdiction over status offenders because of the nature of their offending. Juvenile courts are interested in repeat status offenders because they believe that their offending may become more serious. Continued offending, however, also seems to be associated with the amount of contact youths have with juvenile courts. This is referred to as stigmatization or a labeling effect. Divestiture of jurisdiction and deinstitutionalization of juvenile status offenders have been advocated for as methods by which to reduce the stigmatizing effect of court contact and processing.

3. Understand the jurisdiction of juvenile courts and the influence of parens patriae *on court actions.*

The juvenile justice process has been influenced largely by the doctrine of *parens patriae*, which originated in England during the 1500s. The king of England utilized chancellors in different shires or English counties to make decisions on his behalf relating to all juveniles who committed various offenses. These decisions were most often influenced by what would be in the children's best interests. Today, juvenile courts make decisions according to these same criteria, although bureaucratization and extended legal rights for juveniles have caused these courts to focus more on due process and less on one's best interests. Nevertheless, these courts continue to perpetuate the *parens patriae* doctrine informally, and this practice, the traditional approach to juvenile justice, is largely individualized. Many juvenile courts regard their functions as largely treatment centered rather than punishment centered.

4. Summarize the history of the juvenile court.

Juvenile court history is relatively brief. The first juvenile court in the United States was established in 1899 in Illinois under the Juvenile Court Act. By the 1940s, all states had juvenile courts. Prior to 1899, juveniles were subject to a wide variety of sanctions by different bodies, such as children's tribunals. Many juveniles whose parents worked for long hours in factories to earn a living wandered city streets during daytime hours. Some of these juveniles were institutionalized for short periods as a punishment for vagrancy or begging.

Child savers emerged, largely from the middle and upper classes, and these persons often established shelters or temporary homes where idle juveniles could be accommodated safely and removed from the dangers of the streets. During the late 1800s, many persons and agencies became concerned and involved with child welfare matters, and the gradual progression to a full-fledged juvenile court was realized.

Early juvenile court proceedings were different from criminal court proceedings. These proceedings initiated with a petitioner claiming the juvenile should be declared delinquent, or dependent, or neglected, and a judge who would have the ultimate authority to make decisions about juveniles according to what the judges believed was in their best interest. Juveniles had no rights, no attorneys, and were not permitted to call witnesses or testify on their own behalf.

In recent years, juvenile court processing has become more formalized. Thus, the presence of defense counsel, an adversarial approach, and in some cases jury trials sometimes characterize juvenile court proceedings today. Some have argued that this increased formalization and adherence to Rules of Procedure have led to greater bureaucratization and criminalization which is not in the best interest of juveniles.

5. *Apply your knowledge of influence of due process upon juvenile offender processing to examine the legal rights of juveniles.*

In 1974, the Juvenile Justice and Delinquency Prevention Act was passed that sought to deinstitutionalize status offenders. At the time, it was customary for juvenile courts to institutionalize both delinquents and status offenders, and some states continue to do so. Today, most states have effectively removed status offenders from institutions where they were formerly housed together with qualitatively more serious delinquent offenders. Many juvenile courts have divested themselves of their jurisdiction over status offenders as well, thus giving greater jurisdictional power to social services and social welfare agencies who often supervise those charged with status offenses. During the mid-1960s and for the next 30 years, several Supreme Court cases granted significant rights to juveniles regarding due process. Although the *parens patriae* philosophy continues to be somewhat influential in juvenile proceedings, the U.S. Supreme Court has vested youths with certain constitutional rights.

The *Gault* decision, for example, granted juveniles a right to a notice of charges, the right to counsel, the right to confront and cross-examine witnesses, and the Fifth Amendment right to invoke the privilege against self-incrimination. The *Winship* decision changed the standard of proof to beyond a reasonable doubt to establish guilt for juveniles. The *Kent* decision entitled juveniles to a waiver hearing if their case is going to be transferred to an adult court where they also have the right to have an attorney present. In *Breed v. Jones*, the court ruled that juveniles cannot be adjudicated on a given charge in juvenile court and then sent to criminal court to face the same charge as this would violate the double jeopardy clause. With more due process rights, however, juveniles are also treated like adults in other ways. For example, under the *Schall v. Martin* decision, juveniles can be detained. To date, however, the majority of states do not grant juveniles the right to a jury trial.

Key Terms

children in need of supervision (CHINS) 269
child savers 271
criminalization 270
curfew violators 267
deinstitutionalization 268
deinstitutionalization of status offenders (DSO) 268
divestiture of jurisdiction 268
due process courts 272
Illinois Juvenile Court Act 270
intake 272

intake officer 272
Juveniles 266
juvenile court 266
juvenile court jurisdiction 266
juvenile delinquency 267
juvenile delinquent 267
Juvenile Justice and Delinquency Prevention Act of 1974 (JJDPA) 268
Office of Juvenile Justice and Delinquency Prevention (OJJDP) 268

parens patriae 269
petition 273
prosecutorial waiver 273
referral 272
reformatory 271
runaways 267
Society for the Prevention of Pauperism 271
status offenders 267
stigmatize 268
truants 267
juveniles 266

Critical Thinking Exercises

1. What are some reasons why the Juvenile Justice and Delinquency Prevention Act of 1974 called for the deinstitutionalization of status offenders? What is divestiture of jurisdiction?
2. Why does common law set the minimum age of juveniles at seven years? What would happen if a child younger than seven committed a crime? Why do children in need of supervision fall under juvenile court jurisdiction?
3. What are some arguments for granting juveniles more due process rights and formalization of the juvenile court? What are some of the arguments against this?

Case Study Decision-Making Exercise

Parens patriae affords juvenile court judges with a great deal of discretion in dealing with juvenile offenders under the rehabilitative goals of the juvenile justice system. Of the roughly one and a half million cases that are referred to the juvenile justice system each year, about one-third (450,000) result in dismissals. Another 300,000 are given nominal sanctions. What do you think of these statistics? Does this mean that juvenile court judges are being too lenient or could it mean that schools, parents, and law enforcement are referring too many cases where the offenses are minor or where there is little evidence?

Concept Review Questions

1. Distinguish between a juvenile delinquent and a status offender. What has the federal government done to keep status offenders out of jails?
2. What is the jurisdiction of juvenile courts?
3. What is the doctrine of *parens patriae*? Why is it significant in examining the actions of juvenile courts today? In what ways does *parens patriae* influence judicial decision making?
4. What is a referral? Who can make referrals? What are their purposes?
5. Identify three major cases involving juvenile rights. What are the major rights conveyed in the cases you have identified?
6. What are some general differences between criminal courts and juvenile courts?
7. Under what circumstances can juveniles have jury trials in juvenile courts?

Suggested Readings

1. Catherine Y. Kim, Daniel J. Losen, and Damon T. Hewitt (2010). *The School-to-Prison Pipeline: Structuring Legal Reform.* New York, NY: Oxford University Press.
2. Lynn Bye, Michelle E. Alvarez, Janet Haynes, and Cindy E. Sweigert (2010). *Truancy Prevention and Intervention: A Practical Guide.* New York, NY: Oxford University Press.
3. B. K. Applegate, R. King Davis, and F. T. Cullen (2009). "Reconsidering Child Saving: The Extent and Correlates of Public Support for Excluding Youths From the Juvenile Court." *Crime and Delinquency* **55**:51–77.
4. Charlotte Lyn Bright, Patricia L. Kohl, and Melissa Jonson-Reid (2014). "Females in the Juvenile Justice System: Who are They and How do They Fare?" *Crime and Delinquency* **60**:106–125.
5. Rebecca House (2013). "Seen But Not Heard: Using Judicial Waiver to Save the Juvenile Justice System and Our Kids." *University of Toledo Law Review* **45**:149–179.

Vchalup/Fotolia

12 Juvenile Courts
Adjudication and Disposition

LEARNING OBJECTIVES

As the result of reading this chapter, you will have accomplished the following objectives:

 Examine the role of juvenile court prosecutors and the changing nature of juvenile court proceedings as defense counsels are increasingly used in most jurisdictions.

2 Explain juvenile court adjudicatory proceedings and compare and contrast the different dispositions available to juvenile judges.

3 Understand the waiver, transfer, and certification processes, how these procedures move juveniles to criminal court jurisdiction, and the implications of these decisions for juvenile offenders.

 Understand blended sentencing statutes and how these statutory provisions have changed the nature of juvenile sentencing and rehabilitation.

 Summarize teen courts and their purpose and focus.

 Describe several important trends in juvenile justice that have significance for how juveniles are processed by juvenile courts.

In the crime control era of the 1980s, many states expanded their juvenile transfer laws in an effort to "get tough" on juvenile crime. These expansions included increasing the number of offenses for which juveniles could be transferred to adult court, lowering the age at which juveniles could be transferred to adult court, and increasing prosecutorial discretion in transfer decisions. According to a report by the Office of Juvenile Justice and Delinquency Prevention (OJJDP), the number of juvenile cases transferred to adult court increased from just over 7,000 in 1988 to roughly 11,700 in 1992 which only represented 1.2 and 1.6 percent of juvenile cases, respectively (Butts 1994). The report also cites that of the cases transferred, 66 percent were nonviolent offenders. The theory behind expanding the transfer provisions was based on a deterrence assumption that harsher adult sanctions would deter juveniles from committing future offenses (Redding 2010). Recent studies, comparing the recidivism rates of juveniles who were transferred versus a matched group of those who remained in the juvenile justice system, revealed that the transferred group had higher recidivism rates; 49 percent of the transferred juveniles were rearrested versus only 35 percent of the juveniles who remained in juvenile court (Lanza-Kaduce, Lane, Bishop, and Frazier 2005). When partitioned by offense type, the greatest recidivism differences between the two groups were for violent offenders; 24 percent of those transferred reoffended versus only 16 percent of those who remained in the juvenile court. As such, today, the expansion of transfer policies has been seriously questioned, especially since juveniles housed in adult facilities are more likely to be victimized through assault and sexual assault than adult offenders (Mulvey and Schubert 2012). What do you think? Do harsher punishments and prison time in adult prisons scare juveniles straight? Or does treating juveniles more harshly and opening them up to victimization in adult prison have a criminogenic effect? In other words, make it more likely that they will continue to engage in criminal activity after they are released.

▶ Introduction

Adjudication is a juvenile court judicial decision that the facts alleged against the juvenile, either by petition or by other means, are true or not true. If judges decide that the facts are true and that the juvenile committed one or more delinquent acts, one of several different kinds of dispositions is imposed. This chapter begins with the different types of dispositions that are available to juvenile court judges. These dispositions are nominal, conditional, and custodial. These dispositions roughly equate respectively with verbal warnings, probation, or incarceration in a secure facility. The adjudicatory process is described, as well as the different types of dispositions imposed on juveniles by juvenile court judges.

Juveniles have the right to due process that vests them with many of the same rights as adults charged with crimes. All juveniles are entitled to counsel. If the juvenile or the juvenile's family/guardian is indigent, then an attorney will be appointed to represent the juvenile. Cases against juveniles may be plea bargained in much the same way that adult cases are plea bargained. Thus, many juvenile cases are never brought before the juvenile court judge for a formal adjudicatory hearing. At least 11 states make provisions for jury trials for juveniles if they request them. Jury trials for juveniles are not a matter of right, but rather, certain states extend the jury trial privilege to certain juveniles depending on their age, offense seriousness, and other important and relevant criteria.

About 1 percent of all juveniles referred to the juvenile court each year are transferred, waived, or certified to the jurisdiction of criminal courts, where the juveniles are treated as adults. Transfers, waivers, or certifications make it possible for criminal courts to impose

transfers proceedings where the jurisdiction over juvenile offenders shifts from the juvenile court to criminal court.

waiver, waiver of jurisdiction made by motion, the transfer of jurisdiction over a juvenile to a criminal court where the juvenile is subject to adult criminal penalties. Includes judicial, prosecutorial, and legislative waivers. Also known as "certification" or "transfer."

harsher sanctions against juveniles, such as the death penalty or life imprisonment. Such sanctions are beyond the jurisdiction of juvenile courts. The waiver process is described, and various positive and adverse implications for juveniles are discussed.

There are four major types of waiver actions. These include judicial waivers, prosecutorial waivers, statutory exclusion or legislative or automatic waivers, and demand waivers. Each of these types of waivers is defined and discussed. All juveniles who are transferred to criminal court jurisdiction are entitled to a hearing before they are waived. The implications of such hearings are described.

In recent decades, most states have evolved blended sentencing statutes. The next section of this chapter examines several types of blended sentencing statutes whereby either juvenile court judges or criminal court judges may hear and decide juvenile cases and impose either juvenile sanctions, criminal sentences, or both, depending upon the jurisdiction. The advantages and disadvantages of blended sentencing statutes will be described. The chapter concludes with an examination of several important trends in juvenile justice and a discussion of the favorable and unfavorable implications of these trends for affected juveniles.

▶ Adjudicatory Proceedings

Most of the physical trappings of criminal courts are present in juvenile courts, including the judge's bench, tables for the prosecution and defense, and a witness stand. Juvenile court judges have almost absolute discretion in how their courts are conducted. Juvenile defendants may or may not be granted a trial by jury, if one is requested. Few states permit jury trials for juveniles in juvenile courts, according to legislative mandates. After hearing the evidence presented by both sides in any juvenile proceeding, the judge decides or adjudicates the matter in an adjudication hearing. Adjudication is a judgment or action on the petition filed with the court by others. If the petition alleges delinquency on the part of certain juveniles, the judge determines whether the juveniles are delinquent or not delinquent. If the petition alleges that the juveniles involved are dependent, neglected, or otherwise in need of care by agencies or others, the judge decides the matter. If the adjudicatory proceeding fails to support the facts alleged in the petition filed with the court, the case is dismissed and the youth is freed. If the adjudicatory proceeding supports the allegations, then the judge must sentence the juvenile or order a particular disposition (Harris 2004).

Dispositions

Twelve dispositions are available to juvenile court judges, if the facts alleged in petitions are upheld. These dispositions may be grouped into (1) nominal, (2) conditional, or (3) custodial options. Nominal dispositions are the least punitive of the three major courses of action available to juvenile court judges. These are usually verbal warnings or reprimands. Release to the custody of parents or legal guardians completes the juvenile court action.

All conditional dispositions are probationary options. Youths are placed on probation and required to comply with certain conditions during the probationary period. Conditional options or dispositions usually provide for an act or acts on the part of juveniles to be fulfilled as conditions of the sentence imposed. If juveniles have been adjudicated as delinquent and if the delinquency involved damage to a victim's property or bodily harm, restitution to victims may be required to pay for the property or medical bills (Wood 2004). Various kinds of community services are performed by juveniles, such as cutting courthouse lawns, cleaning up city parks, and cleaning debris from city highways or public areas. Group or individual therapy may be required of certain juveniles who exhibit psychological or social maladjustment. If some juveniles are alcohol or drug dependent, they may be required to participate in various recovery programs.

adjudication hearing formal proceeding involving a prosecuting attorney and a defense attorney where evidence is presented and a juvenile's status or condition is determined by the juvenile court judge.

adjudication legal resolution of a dispute; when a juvenile is declared delinquent or a status offender, the matter has been resolved; when an offender has been convicted or acquitted, the matter at issue (guilt or innocence) has been concluded by either a judge or jury.

nominal dispositions juvenile court outcome in which juvenile is warned or verbally reprimanded, but returned to custody of parents.

conditional dispositions decisions by juvenile court judge authorizing payment of fines, community service, restitution, or some other penalty after an adjudication of delinquency has been made.

custodial dispositions outcomes by juvenile judge following adjudication of juvenile as delinquent. Includes nonsecure custody (in a foster home, community agency, farm, camp) or secure custody (in a detention center, industrial, reform school).

nonsecure custody, confinement a facility that emphasizes the care and treatment of youths without the need to place constraints to ensure public protection.

secure custody, confinement incarceration of juvenile offender in a facility that restricts movement in the community. Similar to an adult penal facility involving total incarceration.

foster home dwelling including family where child is placed, usually where such child is from an abusive household or without parents or legal guardians.

group home facilities for juveniles that provide limited supervision and support. Juveniles live in homelike environment with other juveniles and participate in therapeutic programs and counseling. Considered nonsecure custodial. *See also* foster home.

camp, ranch any of several types of similar correctional confinement facilities for adults or juveniles, usually located in rural areas.

Custodial dispositions are either nonsecure custody or confinement or secure custody. Nonsecure custody consists of placing certain juveniles into a foster home, group home, or camp, ranch, or schools. These are temporary measures often designed to make more permanent arrangements for juvenile placement later. Juveniles have freedom of movement, and they can generally participate in school and other youthful activities. For juveniles, secure custody is often the last resort considered by most juvenile court judges. There is a general reluctance among judges to incarcerate youths because of adverse labeling effects. Furthermore, there are increasing numbers of alternatives to incarceration within communities. Judges are increasingly apprised of these programs and are assigning more youths to them in lieu of industrial school placements (Kupchik 2004).

Changing Juvenile Court Practices

Confidentiality of Juvenile Court Records and Proceedings

Most courts do not allow open hearings in juvenile or family court proceedings to protect the identity of the juvenile. Most states will allow release of the names of the juvenile if he or she is charged with a serious crime or is being transferred to adult court. Most states will release court records to interested parties. In fact, all states currently make available juvenile court records to any party showing a legitimate interest. In such cases, information is ordinarily obtained through a court order. Fingerprinting and photographing of juveniles is conducted routinely in most states. Half the states require registration of all juvenile offenders when they enter new jurisdictions. Also, most states presently have state repositories of juvenile records and other relevant information about juvenile offending. Seventeen states prohibited sealing or expunging juvenile court records after certain dates, such as one's age of majority or adulthood (Champion 2009). Therefore, juveniles today are considerably more likely to have their offenses known to the public in one form or another.

The protections previously enjoyed by juveniles are rapidly disappearing. The greater formality of juvenile proceedings as well as their openness to others may restrict the discretion of juvenile court judges, although this limitation is not particularly an undesirable one. This is because juvenile court judge decision making has often been individualized, and individualized decision making is inherently discriminatory. With more open proceedings, less individualization is evident, thus making due process a greater priority for juvenile court judges. Theoretically, at least, more open proceedings are fairer proceedings.

The Prosecution Decision

The juvenile justice system in general has been slow in its case processing of juvenile offenders. In fact, delays in filing charges against juveniles and the eventual adjudicatory hearing are chronic in many jurisdictions. Juveniles arrested for various types of offenses may wait a year or longer in some jurisdictions before their cases are heard by juvenile court judges. Juvenile court prosecutors may delay filing charges against particular juveniles for a variety of reasons. The most obvious reasons for delays—court case backlogs, crowded court dockets, insufficient prosecutorial staff, too much paperwork—are not always valid reasons. In many instances, the actors themselves are at fault. In short, prosecutors and judges may simply be plodding along at a slow pace, because of their own personal dispositions and work habits. It has been illustrated that in many jurisdictions where prosecutors and judges have aggressively tackled their caseload problems and forced functionaries to work faster, juvenile caseload processing has been greatly accelerated. Thus, the time between a juvenile's arrest and disposition has been greatly shortened because of individual decision making and not because of any organizational constraints or overwork (Champion 2009).

The Sixth Amendment right to a speedy trial does not extend to juvenile court proceedings. A number of states, however, have enacted statutes or put court rules in place to encourage timely case processing (Ridgeway and Listenbee 2014). However, in 30 states in 2005, juvenile court prosecutors were at liberty to file charges against juvenile offenders whenever they decided. No binding legislative provisions were applicable to these actors to force them to act promptly and bring a youth's case before the juvenile court. In the meantime, 20 states have established time limits that cannot be exceeded between the time of a juvenile's court referral and the filing of charges by prosecutors.

Defense Counsels as Advocates for Juveniles

Attorneys for Juveniles as a Matter of Right

Juveniles are entitled to attorneys at all stages of juvenile proceedings. Despite this safeguard, attorney representation for juveniles in juvenile courts in most jurisdictions is less than adequate. Feld and Schaefer (2010) cite that even decades after the *Gault* decision, states have failed to set up provisions for adequate defense representation in juvenile cases.

Defense Counsel and Due Process Rights for Juveniles

The manifest function of defense attorneys in juvenile courts is to ensure that **due process** is fulfilled by all participants. Defense attorneys are the primary advocates of fairness for juveniles who are charged with crimes or other types of offenses (Rodriguez and Armstrong 2004). Minors, particularly very young youths, are more susceptible to the persuasiveness of adults.

> **due process** basic constitutional right to a fair trial, presumption of innocence until guilt is proven beyond a reasonable doubt, the opportunity to be heard, to be aware of a matter that is pending, to make an informed choice whether to acquiesce or contest, and to provide the reasons for such a choice before a judicial official.

Are Attorneys Being Used More by Juvenile Defendants?

Yes. However, adequate defense has still not been achieved as fewer than half of juvenile defendants are represented in some states, and juvenile defenders like their adult counterparts have high caseloads which do not allow them to spend much time with clients.

Do Defense Counsels Make a Difference in Juvenile Case Dispositions?

Having an attorney to represent you generally makes a difference in the case disposition. But not all dispositions are favorable for juveniles. The presence of attorneys may heighten juvenile court formality. In the processing of juveniles, attorney presence may cause intake officers to take sterner measures with juveniles who ordinarily would be dismissed from the system. More than a few intake officers, for instance, are intimidated by attorneys, if present. If an intake officer would be inclined to divert a particular case from the juvenile justice system because of his/her judgment that the youth will probably not reoffend, this diversion decision may not be selected if an attorney is present to represent the juvenile's interests. The intake officer may feel that the prosecutor of juvenile court judge should decide the case. However, in an otherwise attorney-free environment, the intake officer would act differently. Thus, an attorney's presence or absence may cause intake officers to react differently and make decisions that are better or worse for juveniles charged with delinquency or status offenses.

Defense Counsel as Guardians *Ad Litem*

Defense counsels perform additional responsibilities as they attempt to ensure that the best interests of their clients are served in ways that will protect children from parents who abuse them (Kupchik 2004; Ward 2004). A **guardian *ad litem*** may be appointed by the court in which a particular litigation is pending to represent a youth, ward, or unborn person in that particular litigation (Williams, Rodeheaver, and Guerrero 2004). Most juvenile court jurisdictions have guardian *ad litem* programs, where interested persons serve in this capacity. In some cases, defense counsels for youths perform the dual role of defense counsel and the youth's guardian *ad litem*. Guardians *ad litem* are supposed to work in ways that will benefit those they represent, and such guardians provide legal protection from others. Defense counsel working as guardians *ad litem* may act to further the child's best interests, despite a child's contrary requests or demands.

> **guardian *ad litem*** is a person appointed by the court to represent a juvenile in pending litigation.

Juvenile Plea Bargaining and the Role of Defense Counsel

Many juveniles plea bargain with juvenile court prosecutors (Helms et al. 2004). Plea bargaining is an invaluable tool with which to eliminate case backlogs that might occur in some of the larger juvenile courts. Most frequently sought by defense counsel are charge reductions against their clients by prosecutors. Defense counsels are interested in reducing the stigma of a serious, negative juvenile court profile of their youthful clients by seeking reduced charges from prosecutors (Burruss and Kempf-Leonard 2002). Prosecutors benefit because plea agreements would decrease case processing time.

▶ Transfers, Waivers, and Certifications

A transfer means changing the jurisdiction over certain juvenile offenders to another jurisdiction, usually from juvenile court jurisdiction to criminal court jurisdiction. A transfer is also known as a waiver, referring to a change of jurisdiction from the authority of juvenile court judges to criminal court judges. Prosecutors or juvenile court judges decide that in some cases, juveniles should be waived or transferred to the jurisdiction of criminal courts (Bishop et al. 2004).

In Utah, juveniles are waived or transferred to criminal courts through a process known as certification (Listwan and Miethe 2004). A certification is a formal procedure whereby the state declares the juvenile to be an adult for the purpose of a criminal prosecution in a criminal court (Sridharan et al. 2004). The results of certifications are the same as for waivers or transfers. Thus, certifications, waivers, and transfers result in juvenile offenders being subject to the jurisdiction of criminal courts where they can be prosecuted as though they were adult offenders. A 13-year-old murderer, for instance, might be transferred to criminal court for a criminal prosecution on the murder charge (Merlo and Benekos 2004).

The Rationale for Transfers, Waivers, or Certifications

The basic rationale underlying the use of waivers is that the most serious juvenile offenders will be transferred to the jurisdiction of criminal courts where the harshest punishments, including capital punishment, may be imposed as sanctions (Jordan 2004b). A listing of reasons for the use of transfers, waivers, or certifications includes the following:

1. To make it possible for harsher punishments to be imposed.
2. To provide just deserts and proportionately severe punishments on those juveniles who deserve such punishments by their more violent actions.
3. To foster fairness in administering punishments according to one's serious offending.
4. To hold serious or violent offenders more accountable for what they have done.
5. To show other juveniles who contemplate committing serious offenses that the system works and that harsh punishments can be expected if serious offenses are committed.
6. To provide a deterrent to decrease juvenile violence.
7. To overcome the traditional leniency of juvenile courts and provide more realistic sanctions.
8. To make youths realize the seriousness of their offending and induce remorse and acceptance of responsibility.

The Characteristics of Transferred Juveniles

In 2004, there were 13,200 youths who were transferred to criminal court. Most juveniles transferred were male, with only 625 females (4.7 percent) being waived (Bureau of Justice Statistics 2005). About 7,200 (54 percent) of all transferred juveniles were black or other minority, despite the fact that white juveniles comprised about 66 percent of all cases referred to juvenile court. Furthermore, those charged with person offenses and waived to criminal court made up only 41 percent of those transferred (Johnson, Bannister, and Alm 2004). About 44 percent of those charged with property or public order offenses were waived to criminal courts, while about 14 percent of those waived were charged with drug offenses (Bureau of Justice Statistics 2005).

Youngest Ages at Which Juveniles Can Be Transferred to Criminal Court

In 1987, all federal districts and 15 states indicated no specified age for transferring juveniles to criminal courts for processing. One state, Vermont, specified age 10 as the minimum age at which a juvenile could be waived. Montana established age 12 as the earliest age for a juvenile waiver. Fourteen states used age 14 as the youngest transfer age, while seven states and the District of Columbia set the minimum transfer age at 15, and seven states used the minimum transfer age of 16. During the 1990s, however, more states moved to have their juvenile age ranges lowered for transfers or waivers. Table 12-1 ■ shows the various states that have modified or enacted changes in their transfer provisions for juveniles during the 1992–1995 period.

TABLE 12-1 States Modifying or Enacting Transfer Provisions, 1996–2005

Type of transfer provision	Action taken (number of states)	States making changes	Examples
Discretionary waiver	Added crimes (7 states)	DE, KY, LA, MT, NV, RI, WA	Kentucky: 1996 provision permits the juvenile court to transfer a juvenile to criminal court if he/she is 14 years old and charged with a felony committed with a firearm.
	Lowered age limit (4 states)	CO, DE, HI, VA	Hawaii: 1997 provision adds language that allows waiver of a minor at any age (previously 16) if charged with first- or second-degree murder (or attempts) and there is no evidence that the person is committable to an institution for the mentally defective or mentally ill.
	Added or modified prior record provisions (4 states)	FL, HI, IN, KY	Florida: 1997 legislation requires that if the juvenile is 14 at the time of a fourth felony, and certain conditions apply, the state's attorney must ask the court to transfer him or her and certify the child as an adult or must provide written reasons for not making such a request.
Presumptive waiver	Enacted provisions (2 states)	KS, UT	Kansas: 1996 legislation shifts the burden of proof to the child to rebut the presumption that the child is an adult.
Direct file	Enacted or modified (8 states)	AR, AZ, CO, FL, GA, MA, MT, OK	Colorado: 1996 legislation adds vehicular homicide, vehicular assault, and felonious arson to direct file statute.
Statutory exclusion	Enacted provision (2 states)	AZ, MA	Arizona: 1997 legislation establishes exclusion for 15- to 17-year-olds charged with certain violent felonies.
	Added crimes (12 states)	AL, AK, DE, GA, IL, IN, OK, OR, SC, SD, UT, WA	Georgia: 1997 legislation adds crime of battery if victim is a teacher or other school personnel to list of designated felonies.
	Lowered age limit (1 state)	DE	Delaware: 1996 legislation lowers from 16 to 15 the age for which the offense of possession of a firearm during the commission of a felony is automatically prosecuted in criminal court.
	Added lesser-included offense (1 state)	IN	Indiana: 1997 legislation lists exclusion offenses, including any offenses that may be joined with the listed offenses.

Source: Torbet, Patricia and Linda Szymanski (1998). State Legislative Response to Violent Juvenile Crime: 1996–1997 Update. Washington, DC: U.S. Department of Justice, 1998:5. Updated 2005 by author.

Inspecting Table 12-1, under judicial waiver modifications, 11 states lowered the age limit at which juveniles can be transferred to criminal court. One example of a significant age modification is Missouri, where the minimum age for juvenile transfers was lowered from 14 to 12 for any felony. In the case of Texas, the minimum transfer age was lowered from 15 to 10. Virginia lowered the transfer age from 15 to 14. Table 12-1 also shows that other modifications were made to get tough toward juvenile offenders. Ten states added crimes to the list of those qualifying youths for transfer to criminal courts. In six states, the age of criminal accountability was lowered, while 24 states authorized additional crimes to be included that would automatically direct that the criminal court would have jurisdiction rather than the juvenile court.

Types of Waivers

Four types of waiver actions include (1) prosecutorial waivers, (2) judicial/discretionary waivers, (3) demand waivers, and (4) legislative or automatic waivers.

Prosecutorial waivers are also known as direct file or concurrent jurisdiction. Thus, under direct file, the prosecutor has the sole authority to decide whether a particular juvenile case will be heard in criminal court or juvenile court. In Florida, one of the states where prosecutors have concurrent jurisdiction, prosecutors may file extremely serious charges (e.g., murder, rape, aggravated assault, and robbery) against youths in criminal courts and present cases to grand juries for indictment action. Or prosecutors may decide to file the same cases in the juvenile court.

The largest numbers of waivers from juvenile to criminal court annually come about as the result of direct judicial action. Judicial waivers give the juvenile court judge the authority to decide whether to waive jurisdiction and transfer the case to criminal court. Known also as discretionary waivers, judicial waivers typically involve a juvenile court judge's consideration of various criteria, including the juvenile's age, current offense, criminal history, and amenability to rehabilitation. This particular type of transfer is invoked following a motion by the prosecutor (Champion 2004).

Legislative waivers or automatic waivers are statutorily prescribed actions that provide for a specified list of crimes to be excluded from the jurisdiction of juvenile courts, where offending juveniles are within a specified age range, and where the resulting action gives criminal courts immediate jurisdiction over these juveniles. By the mid-1980s, 36 states excluded certain types of offenses from juvenile court jurisdiction. These excluded offenses were either very minor or very serious, ranging from traffic or fishing violations to rape or murder. Also, many state jurisdictions have made provisions for automatic transfers of juveniles to criminal court. Among those states with automatic transfer provisions are Washington, New York, and Illinois (Steiner, Hemmens, and Bell 2004).

Automatic or legislative waivers are also known as statutory exclusion or mandatory transfer. Statutory exclusion generally refers to provisions that automatically exclude certain juvenile offenders from the juvenile court's original jurisdiction (Champion 2009). An example of statutory exclusion is to simply lower the upper age of original juvenile court jurisdiction from 18 to 17 or 16. States with statutory exclusion make provisions for the statutory exclusion of offenders of particular ages and who are alleged to have committed certain types of serious offenses. For instance, a state may prohibit juvenile courts from hearing any case involving a 15-year-old murderer. The age and offense are combined to create the statutory exclusion.

Under certain conditions and in selected jurisdictions, juveniles may submit motions for demand waiver. Demand waiver actions are requests or motions filed by juveniles and their attorneys to have their cases transferred from juvenile courts to criminal courts. If a juvenile's case is heard in a criminal court, the juvenile is entitled to the full range of rights available to adults charged with crimes.

Finally, 13 states, including the District of Columbia, have established presumptive waiver provisions, which require that certain offenders should be waived unless they can prove that they are suited for juvenile rehabilitation (Champion 2009). Essentially, a juvenile is considered waived to criminal court unless he/she can prove to be suitable candidates for rehabilitation. This rebuttable presumptive waiver, where the burden of proving one's rehabilitation potential rests with the juvenile and his/her attorney rather than the prosecutor, is used especially in those instances where juveniles have a history of frequent offending or where they have committed serious or violent offenses. It is difficult for any defense attorney to overcome this presumption if the juvenile client has committed an especially serious offense and has a prior record of violent offending.

Once an Adult/Always an Adult

The once an adult/always an adult provision is perhaps the most serious and long-lasting for affected juvenile offenders. This provision means that once juveniles at any age have been waived to the criminal court for processing, or once juveniles have been convicted and sentenced for one or more crimes by a criminal court, they are forever after considered adults for the purpose of criminal prosecutions.

Waiver and Reverse Waiver Hearings

All juveniles who are waived to criminal court for processing are entitled to a hearing on the waiver if they request one (Champion 2009). A waiver hearing is a formal proceeding designed to determine whether the waiver action taken by the judge or prosecutor is the correct action, and that the juvenile should be transferred to criminal court. Waiver hearings are normally conducted before the juvenile court judge. These hearings are to some extent evidentiary, since a case must be made for why criminal courts should have jurisdiction in any specific instance.

Reverse Waiver Hearings

For those jurisdictions with automatic or legislative waiver provisions, waiver actions may be contested through the use of reverse waiver hearings. Reverse waiver hearings are conducted before criminal court judges to determine whether to send the juvenile's case back to juvenile court. Reverse waiver hearings in those jurisdictions with automatic transfer provisions are also conducted in the presence of judges (Champion 2009).

Implications of Waiver Hearings for Juveniles

Arguments for Having one's Case Heard in Juvenile Court

Among the positive benefits of having one's case heard in juvenile court are the following:

1. Juvenile court proceedings are civil, not criminal; thus, juveniles do not acquire criminal records.
2. Juveniles are less likely to receive sentences of incarceration.
3. Compared with criminal court judges, juvenile court judges have considerably more discretion in influencing a youth's life chances prior to or at the time of adjudication.
4. Juvenile courts are traditionally more lenient than criminal courts.
5. There is considerably more public sympathy extended to those who are processed in the juvenile justice system, despite the general public advocacy for a greater get-tough policy.

---

statutory exclusion provisions that automatically exclude certain juveniles and offenses from the jurisdiction of the juvenile courts; for example, murder, aggravated rape, and armed robbery.

mandatory transfer automatic waiver of certain juveniles to criminal court on the basis of (1) their age and (2) the seriousness of their offense; for example, a 17-year-old in Illinois who allegedly committed homicide would be subject to mandatory transfer to criminal court for the purpose of a criminal prosecution.

demand waiver request by juveniles to have their cases transferred from juvenile courts to criminal courts.

presumptive waiver type of judicial waiver where burden of proof shifts from the state to the juvenile to contest whether youth is transferred to criminal court.

once an adult/ always an adult provision that once a juvenile has been transferred to criminal court to be prosecuted as an adult, regardless of the criminal court outcome, the juvenile can never be subject to the jurisdiction of juvenile courts in the future; in short, the juvenile, once transferred, will always be treated as an adult if future crimes are committed, even though the youth is still not of adult age.

6. Compared with criminal courts, juvenile courts do not have as elaborate an information-exchange apparatus to determine whether certain juveniles have been adjudicated delinquent by juvenile courts in other jurisdictions.

7. Life imprisonment and the death penalty lie beyond the jurisdiction of juvenile court judges, and they cannot impose these harsh sentences.

Arguments Against Having One's Case Heard in Juvenile Court

Juvenile courts are not perfect, however, and they may be disadvantageous to many youthful offenders (Ward 2004). Some of their major limitations are the following:

1. Juvenile court judges have the power to administer lengthy sentences of incarceration, not only for serious and dangerous offenders but also for status offenders as well.

2. In most states, juvenile courts are not required to provide juveniles with a trial by jury.

3. Because of their wide discretion in handling juveniles, judges may underpenalize a large number of those appearing before them on various charges.

4. Juveniles do not enjoy the same range of constitutional rights as adults in criminal courts.

▶ Criminal Court Processing of Juvenile Offenders

Arguments for and Against Having One's Case Tried in Criminal Court

When juveniles are transferred, waived, or certified to criminal court, then all rules and constitutional guarantees attach for them as well as for adults. The primary benefits for juveniles of being processed in criminal courts are as follows. Positively, depending upon the seriousness of the offenses alleged, a jury trial may be a matter of right. Adversely, periods of lengthy incarceration in minimum, medium, and maximum security facilities with adults become a real possibility. Also negatively, criminal courts in a majority of state jurisdictions may impose the death penalty in capital cases. A sensitive subject with most citizens is whether juveniles should receive the death penalty if convicted of capital crimes (Horton 2005). In recent years, the U.S. Supreme Court has addressed this issue specifically and ruled that in those states where the death penalty is imposed, the death penalty may be imposed as a punishment on any juvenile who was age 18 or older at the time the capital offense was committed (*Roper v. Simmons*, 2005). Positively, one's youthfulness works to the benefit of the defense. Jury sympathy is often evoked for a youth who has committed a horrible crime, since it can be shown that one's home life, sexual or physical abuse, and other factors are to blame for one's present plight. Therefore, a jury often favors leniency for young offenders.

What Do You Think?

Are juveniles disadvantaged by having their case waived or transferred to adult court? They are afforded more due process rights but the punishments could be harsher than in juvenile court. Although sometimes juveniles do not have a choice because the prosecutor or judge in the case makes a waiver determination, but what if you were an attorney representing a juvenile accused of a serious crime and the juvenile wanted to file a demand waiver to have the case heard by a jury in adult court. What would you advise the juvenile about the pros and cons of doing that?

► Blended Sentencing Statutes and the Get-Tough Movement

The most significant change in waiver patterns throughout the United States is that between 1992 and 1996, all but 10 states had adopted or modified laws making it easier to prosecute juveniles as adults in criminal courts (Champion 2009). Some of the reasons suggested for this tougher stance toward juvenile offending are that (1) juvenile rehabilitation has not been particularly effective at deterring juveniles from further offending, and (2) that the juvenile justice system is simply not punitive enough to impose the nature and types of punishments deserved by an increasingly violent juvenile offender population (Leiber, Fox, and Johnson 2004).

The major ways of making juveniles more amenable to criminal court punishment are to (1) lower the age at which they can be processed by criminal courts as adults, (2) expand the number of crimes that qualify juvenile offenders as adults for criminal court action, and (3) lower the age at which juveniles can be transferred to criminal courts for various offenses.

Blended Sentencing Statutes

Aaron Kupchik (2004) observes that in recent years, many states have legislatively redefined the juvenile court's purpose and role by diminishing the role of rehabilitation and heightening the importance of public safety, punishment, and accountability in the juvenile justice system. One of the most dramatic changes in the dispositional/sentencing options available to juvenile court judges is blended sentencing. Blended sentencing refers to the imposition of juvenile and/or adult correctional sanctions to cases involving serious and violent juvenile offenders who have been adjudicated in juvenile court or convicted in criminal court. Blended sentencing options are usually based on age or on a combination of age and offense (Champion 2009).

> **blended sentencing** any type of sentencing procedure where either a criminal or juvenile court judge can impose both juvenile and/or adult incarcerative penalties.

There are five basic models of blended sentencing. These include (1) juvenile–exclusive blend, (2) juvenile–inclusive blend, (3) juvenile–contiguous blend, (4) criminal–exclusive blend, and (5) criminal–inclusive blend.

The juvenile–exclusive blend involves a disposition by the juvenile court judge, which is either a disposition to the juvenile correctional system or to the adult correctional system, but not both. Thus, a judge might order a juvenile adjudicated delinquent for aggravated assault to serve three years in a juvenile industrial school; or the judge may order the adjudicated delinquent to serve three years in a prison for adults. The judge cannot impose *both* types of punishment under this model, however. In 1996, only one state, New Mexico, provided such a sentencing option for its juvenile court judges.

The juvenile–inclusive blend involves a disposition by the juvenile court judge, which is both a juvenile correctional sanction and an adult correctional sanction. In cases such as this, suppose the judge had adjudicated a 15-year-old juvenile delinquent on a charge of vehicular theft. The judge might impose a disposition of two years in a juvenile industrial school or reform school. Further, the judge might impose a sentence of three additional years in an adult penitentiary. However, the second sentence to the adult prison would typically be suspended, unless the juvenile violated one or more conditions of his/her original disposition and any conditions accompanying the disposition. Usually, this suspension period would run until the youth reaches age 18 or 21. If the offender were to commit a new offense or violate one or more program conditions, he/she would immediately be placed in the adult prison to serve the second sentence originally imposed.

The juvenile–contiguous blend involves a disposition by a juvenile court judge that may extend beyond the jurisdictional age limit of the offender. When the age limit of the juvenile court jurisdiction is reached, various procedures may be invoked to transfer the case to the jurisdiction of adult corrections. States with this juvenile–contiguous blend include Colorado, Massachusetts, Rhode Island, South Carolina, and Texas. In Texas, for example, a 15-year-old youth who has been adjudicated delinquent on a murder charge can be given an incarcerative term of from 1 to 30 years. At the time of the disposition in juvenile court, the youth is sent to the Texas Youth Commission and incarcerated in one of its facilities (similar to reform or industrial schools). By the time the youth reaches age 17½, the juvenile court must hold a transfer hearing to determine whether the youth should be sent to the Texas Department of Corrections. At this hearing, the youth may present evidence in his/her favor to show why he/she has become rehabilitated and no longer should be confined. However, evidence of institutional misconduct may be presented by the prosecutor to show why the youth should be incarcerated for more years in a Texas prison. This hearing functions as an incentive for the youth to behave and try to improve his/her behavior while confined in the juvenile facility.

The criminal–exclusive blend involves a decision by a criminal court judge to impose either a juvenile court sanction or a criminal court sanction, but not both. For example, a criminal court judge may hear the case of a 15-year-old youth who has been transferred to criminal court on a rape charge. The youth is convicted in a jury trial in criminal court. At this point, the judge has two options: the judge can sentence the offender to a prison term in an adult correctional facility, or the judge can impose an incarcerative sentence for the youth to serve in a juvenile facility. The judge may believe that the 15-year-old would be better off in a juvenile industrial school rather than an adult prison. The judge may impose a sentence of adult incarceration, but he/she may be inclined to place the youth in a facility where there are other youths in the offender's age range.

The criminal–inclusive blend involves a decision by the criminal court judge to impose both a juvenile penalty and a criminal sentence simultaneously. Again, as in the juvenile court–inclusive blend model, the latter criminal sentence may be suspended depending upon the good conduct of the juvenile during the juvenile punishment phase. For example, suppose a 12-year-old boy has been convicted of attempted murder. The boy participated in a drive-by shooting and is a gang member. The criminal court judge sentences the youth to a term of six years in a juvenile facility, such as an industrial school. At the same time, the judge imposes a sentence of 20 years on the youth to be spent in an adult correctional facility, following the 6-year sentence in the juvenile facility. However, the adult portion of the sentence may be suspended, depending upon whether the juvenile behaves or misbehaves during his 6-year industrial school incarceration. There is an additional twist to this blend. If the juvenile violates one or more conditions of his confinement in the juvenile facility, the judge has the power to revoke that sentence and invoke the sentence of incarceration in an adult facility. With good behavior, the youth can be free of the system following the period of juvenile confinement; the adult portion of the sentence is suspended if the youth deserves such leniency. Arkansas has the revocation power and ability to place youths in adult correctional facilities (Champion 2007).

▶ Teen Courts

Increasing numbers of jurisdictions are using **teen courts** as an alternative to juvenile court for determining one's guilt and punishment. Teen court proceedings are informal jury proceedings, where jurors consist of teenagers who hear and decide minor cases. First-offender cases, where status offenses or misdemeanors have been committed, are given priority in a different type of court setting involving one's peers as judges. Judges may divert minor cases to these teen courts. Adults function only as presiding judges, and these persons are often retired judges or lawyers who perform such services voluntarily and in their spare time. The focus of teen courts is upon therapeutic jurisprudence, with a strong emphasis upon rehabilitation (Judith Reed 2004). One objective of such courts is to teach empathy to

teen courts courts where proceedings are conducted by youths who try other youths for nonserious misdemeanors such as shoplifting or mischief; punishments are nonincarcerative and usually involve restitution of some form of victim compensation of community service; an adult supervises the proceedings and the decisions by youths and juries of youths are valid and enforceable.

offenders. Victims are encouraged to take an active role in these courts. Youths become actively involved as advisory juries (Peterson 2005).

Teen courts are also known as youth courts, peer courts, and student courts (Preston and Roots 2004). In 1997, there were 78 active teen courts. By 2005, there were over 1,000 youth court programs operating in juvenile justice systems, schools, and community-based organizations throughout the United States (Peterson 2005). Today, there are over 1,200 programs with over 100 more in the planning stages (Peterson 2009). Beginning in 2000, juvenile courts were handling over 1.5 million cases (Vose and Vannan 2013). Teen courts are responsible for diverting about 9 percent of juvenile cases away from the traditional court resulting in 110,000 to 125,000 juveniles participating in youth courts each year (Schneider 2007). Although these courts are usually reserved for first-time offenders, they are a lot cheaper than processing cases through juvenile courts. It costs $430–$480 per juvenile participant whereas incarcerating a juvenile costs anywhere from $23,000 to $64,000 per year (Schneider 2007). The American Probation and Parole Association has recognized the significance and contributions of teen courts by establishing September as National Youth Court Month to highlight the activities of youth courts and their contributions to the youth justice system (APPA Perspectives 2004a, 8).

The Use of Teen Courts

Among the first cities to establish teen courts were Seattle, Washington, and Denver, Colorado (Rasmussen 2004). Subsequently, teen courts have been established in many other jurisdictions, including Odessa, Texas. In Odessa, for instance, juveniles are referred to teen courts for class C misdemeanors and minor traffic violations. Defendants range in age from 10 to 16. Traffic citation cases result in teen court referrals by municipal judges, who give youths the option of paying their fines or having their cases heard by the teen court. If youths select the teen court for adjudication, then they do not acquire a juvenile record. The teen court listens to all evidence and decides the matter (Peterson 2005).

Teen court dispositions are always related closely to community service as well as jury service (Karp 2001, 2004). Thus, juveniles who are found guilty by teen courts may, in fact, serve on such juries in the future, as one of their conditional punishments (Rasmussen 2004). Or they may be required to perform up to 22 hours of community service, such as working at the animal shelter, library, or nursing home; picking up trash in parks or ball fields; or working with various community agencies. The teen court program in Odessa has been very successful. Prior to using teen courts, the recidivism rate for all juvenile offenders in the city was between 50 and 60 percent. However, teen court adjudications all but eliminated this recidivism figure. Interestingly, juveniles who are tried by the teen court often develop an interest in the legal system. Teen courts place a high priority on educating young people about their responsibilities of being individuals, family members, and citizens (Roberts 2003). As a part of one's diversion, conditional options such as restitution, fines, or community service may be imposed in those cases where property damage was incurred as the result of the juvenile's behavior (Chapman 2005). Juvenile court judges must exercise considerable discretion and impose dispositions that best meet the juvenile's needs and circumstances.

Constructive dispositions are the objective of teen courts in Kentucky. In September, October, and November 1992, teen jurors in a Kentucky teen court heard case details in nine different cases (Williamson, Chalk, and Knepper 1993). Referrals to teen court were made from the regular juvenile court, a division of the state's district court. If juveniles are found guilty by the teen court, then the court imposes constructive dispositions involving community service hours. It should be noted that these teen courts do not determine one's guilt or innocence—rather, they convene and recommend appropriate dispositions. Teenagers act as prosecutors, defense attorneys, clerks, bailiffs, jury forepersons, and jurors as they carry out roles similar to those of their counterparts in criminal courts. The Kentucky teen court variety is interesting because accused and judged teens are themselves recruited subsequently to serve as teen jurors. Thus, all defendants are assigned to jury duty following their teen court appearances. When this study was conducted, no youth had been returned to the teen court for noncompliance. Perhaps seeing how the process works from the other side, as jurors, made these teenagers understand the seriousness of what they had done themselves as victimizers in the past. One example of a teen court is the Anchorage, Alaska Youth Court.

Teen courts have rapidly expanded across the country since the 1990s, and by 2006, there were more than 1,100 operational courts (Vose and Vannan 2013). These courts are not always known as teen courts. In Anchorage, Alaska, for instance, a teen court program was established in 1989 and exists today as the Anchorage Youth Court (AYC). Subsequently, 14 other youth courts have been established in various Alaska cities and modeled after the AYC (Anchorage Youth Court 2005). Funding for youth courts in Alaska varies. AYC receives a third of its funds from federal block grants, United Way, and program fees; a third from fundraising and donations; and a third from the Anchorage Assembly. The AYC targets first-time offenders and makes extensive use of volunteers from the community.

Blue Earth County Teen Court

A contrast to the AYC is the Blue Earth County Teen Court (BECTC), in Makato, Minnesota (Blue Earth County 2005). According to BECTC officials, teen court is an alternative to the district court that handles very serious juvenile offenses. The BECTC is a collaborative effort that involves Blue Earth County officials and citizens. Juveniles are held accountable for their actions by a jury of their peers, and the rights of victims, if any, are respected. BECTC is also an opportunity for teens and adult volunteers to have an active, positive role in the juvenile justice system. The overall goal is to reduce the number of juvenile offenders who offend in Blue Earth County. Targeted are juveniles who commit petty offenses and choose to appear in the BECTC rather than in district court. These youths may have already participated in the Blue Earth County Youth Diversion Program as a result of a prior offense.

Teen Court Variations

Several variations of teen courts have been described (Champion 2007). Four courtroom models of teen courts include (1) adult judge, (2) youth judge, (3) peer jury, and (4) tribunal. Adult judge teen courts use adult judges to preside over all actions. The judge is responsible for managing all courtroom dynamics. Generally, a youth volunteer acting as the prosecutor presents each case against a juvenile to a jury comprised of one's peers. This is similar to a prosecutor in the adult system presenting a case against a defendant in a grand jury action. A juvenile defense counsel offers mitigating evidence, if any, that the jury may consider. The jury is permitted to ask the youthful defendant any question in an effort to determine why the offense was committed and any circumstances surrounding its occurrence. Subsequently, the jury deliberates and determines the most fitting punishment. This is a recommendation only. The suitability of the recommended punishment, which is most often some form of community service and/or victim compensation or restitution, is decided by the judge. About half of all teen courts in the United States use the adult judge model.

The youth judge variation of teen courts uses a juvenile judge instead of an adult judge. Youths are used as prosecutors and defense counsel as well. This teen court variation functions much like the adult judge teen court model. Again, a sentence is recommended by a jury, and the appropriateness of the sentence is determined by the juvenile judge. About a third of all teen courts use this model.

This model is used by the Elko (Nevada) Teen Court (ETC). The ETC uses teens as judges, prosecutors, and defense counsels. The proceedings are conducted in real trial courtrooms. The procedures emulate adult proceedings as much as possible. The average teen court hearing lasts about 20–30 minutes. During the ETC proceedings, the jury is sworn in by a court clerk. The court clerk states to the jury the charge and the plea of guilty entered by the youthful defendant. The prosecutor summarizes the police report, or facts in the case, for the jury. The defense counsel calls one or more witnesses, including the defendant. The defendant's parents may also be called. The prosecutor can cross-examine witnesses. Both the prosecutor and defense counsel make closing arguments to the jury who then receives jury instructions from the judge and retires to reach a verdict. The verdict is returned. The objective of this proceeding is to heighten offender accountability, not deal with the guilt or innocence of the defendant. The teen jury determines the consequences of the juvenile's actions. The jury can require juvenile detention center tours, community service, educational classes, apology letters, and written reports (Elko Teen Court 2005).

In the peer jury model, an adult judge presides, while a jury hears the case against the defendant. There are no youth prosecutors or defense counsels present. After hearing the case, which is usually determined through jury questioning of the defendant directly, the jury deliberates and decides the sentence, which the judge must approve. This model is used by the BECTC example in Minnesota.

Under the tribunal model, one or more youths act as judges, while other youths are designated as prosecutors and defense counsels. The prosecution and defense present their side of the case against the youthful defendant to the judges who subsequently deliberate and return with a sentence. All sentences may be appealed. Again, the sentences usually involve restitution or some form of victim compensation, community service, or a combination of punishments depending upon the circumstances. This tribunal model is the one featured in the AYC example.

The Successfulness of Teen Courts

The growing popularity of teen courts as alternatives to formal juvenile court actions attests to their successfulness in sanctioning first-time low-risk youthful offenders (Patrick et al. 2004). Being judged by one's peers seems to be an effective method of imposing sanctions. Youths who function as judges, prosecutors, and defense counsels usually receive a certain number of hours of training to perform these important roles (Carrington and Schulenberg 2004). In New York, for instance, an average of 16–20 hours of training is required of youth court juvenile officials (Champion 2009). In some instances, written tests are administered following one's training. These are the equivalent of bar exams for youths, to ensure that they understand some basic or fundamental legal principles.

Several national youth court guidelines have been articulated. These guidelines have been developed for (1) program planning and community mobilization, (2) program staffing and funding, (3) legal issues, (4) identified respondent population and referral process, (5) volunteer recruitment and sentencing options, (6) volunteer training, (7) youth court operations and case management, and (8) program evaluation.

Recidivism rates of teen courts have not been studied consistently throughout all jurisdictions. However, available information suggests that the recidivism rates among youthful defendants who have gone through the teen court process are very low, less than 20 percent. In a comparison of past recidivism studies, Vose and Vannan (2013) revealed that completion rates of the participants across 12 studies ranged from a low of 62 percent to 100 percent of juveniles completing their teen court sentence. This analysis also revealed that recidivism rates were lower for youth who completed their sentence versus youth who did not; recidivism rates of those who completed their sentence ranged from 6 to 49 percent across the 12 studies, whereas recidivism rates for those who failed to complete ranged from 32 to 100 percent. One positive consequence that is reported in many jurisdictions is that processed youths emerge with a greater appreciation for the law, a greater understanding of it, and a greater respect for authority figures. They appear to be more law-abiding compared with youths adjudicated in more traditional ways through juvenile courts (Champion 2009). A majority of states have adopted teen court models of one type or another, and many are in the process of considering legislation to establish them (Chapman 2005).

Beyond lowering recidivism rates of justice involved youth, teen or youth court programs also have other benefits, such as reducing juvenile court backlogs, limiting the number of youths who will get a juvenile court record, giving youths the opportunity to learn about responsible citizenship and the law outside the formal juvenile court setting, and increased community service activities for the communities they serve (Schneider 2007). States vary in terms of the eligibility age limits and types of offenses that youth courts may consider. Mostly first-offense, low-level misdemeanors, or status offenses are included. More serious offenses are usually passed along to the juvenile court beyond the intake stage. The accountability of participating youths is heightened considerably inasmuch as youths must admit guilt before participating in teen courts (Champion 2009). Furthermore, they must waive their confidentiality rights in most jurisdictions.

▶ Trends and Implications for Juvenile Offenders

A Summary of Juvenile Justice Trends

The trends discussed in this section pertain to (1) the legal rights of juveniles; (2) law enforcement; (3) the prosecution of juveniles and juvenile courts; (4) diversion, probation, and intermediate punishments; and (5) juvenile corrections and aftercare.

1. The juvenile justice system will experience greater reforms in the area of juvenile rights commensurate with those enjoyed by adult offenders.
2. Attaining constitutional rights commensurate with adult offenders. Currently, there are no speedy trial provisions for juvenile offenders.
3. Greater accountability and responsibility expected from juvenile offenders.
4. The deinstitutionalization of status offenders. As we have seen, there is a general trend toward DSO as a means of diverting less serious offenders from the jurisdiction of juvenile courts.
5. Greater attention to preventing short-term detention of juveniles with adult offenders after arrest.
6. Greater use of transfers and waivers to adult criminal courts.
7. The juvenile court will become increasingly adversarial, in many respects paralleling the adult system.
8. Greater formality of juvenile courts (Guevara and Herz 2004).
9. The increased use of transfers of juveniles to criminal courts will continue, especially for serious offenses, including rape, robbery, and murder.
10. Greater concern for juvenile rights.
11. More stringent standards relating to the admissibility of evidence in juvenile proceedings.
12. Greater use of plea bargaining.
13. Greater use of diversion.
14. Greater innovations in juvenile offender management, including electronic monitoring and/or home confinement (Rodriguez 2004).
15. Greater emphasis on victim restitution and community service.

Summary

1. *Examine the role of juvenile court prosecutors and the changing nature of juvenile court proceedings as defense counsels are increasingly used in most jurisdictions.*

Juvenile court decision making has often been focused on the individual offender rather than stressing equality of defendants in court decisions. Prosecutors, therefore, enjoy a great deal of discretion in the juvenile system to determine what decisions are in the best interest of the individual juvenile. In the past, the juvenile justice system has been criticized as being fraught with racial and gender-based discrimination as individualized decision making is inherently discriminatory. More recently, juvenile justice decisions and proceedings have been more open and therefore less individualization is evident, giving due process more priority in the handling of juvenile cases by both prosecutors and judges. The idea is that in theory, more open processes are fairer ones. Juvenile justice processing in the past has also been slow. Prosecutorial delays in the filing of charges against juveniles are widespread in many jurisdictions. Juvenile court prosecutors may delay filing charges because of court case backlogs, crowded court dockets, and insufficient staff and resources.

Defense counsels for juveniles attempt to ensure that their due process rights are respected. Many juvenile cases are plea bargained similar to criminal cases. Defense counsels perform many of the same functions for juveniles as they do for adults, including representing them in adjudicatory proceedings. In those states where jury trials for juveniles are permitted, defense counsels are advocates for juveniles in every respect, seeking their acquittal of charges against them.

2. *Explain juvenile court adjudicatory proceedings and compare and contrast the different dispositions available to juvenile judges.*

The juvenile justice process has become increasingly legalistic, particularly since the 1960s, when the U.S. Supreme Court commenced hearing juvenile cases and extending various rights to juveniles. Juvenile court judges still, however, have almost absolute discretion in making decisions regarding juvenile dispositions. Dispositions in juvenile court are like sentences in adult court, in that they involve nominal or verbal warnings, conditional punishments such as probation, or custodial sanctions, including incarceration in a juvenile facility for various lengths of time. Relatively few juveniles are actually incarcerated, and the terms of their incarceration are short compared with time served by convicted adults who are incarcerated.

3. *Understand the waiver, transfer, and certification processes, how these procedures move juveniles to criminal court jurisdiction, and the implications of these decisions for juvenile offenders.*

Approximately 1 percent of all juveniles referred to the juvenile justice system each year are transferred, waived, or certified as adults and processed by criminal courts. These transferred juveniles are not always the most serious offenders, despite the fact that the intent of transfers or waivers is to make it possible for criminal courts to impose more serious punishments, which are beyond the jurisdiction of juvenile courts. States vary in the youngest ages at which juveniles may be transferred to criminal court to be processed as though they were adults. Different types of waivers include judicial waivers, where judges on their own waive particular juveniles to the jurisdiction of criminal courts; prosecutorial waivers or concurrent jurisdiction or direct file, where prosecutors decide whether to prosecute juveniles in criminal or juvenile courts; and legislative or automatic waivers, also known as statutory exclusion, where juveniles are automatically waived to the jurisdiction of criminal courts for processing as adults.

All juveniles are entitled to hearings on waiver actions. For those subject to legislative or automatic waivers, these juveniles may obtain hearings to have their cases placed back into juvenile courts for adjudication. These types of actions are known as reverse waiver hearings. Some juveniles may also initiate transfer proceedings through demand waiver actions. Thus, they ask juvenile courts to transfer jurisdiction over them to criminal courts.

The implications of transfers are several and diverse. Not all transferred juveniles are the most serious offenders. About 60 percent of all transferred juveniles are persistent or chronic property offenders or drug users. About 40 percent are violent offenders who are supposedly the most vulnerable to being transferred or waived. About 50 percent of all juvenile cases transferred to criminal court result in dismissals or the charges are downgraded, and probation is usually imposed through plea bargaining.

Even where the remaining cases come to trial, the result for nearly another 40 percent of these offenders is probation. Only 12 percent or fewer juveniles ever serve time as the result of transfers and subsequent convictions in criminal courts. Thus, the transfer process does not necessarily achieve its manifest goals, and this general failure of the waiver process is repeated annually with uncanny similarity.

4. *Understand blended sentencing statutes and how these statutory provisions have changed the nature of juvenile sentencing and rehabilitation.*

Since the early 1990s, increasing numbers of states have designed blended sentencing statutes that authorize either juvenile court or criminal court judges to impose either juvenile sanctions or criminal penalties or both on juvenile offenders. These blended sentencing statutes afford juveniles the full range of constitutional rights, including a trial by jury without having to go through the formal transfer process. Blended sentencing statutes include the juvenile–inclusive blend, the juvenile–exclusive blend, the juvenile–contiguous blend, the criminal–inclusive blend, and the criminal–exclusive blend. Inclusive blends for both juvenile and criminal courts authorize judges to impose both juvenile and criminal punishments.

5. *Summarize teen courts and their purpose and focus.*

Teen courts are an alternative to juvenile court for determining one's guilt and punishment where jurors consist of teenagers who hear and decide minor cases. Teen courts are usually reserved for first-time offenders, and for status offenses, and misdemeanors. Retired judges often oversee the proceedings while the youths do most of the decision making. Teen courts are focused on therapeutic jurisprudence and rehabilitation via teaching the juvenile offenders empathy. Teen courts are sometimes called youth courts, peer courts, or student courts and in the last decade have expanded widely across the country.

Juveniles who have their cases heard by a teen court, ordinarily do not acquire a juvenile record. The dispositions in teen court are almost always community service and a requirement that the juvenile defendant come back as a teen court juror. There are several different types of teen courts but the most common are courts include (1) adult judge, (2) youth judge, (3) peer jury, and (4) tribunal. Although not studied extensively, teen courts have been shown to be successful in that juveniles who participate in teen courts have very low recidivism rates, in some cases less than 20 percent. Jurisdictions that have these courts report that the juveniles who participate have a greater appreciation for the law and a greater respect for authority figures once their case is heard.

6. *Describe several important trends in juvenile justice that have significance for how juveniles are processed by juvenile courts.*

Several trends in juvenile justice include greater reforms in juvenile justice processing; greater emphasis on due process issues; greater accountability among juveniles in terms of sanctions imposed; greater use of waivers and transfers for more serious juvenile offenders; increasingly adversarial juvenile court proceedings; more stringent evidentiary standards; less use of secure confinement; greater use of plea bargaining; greater use of diversion and probation; greater use of innovations in offender supervision, including electronic monitoring, home confinement, and intensive supervised probation with conditions; and greater emphasis upon victim compensation, restitution, and restorative justice as sanctioning options.

Key Terms

adjudication *283*
adjudication hearing *283*
automatic waivers *288*
blended sentencing *291*
camp *284*
conditional dispositions *283*
confinement *284*
custodial dispositions *284*
demand waiver *288*
direct file *288*
discretionary waivers *288*

due process *285*
foster home *284*
group home *284*
guardian *ad litem 285*
judicial waiver *288*
legislative waivers *288*
mandatory transfer *288*
nominal dispositions *283*
nonsecure custody *284*
once an adult/always
   an adult *289*

presumptive waiver *289*
prosecutorial waiver *288*
ranch *284*
reverse waiver
   hearings *289*
secure custody *284*
statutory exclusion *288*
teen courts *292*
transfers *282*
waiver hearing *289*
waivers *282*

Critical Thinking Exercises

1. Despite every state expanding the instances when juvenile offenders can have their cases transferred to adult court, the number of youths actually transferred to adult court is very small, roughly 1 percent of all cases. Given these statistics and research that show that juveniles who are transferred are more likely to be victimized in adult prison, as well as reoffend once they are released, should the Juvenile Justice System reconsider transferring juveniles to adult court and adopt some other programs or alternatives for dealing with serious juvenile offenders in the juvenile court? What could be some alternatives to prosecuting juveniles in adult court and sending them to adult prisons?

2. As juvenile courts have become more formal, juvenile defendants have received more and more due process rights, such as being afforded attorneys and the right to jury trials in some states. Some see this as a good thing in order to protect juveniles accused of crimes from prosecutors and judges who have a great deal of discretion in how to deal with those in the juvenile court system. Other argue that these increased due process rights have also led to juveniles being treated more formally by the juvenile courts, which can often mean being treated more harshly by prosecutors and judges. What do you think, should juveniles enjoy most of the due process rights that adults in the criminal court system are afforded, or should we trust prosecutors and judges to make decisions in the best interest of the juveniles, and allow a more informal, less intrusive process in handling these cases?

3. Teen Courts have been shown to be more cost effective and more successful at reducing recidivism than the traditional juvenile court system. They still only, however, handle very few (10 percent) of juvenile cases and participation in teen courts is usually reserved for low level first-time offenders. Given their success, should teen courts be expanded to allow more juveniles with a broader range of offenses to participate? If more serious offenders were allowed to have their case heard in teen court, would recidivism reductions still be as great?

Case Study Decision-Making Exercise

According to a report by the Office of Juvenile Justice and Delinquency Prevention, there is no national data set to track the juvenile cases that are automatically filed in adult court (Griffin, Addie, Adams, and Firestine 2011). Also according to this report, about 41 percent of the cases transferred were to a statute that automatically waived juvenile court jurisdiction because of the offense involved, 35 percent were transferred by the prosecutor, and another 24 percent were due to a judge's decision to transfer the case. A majority of the transfer cases involved a violent offense (64 percent), where the juvenile was male (96 percent) and African American (62 percent). The authors also point out that despite the fact that every state expanded their transfer laws, these laws vary widely across the states, and that many have very few report statistics on the number of transfers (only about 13), what offenses were transferred, and the demographic characteristics of the juveniles who were transferred. If you were in charge of the Office of Juvenile Justice and Delinquency prevention, would you urge the president to have more uniformity in transfer laws across the states? Do you think the type of case and juvenile that is transferred to adult court should depend on what state the crime was committed in? What are the pros and cons of having more uniform transfer laws and a requirement that the states keep and report their transfer statistics?

Concept Review Questions

1. Identify four types of waivers. Which types of waivers are made by judges? Which types of waivers are made by legislatures?

2. Can juveniles contest waivers? How can these waiver actions be reversed? Describe several methods to accomplish this task.

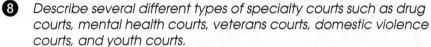

7 *Understand specialty and problem-solving courts and the underlying focus on treatment and rehabilitation of the offender rather than punishment of the offense.*

8 *Describe several different types of specialty courts such as drug courts, mental health courts, veterans courts, domestic violence courts, and youth courts.*

A recent NIJ study of over 400,000 prisoners who were released in 2005 from state prisons revealed that 67.8 percent were rearrested within three years and 76.6 percent were rearrested within five years; also at three-years post release almost 50 percent were sent back to prison and at five years after being released, just under 60 percent were reincarcerated (Durose, Copper, and Snyder 2014). This is causing more than a few jurisdictions around the country to question whether corrections can actually correct an individual's behavior. As such, many states have been looking for alternatives to incarceration, and have been adopting a number of different diversion programs designed to keep certain offenders out of jail and prison and keep them in the community while requiring they attend treatment programs and adhere to certain court conditions. These treatment-based diversion programs are often much cheaper than incarceration and have shown to be more effective at reducing recidivism. A good example is the rapidly expanding phenomenon of veterans treatment courts (VTCs). With the recent return of hundreds of thousands of veterans from the wars in Iraq and Afghanistan, there has been an increase in the number of justice involved veterans who have had difficulties adjusting back to normal life. Due to the post-traumatic stress disorder that many veterans have developed as a result of the death, destruction, grief, and sorrow that they encountered overseas, they are at an increased risk of substance abuse and addiction which can lead to crime.

Congress recently authorized the Comprehensive Addiction and Recovery Act (CARA) that authorizes Department of Justice funding for VTCs. President Obama said he will sign the legislation that will allow funding for evidence-based treatment for those with substance abuse disorders. The purpose of VTCs is to divert offenders from the traditional processes and mandate treatment. If the offender does not comply, they get sent back to regular court. VTC requirements include adherence to treatment, continued appearances (sometimes monthly or bimonthly) at the court and continued interaction with the VTC judge designed to monitor progress, and adherence to other court conditions such as urine analysis testing (Hartley and Baldwin 2016). Critics of VTCs argue that these specialty court programs are giving special treatment to veterans because they divert offenders away from the court without prosecuting and sentencing them. Those who advocate for these types of courts, however, argue that if the goal is crime prevention, treating the underlying conditions facing veterans that led to their criminal involvement is the most practical and cost-effective response. They also argue that those who have risked their lives serving the country should be able to get the treatment they need and deserve, as well as get a second chance to get their lives back to normal. What do you think? Do veterans who have served their country deserve to get a second chance and counseling and treatment rather than jail if their behavior is stemming from problems related to stress and trauma from combat?

▼

▶ Introduction

Several jurisdictions around the country over the past two decades have sought to dispose of certain types of cases using methods other than those traditionally used by the criminal justice system. More state and local court authorities today are using alternative sanctions to deal with certain types of crimes or offenders. Some of these alternative methods of disposing of cases include alternative dispute resolution or ADR, pretrial diversion or community-based corrections, and specialty, or problem-solving, courts.

ADR uses informal processes to dispose of certain types of cases, especially where there is some type of dispute between the offender and victim. This sometimes involves victim–offender mediation or victim–offender reconciliation and has the goal of removing less serious offenders from criminal court jurisdiction and to alleviate the number of these cases in criminal courts. Offenders who agree to participate in ADR do not usually get criminal records and victims are usually compensated for their losses or injuries. Some of these programs may be referred to as restorative justice processes because they aim to achieve justice by restoring or repairing the harm that was done between offender and victim. Advocates say that ADR is beneficial because court dockets are eased, prosecutor caseloads are lessened, and the community may benefit if community service is involved. Some also believe that community service and restitution heighten offender accountability by obligating offenders to pay for the damages they have caused to property, or for the loss of wages if victims are injured.

Pretrial diversion is another option that prosecutors may use to divert cases from the criminal justice process, at least temporarily. Diversion is the temporary stopping of prosecution of someone, who then is required to participate in one or more community programs. If these persons, known as divertees, complete their periods of diversion successfully, they often have the charges against them dismissed and the records of the arrest expunged. There are many functions of diversion that will be discussed in this chapter.

Other types of noncriminal or pretrial sanctions include community service, victim compensation, and restitution. The forms of community service vary from jurisdiction to jurisdiction. Victim compensation is a way of offsetting the damages caused to victims. The nature of victim compensation may also vary; different programs will be described in this chapter, including the financial/community service model, the victim–offender mediation model, the victim/reparations model, and repaying victims through restitution.

Specialty courts are also known as problem-solving courts and are alternative methods of dealing with certain types of offenders. Specialty courts have a philosophy of therapeutic jurisprudence and are focused on rehabilitating the offender rather than simply punishing them for an offense. Certain specialty courts, such as domestic violence courts, also focus on victims to ensure their safety. Drug courts are the most prevalent of the problem-solving courts, but others also include youth or teen courts, mental health courts, and more recently veterans courts.

▶ Decriminalization, Alternative Dispute Resolution (ADR), Diversion, and Restorative Justice: Exploring Alternatives to Criminal Prosecution

It is important to understand that once a criminal case is placed into the criminal justice system, this doesn't necessarily mean that the case will proceed throughout the entire system and be processed fully. Several factors operate to determine whether specific cases will move further into the system or whether they will be removed from it. There is a great deal of pressure on prosecutors to resolve increasing numbers of cases expeditiously. Unfortunately, prosecutor's offices throughout the United States do not have sufficient person power or resources to prosecute all cases brought to their attention. Therefore, prosecutors must often prioritize cases and arrange them from the most to least serious. The most serious cases will likely receive the full attention of prosecutors and move forward. However, there are a massive number of less serious criminal cases that are relegated to lower priority for prosecution.

Several solutions have been devised or proposed to resolve these less serious cases and not consume valuable court time. For instance, a large number of cases involve possession of marijuana and/or recreational drug use. Some cases involve assault and battery or spousal abuse, where persons married or otherwise have physically injured one another. Subsequently, one or both parties have been arrested by police who have intervened. It is clear that while criminal laws have been violated, prosecutors do not always regard these types of offenses with the same degree of seriousness as armed robbery, rape, and murder.

In the case of illegal drug use, some persons have advocated legalizing certain drugs, thus rendering their possession as a noncriminal act. This doesn't mean that prosecutors don't think drug use is harmless. But they might inquire as to whether the criminal justice system is the best place to deal with illicit drug use and punish it. Should drug users be treated rather than punished? No one knows the answer to this question. Certainly there are strong opinions favoring and opposing the legalization of certain drugs.

Accordingly, some types of assault and battery as well as spousal abuse may be regarded as less serious crimes. Again, this doesn't mean that prosecutors are insensitive to the needs of persons who have been assaulted, or that they condone spousal abuse. These are serious offenses deserving of some form of punishment. But should some of these crimes receive the same amount of attention and court time compared with murder, rape, and armed robbery? Again, there are no easy answers to this question. The following section, therefore, explores several strategies devised by legislators and others to reduce the caseloads of prosecutors and accelerate the justice process by focusing on the most serious cases. These strategies for reducing the sheer numbers of criminal cases confronting overworked prosecutor's offices include (1) decriminalization, (2) alternative dispute resolution, and (3) diversion.

Decriminalization

> **decriminalization, decriminalize** legislative action whereby an act or omission, formerly criminal, is made noncriminal and without punitive sanctions.

Decriminalization is removing an act from the category of crime (Sheehy 2004). Decriminalization might occur, for instance, in marijuana use (Jones 2003). In the last few years, as many as 25 states and the District of Columbia have legalized possession of marijuana in some form. Most of these states have legalized marijuana for medical purposes but others, such as Oregon, Washington, Colorado, Alaska and DC, have legalized marijuana for recreational use. In Alaska, for example, if you are 21, you can buy or possess up to an ounce of marijuana or have six plants. In Oregon, the voters approved legalizing the possession of marijuana up to one ounce in public and eight ounces in one's home. Other states are considering putting similar measures on their state ballots to let the people decide whether or not possessing small amounts of marijuana should be legal. When crimes are decriminalized, they may be shifted to civil courts for noncriminal resolution (Coomber, Oliver, and Morris 2003). Thus, a fight at a football game between overly enthusiastic fans from crosstown rival high schools may be shifted from criminal court to some type of civil resolution which entails a process that can restore or repair the harm done. If seeming such as possession of a small amount of drugs is legalized, the police and courts are no longer involved in an enforcement capacity. Obviously, law enforcement is still going to be out policing and ensuring that if persons possess marijuana, it is within the legally allowed limit or weight, or if someone has a prescription to possess marijuana for medicinal purposes. In some jurisdictions, a ticket can be written similar to those for a traffic offense. Some of these alternative methods have been referred to as restorative processes or restorative justice. Restorative justice is gaining more ground as a popular alternative to traditional criminal justice responses; the underlying assumption is that all persons involved or affected by the crime (offender, victim, victim's family, and community) should play a part in the response to it (Miller 2008). At the same time that decriminalization is occurring with certain acts, however, criminalization is occurring with other acts, such as certain types of domestic violence and substance abuse (Sridharan et al. 2004).

Alternative Dispute Resolution

An increasingly used option to settle minor criminal cases is alternative dispute resolution (ADR). ADR is a community-based, informal dispute settlement between offenders and their victims. Most often targeted for participation in these programs are first-time, low-level, or misdemeanor offenders. Some overly excited persons at a football game may get into a fight. One person may assault another, causing minor physical injuries. While criminal charges may be filed against the aggressor, these cases often consume considerable and valuable court time. However, if the offenders and victims agree, ADR may be used to conclude these cases quickly and informally to the mutual satisfaction of both parties involved. Victim–offender mediation or ADR programs originated in the Midwestern United States (Schiff and Bazemore 2004). Umbreit (1994, 25) notes that in most victim–offender programs, the process consists of four phases:

1. Case intake from referral sources.
2. Preparation for mediation, during which the mediator meets separately with the offender and the victim.
3. The mediation session, which consists of a discussion of what occurred and how people felt about it, followed by negotiation of a restitution agreement.
4. Follow-up activities such as monitoring restitution completion.

Umbreit found in a cross-site study that 79 percent of the victims were satisfied with the results of the mediation, 87 percent of the offenders were satisfied, and 83 percent of all parties believed that the mediation process was fair for both the victims and the offenders. Examples of the volume of referrals in specific mediation agencies are 591 mediations in 1991 in Albuquerque, New Mexico; 903 mediations in Minneapolis, Minnesota in 1991; 541 mediations in Oakland, California in 1991; and 1,107 mediations in Austin, Texas in 1991 (Umbreit 1994, 28).

Restorative Justice

Another name for ADR is restorative justice (Braithwaite 2002). Restorative justice seeks to produce a civil remedy between victims and their victimizers (Strang 2004). The roots of restorative justice can be traced to aboriginal courts in other countries, such as Australia and South Africa (Gallinetti, Redpath, and Sloth-Nielsen 2004; Harris 2004). Restorative justice programs or processes emphasize reparation and reintegration (Miller 2008). The intent of restorative justice is not simply to restore to victims that which was lost or the value of services or lost wages due to injuries suffered. An additional objective is to heighten the accountability of the offender by requiring him/her to enter into a bilateral agreement with the victim in an effort to reach a compromise that will be mutually satisfying for both parties (Lemley 2004). Thus, although a criminal case has been transformed into a civil one, ADR involves the direct participation of the victim and offender, with the aim of mutual accommodation for both parties. The emphasis of ADR is upon restitution

restorative justice mediation between victims and offenders whereby offenders accept responsibility for their actions and agree to reimburse victims for their losses; may involve community service and other penalties agreeable to both parties in a form of arbitration with a neutral third party acting as arbiter.

alternative dispute resolution (ADR) procedure whereby a criminal case is redefined as a civil one and the case is decided by an impartial arbiter, where both parties agree to amicable settlement. Usually reserved for minor offenses.

stigmatization social process whereby offenders acquire undesirable characteristics as the result of imprisonment or court appearances. Undesirable criminal or delinquent labels are assigned to those who are processed through the criminal and juvenile justice systems.

mediation informal conflict resolution through the intervention of a trained negotiator who seeks a mutually agreeable resolution between disputing parties.

rather than punishment (Jones 2003). There are small costs associated with it compared with trials, and criminal stigmatization is avoided (Tishler et al. 2004; Tshehla 2004). Many criminal cases are being diverted from the criminal justice system through ADR (Hayes 2004). Mediation is increasingly used. ADR is recognized increasingly as a means by which differences between criminals and their victims can be resolved through civil means (Karp, Bazemore, and Chesire 2004). These usually involve face-to-face meetings between victims and offenders. The model program started in Canada (Grace 2010) but has expanded throughout the United States for both adults and juvenile offenders (Bakker 1994). Mediation services help relieve congested criminal and civil courts. Often volunteers from the community are used as mediators.

States vary in their use of ADR (Tifft 2004); however, ADR programs are operating in every state in some way, shape, or form. That is not to say that these programs are operating extensively and in all corners of every state, but that there are programs in each state. How extensively and exactly the different types of programs are being piloted or implemented, however, is a difficult thing to measure (National Center for State Courts 2010). ADR is most frequently used to settle misdemeanor cases.

Advantages and Disadvantages of ADR

ADR has the following advantages:

1. Offenders do not acquire a criminal record following a successful resolution of the dispute.
2. Victims have the satisfaction of seeing punishment imposed for the criminal act committed.
3. Court dockets are eased because of the diversion of disputes to ADR.
4. Prosecutor caseloads are alleviated.
5. The community benefits where community service orders are issued to perpetrators.
6. Accountability is heightened, since victim compensation and restitution are required of offenders. (Palumbo, Musheno, and Hallett 1994)

The disadvantages of ADR include the following:

1. Offenders who have committed crimes escape criminal convictions. Some persons regard this as unjust and believe that if you commit a crime, you should receive a criminal conviction as a result.
2. ADR is insufficient as a punishment and causes some persons to flaunt the law, knowing that they will not be harshly treated if caught. ADR is perceived as too lenient.
3. Reoffending may occur if perpetrators believe that they can get away with crimes with only civil sanctions being imposed.
4. The criminal justice system image is tainted by excessive leniency from ADR programs.
5. The proportionate punishment is not the same as a criminal conviction and the record an offender would acquire as a result.

impartial arbiters persons such as judges, attorneys, or prominent citizens who are called upon to be objective and neutral third parties in disputes between perpetrators and their victims under conditions of restorative justice or alternative dispute resolution.

▶ Impartial Arbiters and Their Qualifications

Who Are the Impartial Arbiters?

Impartial arbiters in ADR programs may be retired judges, attorneys, or interested citizens. Depending on the jurisdiction, ADR arbiters are appointed on the basis of their fairness and integrity (Deukmedjian 2003). There are no special qualifications for arbiters. They do not have to have a precise and extensive knowledge of the law. Their actions are designed to be fair, and the resolutions they negotiate must be agreeable to both the offender and the victim. In the event that the arbiters cannot settle cases, then prosecutors can always reinstitute criminal charges against defendants and take these cases to court for resolution.

▶ Victim Participation and Input

Victim involvement in offender sentencing and punishments has increased dramatically in recent years in both criminal and juvenile proceedings (Booth 2004; Carr, Logio, and Maier 2003). Testimony from victims can add much emotional appeal to formal proceedings. Victim feedback through direct participation in such proceedings is not always negative. In more than a few cases, victims have spoken on behalf of perpetrators and made requests for leniency (Hayes 2004). However, in ADR, victim participation ensures that all aspects of the offense and its results are brought to the attention of the arbiter. When prosecutors decide to divert cases to ADR, every effort is made to reconcile the dispute between victims and offenders. When victims have such input, often it is in the form of a victim impact statement, or a written and/or oral summary of the damages or injuries suffered from actions of the perpetrator (Roberts and Erez 2004). When the perpetrator and victim agree on the proposed punishment, under the supervision of an impartial arbiter, then victim compensation is discussed (Rojek, Coverdill, and Fors 2003). This is usually a monetary award to be paid by the perpetrator to the victim for the loss of property or work time. Many jurisdictions have victim compensation programs to provide guidelines about how much perpetrators should pay for the suffering and losses they have caused to victims (Myers et al. 2004).

Victim–Offender Reconciliation

Victim–offender reconciliation is another version of ADR (Lightfoot and Umbreit 2004; Presser, Hamilton, and Gaarder 2004). Roy, Sudipto, and Brown (1992) report that victim–offender reconciliation is a specific form of conflict resolution between the victim and the offender. Face-to-face encounter is the basic element in this process. Elkhart County, Indiana, has been the site of the Victim-Offender Reconciliation Project (VORP) since 1987. The primary aims of VORP are to (1) make offenders accountable for their wrongs against victims, (2) reduce recidivism among participating offenders, and (3) heighten responsibility of offenders through victim compensation and repayment for damages inflicted (Roy et al. 1992).

VORP was established in Kitchener, Ontario, in 1974 and was subsequently replicated as PACT, or Prisoner and Community Together, in northern Indiana near Elkhart, Indiana (Bakker 1994). Subsequent replications in various jurisdictions have created different varieties of ADR, each variety spawning embellishments, additions, or program deletions deemed more or less important by the particular jurisdiction (Lightfoot and Umbreit 2004). The Genesee County (Batavia), New York, Sheriff's Department established a VORP in 1983, followed by programs in Valparaiso, Indiana; Quincy, Massachusetts; and Minneapolis, Minnesota in 1985. In Quincy, for instance, the program was named EARN-IT and was operated through the Probation Department (Lightfoot and Umbreit 2004). ADR programs in other jurisdictions have been evaluated, and the results of these evaluations suggest that most victims and offenders are satisfied with the fairness of these proceedings. A high rate of restitution by offenders has been reported by many participating jurisdictions (Lightfoot and Umbreit 2004). But criticisms have been lodged against VORPs that allege both victims and offenders do not benefit in ways originally conceived by this type of programming (Tifft 2004). VORPs are not unique to the United States. Other countries, such as Chile, England, Australia, and Italy, have experimented with such programs in recent years with positive results (Stanley 2004).

victim impact statement information or version of events filed voluntarily by the victim of a crime, appended to the presentence investigation report as a supplement for judicial consideration in sentencing the offender. Describes injuries to victims resulting from convicted offender's actions.

victim compensation programs any plans for assisting crime victims in making social, emotional, and economic adjustments.

victim–offender reconciliation any agreement between the victim and the perpetrator concerning a satisfactory arrangement for compensation for injuries or financial losses sustained.

Victim-Offender Reconciliation Project (VORP) form of alternative dispute resolution, whereby a civil resolution is made by mutual consent between the victim and an offender; objectives are to provide restitution to victims, hold offender accountable for crime committed, and to reduce recidivism.

▶ Pretrial Diversion

Pretrial diversion or simply diversion is the process where criminal defendants are either diverted to a community-based agency for treatment or assigned to a counselor for social and/or psychiatric assistance. Pretrial diversion may involve education, job training, counseling, or some type of psychological or physical therapy (Minor, Wells, and Jones 2004). Diversion officially halts or suspends criminal proceedings against a defendant (Ulrich 2002). The thrust of diversion is toward an informal administrative effort to determine (1) whether nonjudicial processing is warranted; (2) whether treatment is warranted; (3) if treatment is warranted, which one to use; and (4) whether charges against the defendant should be dropped or reinstated (Peters et al. 2004).

Most likely targeted for pretrial diversion programs are first-time petty offenders. If these programs are completed successfully, then the charges against these defendants are either downgraded or dismissed outright. The totality of circumstances of the offender's crime is ascertained by the prosecutor and the court, and a decision about diversion is made. Each case is evaluated and decided on its own merits. Persons charged with possessing marijuana may be diverted and required to attend counseling classes or sessions where drug abuse discussions are featured. Diverted defendants usually pay monthly fees during the period of their diversion in order to defray a portion of the expenses for their supervision (Maxwell and Morris 2002).

The History and Philosophy of Diversion

Diversion originated in the United States through the early juvenile courts in Chicago and New York in the late 1800s. Strong efforts were made by religious groups and reformers to keep children from imprisonment of any kind, since children over eight years of age were considered eligible for adult court processing. Cook County, Illinois, implemented a diversion program for youthful offenders in 1899 (National Association of Pretrial Services Agencies 1995).

The philosophy of diversion is community reintegration and rehabilitation (Proulx 2003). The objective is that offenders can avoid the stigma of incarceration and public notoriety. In most state courts where diversion is condoned, diversion does not entirely remove offenders from court processing, since the court usually must approve prosecutorial recommendations for diversion in each case. Since these approvals are often conducted in less publicized hearings, a divertee's crimes are less likely to be scrutinized publicly.

Functions of Diversion

The functions of diversion are as follows:

1. To permit divertees the opportunity of remaining in their communities where they can receive needed assistance or treatment, depending upon the nature of the crimes charged.
2. To permit divertees the opportunity to make restitution to their victims where monetary damages were suffered and property destroyed.
3. To permit divertees the opportunity of remaining free in their communities to support themselves and their families, and to avoid the stigma of incarceration.
4. To help divertees avoid the stigma of a criminal conviction.
5. To assist corrections officials in reducing prison and jail overcrowding by diverting less serious cases to nonincarcerative alternatives.

6. To save the courts the time, trouble, and expense of formally processing less serious cases and streamlining case dispositions through informal case handling.

7. To make it possible for divertees to participate in self-help, educational, or vocational programs.

8. To preserve the dignity and integrity of divertees by helping them avoid further contact with the criminal justice system and assisting them to be more responsible adults capable of managing their own lives.

9. To preserve the family unit and enhance family solidarity and continuity.

Factors Influencing Pretrial Diversion

Excluded from diversion programs are recidivists with prior records of violent offending. Also, if offenders have drug or alcohol dependencies, they may be excluded from diversion programs. Probation and parole violators are also excluded. In view of these restrictive criteria, diversion is most often granted for low-risk, first-time property offenders. While recidivism rates among property offenders are not particularly different from those of violent offenders and drug traffickers, property offenders pose less public risk and are less dangerous compared with these other types of criminals. Relevant criteria operating in most jurisdictions where diversion exists as an option include the following:

1. The age of the offender.

2. The residency, employment, and familial status of the offender.

3. The prior record of the offender.

4. The seriousness of the offense.

5. Aggravating or mitigating circumstances associated with the commission of the offense.

One's residency, employment, and familial status are important considerations because they are indicators of one's stability. More stable persons are more likely to complete diversion programs successfully. Most diversion programs require at least some regular contact with probation agencies operated by state or local authorities. Unemployed and transient offenders are more likely to flee from the jurisdiction contrasted with those offenders who are gainfully employed and have families in the area.

Criticisms of Diversion

1. Diversion is the wrong punishment for criminals. Criminals ought to be convicted of crimes and sent to jail or prison. Diverting them to community programs is wrong.

2. Diversion assumes guilt without a trial. If prospective divertees accept diversion in lieu of a trial, this is regarded as their admission that they are guilty of the offenses alleged.

3. Diversion leads to net-widening. When diversion programs exist in communities, there is a tendency for prosecutors to assign persons to these programs who otherwise would not be prosecuted because of case backlogs and crowded court dockets.

4. Diversion excludes female offenders. In the 1990s this criticism is no longer a valid one, since many female offenders are diverted from criminal prosecutions.

5. Diversion ignores due process. When a case is diverted, the defendant is deprived of his/her right to a trial by jury, a mechanism where guilt must be established beyond a reasonable doubt. Diversion frustrates due process by avoiding a trial.

6. Diversion is too lenient with criminals. (Mackay and Moody 1996)

▶ Other Noncriminal or Criminal Sanctions

Community Service

community service an alternative sanction requiring offenders to work in the community at such tasks as cleaning public parks or working with handicapped children in lieu of an incarcerative sentence. Restitution involves paying back a victim through money received from one's work.

Community service sentencing is one way of achieving offender accountability (Lo and Harris 2004). Community service is different from restitution in that usually, though not always, offenders perform services for the state or community. The nature of community service to be performed is discretionary with the sentencing judge or paroling authority (Teske and Zhang 2005). Judges may also impose fines as a part of an offender's sentence for almost any crime, but in many jurisdictions, fines are imposed only about a third of the time. Also, when fines are imposed, not all offenders pay them. The Victim and Witness Protection Act of 1982 made restitution to victims a mandatory part of one's sentence. Victim advocates strongly urge that restitution to victims be an integral feature of the sentencing process (Xenos 2003).

What Do You Think?

Is Community Service a Punishment? Community service is considered a punishment and is court-imposed. Many types of projects are undertaken by offenders as community service. Usually, these projects are supervised by probation office staff, although supervisors may be recruited from the private sector. Some amount of offender earnings is allocated to victims as well as to the state or local public or private agencies that provide supervisory services (McCold 2003). Restitution to victims may be through periodic payments from offender earnings while on work release, probation, or parole. Sometimes, restitution takes nonmonetary forms, where offenders rebuild or restore property destroyed earlier by their crimes (Ruback 2002).

Is Community Service Effective?

Because many offenders are released into their communities for the purpose of performing community service, it raises a public risk issue for some people, although those offenders ordinarily selected for community service are low-risk and nonviolent (Ruback 2002). Other criticisms relate to the personal philosophies of judicial and correctional authorities, the offender eligibility and selection criteria used among jurisdictions, organizational arrangements, the nature of supervision over offenders performing community services, and how such services are evaluated. Most researchers regard community service and restitution as just and fitting punishments to accompany whatever incarcerative sentence is imposed by judges.

Restitution and Victim Compensation

restitution stipulation by the court that offenders must compensate victims for their financial losses resulting from crime. Compensation to the victim for psychological, physical, or financial loss. May be imposed as a part of an incarcerative sentence.

Restitution is also a victim-initiated action. Restitution is the practice of requiring offenders to compensate crime victims for damages offenders may have inflicted. If the victim fails to notify the court of financial losses or medical expenses, the restitution order may be neglected. Currently, there are no reliable statistics concerning the proportion of convictions where restitution orders are imposed nor are there statistics showing the extent to which probationers and parolees must make restitution as a part of their probation or parole programs (Ruback 2002). Several models of restitution have been described. These include the following models.

The Financial/Community Service Model

The financial/community service model stresses the offender's financial accountability and community service to pay for damages inflicted upon victims and to defray a portion of the expenses of court prosecutions. It is becoming more commonplace for probationers and divertees to be ordered to pay some restitution to victims *and* to perform some type of community service. Community service may involve clean-up activities in municipal parks, painting projects involving graffiti removal, cutting courthouse lawns, or any other constructive project that can benefit the community. These community service sentences are imposed by judges. Probation officers are largely responsible for overseeing the efforts of convicted offenders in fulfilling their community service obligations. These sentencing provisions are commonly called community service orders. Community service orders involve redress for victims, less severe sanctions for offenders, offender rehabilitation, reduction of demands on the criminal justice system, and a reduction of the need for vengeance in a society, or a combination of these factors (Lutz 1990). Community service orders are found in many different countries and benefit the community directly. Further, where convicted offenders are indigent or unemployed, community service is a way of paying their fines and court costs. Some of the chief benefits of community service are that (1) the community benefits because some form of restitution is paid, (2) offenders benefit because they are given an opportunity to rejoin their communities in law-abiding responsible roles, and (3) the courts benefit because sentencing alternatives are provided (Jaffe and Crooks 2004).

> **community service orders** judicially imposed restitution for those convicted of committing crimes; some form of work must be performed to satisfy restitution requirements.

The Victim–Offender Mediation Model

The victim–offender mediation model focuses upon victim–offender reconciliation. ADR is used as a mediating ground for resolving differences or disputes between victims and perpetrators (Lightfoot and Umbreit 2004).

The Victim/Reparations Model

The victim/reparations model stresses that offenders should compensate their victims directly for their offenses. Many states have provisions that provide reparations or financial payments to victims under a U.S. Victims of Crime Act (VOCA). VOCA is a federally financed program of reparations to persons who suffer personal injury and to dependents of persons killed as the result of certain criminal conduct. In many jurisdictions, a specially constituted board determines, independent of court adjudication, the existence of a crime, the damages caused, and other elements necessary for reparation.

> **reparations** damages assigned to be paid by a defendant found liable in a civil action; may include restitution to victims; usually follow trial showing liability or culpability of defendant in lawsuit filed by plaintiff who is seeking damages.

Repaying Victims and Society Through Restitution

President Ronald Reagan signed Public Law 98-473 on October 12, 1984, which established the Comprehensive Crime Control Act. Chapter 14 of this Act is known as the Victims of Crime Act of 1984 or the Comprehensive Crime Control Act of 1984. Currently, all states and the federal government have victim compensation programs. As a part of offender work release requirements, a certain amount of their earned wages may be allocated to restitution and to a general victim compensation fund. In fact, in the federal system, the federal Victim and Witness Protection Act of 1982 created a statute whereby federal judges should order restitution to the victim in all cases in which the victim has suffered a financial loss, unless they state compelling reasons for a contrary ruling on the record. Thus, fines, restitution, and some form of community service have become common features of federal sentencing (18 U.S.C. Sec. 3563(a)(2), 2005; Keller and Spohn 2005).

> **Victims of Crime Act of 1984, Comprehensive Crime Control Act of 1984** significant act that authorized establishment of U.S. Sentencing Commission, instituted sentencing guidelines, provided for abolition of federal parole, and devised new guidelines and goals of federal corrections.

▶ Specialty Courts

Specialty Courts, sometimes referred to as problem-solving courts have increased rapidly around the country as jurisdictions attempt to find alternative methods of dealing with certain types of offenders. Specialty courts often spring up in jurisdictions where traditional criminal justice processing practices have been ineffective at solving certain types of problematic crimes or behaviors. Drug courts are the most popular and prevalent type of specialty court, but others include domestic violence courts, DWI courts, youth or teen courts, mental health courts, and more recently veterans courts. These different types of specialty courts are more focused on the offender, or in the case of domestic violence courts, the victim, rather than on the offense that has been committed in order that the offender gets the help he/she needs to prevent him/her from committing future offenses.

Problem-solving courts take a different approach; the courts and courtroom actors look at cases as problems to be solved. Berman and Feinblatt (2005, 5–7) outline five elements underlying the problem-solving court agenda:

1. Tailoring justice to the needs of each case—this involves disaggregating the cases to identify the special problems of each and tailoring the courts' approach to better meet these needs.

2. Partnering with other agencies—problem-solving courts work with other agencies not normally involved in the justice process such as community groups, social service agencies, treatment providers, and vocational programs utilizing the expertise of each to help offenders rehabilitate and reintegrate into a normal productive life. This lessens the reliance on the incarcerative and supervisory probation role of the courts.

3. Making informed decisions—problem-solving courts through the above-mentioned methods provide judges and other courtroom actors with more information about offenders' personal background and treatment needs as well as progress so that they may make better informed decisions about sanctions and or future treatment.

4. Accountability—problem-solving courts often monitor offenders very aggressively requiring them to be in front of the judge on a weekly basis, show up for treatment or services, and comply with court orders. Offenders in these programs often sign contracts with the court, giving up their Fourth Amendment rights, meaning that their person, belongings, or residences can be searched at any time for contraband. If offenders miss a court appearance, do not show up for services they need to do, or are found in the possession of illegal substances, the court has the power to use graduated sanctions such as a specific period in jail. Some say this type of accountability is more effective than regular probation or even a jail sentence.

5. Focusing on results—because problem-solving courts tailor services and sanctions to the need of the individual, they are more focused on results than on punishment. This means getting input from a number of sources about offenders' progress and continuing supervision until the offenders are not at risk to relapse or reoffend.

These elements of problem-solving courts make them very successful at lowering recidivism rates and getting offenders the help they need. Some studies also show that these methods are more cost effective in the long run than incarceration and continuing the revolving door of justice. Advocates of these courts say they also provide the benefit of turning offenders into taxpayers again instead of a tax burden on the state which has long-term immeasurable benefits (Alonso 2009).

▼

Drug Courts

Drug courts have been in operation for over 25 years, and in an increasing number of jurisdictions drug courts are being used to process offenders charged with various types of drug offenses (Veneziano 2005b). Drug courts are specialized courts that hear and decide exclusively drug-related charges against defendants who may be either users or traffickers. There is a therapeutic milieu associated with drug courts (Maahs 2005). Often, judges will attempt to place drug abusers into programs where their drug problems can be remedied. These persons receive counseling and other forms of therapy, including drugs of use in assisting them to withdraw from highly addictive substances, such as heroin and methamphetamine (Atkins 2005; Veneziano 2005a). Thus, many drug offenders are more likely to be treated rather than punished, compared with more traditional offender processing in conventional criminal courts (Maahs 2005). These drug courts seem successful in assisting many offenders to overcome and deal with their addiction problems.

The first drug court began in Dade County (Miami) in 1989. Today, there are over 3,000 drug courts across the United States, half of which are adult drug courts, and another 700 are juvenile or family drug courts (National Institute of Justice 2014). Drug courts take the stance that addiction is at the heart of the offender's criminal activity (Berman and Feinblatt 2005). The Office of Justice Programs (1998) states that the reason the drug court movement has been so powerful is due to the human element involved; many of the participants are polydrug users, many have never had drug treatment, and most have not experienced the supervision, care, and concern that the drug court judges, attorneys, and treatment and service providers will exhibit.

The results that drug courts and other problem-solving courts have produced are unparalleled by any other approach. Berman and Feinblatt (2005) point out a few of these results, including reduced drug use and abuse, reductions in recidivism rates, enhanced services, stronger familial ties, and improved confidence by the public in the justice process. The Office of Justice Programs (1998) likewise states that beyond reduced recidivism and drug use rates, drug courts have resulted in hundreds of families being reunified, the regaining of custody of hundreds of children by parents, increases in educational and job training, and fewer babies born to addicted parents. In 2016, Congress passed the Comprehensive Addiction and Recovery Act (CARA) which President Obama has stated he will sign. CARA authorizes Department of Justice funding for VTCs, continues funding for drug courts, and improves funding for evidence-based treatment for substance abuse disorders (National Association of Drug Court Professionals 2016). The passage of this bill signifies that the government and perhaps the criminal justice system are more committed to addition and recovery as part of the response to drug crimes. It is highly likely that due to the results that have been produced, such as lower recidivism rates and reduced costs to jurisdictions in processing of these cases in the long run, drug courts are here to stay and their numbers across the country will likely continue to increase.

Domestic Violence Courts

In the 1990s, many jurisdictions implemented specialized courts to deal with domestic violence because of the problems these types of cases cause for courts regarding both the offenders and victims (Buzawa and Buzawa 2003; Labriola, Bradley, O'Sullivan, Rempel, and Moore 2009). The goals of domestic violence courts revolve around providing consistent responses to cases of domestic violence, coordinating services and advocacy for the victim, and providing accountability for the offender as well as close supervision and monitoring (Labriola et al. 2009).

Traditional criminal justice system approaches to domestic violence have been criticized that they do not reduce domestic violence between the offender and the victim; often the victim (wife) is the person who bails the offender (her husband) out of jail, and the problems associated with court processing and legal fees cause increased domestic violence among the couple. Other criticisms to traditional criminal justice system approaches include that the criminal justice system does a poor job at protecting the victim from further abuse by making it easy to get protection orders (even when protection orders are granted, they are often violated with little response from the court), and that the court has been reluctant to get formally involved in domestic and familial matters, providing only cursory responses to domestic disputes (Tsai 2000). As Ostrom (2006) points out, the traditional approaches of arrest and conviction do nothing to reduce violence. These courts therefore utilize therapeutic jurisprudence to place more attention on the victim, offender, and community to reduce levels of domestic violence (Ostrom 2006).

Youth Courts

Today, there are well over a thousand youth courts operating in jurisdictions around the country. Youth courts are also referred to as teen courts, peer courts, or student courts (Preston and Roots 2004). These jurisdictions are utilizing youth courts as an alternative to traditional juvenile court processing. Youth court proceedings are informal, where other youths act as jurors. These courts usually only hear and decide minor cases. Usually, where a youth has committed a status offense or a misdemeanor, a judge will divert the case to a youth court. The focus of these courts is therapeutic jurisprudence, with a strong emphasis upon rehabilitation (Judith Reed 2004) and teaching empathy to offenders. Youth courts were explained in much more in depth in Chapter 12.

In some teen courts, the jury can ask juveniles questions about the offenses they committed and victims can also have the opportunity to be heard and present any pertinent information. The jury will decide the consequences for the juvenile's behaviors. Some examples of offenses heard by teen courts could include shoplifting, alcohol offenses, smoking, curfew violations, and criminal damage to property or vandalism. Some possible consequences as punishments include community service hours, restitution to victims, fines, completion of offense-related educational programming, and service on teen court juries in the future. Jurisdictions who operate teen courts believe that it is important for former offenders to sit in judgment of subsequent offenders, since this gives them insights into their own prior conduct.

If youth fail to complete the terms of their probation successfully, then they will be referred back to the regular court for processing. In traditional juvenile court, there is the possibility that more serious consequences will be imposed on such juveniles by presiding judges.

Benefits of teen courts are that youth will not acquire a juvenile record if they complete the terms of their program successfully. This is a strong incentive to remain law-abiding and conform to all rules imposed by the teen court.

Mental Health Courts

Problems with mentally ill prisoners are not new to United States' prisons and jails (American Bar Association 1989; Mattick 1975). Prisoners with mental health issues present particularly problematic issues for prison administrators, as well as guards and inmates (Henderson 1998; Steadman and Veysey 1997). The most fundamental problem is that prisons, and specifically jails, are ill equipped to deal with these prisoners by providing adequate mental health services (Wolff 1998). According to James and Glaze (2006), over half of persons in jail and prison have some type of mental health problem; this means there are over 700,000 mentally ill persons in state prisons, close to 79,000 mentally ill persons in federal prisons, and roughly 480,000 persons with mental health problems in jails. These statistics portray that mental health issues are a clear problem for individuals who come into contact with the courts as well as the difficulties that might be encountered by the criminal justice system in dealing with these offenders.

The extent of mental health problems for criminal defendants has prompted calls for the court to do more regarding defendants with mental illnesses. Mental health courts are specialized courts designed to deal with defendants who have diagnoses of mental illness to provide them with a wide range of services in order to stop the cycle of contact with the criminal justice system and help them to be functional, participating members of the community again (Council of State Governments Justice Center 2008). These offenders, as opposed to mentally stable offenders, cause numerous problems for criminal courts. Controlling and supervising jail and prison populations in order to ensure the safety of both prisoners and guards is crucial to corrections officials. The presence of mentally ill prisoners in the nation's jails and prisons, coupled with overcrowding problems, makes supervision and safety increasingly difficult (Goldkamp and Irons-Guynn 2000). First, offenders may not realize the rights that they have as defendants in a court of law, and second, they may not understand the consequences of their actions or the severity of the sanctions they are facing. Often these offenders have dual diagnoses.

Common features among mental health courts include the following: some eligibility requirements for participation (a demonstrable mental health issue), preventing incarceration of the mentally ill and instead providing some form of community-based corrections facilities, ensuring public safety through careful screening and acceptance only of low-level offenders without histories of violent behavior, and early intervention through identification of eligible participants within a short period after their arrest (Goldkamp and Irons-Guynn 2000). Today, there are over 300 mental health courts operating in the United States (Council of State Governments Justice Center 2016). As jurisdictions continue to struggle with the best and most cost-effective ways to resolve criminal cases involving defendants with mental health issues, the number of mental health courts being implemented is likely to increase.

Veterans Courts

As the number of veterans who are returning from Iraq and Afghanistan with severe depression and post-traumatic stress disorder increases, jurisdictions are seeking new ways to deal with those who commit crimes or are addicted to, and abuse, drugs (Haughney 2010). The first VTC was set up in Buffalo, New York, in 2008, and the number of them being implemented around the country has rapidly expanded since. In fact, VTCs are the fastest growing type of specialty court with only one in existence in 2004 and over 250 in 2016 (Baldwin 2016). Veterans courts, like other specialty courts, are run from a therapeutic justice approach. These courts similarly have certain goals and objectives in dealing with and treating their clients, U.S. veterans. Some of these include eligibility for participation related to service in the armed forces and some type of illness related to combat; the court acting as a liaison with the criminal justice system and the Veterans Affairs (VA); treatment, supervision, advocacy, and support for veterans struggling with addiction, depression, and other illnesses related to reintegration back into society after combat (Schaffer 2010).

While the VTC phenomenon is likely to continue in the foreseeable future as returning veterans from the most recent wars in Iraq and Afghanistan endure issues adjusting back to civilian life, not much is known about the operation of VTCs in general, and even less regarding their effects on recidivism (Hartley and Baldwin 2016). Although a few VTCs report data and outcomes, lack of empirical research limits our ability to determine the reliability of these initial results.

Unfortunately today, veterans are overrepresented in statistics relating to "substance abuse, driving under the influence (DUI). . .assaults, intimate partner violence (IPV), family conflicts, homelessness episodes, suicides, post-traumatic stress disorder (PTSD), and other problems" (Schaffer 2010, 22). Veterans are also more likely to commit suicide; these chances might increase if they are incarcerated (Wortzel, Binswanger, Anderson, and Adler 2009). As more and more veterans return from Iraq and Afghanistan and as some of them have difficulties adjusting back to civilian life, veterans courts will become an increasingly important aspect of the criminal justice system in helping those who have served their country to get the help they need (Haughney 2010).

Not every veteran returning from war will have problems adjusting to life back at home, or turn to alcohol, drugs, or crime to deal with their adjustment. Transitioning back to civilian life, however, may be difficult for some veterans returning from war, especially those who have seen a lot of combat time. The nation's courts, the Department of Veterans Affairs, and our prison systems are often lacking resources to adequately deal with offenders who suffer from some of the problems that returning vets will face (Schaffer 2010). Jurisdictions establishing veterans treatment courts to provide a holistic approach in dealing with substance abuse and other crime problems such as domestic violence will give those who have served their country a fighting chance to reintegrate back into society and civilian life.

Summary

1. *Understand the trend in options that prosecutors and judges have when a case comes into the criminal court system and that these vary by type of crime and jurisdiction.*

When a case enters the criminal court system, it does not mean that it will follow through the entire criminal court process. There are many factors that go into determining whether cases will continue onto the next stage in the criminal court process or whether they will be diverted out of the formal system. Prosecutors are under pressure to resolve their cases and to also do that in the most cost effective and expeditiously manner. Obviously a prosecutor's office cannot prosecute all cases and so they must prioritize on the basis of which are the most deserving of prosecution and which are a lower priority and may be dealt with via alternative programs and processes.

Many jurisdictions around the country have passed resolutions to resolve less serious cases in a more informal manner to preserve valuable court time and resources. They have either enacted new statutes or have given prosecutors and judges increased discretion in how to deal with certain types of cases or particular types of offenders. For example, some jurisdictions have resorted to giving fines in possession of marijuana cases. Others have set up specialty court programs to deal with drinking and driving offenders or domestic abuse cases. Other jurisdictions

have gone as far as decriminalizing or legalizing small amounts of certain drugs. There is obviously opposition to this from more crime control oriented opponents but in the last decade, more and more legislators, county judges, and mayors are seeking to alleviate court caseloads and the high cost that comes with processing cases. By diverting certain cases or offenders away from the traditional court process, more time can be spent on prosecuting the most serious cases. The main strategies for reducing the criminal court caseload include (1) decriminalization, (2) alternative dispute resolution, and (3) diversion.

2. *Understand the decriminalization process.*

Several states have sought to decriminalize various laws seeking to lessen the number of defendants charged with minor crimes. Decriminalization means to remove a particular act from the classification of misdemeanor and/or felony. Often when certain crimes are decriminalized, some of these acts, which were previously crimes, fall within civil jurisdiction and are resolved through civil courts.

3. *Examine alternative dispute resolution, including its applications, advantages, and disadvantages.*

Another pretrial option is to use alternative dispute resolution, or ADR. ADR is an informal process of dispute settlement between an offender and a victim, under the supervision of a third party. Sometimes known as restorative justice or victim–offender mediation or victim–offender reconciliation, ADR seeks to remove less serious offenses from the jurisdiction of criminal courts and decrease their case volumes. When ADR is used, offenders ordinarily do not acquire criminal records; victims are compensated for their losses or injuries; court dockets are eased; prosecutor caseloads are alleviated; the community benefits in various ways; and one's accountability is heightened through the restitution process.

Some disadvantages are that ADR permits many persons to escape prosecution as criminals; it may be an insufficient punishment and deterrent to future offending; reoffending may be encouraged if offenders think their crimes will only result in civil resolutions; excessive leniency may be alleged by an increasingly critical public; and the proportionality of punishment may be questioned.

4. *Understand the role and participation of victims in alternative dispute resolution and victim–offender reconciliation projects.*

The goal of ADR is to reconcile the dispute between victims and offenders. Victim participation in ADR allows all aspects of the offense and the impact on the victim to be part of the process. When the victim has input on the punishment and perhaps is able to receive compensation they feel as if the system has their best interest in mind and can also confront the perpetrator to assist in their emotional healing. Several victim–offender reconciliation projects (VORPs) have been used as the basis for experiments designed to heighten offender accountability, reduce offender recidivism, and provide adequate compensation to victims for their losses.

5. *Describe pretrial diversion, its implications for divertees, and the advantages and disadvantages of diversion.*

Pretrial diversion is another option that prosecutors may use to divert cases from the criminal justice process, at least temporarily. Diversion is the temporary cessation of a prosecution against someone, usually a low-risk first offender, who may be required to participate in one or more community programs and complete different types of activities for periods of six months or longer. If persons, known as divertees, complete their periods of diversion successfully, they often have the charges against them dismissed and the records of the arrest expunged.

There are many functions of diversion. These include permitting offenders to remain in their communities and continue earning a living and supporting their dependents; making restitution to victims if appropriate; avoiding the stigma of a criminal conviction; reducing

jail and prison overcrowding; making it possible for offenders to participate in self-help programs and to receive possible individual or group counseling for certain problems they may have; and preserving family unity. Criticisms of diversion are that it sends a leniency message to offenders that they can get away with violating the law and have their records expunged as a result; guilt is assumed without a trial; net-widening is encouraged; some gender bias results, as proportionately greater numbers of men are placed on diversion compared with women; due process is ignored; and the policy of diversion is too lenient.

6. *Describe several sanctioning options available to judges, including community service, fines, restitution to victims, and various types of victim compensation programs.*

Other types of noncriminal or pretrial sanctions include community service, victim compensation, and restitution. The forms of community service vary from maintaining public parks, cutting courthouse lawns, and picking up highway litter, to participating in youth leagues or assisting the elderly in their residences or group homes.

Restitution heightens offender accountability by obligating offenders to pay for the damages they have caused to property or for the loss of wages if victims are injured. Victim compensation is a way of offsetting the damages caused to victims. The nature of victim compensation may vary. Different victim compensation programs have been described. These include the financial/community service model, the victim–offender mediation model, the victim/reparations model, and repaying victims through restitution. Each of these models offers victims some form of compensation or restitution, and perpetrator involvement in such programs is mandatory. Offender accountability is heightened.

7. *Understand specialty and problem-solving courts and the underlying focus on treatment and rehabilitation of the offender rather than punishment of the offense.*

Specialty courts are also known as problem-solving courts and are alternative methods of dealing with certain types of offenders. Specialty courts have a philosophy of therapeutic jurisprudence and are focused on rehabilitating the offender rather than punishment for an offense. Certain specialty courts, such as domestic violence courts, also focus on victims to be sure of their safety and getting them the help they may also need. Drug courts are the most prevalent of these problem-solving courts, but others also include domestic violence courts, youth or teen courts, mental health courts, and more recently, the fastest growing incarnation, veterans treatment courts.

8. *Describe several different types of specialty courts such as drug courts, mental health courts, veterans courts, domestic violence courts, and youth courts.*

The most prevalent type of specialty courts are drug courts. These courts hear exclusively drug-related charges against defendants placing drug users and abusers into programs where their underlying drug problems can be remedied. Drug court participants receive counseling and other forms of therapy and have been successful in assisting many offenders to overcome and deal with their addiction problems.

Domestic violence courts have the goal of assisting jurisdictions to provide consistent responses to cases of domestic violence, provision of services for victims, and providing accountability for offenders via supervision and monitoring. Because the traditional manner in which the courts have dealt with domestic violence have been criticized that they do not reduce domestic violence or provide protection to victims, these courts have been established as a method of placing more attention on the victims in these cases and holding offenders more accountable via supervision and monitoring to reduce future incidents of domestic violence.

Youth courts, also referred to as teen courts, peer courts, or student courts, are informal court proceedings as an alternative to juvenile court for determining one's guilt and punishment. The focus of these courts is rehabilitation and they usually only hear and decide minor cases where a youth has committed a status offense or a misdemeanor. An outcome of these courts is that they teach empathy to juvenile offenders.

Mental health courts are specialized courts designed to deal with persons who have committed offenses but have mental illness. These courts provide these individuals with a wide range of services in order to assist in stabilizing health problems with the hopes of stopping the cycle of contact with law enforcement and the courts. Goals of mental health courts are to deal with offenders who have issues that cause numerous problems for traditional criminal courts, and help them to become functional, participating members of the community again.

Veterans treatment courts are the fastest growing specialty court in the United States, and have goals and objectives to assist and rehabilitate justice involved veterans who have mental health and substance abuse issues. Unfortunately today, post the recent wars in Iraq and Afghanistan, veterans have higher incidents of substance abuse, DUI, assaults, PTSD, homelessness, and suicide. As more and more veterans returning from Iraq and Afghanistan become involved with the criminal justice system because of some of these issues, veterans treatment courts will continue to be established across the country to assist veterans struggling with addiction, depression, and other illnesses related to adjusting back to civilian life.

Key Terms

alternative dispute resolution (ADR) *305*
community service *310*
community service orders *311*
Comprehensive Crime Control Act of 1984 *311*
decriminalization *304*
diversion *308*

diversion programs *308*
impartial arbiters *306*
mediation *306*
pretrial diversion *308*
problem-solving courts *312*
reparations *311*
restitution *310*
restorative justice *305*

specialty courts *312*
stigmatization *306*
victim compensation programs *307*
victim impact statement *307*
victim–offender reconciliation *307*
Victim–Offender Reconciliation Project (VORP) *307*
Victims of Crime Act of 1984 *311*

Critical Thinking Exercises

1. What do you think of the differences in the forms in which states have legalized marijuana? In about half of the states, it is still illegal to possess, and in the other half, it is legal to possess mostly for medical purposes, but at least five states have now legalized possession of small amounts for recreational purposes. Some of these states put it on the ballot and let the people decide whether or not to legalize it. What

do you think about the fact that the people have voted to legalize marijuana but federally it is still illegal? Should anything be done by the federal government to step in and make the laws uniform across the country, either invalidating the ballot votes, or changing federal law to legalize or decriminalize possession?

2. Some people have criticized alternative dispute resolution and diversion programs as picking the least serious offenders for participation and then lauding their success. There have also been criticisms of gender and race disparity in acceptance into these programs. Should these programs attempt to treat and reform more serious offenders? What could be done to the eligibility criteria for these programs to ensure that they are not discriminating with regard to which cases get diverted and which remain in the traditional court system?

Case Study Decision-Making Exercise

Some critics have stated that veterans treatment courts give preferential treatment to justice involved veterans that offenders who are not veterans do not receive. They argue that judges are already able to consider military service at sentencing as a mitigating factor and that veterans courts are diverting certain offenders, veterans, away from the criminal justice system thereby treating them as a special class of citizens. Proponents of veterans treatment courts argue that justice involved veterans have unique needs related to combat deployments such as post-traumatic stress disorder (PTSD) and traumatic brain injuries (TBI) that could be related to their criminal offending and as such deserve to get treatment they need in an alternative setting. What do you think? Because the military doesn't do a good job of assisting veterans to reintegrate and get assistance for issues they may have related to trauma and injuries, do they deserve to get a second chance to be treated if they run afoul of the law? Or do you think that these courts are discriminating by making eligibility for acceptance that the individual be a veterans and therefore giving preferential treatment by the courts to those who have served?

Concept Review Questions

1. What are four types of victim–offender mediation? Describe each briefly.
2. Distinguish between diversion and alternative dispute resolution.
3. What is meant by decriminalization?
4. What are the advantages of alternative dispute resolution? Disadvantages?
5. What is victim–offender mediation? Where did it start and for what type of crime?
6. What is restorative justice? How is it different from traditional methods of criminal case processing?
7. What is special about specialty or problem-solving courts? What is the focus of these courts?
8. Where was the first ever drug court begun? How extensive are drug courts today?
9. List the ways in which specific specialty courts are focused on the offender or victim rather than on the offense.

Suggested Readings

1. Jeremy Prichard (2010). "Net-Widening and the Diversion of Young People From Court: A Longitudinal Analysis With Implications for Restorative Justice." *Australian and New Zealand Journal of Criminology* **43**:112–129.
2. Julie M. Baldwin (2014). "The Veterans Treatment Court Concept in Practice: Issues for *Practitioners." Perspectives* **38**:74–92.
3. Maggie T. Grace (2010). "Criminal Alternative Dispute Resolution: Restoring Justice, Respecting Responsibility, and Renewing Public Norms." *Vermont Law Review* **34**:563–595.
4. Richard D. Schneider (2010). "Mental Health Courts and Diversion Programs: A Global Survey." *International Journal of Law and Psychiatry* **33**:201–206.
5. Kimberly A. Kaiser and Kristy Holtfreter (2015). "An Integrated Theory of Specialized Court Programs: Using Procedural Justice and Therapeutic Jurisprudence to Promote Offender Compliance and Rehabilitation." *Criminal Justice and Behavior* doi: 10.1177/0093854815609642.
6. Greg Berman and John Feinblatt (2005). *Good Courts: The Case for Problem-Solving Justice*. New York: The New Press.

14 Courts, Media, and the Litigation Explosion

LEARNING OBJECTIVES

As a result of reading this chapter, you will have accomplished the following objectives:

1 *Understand how the media have been instrumental in shaping our perceptions of justice, and that the courts and the media are at odds with each other because of competing interests.*

2 *Explain the history of the media and the courts from before the 1800s up until today and the idea of cameras in courtrooms.*

3 *Define the current status of the access granted to the media by the courts in the various jurisdictions throughout the United States.*

4 *Draw appropriate conclusions about pretrial publicity and the effect it has on trials.*

5 *Recognize the types of information that potential jurors consider to be prejudicial, including case-specific and general pretrial publicity.*

6 *Give examples of the different ways in which pretrial publicity can be minimized, including gag orders, jury instructions, change of venues, and jury sequestration.*

7 *Understand the litigation explosion and the reasons why America has become more litigious, including the emergence of industrial capitalism, changing legal doctrines, and the transformation of scholarly legal thought.*

8 *Distinguish among the different arguments for tort reform, such as the fact that the number of tort cases has dramatically increased, and the belief that juries are unable to handle tort cases because they are usually sympathetic to the plaintiff and hand out excessive awards.*

Many cities around the nation face thousands of lawsuits each year, and the cost of resolving these disputes against city workers, police departments, and hospitals has increased in recent years. Some large cities like New York and Chicago will spend close to a $1 billion in tax payer dollars to settle lawsuits against them. These lawsuits range from breach of contract cases to wrongful convictions, but police misconduct and hospital malpractice suits are increasingly comprising a larger share of costs to the nations metropolitan areas (Balko, 2014; Durkin, 2015). A Wall Street Journal report reveals that cities with the ten largest police departments shelled out close to $250 million to settle lawsuits in 2014; New York, Chicago, and Los Angeles paid out the most for police misconduct cases (Elinson and Frosch, 2015). It is likely that mayors and city administrators will have to pay closer attention to the day to day practices and professionalism of city employees as taxpayers will demand greater accountability for prevention of future lawsuits which are an increasing drain on their tax dollars.

Sources: Balko, Radley (2014). "U.S. cities pay out millions to settle police lawsuits." *Washington Post,* October 1, 2014. Retrieved online at: https://www.washingtonpost.com/news/the-watch/wp/2014/10/01/u-s-cities-pay-out-millions-to-settle-police-lawsuits/?utm_term=.880b34c9e4bf.

Durkin, Erin (2015). "New York City paid $550 million for lawsuits in 2014; NYPD was target of most claims." *New York Daily News,* August 27, 2015. Retrieved online at: http://www.nydailynews.com/new-york/new-york-city-paid-550m-lawsuits-2014-report-article-1.2339869.

Elison, Zusha, and Dan Frosch (2015). "Cost of police-misconduct cases soars in big U.S. cities." *The Wall Street Journal,* July 15, 2015. Retrieved online at: http://www.wsj.com/articles/cost-of-police-misconduct-cases-soars-in-big-u-s-cities-1437013834.

▶ Introduction

These awards and many others like them every year are given to plaintiffs by juries in civil cases. They seem exorbitant or out of proportion compared with the harm done in the case. The U.S. society is characterized as being too litigious, so much so that doctors, coaches, teachers, and even ministers have a fear of being sued. It is the reason insurance premiums in some professions are excessive, the reason why some cities have to cut funding to public services, and the reason why the average citizen when wanting to have something as simple as a garage sale has to put up a sign saying that they are not responsible for accidents.

Do these things happen every day? Should we be fearful of litigation against us? Or is the media blowing these things out of proportion by focusing on what constitutes an infinitesimal number of cases? According to the American system of justice, the media coverage given to trials is supposedly irrelevant and should not be viewed by jurors. Jurors take an oath that they will remain impartial and objective. They are obliged to refrain from listening to, reading about, or watching anything related to the trial. In reality, however, many jurors keep in close touch with trial events and the media coverage of them. And most people, including jurors, are affected by what they see and hear. We are in the midst of an era of media news frenzy, and in diverse ways almost everyone is influenced by the media and its news reports and characterizations.

Since the early 1900s, the courts have had an antagonistic relationship with the media. Increasing numbers of courtrooms are permitting limited or extensive television coverage. Such permissiveness is consistent with the public's right to know, about public access to the courts, and about the freedom of speech. However, the media has almost always sought to dramatize court events in different ways so as to stimulate listeners, readers, and viewers. *Court TV* and *CNN Headline News* show pioneered creative and innovative court reporting through the use of experts and panels of experts who debate, criticize, and overanalyze information bits from trial testimony and events. No court actor has escaped the intensive scrutiny of television cameras or the opinions, reactions, and interpretations of events through the eyes and ears of courtroom observers. Hourly reporting of who has testified, what the judge thought or seemed to think about the testimony, juror reactions, and other courtroom banter has riveted millions of television viewers. If the courtroom news has not been sufficiently dramatic, these shows will often create their own news by giving less newsworthy events fictitious spins for audience consumption. Conjectures from guests and "what ifs" from news commentators or legal experts and analysts are often passed off as factual information, when in fact they may simply be their opinion.

Today, the public seems discontent with simple news reporting. Generally, judicial decisions are reported only when they seem newsworthy. When television producers or newspaper reporters determine that a judge has imposed a lenient sentence, or that a jury has failed to convict a guilty-appearing defendant, or if an unusually large monetary award is made in a civil case by a jury, these outcomes are reported on the evening news or in daily newspapers. The selection of the news events to report is not particularly random. Rather, the news selection process is carefully calculated to yield the greatest public impact. The more sensational the news and the way it is reported, the greater the interest and viewership.

The police and prosecutors often have a symbiotic relationship with the media. In exchange for confidential information from the police or district attorney's offices, reporters will slant their stories in ways favorable to police conclusions and prosecutorial theorizing about the crime, how it was committed, and who probably committed it. Seldom is equal time allocated to defendants so that they can give their version of events or their side of the story. The courts have increasingly relied upon technology to assist in processing cases. In many jurisdictions, initial appearances and arraignments are held by means of closed-circuit television. The defendant remains at the jail and enters a plea before the judge across town in the courthouse through closed-circuit television monitoring systems. Jurisdictions have adopted this alternative to minimize security problems and the costs of transporting defendants to and from their jails for short court appearances.

This chapter examines two important issues that shape our perceptions about the American court system. The first issue is the nature of the interplay between the courts and the media. This interplay has prompted much public discourse, especially as the direct result of several high-profile trials during the 1990s. The O. J. Simpson trial focused national attention both on court protocol and on the various personalities involved in the trial. All relevant actors were scrutinized, including the judge, the prosecution and defense counsel, jury members, and witnesses. All persons watching the courtroom drama were active participants who critiqued the actions of the witnesses, attorneys, and the judge.

The second issue is our definition of justice as portrayed by the media. Has the legitimacy of the court system been undermined because our ideals of justice are inconsistent with courtroom reality delivered by the media into our homes through radio or television? Have the courts been effective and acted responsibly in their use of technology? How has the media shaped our perceptions of the "litigation explosion"? We have witnessed seemingly outlandish jury judgments in civil cases extended to persons who have filed lawsuits that appear frivolous. We have seen an array of courtroom tactics used successfully by plaintiff's attorneys against big businesses and corporate giants. The mentality of juries and the racial and ethnic composition of jurors have been analyzed extensively by the media, and we are inclined to view the average juror in a criminal or civil case in disparaging ways. Jurors are perceived both as pawns of the legal system and as self-styled vigilantes with their own political and social agendas. The buzzword of the 1990s was jury nullification, where juries disregard the facts in favor of some alternative and contrary verdict that satisfies political ends rather than legal ones.

This chapter is organized as follows. First, a brief history is provided of the media and its uneasy association with the American justice system. Technological change has modified greatly the nature of courtroom intrusion by the media. Newspapers, radio, and television innovations have been significant in influencing what happens in courtrooms throughout the nation. Increasingly clear is the fact that the behaviors of courtroom actors have undergone a metamorphosis of sorts as courtrooms have been subjected to greater public scrutiny. The implications of these behavioral changes for the justice process are explored.

Several highly visible trials are described, together with the nature of attention given to each by the media. The media has been instrumental in promoting a defendant's guilt or innocence, depending on the specific case. Accordingly, jurors have been responsive to particular types of media coverage, such that it is questionable whether justice has been served in certain cases. Indeed, some jury verdicts have been reversed by the U.S. Supreme Court because of the undue influence of media trial coverage. Often, media coverage has been passed off and labeled as the **court of public opinion**. The media has magnified the popularity of this term over time, and many citizens accept media opinion as factually based and give considerable credence to it.

Next, pretrial publicity is described. Pretrial publicity is almost always prejudicial for the defense or prosecution. Sensationalized coverage of both spectacular and heinous crimes has created an emotionally charged milieu for more than a few defendants. In certain cases, defense counsels have sought to change the site of a trial because of extensive adverse pretrial publicity. The trials of the Oklahoma City Bombers, Timothy McVeigh and Terry Nichols, were transferred from Oklahoma City to Denver because it was believed that the amount of pretrial publicity indicated that they could not receive a fair trial in Oklahoma. This section will also explore the factors that determine whether the prejudice generated by pretrial publicity is sufficient to jeopardize one's right to a fair and impartial trial. Several ways for minimizing the prejudicial effects of pretrial publicity are described.

Besides criminal trials, many civil trials have generated a considerable amount of publicity and coverage by the media. Often these trials involve tort actions, where monetary damages are sought instead of convictions. **Tort actions** may highlight negligence, wrongful death, or product liability. The litigation explosion is also depicted, where the volume of civil cases has burgeoned in recent decades. The media has labeled our society as litigious, emphasizing quite appropriately the increasing interest of persons in seeking monetary awards from their employers or from large corporations. The bases of these increasing numbers of lawsuits may be sexual harassment, product liability, or wrongful death. Many lawsuits are labeled by judges as frivolous and dismissed. Others are decided in civil courtrooms by juries. Again, the media is present and pervasive to assess and interpret what is going on and why. The chapter concludes with a discussion of tort reforms.

court of public opinion informal reactions to legal cases by unofficial pollsters and media broadcasters who cover high-profile cases on television and in the newspapers; independent reactions to court events by persons who may have only a passing interest in cases.

tort actions any legal proceeding where a plaintiff is seeking damages from a defendant for a civil wrong.

▶ Trials and the Court of Public Opinion

The media has been instrumental in shaping our perceptions of justice. The media and the courts are often at odds because of their competing interests. The courts operate in a methodical fashion, following specific criminal or civil protocols that may at times frustrate the observer. A great deal of time is consumed over seemingly trivial details of events, although we are reminded by the experts on television talk shows that the most trivial details have profound importance in shaping trial outcomes. Verdicts are rendered only after juries have given careful review to factual details, expert witness testimony, and an intricate inspection of all relevant evidence. While the case proceeds at a snail's pace, the media has its story to tell. The most innocuous details of a case are given great weight. Thus, an otherwise boring story by the media is converted into an exciting one by creative media spins. The viability of a network television show is critically dependent upon the nature of sensational coverage given to the most mundane courtroom events.

There has been considerable debate about the role and influence of the media and the courts. The O. J. Simpson case brought all the arguments for and against the media access to the courts into the public discourse. For instance, before the O. J. Simpson murder case, the presiding judge, Lance Ito, was initially reluctant to permit television cameras in his courtroom. Judge Ito believed that the presence of television cameras would undermine the justice process and cause viewers to misunderstand the proceedings. He also believed that tabloidization of the judicial process would occur. In retrospect, Judge Ito was right, although he permitted television cameras to cover most aspects of the trial anyway.

Judge Ito's reservations about the intrusion of television cameras and representatives from the media into his courtroom were well-founded and grounded in scientific research. Several scholars and legal experts have provided compelling arguments both for and against television cameras in courtrooms (Hoskins, Ruth, and Ruback 2004). While these arguments are inconclusive and inconsistent, the general sentiment is that television coverage of courtroom drama does influence what goes on in the courtroom. There is extensive debate about whether this influence jeopardizes one's right to a fair trial, however. Media representatives emphasize that their interest in covering courtroom events is based on the public's right to be present inside courtrooms as public events. Thus, a judge's refusal to allow the media into courtrooms is perceived as a violation of the First Amendment. Technological change and the advent of television and closed-circuit broadcasting have done much to change the definition of public access to courtroom activities, however. In order to understand how the definition of public courtroom access has changed, we must first examine the early vestiges of courtroom coverage by the media.

▶ History of the Media and the Courts

Court reaction to media intrusion has gradually changed with changing media technology. In the 1800s, trial outcomes or happenings were relayed by word of mouth. This information dissemination shifted from word of mouth to the printed page with the advent of newspapers. By the 1850s, trial events and court decisions were transmitted throughout the country by use of the telegraph. Those eager to hear the results would often gather at the local telegraph office and wait for the trial results to be announced. The most widely acknowledged example of this process was the murder trial of Harry Thaw. He had killed millionaire Stanford White over the affections of a very young Evelyn Nesbit, also known as the "girl in the red velvet swing."

Soon courtroom photographers and newsreel cameras were common occurrences in the most high-profile cases. The Tennessee trial of teacher John Scopes, known as the "monkey trial," was the first to be broadcast over the radio. Attorneys Clarence Darrow and William Jennings Bryan were well aware of the impact of the media presence and structured their trial tactics not only for the benefit of the jury but also for the benefit of the larger national audience. In fact, compared with today's standards, the media seemed to intrude on court proceedings by making requests similar to those from a movie director to an actor rather than to court officers. For instance, representatives from the media have often made requests for the attorneys and judges to position themselves so that their cameras could get better picture angles.

The problems created by the media during the murder trial of Bartolomeo Vanzetti and Nicola Sacco in 1921 and during the trial of Richard Loeb and Nathan Leopold Jr. in 1924 prompted the American Bar Association to review the issue of news reporting and the courts. It took another "trial of the century" to force the courts to come to terms with the impact of the media on court proceedings.

The trial involved Bruno Hauptmann, a German immigrant. Hauptmann was accused of kidnaping and murdering the baby of Charles Lindberg. The trial started with over 700 representatives of the media, with 120 being cameramen. The trial was chaos. Witnesses were barraged by reporters and blinded by flashbulbs reminiscent of an opening at a Hollywood movie premiere. Hauptmann appealed his conviction, alleging that the extensive media coverage prevented him from receiving a fair trial. He lost his appeal, but the trial prompted the American Bar Association to review their position on camera access to court proceedings. They ultimately ruled in 1937 that photographing and broadcasting court proceedings should be prohibited. Most states adopted the position of the American Bar Association and forbid photographing and broadcasting trials and trial participants. In 1952, the American Bar Association extended the media ban to include television coverage of court proceedings.

Texas was one of the states that ignored the recommendation of the American Bar Association and allowed cameras into the courtroom at the discretion of the judge. In 1962, Texas provided the case that served as the basis for denying cameras into the courtroom. Billie Sol Estes, a friend of President Lyndon B. Johnson, was charged with swindling persons out of large sums of cash. The trial judge decided to allow television cameras into the courtroom, but they were restricted to the back of the courtroom in a specially constructed booth. Like Hauptmann 30 years earlier, Estes argued that the media coverage deprived him of a fair trial. The Texas Court of Appeals declared that his due process rights had not been violated, and Estes appealed to the U.S. Supreme Court. In a 5–4 decision, the U.S. Supreme Court reversed Estes's conviction. In the decision of the majority, the Court held that although no prejudice was actually shown, the circumstances of the case were suspect. Furthermore, Justice Clark believed that the presence of the cameras in the courtroom had a harmful effect on all of those involved in the trial. In its decision, the U.S. Supreme Court did not address the issue of whether the First Amendment extended to the media to broadcast from the courtroom (*Estes v. Texas*, 1965).

After the *Estes* decision, states continued to experiment with media coverage of courts. Judges were generally given the discretion to allow cameras. For the next 12 years, courts individually struggled with the decision to allow cameras. In 1977, the Florida Supreme Court approved a one-year pilot study that allowed the electronic media to cover all of cases in Florida state courts without the consent of the participants. The crucial case that emerged during this year involved a 15-year-old boy who was charged with murdering an elderly neighbor while he and some friends burglarized the victim's house. The circumstances of the offense were not unusual. What attracted the media to the trial was the unusual defense of involuntary television intoxication, which was offered by the boy and his attorneys. The defense alleged that Zamora (the boy) did not know what he was doing because of the massive amounts of crime and violence he had watched on television. The local media broadcast segments of the trial on the nightly news and the worldwide audience was estimated at several million viewers. At the conclusion of the trial, Judge Paul Baker submitted a report, including his observations about the effect of the media on the trial. He believed that the equipment did not produce any distracting noises or light flashes. By contrast, during the *Estes* trial, the camera and lighting equipment created various distractions. In the years between these cases, camera technology had changed significantly, and ultimately it became less intrusive in the courtroom and seemed to have little impact on the courtroom actors.

Judge Baker spoke with jurors about their reactions to the presence of the media. The jurors believed that the presence of the cameras caused only slight distractions. Yet, the actions of the media did not hinder or distract the jurors from following the testimony, arguments of counsel, and judicial instructions. The judge also found no support for the assertion that judges would alter the way that they conduct business with the presence of the cameras.

Considering this information as well as the evidence from other cases, in 1979, the Florida Supreme Court permanently allowed cameras in the courts with the approval of the presiding judge. The new provisions were put to the test with the Ted Bundy murder trial. Ted Bundy defended himself and appeared to enjoy playing to the cameras. However, the trial judge believed that the rules in place were effective and the cameras did not hamper the court process. The court acknowledged that publicity could undermine a defendant's right to a fair trial. However, this risk did not allow for an absolute ban on news reporting and the broadcasting of trials. Essentially, the U.S. Supreme Court left the decision up to the individual states whether to allow the media into their courtrooms.

▶ Current Status of Media Access to the Courts

Currently, all 50 states allow videotaping of court proceedings in some form with certain restrictions. The federal courts, however, including the Supreme Court, do not allow cameras to cover their proceedings. A bill in Congress authored by Senator Chuck Grassley of Iowa would give federal judges the discretion to grant cameras access to court proceedings. Under this legislation, there would be certain restrictions, such as no videotaping of the jury or certain witnesses, and no recording of conferences between the defendant and his or her attorney or conversations between the prosecution, defense, and judge that are not part of the record.

Most states have allowed cameras in their courtrooms on either an experimental or a permanent basis. States that have allowed cameras in the courtroom have developed guidelines for their usage. In most states, the consent of the presiding judge is required. Many states require a written application submitted in advance of the trial. Furthermore, in some states, if the defendant objects, cameras will not be permitted to record the trial proceedings.

Most states do not allow television coverage of cases involving juveniles, and coverage is limited where victims of sex crimes are involved or where cases involve trade secrets of business organizations. Fewer states limit coverage of jurors and the *voir dire* process. And all states ban the coverage of pretrial conferences or sidebars between the judge, prosecutor, and defense counsel in court. States have also developed guidelines that regulate media equipment and personnel. Courts specify which types of cameras are allowed and limit the movement and number of media personnel in the court.

▶ Pretrial Publicity

pretrial publicity any media attention given to a case before it is tried in court.

One of the primary concerns of those who study the relationship between the court and the media is the effect of pretrial publicity. Within this area, there are two different issues. The first is that the extensive pretrial publicity will make it difficult if not impossible to locate jurors who have not heard of the cases and developed some preconceived notions about the defendant's guilt or innocence. The second is that the jurors, as the result of the pretrial publicity, will recognize that their decision will be scrutinized by friends, family, neighbors, and the larger community. This pressure will ultimately influence them to vote on the basis of how their own lives will be affected rather than the actual facts of the case. In the *Estes* decision, this was probably the issue that concerned the U.S. Supreme Court the most. The Court wrote that the potential impact of television on the jurors is perhaps of the greatest significance. They are the nerve center of the fact-finding process. And we must remember that realistically it is only the notorious trial that will be broadcast, because of the necessity of the paid sponsorship. The conscious or unconscious effect that this may have on the juror's judgment cannot be evaluated, but experience indicates that it is not only possible but probable that it will have a direct bearing on his/her vote as to guilt or innocence. Where pretrial publicity of all kinds has created intense public feeling that is aggravated by the telecasting or picturing of the trial, the televised jurors cannot help but feel the pressure of knowing that friends or neighbors have their eyes upon them. If the community is hostile to an accused, then a televised juror, realizing he/she must return to neighbors who saw the trial themselves, may well be led "not to hold the balance nice, clear and true between the State and the accused" (*Estes v. Texas*, 1965:545).

Some persons have argued that juror concerns over the impact of their decisions should not allow for their identity to be concealed. In fact, juror anonymity should only be allowed in the rarest of cases. In fact, jurors in high-profile cases should be regarded as citizen-soldiers in the quest for justice. It may be that the pretrial publicity placed in the context of day-to-day operations of the court should not be a concern. Daily, the courts process thousands of cases, usually in empty courtrooms. Some persons might assert that rather than having a problem with pretrial publicity, the larger problem facing the court is public apathy. When somebody wanders into a courtroom merely to watch the proceedings, the courtroom actors take notice. They assume that the observer must be a defendant, and when this is not the case, they wonder why this person doesn't have anything better to do than watch courtroom proceedings. Researchers have estimated that only about 7 percent of felony arrests are covered by the press (Champion 2005b).

What Do You Think?

Should television cameras be allowed in courtrooms? Advocates of allowing cameras cite the First Amendment right of citizens to see justice in action literally. Some states have very restrictive access policies, and the federal courts mostly oppose cameras on grounds having to do with undue influence of court officers, including the prosecution, defense, and jury. Supreme Court justices have even weighed in citing that allowing cameras into their proceedings would have a negative effect on the participants, causing lawyers, judges, and witnesses to be intimidated and act unnaturally. Although these claims have never been proven in the states where cameras have been allowed to cover trials, there have been a few cases where it appeared as if the judge or other actors were playing to the camera. Proponents of camera access and some broadcasting organizations say that televised court proceedings would give the public a valuable education on the workings of the justice system. They say that the educational benefit could be even greater in the nation's highest court. However, the U.S. Supreme Court has been opposed to televising their work, just as Congress at one time balked at having cameras cover their proceedings. But today, programs such as those on C-Span have given millions of Americans a better understanding of how Senators debate subjects and how laws are made. Does the public also deserve to see how the courts carry out and interpret the law? Should all courts, including the SCOTUS, allow cameras in the courtroom? Should the public be allowed to see their appointed and elected officials, including justices of the highest court, in action firsthand? What harm would cameras cause, if any, to the outcomes of the cases? What do you think?

The concern over pretrial publicity only occurs when there is a high-profile case. The common assumption is that pretrial publicity almost always favors the prosecution and therefore limits the defendant's ability to receive a fair and impartial trial. Researchers have disclosed that most courtroom actors do not believe that pretrial publicity does not significantly affect juror behavior. Judges believe that the *voir dire* process is an effective method for removing jurors who have been prejudiced by the media. Prosecutors acknowledge that pretrial publicity usually works in their favor. Simon and Eimermann (1971), for example, found that 65 percent of those exposed to pretrial publicity had pro-prosecution attitudes compared with 45 percent of those not exposed to pretrial publicity. As prosecutors contend, whether defense attorneys can overcome this bias depends on the type of information prospective jurors are exposed to prior to the trial. Defense attorneys are most inclined to believe that pretrial publicity adversely affects their clients. However, it is believed that pretrial publicity is an insignificant problem. Surveys of the public reveal that while pretrial publicity may affect juror attitudes about the case, they still believe that despite this information, they could render objective and impartial judgments and base their decisions on the facts presented at trial.

BOX 14-1

KEY CASES: PRETRIAL PUBLICITY

Sheppard v. Maxwell 384 U.S. 333, 86 S.Ct. 1507 (1966)

Sheppard claimed that someone unknown to him entered his home in Bay Village, Ohio, and hit him on the head. When he awakened, he saw his wife had been injured and was sitting in a chair, bleeding, and not moving. Early in the case, police suspected Sheppard of killing his wife and later diverting attention from himself to so-called unknown assailants. The police made known their views to the media, which dramatized the event, as Sheppard was a well-respected physician in the community. Front-page headlines in the local newspapers created a media frenzy, with Sheppard at its center. During his subsequent trial, Sheppard was subjected to considerable media attention, and cameras and other media agents and apparatuses were admitted into the courtroom to witness the proceedings. This action by the court further intensified the media frenzy. In this milieu, Sheppard was convicted of murder. He appealed and the U.S. Supreme Court overturned his murder conviction holding that the failure of the state trial judge to protect Sheppard from inherently prejudicial publicity, which saturated the community, and to control disruptive influences in court had deprived Sheppard of a fair trial consistent with due process.

Dobbert v. Florida 432 U.S. 282, 97 S.Ct. 2290 (1977)

Dobbert was convicted of first-degree murder, second-degree murder, child torture, and child abuse and sentenced to death. He appealed, alleging that changes in the jury decision to recommend mercy instead of the death penalty without review by a trial judge had jeopardized his chances of receiving a life sentence. Further, he claimed that there was no death penalty "in effect" in Florida at the time he was convicted, because an earlier death-penalty statute had been held to be invalid when *Furman v. Georgia* (1972) had been decided. Dobbert also claimed that excessive pretrial publicity denied him the right to a fair trial. The U.S. Supreme Court rejected all of his arguments, saying that changes in the death-penalty statute were simply procedural, and thus there was no rights violation. Further, new statutes provided convicted offenders with *more* procedural safeguards rather than fewer of them. Dobbert's equal-protection rights under the Fourteenth Amendment were not violated either, because the new statute did not deny him such protection. Finally, the pretrial publicity, in view of the "totality of circumstances," was insufficient to conclude that he was denied a fair trial. The U.S. Supreme Court upheld his conviction and sentence.

Mu'Min v. Virginia 500 U.S. 415, 111 S.Ct. 1899 (1991)

Mu'Min was charged with and convicted of a murder while he was out on a prison work detail (where he was serving a term on another charge). There was considerable news publicity surrounding the killing, and when the case came to trial, Mu'Min's attorney made a

▼

motion for the judge during *voir dire* to ask whether any specific jurors had any knowledge of the pretrial publicity and if so, what effect it would have on their ability to hear and decide the case fairly. The judge denied the motion, and Mu'Min was subsequently convicted. He appealed, alleging that his right to an impartial jury as provided by the Sixth Amendment had been violated. The U.S. Supreme Court upheld his conviction, holding that the refusal of the judge to question jurors about specific contents of news reports to which they had been exposed had not violated Mu'Min's Sixth or Fourteenth Amendment rights to due process.

▶ What Types of Information Do Potential Jurors Consider Prejudicial?

Researchers have identified two ways that jurors are affected by prejudicial information. The first is **case-specific pretrial publicity**. This is information about a specific case where jurors might make a determination of one's guilt or innocence (Greene 1990). An example of case-specific pretrial publicity might come from the Rodney King state and federal cases. Most Americans were repeatedly exposed to the videotape showing police officers beating King as he lay on the ground. Jurors asked to serve in that case were probably exposed to that videotape numerous times prior to the trial. Their perceptions of the event were only relevant to this individual case.

The second type of pretrial publicity is **general pretrial publicity** which includes information about crime, criminals, and the criminal justice system that is constantly in the media and shapes our perceptions when we are asked to serve as jurors. For example, most of us have probably developed an opinion about the insanity defense based on several cases and stories about the insanity defense presented to us in the media. Jurors with these vague perceptions may have already formed an opinion about whether they might accept insanity as a valid defense before hearing any relevant evidence or testimony about one's sanity in an actual trial. Many jurors may still believe that if they find the defendant guilty but mentally ill, he/she will escape punishment or receive a light sentence.

Research has revealed that when jurors were exposed to pretrial publicity revealing a confession or a prior lengthy criminal record of a particular defendant, they were more likely to believe that the defendant was guilty. Furthermore, when information was released prior to the trial about the defendant failing a lie detector test, jurors were more likely to infer guilt from this event.

Uncovering the effects of general pretrial publicity is more difficult. The best research comes from conducting experiments with mock juries. Greene and Loftus (1984) compared three groups of mock jurors. The first group read newspaper stories about a defendant who was mistakenly identified and convicted of rape. The second group was asked to read stories about how the testimony of an eyewitness led to the conviction of a mass murderer. The final group was exposed to no pretrial publicity and acted as the control group. All three groups were then asked to make a decision about guilt or innocence for the cases involving an alleged armed robbery and murder. The prosecution's case consisted primarily of the testimony of an eyewitness. The first group had a significantly higher acquittal rate than either of the other two groups. From this evidence, we might infer that the story about the miscarriage of justice influenced the jurors and made them more skeptical of law enforcement and increased the probability of acquittal.

Research has also indicated that the entertainment media influences individual's perceptions of criminality and the criminal justice system. Jurors may expect the courtroom to be an exciting and dramatic place if they have watched crime dramas such as *Law and Order* or *Judge Judy*. These shows do not accurately portray what happens in real courtrooms. Court proceedings are typically routine and bland. There are no riveting revelations or courtroom confessions. Jurors are more likely to struggle to find ways to overcome boredom.

case-specific pretrial publicity direct familiarity with actual events that transpired in particular cases where persons are to serve as jurors; example is the Rodney King case, where millions of viewers watched the privately recorded videotape of the Rodney King beating by police on national television newscasts.

general pretrial publicity information about crime and the criminal justice system involving general details of types of crime and offenders and victims covered by the news media regularly which shapes our perceptions.

► How to Minimize the Effects of Pretrial Publicity

gag order official declaration by the judge in a trial proceeding that all parties in the action, including the jurors, must refrain from discussing the case with the media.

Trial judges can minimize the effects of pretrial publicity by various methods. The most radical and least-used approach is to issue a **gag order**. This is the most controversial approach because it raises serious First Amendment questions. Gag orders usually require that the media cannot publish or broadcast any prejudicial information about a case. Sometimes gag orders are extended to include the attorneys involved in the case. When a gag order includes attorneys, they are under court order not to talk about the case; this means that they are prohibited from giving television interviews or appearing on talk shows while the trial is in progress.

change of venue a change in the place of trial, usually from one county or district to another. Changes of venue are often conducted to avoid prejudicial trial proceedings, where it is believed that a fair trial cannot be obtained in the specific jurisdiction where the crime was alleged to have been committed.

Another possible remedy to minimize pretrial publicity is to grant a **change of venue**. A change of venue would shift the trial from one location to another. The objective is that jurors selected from the new trial location have not been exposed to the same degree of pretrial publicity as the potential jurors in the original jurisdiction. This remedy is rarely used because it is quite costly. All the people who have been called to testify have to travel great distances to the new jurisdiction. Family and friends of the victim and the accused have to travel to the new jurisdiction as well, and this hardship increases their emotional and financial stability. Granting continuances is another method judges use to lessen the effect of pretrial publicity. Most high-profile cases only capture public and media attention for a brief period. It is a short time before something new has attracted media attention. Similar to our fleeting attention, memories also fade with time. This allows judges to grant short trial delays in the hope of selecting a jury who has forgotten the media stories about a particular case.

judicial instructions specific admonitions to jurors, prosecutors, and defense counsels to do or refrain from doing different things.

Another method used to minimize pretrial publicity is the use of **judicial instructions**. During the O. J. Simpson trial, Judge Ito gave the jury detailed judicial instructions about what they could and could not do. The question is, do jurors abide by the judge's wishes and follow these judicial instructions? This is one area where much research points to the same conclusion. Judicial warnings do relatively little or nothing to change juror behavior. In fact, judicial warnings seem to make matters worse.

jury selection the process whereby a jury is impaneled for either a civil or criminal trial proceeding.

Many attorneys and judges believe that they can eliminate jurors who have been affected by pretrial publicity through **jury selection**. They assume that an intensive *voir dire* will unmask those prospective jurors who have been unduly influenced by the media. In cases where the publicity has reached most of the potential jurors, lawyers may have to permit some jurors to be seated who have been exposed to stories about the case, although they argue that such information can be disregarded and an impartial verdict can be rendered. While their intentions may be honorable, research does not support their assertion. Jurors exposed to pretrial publicity and who argue that such publicity will not influence their ability to evaluate the facts are much more likely to convict defendants than those who have not been exposed to any pretrial publicity.

Legal scholars have suggested that juries can police themselves during jury deliberations. The belief is that once juries are in the jury room, anyone who begins to depart from the judicial instructions and introduces information that was not presented during trial will be censured by the other members of the jury. The evidence on the jury's ability to police itself has been inconsistent. Some evidence has shown that when jury members who have particular biases join with others with similar biases, this makes the group's determination stronger such that it has a more profound impact on the decision rather than the opinions of any particular juror. When reinforced, individual biases of the group are difficult for juries to overcome. Therefore, it seems that jury deliberations strengthen rather than weaken juror biases.

Overall, these investigations of juror conduct indicate that eliminating biased jurors during *voir dire* is ineffective. The jury is unable to eliminate bias during its deliberations, and judicial instructions simply go unheeded. The most effective option available to judges is granting a continuance until the media fascination with the case has disappeared and people forget case details.

▶ The Litigation Explosion

Texas attorney Joe Jamails likes civil litigation. In his office, he proudly displays the $3 billion bank deposit slip that was his part of the $10.5 billion award to Pennzoil against Texaco. He often urges companies to settle their case rather than to face him in court and suffer the same fate as Texaco. Tort cases have spread a lot of wealth to other attorneys across the country as well. Civil litigation attorneys specialize in product liability cases or injuries as the result of accidents. Similar to the story in the introduction of this chapter, where hospitals and cities and their police departments have to pay out hundreds of millions of dollars a year to settle claims against them, there seems to be no end in sight for such litigation and the enormous financial awards that follow. Attorney Joe Jamails is estimated to be worth $600 million, and many other attorneys like him are looking forward to working out similar settlements with many other companies and city governments.

In recent years, there has been a concerted effort to limit tort litigation. The impetus for this movement has been fueled by allegations that the tort system is careening out of control. The arguments for reform revolve around two central themes. First, there has been a dramatic increase in the number of tort cases. Second, juries are handing out excessive awards. Referendums to reform the tort system and the litigation explosion extend back in time for many decades. For instance, it has been argued that the current trend in litigation will force the collapse of the court system. This sentiment was echoed in the popular press.

BOX 14-2

LEGAL ISSUES: JOURNALISM V. THE COURTS: A COMPROMISE

Journalists, judges, and legal experts have debated the limitations and merits of allowing cameras in the courts. At the heart of the matter is a conflict between the First and Sixth Amendments. Judges and lawyers argue that often the press limits a defendant's Sixth Amendment right for a fair trial. However, journalists argue that free press and free speech protections are equally as important under the First Amendment. The press has argued that journalists should have more access to court proceedings. "The presumption of openness should be the first presumption," says Paul Masters, Freedom Forum First Amendment ombudsman. "When we increase the amount of secrecy, we increase the amount of suspicion and erode confidence in the system," Masters adds.

Legal scholars and lawyers believe that camera access to the courtroom may serve to erode public confidence in legal system. Peter Arenella, professor of UCLA Law School, believes that this occurs when the public acting as the thirteenth juror sees the testimony

Wellphoto/Fotolia

and other coverage, often reaching a different verdict from the jury. Ira Reiner, former Los Angeles district attorney and NBC commentator, believed that some coverage would shed light on courtroom weaknesses. Reiner has declared, "Live TV. . .revealed the single greatest weakness in the court system: inadequate judicial management of criminal trials."

(continued)

Ten recommendations have been developed by the judges, journalists, legal scholars, and lawyers attending the conference.

1. Encourage and establish continuing interdisciplinary educational opportunities and dialogue for judges, journalists, and lawyers to foster an understanding of each other's roles through journalism schools, law schools, and the National Judicial College.

2. Assume accuracy in all court proceedings and records and place the burden of proof for closure on the entity seeking secrecy. Privacy issues may overcome the presumption in appropriate cases.

3. Refrain from imposing gag orders on the news media or attorneys. The court should seek other remedies in lieu of gag orders except in extraordinary cases.

4. Establish and or support bench bar media committees that will meet regularly in every community to address issues of mutual concern.

5. Establish guidelines for trial-press management in high-profile cases. Court officials should confer and consult with media representatives to avoid unanticipated problems and understand each other's legal constraints.

6. Adopt professional standards for journalists that are nonbinding and encourage industry-administered certification.

7. Assume that cameras should be allowed in the courtroom, including the federal system, and that such access should be limited or excluded for only the strongest of reasons.

8. Encourage judges to explain, on the record, the reasons for their rulings.

9. Develop a national model to determine when it may be appropriate to compel reporters to testify or produce notes and tapes, with the understanding that the media cannot serve as an arm of law enforcement.

10. Encourage media organizations to develop an ombudsman system to hear recommendations from the courts and public wherever feasible.

Source: Adapted from Steve Geiman, "Journalism v. Courts," *The Quill*, July–August 1996:46–48.

Newsweek magazine (2003) revealed that Americans from all walks of life are being buried under an avalanche of lawsuits. Doctors are being sued by patients. Lawyers are being sued by clients. Teachers are being sued by students. Merchants, manufacturers, and all levels of government and even cities themselves are being sued by all sorts of persons. The fear of being sued is ubiquitous and no profession is insulated from it.

Even Chief Justice Burger warned that one reason our system has become overburdened is that Americans are increasingly turning to the courts for relief from a range of personal distresses and anxieties. Remedies for personal wrongs were once considered the responsibilities of institutions other than the courts. But now damages for personal wrongs are boldly asserted as legal entitlements. The courts have been expected to fill the void created by the decline of church, family, and neighborhood unity (Burger 1982).

▶ Torts

torts private or civil wrongs or injuries, other than breach of contract, for which the court will provide a remedy in the form of an action for damages. A violation of a duty imposed by law. Existence of a legal duty to plaintiff, breach of that duty, and damage as a result of that breach.

The emergence and development of **torts** and tort law in America can be attributed to three diverse but ultimately related phenomena. These are (1) the emergence of industrial capitalism, (2) changing legal doctrine and legislative intervention, and (3) a transformation of scholarly legal thought. In the following section, a brief description of each of these phenomena is provided.

Industrial Capitalism

Prior to industrial capitalism, interaction and transactions among strangers were governed by contract law. Upon entering into a contract, each individual had a responsibility to uphold his/her obligation or the contract would be declared null and void. This form of law was well suited for governing obligations that occurred between a small number of people. However, the emergence of industrial capitalism greatly reduced face-to-face interaction between producers and consumers. Consumers were inundated with an unprecedented array of products created by an ever-increasing number of manufacturers. Furthermore, because production became more efficient through mechanization, producers were able to sell larger numbers of products to consumers. Capitalism also increased stranger interaction because it increased urbanization. Richard Abel explains why this is problematic when he says that the frequency of interaction among strangers is significant because strangers, unlike acquaintances or intimates, have less incentive to exercise care not to injure one another inadvertently and find it more difficult to resolve differences that arise when such injury occurs (Abel 1990). Industrialization also has the dubious distinction of being directly related to increasing the number of personal injuries. Machines of the Industrial Revolution have had a marvelous capacity for smashing the human body. Increasing the number of accidents is a natural result of increasing the number of persons working with and around dangerous machinery. Because contract law was not developed to deal with these new forms of personal injury, an increasing number of injured persons began to demand some alternative legal solution (Abel 1990).

Changing Legal Doctrine and Legislative Intervention

Initial tort claims brought against organizations in the emerging Industrial Revolution were usually unsuccessful. This was because legal doctrines were generally more supportive of industry than of individuals. Also, the courts were hesitant to support claims that could possibly cause irreparable harm to fledgling industries. Friedman says about this process that lawsuits and damage might injure the health of a precarious enterprise. The machines were the basis for economic growth, for national wealth, and for the greater good of society (Friedman 1985, 468).

Doctrines that have guided American legal decisions had their origins in common law. According to Friedman, this occurred because England had experienced initial forms of the Industrial Revolution prior to those occurring in America. The initial doctrines that guided legal decisions regarding tort law were the doctrine of contributory negligence, the fellow servant rule, and the doctrine of assumptive risk.

The doctrine of contributory negligence essentially held that the defendant was not negligent if the plaintiff was in any degree responsible for his/her own injury. This doctrine was initially developed in England in 1809, and was transplanted in American law to deal with railroad cases. The courts believed that if a person crossing the tracks had any degree of negligence in relation to his/her injury, the railroad could not be held liable.

The doctrine of assumptive risk was equally as problematic for plaintiffs. This doctrine generally held that a person could not recover any damages if he/she willingly placed himself/herself in danger. Initially, this doctrine does not seem restrictive but in reality, it offered no satisfactory remedy for persons who knowingly worked in hazardous occupations.

The first two new legal doctrines that began to chip away at existing legal rules were the doctrines of last clear chance and *res ipsa loquitur* (Friedman 1985). The doctrine of last clear chance was developed in England in the case of *Davies v. Mann* (1842). This doctrine allowed some degree of negligence on the part of plaintiffs while holding defendants responsible for their actions if they had the slightest chance of avoiding the injury. In the *Davies* case, Mann failed to hobble his donkey and it wandered into the path of Davies's approaching wagon, which smashed into the donkey and killed it. It is clear that Mann contributed to the death of his own animal because he failed to control it, but the court ruled that Davies was also negligent because he had the "last clear chance" to avoid hitting the animal but failed to do so. The doctrine of *res ipsa loquitur* or "the thing speaks for itself" originated in *Byrne v. Boadle* (1863). This case is important because it shifted the burden of responsibility from the plaintiff to the defendant where negligence was alleged and damages were sought.

Developing simultaneously with the notion of assumptive risk was the fellow servant doctrine. The fellow servant doctrine was the largest obstacle that faced injured plaintiffs.

doctrine of contributory negligence theory holding that a plaintiff by his/her own actions has brought about injuries for which he/she seeks relief from a defendant.

doctrine of assumptive risk theory holding that plaintiffs who engage in dangerous enterprises must accept some or all of the responsibility when accidents happen to them.

doctrine of last clear chance theory holding that when an accident occurs, the responsibility lies largely with the party who has the last clear chance to avoid the accident; example is a person standing on a railroad track who is subsequently struck by the train; the person is more in the position of avoiding the train than the train is of avoiding the person, even if the train engineer sees the person on the tracks before striking him/her.

doctrine of *res ipsa loquitur* "the thing speaks for itself"; blame in a legal action lies on the part of the defendant, since the instrument(s) bringing about the injury to a plaintiff was within the control of the defendant.

fellow servant doctrine theory holding employer responsible for actions of employees.

However, as the number of industrial accidents increased, so did the number of injured parties bringing suit against organizations rather than specific individuals. The courts began to realize that the plight of the injured worker could not be ignored. This rule held that a servant or employee could not sue his/her master or employer for injuries caused by the negligence of another employee (Friedman 1985, 472). The doctrine essentially left no recourse for employees who were injured in the workplace. They had the option of bringing a lawsuit against the fellow employee who caused the injury. However, this was often a futile effort because the negligent employee was equally as impoverished as the employee bringing suit.

In the 1840s and throughout the 1860s, these doctrines were relatively unchallenged. However, by the 1890s, labor had obtained a collective voice and there was diverse judicial opinion concerning personal injury cases. Furthermore, political and legislative intervention began to erode previously existing legal doctrines. One of the original legal rules that limited the fellow servant rule was the **vice principal doctrine**. This doctrine has been described by Friedman (1985), who says that an employee could sue his/her employer in tort if the careless fellow servant who caused the injury was a supervisor or a boss, more properly compared with an employer than a fellow servant.

Employer immunity for tort law has also been limited by federal and state legislatures. As early as the 1850s, statutes were established that outlined safety regulations for railroads. These regulations forced railroads to ring bells prior to passing through railroad crossings, and railroads were also responsible for any fires caused by their locomotives and had to compensate ranchers for any cattle that were killed by their trains.

> **vice principal doctrine** theory holding that someone may be sued by another if he/she is a supervisor or boss, and not necessarily the owner of an organization.

The Influence of Legal Scholars

Originating and continuing through the middle of the eighteenth century, prominent legal scholars began to rethink the role and purposes of law. Prior to this period, law was believed to have naturalistic and religious origins. These religious foundations seemed less applicable to a world that was experiencing radical social transformations caused by the Industrial Revolution. Consequently, only a few legal scholars believed that order and law had to be based on these new principles. White (1999) explains this process when he indicates that in general, post-Civil War intellectuals were interested in restoring a sense of order and unity that had characterized eighteenth-century thought, but they rejected efforts to derive order and unity from "mythological" religious principles. A particular interest of the intellectuals in the quarter of century after the war was the conceptualization and the transformation of data into theories of universal applicability.

The two leading proponents of this legal reconceptualization were Nicholas St. John Green and Oliver Wendell Holmes, Jr. These scholars rejected the notion that law was static and bound by religious or naturalistic rules. Rather, they believed that law should be evolutionary. Holmes and Green were convinced that life was in constant flux and that laws and the legal system must adapt in order to address these social changes. It is precisely because contract law and the writ system were unable to adequately address the changing social structure that Holmes and Green advocated the expansion of tort law.

More recent expansions of tort law, specifically enterprise liability, were profoundly influenced by twentieth-century legal scholars. In fact, Priest (1985) has rejected the argument that tort expansion was significantly influenced by industrialization, urbanization, mechanization, and expanding intervention of the federal government. Instead, Priest believes that the current form of tort law classified as enterprise liability was the handiwork of three legal scholars: Flemming James, Friedrich Kessler, and William Prosser. The literary and oratory confluence of James's notion of "risk distribution," Kessler's conviction that contract law was inadequate for monopolized capitalism, and Prosser's synthesis of contract and tort law gave rise to the current conception of enterprise liability. Presently, many legal scholars, businesses, and interest groups believe that tort law has expanded too far and is in need of substantial legislative reform.

▼

▶ Arguments for Tort Reform

Advocates of tort reform argue for its necessity because (1) in the last few years the number of tort cases has increased dramatically, and this event can be attributed to the increased litigiousness of American society; and (2) juries are incompetent to handle tort cases because they are sympathetic to plaintiffs and consistently dole out large awards. In the following section each of these arguments will be examined.

> **tort reform** any action taken by an individual or group to revise existing rules governing tort actions in courts, including limiting monetary awards for prevailing in lawsuits.

A Dramatic Increase in the Number of Tort Cases

Until the mid-1960s, most courts never kept records concerning the number and types of cases that they decided. Consequently, gathering statistics for a longitudinal study of American litigiousness is extremely difficult. Within the last two decades a handful of agencies have emerged that compile statistics on litigation rates. These include the National Center for State Courts, the Administrative Office of the U.S. Courts, and the Rand Corporation's Institute for Civil Justice. When investigations were conducted to determine whether we have experienced a litigation explosion, researchers at the Institute for Civil Justice have found that, overall, tort filings in state courts have increased between 2.3 percent and 3.9 percent annually. Federal courts experienced a similar annual increase of 4 percent. Galenter's analysis of tort filings in federal district courts between 1975 and 1984 has shown that these courts had a 46 percent increase during that nine-year period. This percentage may be misleading because the absolute percent increase of tort cases in this nine-year period was only 8.2 percent. During this same time interval, federal government suits against individuals for overpayments comprised 31.6 percent of the entire federal caseload (Galenter 1986).

More recent statistics reveal that civil cases may be decreasing. In 2001, there were 11,908 civil cases in the 75 largest counties, which represent a 47 percent decline from the 22,451 cases in the same counties in 1992. Federally, from 1985 to 2003, tort cases decreased 79 percent (Cohen 2004). More recently, however, from 2006 to 2015, federal civil filings increased 15 percent, however, are down roughly 4 percent from 2011 to 2015 (Administrative Office of the United States Courts 2015). A report by Norton Rose Fulbright (2015) of their annual survey of over 800 corporate counsel in 26 countries reveals that companies in the United States are facing twice as many lawsuits as those in other countries, and that U.S. businesses are worried about the increasing costs of litigation. Other research using a sample of cases from state courts conducted by the National Center for State Courts, however, reveals that high value tort cases represent a very small proportion of the litigation caseload (Hannaford-Agor, Graves, and Miller 2015). So although businesses report that they are worried about an increasing number of class action lawsuits and the costs of a more litigious business environment, data from actual civil case court filings reveals that the number of cases fluctuates up and down, and that just under two-thirds of cases filed are related to contracts, the majority of which are debt collection and landlord/tenant cases. Another 15 percent of cases are small claims disputes where the dollar amount is under $12,000.

Therefore, despite what we see in the media and what business corporations report about increased litigation cases, there is actually a growing movement that argues that the courts do not make access to civil justice accessible enough. In other words, there are many more civil claims that could be filed but are not because either persons are unaware of their right to file a claim or do not have the resources to access attorneys to assist in filing claims. Indeed, the report by the National Center for State Courts also reveals that in over 75 percent of the cases in their study at least one of the parties was self-represented, usually the defendant, and that issues with access to civil courts are cost and the time it takes to resolve cases; over 75 percent of the cases took over a year to dispose (Hannaford-Agor et al. 2015). The implications of this study are that there are many persons whose claims have merit but who are in effect denied access to justice via state courts due to being unable to afford to litigate their case.

In conclusion, on the one hand, we have claims of out of control litigation, and on the other hand, arguments that there is unequal access to justice and that many legitimate civil legal needs are going unmet. It should be noted that statistics reveal as much as they conceal. For example, it may be that the number of people injured by unsafe products has increased, thus causing the rise in the litigation rate. Perhaps large toxic torts, where a large number of claims are processed in a short time period, have caused the litigation rate to be exaggerated. And perhaps this increased rate is an anomaly of the federal system and should not be used as evidence of a litigation explosion, since federal courts handle only 5 percent of all tort cases. Also, if we disaggregate the statistics across the years, we find that case filings increase and then decline again, and then go back up. Several other factors also influence the number of civil case filings. For example, the federal system increased its use of alternative dispute resolution (ADR), steering a number of cases away from the courts. The report compiled by the National Center for State Courts similarly revealed that those with resources abandon the civil justice system and utilize private ADR services (Hannaford-Agor et al. 2015). Finally, it has become increasingly complex and costly to take a civil case to trial (Cohen 2004).

Juries Delivering Excessive Awards

When arguing about whether juries deliver excessive awards, both proponents and opponents of tort reform seem to have the relevant statistics to support their respective positions. This does not mean that one group's statistics are wrong, but rather, they may be the result of applying incorrect statistical techniques. When analyzing data that are extremely skewed (e.g., jury awards), it is inappropriate to use the mean or arithmetic average because a few large cases can severely skew the results. Therefore, it is more appropriate to use the median, or the midpoint of the data, when analyzing jury awards and trends. Using data from San Francisco and Cook County, Illinois, the Institute for Civil Justice has conducted a study of jury awards. Between 1960 and 1979 the median jury award for all tort cases was approximately $30,000. However, in 1979 the awards in Cook County decreased dramatically, while in San Francisco the awards increased dramatically.

The awards declined in Cook County because of a shift to comparative negligence, which may have increased attorney propensity to bring cases involving smaller damage amounts to trial. Conversely, the awards in San Francisco increased because a mandatory arbitration program eliminated most of the smaller cases from reaching courts. When the median tort awards are disaggregated, the median award for auto claims ranges from $5,000 to $40,000. Meanwhile, in product liability cases, the juries award between $180,000 and $200,000 per case. This represents an increase from $70,000 to $150,000 since 1960. When arithmetic means are used as indicators of the average tort award, the picture is quite different. In 1960, for instance, the average award for all tort cases ranged from $50,000 to $75,000. By 1984, this number had increased to between $250,000 and $300,000. When the average award is disaggregated, the data reveal that malpractice awards average about $1.2 million. Average awards for San Francisco automobile accidents and personal injury awards were $150,000 and $250,000, respectively. More recent statistics reveal that the majority of judgments in state civil cases are small, on average, around $10,000; only 0.2 percent of cases had judgments over $500,000 and only 0.1 percent had judgments over 1 million (Hannaford-Agor et al. 2015). Finally, although jury trials with judgments resulted in higher awards, they represented only 3 percent of the trials in state courts.

Proponents of tort reform have utilized mean awards to support their position that juries are delivering excessive awards and that legislative limits should be placed on the amount of these awards, especially in malpractice suits. In this regard, they have been relatively successful because as of 2003, 24 states had passed legislation that limited maximum awards courts would approve. Furthermore, state legislatures have become convinced that tort law is out of control and is in need of reform. In fact, by 2005 about two-thirds of states had passed some form of legislation limiting the amount of awards against the state.

▼

There is little doubt that these reforms have significantly altered the tort system. But scholars are beginning to ask whether these reforms are a benefit to citizens or to businesses.

Who Benefits from Tort Reform?

If reform measures were supportive of citizens, interests, we might assume that when reform measures were passed, insurance availability would increase and insurance premiums would decrease. Research has revealed several instances where reform measures have had no appreciable impact on the availability or affordability of insurance. For example, Florida, Minnesota, Washington, Wisconsin, and Ontario, Canada, have passed legislative reform measures. Despite these reforms, all locations have experienced increased insurance premiums, and many locations are unable to locate any insurance carriers. In fact, allegations by manufacturers and the medical community that reform was necessary because their rates were too high have no basis in fact. Abel (1990) has said that product, occupier, and general liability costs or insurance premiums plus damage payments have totaled less than 0.2 percent of sales; in the manufacturing sector where these costs were highest (e.g., rubber and plastic manufacture), they constituted only 0.58 percent; even among hospitals, these costs were only 2.35 percent of gross income.

The research that focuses on the efficacy of jurors would contradict the notions of jurors portrayed by tort reformers. These reformers allege that juries are sympathetic to plaintiffs simply because they deliver large cash awards. However, research focusing on jury behavior finds the opposite is true. Some jurors are extremely careful and often frugal when deciding cash awards. Sometimes jurors make very precise calculations of medical expenses, repair bills, and other costs when determining awards in order to ensure that the plaintiffs got no more than they were entitled to receive. Furthermore, such careful accounting, particularly in the case of tragic dimensions, contrasts sharply with the common view of juries as overgenerous and free spending.

Legislators are convinced that litigation has increased at a dramatic rate and reform measures (e.g., alternative dispute resolution) might control this problem. Increased litigation rates would indeed be a problem if an increasing number of litigants were bringing frivolous cases while the injury rate remained the same. However, research has revealed the contrary. Abel summarizes research reporting that among those who suffered major permanent partial disability as a result of medical malpractice, less than 17 percent filed claims, and only 6.5 percent received any payment (Abel 1990, 785–788). Regarding workplace injury claims, only 37 percent of the injured workers made worker's compensation claims. These results indicate that contrary to the perception of a litigious public, the majority of persons who have a legitimate injury fail to make a claim. These results seem to indicate that tort reform measures are not intended to help the average citizen. In each of the examples cited, the reform measures have limited the recourse of injured individuals and benefitted insurance companies, businesses, and interest groups.

Summary

1. Understand how the media have been instrumental in shaping our perceptions of justice, and that the courts and the media are at odds with each other because of competing interests.

This chapter has examined some of the major issues that are facing the American court system. The first is the relationship between the courts and the media. The media and the courts have had a relationship dating back to the 1800s. The media has always had a desire to report about certain cases that involve celebrities or are bizarre or unique in some respect. The courts, on the other hand, operate in a more methodical manner, following specific criminal or civil rules of procedure that at times can be very boring. A large amount of trial time is spent on the facts of the case, and specific detail of the events that occurred. Verdicts are rendered only after juries have carefully reviewed all the facts presented in trial, and expert and witness testimony. While this attention to detail and legal procedures may drag out for an extended period of time, the media wants to tell the story now.

The media may also focus on the most trivial aspects of a trial that are not even relevant legally, like the defendant's demeanor, the defendant's appearance or clothing, or missteps that the prosecution has made. Therefore, a boring, drawn-out trial is converted into an exciting media story. The coverage of the trial may even be sensationalized in order to obtain greater viewership. When the ratings of a network are dependent upon the nature of sensational coverage given, the most mundane courtroom events will be blown out of proportion.

2. *Explain the history of media and the courts from before the 1800s up until today and the idea of cameras in courtrooms.*

During the 1900s, there have been many "trials of the century," including the trial of Stanford White, Bruno Hauptmann, Sacco and Vanzetti, John and Lorena Bobbitt, and O. J. Simpson. In each of these cases, the media and the courts have battled to balance the power of the media with the objectives of justice. In most cases, the court has had to determine whether the defendant can have a fair trial because of pretrial publicity generated by the media. Several methods are used to limit pretrial publicity from gag orders to sequestration of the jury. However, with technological advances and the idea of cameras in the courtrooms, there has been some contention about balancing the fact that trials are public with affording the defendant a fair trial by an impartial jury. For instance, in the 1800s, verdicts were relayed by word of mouth. This changed with the advent of newspapers, where verdicts were given on printed page.

By the 1850s, the telegraph was used to transmit trial events and court decisions. Soon courtroom photographers and newsreel cameras became the plague of the most high-profile cases. The Scopes trial was the first to be broadcast over the radio. Attorneys became aware of the impact the media presence could have and used trial tactics that were intended not only for the jury but also for the larger national audience. Media representatives have even made requests for the attorneys and judges to position themselves so that their cameras could get better picture angles. It was during the Hauptmann trial that the court realized the media was not going to go away. Soon,

the American Bar Association would rule that photographing and broadcasting court proceedings should be prohibited. Most states adopted the position of the American Bar Association and forbid photographing and broadcasting trials and trial participants.

In 1952, the American Bar Association extended the media ban to include television coverage of court proceedings. Texas, however, was the first state to allow cameras into court proceedings and in one case, *Estes v. Texas*, in 1965, the judge allowed a camera in the courtroom but it was confined to a box constructed in the back of the courtroom. Estes appealed his conviction all the way to the Supreme Court on the grounds that the media coverage prevented him a fair trial. The SCOTUS did not rule in his favor. In the late 70s, Florida was the next state to experiment with cameras in the courtroom, and in 1979, the Florida Supreme Court permanently allowed cameras in the courts with the approval of the presiding judge. The new provisions were put to the test with the Ted Bundy murder trial. Ted Bundy defended himself and appeared to enjoy playing to the cameras. The court acknowledged that publicity could undermine a defendant's right to a fair trial but this risk did not mean there should be a ban on news reporting and the broadcasting of trials.

The U.S. Supreme Court has essentially left the decision up to the individual states whether to allow the media into their courtrooms. Today, all states allow cameras in their courtrooms to some degree and have developed guidelines for their usage. In most states, the consent of the presiding judge is a requirement, and many states require a written application submitted in advance of the trial. Finally, in some states, if the defendant objects to cameras in the courtroom, they will not be permitted. The federal courts have experimented with cameras from time to time but the Supreme Court still has some concerns over the videotaping of its proceedings.

3. *Define the current status of the access granted to media by the courts in the various jurisdictions throughout the United States.*

All 50 states allow cameras in courtrooms with some restrictions. The federal courts, however, including the Supreme Court, do not allow cameras to cover their proceedings. Congress has authored bills that would allow federal judges the discretion to grant cameras access to court proceedings in their district. There are certain restrictions that most states have adopted, such as no videotaping of the jury or certain witnesses, and no recording of conferences between the defendant and his or her attorney, or pretrial conferences and sidebars between the prosecution, defense, and judge that are not part of the record. In most states, the presiding judge still has to consent to allow cameras in a particular case. Most states also do not allow television coverage of juvenile cases or other sensitive cases, such as where victims of sex crimes are involved, or where business trade secrets might be revealed. Finally, most states have guidelines regarding which types of cameras are allowed and limit the number of media personnel in the court.

4. *Draw appropriate conclusions about pretrial publicity and the effect it has on trials.*

The primary concern of the relationship between the court and the media is the effect of pretrial publicity. Two different issues emerge here—the first is that pretrial publicity will make the process of finding jurors who have not heard of the case very difficult; the second is that because of the pretrial publicity, the jurors will realize their decision could be analyzed by the community, and this will influence them to vote on how their lives will be affected in the aftermath rather than on the facts of the case. A concern is that the effect of pretrial publicity on a juror's decision cannot be known. It should be mentioned, however, that the majority of cases are not subject to media scrutiny and usually it is only the high-profile cases that get coverage. Some research has shown that most courtroom actors say pretrial publicity does not significantly affect juror behavior because they believe that the *voir dire* process is effective at removing those jurors who have been prejudiced by the media.

5. *Recognize the types of information that potential jurors consider to be prejudicial, including case-specific and general pretrial publicity.*

There are two basic ways in which jurors can be affected by pretrial publicity. The first is case specific, which is information about a specific case, and the second is general pretrial publicity, which includes information about crime, criminals, and the criminal justice system that may shape the perceptions of those asked to serve as jurors. Research has shown that when jurors are exposed to pretrial publicity revealing a confession or a prior lengthy criminal record of a particular defendant, they are more likely to believe that the defendant is guilty. The effect of general pretrial publicity is more difficult to ascertain. Some studies have shown that the entertainment media influences our perceptions of criminality and the criminal justice system. Jurors may expect the courtroom to be an exciting and dramatic place if they have watched crime dramas on television. Court proceedings, however, are typically plain and routine, so these television dramas do not accurately represent what happens in real courtrooms. There are no last minute revelations or courtroom confessions as trials are fairly orchestrated so as not to have any surprises.

6. *Give examples of the different ways in which pretrial publicity can be minimized, including gag orders, jury instructions, change of venues, and jury sequestration.*

Pretrial publicity can be minimized in several ways. The least used method is probably for the judge to issue a gag order. Gag orders usually say that the media cannot publish or broadcast any prejudicial information about a case, which borders on fundamentally free speech issues. Another method would be to grant a change of venue, which would change the location of the trial, the idea being that jurors from the new location have not had the same exposure to pretrial publicity as the jurors in the original jurisdiction. Change of venue is, however, rarely used because of the cost involved. Granting continuances can be another method for the judge to minimize pretrial publicity; most cases only get media attention for short periods. In this way, a judge can implement short trial delays in the hope that the jury will have forgotten the media attention for a case. The use of judicial instructions can also minimize the effect of pretrial publicity. Using this method, the judge gives the jury detailed instructions about what they can and cannot do. Lastly, the most common form of eliminating pretrial publicity is through jury selection. This process should reveal those prospective jurors who are no longer impartial because of media publicity. Legal scholars believe that juries also police themselves, and anyone who tries to depart from judicial instructions or uses information that was not presented at trial will be criticized by the other jury members.

7. *Understand the litigation explosion and the reasons why America has become more litigious, including the emergence of industrial capitalism, changing legal doctrines, and the transformation of scholarly legal thought.*

Another issue facing the courts is the perception that juries are out of control and awarding excessive damage awards in civil cases. The evidence suggests that this is more myth than reality. The amount of litigation fluctuates up and down from year to year but appears to be on the decline since the early 2000s. Because of the greater time and monetary resources needed to take a case to trial or the increase in the use of alternative dispute resolution, caseloads do not appear to be overwhelming, and the awards juries are handing out also seem to be declining, although they vary depending on the type of tort. Furthermore, excessive jury awards have been reduced on appeal in more than a few instances. One side believes that due to the emergence of industrial capitalism, changing legal doctrine, legislative intervention, and a legal scholarly thought, torts and litigation have inevitably increased. The other side believes that if we delve into the statistics, litigation is actually on the decline. The increased use of alternative dispute resolution by the federal system and the complexity and costliness of taking a civil case to trial have been a couple of reasons proffered for the steering of a number of cases away from the courts.

8. *Distinguish among the different arguments for tort reform, such as the fact that the number of tort cases has dramatically increased, and the belief that juries are unable to handle tort cases because* *they are usually sympathetic to the plaintiff and hand out excessive awards.*

Several states have, however, started implementing legislation placing caps on monetary damages especially where medical malpractice is concerned. Whether this is because state legislators believe awards given by juries in these cases are out of control, or that medical insurance premiums have skyrocketed, is not known. The media, however, does seem to be still perpetuating a myth that the litigiousness of U.S. society is excessive. One fact that does remain is that doctors, teachers, and state and city officials will continue to be the aim of litigation due to the very nature of the jobs that they hold, and that disputes will arise from human interaction and provision of services.

Key Terms

case-specific pretrial publicity *329*
change of venue *330*
court of public opinion *323*
doctrine of assumptive risk *333*
doctrine of contributory
   negligence *333*

doctrine of last clear chance *333*
doctrine of *res ipsa loquitur* *334*
fellow servant doctrine *334*
gag order *330*
general pretrial publicity *329*
judicial instructions *330*

jury selection *330*
pretrial publicity *326*
tort actions *323*
tort reform *335*
torts *332*
vice principal doctrine *334*

Critical Thinking Exercises

1. Some critics argue that litigation is out of control and that juries are too quick to award large monetary amounts while others argue that many persons have legitimate civil claims for everything from lost benefits and housing and employer discrimination, to health care fraud and faulty products but do not know how to go about accessing attorneys or the courts or simply cannot afford to file a claim. What do you think? How can states attempt to reign in frivolous lawsuits and implement tort reform while also ensuring access to civil justice for those who have legitimate tort claims? Should the population take more responsibility for things that happen to them rather than sue the city or a neighbor? What part do insurance companies and perhaps tort law attorneys play in reform?

2. Most states now allow cameras in the courtroom as long as their guidelines for coverage are followed yet a very small percentage of cases actually receive media coverage. The courts have struggled with the right of the public to gain access to justice in their locale (in most instances, court cases are public record and courtrooms are public venues), and also guarantee the defendant's right to a fair trial. Do you think that all courts should allow television coverage of their proceedings? Could having cameras in the courtroom impinge on the right to a fair trial for a defendant? Why or why not?

Case Study Decision-Making Exercise

Someone filed a $50 million lawsuit against a snack food called *Pirate's Booty*, another person, whose name is Jack Ass sued Viacom the producer of the MTV show Jackass for defaming his character and copyright infringement of his name. The Pirate's Booty lawsuit was filed alleging that the plaintiff had consumed too much of the snack and gained a large amount of weight, and that the company had falsely advertised the caloric content of the snack. The case was eventually settled for $800,000 and $3.5 million in company coupons (Farley, 2002). In the Jack Ass case, Jack Ass, whose earlier name was Bob Craft, had his name changed to "Jack Ass" in 1997 in order to raise awareness about the dangers of drunken driving, and was seeking $10 million in damages (Silverman 2003). The case was eventually dismissed. How should courts respond to frivolous lawsuits such as these? Should such suits be allowed to be filed? What limitations, if any, should be set in place to protect the courts from frivolous lawsuits? Should filers of such suits be held liable for wasting valuable court time? What do you think?

Sources: Farley, Maggie. (2002). "Mom blows whistle on 'booty' snack/Rice puffs contain three times more fat than shown on label," *The Los Angeles Times*, May 20, 2002. Available online at: http://www.sfgate.com/news/article/Mom-blows-whistle-on-booty-snack-Rice-puffs-2820584.php

Silverman, Stephen, M. (2003). "Jack Ass Files Suit Against 'Jackass'" People, January 2, 2003. Available online at: http://people.com/celebrity/jack-assfiles-suit-against-jackass/

Concept Review Questions

1. What is meant by "trials of the century"? What is the relation between the court and the media in so-called trials of the century?
2. How much pretrial publicity is necessary for a change of venue?
3. What are some of the advantages and disadvantages of allowing the media into courtrooms?
4. What are some opposing views regarding frivolous lawsuits and excessive jury awards? Should defendants be allowed millions of dollars in damages for minor injuries or mental suffering? Why or why not?
5. What is tort reform? Who benefits from tort reform?
6. What types of circumstances suggest that pretrial publicity is unfavorable to defendants?
7. What is the litigation explosion? Why do you believe that it has occurred?
8. What is a gag order? Why do judges impose gag orders on jurors and other participants in legal actions?
9. Do media representatives have a constitutional right to enter and record what is going on in U.S. courtrooms? What are your opinions on this issue?

Suggested Readings

1. S. Daniels and J. Martin (2015). *Tort Reform, Plaintiffs' Lawyers, and Access to Justice*. University Press of Kansas.
2. Norton Rose Fulbright (2015). "2015 Litigation Trends Annual Survey." Available online at: http://www.norton-rosefulbright.com/news/128691/norton-rose-fulbright-releases-2015-litigation-trends-annual-survey.
3. Paula Hannaford-Agor, Scott Graves, and Shelley Miller (2015). "The Landscape of Civil Litigation in State Courts." National Center for State Courts. Williamsburg, VA.
4. S. M. Staggs and K. D. Landreville (2016). "The Impact of Pretrial Publicity on 'Eye for an Eye' Retributivist Support and Malicious Perceptions of Criminal Offenders." *Mass Communication and Society*: 1–20.
5. Neil Vidmar (2002). "Case Studies of Pre- and Midtrial Prejudice in Criminal and Civil Litigation." *Law and Human Behavior* **26**:73–105.

ABA Model Code of Professional Responsibility American Bar Association standards of behavior, which are voluntary and intended as self-regulating for lawyer conduct in the courtroom and between lawyers and clients.

Acceptance of responsibility A genuine admission or acknowledgment of wrongdoing. In federal presentence investigation reports, for example, convicted offenders may write an explanation and apology for the crime(s) they committed. A provision that may be considered in deciding whether leniency should be extended to offenders during the sentencing phase of their processing.

Accused Person alleged to have committed a crime; the defendant in any criminal action.

Acquittal Any judgment by the court, considering a jury verdict or a judicial determination of the factual basis for criminal charges, where the defendant is declared not guilty of the offenses alleged.

Action, actions at law A court proceeding; either civil, to enforce a right, or criminal, to punish an offender. Court litigation where opposing parties litigate an issue involving an alleged wrongdoing; may be for the protection of a right or for the prevention of a wrong.

Addams, Jane (circa 1860–1910) Founded Hull House in the 1890s in Chicago, a shelter for runaways and others who were in need of housing, food, and clothing.

Adjudicates To judge, decide a case, conclude a matter.

Adjudication Legal resolution of a dispute; when a juvenile is declared delinquent or a status offender, the matter has been resolved; when an offender has been convicted or acquitted, the matter at issue (guilt or innocence) has been concluded by either a judge or jury.

Adjudication hearing Formal proceeding involving a prosecuting attorney and a defense attorney where evidence is presented and a juvenile's status or condition is determined by the juvenile court judge.

Administrative law The body of laws, rules, orders, and regulations created by an administrative agency.

Administrative Office of United States Courts Organization that hires federal probation officers to supervise federal offenders. Also supervises pretrial divertees; probation officers prepare presentence investigation reports about offenders at the request of a district judge.

Admissible An evidentiary term designating testimony or physical evidence that may be presented to the finders of fact (juries or judges) in criminal proceedings. Restrictions and conditions are usually articulated in federal and state rules of evidence.

Admission A confession; a concession as to the truthfulness of one or more facts, usually associated with a crime that has been committed. May also apply to tort actions.

Admit A plea of guilty, an acknowledgment of culpability, accuracy of the facts alleged in either an adult or a juvenile proceeding.

Adversarial proceedings Opponent-driven court litigation, where one side opposes the other; prosecution seeks to convict or find defendants guilty, while defense counsel seeks to defend its clients and seeks their acquittal.

Adversary system Legal system involving a contest between two opposing parties under a judge who is an impartial arbiter.

Affidavit A statement in writing given under oath before someone who is authorized to administer an oath.

Affirm To uphold the opinion or decision of a lower trial court; usually an action by an appellate court.

Affirmation In courts, an oath, or declaration in place of an oath for persons whose religious beliefs prohibit oaths, to tell the truth and nothing but the truth when giving testimony.

Affirmative defenses Responses to a criminal charge where the defendant bears the burden of proof (e.g., automatism, intoxication, coercion, duress, and mistake), which go beyond simple denial of facts and gives new facts in favor of the defendant, if facts in the original complaint are true.

Affirmative registration Action on the part of women to actively seek to be included on juries that were formerly comprised exclusively of men.

Age of majority Chronological date when one reaches adulthood, usually either 18 or 21; when juveniles are no longer under the jurisdiction of the juvenile courts, but rather the criminal courts; also age of consent.

Aggravating circumstances Events about crime that may intensify the severity of punishment, including bodily injury, death of victim, or the brutality of the act.

Alibi Defense to a criminal allegation that places an accused individual at some place other than the crime scene at the time the crime occurred.

Allegation Assertion or claim made by a party to a legal action.

Allege To aver, assert, claim; usually a prosecutor will allege certain facts in developing a case against a criminal defendant.

Alternate jurors   Jurors who have been selected to replace any of the regular jurors who may become ill and cannot attend the full trial proceeding; these jurors have been vested with the same tasks as regular jurors who will hear and decide cases.

Alternative dispute resolution (ADR)   Procedure whereby a criminal case is redefined as a civil one and the case is decided by an impartial arbiter, where both parties agree to amicable settlement. Usually reserved for minor offenses.

Amendment   A modification, addition, deletion.

American Bar Association (ABA)   National organization of U.S. lawyers headquartered in Chicago, Illinois.

Amicus curiae   A friend of the court. Persons may initiate petitions on behalf of others, perhaps for someone who is in prison. Such *amicus* briefs are designed to present legal arguments or facts on behalf of someone else. Person allowed to appear in court or file a brief even though the person has no right to participate in the litigation otherwise.

Answer   A written response in relation to a filed complaint prepared by a litigant or defendant.

Appeal, appeal proceedings   Any request by the defense or prosecution directed to a higher court to contest a decision or judgment by a lower court.

Appearance   Act of coming into a court and submitting to the authority of that court.

Appellants   Persons who initiate an appeal.

Appellate courts   Courts hearing appeals emanating from lower courts. These courts typically do not try criminal cases.

Appellate jurisdiction   Authority to rehear cases from lower courts and alter, uphold, or overturn lower court decisions.

Appellate review   A comprehensive rehearing of a case in a court other than the one in which it was previously tried.

Appellees   Parties who prevailed in lower court and who argue on appeal against reversing the lower court's decision.

Arraignment   Official proceeding in which defendant is formally confronted by criminal charges and enters a plea; trial date is established.

Arrest   Taking persons into custody and restraining them until they can be brought before court to answer the charges against them.

Arrestees   Persons who have been arrested by police for suspicion of committing a crime.

Assigned counsel system   Program wherein indigent clients charged with crimes may have defense attorneys appointed for them; these defense attorneys may be private attorneys who agree to be rotated to perform such services for a low rate of reimbursement from the city, county, or state.

Assistant state's attorneys   Prosecutors who serve under other prosecutors in local or state jurisdictions; government prosecutors.

Assistant U.S. attorneys (AUSAs)   Government prosecutors who are subordinate to the U.S. attorney who heads the prosecutor's office for each federal district.

Attorney–client confidentiality and privilege   Relation between a counsel and his/her client wherein any information exchanged between parties will not be disclosed to others, such as prosecutors; attorneys are protected from disclosing information about the clients they represent because of this privilege.

Attorney competence   Standards for determining whether clients are fairly and intelligently represented by their lawyers when they are charged with crimes.

Attorney general   Senior U.S. prosecutor in each federal district court. A cabinet member who heads the Justice Department.

Attorney, lawyer, counsel   Anyone trained in the law who has received a law degree from a recognized university and who is authorized to practice law in a given jurisdiction.

Automatic waivers   Jurisdictional laws that provide for automatic waivers of juveniles to criminal court for processing; legislatively prescribed directive to transfer juveniles of specified ages who have committed especially serious offenses to jurisdiction of criminal courts.

Automatism   A set of actions taken during a state of unconsciousness.

Backdooring hearsay evidence   Action by prosecutor where prosecutor comments about or mentions information that is otherwise inadmissible in court; remarks made in front of a jury for their emotional and persuasive effects, which are otherwise barred because of the inadmissibility of evidence.

Backlog   Number of impending cases that exceeds the court's capacity that cannot be acted upon because the court is occupied in acting upon other cases.

Bail   Surety provided by defendants or others to guarantee their subsequent appearance in court to face criminal charges. Available to anyone entitled to it (not everyone is entitled to bail); is denied when suspects are considered dangerous or likely to flee. *See also* preventive detention and *United States v. Salerno* in list of cases.

Bail bond   A written guarantee, often accompanied by money or other securities, that the person charged with an offense will remain within the court's jurisdiction to face trial at a time in the future.

Bail bond companies   Any organization established for the purpose of posting bail for criminal suspects.

Bail bondsperson, bail bondsman   Person who is in the business of posting bail for criminal suspects. Usually charges a percentage of whatever bail has been set.

Bailiff   Court officer who maintains order in the court while it is in session. Bailiff oversees jury during a trial proceeding, sometimes has custody of prisoners while they are in the courtroom. Also known as messengers.

Bail recovery agents   Persons who seek to take into custody a fugitive or someone who has jumped bail by fleeing the jurisdiction before trial; also persons who seek to recover the amount of bail from a fugitive from justice.

Bail Reform Act Original act passed in 1966 to assure that bail practices would be revised to ensure that all persons, regardless of their financial status, shall not needlessly be detained to answer criminal charges.

Bail Reform Act of 1984 Revision of original 1966 Bail Reform Act where changes in bail practices were implemented to assure that all persons, regardless of their financial status, shall not needlessly be detained to answer criminal charges; gave judges and magistrates greater autonomy to decide conditions under which bail would be granted or denied. Does not mean that all persons are entitled to bail regardless of their alleged offense.

Bar Aggregate denoting all attorneys admitted to practice law in every jurisdiction.

Bench trial Tribunal where guilt or innocence of defendant is determined by the judge rather than a jury.

Beyond a reasonable doubt Standard used in criminal courts to establish guilt of criminal defendant.

Bifurcated trial Tribunal in capital cases where jury is asked to make two decisions. First decision is to determine guilt or innocence of defendant; if guilty, jury meets to decide punishment, which may include the death penalty.

Bill of Rights First ten amendments to the U.S. Constitution setting forth certain freedoms and guarantees to U.S. citizens.

Bind over Following a finding of probable cause that a crime has been committed and the defendant has committed it, a court action to cause the defendant to be tried on the charges later in a criminal court.

Blaming A step in the dispute process whereby the victim singles out someone as a potential target for legal action.

Blaming the victim The stereotypical practice of charging the socially and psychologically handicapped with the lack of motivation. An attitude or belief that the adverse conditions and negative characteristics of a group, often of minorities, are the group's own fault.

Blended sentencing Any type of sentencing procedure where either a criminal or juvenile court judge can impose both juvenile and/or adult incarcerative penalties.

Blue-ribbon jury A jury considered by either side, prosecution or defense, to be ideal because of its perceived likelihood of rendering a verdict favorable to that side; jurors often are selected because of their higher educational level and intellectual skills.

Bond Written document indicating that defendants or sureties assure the presence of these defendants at a criminal proceeding; if not, then the bond will be forfeited.

Booking Process of making written report of arrest, including name and address of arrested persons, the alleged crimes, arresting officers, place and time of arrest, physical description of suspect, photographs, sometimes called "mug shots," and fingerprints.

Bounties, bounty hunters Monetary rewards offered for capture of persons who escape prosecution from a given jurisdiction. Often, such persons have posted a bond with a bonding company and the bonding company hires a bounty hunter (person who earns living by apprehending these persons) to track them down so that monies deposited with the courts by the bonding company can be recovered.

Brady materials Exculpatory materials must be disclosed through discovery to defense counsel by the prosecution when the defendant is to be tried for a crime. *See Brady v. Maryland* (1963).

Brady violation Violation of discovery rules when prosecutor fails to turn over exculpatory materials acquired during a criminal investigation to defense counsel. Violation occurs whenever three conditions are met: (1) the evidence at issue must be favorable to the accused, either because it is exculpatory or because it is impeaching; (2) the evidence must have been suppressed by the state, either willfully or inadvertently; and (3) prejudice must have ensued.

Bribery Crime of offering, giving, requesting, soliciting, receiving something of value to influence a decision of a public official.

Brief A document filed by a party to a lawsuit to convince the court of the merits of that party's case.

Burden of proof The requirement to introduce evidence to prove an alleged fact or set of facts.

Camp, ranch Any of several types of similar correctional confinement facilities for adults or juveniles, usually located in rural areas.

Canons of Professional Ethics Part of ABA Model Code of Professional Responsibility formulated in 1908; nine canons pertain to representing clients in a competent way; improving the legal system; avoiding the appearance of impropriety; and observing client confidences.

Capacity Mental state of being legally responsible; having the mental acuity to know the difference between right and wrong and to realize and appreciate the nature and consequences of particular actions.

Capital punishment Imposition of the death penalty for the most serious crimes. May be administered by electrocution, lethal injection, gas, hanging, or shooting.

Career criminals Those offenders who make their living through crime. Usually offenses occur over the lifetime of the offender.

Case Incident investigated by law enforcement officers. A single charging document under the jurisdiction of a court. A single defendant.

Case backlogs Crowded court dockets in either juvenile court or criminal court; a massive buildup of cases, where judges cannot hear all cases in a timely fashion.

Case law Legal opinions having the status of law as enunciated by the courts (e.g., U.S. Supreme Court decisions become case law and governing cases when identical or very similar cases are subsequently heard in lower courts).

Case processing The speed with which cases are heard in either criminal or juvenile court.

Case-specific pretrial publicity Direct familiarity with actual events that transpired in particular cases where persons are to serve as jurors; example is the Rodney King case, where millions of viewers watched the privately recorded videotape of the Rodney King beating by police on national television newscasts.

Cash bail bond Cash payment for situations in which charges are not serious and the scheduled bail is low. Defendants obtain release by paying in cash the full amount, which is recoverable after the required court appearances are made.

Centralization Limited distribution of power among a few top staff members of an organization.

Certification (juvenile) *See* waiver.

Certiorari, **writ of** A writ issued by a higher court directing a lower court to prepare the record of a case and send it to the higher court for review; a means of accessing the U.S. Supreme Court in order for a case to be heard.

Challenge *See* peremptory challenge.

Challenge for cause In jury selection, the method used by either the prosecution or defense attorneys to strike or remove prospective jurors from the available jury pool because of prejudices they might have, either toward the defendant or prosecution. Prospective jurors may also be excused from jury duty because of being law enforcement officers, relatives of law enforcement officers, court officers, or relatives of court officers. Any obvious bias for or against a defendant may result in the exclusion of the biased prospective juror.

Challenges of jurors Questions raised of jurors by the judge, prosecutor, and/or defense attorney relating to their qualifications as impartial finders of fact; a determination of juror bias one way or another for or against the defendant.

Chambers Usually a judge's office in a courthouse.

Chancery court Tribunal of equity rooted in early English common law where civil disputes are resolved. Also responsible for juvenile matters and adjudicating family matters such as divorce. Has jurisdiction over contract disputes, property boundary claims, and exchanges of goods disputes.

Change of venue A change in the place of trial, usually from one county or district to another. Changes of venue are often conducted to avoid prejudicial trial proceedings, where it is believed that a fair trial cannot be obtained in the specific jurisdiction where the crime was alleged to have been committed.

Charge A formal allegation filed against some defendant in which one or more crimes are alleged.

Charge reduction bargaining, charge bargaining Negotiation process between prosecutors and defense attorneys involving dismissal of one or more charges against defendants in exchange for a guilty plea to remaining charges, or in which the prosecutor downgrades the charges in return for a plea of guilty.

Chief justice The presiding or principal judge of a court, possessing nominal authority over the other judges (e.g., the chief justice of the U.S. Supreme Court).

Child savers Groups who promoted rights of minors during the nineteenth century and helped create a separate juvenile court. Their motives have been questioned by modern writers who see their efforts as a form of social control and class conflict.

Children in need of supervision (CHINS) Typically unruly or incorrigible children who cannot be supervised well by their parents. Also includes children from homes where parents are seldom present. State agencies exist to find housing for such children.

Chronic offenders Habitual offenders; repeat offenders; persistent offenders; youths who commit frequent delinquent acts.

Chronic recidivists Persons who continue to commit new crimes after being convicted of former offenses.

Circuit courts Originally, courts that were held by judges who followed a circular path, hearing cases periodically in various communities. The term now refers to courts with several counties or districts within their jurisdiction. In the federal court organization, there are 13 federal circuit courts of appeal, having jurisdiction over U.S. District Courts within specified states.

Circumstantial evidence Material provided by a witness from which a jury must infer a fact.

Citation Any document issued by a law enforcement or court officer directing one to present oneself in court on a specific date and time.

Cite, citation Any legal reference in which a point of law is made. In law enforcement, a summons.

Civil action Any lawsuit brought to enforce private rights and to remedy violations thereof.

Civil law All state and federal law pertaining to noncriminal activities, also referred to as municipal law. Laws pertain to private rights and remedies. A body of formal rules established by any society for its self-regulation.

Civil liability In tort law, the basis for a cause of action to recover damages.

Claiming The process in a dispute where a grievance is expressed and a cause of action is cited.

Class action, class action suit Any lawsuit on behalf of a segment of the population with specific characteristics, namely that they are victims of whatever wrongs are alleged. The class of persons may persist over time and change, but the action is for all current and future members of the class.

Coconspirator Another party besides the defendant who is alleged to have committed the same crime in concert with the defendant.

Code A systematic collection of laws.

Codefendants Two or more defendants charged with the same crime and tried in the same judicial proceeding.

Code of ethics Regulations formulated by major professional societies that outline the specific problems and issues that are frequently encountered in the types of research carried out within a particular profession. Serves as a guide to ethical research practices.

Coercion Affirmative defense similar to duress, wherein defendants allege that they were made or forced to commit an illegal act.

Common law Authority based on court decrees and judgments that recognize, affirm, and enforce certain usages and customs of the people. Laws determined by judges in accordance with their rulings.

Community service An alternative sanction requiring offenders to work in the community at such tasks as cleaning public parks or working with handicapped children in lieu of an incarcerative sentence. Restitution involves paying back a victim through money received from one's work.

Community service orders Judicially imposed restitution for those convicted of committing crimes; some form of work must be performed to satisfy restitution requirements.

Complaint Written statement of essential facts constituting the offense alleged, made under oath before a magistrate or other qualified judicial officer.

Comprehensive Crime Control Act of 1984 Significant act that authorized establishment of U.S. Sentencing Commission, instituted sentencing guidelines, provided for abolition of federal parole, and devised new guidelines and goals of federal corrections.

Concession givers Judges who make plea agreement offers to criminal defendants, wherein the defendants will plead guilty to a criminal charge in exchange for judicial leniency in sentencing.

Conclusive evidence Any compelling evidence that is so strong that it cannot be disputed or discounted. Proof establishing guilt beyond a reasonable doubt.

Concurrent jurisdiction Situation in which offender may be held accountable in several different jurisdictions simultaneously. Courts in the same jurisdiction.

Conditional dispositions Decisions by juvenile court judge authorizing payment of fines, community service, restitution, or some other penalty after an adjudication of delinquency has been made.

Conditions of confinement The nature of jail or prison incarceration; refers to heat and humidity, cleanliness of one's cell and surroundings, and general treatment; often is basis for legal action filed as *habeas corpus* petitions.

Confidentiality Any privileged communication between a client and an attorney.

Confidentiality privilege Right between defendant and his/her attorney where certain information cannot be disclosed to prosecutors or others because of the attorney–client relation; for juveniles, records have been maintained under secure circumstances with limited access, and only then accessed by those in authority with a clear law enforcement purpose.

Conflict stage Either a pretrial or an alternative dispute resolution phase where a plaintiff and a defendant confront one another and an accusation is made; a confrontation where the victim faces an alleged victimizer or defendant; may involve a third-party arbiter.

Constitutional rights Rights guaranteed to all U.S. citizens by the U.S. Constitution and its amendments.

Contract system Providing counsel to indigent offenders by having an attorney under contract to the county to handle some or all of these types of cases.

Conviction State of being judged guilty of a crime in a court, either by the judge or jury.

Corroboration Evidence that strengthens the evidence already given.

Cost–benefit analysis Method of analyzing the costs associated with particular policies and determining whether the benefits or value derived from those policies are justified on the basis of the results.

County prosecutors District attorneys at the county level.

Court Public judiciary body that applies the law to controversies and oversees the administration of justice.

Court administrator Any individual who controls the operations of the court in a particular jurisdiction. May be in charge of scheduling, juries, judicial assignment.

Court-appointed counsel Attorneys who are appointed to represent indigent defendants.

Court calendar Docket; the schedule of events for any judicial official.

Court clerk Court officer who may file pleadings, motions, or judgments, issue process, and may keep general records of court proceedings.

Court of last resort The last court that may hear a case. In the United States the Supreme Court is the court of last resort for many kinds of cases.

Court of limited jurisdiction *See* trial court of limited jurisdiction.

Court of public opinion Informal reactions to legal cases by unofficial pollsters and media broadcasters who cover high-profile cases on television and in the newspapers; independent reactions to court events by persons who may have only a passing interest in cases.

Court order Any judicial proclamation or directive authorizing an officer to act on behalf of the court.

Court reporter Court official who keeps a written word-for-word and/or tape-recorded record of court proceedings. *See also* transcript.

Courtroom workgroup The phrase denoting all parties in the adversary process who work together cooperatively to settle cases with the least amount of effort and conflict.

Courts of general jurisdiction Any court having the power to hear diverse types of cases, both civil and criminal.

Courts of last resort   Either state or federal supreme courts that function as the final stage for appeals from lower courts; the ultimate court of last resort is the U.S. Supreme Court.

Courts of record   Any legal proceedings where a written record is kept of court matters and dialogue.

Crime   Act or omission prohibited by law, by one who is held accountable by that law. Consists of legality, *actus reus, mens rea*, consensus, harm, causation, and prescribed punishment.

Crime Bill of 1994   Legislation supported by President Bill Clinton designed to increase crime prevention measures and put more police officers on city streets; also established truth-in-sentencing laws to maximize the amount of time inmates must serve in relation to their maximum sentences.

Crime prevention   Any overt activity conducted by individuals or groups to deter persons from committing crimes. May include "target hardening" by making businesses and residences more difficult to burglarize; neighborhood watch programs, in which neighborhood residents monitor streets during evening hours for suspicious persons or automobiles and equipping homes and businesses with devices to detect crime.

Criminal courts   Tribunals handling criminal cases. May also handle civil cases, and are then called criminal courts only in reference to the criminal cases that they handle.

Criminal-exclusive blend   Form of sentencing by a criminal court judge where either juvenile or adult sentences of incarceration can be imposed, but not both.

Criminal history   One's prior convictions, indictments, and arrests.

Criminal-inclusive blend   Form of sentencing by a criminal court judge where both juvenile and adult sentences can be imposed simultaneously.

Criminal informations   Written accusations made by a public prosecutor against a person for some criminal offense, usually restricted to minor crimes or misdemeanors, without an indictment.

Criminal law   Body of law that defines criminal offenses and prescribes punishments (substantive law) and that delineates criminal procedure (procedural law).

Criminalization   Transformation of civil proceedings into criminal proceedings; the juvenile court has undergone a transformation toward greater criminalization as juveniles have acquired almost the same number of legal rights as adults.

Criminal trial   An adversarial proceeding within a particular jurisdiction, in which a judicial determination of issues can be made, and in which a defendant's guilt or innocence can be decided impartially.

Critical legal studies   Movement involving an examination of the entire legal system; recognizes that law is subjective rather than objective.

Cross-examination   Questioning of one side's witnesses by the other side's attorney, either the prosecution or defense.

Culpable, culpability   State of mind of persons who have committed an act that makes them liable for prosecution for that act.

Curfew violators   Persons under the legal age of adulthood who roam city streets beyond times when they are supposed to be in their homes; a type of status offender.

Custodial dispositions   Outcomes by juvenile judge following adjudication of juvenile as delinquent. Includes nonsecure custody (in a foster home, community agency, farm, camp) or secure custody (in a detention center, industrial, reform school).

Damages   Monetary sums awarded to prevailing litigants in civil actions.

Death penalty   Imposition of the death as a punishment for the most serious capital crimes. *See also* capital punishment.

Death row   Arrangement of prison cells where inmates who have been sentenced to death are housed.

Decriminalization, decriminalize   Legislative action whereby an act or omission, formerly criminal, is made noncriminal and without punitive sanctions.

Defendant   Person against whom a criminal proceeding is pending.

Defendant dispositions   Any one of several adjudication and dispositional options available to a judge at various places during a criminal proceeding, ranging from dismissal of the case to long-term imprisonment.

Defendant's sentencing memorandum   Version of events leading to conviction offense in the words of the convicted offender. Memorandum may be submitted together with victim impact statement.

Defense   A response by defendants in criminal law or civil cases. May consist only of a denial of the factual allegations of the prosecution (in a criminal case) or of the plaintiff (in a civil case). If defense offers new factual allegations in an effort to negate the charges, this is called an affirmative defense.

Defense attorney, counsel   A lawyer who represents a client accused of a crime.

Defense of property   Affirmative defense to justify illegal conduct, wherein defendants claim that they broke one or more laws to safeguard their property or possessions or the property or possessions of others.

Defense strategy   Approach taken by defense counsel for defending his/her client; usually involves a particular defense to criminal charges.

Deferred prosecution   Temporary halting of a prosecution against a defendant while he/she is subjected to a program with particular requirements for a short period. *See also* diversion.

Deinstitutionalization   Providing programs in community-based settings instead of institutional ones.

Deinstitutionalization of status offenders (DSO)   Movement to remove nondelinquent juveniles from secure facilities by eliminating status offenses from the delinquency category and removing juveniles from or precluding their confinement in juvenile correction facilities. Process of removing status offenses from jurisdiction of juvenile court.

Demand waiver   Request by juveniles to have their cases transferred from juvenile courts to criminal courts.

Demonstrative evidence   Material related to a crime that is apparent to the senses, in contrast to material presented by the testimony of other persons.

De novo   Anew, afresh, as if there had been no earlier decision.

Deponents   Persons who give testimony through a deposition. If someone cannot physically attend a trial and give testimony under oath, then a deposition is taken and read into the court record.

Derivative evidence   Information obtained as the result of previously discovered evidence (e.g., residue from an automobile tire may suggest that a crime was committed in a part of the city where such residue is found and police discover subsequent "derivative" evidence by investigating that area).

Determinate sentencing   Sanctioning scheme in which court sentences offender to incarceration for fixed period, and which must be served in full and without parole intervention, less any good time earned in prison.

Deterrence, general or specific   Actions that are designed to prevent crime before it occurs by threatening severe criminal penalties or sanctions. May include safety measures to discourage potential lawbreakers such as elaborate security systems, electronic monitoring, and greater police officer visibility; influencing by fear, where fear is of apprehension and punishment.

Differential discretion   View that sentencing disparities are more likely to occur during informal charge reduction bargaining than in the final sentencing process following trial and the sentencing hearing.

Direct evidence   Evidence offered by an eyewitness who testifies to what was seen or heard.

Direct examination   Questioning by attorney of one's own (prosecution or defense) witness during a trial.

Direct file   Prosecutorial waiver of jurisdiction to a criminal court; an action taken against a juvenile who has committed an especially serious offense, where that juvenile's case is transferred to criminal court for the purpose of a criminal prosecution.

Directed verdict of acquittal   Order by court declaring that the prosecution has failed to produce sufficient evidence to show defendant guilty beyond a reasonable doubt.

Discovery   Procedure where prosecution shares information with defense attorney and defendant. Specific types of information are made available to defendant before trial, including results of any tests conducted, psychiatric reports, transcripts, and tape-recorded statements made by the defendant. Also known as "Brady materials" after a specific court case.

Discretionary waivers   Transfers of juveniles to criminal courts by judges, at their discretion or in their judgment; also known as judicial waivers.

Disposition   Action by criminal or juvenile justice court or agency signifying that a portion of the justice process is completed and jurisdiction is relinquished or transferred to another agency or signifying that a decision has been reached on one aspect of a case and a different aspect comes under consideration, requiring a different kind of decision.

Disposition hearing   Hearing in juvenile court, conducted after an adjudicatory hearing and a finding of delinquency, status offender, dependent/neglected, to determine the most appropriate punishment/placement/treatment for the juvenile.

Disputants   Opposing sides in a civil action or case.

Dispute resolution   Civil action intended to resolve conflicts between two parties, usually a complainant and a defendant.

Dispute stage   Public revelation of a dispute by filing of a legal action.

Dissenting opinion   Any judicial opinion disavowing or attacking the decision of a collegial court.

District attorneys   City, county, and state prosecutors who are charged with bringing offenders to justice and enforcing the laws of the state.

District court   Trial courts at the state or federal level with general and original jurisdiction. Boundaries of their venue do not conform to standard political unit boundaries, but generally include several states or counties.

Diversion   Removing a case from the criminal justice system, while a defendant is required to comply with various conditions (e.g., attending a school for drunk drivers, undergoing counseling, and performing community service). May result in expungement of record. Conditional removal of the prosecution of a case prior to its adjudication, usually as the result of an arrangement between the prosecutor and judge.

Diversion programs   One of several programs preceding formal court adjudication of charges against defendants; defendants participate in therapeutic, educational, and other helping programs. *See also* diversion.

Divestiture of jurisdiction   Juvenile court relinquishment of control over certain types of juveniles, such as status offenders.

DNA fingerprinting   Deoxyribonucleic acid (DNA) is an essential component of all living matter, which carries hereditary patterning. Suspects can be detected according to their unique DNA patterning, as each person has a different DNA pattern. Similar to fingerprint identification, in which no two persons have identical fingerprints.

Docket   A court record of the cases scheduled to appear before the court.

Doctrine of assumptive risk   Theory holding that plaintiffs who engage in dangerous enterprises must accept some or all of the responsibility when accidents happen to them.

Doctrine of contributory negligence   Theory holding that a plaintiff by his/her own actions has brought about injuries for which he/she seeks relief from a defendant.

Doctrine of last clear chance Theory holding that when an accident occurs, the responsibility lies largely with the party who has the last clear chance to avoid the accident; example is a person standing on a railroad track who is subsequently struck by the train; the person is more in the position of avoiding the train than the train is of avoiding the person, even if the train engineer sees the person on the tracks before striking him/her.

Doctrine of *res ipsa loquitur* "The thing speaks for itself"; blame in a legal action lies on the part of the defendant, since the instrument(s) bringing about the injury to a plaintiff was within the control of the defendant.

Document Any written paper, official or unofficial, having potential evidentiary importance.

Double jeopardy Subjecting persons to prosecution more than once in the same jurisdiction for the same offense, usually without new or vital evidence. Prohibited by the Fifth Amendment.

Dual court system A system consisting of a separate judicial structure for each state in addition to a national structure. Each case is tried in a court of the same jurisdiction as that of the law or laws broken.

Due process Basic constitutional right to a fair trial, presumption of innocence until guilt is proven beyond a reasonable doubt, the opportunity to be heard, to be aware of a matter that is pending, to make an informed choice whether to acquiesce or contest, and to provide the reasons for such a choice before a judicial official. Actual due process rights include timely notice of a hearing or trial that informs the accused of charges, the opportunity to confront one's accusers and to present evidence on one's own behalf before an impartial jury or judge, the presumption of innocence under which guilt must be proved by legally obtained evidence and the verdict must be supported by the evidence presented, the right of accused persons to be warned of their constitutional rights at the earliest stage of the criminal process, protection against self-incrimination, assistance of counsel at every critical stage of the criminal process, and the guarantee that individuals will not be tried more than once for the same offense.

Due process courts Juvenile courts where the emphasis is upon punishment and offender control rather than individualized treatments and assistance.

Due process of law A right guaranteed by the Fifth, Sixth, and Fourteenth Amendments of the U.S. Constitution, and generally understood to mean the due course of legal proceedings according to the rules and forms that have been established for the protection of private rights. *See also* due process.

Duress Affirmative defense used by defendants to show lack of criminal intent, alleging force, psychological or physical, from others as stimulus for otherwise criminal conduct.

Early release *See* parole board.

Electronic monitoring The use of electronic devices (usually anklets or wristlets) which emit electronic signals to monitor offenders, probationers, and parolees. The purpose of their use is to monitor an offender's presence in a given environment where the offender is required to remain or to verify the offender's whereabouts.

En banc "In the bench." Refers to a session of the court, usually an appellate court, where all of the judges assigned to the court participate.

English common law *See* common law.

Entrapment Activity by law enforcement officers that suggests, encourages, or aids others in the commission of crimes, which would ordinarily not have occurred without officer intervention. Defense used by defendants to show otherwise criminal act would not have occurred without police intervention, assistance, and/or encouragement.

Equal protection Clause of Fourteenth Amendment of U.S. Constitution guaranteeing to all citizens equal protection of the law, without regard to race, color, gender, class, origin, or religion.

Equity The concept that the relationships between men, women, and society should be just and fair and in accordance with contemporary morality.

Ethical code Canons of professional responsibility articulated by professional associations such as the American Bar Association.

Evarts Act Introduced in 1891 and sponsored by New Jersey lawyer William M. Evarts, this act created circuit courts of appeal to hear appeals emanating from the U.S. District Courts.

Evidence All materials or means admissible in a court of law to produce in the minds of the court or jury a belief concerning the matter at issue.

Evidence, corroborating Any collateral evidence that enhances the value of other evidence.

Evidence-driven jury Jury that decides to consider all evidence presented as relevant rather than selected evidence based on juror interest or preferences.

Evidentiary Pertaining to the rules of evidence or the evidence in a particular case.

Examination, direct and cross *See* direct examination and cross-examination.

Exception An objection to a ruling, comments made by the judge or attorneys.

Excessive bail Any bail amount that so grossly exceeds the proportionality of the seriousness of the offense so as to be prohibited by the Eighth Amendment.

Exclusionary rule Rule providing that where evidence has been obtained in violation of the privileges guaranteed by the U.S. Constitution, such evidence may be excluded at the trial.

Exclusive jurisdiction Specific jurisdiction over particular kinds of cases. The U.S. Supreme Court has authority to hear matters involving the diplomats of other countries who otherwise enjoy great immunity from most other courts. Family court may have exclusive jurisdiction to hear child custody cases.

Exculpate, exculpatory Tending to exonerate a person of allegations of wrongdoing.

Exculpatory evidence Any information that exonerates a person of allegations of wrongdoing; any information that reflects favorably upon the accused and shows that they are innocent of the crimes with which they are charged.

Ex parte A hearing or examination in the presence of only one party in the case.

Expert testimony Any oral evidence presented in court by someone who is considered proficient and learned in a given field where such evidence is relevant. Testimony provided by an expert witness.

Expert witnesses Witnesses who have expertise or special knowledge in a relevant field pertaining to the case at trial. Witnesses who are qualified under the Federal Rules of Evidence to offer an opinion about the authenticity or accuracy of reports, who have special knowledge relevant to the proceeding. Sometimes called "hired guns."

Expunge, expungement Deletion of one's arrest record from official sources. In most jurisdictions, juvenile delinquency records are expunged when one reaches the age of majority or adulthood.

Extralegal factors Any element of a nonlegal nature. In determining whether law enforcement officers are influenced by particular factors when encountering juveniles on the streets, extralegal factors might include juvenile attitude, politeness, appearance, dress. Legal factors might include age and specific prohibited acts observed by the officers. In reference to adult offenders, these refer to factors not legally relevant to case processing decisions such as race, ethnicity, and sex.

Eyewitnesses Persons who testify in court as to what they saw when the crime was committed.

Fact A true statement. An actual event.

Factual basis for the plea Evidence presented to the judge by the prosecutor that would have been used if a plea-bargained case had gone to trial; evidence of one's guilt beyond a reasonable doubt to substantiate a plea bargain agreement.

Failure to appear When defendants fail to present themselves for trial or some other formal proceeding, such as arraignment or a preliminary hearing/examination.

Federal district courts Basic trial courts for the federal government that try all criminal cases and have extensive jurisdiction. District judges are appointed by the president of the United States with the advice, counsel, and approval of the Senate. Cases from these courts are appealed to particular circuit courts of appeal.

Federal misdemeanor Any federal crime where the maximum punishment is less than one year in prison or jail.

Federal Rules of Criminal Procedure Contained in Title 18 of the U.S. Code, all protocols and regulations that must be followed during offender processing, from arrest to conviction.

Federal Rules of Evidence Official rules governing the introduction of certain types of evidence in U.S. District Courts.

Fellow servant doctrine Theory holding employer responsible for actions of employees.

Felony Crime punishable by incarceration, usually in a state or federal prison, for periods of one year or longer.

Felony property offending Any crime punishable by more than one year in prison or jail and causes property loss or damage (e.g., burglary, larceny/theft, and vehicular theft).

Feminist legal studies View that women use a different type of logic than men when interpreting the law, favoring less litigation and more mediation.

Filing The commencement of criminal proceedings by entering a charging document into a court's official record.

Financial/community service model Restitution model for juveniles that stresses the offender's financial accountability and community service to pay for damages.

Finding A holding or ruling by the court or judge.

Finding of fact Court's determination of the facts presented as evidence in a case, affirmed by one party and denied by the other.

Fines Financial penalties imposed at time of sentencing convicted offenders. Most criminal statutes contain provisions for the imposition of monetary penalties as sentencing options.

Flat term A specific, definite term for a conviction, not necessarily known in advance of sentencing.

Flat time Actual amount of time required to be served by a convicted offender while incarcerated.

Foster home Dwelling including family where child is placed, usually where such child is from an abusive household or without parents or legal guardians; foster home parents are responsible for proper upbringing of child for a period of time.

Frivolous lawsuits Legal actions commenced by one or more parties where there is little hope of a successful outcome; often groundless legal actions without sufficient bases.

Fruits of the poisonous tree doctrine A U.S. Supreme Court decision in *Wong Sun v. United States* (1963) holding that evidence that is spawned or directly derived from an illegal search or an illegal interrogation is generally inadmissible against a defendant because of its original taint.

Fugitive recovery agents One who seeks to return to a jurisdiction a person who has been charged with a crime and has jumped bail or fled the jurisdiction before trial.

Fundamental fairness Legal doctrine supporting the idea that so long as a state's conduct maintains the basic elements of fairness, the Constitution has not been violated.

Gag order Official declaration by the judge in a trial proceeding that all parties in the action, including the jurors, must refrain from discussing the case with the media.

General jurisdiction Power of a court to hear a wide range of cases, both civil and criminal.

General pretrial publicity Information about crime and the criminal justice system involving general details of types of crime and offenders and victims covered by the news media regularly which shapes our perceptions.

General sessions courts Tribunals in particular states with limited jurisdiction to hear misdemeanor cases and some low-level felony cases.

General trial courts Any one of several types of courts, either civil or criminal, with diverse jurisdiction to conduct jury trials and decide cases.

Geographic jurisdiction The power to hear particular kinds of cases depending upon the legally defined boundaries of cities, counties, or states.

Get-tough movement General orientation toward criminals and juvenile delinquents that favors the maximum penalties and punishments for crime and delinquency; any action toward toughening or strengthening sentencing provisions or dispositions involving adults or juveniles.

Going rate Local view of the appropriate sentence or punishment for a particular offense, the defendant's prior record, and other factors; used in implicit plea bargaining.

Good time, good-time credit An amount of time deducted from the period of incarceration of a convicted offender, calculated as so many days per month on the basis of good behavior while incarcerated. Credits earned by prisoners for good behavior. Introduced in the early 1800s by British penal authorities, including Alexander Maconochie and Sir Walter Crofton.

Grand jury Investigative bodies whose numbers vary among states. Duties include determining probable cause regarding commission of a crime and returning formal charges against suspects. *See also* true bill and no true bill.

Grievance, grievance procedure Formalized arrangements, usually involving a neutral hearing board, whereby institutionalized individuals have the opportunity to register complaints about the conditions of their confinement.

Group home Facilities for juveniles that provide limited supervision and support. Juveniles live in homelike environment with other juveniles and participate in therapeutic programs and counseling. Considered nonsecure custodial. *See also* foster home.

Guardian *ad litem* A court-appointed attorney who protects the interests of children in cases involving their welfare and who works with the children during the litigation period.

Guidelines-based sentencing *See* sentencing guidelines.

Guilty plea A defendant's formal affirmation of guilt in court to charges contained in a complaint, information, or indictment claiming that they committed the offenses listed.

Habeas corpus Writ meaning "produce the body"; used by prisoners to challenge the nature and length of their confinement.

Habeas corpus petition Writ filed, usually by inmates, challenging the legitimacy of their confinement and the nature of their confinement. Document commands authorities to show cause why an inmate should be confined in either a prison or jail. Also includes challenges of the nature of confinement. A written order by the court to any person, including a law enforcement officer, directing that person to bring the named individual before the court so that it can determine if there is adequate cause for continued detention.

Habitual offenders Persons who have been convicted of two or more felonies and may be sentenced under the habitual offender statute for an aggravated or longer prison term.

Habitual offender statutes Statutes vary among states. Generally provide life imprisonment as a mandatory sentence for chronic offenders who have been convicted of three or more serious felonies within a specific time period.

Harmful errors Errors made by judges that may be prejudicial to a defendant's case. May lead to reversals of convictions against defendants and to new trials.

Harmless error doctrine Errors of a minor or trivial nature and not deemed sufficient to harm the rights of parties in a legal action. Cases are not reversed on the basis of harmless errors.

Hearing Any formal proceeding in which the court hears evidence from prosecutors and defense and resolves a dispute or issue.

Hearing, probable cause A proceeding in which arguments, evidence, or witnesses are presented and in which it is determined whether there is sufficient cause to hold the accused for trial or whether the case should be dismissed.

Hearsay evidence Evidence that is not firsthand but is based on an account given by another.

Hearsay rule Courtroom precedent that hearsay cannot be used in court. Rather than accepting testimony on hearsay, the trial process asks that persons who were the original source of the hearsay information be brought into court to be questioned and cross-examined. Exceptions to the hearsay rule may occur when persons with direct knowledge are either dead or otherwise unable to testify.

Hierarchical jurisdiction Distinction between courts at different levels, where one court is superior to another and has the power to hear appeals from lower court decisions.

Holding The legal principle drawn from a judicial decision. Whatever a court, usually an appellate court, decides when cases are appealed from lower courts. When an appellate court "holds" a particular decision, this may be to uphold the original conviction, set it aside, overturn in part, and uphold in part.

Home confinement Housing of offenders in their own homes with or without electronic monitoring devices. Reduces prison overcrowding and prisoner costs. Sometimes an intermediate punishment involving the use of offender residences for mandatory incarceration during evening hours after a curfew and on weekends. Also called "house arrest."

Hung jury Jury that cannot agree on a verdict.

Illinois Juvenile Court Act Legislation establishing first juvenile court in United States in 1899.

Impartial arbiters Persons such as judges, attorneys, or prominent citizens who are called upon to be objective and neutral third parties in disputes between perpetrators and their victims under conditions of restorative justice or alternative dispute resolution.

Impeachment Proceeding for the removal of a political officer, such as a governor, president, or judge.

Implicit plea bargaining Occurs when defendant pleads guilty with the expectation of receiving a more lenient sentence. *See also* plea bargaining.

Inadmissible Evidentiary term used to describe something that cannot be used as evidence during a trial.

Incapacitation, isolation Philosophy of corrections espousing loss of freedom proportional to seriousness of offense. Belief that the function of punishment is to separate offenders from other society members and prevent them from committing additional criminal acts.

Inculpatory evidence Any information that places the defendant in an unfavorable light and increases the likelihood of his/her guilt.

Incumbents Political officers who are currently in power, but who are seeking to be re-elected or reappointed.

Indeterminate sentencing Sentencing scheme in which a period is set by judges between the earliest date for a parole decision and the latest date for completion of the sentence. In holding that the time necessary for treatment cannot be set exactly, the indeterminate sentence is closely associated with rehabilitation.

Indictments Charges or written accusations found and presented by a grand jury that a particular defendant probably committed a crime.

Indigent defendants Poor persons; anyone who cannot afford legal services or representation.

Ineffective assistance of counsel Standard for determining whether client is defended in a competent way; guidelines for determining counsel's effectiveness articulated in case of *Strickland v. Washington* (1984), which include (1) whether counsel's behavior undermined the adversarial process to the degree that the trial outcome is unreliable; and (2) the counsel's conduct was unreasonable to the degree that the jury's verdict would have been different otherwise.

Informations Written accusations made by a public prosecutor against a person for some criminal offense, without an indictment. Usually restricted to minor crimes or misdemeanors. Sometimes called criminal informations.

Initial appearance Formal proceeding during which the judge advises the defendant of the charges, including a recitation of the defendant's rights and a bail decision.

In re "In the matter of." Refers to cases being filed for juveniles who must have an adult act on their behalf when filing motions or appeals.

Insanity Degree of mental illness that negates the legal capacity or responsibility of the affected person.

Insanity defense Defense that seeks to exonerate accused persons by showing that they were insane at the time they were believed to have committed a crime.

Insanity plea A plea entered as a defense to a crime. The defendant admits guilt but assigns responsibility for the criminal act to the condition of insanity presumably existing when the crime was committed.

Intake Review of a case by a court (juvenile or criminal) official. Screening of cases includes weeding out weak cases. In juvenile cases, intake involves the reception of a juvenile against whom complaints have been made. Decision to proceed or dismiss the case is made at this stage.

Intake hearings Proceedings, usually presided over by an intake officer, where determinations are made about whether certain juveniles should undergo further processing by the juvenile justice system; a screening mechanism for juvenile offenders.

Intake officer Officer who conducts screening of juveniles. Dispositions include release to parents pending further juvenile court action, dismissal of charges against juvenile, detention, treatment by some community agency.

Intake screening A critical phase where a determination is made by a juvenile probation officer or other official whether to release juveniles to their parent's custody, detain juveniles in formal detention facilities for a later court appearance, or release them to parents pending a later court appearance.

Intensive supervised probation Varies from standard probation and includes more face-to-face visits between probation officers and probationers under community supervision.

Intent A state of mind, the *mens rea*, in which a person seeks to accomplish a given result, such as a crime, through a given course of action.

Interim judges Temporary judge who is appointed following the death, resignation, or retirement of another judge, usually to complete the original judge's term; after the interim judge serves, a new judge is appointed or elected according to the rules of judicial selection in the particular jurisdiction.

Intermittent sentencing Imposed punishment where offender must serve a portion of sentence in jail, perhaps on weekends or specific evenings. Considered similar to probation with limited incarceration. *See also* split sentencing.

Intoxication The state of being incapable of performing certain tasks legally, such as operating motor vehicles or boats. Can be induced through consumption of alcoholic beverages, inhaling toxic fumes from petroleum products, or consumption of drug substances. May also be a defense to criminal conduct, although the courts often rule that it is voluntary.

Ipso facto "By the mere fact." By the fact itself (e.g., "We can assume, *ipso facto*, that if the defendant was observed beating another person in a bar by ten witnesses, then he is likely guilty of the beating inflicted on the victim.").

Isolation A sentencing philosophy seeking to remove the offender from other offenders when confined by placing prisoner in a cell with no communication with others. Also known as solitary confinement, which originated in the Walnut Street Jail in Philadelphia, Pennsylvania in the late 1700s. Another usage of this term is to segregate offenders from society through incarceration.

Jail as a condition of probation Sentence in which judge imposes limited jail time to be served before commencement of probation. *See also* split sentencing.

Jencks materials Discoverable materials available from either the prosecutor or defense counsel prior to trial. *See Jencks v. United States* (1957).

Judge A political officer who has been elected or appointed to preside over a court of law, whose position has been created by statute or by constitution and whose decisions in criminal and juvenile cases may only be reviewed by a judge or a higher court and may not be reviewed *de novo*.

Judgment Final determination of a case. A proclamation stating one's guilt or innocence in relation to criminal offenses alleged. In tort law, a finding in favor of or against the plaintiff. The amount of monetary damages awarded in civil cases.

Judicial activism U.S. Supreme Court's use of its power to accomplish social goals.

Judicial appointments Selections of judges by political figures, such as governors or presidents.

Judicial conduct commission Investigative body created in California in 1960, comprised of other judges, attorneys, and prominent citizens; task was to investigate allegations of judicial misconduct, incompetence, and unfairness.

Judicial instructions Specific admonitions to jurors, prosecutors, and defense counsels to do or refrain from doing different things.

Judicial misconduct Departure of a judge from accepted modes of conduct after becoming a judicial official; forms of misconduct are accepting bribes in exchange for money or services; making biased decisions favoring one side or the other during a trial; engaging in behaviors (e.g., drunkenness, driving while intoxicated, perjury) while serving on the bench.

Judicial plea bargaining Recommended sentence by judge who offers a specific sentence and/or fine in exchange for a guilty plea. *See also* plea bargaining.

Judicial privilege Power of judges to change plea bargain agreements and substitute their own punishments; the power to override prosecutors and defense counsel concerning the agreed upon terms of plea agreements.

Judicial process The sequence of procedures designed to resolve disputes or conclude a criminal case.

Judicial review The authority of a court to limit the power of the executive and legislative branches of government by deciding whether their acts defy rights established by the state and federal constitutions.

Judicial waiver Decision by juvenile judge to waive juvenile to jurisdiction of criminal court.

Judiciary Act of 1789 A congressional act that provided for three levels of courts: (1) 13 federal district courts, each presided over by a district judge; (2) 3 higher circuit courts of appeal, each comprising 2 justices of the Supreme Court and 1 district judge; and (3) a Supreme Court, consisting of a chief justice and 5 associate justices.

Jumping bail Act by defendant of leaving jurisdiction where trial is to be held. Attempt by defendant to avoid prosecution on criminal charges.

Jurisdiction The power of a court to hear and determine a particular type of case. Also refers to territory within which the court may exercise authority, such as a city, county, or state.

Juror misconduct Any impropriety by a juror; acceptance of illegal gratuities in exchange for a favorable vote for or against the defendant; sleeping during the trial; reading newspaper accounts, listening or watching newscasters voice their opinions about the case, and then relating this information to other jurors in attempt to persuade them one way or another for or against the defendant.

Jury *See* petit jury.

Jury deliberations Discussion among jury members concerning the weight and sufficiency of witness testimony and other evidence presented by both the prosecution and defense. An attempt to arrive at a verdict.

Jury misconduct Any impropriety exhibited by one or more jurors, such as sleeping during a trial; attempting to bias other jurors for or against a particular defendant by illegal means; or accepting bribes or gratuities from persons interested in the case.

Jury nullification Jury refuses to accept the validity of evidence at trial and acquits or convicts for a lesser offense (e.g., although all of the elements for murder are proved, a jury may acquit defendants who killed their spouses allegedly as an act of mercy killing).

Jury panel A list of jurors summoned to serve on possible jury duty at a particular court. From the jury panel, the petit jury is selected.

Jury poll A poll conducted by a judicial officer or by the clerk of the court after a jury has stated its verdict but before that verdict has been entered into the record of the court, asking each juror individually whether the stated verdict is his or her own verdict.

Jury pool Aggregate of persons from which a jury is selected; use of voter registration lists, driver's licenses, home ownership records, and other public documents to create such pools; also known as a *venire* or *venireman* list.

Jury selection The process whereby a jury is impaneled for either a civil or criminal trial proceeding.

Jury sequestration The process of isolating a jury from the public during a trial; the objective is to minimize the influence of media publicity and exposure, which might otherwise influence juror opinions about the guilt or innocence of the defendant.

Jury size Traditional 12-member jury at federal level and many state and local levels; may vary between 6-member jury and 12-member jury at state and local levels.

Jury trial Proceeding by which guilt or innocence of defendant is determined by jury instead of by the judge.

Jury waiver system Occurs when defendants waive their constitutional right to a jury trial and enter into a plea bargain agreement with the prosecutor.

Juvenile–contiguous blend Form of blended sentencing by a juvenile court judge where the judge can impose a disposition beyond the normal jurisdictional range for juvenile offenders; for example, a judge may impose a 30-year term on a 14-year-old offender, but the juvenile is entitled to a hearing when he/she reaches the age of majority to determine whether the remainder of the sentence shall be served.

Juvenile court A term for any court with original jurisdiction over persons statutorily defined as juveniles and alleged to be delinquents, status offenders, or dependents.

Juvenile court jurisdiction Power of juvenile courts to hear cases involving persons under the legal age of adulthood.

Juvenile delinquency The violation of criminal laws by juveniles. Any illegal behavior or activity committed by persons who are within a particular age range; subjects them to the jurisdiction of a juvenile court or its equivalent.

Juvenile delinquent Any minor who commits an offense that would be a crime if committed by an adult.

Juvenile–exclusive blend Blended sentencing form where a juvenile court judge can impose either adult or juvenile incarceration as a disposition and sentence but not both.

Juvenile–inclusive blend Form of blended sentencing where a juvenile court judge can impose *both* adult and juvenile incarceration simultaneously.

Juvenile Justice and Delinquency Prevention Act of 1974 (JJDPA) Act passed by Congress in 1974 and amended numerous times, including 1984, encouraging states to deal differently with their juvenile offenders. Promotes community-based treatment programs and discourages incarceration of juveniles in detention centers, industrial schools, or reform schools.

Juvenile justice system, process The system through which juveniles are processed, sentenced, and corrected after arrests for juvenile delinquency.

Juveniles Persons who have not as yet achieved their eighteenth birthday or the age of majority.

Kales Plan The 1914 version of Missouri Plan, in which a committee of experts creates a list of qualified persons for judgeships and makes recommendations to governor. *See also* Missouri Plan.

Labeling theory, labeling Theory attributed to Edwin Lemert that persons acquire self-definitions that are deviant or criminal. Persons perceive themselves as deviant or criminal through labels applied to them by others; thus the more people are involved in the criminal justice system, the more they acquire self-definitions consistent with the criminal label.

Law The body of rules of specific conduct, prescribed by existing, legitimate authority in a particular jurisdiction and at a particular point in time.

Legal realism View that law and society are constantly evolving and that law should be the means to a social end rather than an end in itself.

Legislative waivers Provisions that compel juvenile court to remand certain youths to criminal courts because of specific offenses that have been committed or alleged.

Lex talionis The law of retaliation or retribution. A form of revenge dating back to the Apostle Paul and used up until the Middle Ages.

Lie detectors Apparatuses that record one's blood pressure and various other sensory responses and plot one's reactions by means of a moving pencil and paper. Designed to determine whether one is telling the truth during an interrogation. Also known as polygraphs. Results of tests are not admissible in court.

Life imprisonment Any sentence involving lengthy incarceration, presumably for the life expectancy of the convicted offender.

Life-without-parole sentence Penalty imposed as maximum punishment in states that do not have death penalty; provides for permanent incarceration of offenders in prisons, without parole eligibility; early release may be attained through accumulation of good-time credits.

Limited jurisdiction Court is restricted to handling certain types of cases such as probate matters or juvenile offenses. Also known as special jurisdiction.

Litigation Civil prosecution in which proceedings are maintained against wrongdoers, as opposed to criminal proceedings.

Litigation explosion Sudden increase in inmate suits against administrators and officers in prisons and jails during the late 1960s and continuing through the 1980s. Suits usually challenge nature and length of confinement or torts allegedly committed by administration, usually seek monetary or other forms of relief.

Magistrate A judge who handles cases in pretrial stages. Usually presides over misdemeanor cases. An officer of the lower courts.

Magistrate courts Courts of special jurisdiction, usually urban.

Malfeasance Misconduct by public officials. Engaging in acts that are prohibited while serving in public office.

Malicious prosecution Prosecutorial action against someone without probable cause or reasonable suspicion.

Mandamus *See* writ of *mandamus*.

Mandatory sentencing, mandatory sentence Sentencing where court is required to impose an incarcerative sentence of a specified length, without the option for probation, suspended sentence, or immediate parole eligibility.

Mandatory transfer Automatic waiver of certain juveniles to criminal court on the basis of (1) their age and (2) the seriousness of their offense; for example, a 17-year-old in Illinois who allegedly committed homicide would be subject to mandatory transfer to criminal court for the purpose of a criminal prosecution.

Material witness Any witness who has relevant testimony about a crime.

Mediation Informal conflict resolution through the intervention of a trained negotiator who seeks a mutually agreeable resolution between disputing parties.

Mens rea Intent to commit a crime. Guilty mind.

Merit selection Reform plan in which judges are nominated by a committee and appointed by the governor for a given period. When the term expires, the voters are asked to signify their approval or disapproval of the judge for a succeeding term. If judge is disapproved, the committee nominates a successor for the governor's appointment.

Miranda warning, rights Warning given to suspects by police officers advising suspects of their legal rights to counsel, to refuse to answer questions, to avoid self-incrimination, and other privileges. Named after landmark case of *Miranda v. Arizona* (1966).

Misdemeanor Crime punishable by fines and/or imprisonment, usually in a city or county jail, for periods of less than one year.

Misdemeanor Trial Law Action by New York City passed in 1985 permitting low-level misdemeanor cases involving incarceration of six months or less to be disposed of by bench trials rather than jury trials; a time-saving strategy for more rapid criminal case processing.

Missouri Plan Method of selecting judges in which merit system for appointments is used. Believed to reduce political influence in the selection of judges.

Mistake Affirmative defense that alleges an act was not criminal because the person charged did not know the act was a prohibited one.

Mistake of fact Unconscious ignorance of a fact or the belief in the existence of something that does not exist.

Mistake of law An erroneous opinion of legal principles applied to a given set of facts. A judge may rule on a given court issue and the ruling may be wrong because the judge misunderstands the meaning of the law and how it should be applied.

Mistrial A trial that cannot stand, is invalid. Judges may call a mistrial for reasons such as errors on the part of prosecutors or defense counsel, the death of a juror or counsel, or a hung jury.

Mitigating circumstances Factors about a crime that may lessen the severity of sentence imposed by the judge. Cooperating with police to apprehend others involved, youthfulness or old age of defendant, mental instability, and having no prior record are considered mitigating circumstances.

Mittimus An order by the court to an officer to bring someone named in the order directly to jail.

Mixed sentencing Two or more separate sentences imposed after offenders have been convicted of two or more crimes in the same adjudication proceeding. *See also* split sentencing.

Motion for a bill of particulars An action before the court asking that the details of the state's case against a defendant be made known to the defense. *See also* discovery.

Motion for a change of venue Action requested by either the prosecutor or defense counsel seeking to change the trial site to a different jurisdiction or geographical location, possibly because of extensive pretrial publicity and the belief that prospective jurors might be biased one way or another toward the defendant.

Motion for continuance An action before the court asking that the trial or hearing or proceeding be postponed to a later date.

Motion for determination of competency Action requested by defense counsel where the court is asked to order a psychiatric examination of the defendant to determine whether the defendant is competent to stand trial for a crime.

Motion for discovery Action initiated by either prosecutor or defense counsel entitling either side to certain discoverable evidence, such as police reports and defendant interviews, and any other relevant evidentiary items that might be useful as the basis for case arguments at trial later.

Motion for dismissal of charges Action requested by defense counsel to have charges against the defendant dismissed because of an insufficiency of evidence presented by the prosecutor.

Motion for intention to provide alibi Defense-initiated motion to indicate the intention to use an alibi witness or witnesses, evidence, or some type of rationale to show cause for why defendant was not at the scene of the crime(s) alleged and for which the defendant is being tried.

Motion for severance Action requested by either the prosecutor or defense counsel to have separate trial proceedings for different persons charged with the same offense and who are accused of acting in concert with one another to effect a crime.

Motion for summary judgment Request granted by judges who have read the plaintiff's version and defendant's version of events, and a decision is reached holding for the defendant.

Motion for suppression of evidence Action initiated by prosecutor or defense counsel asking the judge to bar the admission of certain evidence from the trial proceeding.

Motions Oral or written requests to a judge asking the court to make a specific ruling, finding, decision, or order. May be presented at any appropriate point from an arrest until the end of a trial.

Motions *in limine* A pretrial motion, generally to obtain judicial approval to admit certain items into evidence that might otherwise be considered prejudicial or inflammatory.

Motion to dismiss An action before the court requesting that the judge refuse to hear a suit. Usually granted when inmates who file petitions fail to state a claim upon which relief can be granted.

Motion to suppress An action before the court to cause testimony or tangible evidence from being introduced either for or against the accused.

Municipal courts Courts of special jurisdiction whose jurisdiction follows the political boundaries of a municipality or city.

Naming Identifying a party in a legal action as the target of that action.

Narrative A portion of a presentence investigation report prepared by a probation officer or private agency, which provides a description of offense and offender. Culminates in and justifies a recommendation for a specific sentence to be imposed on the offender by judges.

Necessity A condition that compels someone to act because of perceived needs. An affirmative defense (e.g., when someone's automobile breaks down during a snowstorm and an unoccupied cabin is nearby, breaking into the cabin to save oneself from freezing to death is acting out of "necessity" and would be a defense to breaking and entering charges later).

Negligence Liability accruing to prison or correctional program administrators and probation or parole officers as the result of a failure to perform a duty owed to clients or inmates or the improper or inadequate performance of that duty. May include negligent entrustment, negligent training, negligent assignment, negligent retention, or negligent supervision (e.g., providing probation or parole officers with revolvers and not providing them with firearms training).

Negotiated guilty pleas Pleas of guilty entered in exchange for some form of sentencing leniency during plea bargaining.

New trial Tribunal *de novo*. After a hung jury or a case is set aside or overturned by a higher court, a new trial is held to determine one's guilt or innocence.

New York House of Refuge Established in New York City in 1825 by the Society for the Prevention of Pauperism;

school that managed largely status offenders; compulsory education provided; strict prison-like regimen was considered detrimental to youthful clientele.

No bill *See* no true bill.

Nolle prosequi An entry made by the prosecutor on the record in a case and announced in court to indicate that the specified charges will not be prosecuted. In effect, the charges are thereby dismissed.

Nolo contendere Plea of "no contest" to charges. Defendant does not dispute facts, although issue may be taken with the legality or constitutionality of the law allegedly violated. Treated as a guilty plea. Also known as "Alford plea" from leading case of *North Carolina v. Alford* (1970).

Nominal dispositions Juvenile court outcome in which juvenile is warned or verbally reprimanded, but returned to custody of parents.

Nonpartisan elections Voting process in which candidates who are not endorsed by political parties are presented to the voters for selection.

Nonsecure custody, confinement A facility that emphasizes the care and treatment of youths without the need to place constraints to ensure public protection.

Not guilty A defendant's formal contesting of any wrongdoing in court to charges contained in a complaint, information, or indictment claiming that they committed the offenses listed.

Notice An official document advising someone of a proceeding that usually requires his/her attendance.

Notice of appeal Filing a formal document with the court advising the court that the sentence is to be appealed to a higher court or appellate court.

No true bill Grand jury decision that insufficient evidence exists to establish probable cause that a crime was committed and a specific person committed it.

Objections Actions by either the prosecutor or defense requesting that certain questions not be asked of witnesses or that certain evidence should or should not be admitted.

Office of Juvenile Justice and Delinquency Prevention (OJJDP) Established by Congress under the Juvenile Justice and Delinquency Prevention Act of 1974; designed to remove status offenders from jurisdiction of juvenile courts and dispose of their cases less formally.

Once an adult/always an adult Provision that once a juvenile has been transferred to criminal court to be prosecuted as an adult, regardless of the criminal court outcome, the juvenile can never be subject to the jurisdiction of juvenile courts in the future; in short, the juvenile, once transferred, will always be treated as an adult if future crimes are committed, even though the youth is still not of adult age.

Open court Any court where spectators may gather.

Opening statement Remarks made by prosecution and defense attorneys to the jury at the commencement of trial proceedings. Usually these statements set forth what each side intends to show by evidence to be presented.

Opinion of the court Opinion summarizing the views of the majority of judges participating in a judicial decision; a ruling or holding by a court official.

Oral argument Verbal presentation made to an appellate court by the prosecution or the defense in order to persuade the court to affirm, reverse, or modify a lower court decision.

Order Any written declaration or proclamation by a judge authorizing officials to act.

Original jurisdiction First authority over a case or cause, as opposed to appellate jurisdiction.

Overrule To reverse or annul by subsequent action (e.g., judges may overrule objections from prosecutors and defense attorneys in court, nullifying these objections; lower court decisions may be overruled by higher courts when the case is appealed).

Parens patriae "Parent of the country." Refers to doctrine that the state oversees the welfare of youth, originally established by the king of England and administered through chancellors.

Parole board, paroling authority Body of persons either appointed by governors or others or elected, which determines whether those currently incarcerated in prisons should be granted parole or early release.

Partisan elections Elections in which candidates endorsed by political parties are presented to the voters for selection.

Per diem "By the day." The cost per day, for example, the daily cost of housing inmates.

Per se "By itself." In itself (e.g., the death penalty is not unconstitutional *per se*, but a particular method of administering the death penalty may be unconstitutional in some states).

Peremptory challenge Rejection of a juror by either the prosecution or the defense in which no reason needs to be provided for excusing the juror from jury duty. Each side has a limited number of these challenges. The more serious the offense, the more peremptory challenges are given each side.

Perjury Lying under oath in court.

Persistent felony offenders Habitual offenders who commit felonies with a high recidivism rate.

Persistent offender statutes Any law prohibiting someone from being a habitual offender or someone who has been convicted of several serious crimes.

Petit jury The trier of fact in a criminal case. The jury of one's peers called to hear the evidence and decide the defendant's guilt or innocence. Varies in size among states.

Petition A document filed in juvenile court alleging that a juvenile is a delinquent, a status offender, or a dependent and asking that the court assume jurisdiction over the juvenile or that the juvenile be transferred to a criminal court to be prosecuted as an adult.

Petitioner Person who brings a petition before the court.

Petty offenses Minor infractions or crimes, misdemeanors. Usually punishable by fines or short terms of imprisonment.

Philadelphia Experiment Study conducted involving setting bail guidelines in Philadelphia, Pennsylvania, during 1981–1982 and the use of release on one's own recognizance (ROR); experiment led to greater equity in bail decision making for persons of different socioeconomic statuses.

Pickpocketing The theft of money or valuables directly from the garments of the victim.

Plea Answer to charges by defendant. Pleas vary among jurisdictions. Not guilty, guilty, *nolo contendere*, not guilty by reason of insanity, and guilty but mentally ill are possible pleas.

Plea agreement hearing Meeting presided over by a trial judge to determine the accuracy of a guilty plea and acceptability of general conditions of a plea bargain agreement between the prosecution and defense attorneys.

Plea bargaining A preconviction deal-making process between the state and the accused in which the defendant exchanges a plea of guilty or *nolo contendere* for a reduction in charges, a promise of sentencing leniency, or some other concession from full, maximum implementation of the conviction and sentencing authority of the court. Includes implicit plea bargaining, charge reduction bargaining, sentence recommendation bargaining, and judicial plea bargaining.

Plea bargain agreement Formal agreement between prosecutor and defense counsel wherein the defendant enters a guilty plea to one or more criminal charges in exchange for some form of sentencing leniency.

Plea bargains Formal agreements between the prosecutors and defense concerning the defendant offering a guilty plea in exchange for some form of sentencing leniency.

Plea, guilty A defendant's formal answer in court to the charges in a complaint, information, or an indictment where the defendant states that the charges are true and that he or she has committed the offense(s) as charged.

Plea, initial The first plea entered in response to a given charge entered in a court record by or for a defendant.

Plea, not guilty A defendant's formal answer in court to the charges in a complaint or information or indictment, in which the defendant states that he or she has not committed the offense(s) as charged.

Plead To respond to a criminal charge.

Plea negotiation *See plea bargaining.*

Plea *nolo contendere* See nolo contendere.

Polling jurors A direct method of asking jurors to state whether they have voted in a particular way.

Polygraph tests *See* lie detectors.

Postconviction relief   Term applied to various mechanisms whereby offenders may challenge their conviction after other appeal attempts have been exhausted.

Pound's model   Plan of court organization with three tiers: supreme court, major trial court, and minor trial court.

Precedent   Principle that the way a case was decided previously should serve as a guide for how a similar case currently under consideration ought to be decided.

Pre-conflict stage   Perception by individuals or groups that they are involved in a conflict situation where a legal resolution is sought.

Preliminary examinations   See preliminary hearings.

Preliminary hearings, preliminary examinations   Hearings by magistrate or other judicial officer to determine if person charged with a crime should be held for trial. Proceedings to establish probable cause. They do not determine guilt or innocence.

Preponderance of the evidence   Civil standard whereby the weight of the exculpatory or inculpatory information is in favor of or against the defendant; the greater the weight of information favoring the defendant, the greater the likelihood of a finding in favor of the defendant.

Presentence investigation reports, presentence reports (PSIs)   Reports filed by probation or parole officer appointed by the court containing background information, socioeconomic data, and demographic data relative to defendant. Facts in the case are included. Used to influence the sentence imposed by the judge and by the parole board considering an inmate for early release.

Presentment   An accusation, initiated by the grand jury on its own authority, from jurors' own knowledge or observation, which functions as an instruction for the preparation of an indictment.

Presiding judge   The title of the judicial officer formally designated for some period as the chief judicial officer of the court.

Presumption of innocence   Premise that a defendant is innocent unless proven guilty beyond a reasonable doubt. Fundamental to the adversary system.

Presumptive sentencing, presumptive sentences   Statutory sentencing method that specifies normal sentences of particular lengths with limited judicial leeway to shorten or lengthen the term of the sentence.

Presumptive waiver   Type of judicial waiver where burden of proof shifts from the state to the juvenile to contest whether youth is transferred to criminal court.

Pretrial conference   A meeting between opposing parties in a lawsuit or criminal trial, for purposes of stipulating things that are agreed upon and thus narrowing the trial to the things that are in dispute, disclosing the required information about witnesses and evidence, making motions, and generally organizing the presentation of motions, witnesses, and evidence.

Pretrial diversion   See diversion.

Pretrial motions   See motions in limine.

Pretrial publicity   Any media attention given to a case before it is tried in court.

Prima facie case   A case for which there is as much evidence as would warrant the conviction of defendants if properly proved in court. A case that meets the evidentiary requirements for a grand jury indictment.

Pro se   Acting as one's own defense attorney in criminal proceedings. Representing oneself.

Probable cause   Reasonable suspicion or belief that a crime has been committed and that a particular person committed it.

Probation officer   Professional who supervises probationers.

Procedural law   Rules that specify how statutes should be applied against those who violate the law. Procedures whereby the substantive laws may be implemented.

Process   A summons requiring the appearance of someone in court.

Proof beyond a reasonable doubt   Standard of proof to convict in criminal case.

Prosecuting attorney   See prosecutor.

Prosecution   Carrying forth of criminal proceedings against a person, culminating in a trial or other final disposition such as a plea of guilty in lieu of trial.

Prosecution agency, prosecutorial agency   Any local, state, or federal body charged with carrying forth actions against criminals. State legal representatives, such as district attorneys or U.S. attorneys and their assistants, who seek to convict persons charged with crimes.

Prosecutor   Court official who commences civil and criminal proceedings against defendants. Represents state or government interest, prosecuting defendants on behalf of state or government.

Prosecutorial bluffing   Attempt by prosecution to bluff the defendant into believing the case is much stronger than it really is. Used to elicit a guilty plea from a defendant to avoid a lengthy trial where the proof of a defendant's guilt may be difficult to establish.

Prosecutorial discretion   The decision-making power of prosecutors based upon the wide range of choices available to them in the handling of criminal defendants, the scheduling of cases for trial, and the acceptance of bargained pleas. The most important form of prosecutorial discretion lies in the power to charge or not to charge a person with an offense.

Prosecutorial misconduct   Any deliberate action that violates ethical codes or standards governing the role of prosecutors; usually the action is intended to injure defendants and illegally or unethically strengthen the case of prosecutors.

Prosecutorial waiver   Authority of prosecutors in juvenile cases to have those cases transferred to the jurisdiction of criminal court.

Public defender system   Means whereby attorneys are appointed by the court to represent indigent defendants.

Punishment   Any sanction imposed for committing a crime; usually a sentence imposed for being convicted of either a felony or misdemeanor.

Reasonable doubt   Standard used by jurors to decide if the prosecution has provided sufficient evidence for conviction. Jurors vote for acquittal if they have reasonable doubt that the accused committed the crime.

Reasonable suspicion   Warranted suspicion (short of probable cause) that a person may be engaged in criminal conduct.

Recall election   Special election called to remove a politician or judge from his/her office.

Recognizance   Personal responsibility to return to court on a given date and at a given time.

Re-cross-examination   Opposing counsel further examines an opposing witness who has already testified.

Re-direct examination   Questioning of a witness following the adversary's questioning under cross-examination.

Referral   Any citation of a juvenile to juvenile court by a law enforcement officer, interested citizen, family member, or school official; usually based upon law violations, delinquency, or unruly conduct.

Reformatory   Detention facility designed to change criminal behavior or reform it.

Rehabilitation, rehabilitative ideal   Correcting criminal behavior through educational and other means, usually associated with prisons.

Reintegration   Punishment philosophy that promotes programs that lead offenders back into their communities. Reintegrative programs include furloughs, work release, and halfway houses.

Release on their own recognizance (ROR)   Arrangement where defendants are able to be set free temporarily to await a later trial without having to post a bail bond; persons released on ROR are usually well known or have strong ties to the community and have not been charged with serious crimes.

Remand   To send back (e.g., the U.S. Supreme Court may remand a case back to the lower trial court where the case was originally tried).

Remedy   Any declared solution to a dispute between parties (e.g., if someone is found guilty of slashing another's automobile tires, the remedy may be to cause the convicted offender to compensate the victim with money for the full value of the destroyed tires).

Reparations   Damages assigned to be paid by a defendant found liable in a civil action; may include restitution to victims; usually follow trial showing liability or culpability of defendant in lawsuit filed by plaintiff who is seeking damages.

Respondent   A person asked to respond in a lawsuit or writ.

Responsible   Legally accountable for one's actions and obligations.

Restitution   Stipulation by the court that offenders must compensate victims for their financial losses resulting from crime. Compensation to the victim for psychological, physical, or financial loss. May be imposed as a part of an incarcerative sentence.

Restorative justice   Mediation between victims and offenders whereby offenders accept responsibility for their actions and agree to reimburse victims for their losses; may involve community service and other penalties agreeable to both parties in a form of arbitration with a neutral third party acting as arbiter.

Reverse waiver hearings   Formal proceedings, usually conducted by a criminal court judge, to determine whether a transferred juvenile should be sent back to be tried for his/her crimes in juvenile court rather than criminal court.

Reversed and remanded   Decision by the appellate court to set aside or overturn the verdict of a lower trial court with instructions to the trial court to rehear the case with suggested modifications.

Reversible errors   Mistakes committed by judges during a trial that may result in reversal of convictions against defendants.

Review   The procedure whereby a higher court examines one or more issues emanating from a lower court on an appeal by the prosecution or defense.

Rights of defendant   Constitutional guarantees to all persons charged with crimes. Includes representation by counsel at various critical stages, such as being charged with crimes, preliminary hearings, arraignments, trial, and appeals.

Right to counsel   Right to be represented by an attorney at critical stages of the criminal justice system. Indigent defendants have the right to counsel provided by the state.

ROR   *See* release on their own recognizance.

Rule of Four   U.S. Supreme Court rule whereby the Court grants *certiorari* only on the agreement of at least four justices.

Rule of law   Describes willingness of persons to accept and order their behavior according to rules and procedures that are prescribed by political and social institutions.

Rules of criminal procedure   Rules legislatively established by which a criminal case is conducted. Law enforcement officers, prosecutors, and judges use rules of criminal procedure in discretionary actions against suspects and defendants.

Runaways   Juveniles who abscond from their homes or residences without parental permission; often these youths seek a free life in another city away from parental control; a type of status offender.

Scientific jury selection   Applying the scientific method to select jurors who it is believed will render favorable decisions for or against defendants.

Screening   Process of jury selection by attempting to remove biased jurors and select only the most competent and objective ones.

Screening cases Procedure used by prosecutor to define which cases have prosecutive merit and which ones do not. Some screening bureaus are made up of police and lawyers with trial experience.

Seal To close from public inspection any record of an arrest, judgment, or adjudication, either criminal or juvenile.

Secure custody, confinement Incarceration of juvenile offender in a facility that restricts movement in the community. Similar to an adult penal facility involving total incarceration.

Selective chivalry View that judges tend to favor white females in their sentencing decisions compared with females of other races or ethnicities or males.

Self-defense Affirmative defense in which defendants explain otherwise criminal conduct by showing necessity to defend themselves against aggressive victims.

Self-incrimination The act of exposing oneself to prosecution by answering questions that may demonstrate involvement in illegal behavior. Coerced self-incrimination is not allowed under the Fifth Amendment. In any criminal proceeding, the prosecution must prove the charges by means of evidence other than the testimony of the accused.

Self-representation See pro se.

Sentence Penalty imposed upon a convicted person for a crime. May include incarceration, fine, both, or some other alternative. See also mandatory sentencing, presumptive sentencing, indeterminate sentencing, determinate sentencing.

Sentence disparity See sentencing disparity.

Sentence hearing See sentencing hearing.

Sentence recommendation bargaining Negotiation in which the prosecutor proposes a sentence in exchange for a guilty plea. See also plea bargaining.

Sentencing Process of imposing a punishment on a convicted person following a criminal conviction.

Sentencing disparity Inconsistency in sentencing of convicted offenders, in which those committing similar crimes under similar circumstances are given widely disparate sentences by the same judge. Usually based on gender, race, ethnic, or socioeconomic factors.

Sentencing guidelines Instruments developed by the federal government and various states to assist judges in assessing fair and consistent lengths of incarceration for various crimes and past criminal histories. Referred to as presumptive sentencing in some jurisdictions.

Sentencing hearing Optional hearing held in many jurisdictions in which defendants and victims can hear contents of presentence investigation reports prepared by probation officers. Defendants and/or victims may respond to the report orally, in writing, or both. This hearing precedes the sentence imposed by the judge.

Sentencing memorandum Court decision that furnishes ruling or finding and orders to be implemented relative to convicted offenders. Does not necessarily include reasons or rationale for the sentence imposed.

Sentencing Reform Act of 1984 Act that provided federal judges and others with considerable discretionary powers to provide alternative sentencing and other provisions in their sentencing of various offenders.

Sequester, sequestration The insulation of jurors from the outside world so that their decision making cannot be influenced or affected by extralegal factors.

Sequestered jury A jury that is isolated from the public during the course of a trial and throughout the deliberation process.

Serious felonies Any crime punishable by more than a year in prison or jail that causes substantial property loss or fraud; may include some crimes against persons, such as robbery.

Severance Separation of related cases so that they can be tried separately in different courts.

Sexual predator laws Somewhat ambiguous laws enacted in various states to identify and control previously convicted sex offenders; may include listing such persons in public announcements or bulletins, or some other form of community notification.

Shock incarceration See shock probation.

Shock parole See shock probation.

Shock probation Sentencing offenders to prison or jail for a brief period, primarily to give them a taste or "shock" of prison or jail life, and then releasing them into the custody of a probation or parole officer through a resentencing project.

Sides Opposing parties in an adversarial relation, usually in the courtroom; prosecutors and defense counsel are considered "sides" in the adversarial system of U.S. justice.

Social change Process whereby ideas and/or practices are modified either actively or passively or naturally.

Social control Informal and formal methods of getting members of society to conform to norms, folkways, and mores.

Society for the Prevention of Pauperism Philanthropic society that established first public reformatory in New York in 1825, the New York House of Refuge.

Sociological jurisprudence View that holds that part of law should be devoted to making or shaping public policy and social rules.

Solitary confinement See isolation.

Specialty courts Courts set up as alternatives to traditional criminal court processing and that focus on specific types of offenses or offenders. These courts use a nonadversarial approach and utilize an approach referred to as therapeutic jurisprudence which requires that offenders engage in treatment and adhere to court conditions and are accountable to a judge via frequent docket appearances.

Speedy trial Defined by federal law and applicable to federal district courts, where a defendant must be tried within 100 days of an arrest. Every state has speedy trial provisions that are within reasonable ranges of the federal standard. Originally designed to comply with the Sixth Amendment of the U.S.

Constitution. The longest state speedy trial provision is in New Mexico, which is 180 days.

Speedy Trial Act of 1974 (amended 1979, 1984) Compliance with Sixth Amendment provision for a citizen to be brought to trial without undue delay of 30–70 days from date of formal specification of charges, usually in arraignment proceeding.

Spirit of the law Efforts by police officers to exhibit leniency where law violations are observed. Usually first offenders may receive leniency because of extenuating circumstances.

Split sentencing Procedure whereby a judge imposes a sentence of incarceration for a fixed period, followed by a probationary period of a fixed duration. Similar to shock probation.

Standard of proof Norms used by courts to determine validity of claims or allegations of wrongdoing against offenders; civil standards of proof are "clear and convincing evidence" and "preponderance of evidence," while criminal standard is "beyond a reasonable doubt."

Standing A doctrine mandating that courts may not recognize a party to a suit unless that person has a personal stake or direct interest in the outcome of the suit.

Stare decisis Legal precedent. Principle whereby lower courts issue rulings consistent with those of higher courts, where the same types of cases and facts are at issue. The principle of leaving undisturbed a settled point of law or particular precedent.

State bar associations Professional organizations of lawyers bound to observe the laws of the various states where they reside; state affiliate organizations in relation to national American Bar Association.

State's attorneys Government prosecutors.

Status offenders Juveniles who have committed an offense that would not be considered a crime if committed by an adult (e.g., a curfew violation would not be criminal action if committed by an adult, but such an act is a status offense if engaged in by a juvenile).

Status offense Any act committed by a juvenile that would not be a crime if committed by an adult.

Statute of limitations Period of time after which a crime that has been committed cannot be prosecuted. No statute of limitations exists for capital crimes.

Statutes Laws passed by legislatures. Statutory definitions of criminal offenses are embodied in penal codes.

Statutory exclusion Provisions that automatically exclude certain juveniles and offenses from the jurisdiction of the juvenile courts; for example, murder, aggravated rape, and armed robbery.

Statutory law Authority based on enactments of state legislatures. Laws passed by legislatures.

Stigmas The result of the process of being labeled as a delinquent or unruly child by others.

Stigmatization Social process whereby offenders acquire undesirable characteristics as the result of

imprisonment or court appearances. Undesirable criminal or delinquent labels are assigned to those who are processed through the criminal and juvenile justice systems.

Stigmatize The process of labeling someone as a delinquent or a criminal on the basis of their exhibited behavior.

Strike for cause *See* challenge for cause.

Subject matter jurisdiction Term applied when certain judges have exclusive jurisdiction over particular crimes.

Subornation of perjury The crime of procuring someone to lie under oath.

Subpoena Document issued by a judge ordering a named person to appear in court at a particular time to either answer to charges or to testify in a case.

Substantive criminal law Legislated rule that governs behaviors that are required or prohibited. Usually enacted by legislatures. Such law also specifies punishments accompanying such law violations.

Substantive law Body of law that creates, discovers, and defines the rights and obligations of each person in society. Prescribes behavior, whereas procedural law prescribes how harmful behavior is handled.

Summary judgment Any granted motion following the presentation of a case against a defendant in a civil court. Any argument countering the plaintiff's presented evidence. Usually the result of failing to state a claim upon which relief can be granted.

Summation Conclusionary remarks made by the prosecutor and defense counsel at the end of a trial before the jury.

Summons Same form as a warrant, except it commands a defendant to appear before the magistrate at a particular time and place.

Superior courts The courts of record or trial courts.

Supreme Court The federal court of last resort as specified by the U.S. Constitution; at the state level, any court of last resort in most kinds of cases.

Surety bond A sum of money or property that is posted or guaranteed by a party to ensure the future court appearance of another person. *See also* bail bond.

Sustain To uphold (e.g., the conviction was sustained by a higher appellate court).

Sworn in The process whereby persons who offer testimony in court swear to tell the truth and nothing but the truth, usually by oath upon the Bible.

Teen courts Courts where proceedings are conducted by youths who try other youths for nonserious misdemeanors such as shoplifting or mischief; punishments are nonincarcerative and usually involve restitution of some form of victim compensation of community service; an adult supervises the proceedings and the decisions by youths and juries of youths are valid and enforceable.

Texas model Also known as the "traditional" model of state court organization. Two "supreme" courts, one for civil appeals, one for criminal appeals. Has five tiers of district, county, and municipal courts.

Three-strikes-and-you're-out Legislation designed to prevent offenders from becoming recidivists; provides that persons who commit three or more serious felonies are in jeopardy of being incarcerated for life terms.

Three-strikes-and-you're-out policies A crime prevention and control strategy that proposes to incarcerate those offenders who commit and are convicted of three or more serious or violent offenses; usual penalty is life imprisonment or the life-without-parole option. Intent is to incarcerate high-rate offenders to reduce crime in society. *See also* habitual offender statutes.

Tiers Different floor levels in prisons and jails where inmates are housed; usually, different tiers house different types of offenders according to their conviction offenses and offense seriousness.

Tort actions Any legal proceeding where a plaintiff is seeking damages from a defendant for a civil wrong.

Tort reform Any action taken by an individual or group to revise existing rules governing tort actions in courts, including limiting monetary awards for prevailing in lawsuits.

Torts Private or civil wrongs or injuries, other than breach of contract, for which the court will provide a remedy in the form of an action for damages. A violation of a duty imposed by law. Existence of a legal duty to plaintiff, breach of that duty, and damage as a result of that breach.

Totality of circumstances Exception to exclusionary rule, whereby officers may make warrantless searches of property and seizures of illegal contraband on the basis of the entire set of suspicious circumstances; sometimes applied to bail decision making, where the entire set of circumstances is considered for persons considered bail-eligible.

Traditional courts Courts where juvenile proceedings are characterized by individualized treatments and proscriptions for assistance; the opposite of due process courts.

Transcript A written record of a trial or hearing.

Transfer Proceeding to determine whether juveniles should be certified as adults for purposes of being subjected to jurisdiction of adult criminal courts, where more severe penalties may be imposed. Also known as "certification" or "waiver."

Transfers Proceedings where the jurisdiction over juvenile offenders shifts from the juvenile court to criminal court.

Trial An adversarial proceeding within a particular jurisdiction, in which a judicial examination and determination of issues can be made, and in which a criminal defendant's guilt or innocence can be decided impartially by either a judge or jury. See also bench trial, jury trial.

Trial by the court *See* bench trial.

Trial by the judge *See* bench trial.

Trial courts Courts where guilt or innocence of defendants is established; may be criminal or civil, depending on the nature of the charge; criminal courts try defendants charged with crimes; civil courts seek to resolve disputes between plaintiffs, who seek damages, against named defendants who claim they should not be held liable.

Trial court of general jurisdiction Criminal court that has jurisdiction over all offenses, including felonies, and may in some states also hear appeals from lower courts.

Trial court of limited jurisdiction Criminal court where trial jurisdiction either includes no felonies or is limited to some category of felony. Such courts have jurisdiction over misdemeanor cases, probable-cause hearings in felony cases, and sometimes, felony trials that may result in penalties below a specific limit.

Trial delays Any one of several legitimate reasons that may contribute to delaying or prolonging the occasion that a trial commences; may be due to crowded court dockets; requests from the defense or prosecution for more time in case preparation; or the health of different courtroom actors, such as the prosecutor, defense counsel, or defendant.

Trial judge *See* judge.

Trial jury *See* petit jury.

Tribunal A court. A place where judges sit. A judicial weighing of information leading to a decision about a case.

Truants Juveniles who absent themselves from school during school hours and without excuse of parental or school consent; a type of status offender.

True bills Grand jury decisions that sufficient evidence exists that a crime has been committed and that a specific suspect committed it.

Truth in sentencing Policy of imposing a sentence, most of which must be served in prison or jail; maximizing one's incarceration under the law.

Truth-in-sentencing laws Any legislation intended to maximize one's sentence and time served for committing a crime; intent is to compel offenders to serve at least 80 or 90 percent of their maximum sentences before they become eligible for parole or early release.

Typicality hypothesis View that judges give women greater consideration than men during sentencing, but only when their criminal charges are consistent with stereotypes of female offenders.

United States Sentencing Commission Body of persons originating from Sentencing Reform Act of 1984 and promulgated sentencing guidelines for all federal crimes.

United States Sentencing Guidelines Rules implemented by federal courts in November 1987 obligating federal judges to impose presumptive sentences on all convicted offenders. Guidelines are based upon offense seriousness and offender characteristics. Although several Supreme Court cases have altered their original proscriptive nature, ordinarily, judges may depart from guidelines only by justifying their departures in writing.

U.S. attorney Official responsible for the prosecution of crimes that violate the laws of the United States. Appointed by the president and assigned to a U.S. District Court jurisdiction.

U.S. attorney's office Chief prosecuting body affiliated with each U.S. District Court in the federal court system.

U.S. Circuit Courts of Appeal Appellate courts from which U.S. District Court decisions are appealed; cases appealed from the U.S. Circuit Courts of Appeal are appealed directly to the U.S. Supreme Court; there are 13 circuit courts of appeal.

U.S. Courts of Appeal The federal circuit courts of appellate jurisdiction. There are 13 circuit courts of appeal zoned throughout the United States and its territories.

U.S. District Courts The basic trial courts for federal civil and criminal actions.

U.S. magistrate judges Judges who fulfill the pretrial judicial obligations of the federal courts.

U.S. Supreme Court Court of last resort; final and highest court that decides particular issues, usually issues with constitutional significance.

Vacate To annul, set aside, or rescind.

Vacated sentence Any sentence that has been declared nullified by action of a court.

***Venire*, venireman list, veniremen** List of prospective jurors made up from registered voters, vehicle driver's licenses, tax assessors' records. Persons must reside within the particular jurisdiction where the jury trial is held. Persons who are potential jurors in a given jurisdiction.

Venue Area over which a judge exercises authority to act in an official capacity. Place where a trial is held.

Venue, change of Relocation of a trial from one site to another, usually because of some pretrial publicity making it possible that a jury might be biased and that a fair trial will be difficult to obtain.

Verdict Decision by judge or jury concerning the guilt or innocence of a defendant.

Verdict-driven jury Jury that decides guilt or innocence first without considering adequately the relevant evidence in the case; jurors are polled initially to see to what extent they agree or disagree among themselves; if most or all of the jurors vote the same way, then they conclude their deliberations without further consideration of the evidence.

Verdict, guilty In criminal proceedings, the decision made by a jury in a jury trial, or by a judicial officer in a bench trial, that defendants are guilty of the offense(s) for which they have been tried.

Verdict, not guilty In criminal proceedings, the decision made by a jury in a jury trial, or by the judge in a bench trial, that defendants are not guilty of the offense(s) for which they have been tried.

Vice principal doctrine Theory holding that someone may be sued by another if he/she is a supervisor or boss, and not necessarily the owner of an organization.

Victim Person who has either suffered death or serious physical or mental suffering, or loss of property resulting from actual or attempted criminal actions committed by others.

Victim compensation Any financial restitution payable to victims by either the state or convicted offenders.

Victim compensation programs Any plans for assisting crime victims in making social, emotional, and economic adjustments.

Victim impact statement Information or version of events filed voluntarily by the victim of a crime, appended to the presentence investigation report as a supplement for judicial consideration in sentencing the offender. Describes injuries to victims resulting from convicted offender's actions.

Victim–offender mediation model Meeting between criminal and person suffering loss or injury from criminal whereby third-party arbiter, such as a judge, attorney, or other neutral party decides what is best for all parties. All parties must agree to decision of third-party arbiter. Used for both juvenile and adult offenders.

Victim–offender reconciliation Any agreement between the victim and the perpetrator concerning a satisfactory arrangement for compensation for injuries or financial losses sustained.

Victim–Offender Reconciliation Project (VORP) Form of alternative dispute resolution, whereby a civil resolution is made by mutual consent between the victim and an offender; objectives are to provide restitution to victims, hold offender accountable for crime committed, and to reduce recidivism.

Victim/reparations model Restitution model for juveniles in which juveniles compensate their victims directly for their offenses.

Victims of Crime Act of 1984 Also known as the Comprehensive Crime Control Act of 1984, includes sanctions against offenders such as victim compensation, community service, and/or restitution.

Victim-witness assistance programs Plans available to prospective witnesses to explain court procedures and inform them of court dates, and to assist witnesses in providing better testimony in court.

Violent felonies Any crime that is punishable by more than one year in a prison or jail and causes serious bodily injury or death (e.g., rape, aggravated assault, murder, and armed robbery).

Voir dire "To speak the truth." Interrogation process whereby prospective jurors are questioned by either the judge or by the prosecution or defense attorneys to determine their biases and prejudices.

Voluntariness Willingness of defendant to enter a plea or make an agreement in a plea bargain proceeding. Judges must determine the voluntariness of the plea to determine that it was not coerced.

Waiver, waiver of jurisdiction Made by motion, the transfer of jurisdiction over a juvenile to a criminal court where the juvenile is subject to adult criminal penalties. Includes judicial, prosecutorial, and legislative waivers. Also known as "certification" or "transfer."

Waiver hearing Motion by prosecutor to transfer juvenile charged with various offenses to a criminal or adult court for prosecution, making it possible to sustain adult criminal penalties.

Warrant A written order directing a suspect's arrest and issued by an official with the authority to issue the warrant. Commands suspect to be arrested and brought before the nearest magistrate.

Warrant, arrest   Document issued by a judge that directs a law enforcement officer to arrest a person who has been accused of an offense.

Warrant, bench   Document issued by a judge directing that a person who has failed to obey an order or notice to appear be brought before the court without undue delay.

Warrant, search   Any document issued by a judicial official, based upon probable cause, directing law enforcement officers to conduct an inspection of an individual, automobile, or building with the intent of locating particular contraband or incriminating evidence as set forth in the document.

With prejudice   To dismiss charges, but those same charges cannot be brought again later against the same defendant.

Without prejudice   To dismiss charges, but those same charges can be brought again later against the same defendant.

Without undue delay or unnecessary delay   Standard used to determine whether suspect has been brought in a timely manner before a magistrate or other judicial authority after arrested. Definition of undue delay varies among jurisdictions. Circumstances of arrest, availability of judge, and time of arrest are factors that determine reasonableness of delay.

Witnesses   Persons who have relevant information about the commission of a crime; persons who have seen or heard inculpatory or exculpatory evidence that may incriminate or exonerate a defendant.

Writ   A document issued by a judicial officer ordering or forbidding the performance of a specific act.

Writ of *certiorari*   An order of a superior court requesting that the record of an inferior court (or administrative body) be brought forward for review or inspection. Literally, "to be more fully informed."

Writ of *habeas corpus*   *See habeas corpus.*

Writ of *mandamus*   An order of a superior court commanding that a lower court, administrative body, or executive body perform a specific function. Commonly used to restore rights and privileges lost to a defendant through illegal means.

Wrongful convictions   Adjudications of guilt by either a judge or jury and where the convicted offender is actually innocent of the charges alleged.

References

Aas, Katja Franko (2004). "Sentencing Transparency in the Information Age." *Journal of Scandinavian Studies in Criminology and Crime Prevention* **5:**48–61.

Abel, Richard (1990). "A Critique of Torts." *UCLA Law Review* **37:**785–831.

Abrams, Stan (1995). "False Memory Syndrome vs. Total Repression." *Journal of Psychiatry and Law* 23:283–293.

Adamson, Hoebel E. (1954). *The Law of Primitive Man: A Study in Comparative Legal Dynamic*. Cambridge, MA: Harvard University Press.

Adler, Stephen J. (1995). *The Jury: Disorder in the Court*. New York: Doubleday.

Administrative Office of the United States Courts (2015). *Federal Judicial Caseload Statistics 2015*. Available online at: http://www.uscourts.gov/statistics-reports/federal-judicial-caseload-statistics-2015.

Administrative Office of the United States Courts (2016). *Defender Services*. Available online at: http://www.uscourts.gov/services-forms/defender-services.

Ajzenstadt, Mimi, and Odeda Steinberg (2001). "Never Mind the Law: Legal Discourse and Rape Reform in Israel." *Affilia* **16:**337–259.

Albonetti, Celesta A., and Chana Barron (2004). "On the Way to Settled Law: An Examination of Law Making and Law Finding in Federal Appellate Decisions." Unpublished paper presented at the annual meeting of the American Society of Criminology, November (Nashville, TN).

Alfini, James J. (1981). "Mississippi Judicial Selection: Election, Appointment, and Bar Anointment." In *Courts and Judges*, James A. Cramer (ed.). Beverly Hills, CA: Sage.

Alexander, R. (2004). "The United States Supreme Court and the Civil Commitment of Sex Offenders." *The Prison Journal* **84:**33–54.

Alonso, Alfonso (2009). "Best Practices for Drug Courts." Unpublished thesis, University of Nevada at Reno.

Ambos, Kai (2003). "International Criminal Procedure: 'Adversarial,' 'Inquisitorial,' or 'Mixed'?" *International Criminal Law Review* **3:**1–27.

American Bar Association (1989). *Criminal Justice Mental Health Standards*. Washington, DC: American Bar Association.

American Bar Association (2008). *Judicial Selection: The Process of Choosing Judges*. American Bar Association, Coalition for Justice. Washington, DC.

American Judicature Society (2008a). "Judicial Selection in the States: How it works and why it matters." Nashville, TN: American Judicature Society.

American Judicature Society (2008b). "Model Judicial Selection Provisions." Nashville, TN: American Judicature Society.

Anchorage Youth Court (2005). "Youth Courts Strive for Sustainability." *Gavel* **16:**1–4.

APPA Perspectives (2004a). "APPA Resolves Support for Youth Courts." *APPA Perspectives* **28:**8.

Arpey, Andrew W. (2003). *The William Freeman Murder Trial: Insanity, Politics and Race*. Syracuse, NY: Syracuse University Press.

Arrigo, B. A., and M. C. Bardwell (2000). "Law, Psychology, and Competency to Stand Trial: Problems with and Implications for High-profile Cases." *Criminal Justice Policy Review* **11:**16–43.

Asch, Solomon E. (1966). "Effect of Group Pressure Upon the Modification and Distortion of Judgments." *Group Dynamics* **14:**189–199.

Associated Press (1998). "Judge Who Drank after Trial Quits." *Minot (N.D.) Daily News*, April 8, 1998:A2.

Atherton, Matthew (2004). "Study of Hispanic Outcomes in U.S. Federal Courts." Unpublished paper presented at the annual meeting of the American Society of Criminology meeting, November (Nashville, TN).

Atkins, Holly (2005). "Evaluation of a Large Urban Drug Court." Unpublished paper presented at the annual meeting of the Academy of Criminal Justice Sciences, March (Chicago).

Auerhahn, Kathleen (2004). "Homicide Sentencing and the Behavior of Law." Unpublished paper presented at the annual meeting of the American Society of Criminology, November (Nashville, TN).

Austin, James et al. (1995). *National Assessment of Structured Sentencing*. Washington, DC: U.S. Bureau of Justice Statistics.

Austin, James, and John Irwin (2001). *It's About Time: America's Imprisonment Binge* (3rd ed). Toronto, ON: Wadsworth Thompson.

Austin, James, John Clark, Patricia Hardyman, and Alan Henry (1999). "The Impact of Three Strikes and You're Out." *Punishment and Society* **1:**131–162.

Bakker, Mark William (1994). "Repairing the Breach and Reconciling the Discordant: Mediation in the Criminal Justice System." *North Carolina Law Review* **71:**1479–1483.

Baldwin, J. M. (2016). "Investigating the programmatic attack: A National Survey of Veterans Treatment Courts." *The Journal of Criminal Law and Criminology* **105:**101–148.

Ball, Jeremy D. (2005). "Does Race Matter? Assessing Racial and Ethnic Bias." Unpublished paper presented at the annual meeting of the Academy of Criminal Justice Sciences, March (Chicago).

Barrile, Leo G., and Neal Slone (2005). "Punishing Environmental Criminals: Extra Legal Factors and the Sentencing Guidelines." Unpublished paper presented at the annual meeting of the Academy of Criminal Justice Sciences, March (Chicago).

Beechen, Paul D. (1974). "Can Judicial Elections Express the People's Choice?" *Judicature* **57:**242–256.

Beger, Randall R. (2003). "The Worst of Both Worlds: School Security and the Disappearing Fourth Amendment Rights of Students." *Criminal Justice Review* **28:**336–354.

Belbot, Barbara et al. (2004). "Legal Issues in Corrections." *Prison Journal* **84:**287–410.

Bell, Bernard P. (1983). "Closure of Pretrial Suppression Hearings: Resolving the Fair Trial/Free Press Conflict." *Fordham Law Review* **51:**1297–1316.

Bensinger, Gad J. (1988). "Operation Greylord and Its Aftermath." *International Journal of Comparative and Applied Criminal Justice* **12:**111–118.

Berkson, L., Rachel Caufield, and Malia Reddick (2010). "Judicial Selection in the United States: A Special Report." American Judicature Society.

Berman, Greg, and John Feinblatt (2005). *Good Courts: The Case for Problem Solving Justice.* New York: Free Press.

Bernard, Thomas, J., Jeffrey B. Snipes, and Alexander L. Gerould (2009). *Vold's Theoretical Criminology.* New York, NY: Oxford University Press.

Besley, T., and Payne, A. (2003). "Judicial Accountability and Economic Policy Outcomes: Evidence from Employment Discrimination Charges" The Institute for Fiscal Studies, London School of Economics.

Birzer, Michael L., and Ronald Tannehill (2003). "Criminal Justice Practitioners' Perceptions of Themselves, Each Other, and Selected Criminal Justice Practices." *Journal of Crime and Justice* **26:**77–100.

Bishop, Donna M. et al. (2004). "Prosecutorial Charging Decisions in Transfer Cases." Unpublished paper presented at the annual meeting of the American Society of Criminology, November (Nashville, TN).

Black, Donald (1973). "The Mobilization of Law." *The Journal of Legal Studies* **2:**125–149.

Black, Henry Campbell (1990). *Black's Law Dictionary.* St. Paul, MN: West Publishing Company.

Blackmore, John, Marci Brown, and Barry Krisberg (1988). *Juvenile Justice Reform: The Bellwether States.* Ann Arbor, MI: University of Michigan.

Blackwell, Kevin R. (2004). "Is There a Penalty for Going to Trial in Federal Court?" Unpublished paper presented at the annual meeting of the American Society of Criminology, November (Nashville, TN).

Blankenship, Michael B., Jerry B. Sparger, and W. Richard Janikowski (1994). "Accountability v. Independence: Myths of Judicial Selection." *Criminal Justice Policy Review* **6:**69–79.

Blue Earth County (2005). *Blue Earth County Teen Court.* Mankato, MN: Blue Earth County Teen Court.

Blumstein, Alfred (1982). "Racial Disproportionality of U.S. Prison Populations Revisited." *University of Colorado Law Review* **64:**743–760.

Boari, Nicola, and Gianluca Fiorentini (2001). "An Economic Analysis of Plea Bargaining: The Incentives of the Parties in a Mixed Penal System." *International Review of Law and Economics* **21:**213–231.

Boller, Kelley G. (2005). "Wrongful Convictions: Theoretical Explanations for the Differing Perceptions of Criminal Justice Actors." Unpublished paper presented at the annual meeting of the Academy of Criminal Justice Sciences, March (Chicago).

Bontrager, Stephanie, Kelle Barrick, and Elizabeth Stupi (2013). "Gender and Sentencing: A Meta-Analysis of Contemporary Research." *The Journal of Gender, Race, and Justice* **16:**349–635.

Booth, Tracey (2004). "Homicide, Family Victims and Sentencing: Continuing the Debate about Victim Impact Statements." *Current Issues in Criminal Justice* **15:**253–257.

Borton, Ian M. (2008). "Victim Offender Communication in Felony Cases: An Archival Analysis of Ohio's Office of Victim Services Dialogue Program." Doctoral Dissertation. Bowling Green State University.

Boyle, Robert, Donna R. Newman, and Sam A. Schmidt (2003). "Center for Professional Values and Practice Symposium: Criminal Defense in the Age of Terrorism." *New York Law School Law Review* **48:**3–384.

Bradfield, A., and D. E. McQuiston (2004). "When Does Evidence of Eyewitness Confidence Inflation Affect Judgments in a Criminal Trial?" *Law and Human Behavior* **28:**369–387.

Braithwaite, John (1998). "Restorative Justice." In *The Handbook of Crime and Punishment,* Michael Tonry (ed.). New York, NY: Oxford University Press.

Braithwaite, John (2002). *Restorative Justice and Responsive Regulation.* Oxford, UK: Oxford University Press.

Breckenridge, Sophonisba P. (1906). "Legislative Control of Women's Work." *Journal of Political Economy* **14:**115–120.

Brocke, Michaela et al. (2004). "Attitudes Toward the Severity of Punishment: A Conjoint Analytic Approach." *Psychology, Crime and Law* **10:**205–219.

Brown, Gary (1998). "Characteristics of Elected Versus Merit-Selected New York City Judges 1992–1997." New York, Fund for Modern Courts.

Bullock, Jennifer Leslie (2002). "Involuntary Treatment of Defendants Found Incompetent to Stand Trial." *Journal of Forensic Psychology Practice* **2:**1–34.

Bureau of Justice Statistics. (2005). *Annual Reports.* Washington, DC: U.S. Department of Justice, Bureau of Justice Statistics.

Burger, Warren (1982). "Isn't There a Better Way?" *American Bar Association Journal* **68:**274–275.

Burnett, Cathleen (2005). "Restorative Justice and Wrongful Capital Convictions." *Journal of Contemporary Criminal Justice* **21:**272–289.

Burrow, John D. (2004). "The Death of Innocence: Factual and Procedural Errors that Result in Wrongful Convictions." Unpublished paper presented at the annual meeting of the American Society of Criminology, November (Nashville, TN).

Burruss, George W., and Kimberly Kempf-Leonard (2002). "The Questionable Advantage of Defense Counsel in Juvenile Court." *Justice Quarterly* **19:**37–67.

Butts, Jeffrey A. (1994). "Offenders in Juvenile Court, 1992." U.S. Department of Justice, Office of Juvenile Justice and Delinquency Prevention.

Buzawa, Eve S., and Carl G. Buzawa (2003). *Domestic Violence: The Criminal Justice Response.* Thousand Oaks, CA: Sage.

Carey, Bryan A. (2001). "Should American Courts Listen to What Foreign Courts Hear? The Confrontation and Hearsay Problems of Prior Testimony Taken Abroad in Criminal Proceedings." *American Journal of Criminal Law* **29:**29–58.

Carr, Patrick J., Kim A. Logio, and Shana Maier (2003). "Keep Me Informed: What Matters for Victims as They Navigate the Juvenile Criminal Justice System in Philadelphia." *International Review of Victimology* **10:**117–136.

Carrington, Peter J., and Jennifer L. Schulenberg (eds.) (2004). "The Youth Criminal Justice Act." *Canadian Journal of Criminology and Criminal Justice* **46:**219–389.

Carter, Linda E. (2001). "The Sporting Approach to Harmless Error in Criminal Cases: The Supreme Court's 'No Harm, No Foul' Debacle in *Neder v. United States.*" *American Journal of Criminal Law* **28:**229–246.

Casper, Jonathan D. (1972). *American Criminal Justice: The Defendant's Perspective.* Englewood Cliffs, NJ: Prentice Hall.

Cassell, Paul G. (2009). "In Defense of Victim Impact Statements." *Ohio State Journal of Criminal Law* **6:**611–648.

Caulkins, Jonathan P., C. Peter Rydell, William L. Schwabe, and James Chiesa (1998). "Are Mandatory Minimum Drug Sentences Cost Effective?" *Corrections Management Quarterly* **2:**8–73.

Ceci, Stephen J., and Maggie Bruck (1995). *Jeopardy in the Courtroom: A Scientific Analysis of Children's Testimony.* Washington, DC: American Psychological Association.

Chambers, Rex L. (1989). "Comparative Performance of Women in Law School." *Excelsior Law Review* **22:**196–222.

Champion, Dean J. (2004). "Juvenile Felons and Waivers, 1990–1999: Bursting the 'Get Tough' Bubble." Unpublished paper presented at the annual meeting of the American Society of Criminology, November (Nashville, TN).

Champion, Dean J. (2005a). "Plea Bargaining in Texas 2000–2001: A View from Prosecutors." Unpublished paper presented at the annual meeting of the Academy of Criminal Justice Sciences, March (Chicago).

Champion, Dean J. (2005b). *Probation, Parole, and Community Corrections* (5th ed). Upper Saddle River, NJ: Prentice Hall.

Champion, Dean J. (2007). *The Juvenile Justice System: Delinquency, Processing and the Law* (5th ed). Upper Saddle River, NJ: Prentice Hall/Pearson.

Champion, Dean J. (2009). *The Juvenile Justice System: Delinquency, Processing and the Law.* Upper Saddle River, NJ: Prentice Hall.

Chapman, Yvonne K. (2005). "Teen Courts and Restorative Justice." Unpublished paper presented at the annual meeting of the Academy of Criminal Justice Sciences, Chicago (March).

Charish, Courtney L. (2004). "Gender Effects on Juvenile Justice System Processing." Unpublished paper presented at the annual meeting of the American Society of Criminology, November (Nashville, TN).

Chiricos, T., and B. Bales (1991). "Unemployment and Punishment: An Empirical Assessment." *Criminology* **29:**701–724.

Choi, Stephen, G. Mity Gulati, and Eric A. Posner (2010). "Professionals or Politicians: The Uncertain Empire Case for an Elected Rather Than Appointed judiciary." *Journal of Law, Economics, and Organizations,* **26:**290–336.

Church, Thomas (1976). "Plea Bargains, Concessions and the Courts: Analysis of a Quasi-Experiment." *Law and Society Review* **10:**377–401.

Clark, James D. (2004a). "Racial, Ethnic, and Citizenship Disparity in Sentencing Under Federal Sentencing Guidelines: A Comparison of Two Judicial Districts." Unpublished paper presented at the annual meeting of the American Society of Criminology, November (Nashville, TN).

Clark, John W. III (2004b). "The Utility of Jury Consultants in the Twenty-First Century." Unpublished paper presented at the annual meeting of the American Society of Criminology, November (Nashville, TN).

Cohen, Thomas H. (2004). "The Impact of Bench Trial Convictions on Sentencing." Unpublished paper presented at the annual meeting of the American Society of Criminology, November (Nashville, TN).

Connell, Nadine M. (2004). "The Power of the Prosecutor: Understanding Prosecutorial Discretion in a Social Network Analysis Framework." Unpublished paper presented at the annual meeting of the American Society of Criminology, November (Nashville, TN).

Cook, Alison, Jamie Arndt, and Joel D. Lieberman (2004). "Firing Back at the Backfire Effect: The Influence of Mortality Salience and Nullification Beliefs on Reactions to Inadmissible Evidence." *Law and Human Behavior* **28:**389–410.

Coomber, Ross, Michael Oliver, and Craig Morris (2003). "Using Cannabis Therapeutically in the United Kingdom: A Qualitative Analysis." *Journal of Drug Issues* **33:**325–356.

Correctional Association of New York (1993). *Court Case Processing in New York: Problems and Solutions.* New York: Correctional Association of New York.

Cossins, Anne (2003). "Saints, Sluts, and Sexual Assault: Rethinking the Relationship Between Sex, Race, and Gender." *Social and Legal Studies* **12:**77–103.

Council of State Governments Justice Center (2008). *Mental Health Courts: A Primer for Policymakers and Practitioners.* New York, NY: Council of State Governments.

Council of State Governments Justice Center (2016). "Mental Health Courts." Available online at: https://csgjusticecenter.org/mental-health-court-project/

Crow, Matthew S. (2004). "The Impact of Sentencing Guidelines Policy Reform: Florida's 1994 Sentencing Guidelines." Unpublished paper presented at the annual meeting of the American Society of Criminology, November (Nashville, TN).

Crow, Matthew S., and Katherine A. Johnson (2008). "Race, Ethnicity, and Habitual-Offender Sentencing: A Multilevel Analysis of Individual and Contextual Threat." *Criminal Justice Policy Review* **19:**63–83.

Cunningham, Mark D., and Mark P. Vigen (1999). "Without Appointed Counsel in Capital Postconviction Proceedings: The Self-Representation Competency of Mississippi Death Row Inmates." *Criminal Justice and Behavior* **26:**293–321.

Cummingham, Scott (2005). "Perspectives on Prosecutors, Community Prosecution, and Collective Bargaining Issues." Unpublished paper presented at the annual meeting of the Academy of Criminal Justice Sciences, March (Chicago).

Dabney, Dean, Sue Carter Collins, and Volkan Topalli (2004). "Statutory Provisions and Legal Precedents in the Area of Bail Bondsmen and Bail Recovery Agents: Assessing a Fringe Element of the Criminal Justice System." Unpublished paper presented at the annual meeting of the American Society of Criminology, November (Nashville, TN).

D'Allessio, Stewart J., and Lisa Stolzenberg (1993). "Socioeconomic Status and the Sentencing of the Traditional Offender." *Journal of Criminal Justice* **21:**61–77.

Daly, Kathleen (1989). "Neither Conflict Nor Labeling Nor Paternalism Will Suffice: Intersections of Race, Ethnicity, Gender, and Family in Criminal Court Decisions." *Crime & Delinquency* **35:**136–168.

Daly, Kathleen, and Rebecca L. Bordt (1995). "Sex Effects and Sentencing: An Analysis of the Statistical Literature." *Justice Quarterly* **12:**141–175.

Davies, Graham M. et al. (1995). "Seminar: A New Look at Eyewitness Testimony: Papers presented at the BAFS Joint Seminar on 12 October 1994." *Medicine Science and the Law* **35:**95–149.

Davis-Frenzel, Erika, and Cassia Spohn (2004). "Questioning the Measurement of the Dependent Variable Used in Sex Disparity Research." Unpublished paper presented at the annual meeting of the American Society of Criminology, November (Nashville, TN).

Davis, Jacqueline (2005). "Texas Landmark Cases: An Analysis and Comparison of *Ruiz v. Estelle* and *Morales v. Turman.*" Unpublished paper presented at the annual meeting of the Academy of Criminal Justice Sciences, March (Chicago).

Death Penalty Information Center. (2014). Facts. Death Penalty Information Center. Available online at: http://www.deathpenaltyinfo.org/node/5623/4.

DeFrances, Carol J. (2001). *State-funded Indigent Defense Services, 1999.* U.S. Department of Justice, Bureau of Justice Statistics.

DeLone, Miriam A., and Keith A. Wilmot (2004). "Minnesota Sentencing Guidelines Revisited: Does Race Matter for Native American Offenders?" Unpublished paper presented at the annual meeting of the American Society of Criminology, November (Nashville, TN).

Demuth, Stephen (2003). "Racial and Ethnic Differences in Pretrial Release Decisions and Outcomes: A Comparison of Hispanic, Black, and White Felony Arrestees." *Criminology* 41:873–907.

Denov, Myriam S., and Kathryn M. Campbell (2005). "Understanding the Causes, Effects, and Responses to Wrongful Conviction in Canada." *Journal of Contemporary Criminal Justice* 21:224–249.

Dent, Helen, and Rhona Flin (eds.) (1992). *Children as Witnesses.* Chichester, UK: Wiley.

Deukmedjian, John Edward (2003). "Reshaping Organizational Objectives in Canada's National Police Force: The Development of the RCMP Alternative Dispute Resolution." *Policing and Society* 13:331–348.

DiCristina, Bruce (2004). "Durkheim's Theory of Homicide and the Confusion of the Empirical Literature." *Theoretical Criminology* 8:57–91.

Ditton, Paula M., and Doris James Wilson (1999). *Truth in Sentencing in State Prisons.* Washington, DC: U.S. Department of Justice, Bureau of Justice Statistics.

Dixon, Jo (1995). "The organizational context of criminal sentencing." *American Journal of Sociology* 100:1157–1198.

Doerner, Jill K., and Stephen Demuth (2010). "The Independent and Joint Effects of Race/Ethnicity, Gender, and Age on Sentencing Outcomes in U.S. Federal Courts." *Justice Quarterly* 27:1–27.

Doerner, Jill K., and Stephen Demuth. (2014). "Gender and Sentencing in the Federal Courts: Are Women Treated More Leniently?" *Criminal Justice Policy Review* 25:242–269.

Dubois, Philip L. (1990). "Voter Responses to Court Reform: Merit Judicial Selection on the Ballot." *Judicature* 73:238–247.

Durose, Matthew R., Alexia D. Cooper, and Howard N. Snyder (2014). *Recidivism of Prisoners Released in 30 States in 2005: Patterns from 2005 to 2010.* Washington, DC: U.S. Department of Justice, Bureau of Justice Statistics.

Dynia, Paul A. (1987). *Misdemeanor Trial Law Study: Final Report.* New York: New York City Criminal Justice Agency.

Dynia, Paul A. (1990). *Misdemeanor Trial Law: Is It Working?* New York: New York City Criminal Justice Agency.

Edwards, T. (2004). *Judicial Selection in the Southern States.* Atlanta, GA: The Council of State Governments.

Eisenstein, J., and H. Jacob (1977). *Felony Justice: An Organizational Analysis of Criminal Courts.* Boston: Little, Brown.

Elko Teen Court. (2005). *Elko, Nevada Teen Court.* Elko, NV: Elko Teen Court.

Emmelman, Deborah S. (2003). *Justice for the Poor: A Study of Criminal Defense Work.* Burlington, VT: Ashgate Publishing Company.

Enriquez, Roger (2005). "Courts and Juries." Unpublished paper presented at the annual meeting of the Academy of Criminal Justice Sciences, March (Chicago).

Enriquez, Roger, and John W. Clark (2005). "The Relationship Between Personality and Jury Selection: An Exploratory Study of Jurors in Bexar County, Texas." Unpublished paper presented at the annual meeting of the Academy of Criminal Justice Sciences, March (Chicago).

Erez, Edna, and Peter R. Ibarra (2004). "Making Your Home a Shelter: The Electronic Monitoring of Domestic Violence Cases." Unpublished paper presented at the American Society of Criminology, November (Nashville, TN).

Fearn, Noelle (2004). "The Main and Conditioning Effects of Community Characteristics on Sentencing: A Multilevel Analysis." Unpublished paper presented at the annual meeting of the American Society of Criminology, November (Nashville, TN).

Federman, C. (2004). "Who Has the Body? The Paths to Habeas Corpus Reform." *The Prison Journal* 84:317–339.

Feld, Barry C. (2000). *Cases and Materials on Juvenile Justice Administration.* St. Paul, MN: West Group.

Feld, Barry C. (2001). "Race, Youth Violence, and the Changing Jurisprudence of Waiver." *Behavioral Sciences and the Law* 19:3–22.

Feld, Barry C. (2003). "The Constitutional Tension Between *Apprendi* and *McKeiver*: Sentence Enhancements Based on Delinquency Convictions and the Quality of Justice in Juvenile Courts." *Wake Forest Law Review* 38:1111–1224.

Feld, Barry C., and Shelly Schaefer (2010). "The Right to Counsel in Juvenile Court: Law Reform to Deliver Legal Services and Reduce Justice by Geography." *Criminology and Public Policy* 9:327–256.

Felstiner, William, Richard Abel, and Austin Sarat (1980). "The Emergence of Disputes: Naming, Blaming, and Claiming." *Law and Society Review* 15:631–634.

Ferdinand, Theodore (1992). *Boston's Lower Criminal Courts, 1814–1850.* Newark, DE: University of Delaware Press.

Finn, Peter, and B. Lee (1985). "Collaboration with Victim-Witness Assistance Programs: Payoffs and Concerns for Prosecutors." *Prosecutor* 18:27–36.

Findlay, Mark, and Peter Duff (eds.) (1988). *The Jury Under Attack.* Sydney, Australia: Butterworths.

Fischer, Gloria J. (1997). "Gender Effects on Individual Verdicts and on Mock Jury Verdicts in a Simulated Acquaintance Rape Trial." *Sex Roles: A Journal of Research* 36:491–502.

Fisher, George (2000). "Plea Bargaining's Triumph." *Yale Law Journal* 109:868–1086.

Fisher, Jim (1999). *The Ghosts of Hopewell: Setting the Record Straight in the Lindbergh Case.* Carbondale, IL: Southern Illinois University Press.

Fletcher, George P. (2004). "Black Hole in Guantanamo Bay." *Journal of International Criminal Justice* 2:121–132.

Florida Joint Legislative Management Committee. (1992). *An Empirical Examination of the Application of Florida's Habitual Offender Statute.* Tallahassee, FL: Florida Joint Legislative Management Committee Economic and Demographic Research Division.

Foley, Michael A. (ed.) (2003). *The Supreme Court, the Constitution, and the Death Penalty.* Westport, CT: Praeger.

Forst, Brian (2004). "Minimizing Errors of Justice: The Role of the Prosecutor." Unpublished paper presented at the annual meeting of the American Society of Criminology, November (Nashville, TN).

Freedman, Eric M. (2001). *Habeas Corpus: Rethinking the Great Writ of Liberty.* New York: New York University Press.

Freiburger, Tina L. (2011). "The Impact of Gender, Offense Type, and Familial Role on the Decision to Incarcerate." *Social Justice Research* 24:143–167.

Friedman, Lawrence (1985). *History of American Law* (2nd ed). New York: Simon and Schuster.

Fryling, Tina M. (2005). "Mitigating and Aggravating Factors in Death Penalty Cases: A Review of State Law." Unpublished paper presented at the annual meeting of the Academy of Criminal Justice Sciences, March (Chicago).

Fulbright Norton Rose (2015). "2015 Litigation Trends Annual Survey." Available online at: http://www.nortonrosefulbright.com/news/128691/norton-rose-fulbright-releases-2015-litigation-trends-annual-survey.

Galenter, Marc (1986). "The Day After the Litigation Explosion." *Maryland Law Review* 46:3–39.

Gallinetti, J., J. Redpath, and J. Sloth-Nielsen (2004). "Race, Class and Restorative Justice in South Africa: Achilles Heel, Glass Ceiling, or Crowning Glory?" *South African Journal of Criminal Justice* **17**:17–40.

Gallup. (2014). "Death penalty." Available online at: http://www.gallup.com/poll/1606/death-penalty.aspx.

Gants, Earl III (2005). "Why Do You People Always Think About Race? Historically African-Americans and Courts." Unpublished paper presented at the annual meeting of the Academy of Criminal Justice Sciences, March (Chicago).

Gerwitz, Marian (1987). *Court-Ordered Releases—November 1983.* New York: New York City Criminal Justice Agency.

Gilbertson, D. Lee (2005). "Gangs in the Law." *Journal of Gang Research* **13**:1–16.

Glaze, Lauren E., and Thomas P. Bonczar (2009). *Probation and Parole in the United States in 2009.* Washington, DC: U.S. Department of Justice, Bureau of Justice Statistics.

Glaze, Lauren E., and Erinn J. Herberman (2013). *Correctional Populations in the United States, 2012.* Washington, DC: U.S. Department of Justice, Bureau of Justice Statistics.

Glick, Henry R., and Craig F. Emmert (1987). "Selection Systems and Judicial Characteristics: The Recruitment of State Supreme Court Judges." *Judicature* **70**:228–235.

Goldkamp, John S., and Cheryl Irons-guynn (2000). Emerging Judicial Strategies for the Mentally Ill in the Criminal Caseload: Mental Health Courts in Fort Lauderdale, Seattle, San Bernardino, and Anchorage. Washington, DC: Bureau of Justice Statistics.

Goldkamp, John S., and Michael R. Gottfredson (1984). *Judicial Guidelines for Bail: The Philadelphia Experiment.* Washington, DC: U.S. Government Printing Office.

Goldman, Sheldon, Elliot Slotnick, and Sara Schiavoni (2013). "Obama's First Term Judiciary: Picking Judges in the Minefield of Obstructionism." *Judicature* **97**:7–47.

Goldschmidt, Jona, David Olson, and Margaret Ekman (2009). "The Relationship Between Method of Judicial Selection and Judicial Misconduct." *Widener Law Journal* **18**:455–490.

Gonsoulin, Simon, Mark Zablocki, and Peter E. Leone (2012). "Safe Schools, Staff Development, and the School-to-Prison Pipeline." *Teacher Education and Special Education: The Journal of the Teacher Education Division of the Council for Exceptional Children* **35**:309–319.

Goodman, John C., and Philip Porter (2002). "Is the Criminal Justice System Just?" *International Review of Law and Economics* **22**:25–39.

Gould, Jon B. (2004). "A First Try: The Innocence Commission for Virginia." Unpublished paper presented at the annual meeting of the American Society of Criminology, November (Nashville, TN).

Grace, Maggie T. (2010). "Criminal Alternative Dispute Resolution: Restoring Justice, Respecting, Responsibility, and Renewing Public Norms." *Vermont Law Review* **34**:563–595.

Graham, Michael H. (1985). *Witness Intimidation: The Law's Response.* Westport, CT: Quorum.

Greene, J. (1990). "Media Effects on Jurors." *Law and Human Behavior* **14**:439–450.

Greene, J., and C. Loftus (1984). "What's News in the News? The Influence of Well-Publicized News Events on Psychological Research and Courtroom Trials." *Basic and Applied Social Psychology* **5**:123–135.

Greenstein, Marla N., and Kate Sampson (2004). *A National Symposium on Sentencing: Report and Policy Guide.* Des Moines, IA: American Judicature Society.

Greenstein, Steven C. (1994). *The Impact of Restrictions on Post-Indictment Plea Bargaining in Bronx County: The Processing of Indictments Already Pending.* Albany, NY: New York State Division of Criminal Justice.

Griffin, Patrick, Sean Addie, Benjamin Adams, and Kathy Firestine (2011). *Trying Juveniles as Adults: An Analysis of State Transfer Laws and Reporting.* U.S. Department of Justice, Office of Juvenile Justice and Delinquency Prevention.

Gubanski, Jakub (2004). "Comparative Criminal Justice: Special Investigation Techniques During the Criminal Trial: Disclosure Issues in Polish and American Legal Systems." *Crime, Law, and Social Change: An Interdisciplinary Journal* **41**:15–32.

Guerino, Paul, Paige M. Harrison, and William J. Sabol (2011). *Prisoners in 2010.* Washington, DC: U.S. Department of Justice, Bureau of Justice Statistics.

Guevara, Lori, and Denise C. Herz (2004). "Race, Gender, and Juvenile Justice: Differences in Dispositional Outcomes." Unpublished paper presented at the annual meeting of the American Society of Criminology, November (Nashville, TN).

Gustafson, Kaaryn (2009). "Criminal Law: The Criminalization of Poverty." *Journal of Criminal Law and Criminology* **99**:643–716.

Hack, Peter (2003). "The Roads Less Traveled: Post-Conviction Relief Alternatives and the Antiterrorism and Effective Death Penalty Act of 1996." *American Journal of Criminal Law* **30**:171–223.

Haist, Matthew (2009). "Deterrence in a Sea of Just Deserts: Are utilitarian Goals Achievable in a World of Limiting Retributivism" *The Journal of Criminal Law and Criminology* **99**:789–821.

Hanke, Penelope J. (1995). "Sentencing Disparities by Race of Offender and Victim: Women Homicide Offenders in Alabama, 1929–1985." *Sociological Spectrum* **15**:277–297.

Hannaford-Agor, Paula, Scott Graves, and Shelley Miller (2015). *The Landscape of Civil Litigation in State Courts.* Williamsburg, VA: National Center for State Courts.

Harlow, Caroline W. (2000). *Defense Counsel in Criminal Cases.* U.S. Department of Justice, Bureau of Justice Statistics.

Harmon, Talia Roitberg (2000). *Overturned Convictions in Capital Cases.* Ann Arbor, MI: University Microfilms International.

Harmon, Talia Roitberg (2001). "Guilty Until Proven Innocent: An Analysis of Post-Furman Capital Errors." *Criminal Justice Policy Review* **12**:113–139.

Harmon, Talia Roitberg (2004). "Close Calls: Exonerations in Capital Cases in the Post-Furman Era." Unpublished paper presented at the annual meeting of the American Society of Criminology, November (Nashville, TN).

Harris, Alexes (2004). "The Institutional Careers of Juvenile Delinquents: Offending and Processing Patterns of a Sample of Violent and Chronic Offenders." Unpublished paper presented at the annual meeting of the American Society of Criminology, November (Nashville, TN).

Harris, M. (2004). "From Australian Courts to Aboriginal Courts in Australia: Bridging the Gap?" *Current Issues in Criminal Justice: Journal of the Institute of Criminology* **16**:26–41.

Harris, Victoria, and Christos Dagadakis (2004). "Length of Incarceration: Was There Parity for Mentally Ill Offenders?" *International Journal of Law and Psychiatry* **27**:387–393.

Hartley, Richard D. (2008). "Sentencing Reforms and the War on Drugs: An Analysis of Sentencing Outcomes for Narcotics Offenders Adjudicated in U.S. District Courts on the Southwest Border." *Journal of Contemporary Criminal Justice* **24**:437–461.

Hartley, Richard D., Holly V. Miller, and Cassia Spohn (2010). "Do You Get What You Pay For? Type of Counsel and Its Effect on Criminal Court Outcomes." *Journal of Criminal Justice* **38**:1063–1070.

Hartley, Richard D., and Julie Marie Baldwin (2016). "Waging War on Recidivism Among Justice-Involved Veterans: An Impact Evaluation of a Large Urban Veterans Treatment Court." *Criminal Justice Policy Review*. doi: 10.1177/0887403416650490.

Haughney, Kathleen (2010). "Senate Report Suggests Veterans Court." The St. Augustine Record, October 20.

Hayes, Hennessey D. (2004). "Effectiveness of Restorative Justice." Unpublished paper presented at the annual meeting of the American Society of Criminology, November (Nashville, TN).

Haynes, Andrew (2000). "The Struggle Against Corruption: A Comparative Analysis." *Journal of Financial Crime* 8:123–135.

Helland, E., and Tabarrok, A. (2002). "The Effect of Electoral Institutions on Tort Awards." *American Law and Economics Review* 4:341–370.

Helms, Michael et al. (2004). "Waiver of Counsel among Young Offenders: Variability Between the Juvenile and Criminal Justice Systems." Unpublished paper presented at the annual meeting of the American Society of Criminology, November (Nashville, TN).

Hemenway, David (2004). *Private Guns, Public Health*. Ann Arbor, MI: University of Michigan Press.

Henderson, D. (1998). "Gender Appropriate Mental Health Services for Incarcerated Women: Issues and Challenges." *Family Community Health* 21:42–53.

Henrichson, Christian, and Ruth Delaney (2012). *The Price of Prisons: What incarceration Costs Taxpayers*. New York, NY: Vera Institute of Justice, Center on Sentencing and Corrections.

Hermida, Julian (2005). "Comparative Analysis of the Theory of Offense in Common Law and Civil Law Criminal Justice Systems." Unpublished paper presented at the annual meeting of the Academy of Criminal Justice Sciences, March (Chicago).

Herzog, Sergio (2003). "The Relationship Between Public Perceptions of Crime Seriousness and Support for Plea Bargaining in Israel: A Factorial-Survey Approach." *Journal of Criminal Law and Criminology* 94:103–131.

Herzog, Sergio (2004). "Plea Bargaining Practices: Less Covert, More Public Support?" *Crime & Delinquency* 50:590–614.

Hewitt, William E. (1995). *Court Interpretation: Model Guides for Policy and Practice in the State Courts*. Williamsburg, VA: National Center for State Courts.

Hirschfield, Paul J. (2008). "Preparing for Prison? The Criminalization of School Discipline in the USA" *Theoretical Criminology* 12:79–101.

Hodge, John L. (1986). "Deadlocked Jury Mistrials, Lesser Included Offenses, and Double Jeopardy: A Proposal to Strengthen the Manifest Necessity Requirement." *Criminal Justice Journal* 9:9–44.

Hollander, Jocelyn A. (2004). " 'I Can Take Care of Myself': The Impact of Self-Defense Training on Women's Lives." *Violence Against Women* 10:205–235.

Holmes, Malcolm D. et al. (1992). "Plea Bargaining Policy and State District Court Caseloads: An Interrupted Time Series Analysis." *Law and Society Review* 26:139–159.

Holmes, Oliver Wendell (1897). *Courts and the Law*. New York: Knopf.

Horton, Candace L. (2005). "America's Stance." Unpublished paper presented at the annual meeting of the Academy of Criminal Justice Sciences, March (Chicago).

Hoskins, Stacy N., Gretchen R. Ruth, and R. Barry Ruback (2004). "Courtroom Workgroups: A Quantitative Description and Analysis of Their Effect on Sentencing." Unpublished paper presented at the annual meeting of the American Society of Criminology, November (Nashville, TN).

Hospers, John (1977). "Punishment, Protection and Rehabilitation." In *Justice and Punishment*, J. Cederblom and W. L. Blizek (eds.). Cambridge, MA: Ballinger.

Hunzeker, Donna (1985). "Habitual Offender Statutes." *Corrections Compendium* 10:1–15.

Hurwitz, M. and Drew Lanier (2008). "Diversity in State and Federal Appellate Courts: Change and Continuity Across 20 Years." *Justice System Journal* 29:47–70.

Inciardi, James A. et al. (2004). "Sentencing Drug Offenders." *Criminology and Public Policy* 3:397–492.

Innocence Project (2014a). DNA Exonerations Nationwide. Available online at: http://www.innocenceproject.org/Content/DNA_Exonerations_Nationwide.php.

Innocence Project (2014b). "Making up for Lost Time: What the Wrongfully Convicted Endure and How to Provide Fair Compensation." Innocence Project, Benjamin Cardozo School of Law, Yeshiva University.

Institute for Court Management (1983). *Evaluation of Telephone Conferencing in Civil and Criminal Court Cases*. Denver: Prepared for the National Institute of Justice and the National Science Foundation; American Bar Association Action Commission to Reduce Court Costs and Delay.

Jaffe, P. G., and C. V. Crooks (2004). "Partner Violence and Child Custody Cases: A Cross-National Comparison of Legal Reforms and Issues." *Violence Against Women* 10:917–934.

James, D. J., and L. E. Glaze (2006). *Mental Health Problems of Prison and Jail Inmates*. Washington, DC: U.S. Department of Justice, Bureau of Justice Statistics.

Johnson, Brian D. (2004). "Judges on Trial: The Impact of Judge Characteristics Across Modes of Conviction." Unpublished paper presented at the annual meeting of the American Society of Criminology, November (Nashville, TN).

Johnson, Brian, Jeff Ulmer, and John Kramer (2008). "The Social Context of Guideline Circumvention: The Case of Federal District Courts." *Criminology* 44:259–298.

Johnson, Deborah L., Debra Bannister, and Michelle Alm (2004). "The Violent Youth Offender and Juvenile Transfer to the Adult Criminal Court." Unpublished paper presented at the annual meeting of the American Society of Criminology, November (Nashville, TN).

Jones, Marilyn J. (2003). "Jamaica: Marijuana Decriminalization Conundrum." *Canadian Journal of Law and Society* 18:91–114.

Jordan, C. E. (2004a). "Intimate Partner Violence and the Justice System: An Examination of the Interface." *Journal of Interpersonal Violence* 19:1412–1434.

Jordan, Kareem L. (2004b). "Youth in Adult Court: Examining the Predictors of Juvenile Decertification." Unpublished paper presented at the annual meeting of the American Society of Criminology, November (Nashville, TN).

Jordan, Kareem L., and David L. Meyers (2003). "Attorneys, Psychiatrists, and Psychologists: Predictors of Attitudes Toward the Insanity Defense." *Criminal Justice Studies* 16:77–86.

Kakar, Suman (2004). "Causes of Disproportionate Minority Representation: A Pilot Study." Unpublished paper presented at the annual meeting of the American Society of Criminology, November (Nashville, TN).

Kales, Albert H. (1914). *Unpopular Government in the United States*. Chicago: University of Chicago Press.

Kalven, Harry Jr., and Hans Ziesel (1966). *The American Jury*. Chicago: University of Chicago.

Karp, David R. (2001). "Harm and Repair: Observing Restorative Justice in Vermont." *Justice Quarterly* 18:727–757.

Karp, David R. (2004). "Teen Courts." *APPA Perspectives* **28**:18–20.

Karp, David R., G. Bazemore, and J. D. Cheshire (2004). "The Role and Attitudes of Restorative Board Members: A Case Study of Volunteers in Community Justice." *Crime & Delinquency* **50**:487–515.

Katz, Charles M., and Cassia Spohn (1995). "The Effect of Race and Gender on Bail Outcomes: A Test of an Interactive Model." *American Journal of Criminal Justice* **19**:161–184.

Kauder, Neal B., and Brian J. Ostrom (2008). *State Sentencing Guidelines: Profiles and Continuum.* Williamsburg, VA: National Center for State Courts.

Kaufman, Whitley (2004). "Is There a 'Right' to Self-Defense?" *Criminal Justice Ethics* **23**:20–32.

Keil, K. Douglas et al. (1994). "Election, Selection, and Retention." *Judicature* **77**:290–321.

Keller, Elizabeth M. (2005). "Security and Prosecution Issues." Unpublished paper presented at the annual meeting of the Academy of Criminal Justice Sciences, March (Chicago).

Keller, Elizabeth M., and Cassia Spohn (2005). "Focal Concerns in Federal Sentencing Decisions." Unpublished paper presented at the annual meeting of the Academy of Criminal Justice Sciences, March (Chicago).

Kellough, Gail, and Scot Wortley (2002). "Remand for Plea: Bail Decisions and Plea Bargaining as Commensurate Decisions." *The British Journal of Criminology* **42**:186–210.

Kerbs, John J., Mark Jones, and Jennifer M. Jolley (2009). "Discretionary Decision Making by Probation and Parole Officers: The role of Extralegal Variables as Predictors of Responses to Technical Violations." *Journal of Contemporary Criminal Justice* **25**:424–441.

Kerr, Norbert L. (1994). "The Effects of Pretrial Publicity on Jurors." *Judicature* **78**:120–127.

Kerr, Norbert L., and Robert J. MacCoun (1985). "The Effects of Jury Size and Polling Method on the Process and Product of Jury Deliberation." *Journal of Personality and Social Psychology* **48**:349–363.

Ketchum, Paul Robert, and David Geronimo Embrick (2004). "Where Are All the White Kids? An Analysis of the Effects of Race in Juvenile Court." Unpublished paper presented at the annual meeting of the American Society of Criminology, November (Nashville, TN).

Kirschner, Stuart M., and Gary J. Galperin (2001). "Psychiatric Defenses in New York County: Pleas and Results." *Journal of the American Academy of Psychiatry and the Law* **29**:194–201.

Klein, Richard, and Robert Spangenberg (1993). *The Indigent Defense Crisis.* Washington, DC: Section of Criminal Justice, American Bar Association.

Kleinig, John (ed.) (1989). "Ethics in Context: The Selling of Jury Deliberations." *Criminal Justice Ethics* **8**:26–34.

Knab, Karen M. (ed.) (1977). *Courts of Limited Jurisdiction: A National Survey.* Washington, DC: U.S. National Institute of Law Enforcement and Criminal Justice.

Kovandzic, Tom V. (2001). "The Impact of Florida's Habitual Offender Law on Crime." *Criminology* **39**:179–203.

Kramer, John H., and Brian D. Johnson (2004). "Guideline Revisions and Courtroom Actor Decision-Making: Assessing the Influence of Legislative Changes in Pennsylvania, 1991–2000." Unpublished paper presented at the annual meeting of the American Society of Criminology, November (Nashville, TN).

Kramer, John H., and Jeffrey T. Ulmer (1996). "Sentencing Disparities and Guidelines Departures." *Justice Quarterly* **13**:401–426.

Kremling, Janine (2004). "An Empirical Analysis of the Role of Mitigation on Capital Sentencing in North Carolina Before and After *McKoy v. North Carolina* (1990)." Unpublished paper presented at the annual meeting of the American Society of Criminology, November (Nashville, TN).

Kuckes, N. (2004). "The Useful, Dangerous Fiction of Grand Jury Independence." *American Criminal Law Review* **41**:1–66.

Kupchik, Aaron (2004). "The Negotiated Balance of Care and Control in the Juvenile Court." Unpublished paper presented at the annual meeting of the American Society of Criminology, November (Nashville, TN).

Labriola, Melissa, Sarah Bradley, Chris S. O'Sullivan, Michael Rempel, and Samantha Moore (2009). *A National Portrait of Domestic Violence Courts.* Washington, DC: National Institute of Justice, Center for Court Innovation.

Lafferty, Elaine (1994). "Now, a Jury of His Peers." *Time*, November 14, 1994.

LaFountain, R., R. Schauffler, S. Strickland, S. Gibson, and A. Mason (2011). *Examining the Work of State Courts: An Analysis of 2009 State Court Caseloads.* Williamsburg, VA: National Center for State Courts.

LaFree, Gary D. (1985). "Official Reactions to Hispanic Defendants in the Southwest." *Journal of Research in Crime & Delinquency* **22**:213–237.

Langton, Lynn, and Donald Farole (2010). "Special Report: State Public Defender Programs, 2007." U.S. Department of Justice, Bureau of Justice Statistics.

Lanza-Kaduce, Lonn, Jodi Lane, Donna M. Bishop, and Charles E. Frazier. (2005). "Juvenile Offenders and Adult Felony Recidivism: The Impact of Transfer." *Journal of Crime and Justice* **28**:59–77.

Lawrence, Richard, and Marop Hesse (2010). *Juvenile Justice: The Essentials.* Thousand Oaks, CA: Sage.

Leiber, Michael J., Kristan Fox, and Joe Johnson (2004). "Race, Gender, and Juvenile Justice: Differences in Disposition Outcomes." Unpublished paper presented at the annual meeting of the American Society of Criminology, November (Nashville, TN).

Lemley, Ellen C. (2004). "Restorative and Perceived Fairness: A Gateway Variable." Unpublished paper presented at the annual meeting of the American Society of Criminology, November (Nashville, TN).

Leo, Richard A. (1994). "Police Interrogation and Social Control." *Social and Legal Studies* **3**:93–120.

Leo, Richard A. (2005). "Rethinking the Study of Miscarriages of Justice: Developing a Criminology of Wrongful Conviction." *Journal of Contemporary Criminal Justice* **21**:201–223.

Levenson, J. S. (2004). "Reliability of Sexually Violent Predator Civil Commitment Criteria in Florida." *Law and Human Behavior* **28**:357–368.

Levin, Martin H. (1988). "The Jury in a Criminal Case: Obstacles to Impartiality." *Criminal Law Bulletin* **24**:492–520.

Levine, James P. (2005). "Race, American Courts and Their Quest for Equal Protection." Unpublished paper presented at the annual meeting of the Academy of Criminal Justice Sciences, March (Chicago).

Levine, James P., and J. Petitt (2005). "The Impact of Excluding Convicted Felons from Jury Service on the Racial Composition of Juries." Unpublished paper presented at the annual meeting of the Academy of Criminal Justice Sciences, March (Chicago).

Lightfoot, E., and Umbreit, M. (2004). "An Analysis of State Statutory Provisions for Victim–Offender Mediation." *Criminal Justice Policy Review* **15**:418–436.

Lindsey, Samuel C., and Monica K. Miller (2011). "Discretionary Release Decisions of Actual and Mock Parole Board Members: Implications for Community Sentiment and Parole Decision-Making Research." *Psychiatry, Psychology and Law* **18:**498–516.

Liptak, Adam (2008). "Inmate Count in U.S. Dwarfs Other Nations." *New York Times*, April 23.

Listwan, Shelley Johnson, and Terance D. Miethe (2004). "Adult Certification and Juvenile Justice: A Comparative Analysis of Differential Treatment." Unpublished paper presented at the annual meeting of the American Society of Criminology, November (Nashville, TN).

Litwack, Thomas R. (2003). "The Competency of Criminal Defendants to Refuse, for Delusional Reasons, a Visible Insanity Defense Recommended by Counsel." *Behavioral Sciences and the Law* **21:**135–156.

Llewellyn, Karl (1931). "Some Realism about Realism: Responding to Dean Pound." *Harvard Law Review* **44:**1222–1235.

Lo, T. Wing, and Robert J. Harris (2004). "Community Service Orders in Hong Kong, England, and Wales: Twins or Cousins?" *International Journal of Offender Therapy and Comparative Criminology* **48:**373–388.

Lobo-Antunes, M. J. (2004). "Racial and Gender Discrimination in Federal Court Pretrial Processing." Unpublished paper presented at the annual meeting of the American Society of Criminology, November (Nashville, TN).

Loftus, Elizabeth F. (1996). *Eyewitness Testimony*. Cambridge, MA: Harvard University Press.

Lovrich, Nicholas P. Jr., and Charles H. Sheldon (1994). "Is Voting for State Judges a Flight or Fancy or a Reflection of Policy and Value Preferences?" *Justice System Journal* **16:**57–71.

Lutz, R. (1990). *Community Service Orders and Restitution*. Washington, DC: U.S. Government Printing Office.

Ma, Yue (2002). "Prosecutorial Discretion and Plea Bargaining in the United States, France, Germany, and Italy: A Comparative Analysis." *International Criminal Justice Review* **12:**23–52.

Maahs, Jeff (2005). "Evaluation of a Large Urban Drug Court." Unpublished paper presented at the annual meeting of the Academy of Criminal Justice Sciences, March (Chicago).

Mackay, Robert E., and Susan R. Moody (1996). "Diversion of Neighbourhood Disputes in Community Mediation." *Howard Journal of Criminal Justice* **35:**299–313.

Maguire, Kathleen, and Ann L. Pastore (2005). *Sourcebook of Criminal Justice Statistics 2004*. Albany, NY: The Hindelang Criminal Justice Research Center.

Martin, Jamie S., and Jennifer Roberts (2005). "To Die or Not To Die: Factors Influencing Death Sentences." Unpublished paper presented at the annual meeting of the Academy of Criminal Justice Sciences, March (Chicago).

Mason, Mary Ann (1991). "A Judicial Dilemma: Expert Witness Testimony in Child Sex Abuse Cases." *Journal of Psychiatry and Law* **19:**185–219.

Matthews, Roger, Catherine Pease, and Ken Pease (2001). "Repeated Bank Robbery: Theme and Variations." In *Repeat Victimization*, Graham Farrell and Ken Pease (eds.). Monsey, NY: Criminal Justice Press.

Mattick, H. (1975). "The Contemporary Jails of the United States." In *Handbook of Criminology*, Daniel Glaser (ed.). Chicago, IL: Rand McNally.

Mauer, Marc (1999). *Race to Incarcerate*. New York, NY: The New Press.

Maxwell, Christopher D., Steven B. Dow, and Sheila Royo Maxwell (2004). "The Impact of Defense Counsel on the Processing and Disposition of Felony Court Cases." Unpublished paper presented at the annual meeting of the American Society of Criminology, November (Nashville, TN).

Maxwell, Gabrielle, and Allison Morris (2002). "Restorative Justice and Reconviction." *Contemporary Justice Review* **5:**133–146.

McCart, Samuel W. (1964). *Trial by Jury: A Complete Guide to the Jury System*. New York: Chilton Books.

McCold, Paul (2003). "An Experiment in Police-Based Restorative Justice: The Bethlehem Pennsylvania Project." *Police Practice and Research* **4:**379–390.

McConville, Mike, and Chester Mirsky (2005). *Jury Trials and Plea Bargaining: A True History*. Oxford, UK: Hart.

McDonald, William F. (1985). *Plea Bargaining: Critical Issues and Common Practices*. Washington, DC: U.S. National Institute of Justice by the Institute of Criminal Law and Procedure, Georgetown University.

McGough, Lucy S. (1994). *Fragile Voices in the American Legal System*. New Haven, CT: Yale University Press.

McKimmie, B. M. et al. (2004). "Jurors' Responses to Expert Witness Testimony: The Effects of Gender Stereo-types." *Group Processes and Intergroup Relations* **7:**131–143.

McLean, Sarah J., Joseph Cocozza, and Kathy Skowyra (2004). "Understanding the Diversity of Juvenile Diversion Programs." Unpublished paper presented at the annual meeting of the American Society of Criminology, November (Nashville, TN).

McManimon, Patrick F. (2005a). "Effects of Truth-in-Sentencing on Inmate Conduct: The Good-Time Myth." Unpublished paper presented at the annual meeting of the Academy of Criminal Justice Sciences, March (Chicago).

McManimon, Patrick F. (2005b). "The Role of Sentencing Policy in the Corrections System." Unpublished paper presented at the annual meeting of the Academy of Criminal Justice Sciences, March (Chicago).

McSherry, B. (2004). "Criminal Responsibility: Fleeting States of Mental Impairment, and the Power of Self-Control." *International Journal of Law and Psychiatry* **27:**445–457.

Menkel-Meadow, Carrie (1986). "The Comparative Sociology of Women Lawyers." *Osgood Law Journal* **24:**897–918.

Merlo, Alida V., and Peter J. Benekos (2004). "The Constitution and the Death Penalty for Juveniles: Assessing Standards of Decency." Unpublished paper presented at the annual meeting of the American Society of Criminology, November (Nashville, TN).

Miley, Cynthia (2014). "Federal Judges Grant California Extension to Reduce Prison Overcrowding." Jurist, University of Pittsburgh Law School. Available online at: http://jurist.org/paperchase/2014/02/panel-of-federal-judges-grants-california-two-year-extension-to-reduce-prison-overcrowding.php.

Miller, Holly Ventura (2008). "Restorative Justice: From Theory to Practice." *Sociology of Crime Law and Deviance* (Vol. 11). Bingley, UK: Emerald/ JAI Press.

Minor, Kevin I., James B. Wells, and Brandi Jones (2004). "Staff Perceptions of the Work Environment in Juvenile Group Home Settings: A Study of Social Climate." *Journal of Offender Rehabilitation* **38:**17–30.

Mirande, Alfredo (1987). *Gringo Justice*. Notre Dame, IN: University of Notre Dame Press.

Mitchell, Edward W. (2003). *Self-Made Madness: Rethinking Illness and Criminal Responsibility*. Aldershot, UK: Ashgate.

Morgan, Thomas D. (1983). *Legal Ethics*. Chicago: Harcourt Brace Jovanovich Legal and Professional Publications, Inc.

Morris, Norval, and Michael Tonry (1990). *Between Prison and Probation: Intermediate Punishments in a Rational Sentencing System*. New York, NY: Oxford University Press.

Mukoro, Saliba D. (2005). "Disproportionate Minority Confinement: What Way Forward?" Unpublished paper presented at the annual meeting of the Academy of Criminal Justice Sciences, March (Chicago).

Mulford, Carrie Fried et al. (2004). "Legal Issues Affecting Mentally Disordered and Developmentally Delayed Youth in the Justice System." *International Journal of Forensic Mental Health* **3**:3–22.

Mulvey, Edward P., and Carol A. Schubert. (2012). *Transfer of Juveniles to Adult Court: Effects of a Broad Policy in One Court*. U.S. Department of Justice, Office of Juvenile Justice and Delinquency Prevention.

Mustard, D. B. (2001). "Racial, Ethnic, and Gender Disparities in Sentencing: Evidence from the U.S. Federal Courts. *Journal of Law and Economics* **44**:285–314.

Myers, Bryan et al. (2004). "Victim Impact Statements and Mock Juror Sentencing: The Impact of Dehumanizing Language on a Death Qualified Sample." *American Journal of Forensic Psychology* **22**:39–55.

Myers, K. O. (2013). "Merit Selection and Diversity on the Bench." *Indiana Law Review* **46**:43–57.

Myers, Laura B., and Sue Titus Reid (1995). "The Importance of County Context in the Measurement of Sentence Disparity." *Journal of Criminal Justice* **23**:223–241.

Nadeau, Sarah, Melissa W. Burek, and Marian R. Williams (2005). "Quit Mocking Me: An Examination of Racial Composition of Juries on Non-Capital Felony Case Outcomes." Unpublished paper presented at the annual meeting of the Academy of Criminal Justice Sciences, March (Chicago).

Nader, Laura (1979). "Disputing within the Force of the Law." *Yale Law Journal* **88**:998–1043.

Nader, Laura, and Harry F. Todd (eds.) (1978). "Introduction." In *The Disputing Process: Law in Ten Societies*. New York: Columbia University Press.

National Association of Drug Court Professionals (2016). "CARA Bill Authorizes Drug Court and Veterans Treatment Court Expansion!" National Association of Drug Court Professionals. Available online at: http://www.nadcp.org/CARA.

National Association of Pretrial Services Agencies (1995). *Performance Standards and Goals for Pretrial Release and Diversion*. Frankfort, KY: National Association of Pretrial Services Agencies.

National Center for State Courts (2010). "Alternative Dispute Resolution." Available online at: http://www.ncsconline.org/WC/Publications/ADR/default.htm.

National Center for State Courts (2012). "Survey of Judicial Salaries." Available online at: http://www.ncsc.org/~/media/Files/PDF/Information%20and%20Resources/Judicial%20Salary/judicialsalaries.ashx.

National Center for Victims of Crime (1996). *Statutory and Constitutional Protection of Victim's Rights: Implementation and Impact on Crime Victims, Final Report*. Arlington, VA.

National Institute of Justice (2014). "Drug Courts." Department of Justice, National institute of Justice. Available online at: http://www.nij.gov/topics/courts/drug-courts/pages/welcome.aspx

Newsweek (2003). "Lawsuits Out of Control in Major Cities." Editorial, *Newsweek*, November 3, 2003:61.

Nicholson, Marlene Arnold, and Bradley Scott Weiss (1986). "Funding Judicial Campaigns in the Circuit Court of Cook County." *Judicature* **70**:17–25.

Norris, R. J. (2012). "Assessing Compensation Statutes for the Wrongly Convicted." *Criminal Justice Policy Review* **23**(3): 352–374.

Nunn, Samuel (2003). "Seeking Tools for the War on Terror: A Critical Assessment of Emerging Technologies in Law Enforcement." *Policing* **26**:454–473.

Office of Justice Programs (1998). *Looking at a Decade of Drug Courts*. Washington, DC: U.S. Department of Justice.

Office of Juvenile Justice and Delinquency Prevention (2014). *State Compliance with JJDP Act Core Requirements*. U.S. Department of Justice, OJJDP. Available online at: http://www.ojjdp.gov/compliance/compliancedata.html.

Ogletree, C. (2004). "Discriminatory Impact of Mandatory Minimum Sentences in the United States." *Federal Sentencing Reporter* **18**:273–278.

Ostrom, Brian J. (2006). "Domestic Violence Courts." *Criminology and Public Policy* **3**:105–108.

O'Sullivan, Julie R. (2001). *Federal White Collar Crime: Cases and Materials*. St. Paul, MN: West Group.

Palermo, George B. (2004). "Tattooing and Tattooed Criminals." *Journal of Forensic Psychology Practice* **4**:1–25.

Palumbo, Dennis J., Michael Musheno, and Michael Hallett (1994). "The Political Construction of Alternative Dispute Resolution and Alternatives to Incarceration." *Evaluation and Program Planning* **17**:197–203.

Park, Mirang (2005). "Racial Disparity in Drug Sentencing: Focusing on Hispanic." Unpublished paper presented at the annual meeting of the Academy of Criminal Justice Sciences, March (Chicago).

Patrick, Steven et al. (2004). "Control Group Study of Juvenile Diversion Programs." *Social Science Journal* **41**:129–135.

Pearce, Matt. (2014). "Indiana Judge Assailed for Light Sentence in Husband-Wife Rape Case" *The Los Angeles Times Nation Now*. Available online at: http://www.latimes.com/nation/nationnow/la-na-nn-indiana-rape-judge-20140520-story.html.

Pearce, Matt. (2014). "No Prison Time for Indiana Man Convicted of Drugging, Raping Wife" *The Los Angeles Times Nation Now*. Available online at: http://www.latimes.com/nation/nationnow/la-na-nn-indianapolis-rape-sentence-20140519-story.html#page=1.

Penrod, Steven D., Solomon M. Fulero, and Brian L. Cutler (1995). "Expert Psychological Testimony on Eyewitness Reliability Before and After Daubert: The State of the Law and Science." *Behavioral Sciences and the Law* **13**:229–259.

Peters, Roger H. et al. (2004). "Co-Occurring Disorders and the Criminal Justice System." *Behavioral Sciences and the Law* **22**:427–610.

Petersilia, Joan (2003). *When Prisoners Come Home: Parole and Prisoner Reentry*. New York, NY: Oxford University Press.

Peterson, Scott (2005). *The Growth of Teen Courts in the United States*. Washington, DC: Office of Juvenile Justice and Delinquency Prevention.

Peterson, Scott (2009). "Made in America: The Global Youth Justice Movement." *Reclaiming Children and Youth: The Journal of Emotional and Behavioral Problems* **18**:48–52.

Pew Charitable Trusts (2012). "Public Opinion on sentencing and corrections policy in America." Available online at: http://www.pewstates.org/uploadedFiles/PCS_Assets/2012/PEW_NationalSurveyResearchPaper_FINAL.pdf.

Pew Charitable Trusts (2014). "Max Out: The rise in prison inmates released without supervision." Available online at: http://www.pewtrusts.org/~/media/assets/2014/06/04/maxout_report.pdf.

Phillips, Amy K. (1997). "Thou Shalt Not Kill Any Nice People: The Problem of Victim Impact Statements in Capital Sentencing." *American Criminal Law Review* **35**:93–118.

Pickles, James (1987). *Straight from the Bench*. London, UK: Dent and Sons.

Pinello, Daniel R. (1995). *The Impact of Judicial Selection Method on State Supreme Court Policy: Innovation, Reaction, and Atrophy.* Westport, CT: Greenwood Press.

Piquero, A. R., T. Brezina, and M. G. Turner (2005). "Testing Moffit's Account of Delinquency Abstention." *Journal of Research in Crime & Delinquency* **42**:27–54.

Pohlman, H. L. (1995). *Constitutional Debate in Action: Criminal Justice.* New York: HarperCollins College Publishers.

Posey, Amy J., and Lisa M. Dahl (2002). "Beyond Pretrial Publicity: Legal and Ethical Issues Associated with Change of Venue Surveys." *Law and Human Behavior* **26**:107–125.

Pound, Roscoe (1912). "The Scope and Purpose of Sociological Jurisprudence." *Journal of Political Economy* **25**:489–500.

Prentice, Melissa A. (2001). "Prosecuting Mothers Who Maim and Kill: The Profile of Munchausen Syndrome by Proxy Litigation in the Late 1990s." *American Journal of Criminal Law* **28**:373–412.

President's Commission on Law Enforcement. (1967). *President's Commission on Law Enforcement and the Administration of Justice.* Washington, DC: U.S. Government Printing Office.

Presser, Lis, Cynthia Hamilton, and Emily Gaarder (2004). "Power Dynamics of Victim-Offender Mediation." Unpublished paper presented at the annual meeting of the American Society of Criminology, November (Nashville, TN).

Preston, Frederick W., and Roger I. Roots (eds.) (2004). "When Laws Backfire: Unintended Impacts of Public Policy." *American Behavioral Scientist* **47**:1371–1466.

Priest, George (1985). "The Invention of Enterprise Liability: A Critical History of the Intellectual Foundations of Modern Tort Law." *Journal of Legal Studies* **14**:461–527.

Proulx, Craig (2003). *Reclaiming Aboriginal Justice, Identity, and Community.* Saskatoon, Canada: Purich Publishing.

Puzzanchera, Charles (2013). *Juvenile Arrests 2011.* Washington, DC: U.S. Department of Justice, Office of Juvenile Justice and Delinquency Prevention.

Puzzanchera, Charles, Benjamin Adams, and Sarah Hockenberry (2012). *Juvenile Court Statistics 2009.* Pittsburgh, PA: National Center for Juvenile Justice.

Puzzanchera, Charles, and Crystal Robson (2014). *Delinquency Cases in Juvenile Court, 2010.* Washington, DC. U.S. Department of Justice, Office of Juvenile Justice and Delinquency Prevention.

Rasmussen, A. (2004). "Teen Court Referral, Sentencing, and Subsequent Recidivism: Two Proportional Hazards Models and a Little Speculation." *Crime & Delinquency* **50**:615–635.

Read, J. Don, John C. Yuille, and Patricia Tollestrup (1992). "Recollections of a Robbery: Effects of Arousal and Alcohol Upon Recall and Person Identification." *Law and Human Behavior* **16**:425–446.

Reddick, M. (n.d.). "Judging the Quality of Judicial Selection Methods: Merit Selection, Elections, and Judicial Discipline." Retrieved from http://www.judicialselection.us/uploads/documents/Judging_the_Quality_of_Judicial_Sel_8EF0DC3806ED8.pdf.

Reddick, M., Michael J. Nelson, and Rachel Paine Caufield (2009). "Racial and Gender Diversity on State Courts." *The Judges' Journal* **48**:29–32.

Redding, Richard E. (2010). *Juvenile Transfer Laws: An Effective Deterrent to Delinquency?* U.S. Department of Justice, Office of Juvenile Justice and Delinquency Prevention.

Reed, Judith (2004). *Teen Courts.* Albuquerque, NM: Youth Development and Diagnostic Center.

Ridgeway, Greg, and Robert L. Listenbee (2014). *Delays in Youth Justice.* National Institute of Justice, Office of Juvenile Justice and Delinquency Prevention.

Roberts, Albert R. (ed.) (2003). *Critical Issues in Crime and Justice* (2nd ed.). Thousand Oaks, CA: Sage.

Roberts, Julian V., and Edna Erez (2004). "Communication in Sentencing: Exploring the Expressive Function of Victim Impact Statements." *International Review of Victimology* **10**:223–244.

Roberts, Melinda, Jacinta M. Gau, and David C. Brody (2004). "Eligible Jurors' Knowledge, Information Sources, and Attitudes About the Jury System." Unpublished paper presented at the annual meeting of the American Society of Criminology, November (Nashville, TN).

Robinson, Paul H., and J. M. Darley (2004). "Does Criminal Law Deter? A Behavioral Science Investigation." *Oxford Journal of Legal Studies* **24**:173–205.

Rockwell, P., and A. E. Hubbard (2004). "The Effect of Attorneys' Nonverbal Communication on Perceived Credibility." *Polygraph* **33**:102–114.

Rodriguez, Nancy (2004). "Examining the Influence of Community Racial/Ethnic Composition in Juvenile Detention Decisions: The Mediating Role of Community Characteristics in Juvenile Court." Unpublished paper presented at the annual meeting of the American Society of Criminology, November (Nashville, TN).

Rodriguez, Fernando S., Theodore R. Curry, and Gang Lee (2006). "Gender Differences in Criminal Sentencing: Do Effects Vary Across Violent, Property, and Drug Offenses?" *Social Science Quarterly* **87**:318–339.

Rodriguez, Nancy, and Gaylene S. Armstrong (2004). "The Relationship Between Offense Type and Attorney Presence in Juvenile Court Disposition Decisions." Unpublished paper presented at the annual meeting of the American Society of Criminology, November (Nashville, TN).

Rogers, Patrick, Sharon Cotliar, and Steve Erwin (2000). "Judgment Day." *People*, November 6, 2000:87–91.

Rojek, Dean G., James E. Coverdill, and Stuart W. Fors (2003). "The Effect of Victim Impact Panels on DUI Rearrest Rates: A Five-Year Follow-up." *Criminology* **41**:1319–1340.

Rosay, Andre B., and Brad A. Myrstol (2004). "Gender Effects in the Alaska Juvenile Justice System." Unpublished paper presented at the annual meeting of the American Society of Criminology, November (Nashville, TN).

Rose-Ackerman, Susan (2002). "Corruption and the Criminal Law." *Forum on Crime and Society* **2**:3–21.

Ross, David Frank, J. Don Read, and Michael P. Toglia (1994). *Adult Eyewitness Testimony: Current Trends and Developments.* Cambridge: Cambridge University Press.

Rottman, David B., Carol R. Flango, Melissa Cantrell, Randall Hansen, and Neil LaFountain (2000). *State Court Organization, 1998.* Washington, DC: Bureau of Justice Statistics.

Rottman, David B., and Shauna M. Strickland (2006). *State Court Organization, 2004.* Washington, DC: U.S. Department of Justice, Bureau of Justice Statistics.

Roy, Dina (2004). "Age Disparity in Criminal Court Sentencing." Unpublished paper presented at the annual meeting of the American Society of Criminology, November (Nashville, TN).

Roy, Sudipto, and Michael Brown (1992). "Victim-Offender Reconciliation Project for Adults and Juveniles: A Comparative Study in Elkhart County, Indiana." Unpublished paper presented at the annual meetings of the American Society of Criminology, November (San Francisco, CA).

Ruback, R. Barry (2002). *Restitution in Pennsylvania: A Multimethod Investigation.* Erie, PA: Pennsylvania Commission on Crime and Delinquency.

Sabelli, Martin, and Stacey Leyton (2000). "Train Wrecks and Freeway Crashes: An Argument for Fairness and Against Self-Representation in the Criminal Justice System." *Journal of Criminal Law and Criminology* **91**:161–235.

Sacks, Stanley, and Frank S. Pearson (2003). "Co-Occurring Substance Use and Mental Disorders in Offenders: Approaches, Findings, and Recommendations." *Federal Probation* **67**:32–39.

Saltzburg, Stephen A., and Kenneth R. Redden (1994). *Federal Rules of Evidence Manual.* Charlottesville, VA: Michie.

Schaffer, B. (2010). "Veterans Courts and Diversion Alternatives." *American Jails*, January/February 2010:21–24.

Schauffler, Richard Y., Robert C. LaFountain, Neal B. Kauder, and Shauna M. Strickland (2004). *Examining the Work of State Courts*, 2004. Washington, DC: Bureau of Justice Statistics.

Scheb, John M. II (1988). "State Appellate Judges' Attitudes Toward Judicial Merit Selection and Retention: Results of a National Survey." *Judicature* **62**:170–174.

Schiff, Mara F., and Gordon Bazemore (2004). "Why Restorative Justice Works: Building and Testing Intervention Theories." Unpublished paper presented at the annual meeting of the American Society of Criminology, November (Nashville, TN).

Schmid, Karl H. (2002). "Journalist's Privilege in Criminal Proceedings: An Analysis of United States Courts of Appeals' Decisions from 1973–1999." *American Criminal Law Review* **39**:1441–1499.

Schneider, Jeffery M. (2007). "Youth Courts: An Empirical Update and Analysis of Future Organizational and Research Needs." *Hamilton Fish Institute Reports and Essays Serial.* Washington, DC: Hamilton Fish Institute on School and Community Violence, The George Washington University.

Schoenfeld, Heather (2005). "Violated Trust: Conceptualizing Prosecutorial Misconduct." *Journal of Contemporary Criminal Justice* **21**:250–271.

Schram, Pamela J., Barbara A. Koons-Witt, and Merry Morash (2004). "Management Strategies When Working with Female Prisoners." *Women and Criminal Justice* **15**:25–50.

Schulman, William L. (2005). "Videotaping the Process: Technology in America's Jails and Courtrooms." Unpublished paper presented at the annual meeting of the Academy of Criminal Justice Sciences, March (2005).

Sheehy, Elizabeth (2004). "Advancing Social Inclusion: The Implications for Criminal Law and Policy." *Canadian Journal of Criminology and Criminal Justice* **46**:73–95.

Shelden, Randall G. (2010). *The Prison Industry.* San Francisco, CA: Center on Juvenile and Criminal Justice.

Simon, Rita J., and Thomas Eimermann (1971). "The Jury Finds Not Guilty: Another Look at Media Influence on the Jury." *Journalism Quarterly* **48**:343–344.

Smith, Alisa (2004). *Law, Social Science, and the Criminal Courts.* Durham, NC: Carolina Academic Press.

Smith, Steven K., and Carol J. DeFrances (1996). *Indigent Defense.* Washington, DC: U.S. Department of Justice.

Sobel, R., and Hall, J. (2007). "The Effect of Judicial Selection processes on Judicial Quality: The Role of Partisan Politics." *Cato Journal* **27**:69–82.

Sourcebook of Criminal Justice Statistics (2010). "Characteristics of Presidential Appointees to U.S. District Court Judgeships." Retrieved online at: http://www.albany.edu/sourcebook/pdf/t1812010.pdf.

Sourcebook of Criminal Justice Statistics (2013). University of Albany, Hindelang Criminal Justice Research Center.

Spangenberg, Robert L. et al. (1999). *Indigent Defense and Technology: A Progress Report.* Washington, DC: Bureau of Justice Assistance.

Spohn, Cassia C. (1999). "Gender and Sentencing of Drug Offenders: is Chivalry Dead?" *Criminal Justice Policy Review* **9**:365–399.

Spohn, Cassia C. (2000). *Thirty Years of Sentencing Reform: The Quest for a Racially Neutral Sentencing Process.* Washington, DC: National Institute of Justice, Criminal Justice.

Spohn, Cassia C. (2004). "Sentencing Decisions in Three U.S. District Courts: Testing the Assumption of Uniformity in the Federal Sentencing Process." Unpublished paper presented at the annual meeting of the American Society of Criminology, November (Nashville, TN).

Spohn, Cassia C. (2005). "Sentencing Decisions in Three U.S. District Courts: Testing the Assumption of National Uniformity in the Federal Sentencing Process." *Justice Research and Policy* **7**:1–28.

Spohn, Cassia C. (2009). *How Do Judges Decide: The Search for Fairness and Justice in Punishment.* Thousand Oaks, CA: Sage.

Spohn, Cassia C., and David Holleran (2000). "The Imprisonment Penalty Paid by Young, Unemployed Black and Hispanic Male Offenders." *Criminology* **38**:281–306.

Spohn, Cassia C., and Elizabeth Keller (2005). "U.S. Attorneys and the Federal Sentencing Process: A Test of Inter-Prosecutor Disparity." Unpublished paper presented at the annual meeting of the American Society of Criminology, November (Toronto, CAN).

Sridharan, S. et al. (2004). "Juvenile Transfer." *Criminology and Public Policy* **3**:599–649.

Stacey, Lynn R., and P. E. Dayton (1988). *Jury Deliberations and Judicial Opinions.* Washington, DC: U.S. Department of Justice.

Stalans, Loretta J. et al. (2004). "Identifying Three Types of Violent Offenders and Predicting Violent Recidivism While on Probation: A Classification Tree Analysis." *Law and Human Behavior* **28**:253–271.

Stalmaster, Irvin (1931). *What Price Jury Trials?* New York: Penguin.

Stacy, Ann Martin, and Cassia Spohn (2006). "Gender and the Social Costs of Sentencing: An Analysis of Sentences Imposed on Male and Female Offenders in Three U.S. District Courts." *Berkeley Journal of Criminal Law* **11**:43–76.

Stanley, Steve (2004). " 'What Works'? Revisiting the Evidence in England and Wales." *Journal of Community and Criminal Justice* **51**:7–20.

Starr, Sonja, B. (2012). "Estimating Gender Disparities in Federal Criminal Cases." *The Social Science Research Network Electronic Paper Collection.* Paper No. 12-018.

Steadman, Henry J., and Bonita M. Veysey (1997). *Providing Services for Jail Inmates with Mental Disorders.* Washington, DC: National Institute of Justice.

Steelman, David C., and Samuel D. Conti (1987). *Representation of Indigent Criminal Defendants in the Courts of Hamilton County, Ohio.* North Andover, MA: National Center for State Courts.

Steffensmeier, D., and S. Demuth (2000). "Ethnicity and Sentencing Outcomes in U.S. Federal Courts: Who Is Punished More Harshly?" *American Sociological Review* **65**:705–729.

Steffensmeier, D., J. Kramer, and C. Steifel (1993). "Gender and Imprisonment Decisions." *Criminology* **31**:411–446.

Steffensmeier, D., J. T. Ulmer, and J. H. Kramer (1998). "The Interaction of Race, Gender, and Age in Criminal Sentencing: The Punishment Cost of Being Young, Black, and Male." *Criminology* **36**:763–797.

Steiner, Benjamin, Craig Hemmens, and Valerie Bell (2004). "Legislative Waiver Reconsidered: An Examination of General Deterrence." Unpublished paper presented at the annual meeting of the American Society of Criminology, November (Nashville, TN).

Stemen, Donald (2004). "Policies of Imprisonment: The Adoption of Determinate Sentencing and Sentencing Guidelines in the United States, 1975–2002." Unpublished paper presented at the annual meeting of the American Society of Criminology, November (Nashville, TN).

Stemen, Donald, James A. Wilson, and Andres Rengifo (2004). "Of Fragmentation and Ferment: The Impact of Sentencing Policies on State-Level Incarceration Rates and Admissions to Prison, 1970–2002." Unpublished paper presented at the annual meeting of the American Society of Criminology, November (Nashville, TN).

Stephenson-Lang, Juli (2005). "Tipping the Scales of Justice: The Importance of Proportionality in a Balanced Sentencing Scheme." Unpublished paper presented at the annual meeting of the Academy of Criminal Justice Sciences, March (Chicago).

Stevens, Holly, R., Colleen E. Sheppard, Robert Spangenberg, Aimee Wickman, and Jon B. Gould (2010). "State, County, and Local Expenditures for Indigent Defense Services: Fiscal Year 2008." The American Bar Association Standing Committee on Legal Aid and Indigent Defendants.

Stith, Kate, and Jose A. Cabranes (1998). *Fear of Judging Sentencing Guidelines in Federal Court*. Chicago: University of Chicago Press.

Strang, Heather (2004). "Effectiveness in Restorative Justice: First Doing No Harm." Unpublished paper presented at the annual meeting of the American Society of Criminology, November (Nashville, TN).

Suggs, David, and Bruce Sales (1981). "Juror Self-Disclosure in the Voir Dire: A Social Science Analysis." *Indiana Law Journal* **56**:245–271.

Swain, F. W. (1985). *Of God and His Conscience: Judicial Selection in Louisiana*. Baton Rouge, LA: Louisiana State Legislature.

Szymanski, L. (2008). "Juvenile Delinquent's Right to a Jury Trial." *NCJJ Snapshot* 13 (2). Pittsburgh, PA: National Center for Juvenile Justice.

Tague, Peter W. (1999). "Representing Indigents in Serious Criminal Cases in England's Crown Court: The Advocates' Performance and Incentives." *American Criminal Law Review* **36**:171–222.

Tappan, Christy (2005). "The New Face of Prosecution: Structural Characteristics and Outcomes Associated with Community Prosecution." Unpublished paper presented at the annual meeting of the Academy of Criminal Justice Sciences, March (Chicago).

Taylor, Humphrey, Michael Kagay, and Stuart Leichenko (1987). *Public Attitudes Toward the Civil Justice System and Tort Law Reform*. New York: Louis Harris and Associates for Aetna Life and Casualty Insurance Company.

Technology Review. (2005). "The DNA Defense." *Technology Review* **108**:20.

Teske, Raymond H. C. Jr., and C. Zhang (2005). "Disposition of Defendants Charged with Felony-Level Violation of Protective Orders in Harris County, Texas." Unpublished paper presented at the annual meeting of the Academy of Criminal Justice Sciences, March (Chicago).

The Center for Public Integrity (2003). Harmful Error: Investigating America's Local Prosecutors.

The 1215 Magna Carta: Clause 39'. *The Magna Carta Project*, trans. H. Summerson et al. [http://magnacartaresearch.org/read/magna_carta_1215/Clause_39 accessed 25 November 2016].

Thomas, Cheryl (2006). "Review of Judicial Training and Education in Other Jurisdictions." Retrieved online at: http://www.ucl.ac.uk/laws/socio-legal/docs/Review_of_Judicial_Train.pdf.

Thomas, Wayne (1976). *Bail Reform in America*. Berkeley: University of California Press.

Thomas, Wayne (1977). *National Evaluation Program: Pretrial Release Programs*. Washington, DC: Law Enforcement Assistance Administration.

Thompson, R. Alan (2005). "Results of the 2004 Mississippi Crime Poll." Unpublished paper presented at the annual meeting of the Academy of Criminal Justice Sciences, March (Chicago).

Tifft, Larry (2004). "A Critique of Restorative Justice Evaluation Research." Unpublished paper presented at the annual meeting of the Academy of Criminal Justice Sciences, November (Nashville, TN).

Tillyer, Robert, Richard D. Hartley, and Jeffrey T. Ward (2013). "Gender and criminal court outcomes: Does previous criminal history matter?" Paper presented at the American Society of Criminology Annual Meeting; Atlanta, GA: November, 2013.

Tishler, C. L. et al. (2004). "Is Domestic Violence Relevant? An Exploratory Analysis of Couples Referred for Mediation in Family Court." *Journal of Interpersonal Violence* **19**:1042–1062.

Tomasi, Timothy B., and Jess A. Velona (1987). "All the President's Men: A Study of Ronald Reagan's Appointments to the U.S. Courts of Appeals." *Columbia Law Review* **87**:766–793.

Tonry, Michael (1995). *Malign Neglect*. New York, NY: Oxford University Press.

Tonry, Michael (1996). *Sentencing Matters*. New York, NY: Oxford University Press.

Tonry, Michael (2004). *Punishment and Politics: Evidence and Emulation in the Making of English Crime Control Policy*. Cullompton, Devon, UK: Willan Publishing.

Torres-Spelliscy, Ciara, Monique Chase, and Emma Greenman (2010). "Improving Judicial Diversity." Brennan Center for Justice, New York University School of Law.

Tsai, B. (2000). "The Trend Toward Specialized Domestic Violence Courts: Improvements on an Effective Innovation." *Fordham Law Review* **68**:1285–1327.

Tshehla, B. (2004). "The Restorative Justice Bug Bites the South African Criminal Justice System." *South African Journal of Criminal Justice* **17**:1–16.

Tuckness, Alex (2010). "Retribution and Restitution in Locke's Theory of Punishment." *The Journal of Politics* **72**:720–732.

Ueckert, Edwin (2005). "The Issue of Civil Commitment of Habitual Violent Offenders." Unpublished paper presented at the annual meeting of the Academy of Criminal Justice Sciences, March (Chicago).

Ulmer, Jeffery T. (2004). "Differences in Guideline Departures and Sentencing Among Seven Federal District Courts." Unpublished paper presented at the annual meeting of the American Society of Criminology, November (Nashville, TN).

Ulmer, Jeffery T. (2005). "The Localized Uses of Federal Sentencing Guidelines in Four U.S. District Courts: Evidence of Processual Order." *Symbolic Interaction* **28**:255–279.

Ulmer, Jeffery T., and Keri B. Burchfield (2004). "Charge Manipulation and Relevant Conduct in Federal Criminal Case Processing." Unpublished paper presented at the annual meeting of the American Society of Criminology, November (Nashville, TN).

Ulrich, Thomas E. (2002). "Pretrial Diversion in the Federal Court System." *Federal Probation* **66**:30–37.

Umbreit, Mark S. (1994). "Victim Empowerment Through Mediation." *APPA Perspectives* **18**:25–28.

Umbreit, Mark S. (2001). *The Handbook of Victim Offender Mediation: An Essential Guide to Practice and Research*. San Francisco: Jossey-Bass.

Umbreit, Mark S., and B. Vos (2000). "Homicide Survivors Meet the Offender Prior to Execution: Restorative Justice Through Dialogue." *International Review of Victimology* **13**:27–48.

Unnever, James D., and Francis T. Cullen (2004). "Readdressing the Racial Divide in Support for Capital Punishment." Unpublished paper presented at the annual meeting of the American Society of Criminology, November (Nashville, TN).

Urban, Lynn S. (2005). "The Effect of a Curfew Check Program on Juvenile Opportunities for Delinquent Activity." Unpublished paper presented at the annual meeting of the Academy of Criminal Justice Sciences, Chicago (March).

Urban, Lynn, S., Jeananne Markway, and Kay Crockett (2011). "Evaluating Victim-Offender Dialogue (VOD) for Serious Cases Using Umbreit's 2001 Handbook: A Case Study." *Conflict Resolution Quarterly* **29:**3–23.

Urbina, I. (2009). "Pennsylvania Overturns Many Youths' Convictions" New York Times, October 30, p. A18.

U.S. Advisory Commission on Intergovernmental Relations (1971). *For a More Perfect Union—Court Reform*. Washington, DC: U.S. Government Printing Office.

U.S. Department of Justice (2005). Justice Statistics. Washington, DC: U.S. Department of Justice, Bureau of Justice Statistics.

U.S. Department of Justice (2013). *Crime in the United States, 2012: Percent of Offenses Cleared by Arrest of Exceptional Means*. U.S. Department of Justice, Federal Bureau of Investigation.

U.S. Office of Personnel Management (2010). Personal Communication.

U.S. Sentencing Commission (2003). *Downward Departures from the Federal Sentencing Guidelines*. Washington, DC: U.S. Sentencing Commission.

U.S. Sentencing Commission (2010). *Demographic Differences in Federal Sentencing Practices: An Update of the Booker Report's Multivariate Regression Analysis*. Washington, DC: Author.

U.S. Sentencing Commission (2013). *2013 USSC Guidelines Manual*. Washington, DC: Author.

U.S. Sentencing Commission (2015). *Overview of Federal Criminal Cases Fiscal Year 2014*. Washington, DC: Author.

Vago, Steven (2006). *Law and Society* (6th ed.). Upper Saddle River, NJ: Prentice Hall.

van Koppen, Peter J., and Steven D. Penrod (2003). *Adversarial Versus Inquisitorial Justice: Psychological Perspectives on Criminal Justice Systems*. New York: Kluwer.

Van Zyl Smit, D., and A. Ashworth (2004). "Disproportionate Sentences as Human Rights Violations." *Modern Law Review* **67:**541–560.

Vaughn, Michael S., Volkan Topalli, and Sarah Pierre (2004). "Legal Issues Involving Show-Ups, Line-Ups, and Photographic Identification." Unpublished paper presented at the annual meeting of the American Society of Criminology, November (Nashville, TN).

Veneziano, Carol (2005a). "An Evaluation of a Rural Drug Court Program." Unpublished paper presented at the annual meeting of the Academy of Criminal Justice Sciences, March (Chicago).

Veneziano, Carol (2005b). "Evaluating Drug Courts." Unpublished paper presented at the annual meeting of the Academy of Criminal Justice Sciences, March (Chicago).

Vidmar, Neil (2000). "Juries and Expert Evidence." *Brooklyn Law Review* **66:**1121–1180.

Villanova Law Review (1982). "Judicial Selection in Pennsylvania: A Proposal." *Villanova Law Review* **27:**1163–1178.

Vincent, Barbara S., and Paul J. Hofer (1994). *The Consequences of Mandatory Minimum Prison Terms: A Summary of Recent Findings*. Washington, DC: U.S. Government Printing Office.

Vito, Gennaro F. (1984). "Developments in Shock Probation: A Review of Research Findings." *Federal Probation* **48:**22–27.

Volcansek, Mary L., Maria Eisabetta DeFranciscis, and Jacqueline Lucienne Lafron (1996). *Judicial Misconduct: A Cross-National Comparison*. Gainesville, FL: University Press of Florida.

Vose, Brenda, and Kelly Vannan (2013). "A Jury of Your Peers: Recidivism Among Teen Court Participants." *Journal of Juvenile Justice* **3:**97–109.

Wagner, Meg. (2014). "Wife outraged when husband who drugged, raped her avoids jail time: 'I was told that I needed to forgive my attacker'" *The New York Daily News*. Available online at: http://www.nydailynews.com/news/national/man-guilty-drugging-raping-wife-avoids-jail-time-article-1.1798871.

Walker, Sam, Cassia Spohn, and Miriam DeLone (2000). *The Color of Justice: Race, Ethnicity and Crime in America*. Belmont, CA: Wadsworth.

Wanamaker, John L. (1978). "Computers and Scientific Jury Selection: A Calculated Risk." *Journal of Urban Law* **55:**345–370.

Ward, Geoff (2004). "Custody Against Care in the Concept of Accountability: Shifting Policies and Stubborn Priorities in Juvenile Court Organizations." Unpublished paper presented at the annual meeting of the American Society of Criminology, November (Nashville, TN).

Warden, Rob (2004). "DNA and Justice." *Newsfeed*. Evanston, IL: Northwestern University, May 3, 2004.

Washington, L. (1994). *Black Judges on Justice: Perspectives from the Bench*. New York: The New Press.

Weinberg, S., N. Gordon, and B. Williams (2005). *Harmful Error: Investigating America's Local Prosecutors*. Washington, DC: Center for Public Integrity.

Weisburd, David, Elin Waring, and Stanton Wheeler (1990). "Class, Status, and the Punishment of White-Collar Criminals." *Law and Social Inquiry* **15:**223–243.

Weiss, Michael Scott (2004). "Public Defenders' Pragmatic Motivations: A Qualitative and Inductive Study." Unpublished paper presented at the annual meeting of the American Society of Criminology, November (Nashville, TN).

Wely, Theodore (1904). *Hygiene of Occupation*. New York: Jena.

Westervelt, Saundra D., and Kimberly J. Cook (2004). "Life After Death: Life Histories of Innocents Released from Death Row." Unpublished paper presented at the annual meeting of the American Society of Criminology, November (Nashville, TN).

Wettstein, Robert M. (ed.) (1992). "Cults and the Law." *Behavioral Sciences and the Law* **10:**1–140.

Whitcomb, Debra et al. (1994). *The Child Victim as a Witness*. Washington, DC: U.S. Office of Juvenile Justice and Delinquency Prevention.

White, E.W. (1999). *History of Law in American Society*. New York: Cakewalk Books.

White, Welsh S. (2002). "Curbing Prosecutorial Misconduct in Capital Cases: Imposing Prohibitions on Improper Penalty Trial Arguments." *American Criminal Law Review* **39:**1147–1185.

Williams, James J., Daniel G. Rodeheaver, and Felicia Guerrero (2004). "Processing Offenders in Texas Juvenile Courts: Trends and Patterns." Unpublished paper presented at the annual meeting of the American Society of Criminology, November (Nashville, TN).

Williams, L. Susan, Delores E. Craig-Moreland, and A. Elizabeth Cauble (2004). "Chivalry Revisited: The Case of Girls in Rural Areas." Unpublished paper presented at the annual meeting of the American Society of Criminology, November (Nashville, TN).

Williams, M. R., and J. E. Holcomb (2004). "The Interactive Effects of Victim Race and Gender on Death Penalty Disparity Findings." *Homicide Studies* **8:**350–376.

Williamson, Deborah, Michelle Chalk, and Paul Knepper (1993). "Teen Court: Juvenile Justice for the 21st Century?" *Federal Probation* **57:**54–58.

Wilmot, Keith Alan, and Cassia C. Spohn (2004). "Prosecutorial Discretion and Real-Offense Sentencing: An Analysis of Relevant Conduct Under the Federal Sentencing Guidelines." *Criminal Justice Policy Review* **15:**324–343.

Winston, Norma A., and William E. Winston (1980). "The Use of Sociological Techniques in the Jury Selection Process." *National Journal of Criminal Defense* **6:**79–97.

Wolff, N. (1998). "Interactions Between Mental Health and Law Enforcement Systems: Problems and Prospects for Cooperation." *Journal of Health, Politics, Policy and Law* **23:**133–174.

Wood, William R. (2004). "Defining Success in Juvenile Restorative Justice: A Community Based Approach in Clark County, WA." Unpublished paper presented at the annual meeting of the American Society of Criminology, November (Nashville, TN).

Wooldredge, John, and Tim Griffin (2004). "Neighborhood Level Disparities in Court Dispositions Before and After the Implementation of Sentencing Guidelines in Ohio." Unpublished paper presented at the annual meeting of the American Society of Criminology, November (Nashville, TN).

Worden, Alissa Pollitz (1995). "The Judge's Role in Plea Bargaining: An Analysis of Judges' Agreement with Prosecutor's Sentencing Recommendations." *Justice Quarterly* **12:**257–278.

Worling, James R. (1995). "Adolescent Sex Offenders Against Females: Differences Based on the Age of Their Victims." *International Journal of Offender Therapy and Comparative Criminology* **39:**276–293.

Wortzel, H. S., L. A. Binswanger, C. A. Anderson, and L. E. Adler (2009). "Suicide Among Incarcerated Veterans." *Journal of American Academy of Psychiatry and the Law* **37:**82–91.

Xenos, Nicholas (ed.) (2003). "Restorative Justice." *Polity* **36:**1–90.

Zalman, Marvin (2004). "The Adversary Jury Trial and Wrongful Conviction." Unpublished paper presented at the annual meeting of the American Society of Criminology, November (Nashville, TN).

Zaragoza, Maria S. (1995). *Memory and Testimony in the Child Witness.* Thousand Oaks, CA: Sage.

Zingraff, Matthew, and Randall Thompson (1984). "Differential Sentencing of Women and Men in the USA." *International Journal of the Sociology of Law* **12:**401–413.

Cases Cited Index

Name Index

Subject Index

Note: The locators followed by f and t are referred to figures and tables, respectively.

Impeaching witnesses, 166
Impeachment, 111–112, 166
    defined, 111, 166
Implicit plea bargaining, 193–195
Inadmissible evidence, 57–58
Incapacitation, 220
    sentencing, 220
Incarceration
    by gender and race/ethnicity, 252t
    by gender and race/ethnicity for various
        age groups, 253t
Inculpatory evidence, 49
Incumbent judges, 102
Incumbents, 102
Indeterminate sentencing, 210, 224
    defined, 224
    extralegal factors, 225
Indictments, 150, 151, 259
    incriminating nature of, 259
Indigent defendants, 67, 258, 282
    juveniles, 282
Ineffective assistance of counsel, 71, 83
    reasonableness standard, 75–76
Informations, 53, 151
Initial appearance, 144–145
    defined, 144
Innocence Project, 260
Intake, 272
Intake hearings, 272
Intake officer, 272
    functions, 272
Intensive supervised probation, 200
Interim judges, 102
Intermediate courts of appeal, 39
Intermittent sentencing, 244
Interviewing witnesses, 46
Intoxication, 87
Investigative grand juries, 151
Isolation as cruel and unusual
    punishment, 256
Ito, Judge Lance, 324

J

Jail as a condition of probation, 244
Jamails, Joe, 331
James, Flemming, 334
Johnson, Lyndon B., 325
Judges, 95–112
    court delays, 109–110
    criticisms, 109–110
    disparate sentencing, 110
    federal selection methods, 104–107
    gender bias, 95, 198
    incompetence, 109
    politicalization of judicial selection,
        97–98
    qualifications, 96–97
    racial bias, 95
    rejecting guilty pleas in plea
        bargaining, 202
    removing judges from the office, 110–111
    reversible errors, 109

selection methods by jurisdiction, 98–99
Judicial activism, 8, 14
Judicial applicants
    qualities of, 98
    selection criteria, 98
Judicial appointments, 96
Judicial circuits
    composition, and number of circuit
        judges, 29t
Judicial conduct commissions, 113
Judicial discretion, 96
Judicial instructions, 330
for accepting guilty pleas, 206–210
Judicial misconduct, 108–109
    aggravating or mitigating sentences,
        108–109
    bribes, 109
    corruption, 109
    forms, 108–109
    Operation Greylord, 157
    prejudice in rulings, 108
Judicial participation in plea bargaining, 209
Judicial plea bargaining, 196–197
Judicial privilege, 201
Judicial process, 96–97
    defined, 96
    political influence in, 97–98
Judicial review, 31
Judicial selection
    reforms in, 98–99
Judicial training, 107–108
Judicial waivers, 288
    defined, 288
Judiciary Act of 1789, 26
Judiciary Act of 1891, 29
Jumping bail, 149
    defined, 149
Juries, 116–135
    evidence-driven, 131
    history, 118
    verdict-driven, 132
Jurisdiction, 24
    concurrent, 27
    defined, 266
    geographic, 25–26
    hierarchical, 26
    limited, 24
    defined, 266
Juror exclusion, 57, 121–125
Juror misconduct, 134–135
    defined, 134
Jury consultants, 126–127
    defined, 126
Jury decision-making, 131–132
Jury deliberations, 170–171
    agreement on verdict, 171–172
    polling the jurors, 172
    selling jury votes, 172
    voting, 172
Jury misconduct, 134–135
Jury nullification, 133–134
Jury reform, 132

Jury selection, 120–121, 330
    challenges for cause, 122–123
    exclusion of women, 120–121
    peremptory challenges, 122–125
    venire, 120–121
    voir dire, 121
Jury sequestration, 130–131
    defined, 130
    purposes, 130
Jury size, 127–130
    determining, 127
    limits, 127
    maximums, 127–130
    minimums, 130
Jury trials, 72–73, 158, 286
    contrasted with bench trials, 156–158
    defined, 72
    petty offenses, 73
Jury trials, juvenile courts
Jury verdicts, 128–129, 132
    nonunanimous, 132
Jury voting, 131–132, 172
Jury waiver system, 197
Juvenile-contiguous blend, 291, 291–292
Juvenile court prosecutors, 273
Juvenile courts, 266–272
    adjudicatory proceedings, 283–286
    age jurisdiction, 269
    blended sentencing statute models,
        291–292
    changing practices in, 284–285
    confidentiality, 284
    contrasted with criminal courts, 270
    defense counsels at, 285
    dispositions at, 283–284
    fingerprinting and photographing, 284
    history, 270–272
    jurisdiction, 266, 269
    labeling, 284
    lack of uniformity, 271
    minimum age jurisdiction, 266
    offenders, trends and implications, 296
    parens patriae, 269–270
    proceedings, 271–272
    reverse waiver hearings, 289
    standard of proof, 278
    transfers in, 286–288
    treatment and punishment functions, 269
    uniformity, 271
    waiver hearings in, 289–290
    waivers in, 288
Juvenile delinquency, 267
    contrasted with status offenders, 267–268
    defined, 267
Juvenile delinquents, 266–267
    defined, 267
Juvenile-exclusive blend, 291
Juvenile-inclusive blend, 291
Juvenile Justice and Delinquency Prevention
    Act of 1974, 268
    changes and modifications, 268
    defined, 268

Juvenile justice trends, 296
Juvenile offenders
    trends and implications, 296–297
Juvenile processing
    variation in criminal processing and,
        277–278
Juvenile rights, 274–276
    case examples, 275–276
    contrasted with adult rights, 276t–277t
Juveniles, 267–268
    defined, 266
    stigmatize, 268

K

Kales Plan for judicial selection, 101
    defined, 101
Kessler, Friedrich, 334
King, Rodney, 162, 329

L

Lackland Air Force Base, 25
Last clear chance, 333
Law, 254–255
    administrative, 13
    civil, 12
    common, 10–12
    courts and criminal justice system, 4–6
    criminal, 12–13
    defined, 4
    Dred Scott case and, 4
    functions, 6–8, 46–47
    procedural, 9
    sociolegal perspectives, 13–16
    substantive, 9
    types, 9–13
    women, 38
Law enforcement officers, 47
    working with prosecutors, 47
Legal aid for indigents, 67–70, 74–75
    forms, 67–70
Legal ethics, 66–67
Legal factors, 110
Legal realism, 15
    defined, 15
Legal training for new judges, 36
Legislative appointments of judges, 100–101
    contrasts with other selection methods,
        100–101
Legislative waivers, 288
Lie detectors, 79
Life-without-parole sentences, 229
Limited jurisdiction, 24
    defined, 24
Lindberg, Charles, 325
Litigation explosion, 331–332
Litigation sciences, 127
Llewellyn, Karl, 15
Loiterers, 269

M

Magna Carta, 119, 128
Malicious prosecution, 58

Mandatory punishments, 202–203
Mandatory sentencing, 229
    defined, 229
Mandatory transfers, 289
Marbury v. Madison (1803), 31–32
Media and courts, 324–326
    history, 324–326
Mediation, 306
Mens rea, 86
Mental health courts
    common features of, 314–315
    demographic data, prisoners, 315
Merit selection of judges, 101
    compared with other judicial selection
        methods, 102–103
    defined, 101
Miranda rights, 257
Misconduct risks and sanctions, 58
Misdemeanors, 143
Misdemeanor Trial Law, 157
Missouri Plan for judicial selection, 101–104
Mistake, 89
Mistrials, 49, 172, 256
Mitigating circumstances, 246, 247
    bifurcated trials, 246
Mixed sentencing, 244
Monkey Trial, 324
Motion for a bill of particulars, 161
Motion for a change of venue, 161
Motion for continuance, 161
Motion for determination of
    competency, 161
Motion for discovery, 161
Motion for dismissal of charges, 161
Motion for intention to provide alibi, 161
Motion for severance, 161
Motion for summary judgment, 161
Motion for suppression of evidence, 161
Motions, 161
Motions in limine, 160
Motion to dismiss, 161
Motion to suppress, 160

N

Naming, 8
Narrative, 248
    PSI reports, 248
National Bail Study, 148
National Center for State Courts, 98, 335
National Reporter System, 15
Necessity, 87
Negotiated guilty pleas, 200
Net-widening and diversion, 309
New York City Department of
    Corrections, 149
New York House of Refuge, 271
Nineteenth Amendment, 120
Nixon, President Richard M., 105
No bill, 151
Nolle prosequi, 186
Nolo contendere pleas, 152–153, 156, 190
    avoiding civil liability, 152

Nominal dispositions, 283
Nominating commissions, 98
Nonpartisan elections of judges, 99
Nonsecure custody, 284
Not guilty pleas, 152
Notice of appeal, 57

O

Obama administration
    female and minority judges, 105
    judicial reforms, 105
Objections, 162
O'Connor, Sandra Day, 105
Offender's
    sentencing memorandum, 249
Office of Juvenile Justice and Delinquency
    Prevention (OJJDP), 268
Once an adult, always an adult, 289
Opening arguments, 162–163
Operation Greylord, 157
Oral argument, 258
Original jurisdiction, 30

P

Pardons, 260–261
Parens patriae, 269–270
    defined, 269–270
    modern applications, 270
Parole board, 224
Partisan elections of judges, 98
Peer courts, 293
Peer jury model, 295
Penn, William, 133
Peremptory challenges, 122–125
    defined, 122
    limited number, 122
Persistent felony offenders, 220, 229–230
Petitions, 273
    juvenile delinquents, 273
Petit juries, 119
    history and function, 119–120
Petty offenses, 73, 143
    booking, 143
Philadelphia Experiment, 149
Philadelphia Municipal Court, 149
Photographing juveniles, 284
Pickpocketing, 73
Plea bargaining, 38, 168, 182–213, 259, 286
    amount in United States, 188–189
    avoiding habitual offender statutes,
        202–203
    banning, 188, 206
    bureaucratization, 205
    coerciveness, 190
    convictions, 199–200
    defined, 183
    factual basis for, 199
    going rates, 182, 193
    history, 186–188
    indigent defendants, 197
    judicial participation in, 209
    judicial responsibilities, 206–210